ECONOMIC EMPOWERMENT OF WOMEN IN THE ISLAMIC WORLD

Theory and Practice

Advances in Research on Islamic Economics and Finance

Series Editor: Toseef Azid
(Qassim University, Saudi Arabia & Wayne State University, USA)

Published

Vol. 1: *Economic Empowerment of Women in the Islamic World: Theory and Practice*
edited by Toseef Azid & Jennifer L Ward-Batts

Advances in Research on Islamic Economics and Finance – Vol. 1

ECONOMIC EMPOWERMENT OF WOMEN IN THE ISLAMIC WORLD

Theory and Practice

Editors

Toseef Azid
Qassim University, Saudi Arabia

Jennifer L Ward-Batts
Pomona College, USA

World Scientific

NEW JERSEY • LONDON • SINGAPORE • BEIJING • SHANGHAI • HONG KONG • TAIPEI • CHENNAI • TOKYO

Published by

World Scientific Publishing Co. Pte. Ltd.

5 Toh Tuck Link, Singapore 596224

USA office: 27 Warren Street, Suite 401-402, Hackensack, NJ 07601

UK office: 57 Shelton Street, Covent Garden, London WC2H 9HE

Library of Congress Cataloging-in-Publication Data
Names: Azid, Toseef, editor. | Ward-Batts, Jennifer L, editor.
Title: Economic empowerment of women in the islamic world : theory and practice / edited by Toseef Azid (Qassim University, Saudi Arabia), Jennifer L Ward-Batts (Pomona College, USA).
Other titles: Advances in research on islamic economics and finance ; v. 1.
Description: USA : World Scientific, 2020 | Series: Advances in research on islamic economics and finance ; v. 1 | Includes bibliographical references and index.
Identifiers: LCCN 2020938172 | ISBN 9789811212147 (hardcover) | ISBN 9789811212154 (ebook) | ISBN 9789811212161 (ebook other)
LC record available at https://lccn.loc.gov/20209381722

British Library Cataloguing-in-Publication Data
A catalogue record for this book is available from the British Library.

For any available supplementary material, please visit
https://www.worldscientific.com/worldscibooks/10.1142/11603#t=suppl

Desk Editors: Aanand Jayaraman/Karimah Samsudin

Typeset by Stallion Press
Email: enquiries@stallionpress.com

Foreword

Economic development has implications for social relationships, not least gender roles and status within households. Whether economic empowerment of women is a prerequisite for faster economic development or a consequence depends on the direction of causation, an issue that can only be resolved by empirical evidence rather than simply through opinions. The strength of this book, as the title suggests, is that it concerns practice as well as theory. For example, the contributors provide concrete evidence that education is the key to the economic empowerment of women, a hypothesis which is widely supported by other empirical research focused on gender issues.

The influence of religious teaching on the economic empowerment of women has been less studied from a Christian or Hindu viewpoint than from an Islamic perspective, possibly because it is difficult to separate culture from religion among non-Muslims. Nevertheless, despite the greater interest in the effect of Islamic teaching on women's economic empowerment, the literature remains limited. This book represents the first comprehensive work in this field, and deserves to be read by those researching on Islamic and religious studies, as well as those engaged in gender studies and women's rights. Labor economists and human relations specialists will also find much of value in the book.

There is more guidance on specifically gender issues in the *Qur'an* and the *Sunnah* than in other religious texts, much of it being concerned with the protection of women and male family responsibilities. The first eight chapters of this volume focus on the position of women at the time of the Prophet, as well as provide contemporary perspectives. Contentious issues are covered, including the potential conflict between patriarchal fundamentalism and Islamic feminism. The role of women in the workplace is changing, not least because of the desire, or perhaps necessity, to increase household income. For some participation in the workforce and the quest for promotion reflects individual aspiration at least as much as the satisfaction from social recognition. The contributions in the section on development perspectives cover a wide range of issues from globalization and women's empowerment to the influence of press freedoms on perceptions. Islamic microfinance is also included; its significance to this book being that most of those involved with such financing are women.

Perhaps the most valuable section is the country studies covering eight economies including Indonesia, Malaysia, Singapore, Pakistan, Iran, Turkey and Saudi Arabia. The readers can draw on the wealth of experiences in these diverse economies, including the very long-term changes in Turkey from the position of women in Ottoman times to their contemporary economic status. A second contribution on Turkey highlights the move of women from the private domain to the public sphere, a development which is being followed in the other Muslim countries covered.

Much can be learned from the experiences discussed and analyzed, but the major conclusion is that there is no necessity for any conflict between women's empowerment and religious teachings in Muslim economies. The obvious recognition that women and men are different can actually facilitate women's economic empowerment rather than hindering it.

Rodney Wilson
Emeritus Professor, Durham University, U.K.

Preface

When claims are made arguing that Muslim women are empowered, or that Islam women have equal rights within Islam, Western feminist naysayers are quick to dismiss such claims. They tend to stereotype Muslim women based on their own ethnocentric views of Islam, and to blame the religion itself for the lack of empowerment of women in the Islamic world. Many critiques of Islam as it relates to empowerment of women are misguided and lacking in understanding of Islam. Much of the Western media paints a dreary picture of Muslim women as underprivileged, under-educated, suppressed, neglected, deprived, not permitted to participate in economic and social activities, dominated by their male counterparts, etc. In this volume, we seek to examine the state of and potential for Muslim women's empowerment and their roles in the family and in society from a less hostile and more objective perspective. We seek to address issues that promote and support empowerment of Muslim women, as well as those that hamper their empowerment. We do not begin with an automatic presumption that Muslim women are dissatisfied with their roles. Rather, we seek to stimulate and encourage discourse on this important issue in a manner that respects cultural and religious relativism. As such, the editors of this volume view our role as providing a venue to begin this discourse, and not to censor or mold the points of view of the scholars who have contributed, or to take credit for those views. The viewpoints of each is his or her own, and we simply ask of our reader to come to this discourse with an open mind. Our hope is that this volume will spur both a better understanding of the issues, and a more fruitful discussion going forward regarding whether and how Muslim women's empowerment might be further advanced in ways that improves the well-being of those women from their own perspectives, not just from the perspectives of outsiders with preconceived notions about what those women *should* desire for themselves.

An understanding of the state of empowerment among Muslim women cannot arise without careful examination of religious, cultural, social and economic context, events and influences. Arriving at a better understanding of the state and trajectory of Muslim women's empowerment requires delving into both philosophical background in Islam and real-world socio-economic settings prevalent in Muslim communities at a given time and place. In this volume, we tried to provide a platform for scholars to present various theoretical and practical information and viewpoints relating to Muslim women's empowerment. Our goal is to bring these points to light for the purpose of generating further discussion among a wider audience of scholars and readers who wish to have a deeper, broader and more complete understanding of the issues affecting Muslim women's empowerment.

An understanding of Muslim women's empowerment is enriched by discussion of the early, middle and current periods of Islamic history. We believe readers of this volume will find that Islam, in its true form, empowers women, both historically and today. However, other elements of culture, governments, social and economic conditions, etc. also have important practical impacts on women's empowerment.

Following the introduction, the remainder of this volume is divided into four parts: Part A discusses theoretical underpinnings, Part B analyzes development perspectives, Part C explores the conditions of Muslim women in different Muslim countries, and Part D discusses special issues.

Chapter 2 by Islahi uses a wealth of historically, politically, sociologically and culturally specific data to provide detailed insight into various dimensions of women's empowerment. He emphasizes that Islam recognizes separate and independent identity of women and gives them numerous economic rights, such as rights to own property, share in inheritance, engage in various economic activities to increase their fortune. Men are tasked with affairs outside the home while women are tasked with those inside the home. All are accountable in their own sphere of jurisdiction. A woman's services have economic value no less than a man's. It is therefore obligatory for husbands to spend on their wives. The division of work and different sphere of activities prescribed by Islam is applicable in general and in normal conditions. In emergencies and special circumstances there may be change of their roles or they can join hands to share responsibilities of one another. However, a woman is never required to spend on herself or her family.

Her economic support is the responsibility of her father before marriage and her husband after marriage. In their absence, another close relative has to take care of her expenses. Failing that, the society, and finally the state, have to take this responsibility.

Building on this, in Chapter 3, Osmani *et al.* clarify the saying of Prophet (pbuh), "Never will succeed such a nation as lets their affairs carried out by a woman". They critically evaluated the validity of the quoted *hadith*, and examined its contexts in order to understand how and why the Prophet (pbuh) would have stated this. This analysis is crucial to address present day realities, as a significant number of Muslim women have competently led their nations by holding topmost offices. They also shed light on what the real political status of Muslim women should be today in light of the *Qur'an*, *Sunnah*, and juristic discourse. Resolution of questions about leadership can significantly impact women's empowerment from Islamic perspectives.

In Chapter 4, Abdullah asserts that the vision of the Prophet on women's empowerment can be best analyzed by examining the status of the closest female members of his own family. Among the female family members of the Prophet Muhammad (pbuh) with whom he had an opportunity to repeatedly interact for a considerable period of time were his wives, daughters and granddaughters. Abdullah critically analyses the treatment of the Prophet to one of these three main categories of his female family members i.e., his wives, in terms of their empowerment.

The remaining chapters in Part A represent the great diversity of points in the debate about women's empowerment in Islam. In Chapter 5, Saba and Bari examine the role of business woman among Muslim women, and relate this to the role of the Prophet's (pbuh) first wife Khadija as a rich business woman. In Chapter 6, Kamali provides a thoughtful analysis about women in the workplace under the umbrella of *Shari'ah* and a contemporary perspective. Kamali also presents the case of Malaysia. In Chapter 7, Mohamed navigates between the contending waves of patriarchal fundamentalism and feminism, and moves to the shores of a moderate discourse toward women's empowerment, namely, Islamic femininity. He also interrogates the literalist and decontextualized readings of the religious tradition which encourages cultural chauvinism and leads to erroneous religious expressions. Navigating the genealogy of Western secular feminism, Mohamed notes how the term "feminism" has become loaded with the baggage of imperialism, capitalism, homogenization of womanhood, and negative incursions on Muslim women. In Chapter 8, Akhmetova discusses women rights in Islam, and asserts that Muslim women have the potential to play a fundamental role in curbing corruption, social ills, violence and crime in the Muslim world. Therefore, in order to achieve stability and prosperity, the government must ensure a platform for women to participate in decision-making, and allow them to benefit from the rights they are accorded in Islam.

In Part B, several authors examine development perspectives related to empowerment of Muslim women. In Chapter 9, Choudhury *et al.* develop a relational well-being (*MASLAHA*) index of gender development and socio-economic development sustainability. The inception of *maqasid as-shari'ah al-Tawhid* index of socio-economic development sustainability is presented in its generalized form. The resulting model is that of well-being, which in Islamic context is referred to as *maslaha*. The authors examine complementarities and trade-offs between components of the index and make some policy recommendations about where we should efforts should be concentrated.

In Chapter 10, Majeed measures women's empowerment as a function of economic, political and social rights of women. The results of the ordered-logit-based empirical analysis show that globalization in the form of trade improves women's economic, political and social rights, while the favorable effect of foreign direct investment (FDI) is limited to only political rights of women. In Chapter 11, Anjum compares women's outcomes, as measured by some World Bank World Development Indicators, in predominantly Islamic countries to those in other countries. He discusses the relative merits of Islamic law versus other systems of law in achieving both human and women's empowerment and development. In Chapter 12, Majeed empirically investigates the relationship of press freedom to women's empowerment using panel data from 52 Organisation of Islamic Cooperation (OIC) countries from 1996 to 2011. Empirical findings from ordered-logit estimations show that press freedom is an effective tool to empower women, as it has significant positive impacts on both economic and political empowerment. In Chapter 13, Musari promotes Islamic nano-finance as an answer to the unmet need for Islamic microfinance available to the very poor segment of society. The existence of conventional microfinance institutions and some countries' focus on nano-finance should be a reflection for Islamic finance to engage in this society. Microfinance helps poor households by empowering women to contribute to the economic growth and sustainable livelihoods of their families and communities.

Part C includes 13 chapters presenting new evidence on issues affecting women's empowerment in Muslim countries, their rights, and their participation in socio-economic activities. In Chapter 14, Çaha chronicles the development of the Muslim women's movement in Turkey. He traces the historical roots of this movement and its evolution toward two different understandings of women. He describes two main views of the role of women among Islamic groups: the traditional Islamic faction strives to maintain women's traditional roles but advocates for rights to modern education, while the other group challenges this and seeks to secure a place for women in public life. The author also details the story of how Muslim women have attempted to be articulated in the public sphere, their 50-year struggle to achieve that goal, as well as the discourses, values and symbols that have generally been centered on the "headscarf debates".

In Chapter 15, Husin explores the concept of peace from a broader sense than merely the absence of war, through the eyes of Acehnese women in Indonesia, who continue to strive for better political representation and social justice based on Islam. She analyses Islamic principles of peace, cultural beliefs and practices, as well as the political environment, which engulfed Aceh. Historical accounts and academic research form a theoretical base for her analysis, while interviews with influential women, *Ulama* leaders, political figures and community activists provide integral content for her survey. This inquiry concludes that in spite of widespread political conservatism being promoted by the GAM political party of Partai Aceh and parochial religious fanaticism being advocated by certain transnational groupings, women themselves provide hope for gender equality and empowerment. Women of the *dayah* (Islamic boarding school) and NGO activists may work together to pursue their Islamic endowment of peace and accomplish pragmatic actualization of equality and justice.

In Chapter 16, Yildirim describes changes over many decades in the labor market outcomes of women in Turkey, including at the end of the Ottoman period, and explores some causes for these changes and the persistent low labor force participation rate (LFPR) of women over the past few decades. At the birth of the Turkish Republic in the early 1920s, 90% of the workforce was employed in agriculture. Migration to cities from agricultural areas in the latter half of the 20th century has deeply affected Turkey's labor markets, as well as its political and social structure. This migration especially affected women, who had previously worked in agriculture or small-scale production. Both low levels of education among women migrating from rural areas and discrimination decreases their job opportunities in cities. The relatively high rate of female LFPR of 70% in the mid-1950s, dropped to 26% by 2000, a rate far below the world average, and has increased very little (it was 30% in 2015). Yildirim chronicles social changes over a long period in the forces influencing what activities were socially accepted for women. He asserts that social norms relegating women's place to the domestic sphere allow for women working in the family's fields, as this is considered domestic work. However, women working in cities, in a foreign environment that cannot be controlled by the family, is much less acceptable.

In Chapter 17, Soleimani and Kiaee explain that a large proportion of the population of Iranian women, especially women with academic achievements, are not actively engaged in public life, and that this valuable resource is not adequately utilized within the economy. The non-economic attitude toward education, lack of success in finding suitable jobs, the inconsistency of education with the needs of the market, and low wages seem to be among the barriers in this area. Nevertheless, it is expected that Iranian women's participation in economic and social activities will be enhanced by taking appropriate measures in the area of entrepreneurship development and empowerment of women. In Chapter 18, Suhaimi and Ab Rahman analyze women's involvement in the development of waqf in Malaysia. Property donated by women is in the form of land, houses, buildings and cash. The *waqf* property has value and can generate rental revenue. It can also boost economic activities in an area as in the case of Seetee Aishah and Toh Puan Chah *waqfs*. Moreover, in Malaysia, there is vast potential for women in developing *waqf*. It was found that *waqf* funding obtained either through money, land and buildings could contribute to socio-economic development in Malaysia.

In Chapter 19, Saba and Bari explain that, in order to promote gender equality and women empowerment, the federal government of Pakistan has agreed to many international and nationwide commitments, such as the Convention on Elimination of all Forms of Discrimination Against Women (CEDAW), National Plan of Action (NPA) and Millennium Development Goals (MDGs). The authors highlight various women who made history in Pakistan. In Chapter 20, Suratman examines gender relations in Singapore Malay dual-income households. She shows that there are existing cultural perceptions of Malays regarding the roles of women and men in the family i.e., women see to care-giving and men see to breadwinning. She also argues that parallels of this perception can be found at the state level as well. The Singapore government too is of the view that the primary caregiver in the family is the woman. The author illustrates this by using the example of the discourse on the "supermom" in Singapore to show the government's expectations of women's role as mother. There is external support which makes Malay women affirm their maternal role. In conclusion, the author suggests that Malay women and men's decisions around the division of labor must be conceived within the wider framework of society. Explanations for persistence of unequal division of labor in Malay dual-income households must take into account state views of gender roles.

In Chapter 21, Azahari *et al.* opine that dower-giving symbolizes the love that a husband holds for a wife, and in Islamic teaching it is also a type of socio-economic guarantee for the wife. They investigate the practice of dower-giving among Muslims in Malaysia. The interview method was used to collect data that could be used to identify dower practices among Muslims in Sabah, a state in Malaysia. It was found that, notwithstanding the fact that a dower, according to the religion of Islam, should be a form of economic security for women in their marriage contract, this is not the case in practice in Malaysia.

In Chapter 22, Khan and Raza discuss different measures of women's empowerment and the impact of women's empowerment on an index of nutritional status of children in Bangladesh. The Composite Index of Anthropometric Failure (CIAF) has been calculated from Bangladesh Demographic and Health Survey 2007 (BDHS). The binary logistic regression results show that women's empowerment has no significant effect on child's nutritional status in these data. It may be conferred that the measure of women's empowerment has some flaws. The other explanatory variables, child's birth order and age, duration of breastfeeding, mother's education, mother's BMI, incidence of diarrhea and fever, household wealth and number of children (aged five or less) in the household have significant impacts on nutritional status of children. If a better measure of women's empowerment were available, it may prove to be related with child's nutritional status, as well as with other women and child welfare outcomes.

In Chapter 23, Azid and Aldowsari discuss the phenomenon of intergenerational transmission of education inequality in Saudi Arabia. Saudi Arabia has a unique position in the world, particularly in the Islamic World. This is the first study on this topic. It addresses separately the effect of father's and mother's education on educational attainment of daughters, as well as whether there is an interactive effect of mother and father on daughters' outcomes, in order to address the possibility of assortative mating, and thus the endogeneity of the wife's education with respect to her husband's education. Findings indicate that, while both mothers' and fathers' education influence daughters' educational outcomes, mothers' education has a stronger impact. Conversely, fathers' education has a stronger impact on sons.

Chapter 24 by Shaikh discusses the current state of women rights and their socio-economic participation in the Muslim majority countries and sheds light on effective legislation for promoting gender equality. It also presents the Islamic perspective of the gender equality and highlights the Islamic teachings, required social attitudes and the rationale for having certain prescribed differences in assigning roles to both the genders in the Islamic institution of family. It was observed that there is difference in relative importance and strength of the institution in family in OIC and non-OIC countries. Nevertheless, in some of the conservative OIC countries in GCC and Africa, there are specific attitudes toward their socio-economic participation and mobility, which requires a revisit. It was also observed that the labor force participation and the upward mobility in the corporate hierarchy are lower for women than men; however.

Compulsory schooling in Turkey was increased in 1997 from 5 years to 8 years. In Chapter 25, Ward-Batts and Nowacki examine the effect of this change on educational attainment, and in particular investigate whether there was a differential effect of this change on females relative to males. Using 2003 Demographic and Health Surveys data, the authors find an overall positive effect on the probability of completion of 8 years of school, as well as a positive differential effect for females of the change on both years of education and on the probability of completion of 8 years, narrowing the gender gap in both measures. They also find, as predicted, that the gender gap narrowed in low wealth families in particular. However, there appears to be a persistent gender gap in the country's more traditional, less-developed eastern region.

In Chapter 26, Hassan *et al.* show that the growth in women's revenues and resources plays an important role in improving women's financial freedom and sense of self-possession in Bangladesh. A significant policy lesson from this study is that, it is essential to redirect Islamic microfinance to more sectors and more beneficiaries, in order to spread its benefits in the developmental activities, which will drive the contribution towards the socio-economic empowerment of the recipients and toward the socio-economic development of the country in the long-run.

Part D of this volume presents the study by Jalajel in Chapter 27. Verse 4:34 of the *Qur'an* is the primary source of evidence cited in Islamic legal literature to permit wife beating. The injunction *wa-ḍribūhunna* (literally: "and hit them") is seen as giving the husband permission to hit his wife in response to her rebellion. This interpretation has been challenged by contemporary thinkers who argue that the interpretive community's biases precluded other interpretive possibilities. Attention has been given to interpreting the verb in question, *ḍaraba*, to mean something other than "to hit". Problems have arisen with this approach, since the interpretations suggested have required the use of dependent prepositions before the object of the verb which are absent in the verse. However, classical Islamic legal scholars have recognized that the imperative verb tense has a wide range of senses, listing several possibilities which are determined by context, some of which are far removed from the issuing of commands. Evaluating the function of the verb from this angle allows for a viable, robust interpretation of the verse that disallows wife beating while remaining faithful to classical interpretive methods. As a result, it can be argued that the insistence of classical scholars on asserting the husband's right to beat the wife is a result of cultural perspectives limiting interpretive possibilities.

Finally, the editors present conclusions and highlight some possibilities for further research.

About the Editors

Toseef Azid, is Professor of Economics at College of Business and Economics, Qassim University, Saudi Arabia. He holds PhD in Economics from University College of Wales (UCW), Aberystwyth, U.K. (1993), Master's in Economics from Quaid-i-Azam University (1979). He received COT Scholarship from government of Pakistan to study at UCW, Overseas Research Scholarship from British government, and a Fulbright Award Scholar in Residence (2006) where he worked on a research project titled *Economics of Middle Eastern Countries*. He taught at the Markfield Institute of Higher Education U.K. (2005–2006, 2007, 2012). He taught in Pakistan, Brunei, U.K., U.S.A. and Saudi Arabia. His research focuses on technological change, development Economics, labor economics, Islamic economics and Islamic finance. He published more than 60 papers in local and international journals. He participated in several conferences held in Iran, Saudi Arabia, Turkey, Canada, Australia, Indonesia, Malaysia, Bahrain, Qatar and Pakistan. He has published four books, one is in Pakistan (*Some Basic Principles of Islamic Economics*) and the other two are published by Routledge, U.K. (*Labor in Islamic Setting: Theory* and *Practice & Social Justice and Islamic Economics*: *Theory, Issues and Practice*) and the fourth one is published by Emerald (*Corporate and Shari'ah Governance in the Muslim World*: *Theory and Practice*).

Jennifer Ward-Batts is Visiting Faculty in Economics at Pomona College in Claremont, California, United States. She earned a PhD in Economics from the University of Washington in Seattle, and a Bachelor of Arts in Economics from the University of North Carolina at Asheville. She did postdoctoral study in economic demography at the University of Michigan. She received a Sloan Doctoral Dissertation Fellowship for dissertation work examining intra-household allocation in the U.K. before and after a policy change affecting government benefits to families with children. She was awarded a postdoctoral fellowship from the U.S. National Institute on Aging (1999–2001), and a Fulbright Fellowship to conduct research at Middle East Technical University in Ankara, Turkey (2008–2009). She has previously taught at University of Washington, University of Michigan, Claremont McKenna College (California, U.S.), and Wayne State University. Her research focuses on individual and household decision-making regarding outcomes affecting welfare of families, women, and children, including household spending patterns, saving for retirement, inter-household transfers, time allocation, residence location choice, educational investments and labor supply. She has published papers in the *Journal of Human Resources*, the *Journal of Public Economics*, the *American Economic Review*, and *Cuestiones Economicas.* She contributed a chapter to *How Do We Spend Our Time? Evidence from the American Time Use Survey.* She has presented work at numerous conferences and at universities in the U.S., Canada, U.K., France, Italy, Switzerland, and Turkey.

About the Contributors

Mohammad Abdullah, PhD, is an expert in the theory and practice of Islamic Sciences, Islamic Jurisprudence and Islamic finance. Abdullah is a well-trained and highly experienced Shariah Scholar, providing Shariah consultancy and advisory services to various Islamic financial institutions in Europe, South America and the UAE. He is a reputed researcher and has produced a number of research papers and Book chapters on the comparative study of Waqf and English trust, Shariah governance, Islamic finance and development studies. Dr. Abdullah holds a Bachelor degree in Shariah Sciences from Darul Uloom Nadwatul Ulama, Lucknow, India, and Masters in Islamic Banking, Finance and Management from the Markfieled Institute of Higher Education, U.K. Abdullah received his PhD at the University of Gloucestershire (U.K.) and he is a Certified Shariah Advisor and Auditor (CSSA) by the AAOIFI. Abdullah is frequent presenter of research papers and he has presented a number of research papers on different aspects of Islamic banking and finance in different American, European and Asian countries including Germany, Norway, Italy, Ireland, Scotland, U.K. Trinidad & Tobago, Indonesia, Malaysia, India and Dubai. He is currently based in Dubai. Scotland, U.K. Trinidad & Tobago, Indonesia, Malaysia, India and Dubai. He is currently based in Dubai.

Faezy Adenan is a doctoral student in the Department of *Shari'ah* and Economics, Institute of Islamic Studies, University of Malaya, Kuala Lumpur, Malaysia.

Abu Umar Faruq Ahmad, PhD, is currently an Associate Professor at Islamic Economic Institute in King Abdulaziz University, Jeddah.

He has a significant number of published peer-reviewed refereed journal articles, books, chapters in edited books, conference proceedings and other intellectual contributions to his credit on *Shari'ah* compliance of Islamic banks' products and structures, Islamic economics, the opportunities and challenges of Islamic finance, case studies of Islamic banks and financial institutions, Islamic insurance and reinsurance, Islamic microfinance, *Sukuk*, and dispute resolution in Islamic banking and finance, among others. He has presented over 50 scholarly research papers at international conferences held in the U.S.A., Ireland, Australia, U.A.E., Saudi Arabia, Turkey, Brunei, Qatar, Sudan, Nigeria, Malaysia, Indonesia, Bangladesh and Pakistan. His current editorial roles include serving as founding editor, senior editor, editorial advisory board member of a plethora of internationally reputed refereed journals including some of those published by Emerald Group Publishing, U.K.

Elmira Akhmetova a Tatar scholar from Russia, is an Associate Professor at Department of History and Civilization, International Islamic University Malaysia (IIUM), and an Adjunct Associate Professor at University of South Australia. Before joining IIUM, she served as Research Fellow at International Institute of Advanced Islamic Studies (IAIS) Malaysia. Akhmetova is the author, editor and translator of several books in the areas of Islam in Russia, Islamic Civilization, Islamic Political Thought, Diplomacy in Islam and Nationalism in the Muslim World, and has several dozens of articles and book chapters to her credit. She annually prepares reports on Islam in Russia for the prominent Brill Publications volume of Yearbook of Muslims in Europe since 2009.

Sarah Aldowsari is working as a lecturer of Marketing at College of Business and Economics, Qassim University, Saudi Arabia. She earned her Master's degree in Marketing from Newcastle University, Australia. And her Bachelor of Business Administration is from Qassim University, Saudi Arabia. She is an active researcher and published papers in the local journals.

Hasbi Muh Ali graduated from the Department of Fiqh and Usul, Academy of Islamic Studies, University of Malaya, Kuala Lumpur. Received Bachelor of Syariah (*Fiqh* and *Usul*) and Master of Syariah from Academy of Islamic Studies, University of Malaya. His research focuses on *Mahr* and its application in Sabah.

Muhammad Iqbal Anjum, PhD, is Assistant Professor of Economics at the International Institute of Islamic Economics, International Islamic University Islamabad (IIUI), Pakistan. Anjum was educated at IIUI (BSc (Hons) Economics (1982–1986) and MSc Economics (1987)), Kansas State University, Manhattan, U.S.A. (MA Economics (1990–1992)), and Deakin University, Melbourne, Australia (PhD Economics (2009–2013)). Anjum has at least 19 publications/research papers published in journals of international repute and books of proceedings of international conferences/seminars in Bangladesh, the United Kingdom, Brunei, Indonesia, Malaysia, Pakistan, Saudi Arabia, Turkey and the United States of America.

Raihanah Azahari, PhD, is an Associate Professor at the Department of Fiqh and Usul, Academy of Islamic Studies, University of Malaya. Studied at University of Malaya. Received Bachelor of Shariah (Islamic Law) in 1987 from University of Malaya. Obtained MA in 1994 from University of Jordan and PhD in 2005 from University of Malaya. Area of specialization are Islamic Family Law, Islamic Law of Inheritance, Contemporary Islamic Law and Dispute Resolution in Islam. Published a few books (includes chapter in books) and articles in the internationally recognized refereed journals such as *European Journal of Social Sciences*, *Arab Law Quarterly*, *Man and Society Journal*, *Journal Syariah* and *Journal Fiqh*. Presented more than 30 papers in conference both locally and internationally. Awarded a number of government and university research fund with the accumulative amount of RM500,000 as a principal investigator and co-investigator.

Khadija Bari has been associated with the Institute of Business Administration (IBA), Karachi. Pakistan, since 2002. She earned her PhD in Business Administration from University of Strathclyde, Glasgow, UK (2004) and MBA from the same university in 1995. She has chaired the Department of Economics and Finance at IBA from 2011 to 2018. She has been a member of the Academic Committee at IBA from 2011 to date. Dr. Bari is a certified director duly approved by SECP. She represents IBA on various government platforms. She was selected as a member of National Textile Strategy committee constituted in 2005 by the then Prime Minister of Pakistan Mr. Shaukat Aziz. She is member of the Standing Committee of Research and Policy at the Federation of Chambers of Commerce and Industry (FPCCI). Dr. Bari has authored various research papers. Her key research interests involve empowerment of women and their socioeconomic status.

Ömer Çaha (Professor of Political Science) is actually teaching at Istanbul Sabahattin Zaim University, Department of Political Science and International Relations, Istanbul, Turkey. He has been specialized on such issues as women's movement, political theory and theory of democracy and he has several books and articles in English and in Turkish on these issues. *Women and Civil Society in Turkey: Women's Movements in a Muslim Society*, published by the Ashgate, is one of his studies related to the topic of this book

Masudul Alam Choudhury, PhD, is Adjunct Professor and International Chair of the Post-Graduate Program in Islamic Economics and Finance, Trisakti University, Jakarta, Indonesia. He served as Professor of Economics in Cape Breton University, Canada. He also served as Professor of Economics in Sultan Qaboos University, Muscat, Oman. Choudhury's specialization in the field of economics and finance is analytical methodology derived from the *Qur'an* and *sunnah* in the socio-scientific field with special focus in Islamic economics and finance studied from the *Qur'anic* worldview of monotheism. He earned his Master of Economics and PhD (Political Economy) from University of Toronto. He is Editor-in-Chief of *Humanomics: International Journal of Systems & Ethics.*

Yaser Ahmad Fallatah is an Assistant Professor in Accounting at the College of Industrial Management, King Fahd University of Petroleum and Minerals, Dhahran, Saudi Arabia. Fallatah presented his papers at the different International conferences. He is also a member of the American Accounting Association.

Mohammad Omar Farooq earned his PhD in Economics from the University of Tennessee, Knoxville. He was a Ciriacy-Wantrup post-doctoral fellow at the University of California, Berkeley. He is an Associate Professor of Economics and Finance at University of Bahrain. His primary research interests are economic development, financial institutions, history of economic thoughts and Islamic economics/finance/banking/law. His works have been published in *Journal of Economic Issues*, *International Journal of Islamic and Middle Eastern Finance and Management*, *International Journal of Social Economics*, *Review of Islamic Economy*, *Arab Law Quarterly* and more. In addition to academic research, he frequently contributes to various Islamic media outlets on a wide range of Islamic issues. He also has a keen interest in gender economics and genocide studies.

Abul Hassan, PhD, is Research Scientist II/Associate Professor in Finance King Fahd University of Petroleum and Minerals, Dhahran, Saudi Arabia. Earlier he taught at the Markfield Institute of Higher Education (U.K.), Staffordshire University (U.K.) and University of Brunei Darussalam. Hassan has published more than 30 papers in the area Finance, Islamic Economics and Finance.

Mohammad Shahadat Hossain, PhD, is with the Department of Computer Science and Engineering, University of Chittagong, Bangladesh.

Asna Husin, PhD, teaches Philosophy of Education and Islamic Civilization at the Ar-Raniry State Islamic University Darussalam in Banda Aceh, Indonesia. She currently serves as a senior researcher at Nonviolence International in Washington D.C. working on Cultural Resources for Islamic Peace Building and History of Indonesian Muslim Communities in America. Dr. Husin gained a Masters Degree in Middle Eastern Studies from Harvard University and her Doctorate in Religious Studies from Columbia University. She participates in academic conferences worldwide and writes on Islamic peace, human rights and gender equity, Ulama institutions and civilizational heritage.

Abdul Azim Islahi, PhD, is Professor at the Islamic Economics Institute and the Editor in Chief of the Journal of King Abdulaziz University-Islamic Economics, the first professional journal in the field of Islamic economics. He has spent more than 40 years in research, teaching and expanding the frontiers of the discipline of Islamic economics. He has to his credit 16 books and more than 100 research papers, reviews and article in English, Arabic and Urdu. Some of his works have been translated into French, Turkish and Bahasa Indonesia. He is a world authority on history of Islamic economic thought. His distinct contribution is filling the research gap in this area by conducting series of studies covering the entire period from the 1st century Hijrah (7th CE Century) to the 13th century Hijrah (19th CE Century).

David Solomon Jalajel, PhD, is a consultant with the Prince Sultan Research Institute at King Saud University and holds a PhD in Arabic and Islamic Studies from the University of the Western Cape Town. Formerly, he was a lecturer in Islamic theology and legal theory at the Dar al-Uloom in Cape Town, South Africa. His research interests concern how traditional approaches to Islamic theology and law relate to contemporary Muslim society. He has published *Women and Leadership in Islamic Law: A Critical Survey of Classical Legal Texts* (Routledge), *Islam and Biological Evolution:*

Exploring Classical Sources and Methodologies (UWC) and *Expressing I'rāb: The Presentation of Arabic Grammatical Analysis* (UWC).

Mohammad Hashim Kamali, PhD, Founding CEO of IAIS Malaysia, graduated from Kabul University, and took his PhD in Islamic and Middle Eastern Law at the University of London in 1969. Kamali served as Professor of Islamic Law and Jurisprudence at the International Islamic University Malaysia (IIUM, 1985–2007), then Dean of the International Institute of Islamic Thought and Civilization (ISTAC). He also held Visiting Professorships at McGill University's Institute of Islamic Studies; Capital University, Ohio; and the Wissenschaftskolleg, Berlin. A member of the Constitution Review Commission of Afghanistan (2003), he has provided expert legal consultation to the new constitutions of Iraq, the Maldives and Somalia. He is an eminent authority on Islamic legal studies, and has published over 170 academic articles and 35 texts, including standard textbooks at universities worldwide.

Rana Ejaz Ali Khan, PhD, is working as Professor/Chairman in Department of Economics, The Islamia University of Bahawalpur, Bahawalpur, Pakistan. He completed his PhD in Economics from Bahauddin Zakarya University, Multan, Pakistan in 2005. His major research area is Development Economics. Khan's research interests include; poverty, child labor, informal sector, women employment, and malnutrition. He has published 76 articles in different national and international journals. Khan has also published a book entitled *Child Labor in Pakistan: Estimates and Determinants*. He has supervised 43 M.Phil and 8 PhD students. Currently, 5 PhD students are working under his supervision. Khan is Chief Editor of *Journal of Agriculture and Rural Development* since 2011. He is also member of editorial advisory board of Pakistan *Journal of Commerce and Social Sciences*, *Pakistan Social and Economic Review Journal* and *Asian Economic and Social Society Journal*.

Hasan Kiaee, PhD, Faculty Member, Islamic Studies and Economics Faculty, Imam Sadiq University, Tehran, Iran. Hasan Kiaee started to study Islamic Studies and Economics at Imam Sadiq University in 2001. By writing his dissertation about monetary policy instruments in Islamic Economic framework, he finished his master education in 2008. At the same year, he was accepted in University of Tehran for PhD level and continued his education in the financial and mathematical economics. He finished his PhD at 2013 while his PhD thesis was about using stochastic optimal control theory in modeling the Islamic banking behavior. He is now Assistant Professor of Economics at faculty of Islamic Studies and Economics at Imam Sadiq University and specially focused on quantitative area of Islamic economics and finance. In addition to contributing in some papers and books in this field, he actively participates in the Islamic banking and finance conferences inside and outside of Iran. Beside this academic background, he has a good practical knowledge in Islamic finance, as he has the experience of working as an advisor for a number of banks and financial institutions in Iran.

Muhammad Tariq Majeed, PhD, is working as Associate Professor of Economics in Quaid-i-Azam University, Islamabad, Pakistan. He did his PhD in Economics from the University of Glasgow, U.K. in 2012. He has published many research papers in national and international journals. He has written chapters in seven different research books. Moreover, he has presented his research at various international forums such as Royal Economic Society and Scottish Economic Society. He has more than 14 years of research supervision experience. He has supervised 40 plus MPhil theses. His research interests include: Islamic economics, financial development, corruption, inequality, poverty and economic growth. He has also worked as Research Associate in Punjab Economic Research Institute; Assistant Director in National Tariff Commission of Pakistan; Lecturer in University College Islamabad; Alama Iqbal Open University. He has also worked as research consultant with International Growth Center, HEC, Planning Commission, SDPI and Lead. Moreover, he has delivered various capacity building trainings related to applied research in social sciences. He has delivered honorary lectures to the executives of Intelligence Bureau, Civil Servants, MNAs and Senators.

Nabil Yasien Mohamed is currently a post-graduate candidate at the University of the Western Cape (UWC) in Arabic and Islamic Studies, engineer and entrepreneur. Nabil Mohamed holds a BSc Honors degree in Mechanical Engineering from the University of Cape Town (UCT), a BA degree in Politics, Philosophy and Economics from the University of South Africa (UNISA), and a post-graduate qualification in Islamic Studies at the Islamic Peace College of South Africa (IPSA). He is the co-founder and president of the REED Society.

Khairunnisa Musari, PhD, is a lecturer of Department of Islamic Economics at Postgraduate Program and Faculty of Islamic Economics & Business (FEBI), State Institute for Islamic Studies (IAIN) of Jember. She is an Editor-in-Chief of Indonesian Journal of Islamic Economics and

Finance (IJIEF). She is also a Secretary II of The Indonesian Association of Islamic Economist (IAEI) for Provincial Board of East Java and a General Secretary of Indonesian Economist Association (ISEI) of Jember. Her work concerns about *sukuk*, *waqf*, *waqf-sukuk*, fiscal and monetary policies, and Islamic microfinance and nano-finance. Her writings and papers are published in local and national daily newspapers, magazines, and international journals. She is a reviewer for some national journals, international conferences, and also reviewer of research for Islamic higher education from General Directorate of Islamic Education, Ministry of Religious Affairs of Republic of Indonesia. She has been presenting some papers abroad, particularly for international Islamic economics and finance conference sponsored by Islamic Research & Training Institution (IRTI) — Islamic Development Bank (IDB). She has experiences also as Senior Specialist for Islamic Finance of United Nations Development Programme (UNDP) Indonesia.

Kaitlin Nowacki earned a Bachelor of Arts degree with honors in Economics from the Department of Economics at Wayne State University in Detroit, Michigan, U.S. She presently works for a private sector marketing firm.

Noor Mohammad Osmani, PhD, is an Associate Professor in the Department of *Qur'an* and Sunnah Studies at the International Islamic University Malaysia (IIUM), obtained his PhD in 2002 from IIUM. He obtained his BA and MA degrees from Bangladesh Islamic University Kushtia. Osmani has natural ability of translation from Arabic to English. His research interest includes in *Qur'an* and *Sunnah* issues, inter-religious faiths, comparative studies on *Qur'an* and earlier divine scriptures, women issues and so on. He has published a good number of articles in the reputed journals and presented papers in the conferences. He speaks and writes in four different languages, namely Arabic, English, Urdu and Bengali (native speaker).

Ari Pratiwi is Lecturer in the Faculty of Management, Paramadina University, Jakarta, Indonesia; and Human Resource Development Officer with IBM Indonesia. She is an expert in non-linear econometric estimation using VAR and VECM methods.

Asmak Ab Rahman, PhD, is currently a Associate Professor at the Department of Shariah and Economics, Academy of Islamic Studies, University of Malaya. Her areas of specialization are *takaful*, Islamic economics,

Islamic law and *waqf*. She has been teaching at the University of Malaya since 2005. Asmak has published a few books (which also includes chapters in books) and she has also published some of her works in the internationally recognized refereed journals such as *Arab Law Quarterly*, *Humanomics*, *Journal of Islamic Marketing*, *International Journal of Islamic and Middle Eastern Finance and Management* and *Jurnal Syariah*, She has presented papers at local and several international conferences. She has been awarded a number of government and university research funds as a principal investigator and co-investigator such as LRGS, FRGS and UMRG.

Muhammad Ali Raza is working as Data Processing Manager at National Institute of Population Studies, Islamabad, Pakistan. He earned his MS in Economics from Institute of Business Administration, Karachi, Pakistan. He has experience of working in many consultancy firms as well as in academic institutes. Raza has published seven research articles in different national and international scientific journals. He has participated in different conferences, training workshops, and courses at national and international level. Raza has also co-authored a book chapter entitled *Levels and Trends of Health Care Services Utilization among Married Women in Pakistan*. His research interests include health economics, poverty, child and maternal health.

Irum Saba, PhD, is Assistant Professor in the Department of Economics and Finance and Program Director of MS Islamic Banking and Finance at Institute of Business Administration (IBA), Karachi Pakistan and also member of grand council of the Chartered Institute of Islamic Finance Professionals (CIIF), Malaysia. She is sub-editor of *Journal of Islamic Finance Accountancy* (*JOIFA*), *AAOIFI*, Bahrain and Vice President of Asia Pacific Applied Economics Association (APEA), Australia. She earned her PhD from INCEIF. Her areas of interests are political economy, management, *Shari'ah*, wealth planning and management, Islamic microfinance, corporate governance and Islamic finance.

Salman Ahmed Shaikh holds PhD in Economics from the National University of Malaysia. In Islamic Economics, he has published research papers in top international journals, presented researches in research conferences held in Malaysia, Turkey, Brunei, Indonesia and Pakistan and has also contributed several book chapters in book publications by Routledge, Springer, Palgrave, Edward Elgar and Gower Publishing. He is also on Editorial Advisory Board of several research journals. He also worked as Editor for the 2019 Global Islamic Finance Report for Cambridge

Islamic Institute of Islamic Finance. Furthermore, Emerald editorial team selected two of his papers for two separate journals as Highly Commended Paper in the 2018 Emerald Literati Awards. He had also won paper prize in World Islamic Finance Forum 2018.

Salah Al Shalhoob is an Assistant Professor and Director of the Centre of Research Excellence for Islamic Banking and Finance, King Fahd University of Petroleum and Minerals, Dhahran, Saudi Arabia. He earned his PhD degree in Islamic Finance ad Law from the University of Edinburgh, U.K. He is a well-renowned scholar in Islamic Finance in Saudi Arabia.

Mohammad Soleimani, PhD, Faculty Member, Islamic Studies and Economics Faculty, Imam Sadiq University, Tehran, Iran. Mohammad Soleimani was born in Qom, Iran 1984. He received his MA degree in Islamic studies and Economics from the University of Imam Sadiq University, Iran, in 2008, and PhD degree in Economics from Tarbiat Modares University, Tehran, Iran 2013. His PhD thesis is about the effect of social capital on elite's innovations in Iran. In 2014, he joined the faculty of Islamic Science and Economics, University of Imam Sadiq University. He is an Assistant Professor in this university. His current research interests include financial economics (especially Islamic securitization, financial crisis and derivatives) and development economics. He has some articles published in the area of social capital, financial crisis, income distributions and he is the author or supervisor of many of policy papers in Islamic Parliament Research Center of Iran in the area of banking system, capital market and central banking.

Farhana Mohamad Suhaimi, PhD, is a Senior Lecturer at the Faculty of Shariah and Law, Universiti Sains Islam Malaysia (USIM), Malaysia. She graduated from University of Mu'tah, Jordan with Bachelor's degree in *Shariah*. She later obtained a Master's degree in *Shariah* (University of Malaya, UM). In the year 2016, she was awarded a PhD in economics of *waqf* (UM). Her research interests are related to *waqf*, economics of *waqf*, Islamic economics and principles of Islamic jurisprudence. She has published several articles in scholarly journals and presented papers in both national and international conferences. She has published books with well-known publishers on *waqf* in Malaysia.

Suriani Suratman, PhD, is Senior Lecturer at Department of Malay Studies, faculty of Arts and Social Sciences, the National University of Singapore. Her research focuses on Malay ethnic identity and the (re)production of portrayals of Malays and gender relations and the issue of (in)equalities in Malay families and households. As an artist, she studied pottery under the tutorship of master potter Iskandar Jalil between 2001 to 2005 and now has her own studio space at the Jalan Bahar Clay Studios. Suriani is currently a Board Member of the National Heritage Board, National Gallery Singapore and NParks.

Kadir Yildirim, PhD, is Associate Professor of Economic History. He received his PhD at the Department of Labour Economics at the Istanbul University. He is currently a research fellow at the University of Duisburg-Essen. His primary research interests are labor history, social and economic history of the Ottoman Middle East, and Islamic economics. His book, *Workers in Ottoman Empire* (*Osmanli'da Isciler*), was published in 2013 and he has published several articles about Ottoman labor history, social classes in the Ottoman Middle East, female workers, industrialization efforts, and other issues. He gives courses such as history of economic thought, economic history and labor history.

Zalina Zakaria, PhD, is currently is a Senior Lecturer at Shariah and Law Department, Academy of Islamic Studies, University of Malaya, Kuala Lumpur, Malaysia. Received Bachelor of Law (Hons.) — LL.B and Master of Comparative Laws (MCL) from Ahmad Ibrahim Kulliyyah of Laws, International Islamic University Malaysia. Later, in 2012 obtained PhD from University of Manchester. Her area of specialization is consumer law and issues in Malaysia. Has been teaching at the University of Malaya since 2003 both at postgraduate and undergraduate levels. Awarded a number of governmental research fund. Has successfully supervised postgraduate thesis and dissertations relating to consumer law and issues, product safety, pharmaceutical safety and *halal* regulation. Currently is a coordinator of International Halal Research Centre, University of Malaya. Appointed as external program reviewer to a few halal programs, a committee in Halal Cosmetic Standard working group by the Department of Standard of Malaysia, and an active researcher in Consumer Law Research Asia sponsored by City University of Hong Kong.

Acknowledgments

This project was initiated while Professor Toseef Azid was on a sabbatical when he was working at the Economics Department at Wayne State University, Detroit, Michigan, USA and Dr. Jennifer Ward-Batts was Assistant Professor in the same department. The authors are greatly indebted to the faculty and staff of the Economics Department, Wayne State University, particularly to Professors Kevin Cotter, Allen Goodman, Stephen Spurr, Gail Jensen Summers, Li Way Lee, Ralph Braid and Janet Hankin, and to the late Professor Robert Rosanna as well as to staff members Delores Tennille and Sharon Miller. Azid is grateful for the support provided by Qassim University, Saudi Arabia. Ward-Batts is grateful for the support she received from Pomona College in Claremont, California. The authors also wish to extend heartfelt thanks to their students for making their academic work more rewarding and to their families for their kind support during the completion of this project.

Contents

List of Illustrations

List of Tables

Chapter 1

Empowerment of Women in Islam: An Introduction

Toseef Azid and Jennifer Ward-Batts

More than half a billion Muslim women are living in 45 Muslim majority countries and more than 30 countries have a significant Muslim minority population. "Muslim women aged between 15 to 64 make [up] about 8% of the world's total population." Muslim women and girls of all ages make up approximately 12% of the world's 7.3 billion population as of 2015 (Enriquez, 2016). According to Pew Research Center projections, "Muslims are the fastest-growing religious group in the world" (Lipka, 2017). Due to their sheer number, it is obvious that Muslim women can play a significant role in the development of their economies and societies.

The contributions of women in society are realized in many different ways. For example, due to their role in creating human capital through child rearing, women make a profound impact on the next generation. When they enter the labor market in greater numbers, they contribute to growth in GDP per capita. This list could go on and on. As a result of the important and myriad roles of women, they and their empowerment have become a focal point for development-focused NGOs and government policies.

In this volume, we seek to examine the state of empowerment of Muslim women, what role religion, versus other factors, plays in determining that status. Much of the current literature is somewhat biased (especially in the Western world) as both a cause and consequence of stereotypes about the status of Muslim women, insinuating that Muslim women have little opportunity to involve themselves in economic activities, especially in the private sector (Thompson and Hickey, 2005; Andrews, 2006; Rettig, 2011). Most studies on the issue conclude that, in the Muslim world, women have a low participation rate in the labor market and receive low wages compared to their male counter parts, and that the number of female executives in large companies is very small (Rizzo *et al.*, 2007; Moghadam, 1991). With that in mind, a number of national and international agencies are trying to collect data about these issues (United Nations Statistics Division, 2002; World Bank, 2011; Radelet *et al.*, 2006). There is a lot of misconception and misunderstanding about Muslim society, and in particular about Islam itself.

There is apparently a lot of misunderstanding between Muslims and Westerners about the status of women within the other group relative to their own ideals. A 2011 Pew Research Center survey asked non-Muslims in Western countries and Muslims in predominantly Muslim countries their opinions about the other group. Only 44% of Muslims in Muslim countries said that Westerners are respectful of women, while only 22% of non-Muslims in the U.S., Russia and Western Europe responded that Muslims are respectful of women (Lipka, 2017). This suggests potentially both a lack of knowledge of what the status of women really is in the other group, and that different criteria are being applied by each group to evaluating the other. Ethnocentrism is a common problem, and it often leads to prejudice, distrust and hatred between groups. We will focus here on trying to dispel some of the prejudice of Westerners toward Muslim societies and Muslim individuals, in particular regarding the role and status of women within Muslim groups.

In this volume, we and the contributing authors examine both the religion of Islam itself, as well as practical and cultural considerations that affect the status of Muslim women in various settings. One point we emphasize, as alluded to the aforesaid point, is that one should judge others according to measures that those being judged would view as appropriate, i.e., not take an ethnocentric view when evaluating outcomes from a culture or religion other than one's own. For example, in a free and democratic Western country, we would *generally* not criticize an individual non-Muslim woman for dressing conservatively if she chooses to do so. However, there tends to be much more criticism (by Westerners) of Muslim women for dressing on the conservative end of their own spectrum. A second point that we will emphasize is that the religion and the cultural and practical considerations often have contrasting effects on the status of women.

While we may observe systematically different outcomes for women in predominantly Muslim countries than in other countries, there are many factors besides religion that affect those outcomes, including but not limited to the level of economic development; local and regional culture, which evolves very slowly over time; and law and policies of the government.

Both the *Qur'an* itself and observations of the life of Prophet Muhammad (saw) indicate that, unlike in some other societies and religions, Muslim women have property rights, they are entitled to their share in inheritance, they are allowed to participate actively in economic and social activities, and in many situations they have equal rights with their male counterparts. Mothers are revered in Islam more than fathers, and it is the duty of the husband and the father to provide the basic necessities for his wife and children. It is very difficult to show statistics to indicate the value of care-taking work, primarily done by women as wives, mothers and daughters, since this work is typically unpaid. However, in many countries, time-use studies are being used now to show the incredible contribution made by women in these unpaid roles.

Comparing religious texts, the *Qur'an* does not imply the female is inferior and secondary in ways in which the *Torah* and the *Bible* do. Hassan (2001) and Çevi (2013) consider the three primary prejudices against women in Jewish and Christian religious tradition: (1) that Allah first created man, and then created woman from man's rib, implying that women are secondary and not equal to men, (2) that woman was primarily responsible for the expulsion of humans from the Garden of Eden, and (3) that woman was created for man, again implying her inferiority to man. The secondary creation of woman from man "has no basis whatever in the Qur'an, which describes the creation of humanity in completely egalitarian terms ... [T]he Qur'an uses generic terms for humanity [in passages about creation]. The word 'Adam' occurs twenty-five times in the Qur'an, but ... is used in twenty-one cases as a symbol for self-conscious humanity ... [T]he word 'Adam' is a Hebrew word ... [which] functions generally as a collective noun referring to 'the human' rather than to a male person. In the *Qur'an*, the word 'Adam' does not refer to a particular human being. Rather, it refers to human beings..." (Hassan, 2001, p. 60). Hassan (2001) argues that it is "likely that the rib story entered Islamic tradition [from Jewish and Christian accounts] through incorporation in the ... Hadith literature (p. 61). Equality of male and female in creation would also dispel the third point mentioned earlier.

Çevi (2013) asserts that women being the "cause of humans being thrown out from paradise, is [also] not ... indicated anywhere in the *Qur'an.*" (p. 7). He also argues that Arabic, like many languages, uses gendered pronouns, with the male pronoun as the default in the case of plural, mixed or neutral gender. Therefore, we cannot presume "he" and "his" to necessarily always indicate male gender in the *Qur'an*.

"The believers, men and women, are protectors and supporters of each other. They enjoin what is just and prevent what is evil, perform regular prayers, practice regular charity, and obey Allah and His messenger. On them shall Allah spread his mercy. Truly Allah is almighty and all wise" (*Qur'an* 9:71). This verse also indicates the overall neutral voice of the *Qur'an* regarding the position of men and women relative to one another.

The Prophet (saw) said, "Seeking knowledge is an obligation upon every Muslim."[1] No gender distinction is made here. Nevertheless, many local customs and national laws in predominantly Muslim countries are restrictive regarding education of females, or are biased in ways that result in greater educational attainment of males. Laws may indirectly affect educational attainment of the genders differently, whether or not such effects were intended. An example is a former rule in Turkey forbidding the wearing of *hijab* in public buildings (Headscarf restrictions were lifted in late 2013[2]). Mustafa Kemal Atatürk, the founder of the Turkish Republic, discouraged wearing of a headscarf in public buildings. After the 1980 military coup, wearing a headscarf in government buildings, including schools and universities, was explicitly forbidden. Thus, many girls and young women ceased their education earlier than they would have due to a conflict between their desired expression of faith (wearing the *hijab*) and their desire for education. Others continued their education, but removed their headscarf when arriving at the boundary of the university campus and replaced it upon leaving. This undoubtedly generated feelings of resentment among some. This rule also discouraged women who choose to wear the *hijab* from seeking government jobs, including jobs as teachers. This dress-code restriction helped to create a social wedge in Turkey between girls and women who choose to wear the *hijab* versus those who do not, even though many of the latter consider themselves as following Islam.

[1] Hadith on Knowledge, *Source*: Sunan Ibn Mājah, 224.

[2] See https://en.wikipedia.org/wiki/Headscarf_rights_in_Turkey for further discussion and some supporting sources.

This contributed to more stark divisions between groups, which in turn affects entire families, communities and politics. Interestingly, we can see much more social interaction between Muslim women who wear a headscarf and those who do not in more developed countries with minority Muslim populations, such as the U.S. Both Muslim majority and Muslim minority countries with dress-code restrictions should carefully consider the possible effects of these restrictions, as the effects may be the reverse of what is desired. If one fears that some women wear the *hijab* not of their own choosing, then educating them and not ostracizing them would surely produce better results in empowering them. Once they are educated and empowered in other ways, if they still choose to wear the headscarf, we cannot claim it is because they are oppressed.

Now we turn to the past and current status of women in Muslim majority countries. In cases where Muslim women have low status, is it due to religion *per se*, or to other factors, such as cultural norms and economic conditions? There are different interpretations of religious doctrine among countries, as well as among individuals, and among local communities. Often, religion is cited when trying to rationalize rules or actions, but these rules or actions are often inconsistent with religious doctrine, or at least not necessarily indicated by all reasonable interpretations, and this is certainly true in countless cases with respect to the *Qur'an*. Local and regional customs that predate Islam are sometimes claimed to be something people do in the name of religion. Some authors will evaluate some such issues in this volume. Culture changes very slowly, while technology and economic conditions can change much more quickly.

In order to maximize the welfare of the population, any economy cannot afford for half its population to be unable to participate in economic activities. In early agrarian societies, most production was done within small family groups, so women's productive activities were much less restricted. As the nature of productive economic activities has changed over time, largely due to changes in technology, societies have faced questions regarding what women should or should not do regarding work beyond their domestic sphere. The answers have varied considerably over time and space, but one regularity persists over time and across religious groups: poor women tend to work beyond their domestic sphere in order to contribute to the well-being of themselves and their children. There tends to be a U-shaped relationship between the level of economic development and women's participation rate in the labor market. As economies become richer, families can better afford for women not to work outside the home, so their participation declines as income rises. But as economies develop further, for myriad reasons, the participation of women in the labor market rises as income per capita rises. We will want to keep this pattern in mind as we consider experiences of Muslim women in particular.

We will first examine the status of women at the time of the Prophet (saw) and his successors (Khulfa-i-Rashdun — Rightly Guided Caliphs), followed by the role of Muslim women in the medieval period, and then we will be able to analyze the current period.

1.1 Early period of Islam

We can find different stories related to the role of Muslim women in the early period of Islam. Such stories generally address their societal roles, for example their role as a mother, as wife or as a pious woman. In history, we find that many Muslim women played a very significant role, especially at the time of Prophet Muhammad (saw) and his "Rightly Guided Caliphs". The most prominent woman was his first and beloved wife, Khadija bint Khuwailid, who was the first Muslim woman to embrace Islam. She was a prominent business woman in Mecca (Makkah). In Islamic history, most of the literature did not mention her managerial skills and abilities, i.e., how she was able to manage her business in a tribal society. We might like to know how it was possible for a woman to become a rich businesswoman in such a society. That she did so indicates that she had knowledge about different dimensions of conducting a successful business. She was apparently a very forward-looking businessperson. She collected information about the qualities of Muhammad (saw). After concluding that he is was truthful and honest person, she made an offer to him to be her working partner (which was known as *Mudharabah*[3]; partnership). As businesspeople know even today, a high degree of trust and reliability among the partners make the firm more efficient and productive. Despite her prior knowledge of his trustworthiness, Khadija sent one of her servants with Muhammad (saw) along with the trade convoy to Syria. After the end of this business trip she learned from her servant about the Prophet's (saw) behavior. From this account, we can deduce that she was an intelligent businesswoman, with

[3] *Mudharabah* is a kind of partnership where one party supplies the capital and other party supplies the labor. Profit is distributed among the partners based on predetermined conditions. However, if there is loss then only the capital provider will take a loss, not the supplier of labor.

the skills and knowledge to be successful in the import–export trade, while circumventing problems arising from asymmetric information and making very careful personnel decisions. It is also worthwhile to note that she had a sense of social responsibility. While she was running a profitable business, she was also running a hospital for patients with plague, and she was also looking after the poor members of society. Both she and the Prophet (saw) were members of a charitable organization known as "*Half ul Fudhul*", which was established in Mecca for helping unprivileged people. After a good report about the Prophet (saw) from her servant who accompanied the trade convoy to Syria, Khadija (ra) sent an offer of marriage to Muhammad.

There are other stories in different parts of the Islamic world in which women actively managed their own properties and businesses, either directly or through their agents (Krausen, 2008). Similarly Aysha (the wife of the Prophet) was a scholar with authority on Islamic jurisprudence. She gave a number of verdicts which have a central place in Islamic law. A number of companions of the Prophet (saw) consulted her on various issues after the death of the Prophet (saw). Islamic jurisprudence and theology would be incomplete without the contribution of Aysha (ra).

Another important Muslim woman was Hind bint Uqba, the wife of Abu Sufyan. She embraced Islam when Mecca was conquered by the Muslims under the leadership of Muhammad (saw). She complained to the Prophet (saw) that her husband was a miser, who did not give her and her children enough money to spend. She asked the Prophet (saw) to allow her to take her husband's money from his wallet without his permission. The Prophet replied that she may take a reasonable amount. Krausen (2008) claims this to mean that wives have the legal right to take a reasonable amount of money from the wallet of their husbands to meet the needs of themselves and their children. Later, Hind obtained an interest-free loan from *Baitul Ma'al* (treasury office of the Muslim Government) for starting a new business. The treasury office considered that, if the business is successful, it will provide additional job opportunities, and at the end she will be able to repay the loan. It was not considered whether the borrower is male or female, but rather whether the entrepreneurial and managerial skills of the borrower will result in a successful enterprise. Apparently, the office of *Baitul Ma'al* had confidence in the managerial skills of Hind. Moreover, as we have mentioned earlier there was also the prevailing sense of social responsibility so it may be helpful for the promotion of different social projects.

Zaynab bint Abi Mu'awiya was the wife of a very famous companion of the Prophet (saw), Abdullah bin Masood. Zaynab was a business woman. Her business produced and sold handicrafts, and her income was enough to support her family. However, in Islam, it is the duty of the husband to provide financially for his family, but Abdullah bin Masood was unable to do so. So Zaynab asked the Prophet (saw) whether she may give her *zakat* (religious tax) to her husband and other family members, and the Prophet (saw) said this was allowed. This indicates that if, in some families, the wife is able to earn income to support the family and the husband is not, the wife's financial support of the family is not inconsistent with Islam.

In the early period of Islamic history another very prominent woman was Shifa. Among other things, she taught the Prophet's wife, Hafsa (ra), to read and write. Shifa was also knowledgeable about the market, and so was appointed by Hafsa's father, Umar (ra), as market controller. Her duties were to enforce the rules and regulations of the market, and ensure that there was no cheating or trickery, and that transactions were consistent with Islam. Even though she was female, Umar (ra) offered her this duty based on her merit.

Acquiring knowledge is the duty of both men and women. There are numerous historical examples of male students learning from female teachers. A key example is that of one of the four great Imams, Ash-Shafi, who was the student of a female teacher, Nafisa. Similarly, a famous Muslim traveler, Ibn Battuta, was the student of many women teachers from different parts of the Islamic world. Furthermore, two of the greatest Muslim scholars, at-Tabri and Abu Hanifa, had the opinion that women can be appointed as judges.

If we examine the *hadith* (practices of the Prophet) literature, we can find women working in many different occupations. They were involved, for example, in agricultural, fabric and rug manufacturing, and trade, among other areas.

1.2 Participation of women in the economic activities during the Islamic Medieval Period

Shatzmiller (1997) states that from the 11th to the 15th century, evidence tells us that the participation of women and girls in the labor market in the Islamic world was significant and diversified. She further comments that during this period, the state of skill, degree of specialization, division of labor, degree of participation and range of occupations among Muslim women was greater than among European women at the same time. The Muslim women were involved in manufacturing as well as in the services sector and especially they were heavily involved in the textile sector. In the Islamic states during this period textile industry was the "most specialized" and "market-oriented industry". Shatzmiller (1997, p. 177) stated, "An analysis of the economic activity in which women were involved, shows that gender division of labour was prevalent and that they were employed in the industrial and service sectors, with the strongest showing in the textile industry. There women monopolized several manufacturing occupations including spinning, dying and embroidery within an industry." Generally, it was the tradition of that time that traders or farmers supplied the raw materials to the women, they made the finished goods and in this way they were directly linked with the market and had awareness about the fashion and trends of the market. The Islamic jurisprudence discusses the property rights of women, but wage contracts for women were not as available as for men. In the *Qur'an*, a wage contract for women is only mentioned for lactation: "and if you wish to engage a wet nurse you may do so if you pay her an agreed amount as is customary" (*al-Qur'an*, 2:233), implying it is not compulsory for the mother to lactate. Shatzmiller (1997) explores contracts in medieval times to which Muslim women were a party. A woman had the right to receive wages for suckling a baby even if her husband was not aware about this contract. He had no right to claim those wages. According to Granada jurist Ibn Juzayy, the status of wet nurse is like that of a hired servant. In his opinion, it is not the duty of the mother to lactate but she has to perform other household duties "*al-khidma al-batina'*, such as baking, cooking, sweeping and spreading the carpets and drawing water, but not income generating jobs such as spinning, weaving, etc." (Shatzmiller, 1997, p. 183). The wet nurse contract is considered as *ijara*. According to Islamic *fiqh*, the husband has no legal right to the income of his wife, only to the benefits of her domestic chores; it is not the responsibility of the wife to earn for her husband, whereas he has an obligation to earn in order to support her. Another early profession which was popular among women was hairdressing (beautician), for which there was great demand, especially for weddings. From an earnings point of view, at that time, hairdressing was an attractive profession for women.

During this period women also performed as an entrepreneur. There were evidences that women hired professionals, journeymen and also in some cases they hired their husbands on wages for the completion of their tasks. Women also worked as brokers, with a contract equivalent to a wage contract. They received the specified commission and also received an extra amount according to the *urf* (common law) if they performed extra tasks.

Ijliya bint al Ijli Al-Aturlabi (944–967) made significant contributions in designing and building *astrolabiya* in Syria. She learned first from her father, and then made significant contributions in the design of these scientific instruments, as well as additional contributions in navigation and timekeeping techniques. She is both an example of Islam encouraging scientific advances, and of Islam encouraging knowledge acquisition by women as well as men. In addition to her scientific contributions, she looked after the business of her father and worked in the court of Saif ad-Dawla.

During the regime of Mamluks in Egypt, the wives of soldiers were used to manage their properties. Ottoman Empire provided the management training to the women and also provided the facilities of education to the women. It is evident from the history that during that period a number of women opened *waqf* (welfare trust or charity) institutions for the poor, widows, orphans, hospitals, hostels for the students, mosques, libraries and many others. It can be concluded from the aforesaid discussion that many Muslim women were freely participating in the economy during the medieval era.[4]

In addition to wage contracts, we can also examine marriage contracts from that time. It was the verdict of the jurists of that time that a husband has no right to take all or part of his wife's wages. Wives were allowed to continue their pre-marriage professions, provided these were consistent with both the law of the land and Islamic moral standards. However, if these were unlawful and not according to the Islamic moral standards, then the husband had the right to prevent her from working. Abu Muhamad bin Abi Zayd, a jurist of the 10th century gave a *fatwa* about the wages of a slave girl who was marrying her master. While he owned the product of her labors while she was a slave, he would have no claim on the value of that product after she became his wife.[5]

1.3 Women empowerment in this modern world

At present more than 45 countries are Muslim majority countries. At present, a number of Muslim women have high-ranking positions or had

[4]For more detail see Chapter 2 of this volume.

[5]Note that the *Qu'ran* does not condone the practice of slavery, and encourages freeing of slaves in several passages, but as it was common at the time, some *fatwa* and *hadith* address slavery, marriage to slaves, the value of production of slaves, etc.

high ranks in the recent past in various Muslim countries. For example, Benazir Bhutto, Prime Minister of Pakistan; Khaleda Zia, Prime Minister of Bangladesh; Haseena Wazed, Prime Minister of Bangladesh; Tansu Çiller, Prime Minster of Turkey; Megawati Sukarnoputri, President of Indonesia; Dr Zeti Akhtar Aziz, Governor of Bank Negara, Malaysia; Dr Rabiah Adawiah, Islamic Finance Shariah Adviser with Securities Commission of Malaysia; Dr Shamshad Akhtar, Governor of Bank of Pakistan; Her Excellency Reem Ibrahim Al Hashimi, Minister of State of the UAE; Mona Al-Shinnawy, UAE, founding member of Durra; Lama Al-Sulaiman, Saudi Arabia: on board of conglomerate Rolaco, elected to Jeddah Chamber of Commerce; Thaira Karajeh, Palestine, who operates the only shopping center in the West Bank; Hanan Saab, Lebanon, founder of Pharmamed, pharmaceutical and medical supply company, and many others.

Among those countries, women are reasonably wealthy in the Gulf Cooperation Council (GCC) states.[6] More than $40 billion are owned by women in these states. However, more than 60% of this wealth is in the form of cash. Educated Muslim women are becoming more active in the economy as incomes in these countries rise. Among these states Saudi Arabia has the largest market and women in this country also have significant economic power, holding approximately $12 billion as cash funds. Currently women are involved in the manufacturing and retail sector of the economy. Approximately 55% of the university graduates are female. In Riyadh, a hotel is established for the business women. And also due to the socio-religious culture the separate office complexes for women are established in the different cities. In the finance sector of Bahrain, 30% of the employees are women, whereas in Kuwait, 40% of the employees in finance and real-estate sector are female. "The ratio of female to male tertiary enrollment in the Arab world is 108 percent" (Kazranian, 2016). Whereas the female workforce participation was also comparable to the Western world, for example, the rate in UAE is 51%, in Kuwait it is 47% and in Qatar the female participation rate is 43%. The governments of the Middle East and North Africa (MENA) region are trying to increase the female labor force participation. It is worthwhile to note that the percentage of female entrepreneurs has been increased from 4% to 10% from 2011 to 2014. Al Awar (2016, p. 15) said, "According to figures from the Dubai Women Establishment and the UAE Gender Balance

[6]Political and economic alliance of six Middle Eastern countries — Saudi Arabia, Kuwait, the United Arab Emirates, Qatar, Bahrain and Oman.

Council, ... 66% of government jobs in the Emirates are held by women as of 2015. Emirati women represent 71% of all university graduates in the country and more than 1,500 Emirati women serve in Dubai Police, 93 of whom hold leadership positions." In UAE, the composition of ministers on the basis of gender is very impressive, out of eight new ministers five are women, Her Excellency Ohood Al Roumi was appointed as Minister of State for Happiness, Her Highness Sheikha Lubna bint Khalid bin Sultan Al Qasimi appointed as Minister of International Cooperation and Development whereas 22-year-old Shamma Al Mazrui was appointed as Minister of State for Youth. Dubai Women Establishment (DWE) was formed in 2006 and its objective is to increase the involvement of the women in the socio-economic sphere. The President of DWE is Her Highness Sheikha Manal bint Mohammed bin Rashid Al Maktoum (Al Ghurair, 2016). In the MENA region, the female financial inclusion is also focused by the financial sector, for example, Kuwait Finance House, UAE's Dubai Islamic Bank and Saudi Arabia's Riyad Bank, opened female only special branches in these banks. Islamic Development Bank (IDB) is also trying to improve the conditions of Muslim women through its different strategies and plans, for example, "Women in Development Unit" established in 1998 and "Women's Advisory Panel" was established in 2004 and for the effective women empowerment "Social Capacity Development Division" (SCDD is recently established in IDB. In 2005, IDB has taken two initiatives, such as IDB Prize for Women's Contribution to Development in 2005 and the "IDB Group's Strategy for Mainstreaming Women" in 2005. The Arab Women's Enterprise Fund (AWEF) was established with the cooperation of DFID for the support of female entrepreneurs belonging to Egypt, Jordan, Libya, Morocco, Tunisia, Yemen and Palestine (Omar, 2016).

In Malaysia, Jamelah Jamaluddin was appointed as CEO in 2007 of RHB Islamic Bank and Zarinah Anwar appointed as Chairperson of Security Commission Malaysia. Hajra Adeola was the founder CEO and Managing Director of Lotus Capital (provider of *sahri'ah* compliant investment). In Maldives, Dr Aishath Muneeza (Minister, teacher, scholar and speaker) as a Deputy Finance Minister of the Maldives provided her expertise in the building of Islamic money market and Islamic capital market. She was appointed as Chairperson of the Capital Market Shari'ah Advisory Committee in 2011 and she also started the process of introducing *Sukuk* in the financial market of Maldives (Muneeza, 2016). The Chairperson and Managing Director of the Islamic Finance Centre,

Khazana Maldives, and the Islamic finance window of the Bank of Maldives is are both headed by women (Shafeega, 2016). Similarly, in Pakistan, millions of women is participating in the different socio-economic activities despite many odds in the society and their achievements are marvelous. For example, Nobel Peace Prize winner Malala Yousafzai, winner of Oscar Sharmeen Obaid-Chinoy; Khalida Brohi, founder of Sughar Foundation; Jehan Ara, President of the Pakistan Software Houses Association for IT and ITES; Anita Ghulam Ali, teacher and provincial minister; Deena M. Mistri is the first Pakistani woman who won the Fulbright Scholarship; Perween Rehman and Sabeen Mahmud are the social activists working for the Pakistan's poor women. And Dr Shamshad was appointed as the Governor of the state bank. The participation of women in the labor market is still 25%. According to the World Economic Forum 2015, Pakistan is ranked at 144 out of 145 countries (Hasan, 2016).

At the global level there are different organizations which are trying to improve the women empowerment. "Women's Islamic Initiative in Spirituality and Equality" (WISE) is an initiative which was established for increasing the participation rate of the Muslim women at the global level.

A 2016 Pew Research Center study found that Muslims worldwide (not just those in Muslim-majority countries) have 5.6 years of schooling on average, with higher levels in Europe and North America and lower levels in sub-Saharan Africa. In Muslims-majority countries, the average is 6 years of schooling (compared to a global average of 7.7 years). These figures are based on individuals aged 25 and older, and so might be expected to be low due to the low levels of education among older people. However, among those aged 25–34, Muslims still have the lowest average among major religious groups, at 6.7 years, compared to a global average of 8.6 years for this age group. The study found that Muslims worldwide have a significant gender gap in education, with an average of 4.9 years for women and 6.4 years for men. But again, there is a lot of variation in that across countries, with the largest gap (in average years) in the MENA region. This study also examines Muslim versus non-Muslim educational outcomes, and allows us to compare gender gaps between those two groups, in various regions of the world. While there are gender gaps, with men having higher education than women, in all regions, Muslims have a smaller gap than non-Muslims in Sub-Saharan Africa, and have the same gap as others in the Asia-Pacific region, with the largest gender gap in the MENA region also translating to a large gender gap for Muslims relative to non-Muslims. Again, these figures include individuals aged 25 and over, so we might hope for a more favorable picture if we examine younger cohorts.

We could look at recent educational attainment and enrollment rates at various levels to discern whether there is hope to change these statistics. Ward-Batts and Nowacki (Chapter 25 in this book) examines the impact of a change in compulsory education in Turkey in 1997 and finds that, even though the rule was gender neutral, the change resulted in a reduction in the gender gap in most parts of the country. UNICEF has had programs in various less-developed areas in recent decades aimed at increasing the enrollment at school attendance of children, but especially girls.

The combined per capita income in Muslim-majority countries overall is only about 40% of that of the world, and only about 11% of that in the high-income countries (Sherani, 2013). The rich oil-producing countries obviously have much higher per capita incomes, pulling up the average. This suggests that the remaining Muslim countries are on average quite poor. In 2016, The Federation of Pakistan Chambers of Commerce and Industry President, Abdul Rauf Alam, was quoted as saying, Muslim nations "constitute 23% of the world's population and 21.7% of the world's land mass with gross domestic product (GDP) of around $7 trillion, which is only 8% of the global GDP. Non-oil GDP of the Islamic world is a paltry 4% of the world GDP" (*The Express Tribune*, 2016).

Table 1.1 presents the labor force participation rates by gender for some selected Muslim countries. The picture painted by the labor force participation rates is a bit gloomier, but again, note that these rates include older individuals, and we expect much larger gaps among older cohorts than among younger ones. For comparison, note that the ratio of female to male labor force participation rate (modeled ILO estimate) for the world is ~0.67 in 2017.[7] That includes both rich and poor countries, and most of the example countries we have listed here are significantly below this. The silver lining behind this cloud is that by increasing the participation of women in the economy, we could substantially increase the total output of these economies. A good portion of economic growth in rich countries over the past few decades has come from the large-scale entry of women into

[7]Ratio of female to male labor force participation rate (%) (modeled ILO estimate), available at https://data.worldbank.org/indicator/SL.TLF.CACT.FM.ZS. Retrieved on 4 June 2019.

Table 1.1 Labor force participation rates of men and women aged 15–64, selected Muslim countries (%).

Country	Men	Women	Ratio (female/male)
Algeria	16.7	73	0.229
Bahrain	45.6	88.1	0.518
Egypt	24.1	77.7	0.31
Indonesia	52.9	83.7	0.632
Iran	17.9	75.2	0.238
Jordan	14.9	67.1	0.222
Kuwait	48.7	85.6	0.569
Lebanon	25.9	76.2	0.34
Malaysia	54.7	80.6	0.679
Maldives	44.9	85.1	0.528
Morocco	26.8	78.9	0.34
Oman	31.7	88.6	0.358
Pakistan	26.3	85.8	0.307
Qatar	59.2	95	0.623
Saudi Arabia	23.4	81.6	0.287
Tunisia	27.1	76.6	0.354
Turkey	36.1	77.4	0.466
UAE	41.6	92.8	0.448

Source: World Economic Forum (2018). Ratio calculated by Jennifer Ward-Batts.

the paid labor force, so countries with low female participation rates, with appropriate policies and programs, could use such an increase as a vehicle for growth.

We believe that the forces that constrain women in the Muslim world are not religion itself, but culture, social norms, laws and simply lack of opportunities due to low levels of economic development. We invite the reader to form his or her own opinion after reading and carefully considering the chapters herein.

References

Al Awar, A. M. (2016), *The Islamic Economy: Creation of Opportunities for Women in 2016 Women in Islamic Finance and Islamic Economy Report*, London: Simply Shari'ah Human Capital.

Al Ghurair, M. S. (2016), *Emirati Women: Chipping Away at the Glass Ceiling in 2016 Women in Islamic Finance and Islamic Economy Report*, London: Simply Shari'ah Human Capital.

Andrews, Helena (2006), "Muslim Women Don't See Themselves as Oppressed, Survey Finds." *New York Times*, 8 June.

Baden, Sally (1992), The position of women in Islamic countries: possibilities, constraints and strategies for change [Report prepared for the Special Programme WID, Netherlands Ministry of Foreign Affairs (DGIS)], Institute of Development Studies, Brighton, UK.

Çevi, Mustafa (2013), God and gender in Islam. *Beytulhikme An International Journal of Philosophy*, 3(2), 1–12.

Enriquez, J. (2016), *Case Study: Muslim Women Tech (MWT) in Islamic Finance and Islamic Economy Report*, London: Simply Shari'ah Human Capital.

Hasan, S. (2016), *Women in Business: Pakistan's Inspiring Entrepreneurs in Islamic Finance and Islamic Economy Report*, London: Simply Shari'ah Human Capital.

Hassan, Riffat (2001), Challenging the stereotypes of fundamentalism: An Islamic feminist perspective. *The Muslim World*, 91, 1–2.

Kazranian, S. (2016), *Aspirations and Challenges: Women's Leadership in the Middle East & North Africa in 2016 Women in Islamic Finance and Islamic Economy Report*, London: Simply Shari'ah Human Capital.

Krausen, S. H. (2008), The History of Women in Islamic Trade and Finance. *Proceedings of the Seminar: Women in Islamic Finance*, London: Norton Rose LLP.

Lipka, Michael, (2017), "Muslims and Islam: Key Findings in the U.S. and Around the World", available at https://www.pewresearch.org/fact-tank/2017/08/09/muslims-and-islam-key-findings-in-the-u-s-and-around-the-world/. Retrieved on 30 April 2019.

Moghadam, Valentine M. (1991), The reproduction of gender inequality in Muslim societies: A case study of Iran in the 1980s. *World Development*, 19(10), 1335–1349.

Muneeza, A. (2016), *Islamic Finance: A Journey of Commitment in Islamic Finance and Islamic Economy Report*, London: Simply Shari'ah Human Capital.

Omar, M. A. (2016), *Case Study: Islamic Development Bank Financial Inclusion & Promoting Women in Islamic Finance and Islamic Economy Report*, London: Simply Shari'ah Human Capital.

Perkins, Dwight H., Radelet, Steven and Lindauer, David L. (2006), *Economics of Development*. 6th ed., New York: W.W. Norton & Company.

Pew Research Center (2016), "Religion and Education around the World", available at http://assets.pewresearch.org/wp-content/uploads/sites/11/2016/12/21094148/Religion-Education-ONLINE-FINAL.pdf. Retrieved on 30 April 2019.

Rachidi, S. (2016), *Millennial Generation: Female Expectations in 2016 Women in Islamic Finance and Islamic Economy Report*, London: Simply Shari'ah Human Capital.

Rettig, Jessica (2011), "Women Could Promote Rights Through Islam". *US News & World Report*. Retrieved on 12 January 2019.

Rizzo, Helen, Meyere, Katherine and Abdel-Latif, Abdel-Hamid (2007), The relationship between gender equality and democracy: A comparison of Arab vs. Non-Arab Muslim societies. *Sociology*, 41, 1151–170.

Shafeega, F. (2016), *Women in Islamic Finance: Creating the Leadership Pipelines in Islamic Finance and Islamic Economy Report*, London: Simply Shari'ah Human Capital.

Shatzmiller, M. (1997), Women and wage labour in the Medieval Islamic west: Legal issues in an economic context. *Journal of the Economic and Social History of the Orient*, 40(2), 174–206.

Sherani, Sakib (2013), "Economies of the Ummah" *Dawn*, available at https://www.dawn.com/news/1035026. Retrieved on 30 April 2019.

The Express Tribune (2016), "Muslim States Make Thin Contribution to Global Economy" 22 September 2016, available at https://tribune.com.pk/story/1186109/trailing-behind-muslim-states-make-thin-contribution-global-economy/. Retrieved on 30 April 2019.

Thompson, William and Hickey, Joseph (2005), *Society in Focus*, Pearson: Boston, MA.

United Nations Statistics Division (2002), "United Nations Statistics Division — Classifications Registry: International Standard Industrial Classification of All Economic Activities, Rev. 3, Gender, Research Guides", available at unstats.un.org/unsd. Retrieved on 12 January 2019.

World Bank (2011), *World Development Report 2012: Gender Equality and Development*, Washington DC: World Bank.

World Economic Forum (2018), "Global Gender Gap Report 2018", available at http://www3.weforum.org/docs/WEF_GGGR_2018.pdf. Retrieved on 6 June 2019.

PART A
Theoretical Issues

Chapter 2

Economic Empowerment of Women in Islam

Abdul Azim Islahi

Abstract

The most important aspect of women's economic empowerment in Islam is that it has recognized their separate and independent identity and gave them numerous economic rights such as right to own property, share inheritance, engage in various economic activities to increase their fortune, etc. Their economic roles in Islam are governed by the broad principle of division of labor. This division of labor is based on their natural comparative advantages. Man has to look after the affairs outside the home while woman has to take care of the inside. All are accountable in his or her sphere of jurisdiction. Her services have economic value no less than man's. It is therefore obligatory for husbands to spend on their wives. The division of work and different sphere of activities prescribed by Islam is applicable in general and in normal conditions. In emergencies and special circumstances there may be change of their roles or they can join hands to share responsibilities of one another. However, a woman is never required to spend on herself or her family. Her economic support is responsibility of her father before marriage and her husband after marriage. In their absence, other near relative has to take care of her expenses. Failing that the society and finally the state will have to take this responsibility.

Keywords: Women and Islam, Economic empowerment, Property rights, Inheritance, Dowry, Waqf and women

Economic empowerment of women is the most important aspect of the debate on overall empowerment of a Muslim woman. Economic roles of man and woman in Islam are strictly based on the broad principle of division of labor so that a practical, durable pattern of peaceful family life may be established which assigns to every part its place in a well-organized whole. Man has to look after the affairs outside the home while woman has to take care of the inside. This division of labor is based on their natural characteristics.[1] Man can do hard work. He is physically powerful and more suitable to head the family. He has strong willpower and is capable to exercise authority, while a woman is by nature very emotional and vulnerable to external influences. She is ill-equipped for the hardship of life and burden of management and control of the family. She is more suitable to look after household affairs. However, all are accountable in his or her sphere of jurisdiction. A man is the guardian of his family and is responsible for them. A woman is the guardian of her husband's house and is responsible for it (Al-Bukhari, 2002, 2:6, *hadith* no. 593; 7:34, *hadith* no. 5188).

It must be remembered that her services have economic value exactly as man's. It is therefore obligatory for husbands to spend on their wives. Additionally, they have been given economic rights such as independent ownership, inheritance, etc. without being responsible to spend on themselves and the household.

The *Qur'an* has made clear that both men and women are equal in the sight of the Creator. It declared: "O Mankind, keep your duty to your Lord who created you from a single soul and from it created its mate (of same kind) and from them twain has spread a multitude of men and women..." (*Qur'an* 4:1). Men and women are equal human being as they have been created of the same species and they have the same origin.

However, like all species, there are certain differences in their natural qualities. And by nature, generally, they choose different roles in the family while living together. Islam has taken into account these natural differences while assigning duties and rights to men and women. Their roles are equally valuable. They are not mutually exclusive. Rather they are complementary to each other. Allah Almighty says: "And do not covet that by which Allah has made some of you excel others; men shall have the benefit of what they earn and women shall have the benefit of what they earn; and ask Allah of His grace; surely Allah knows all things" (*Qur'an* 4:32). They are considered partners (*awliya'*) of one another. "The Believers, men and women, are protectors one of another: they enjoin what is just and forbid what is evil: they observe regular prayers, practise regular charity, and obey

[1]That the male and female are not equal by nature in their physical and psychological constituents is too obvious to prove it by evidence. It is not specific to human being. One can easily observe it among other species around us.

Allah and His Messenger. On them will Allah pour His mercy: for Allah is Exalted in power, Wise" (*Qur'an* 9:71).

Man is financially responsible for his family. "Men are the protectors and maintainers of women, because Allah has given the one more (strength) than the other, and because they support them from their means. Therefore the righteous women are devoutly obedient, and guard in (the husband's) absence what Allah would have them guard..." (*Qur'an* 4:34). Thus, Islam makes women free from the stress of earning money for the maintenance of household, so that they can fully devote themselves to nurturing children and taking care of family affairs.

It may be noted that the division of work and different sphere of activities prescribed by Islam is enforceable in normal conditions. In emergencies and special circumstances, there may be the change of their roles or they can join hands to share responsibilities of one another. As we shall discuss in the following pages, Islam gave women various economic rights such as right to inheritance, right to do business and participate in trade, right to dowry, and other avenues are clear proofs that women can participate in socio-economic activities if so needed. Thus, this *division of labor* is not a watertight compartment. A lady companion of the Prophet used to help her husband in agricultural activities (Al-Bukhari, 1987, 7: 45–46, *hadith* no. 5224). Similarly, for men also it is not only permissible but also praiseworthy to help in domestic works. There are reports that the Prophet (pbuh) used to help his family in preparation of flour for bread, sewing the cloth, milking the goat, cleaning the house, etc. (Ibn Sayyid al-Nas, 1986, 2:426).

2.1 Guarantee of expenses of women's maintenance

In Islam, women are not obligated to earn or spend any money on housing, food or general expenses. Before marriage, responsibility of raising the daughter, her education and training rests on the shoulder of the father. In the absence of father, this responsibility belongs to her closest male relative (brother, uncle, etc.). After marriage her husband must fully support her financially.

It is obligatory on the husband to provide his wife with reasonable accommodation according to his means and ability and to spend on her food and other needs. This is the requirement of the husband being head of the family and its maintainer (*qawwam*) as mentioned in the following

Qur'anic verse: "Men are the protectors and maintainers (*qawwam*) of women, because Allah has made one of them to excel the other, and because they spend (to support them) from their means" (*Qur'an* 4:34). If a husband does not spend on his wife and children reasonably, the wife has been permitted to take what is reasonably sufficient for her and her children from his assets without his permission. It is reported that the Prophet (pbuh) said to Hind bint 'Utbah when she complained to him that her husband Abu Sufyan was falling short in his spending on her and on her children "Take what is sufficient for you and your children on a reasonable basis" (Al-Bukhari, 1987, 3:103, *hadith* no. 2211; 7:85, *hadith* no. 5364).

If a husband cannot spend on his wife, then she has the right to get a separation from him, according to a number of scholars like Imam Malik, Shafi'i, Ahmad b. Hanbal among others (Al-Qurtubi, 2003, 3:155). Even after divorce he cannot turn the divorcee out. He has to provide her with fooding, lodging and other expenses for a certain period called "*iddah*". "Lodge them (the divorced women) where you dwell, according to your means" (*Qur'an* 65:6). It is because of this reason that they are a degree above their wives though both have rights and duties over each other. Almighty Allah says, "... And they (women) have rights similar to those (of men) over them according to what is equitable, and men are a degree above them. Allah is Mighty, Wise" (*Qur'an* 2:228).

Although Islam does not impose on a woman any expenditure on household, she can spend on the family including her husband voluntarily if he is financially very weak or unable to work. No doubt she has right, as noted earlier, to get rid of such a penniless husband.

2.2 Property right

In economic empowerment the first and the most important thing is right to own property. In many systems women's independent entity is not recognized. No question of independent property rights. After marriage, a woman even loses her maiden name. In Islam, the case is quite different. She can retain her maiden name as she has been given a separate identity in spite of being a wife. She has also been given property rights which is meant to provide her double security in the sense that fulfillment of her all needs has already been guaranteed in the Islamic family system. A husband cannot take anything away from her belonging without her consent. He is still required to bear her financial burden as if she had nothing in her possession to support herself with.

A woman can own, acquire and dispose property as a man does. She is free to mortgage, to give it in lease, or bequeath it, sell or buy it or exploit it for her own benefit. Her property rights is clearly understood from various *Qur'anic* verses.[2]

Since women have property rights independent from their husbands', and they have various source of income, they are equally demanded to fulfill various monetary obligation such as payment of *zakah*, help of poor, voluntary expenditure in deeds of piety and social welfare, bearing different financial penalty on certain religious offenses (*kaffarat*). These are in turn further proofs of their separate and independent property rights. However, their normal living expenses will be still duty of their husbands or other nearest relatives.

2.3 Dowry and gift

The marriage stage is very decisive in the life of a woman. She leaves her parental home for a new world, almost strange to her. She comes out from her parents and relative's guardianship to a new guard — her husband. This requires strong and assured security for her. Islam made her husband responsible for her protection and to meet her all necessary requirements — fooding, lodging, clothing and cure. Along with this guarantee she must have some resources to have further feeling of economic strength. Islam has considered this aspect of her life as well and made her entitled to a financial payment called *mahr* or *sidaq* (dowry)[3] from her husband at the time of marriage. "And give to the women (whom you marry) their dowry with a good heart, but if they, of their own good pleasure, give up any part of it to you, then take it, and enjoy it with pleasure and good cheer" (*Qur'an* 4:4).

The amount of dowry can be decided mutually and depending on the financial conditions of the husband and social status of the wife. It may

---

[2]For example see the following two verses of the *Qur'an* that clearly reveals property right of women:
"From what is left by parents and those nearest related there is a share for men and a share for women, whether the property be small or large, — a determinate share" (4:7), and
"Men shall have a share of that which they have earned, and women a share of that which they have earned. And ask Allah of His bounty. Surely, Allah has perfect knowledge of all things" (4:32).
[3]It is defined as obligatory valuable objects — such as money, precious metals, etc. — fixed at the time of marriage to be given by the husband to his wife.

be a very small amount or a very huge. However, an exorbitant amount may create some social problems. Men with limited resources may not find wherewithal to marry causing delay in wedding and some men and women remaining unmarried. It is therefore the second Caliph Umar b. al-Khattab once announced that he wanted to fix the ceiling of dowry to be 400 dirhams. However, he refrained because of an objection raised by a woman who questioned him how should you fix it while Almighty Allah said, "Do not take back from divorced woman even if you have given any one of them a *qintar* of gold" (*Qur'an* 4:20). There are various interpretation of the word *qintar* ranging from 1,000 gold dinar to 80,000 gold dinar. It is also said that *qintar* here means a mountain of gold (Abi Hatim, n.d., 3:906–907).

As far the time of payment is concerned, it may be cash or credit. Marriage will be valid even if the *mahr* is not mentioned at the time of marriage. This does not mean that the husband can deny it. It will remain due. In this case, she will be entitled of *mahr mithl* (dowry of the equivalent). That is, equal to the amount of *mahr* which is commonly fixed for similar ladies among her relatives or similar other women (Al-Sughdi, 1984, 1:298). If a marriage is broken at the very outset without establishing physical relations, she has to be paid half of the fixed *mahr* as mentioned in the *Qur'an* (33:49).

It is established from various *Qur'anic* verses (*Qur'an*, 4:24; 5:5; 60:10) that the *mahr* is an undeniable right of women and no husband can interfere with it. It is legally owned by her. Neither her parents nor the husband can take any part of it without her approval and consent. Muslim jurists are of the opinion that if the dowry was not paid at the time of marriage, the wife has right to demand the same from the husband any time. In case of delay or denial of the payment she is fully allowed to appeal to the *qadi* (judge) or to a court (Islahi, 2010, p. 11).

2.4 Inheritance

One of the most important aspects of economic empowerment of women by Islam is holding them entitled of inheritance. In the pre-Islamic period, they had no such right because they were not considered as the earning member of the family (Al-Suyuti, 2003, 4:286). Inheritance rights was confined among the male members of the family only. Surprisingly enough, in many cases women themselves were considered as an object of inheritance. The *Qur'an* says, "O you who believe! You are forbidden to inherit women against their will ..." (4:20). In the interpretation of this verse, a number of scholars have reported that in the pre-Islamic period when a person died, his heirs had the right to marry his wife (Al-Bukhari, 1987, 6:55, hadith no. 4579; 9:27, *hadith* no. 6948). Islam abolished this unjust pre-Islamic tradition and gave them honor and economic power by giving them the right to ownership and inherit property from parents and relatives. "For men is a share of that which parents and near relatives leave; and for women is a share of that which parents and near relatives leave, whether there is little or much of it — a determined share" (*Qur'an* 4:7). No doubt it was a revolutionary step at the time when it was declared and for many centuries to come. Many societies around the world still deny women's inheritance rights.

Attention may be drawn to the aforementioned *Qur'anic* verse. It did not say that men and women have share of what parents and near relatives leave. Rather it stated, "For men is a share of that which parents and near relatives leave; and for women is a share of that which parents and near relatives leave." This repetition is clearly for emphasis and to remind that women's share is independent and they are not appended to men. This reiteration is also meant to reject pre-Islamic practice of Arabs who denied inheritance rights of women and children (Al-Suyuti, 2003, 4:375). According to a contemporary scholar the *Qur'an* pays more attention to and is more emphatic on women's share in inheritance than men's share (Subhani, 2011, 240). Nadwi (2011, 188–193) shows that in distribution of inheritance, the *Qur'an* mentions women many times more than men.

A woman receives a certain share of her deceased relative's property as a daughter, wife, mother or sister. The size of the share depends on how closely she is related to the deceased and how many heirs are there. A closer look into the Islamic system of inheritance would reveal that the shares of inheritors have been decided based on one or more of the following factors:

(1) Nearness with the deceased person. A closer relative has more entitlement of inheritance than a distant. The former may eliminate sometimes the latter from getting a share.
(2) Stage of the life — whether one is in his/her young age of career or he/she is in retiring age where one has no obligation of supporting others.
(3) Financial responsibilities that one has to bear in the family.

One can see easily that in the aforementioned causations, (2) and (3) are related to economic reasoning. Only those who are ignorant of these factors, raise objections against the Islamic system of inheritance distribution. Again, based on sheer ignorance generally it is alleged that Islamic rule is to give women half of a man's share in inheritance. It is interesting to point out that in this distribution the term of reference is woman's share. It has been said that the son shall get a portion equal to that of two daughters. "Allah (thus) directs you as regards your Children's (inheritance): to the male, a portion equal to that of two females" (*Qur'an*, 4:11). It never says that a woman shall get "half" of a man. There is much difference between the two statements. While former may not hurt the feeling of a woman, the latter statement is contemptuous to her. Moreover, it must be remembered that to allocate a male twice as much as a female is *not* a general rule. It has been ordained only where the male's financial responsibilities are much greater than the female which is quite natural and justified. For example, among the deceased's son and daughter, the son gets twice as much as the daughter because man alone has to bear the expenses of family maintenance. The woman is under no such obligation. It can be easily assumed that the half which is received by the daughter will remain intact as she has no financial responsibility. Rather it may increase getting money from other sources, while the share of the son will start diminishing due to his financial obligations.[4] Thus, it is not correct to say that in inheritance woman receives a share less than that of man, as in view of his obligations it is the requirement of justice that male should get here double of what a woman gets. It is not discrimination; it is fairness. A very important economic reasoning has been observed in the fixation of shares in inheritance as noted previously. Where no such reason exists, Islam awards female a share in inheritance equal to male. For instance, in case there is no son of the deceased, and "if only daughters, two or more, their share is two-thirds of the inheritance; if only one, her share is a half" (*Qur'an*, 4:11). In this very situation (i.e., no son, only daughter) if the deceased left the parents also, then each father and the mother shall get "a sixth of the inheritance" (*Qur'an*, 4:11) — *equal share*. It is interesting to note that in some cases *a female can get even more than a male*. For example, if heirs

[4]How quickly a woman's assets may increase and that of a man may diminish can be illustrated with an interesting example. Suppose a man dies leaving a legacy of $45,000. His heirs comprise unmarried daughter and son. The daughter gets $15,000, while the son of the deceased gets $30,000. Soon they marry and the dower of each is fixed $20,000. That is, the woman shall get from her husband $20,000 while the man will pay $20,000 to his bride. Now the daughter's asset will become $35,000, while the son's balance from the inheritance will remain $10,000 only. In addition, he has to bear the maintenance expenditure of the family.

consist of a daughter, a brother and the husband, in this case the daughter of the deceased shall get 50% and the husband and the brother each shall get 25%. Of course, here the category of the female is different from the two males. The factor of nearness with the deceased has worked, mentioned earlier as (1).

2.5 Right to work and earn

The *Qur'an* has strengthened the economic position of women by permitting them to work and keep the amount earned from their work. It emphatically said this by separately mentioning that "women shall have a portion of that which they earn" as it mentioned about men that they shall have "a portion of that which they earn" (*Qur'an*, 4:33). It is worthwhile to reiterate, if a Muslim female earns, then she is not responsible for supporting the family and she can use and spend her earning as she likes, whereas a Muslim man is under an obligation to take care of the entire family and spend on his all dependents. Perhaps one may not be incorrect if he thinks that in economic empowerment Islamic teachings are highly biased toward women!

No injustice or discrimination is allowed with women if she is employed. Muhammad Qutb has rightly said: "... so far as their earnings are concerned, there is no difference between man and woman; nor in their wages for a work, nor in the profit gained in trade, nor in revenues from land etc., for, in these matters Islam follows another law, the law treating on a perfectly equal footing man and woman with regard to their labors and the wages thereof. No injustice is to be done to either of them" (Qutb, 1978, p. 126).

As we mentioned at the outset, based on division of labor in view of comparative natural advantage, the most suitable scope of work for women is household management. However, Islam does not forbid them from working outside, without any controversy, whenever it is unavoidable. In the story of Moses it is said: "when he arrived at the water of Madyan (Midian), he found there a party of men, watering their flocks. And he found beside them two women holding back their flocks. He said, 'What is your problem?' They replied, 'We cannot water our flocks until the shepherds depart with their flocks, and our father is a very old man"' (28:23). It is clear from this story that if it is necessary for women to go out for work, they can do it, provided they avoid mixing with men and observe rules prescribed for them.

Engagement in economic activities and carrying business may not be always out of necessity. It may be done for empowerment of oneself which is accepted in Islam. It has been reported that during the days of the Prophet (pbuh) there were many women who engaged in economic activities and enhanced their own income and the income of their families. For example, Umm al-Muminin Khadijah had international trading in pre-Islamic period (Ibn Kathir, 1:262–263) which she continued after Islam. Qilah al-Anmariyah was also a business lady. She inquired Prophet (pbuh) about bargaining in sale and purchase. He advised her to avoid quoting unrealistic prices (Ibn Athir, n.d., 5:535). Al-Rubayyi bint al-Muawwadh also was engaged in perfume trading in Madinah (Ibn Abd al-Barr, 2002, p. 396). Hawla' had such a famous perfume business that she was known as *al-attarah* (one who sells *itr*, i.e., perfume) (Ibn Abd al-Barr, 2002, 5: 532–533). Umm al-Muminin Zaynab bint Jahsh was an expert of handicraft. She used to manufacture various items to sell and spend income in the way of Allah as she did not need money for her own expenses (Ibn Athir, n.d., 5:465). Abu Mas'ud Ansari's wife Zaynab was also an expert of handicraft. She voluntarily spent money on her husband and children as he was unable to earn money (Ibn Athir, n.d., 5:463).

We find many examples of ladies who worked in the battle field performing works of their talents such as nursing, store-keeping, supplying drinking water, etc. They received shares in the booty (Waqidi, 1966, 2:685–687). In the battle of Khaybar, 20 women accompanied the Muslim fighters (Waqidi, 1966, p. 685).

Breast feeding and nursing children was also considered a noble job for ladies since ancient days.[5] We know how Halimah Sadiyah and many other women from Taif came to Makkah in search of babies to feed them. Mother Halimah was the luckiest woman to get baby Muhammad who was going to be prophet one day (pbuh) (Ibn Hisham, n.d., pp. 160–164). It is reported that a woman named Umm Atiyah used to perform circumscription for women (Al-Baghawi, 1983, 12:111).

Even a few women engaged in cultivation. Jabir b. Abdullah reports that the Prophet (pbuh) allowed his maternal aunt (*khalah*) to go to work in the garden of dates instead of staying at home after divorce so that she might spend her earning in some charitable deeds (Al-Qushayri (n.d.),

[5]The job of breastfeeding was common in Egypt during Pharaoh's time. Due to this practice, baby Moses could be returned to his mother (cf. *Qur'an* 28:12–13).

4:200, *hadith* no. 3794). We have already noted that Asma bt. Abu Bakr used to help her husband Zubayr b. al-Awwam in agricultural work (Al-Bukhari, 2002, 3:1679–80, *hadith* no. 5224). There was arrangement of financing by the *bayt al-mal* (public treasury) and women also could borrow from it. Hind the wife of Abu Sufyan borrowed 4,000 dirham from *bayt al-mal* for trading purpose (Al-Tabari, 1407H, pp. 576–577). Muslim governments or voluntary organizations can come forward to extend finance to women to improve their economic conditions. They are mostly in need of microfinance.[6]

These examples can be multiplied if we go in detailed search of early sources of Islamic history. However, the evidences presented here are enough to show that in Islam women are free to engage in various economic activities to increase their fortune. They can decide, depending on the individual circumstances and with mutual consultation, to stay at home managing its affairs or to work outside it. Of course, remaining under the Shariah limitations.

2.6 Measures prescribed for economic empowerment after divorce

Divorce affects the whole family tremendously, especially the woman. Therefore, it has been considered in Islam as the worst kind of *halal* (permitted rule) (Abu Dawud, n.d., 2:220, *hadith* no. 2180). Hence, Islam prescribed measures that could check or minimize its occurrence in the Muslim society.[7] To provide a divorce woman with financial security and self-reliance, Islam allows her to keep whatever she owned before marriage and whatsoever she earned after it. The former husband has no right to take back any of her belongings including dowry and gifts. In addition, the divorced woman is entitled of accommodation and expenses for interim period, provision (*mut'ah*) at departure, and payment for feeding the child.

[6]Bangladesh Gramin Bank has played a revolutionary role in this respect. But unfortunately, it is an interest-based financing, sometimes charging interest up to 20%.

[7]Like emphasis to solve disputes mutually and graciously involving mediators from both sides (*Qur'an* 4:35); if decided, divorce acts in three stages — in the first stage he can withdraw; in the second stage, the two have equal rights to decide reunion after fresh *nikah* (for details see any book of exegesis); in the third stage, they lose all opportunities except that she marries to someone else and he also divorces her (*Qur'an* 2:230). Of course, this should not be pre-planned. For details one can refer to any book of jurisprudence chapter on *al-talaq* (the divorce). All these measures are meant to be taken seriously.

All these are related to her economic empowerment as discussed in the following paragraphs:

Accommodation and expenditure upon her: After divorce during the counting or waiting period (*iddah*) the former husband cannot force her out of the house, nor should she get out of the house on her own (*Qur'an* 65:1). She should stay there as if it is her own house and the husband has to bear her expenses. If she gets out on her own, then she will deprive herself from expenses as well (*Qur'an* 2:240). The husband has to keep her in his dwelling according to his means and he must not harm her (*Qur'an* 65:6). "Let the man of means spend according to his means: and the man whose resources are restricted, let him spend according to what Allah has given him. Allah puts no burden on any person beyond what He has given him. After a difficulty, Allah will soon grant relief" (*Qur'an* 65:7). It is generally mentioned that the reason for this is that the husband may withdraw his words if he has pronounced single *talaq* (the Arabic word for divorce), or they may decide to reunion if he has pronounced twice. Therefore, some *ulama* have suggested that she should stay there with full makeup (Al-Haskafi, 1386H, 3:408). Apart from this clear reasoning, it may be said that the additional objective is that the woman should not be on the street the next day. She should get enough time to manage her affairs.

Provision (*mut'ah*): Islam asks the former husband to part with the divorced woman in kindness and let her go amicably (*Qur'an* 65:2; 2:229, 231). If anything is outstanding from her dowry, he must pay it to her before departure. He should also arrange some provisions (*mut'ah*) for her (*Qur'an* 2:241), especially those women with whom he has not established consummation relations and even *mahr* was not fixed: "O ye who believe! When ye marry believing women, and then divorce them, then there is no period (of waiting) that you should reckon. So make some provision for them and let them go amicably" (*Qur'an* 33:49). A similar verse has occurred in *Surat al-Baqarah* verse number 236. "It is no sin for you if you divorce women while yet you have not touched them, nor appointed unto them their *mahr*. Provide for them, the rich according to his means, and the straitened according to his means, a fair provision. (This is) a bounden duty for those who do good".

The *Qur'an* further says: "And if ye divorce them before consummation, but after the fixation of a dower for them, then the half of the dower (is due to them), unless they remit it or (the man's half) is remitted by him in whose hands is the marriage tie; and the remission (of the man's half) is the nearest to righteousness. And do not forget liberality between yourselves. For Allah sees well all that ye do" (2:237). In this way the *Qur'an* emphasizes that both the solemnizing marriage and severance of marital relation have to be concluded handsomely and in both cases some provisions have to be made for the woman.

Not only at the time of divorce, but even in the case of his last illness in which the husband is about to die, the *Qur'an* advised that "those of you who are about to die and leave behind them wives, they should bequeath unto their wives a provision for the year without turning them out, but if they go out (of their own accord) there is no sin for you in that which they do of themselves within their rights. Allah is Mighty, Wise" (2:240). However, it is said that later Almighty Allah Himself took care of it and prescribed a share for her in the legacy of the dying husband (Al-Qurtubi, 2003, 3:174, 226–228). Therefore, this order stands abrogated.[8]

Payment for breastfeeding: After divorce the father cannot compel the mother for breast feeding to the delivered baby or the infant who is in the milk-sucking age. The mother is the owner of her milk. If he wants her to feed his baby, he has to pay her for it. The *Qur'an* says "Lodge them (the divorced women) where you dwell, according to your means, and harass them not so as to straiten life for them. And if they are pregnant, then spend (your substance) on them until they deliver their burden: and if they give suck for you, give them their due payment and consult together, according to what is just and reasonable. But if you make difficulties for one another, then let some other woman give suck for him (the father of the child)" (65:6). At another occasion it has given detailed instructions on the issue of suckling the child:

"Mothers shall suckle their children for two whole years; (that is) for those who wish to complete the suckling. The duty of feeding and clothing nursing mothers in a seemly manner is upon the father of the child. No-one should be charged beyond his capacity. A mother should not be made to suffer because of her child, nor should he to whom the child is born (be made to suffer) because of his child. And on the (father's) heir is incumbent the like of that (which was incumbent on the father). If they desire to wean the child by mutual consent and (after) consultation, it is no sin for them; and if ye wish to give your children out to nurse, it is no sin for you, provided that ye pay what is due from you in kindness. Observe your duty to Allah, and know that Allah is Seer of what ye do" (2:233).

---

[8]It may be noted that Almighty Allah Himself used the verb "*yusī*" (He bequeaths) whose root is "*wasiyah*" (bequest) (see *Qur'an* 4:11).

2.7 Marriage — an institution to economically support and empower a woman

We have seen previously how at marriage a woman gets a handsome amount in the form of dowry in addition to guarantee of all her expenses by her husband. To see from this angle, one can rightly conclude that in Islam marriage is a very important source to empower women economically. Almighty Allah has also assured it:

"And arrange marriages for widows from among you, and for your male slaves and female slaves who are fit for marriage. *If they be poor, Allah will grant them means out of His bounty*; and Allah is Bountiful, All-Knowing" (24:32).

In a *hadith* it has been said, "A woman may be married for four things: her wealth, her lineage, her beauty or her religious commitment. Choose the one who is religious, may your hands be rubbed with dust [i.e., may you prosper]!" (Al-Bukhari, 1987, 7:9, *hadith* no. 5090). The emphasis in this *hadith* to prefer religious girl over the rich one, no doubt, shows importance of the religion in Muslim life. But at the same time, it is also understood from this *hadith* that one should marry a poor but religious to become her economic support, rather than marrying a rich lady to be dependent on her wealth.

2.8 Some voluntary measures

Various forms of economic empowerment noted earlier are generally in the framework of family life. No doubt, a woman's economic support is responsibility of her father before marriage and husband after marriage. In their absence, other near relatives have to take care of her expenses and support her financially. Failing that the society and finally the state has to play its role in economic empowerment of women. State is not to provide stipend only to poor and destitute women, it has to support them financially for economic enterprises if they wish and have capabilities, as we have seen previously in case of Hind bint Utbah.

In the Muslim society, there are various institutions for this purpose such as *zakah*, *awqaf* and *jama'iyat khayriyah* (voluntary welfare societies). From the *zakah* a woman can be helped to the extent that she becomes rich, as it is reported from 'Umar, who declared, "When you give, make [the recipient] rich" (Al-Bayhaqi, 1344H, 7:23; Abu Ubayd, 2010, p. 676.).

Especially, the *waqf* has been a very effective source for women's financial help in Islam. In Islamic history, there had been *awqaf* particularly for the help of women. Zubayr ibn al-Awwam dedicated houses for his non-accepted (*al-mardudah*) daughters (Al-Darimi, 1407H. 2:518, *hadith* no. 3300). Ibn Battutah has reported that he found *waqf* in Tunis and Syria for marriage of poor girls (Ibn Battutah, 1985, p. 104).

Resourceful ladies have also participated in establishment of *awqaf* throughout Islamic history. Al-Khassaf (d. 261H), reports that the Prophet's (pbuh) wives — Aishah, Umm Salmah, Umm Habibah, Safiyah and Hafsah (may Almighty Allah be pleased with all of them) — established *awqaf* (Al-Khassaf, n.d., pp. 13–14). Afifi (1991, pp. 183, 240), reports that during the Mamluk period women also participated actively in establishment of waqf foundations. The Ottoman history of awqaf is full of such examples.[9]

A woman can be caretaker or supervisor of a *waqf* (Al-Tarabulusi, 1902, p. 49). Umm al-Muminin Hafsah bint Umar looked after the *waqf* of her father Umar (Abu Dawud, n.d., 3:79, *hadith* no. 2881). In practice many women performed this function in the 16th century (el-Zawahreh, 1992, pp. 118–119, 138; Afifi, p. 243). It may be noted that in the inheritance of a deceased person the male gets double of female but if he establishes a family *waqf*, he is allowed to stipulate equal benefits for both male and female progeny (Ibn Qudamah, 1405H, 8:206). Jurists have also made it clear, if someone creates a *waqf* for his children, his female progeny shall be included without discrimination. Everyone shall be paid equally (Al-Mirdawi, 1419H, 7:25). Thus, *waqf* institution provides women with great opportunity to financially support themselves and contribute to the economic empowerment of other women.

2.9 Concluding remarks

The most important aspect of women's economic empowerment is that Islam has recognized their separate and independent personality which is not merged with men on account of birth or marriage. There is no doubt that someone can be empowered only if he or she has independent entity. A slave girl cannot be empowered. Islam guarantees women fulfillment of their basic needs — before marriage, after marriage and even after divorce. So far, if a woman has got a relative, howsoever distant, she need not take upon herself the support of her family. In addition, she has been granted many economic rights such as proprietary rights over her valuables

[9]See the tract *Dawr al-mar'ah fi'l-waqf* (role of women in *waqf*), pp. 14–19, which is a chapter of a master dissertation entitled *Athar al-waqf ala al-dawah al-nisaiyah* (impact of *waqf* on women's preaching) by al-Uthman (n.d.).

and belongings, inheritance rights in different capacities — daughter, wife, mother, sister, etc. She also has the right to engage in earning money activities, if she desires so or circumstances demand it. She is the sole owner of whatever income she earns and full authority to use them. None is allowed to take anything from her assets without her consent, not even her husband. The maintenance of the family is the full responsibility of the husband even if the wife is better off than her husband. These rights bring immense social gains to women and strengthen their position.

Although it is not obligatory for a woman to spend on upkeep of the household, it is but natural that she would contribute voluntarily toward the maintenance of the family if man is helpless.[10] In totality men and women are partners in maintaining family. In this it is duty of men to work to provide for the family and women are to manage household and take care of the domestic work, to devote to the upbringing and educational development of their children and to look after the comfort of the family. Muslim women believe that their role in household management and rearing children is no less than genuine economic activity in addition to being good deed to be rewarded in the Hereafter. This is the reason that there has been never a general trend among them to do jobs outside the home or manage businesses. They believe that the contribution they make to household administration and education and training of children is no less important than any economic enterprise and the love, affection and enjoyment that they get from their husbands and other family members are much more valuable than earning money. Thus, there is a need to strike balance between permission and obligation, between rights and duties.

Lastly, looking into the fact that Islam gives women all economic rights, without financial obligation, and guarantee fulfillment of their needs at all stages of life — before marriage, after marriage and at separation from their husbands — one may not be wrong to think that Islam has given women extraordinary importance and unprecedented favor. However, it is also a fact that in a larger part of Muslim world, women are prevented from exercising their right to work outside and earn money. They are deprived from acquiring property. They are hardly given their shares in inheritance. Ironically in many parts of the Muslim world, contrary to Islamic teachings,

[10]Zainab, the wife of a well-known companion Abdullah bin Masud, came to the Prophet and told him that her husband is a poor man, but that she in her own right was better off. Would it be an act of spiritual merit if she assisted her husband out of her own means? The Holy Prophet told her that spending on her husband would be doubly meritorious, as it would rank both as charity and as graciousness (Ibn Athir, n.d., 5:463).

husbands demand dowry or offering from the parents of the girls. The *mahr* is fixed only to get it from the wives. In some countries, parents of the girl agree to be a part of it.

These un-Islamic practices show the gap between Islamic teachings and practice in Muslim families and create an impression that Muslim women are the most backward and oppressed ones. And Islam is blamed ignorantly or deliberately for their un-Islamic acts. The change in this deplorable condition can be brought only through a process of re-education, enlightenment, and inculcation of piety and fear of Allah in the heart.

References

Arabic

Abu Dawud (n.d.), *Sunan Abi Dawud*, Beirut: Dar al-Kitab al-Arabi.

Abu Ubayd (2010), *Kitab al-Amwal*, Beirut: Dar al-Fikr.

Afifi, Muhammad (1991), *Al-Awqaf wa'l Hayat al-Iqtisadiyah fi Misr fi'l-Asr al-Uthmani*, n. p. al-Hay'at al-Misriyah al-Ammah li'l-Kitab.

Al-Baghawi, Husayn b, Masud (1983), *Sharh a-Sunnah*, Beirut and Damascus: al-Maktab al-Islami.

Al-Bayhaqi, Abu Bakr Ahmad b. Husayn (1344H), *al-Sunan al-Kubra*, Hyderabad: Dairat al-Ma'arif al-Nizamiyah.

Al-Bukhari, Muhammad b. Ismail, (2002), *al-Jami' al-Sahih*, 9 vols., Cairo: Dar al-Shab.

Al-Darimi, Abd-Allah b. Abd al-Rahman (1407H), *Sunan al-Darimi* (Vol. 2), Beirut: Dar al-Kitab al-Arabi, 518.

Al-Haskafi, Muhammad Ala al-Din (1386H), *Al-Durr al-Mukhtar Sharh Tanwir al-Absar*, Beirut: Dar al-Fikr.

Al-Sughdi, Abu al-Hasan Ali (1984), *Al-Nutf fi al-Fatawa*, Beirut: Mu'assasah al-Risalah.

Al-Suyuti, Abd al-Rahman Abu Bakr (2003), *al-Durr al-Manthur fi al-Tafsir bi al-Mathur*, Beirut: Dar Hajr.

Al-Tabari, Abu Ja'far Muhammad Ibn Jarir (1407H), *Tarikh al-Tabari–Tarikh al-Mulukwa al-Umam* (Vol. 2), Beirut: Dar al Kutub al-Ilmiyah.

Al-Tarabulusi, Burhan al-Din Ibrahim b. Musa (1902), *Kitab al-Is'af fi Ahkam al-Awqaf*, Cairo: Matba'ah Hindiyah.

Al-Uthman, Ali b. Abdullah (n.d.), *Dawr al-mar'ah fi'l-waqf* (Role of Women in waqf), Riyad: Shirkah al-Thibat li Tatwir Idarah al-Awqaf.

Al-Waqidi, Muhammad b. Umar (1966), *Kitab al-Maghazi*, Marden Jones (ed.), Beirut, al-Alami Library, London: Oxford University Press.

Al-Khassaf, Abu Bakr Ahmad (n.d.), *Kitab Ahkam al-Awqaf*, Cairo: Maktabah al-Thiqafah al-Diniyah.

Al-Mirdawi, Ali b. Sulaiman (1419 H), *Al-Insaf fi Ma'rifat al-Rajih min al-Khilaf*, Beirut: Dar Ihya' al-Turath al-Arabi.

Al-Qurtubi, Abu Abd Allah Muhammad (1964), *Al-Jami' li Ahkam al-Qur'an*, Cairo: Dar al-Kutub al-Misriyah.

Al-Qurtubi, Abu Abdullah (2003), *al-Jami' li Ahkam al-Quran*, Riyadh, Dar Alam al-Kutub, 24 vols.

Al-Qushayri, Abu al-Husayn Muslim (n.d.), *Al-Jami' al-Sahih* or *Sahih Muslim*, Beirut: Dar al-Jil and Dar al-Afaq al-Jadidah.

Ibn Battutah (1985), *Rihlah Ibn Battutah*, Beirut: Dar Beirut li al-Tiba'ah wa al-Nashr.

Ibn Abd al-Barr, Abu Umar al-Qurtubi (2002), *Al-Isti'ab fi Ma'rifat al-As'hab*, Beirut: Dar al-Kutub al-Ilmiyah.

Ibn Abi Hatim, Abu Muhammad Abd al-Rahman (n.d.), *Tafsir Ibn Abi Hatim*, Saida: al-Maktabah al-Asriyah.

Ibn Athir (n.d.), *Usud al-Ghabah fi Tamyiz al-Sahabah* (Vol. 5), Beirut: DarIhya' al-Turthal-Arabi.

Ibn Hisham (n.d.), *al-Sirah al-Nabawiyyah*, Beirut, Dar al-Ma'rifah, 2 parts in one volume.

Ibn Kathir (19710), A *al-Sirah al-Nabawiyah*, Beirut: Dar al-Ma'rifah.

Ibn Qudamah (1405H), *Al-Mughni*, Beirut: Dar al-Fikr.

Ibn Sayyid al-Nas, Muhammad b. Abd Allah (1986), *Uyun al-Athar fi al-Maghazi was l-Shama'il wa al-Siyar*, Beirut: Muassasah Izz al-Din.

Islahi, Zafarul Islam (2010), Aurat ki ma'ashi tamkin Quran-e Karim ki roshani mein (Economic Empowerment of Women in the light of the Holy Qur'an). *Shashmahi Ulum al-Qur'an*, 25(2), 5–26.

Qutb, Muhammad (1978), *Shubhat hawl al-Islam*, Beirut: The Holy Quran Publishing House.

Subhani, M. Inayatullah Asad (2011), "*Nizam al-mirath fi'l-Qur'an*" in Ausaf Ahmad and Abdul Azim Islahi (ed.), *Ma'ashi Masa'il aur Qurani Talimat* (Economic Problems and Qur'anic Teachings), Aligarh: Idarah Ulum al-Quran, pp. 200–254.

Urdu

Islahi, Zafarul Islam (2010), "Aurat ki ma'ashi tamkin Quran-e Karim ki roshani mein (Economic Empowerment of Women in the light of the Holy Qur'an)", *Shashmahi Ulum al-Qur'an*, 25(2), 5–26.

Nadwi, Raziul Islam (2011), "Islami Nizam-e warasat mein aurat ka hissah (Woman's share in Islamic inheritance system)" in Ausaf Ahmad and Abdul Azim Islahi (eds.). *Ma'ashi Masa'il aur Qurani Talimat (Economic Problems and Qur'anic Teachings)*, Aligarh: Idarah Ulum al-Quran, pp. 199–200.

English

El-Zawahreh, Taisir Khalil Muhammad (1995), *Religious Endowments and Social Life in the Ottoman Province of Damascus in the Sixteenth and Seventeenth Centuries*, Karak (Jordan): Mutah University.

Chapter 3

Women Empowerment and Leadership in Islam between Myth and Reality*

Noor Mohammad Osmani, Mohammad Omar Farooq and Abu Umar Faruq Ahmad

Abstract

Orthodox Muslim scholars are in general agreement that women are not entitled to hold the leadership or the topmost public office of a nation. Many scholars hold even a more restrictive view on the issue as to whether it is due to *Qur'anic* texts and Prophetic traditions (*ahadith*) that women are barred from key positions, or it is largely due to socio-cultural and economic settings of a society. The *Qur'an* urges the Prophet's wives (*nisa an-nabiyy*) to stay quietly at their homes and not to make dazzling displays like that of the time of primitive ignorance (33:33). It is also commonly cited from the *Qur'an* that men are the caretakers/guardians in charge (*qawwamun*) of women (4:34). The only Prophetic tradition regarding women's leadership is that the Prophet (S) is reported to have said, "Never will succeed such a nation as lets their affairs carried out by a woman" (Sahih al-Bukhari, 4425; Sunan of An-Nasai, 8/227). On the other hand, the *Qur'an* also affirms that the believers, both men and women, are guardians (*awliya'*) of one another (9:71). Also, since the *Qur'an* acclaims the Queen of Sheba for her just rule, such prominent scholars as Imam Abu Hanifa, Imam al-Tabari and Ibn Hazm support that women could hold the topmost judicial position. Ibn Hazm also asserts that there is no theoretical prohibition for women to carry out the mission of Prophethood. Naturally, if they could be Prophets, they could also be the leaders, for the Prophets are the leaders. This chapter aims to explore these issues and examine by primarily analyzing the *Qur'anic* verses, Prophetic traditions, the heritage of the Rightly-Guided Caliphs and the rulings of Muslim jurists. In modern times, the quest for women empowerment is integrally related to the issue of leadership. This chapter will critically evaluate the validity of the quoted *hadith*, and examine

*An earlier version of this chapter was presented at the 38th Annual Conference of the Association of Muslim Social Scientists, Charlottesville, VA, 25–26 September 2009.

its contexts in order to understand how and why the Prophet (S) would have stated as such. This analysis is crucial to address present-day realities, as a significant number of Muslim women have competently led their nations by holding topmost offices. Finally, this presentation hopes to shed light on what the real political status of Muslim women should be today in light of the *Qur'an*, Sunnah and juristic discourse. Resolution of the issue of leadership can significantly impact the women empowerment from Islamic perspectives.

Keywords: Women empowerment, Leadership, Current realities, Political status, Islam

In modern times, one of the key issues facing the Muslim world and that which occupies a prominent position in Islamic discourse is the empowerment of women. Muslim women are asserting themselves claiming that they had been denied the rights that Islam has granted them, the rights that were part of the social reality as part of the Prophetic legacy and heritage. The quest for women empowerment is integrally related to the political status of Muslim women, which is debated by Muslims and non-Muslims alike.

Non-Muslim writers assert that Islam has not only deprived women of political rights but they are also broadly neglected in Islam socially, economically and culturally. From the perspective of Islamic orthodoxy, Islam raised the status of women in all aspects; but the focus of the orthodoxy is only limited to social status of women. Orthodox Muslim scholars do not accept that a woman can hold the leadership role or the topmost public office of a nation, claiming that it was extremely discouraged in a *hadith* of the Prophet (S), "Never will succeed such a nation as lets their affairs carried out by a woman."[1] Many of them also express reservations about women running independent business activities. At the extreme, there are those who do not want women outside their homes at all. Referring to 33:33–34, ultra-conservatives hold that "the general rule is that they should remain at home. This is better for them, more appropriate, and further removed from fitnah" (El Fald, 2014, p. 580).

In contrast, the women's rights advocates among Muslims support women vigorously, and feel that women should have presence outside their homes and be able to participate, as appropriate and relevant, in all affairs alongside their male counterparts (Barlas, 2009). In this respect, some Muslim writers also take a more relaxed view of Islamic ruling of

[1] *Sahih al-Bukhari*, Kitab al-Maghazi, The Prophet's letter to Caesar and Kaiser (732/7), no. 4425.

hijab,[2] let alone *niqab*,[3] and also hold that Islamic ruling of distinction in inheritance among male and female was a transitory affair (Wadud, 2006). The issues of *hijab*/*niqab* and inheritance are part of broader gender-related discourse, but the core issue of this chapter is leadership, which might have implications for other issues related to women empowerment as well. Thus, the issue of women's leadership can be viewed as an apex question for women empowerment in the sense that if this issue can be effectively addressed or resolved, many ancillary issues would be sorted out or reformulated in light of that resolution.

An analytical reading of this widely discussed topic of leadership in the Western discourse indicates sweeping generalizations based often on cases from Middle Eastern Arab nations, and ignoring many larger Muslim majority countries, such as Indonesia, Pakistan, Bangladesh, Turkey, Malaysia and so on. So, in studying these issues, one must make a clear distinction between cultural and religious behaviors and principles, and emphasize on correct methodology of reading and interpreting the Islamic texts, e.g., *Qur'anic* verses and Prophetic traditions as the primary sources along with the views of the classical and contemporary Muslim jurists, while taking into consideration the ever-changing realities.

Historically, women's role has been primarily connected with home except in some rare matriarchal social systems. Of course, in many societies women also used to participate in farming and other activities to support families. The idea of less suitability of women for leadership is not new, or limited to Muslim orthodoxy. Regarding the political role of women, Aristotle (d. 322 G.) said: "Men are more compatible for leadership than women, so the control of men over women is a natural matter" (Everson, 1988, p. 1259). Notwithstanding the fact that there were women leaders at various times, throughout history in different religions, cultures and societies, women were generally discriminated, looked down upon and even subjected to ownership and treated as a property.

The reality in the modern times has gone far beyond the legally conceived restricted space for women, as whether the orthodoxy likes or

[2]*Hijab*: An Arabic word refers to a "partition" or "curtain" in the *literal* or metaphorical sense. It is an Islamic dress code for women to cover their whole body except face and hands. Islam has introduced *hijab* as part of the decency and modesty in interaction between members of the opposite sex. Christian and Jewish women in some traditions also cover their heads as a cultural practice or commitment to modesty or piety.

[3]*Niqab*: Literally, "covering up". A veil for covering the hair and face that is worn by some Muslim females in public.

agrees with, many Muslim majority countries have been experiencing rapid pace in women empowerment and also the rise of women to national leadership. While there is a tendency to argue that these modern realities are deviation from Islam, Muslim women in the quest of their empowerment are also asserting that their participation in leadership roles is fully in harmony with Islam.

In this chapter, the main focus is on the political rights of women as part of their quest for empowerment, whether the women are allowed to run for election for public offices and/or be the head of a state. The study will draw on the texts from the *Qur'an*, the sayings of the Prophet (S) and the juristic opinions of classical and modern Muslim jurists in light of the realities the modern world.

3.1 Women's political role in the *Qur'an*

In the *Qur'an*, Allah made no distinction between men and women in general activities. Rather men and women are placed at par, and it is stated that they belong to one another. Allah mentions very clearly that the entire mankind, whether male or female, will be rewarded for their virtuous deeds in the life hereafter:

> Whoever works righteousness, man or woman, and has Faith, verily, to him will We give a new Life, a life that is good and pure and We will bestow on such their reward according to the best of their actions. (16:97)
>
> And their Lord has accepted of them, and answered them: "Never will I suffer to be lost the work of any of you, be he male or female: You are members, one of another." (3:195)

Women were also charged to discharge duties, with political implications, side by side with men. *Amr bi al-ma'ruf* and *nahy 'an al-munkar* (enjoining virtue and forbidding vice), a duty with political implications, as primarily the people of power and authority can discharge this duty effectively, was assigned to both men and women.

> The Believers, men and women, are *awliya'* (protectors/guardians) of another: they enjoin what is just, and forbid what is evil: they observe regular prayers, practise regular charity, and obey Allah and His Messenger. On them will Allah pour His mercy: for Allah is Exalted in power, Wise. (9:71)

Modern Islamic movements view the role of *amr bi al-ma'ruf* and *nahy 'an al-munkar* as a collective responsibility both at the community and state levels, and thus inseparable from political involvement and pursuit (Jamal, 2013). However, when it comes to women's issues, though the *Qur'an* specifically emphasizes that this role is inclusive of both men and women, somehow women's role is approached by the orthodoxy with a significantly restricted view. Indeed, this role of *amr bi al-ma'ruf* and *nahy 'an al-munkar* is so central to Islam that this role is presented as the *raison d'être* for Muslim *ummah.*

> You are indeed the best community (*ummah*) that has ever been brought forth evolved for [the good of] mankind (*an-nas*). You enjoin the doing of what is right and forbid the doing of what is wrong, and you believe in Allah ... (3:110)

These verses of the *Qur'an* clearly indicate that in assigning the most important job of enjoining virtue and forbidding evil, Allah made no distinction in assigning it to both men and women. Muhammad Rashid Rida (d. 1935), a prominent Islamic scholar, mentioned that the verse made it obligatory on both the men and women to command for virtues, and prohibit from vices. It could be done through one's words and actions. It also includes criticism of the un-Islamic acts of the rulers or those in authority (*'ulu al-'amr*). The women at the time of the Prophet (S) knew this, and participated in this actively and fearlessly (Rida, 1367H, p. 20).

A few verses earlier (9:67), Allah says:

> The Hypocrites, men and women, (have an understanding) with each other: They enjoin evil, and forbid what is just, and withhold with their hands (from spending for the cause of Allah). They have forgotten Allah; so, He has forgotten them. Verily the Hypocrites are rebellious and perverse. (9:67)

So, if the Muslim men and women do not perform their duty, the hypocrite (*munafiqun*) men and women will continue to do their acts as the agents of Satan. During the lifetime of the Prophet (S), we find that there were women who put thorns in the path of the Prophet (S), for whom Surah *al-Masad* (The Palm Fiber) was revealed in the *Qur'an.* So, in this soul-winning and soul-saving struggle, to counteract the negative influence, action and agenda of others, the believing women need to be duly politically active as well.

The *Qur'an* also reports the stories of believing and disbelieving women even in the family of the Prophets, such as the wife of Nuh (A) and Lut (A), who worked against the Prophets. On the other hand, there were contrasting example of the wife of Pharaoh who believed in Allah and led a virtuous life.

3.1.1 *Bay'ah* (allegiance) of women

The *Qur'an* mentions about how the Prophet (S) should take the oath of allegiance from both men and women. They made *bay'ah* to the leader of the state for allegiance. As part of women's empowerment during the era of Prophet Muhammad (S), Islam did not assume or take for granted the women's *bay'ah* (allegiance). In other words, husband's *bay'ah* did not cover the wife's or father's *bay'ah* for the daughter's. Unfortunately, this right and duty of women as an independent person was compromised or even altogether denied over time. Indeed, "The individuality of a woman is a principle in religion," (Al-Turabi, 1991, p. 8) but it cannot be said that the development of Islamic law has been able to uphold this principle. Islam also recognized independent status of women in seeking asylum. Indeed, a Muslim woman could grant asylum to her non-Muslim husband as was in the case with Zainab, the daughter of the Prophet (S), granting asylum to her husband Abu al-'Aas Ibn al-Rabi'I (Ashiq Ilahi, 2005). Allah asked the Prophet (S) not to return the Muslim immigrant women who ran away from persecution of the polytheist leaders and took refuge in Islamic society.

> O ye who believe! When there come to you believing women refugees, examine (and test) them: Allah knows best as to their Faith: if you ascertain that they are Believers, then send them not back to the Unbelievers... (60:10)

> O Prophet! When believing women come to you to take the oath of fealty to you, that they will not associate in worship any other thing whatever with Allah, that they will not steal, that they will not commit adultery (or fornication), that they will not kill their children, that they will not utter slander, intentionally forging falsehood, and that they will not disobey you in any just matter,- then receive their fealty, and pray to Allah for the forgiveness (of their sins): for Allah is Oft-Forgiving, Most Merciful. (60:12)

3.1.2 Queen of Sheba (also known as Bilqis)

The *Qur'an* mentions the story of an important woman who ruled her nation with justice, fairness and reached decisions through consultation. She was the Queen of Sheba. Allah says:

> [Her anxiety prompted her to consult with her counselors]. She said: "O you counsellors! Give me your opinion on the problem with which I am now faced; I would never make a [weighty] decision unless you are present with me." (27:32)

Her just rule was praised in the *Qur'an* that ultimately led the majority of her nation to believe in Allah through Sulayman (Solomon), another Prophet. Were women's leadership in general to be shunned, let alone prohibited, the *Qur'an* would have either stated or suggested.

3.1.3 Men as the caretakers of women

It is claimed by many scholars that the *Qur'an* made the men caretakers and guardians of women, and thus, she is not qualified to rule over them.

> Men are the caretakers and guardians (*qawwamun*) of women, because Allah has given the one more (strength) than the other, and because they support them from their means... (4:34)

Sweeping and one-sided rulings regarding women's subordinate status have been derived from this verse. However, the following verse strikes a strikingly different note:

> ......but, in accordance with justice, the rights of the wives [with regard to their husbands] are equal to the [husbands'] rights with regard to them, although men have a degree [of precedence] over them [in this respect]. And Allah is Exalted in Power, Wise. (2:228)

Unfortunately, the preceding verse where "men have a degree [of precedence]" is mentioned, in practice beyond just "a degree or notch" advantages seem to have been disproportionately and overwhelmingly accorded to or secured by men.

Verse 4:34 where men are identified as caretakers and guardians might be better understood in the context of family matters (Qutb, 2001, pp. 108–114). In the historical context of the society where these verses were revealed, one can view these verses referring specifically to the family matters where man is given the authoritative role. One person should be the leader in the family, who through due consultation with the others come to decisions, and not through dictatorial rule. Of course, that even at family level there is a role of *shura* or mutual consultation is a long-forgotten and neglected norm. This *qiwamah* or guardianship that comes from the word *qawwamun*, which is mentioned in 4:34 was also accorded due to husband's role in the family and the expenses he makes (Sayyid Tantawi, 1997, 1/512, 3/136–137). Wife can be the Dean, Director, Vice Chancellor, Bank Governor, or even the Minister, Speaker of a Parliament, and constitutional head of a country like President, or Prime Minister, and the husband may be a simple officer in the same institution, but at home, the traditional model is that the husband/father is in charge. Since family cannot be a democracy, the guardian should avail the benefits of relevant consultation, but the family members should obey the head of the family.

However, notably, this verse has been used to advance the notion that women are inferior to men (Adnan, 2004, p. 6) and thus they are meant to be subordinated and also to legitimize and condone wife-beating. While rulings pertaining to wife-beating come with clarification that such beating is merely symbolic and must not be physically injurious to the wife, sometimes the male-dominated orthodox interpretive domain has pushed the ruling to such extreme that "retaliation is not permitted for anything short of death, even if a man fractures his wife's skull" (Geissinger, 2015, p. 42). Thus, the ground reality is that the orthodox and literal interpretation of the verse has created a permissive and lenient space and environment for men to be violent to their wives.

However, even this traditional view about family and its framework needs to be tempered by at least two aspects.

First, the role of men as *qawwamun* (4:34) needs to be tempered by and reconciled with the role of men and women as mutual *awliya'* (guardians) (9:71). One way to reconcile is that 4:34 is transitional, while 9:71 is normative. This is similar to the gradual prohibition of alcohol/intoxicants (*khamr*), where the verses about relative benefits and harms of intoxicants (2:221), or asking not to approach prayer while someone is intoxicated are transitional (4:43), while the categorical verse of prohibition (5:90) is normative (Mejia, 2007, pp. 1–24). Second, if 4:34 is to be taken as normative, then the family structure must be such that men alone must take care of the family. However, what about social conditions where both spouses work and share in family finances? In modern times, more and more families are typified by both spouses working, earning and sharing expenses. Unless it is argued and legally barred that women cannot go out, not get educated or cannot work, 4:34 evidently cannot serve as normative. Furthermore, 9:71 is more consistent with the egalitarian view about gender in the *Qur'an* and closer to the legacy and heritage of the time of the Prophet Muhammad (Al-Hibri, 1982, 1997).

3.2 Women's leadership role in the *sunnah* of the Prophet (SAW)

As reflected in the *ahadith* of the Prophet (S) as well as the biographies and historical works, the women were not isolated from the political activities of the state. They were part and parcel of the polity in Madinah. They participated not only in *da'wah*, the role of inviting people toward Allah, but also migrated to Abyssinia (Ethiopia) and finally to Madinah to escape persecution and preserve their Islamic identity and faith. They sacrificed utmost in this regard, not necessarily any less than their male counterparts. Some of them were tortured by their own family members and others due to embracing Islam. Some of them became martyrs preserving their Islamic identity. Some of them remained steadfast to Islam, even after their husbands turned apostates, such as the case of Umm Habibah (R). Some of the women had also participated in war, provided medical services to the warriors and carried the injured to Madinah. Some of them even fought the battles.

For example, when the Prophet (S) told Umm Haram bint Malhan that her *ummah* will be crossing the sea to raise the banner of Islam in other parts of the world, she asked the Prophet (S) to pray for her so she can be one of them. The Prophet (S) prayed for her.[4] Rubayyi'i bint Mu'awwidh, a prominent Ansari woman is also reported to have participated in the battles against polytheists and served the wounded warriors.[5] Umm Sulaym bint Malhan was reported to have guarded the Prophet (S) during the battle of Uhud in Madinah with a dagger. She also carried a dagger with her in the battle of Hunayn and remained firm with the Prophet (S) while many Muslim male warriors were forced to flee.[6] Later, when Umm Sulaym was asked by Abu Talha, who had not yet reverted to Islam, if *she would marry* him should he *revert* to *Islam, she said she would* and *she said* that his acceptance of *Islam* could be *her mahr* (*dowry*).[7] This was an excellent *dowry* and this is a unique sacrifice by a female Muslim in the history of *Islam.* These women were side by side with their husbands, brothers and fellow Muslims in the path of Islam, in the quest of the survival and victory of the earliest generation of Muslims.

---

[4] *Sahih al-Bukhari*, 2788, Book: al-Jihad wa al-Siyar, Chapter: Al-Du'a bi al-Jihad wa ash-shahadah; *Sahih Muslim*, 1912, Book: al-Imarah, Chapter: Fadl al-Ghazw fi al-Bahr.
[5] *Sahih al-Bukhari*, 2883, Book: al-Jihad wa al-Siyar, Chapter: Mudawat al-Nisa' al-Jarha.
[6] *Sahih Muslim*, 1809, Book: Al-Jihad wa al-Siyar, Chapter: Ghazw al-Nisa' ma'a al-Rijal.
[7] *Sunan an-Nasa'i*, 3341, Book: al-Nikah, Chapter: Al-Tazwij 'ala al-Islam.

3.2.1 Umm Salamah (R.A.) advises the Prophet (SAW)

During the peace treaty of Hudaybiyyah, after the apparent unfavorable treaty with the polytheists of Makkah, the companions were very much upset and Umar (R) aggressively asked the Prophet (S) some questions, for which he later repented. The treaty was made as per the Prophet's decision. However, Muslims were unhappy due to the humiliating stipulations in the treaty. After concluding the treaty, the Prophet (S) asked them to rise, slaughter their animals and shave their heads. They did not move even though the Prophet (S) asked them thrice to do so. Being disappointed, he came to Umm Salamah (R), his wife, and told her about the incident. Upset with the incident, the Prophet (S) listened to the advice of Umm Salamah (R) that rather he should go out to slaughter his own camel, shave his head without saying a single word to any. He complied, and seeing his action, the companions quickly rose, and did the same as commanded earlier by the Prophet (S). Umm Salamah (R) was among the wives of the Prophet (S), whom the Prophet (S) consulted on various occasions and she demonstrated her knack as an intelligent advisor to the Prophet.[8]

3.2.2 Umm Hani's granting of political asylum

On the day of the conquest of Makkah, the Prophet (S) was taking a bath, while Umm Hani bint Abu Talib (R) came. She complained about her brother Ali bin Abu Talib (R) that he wanted to kill a person whom she gave refuge, son of Hubairah. The Prophet (S) said, "*O Umm Hani, we too have granted asylum (protection) to whoever you have granted asylum to.*"[9] The incident validates the status and right of women in regard to making such independent decisions of political or administrative implications.

3.2.3 'Ā'isha (R) leads the Battle of the Camel

'Ā'isha (R) was the Prophet's (S) wife and played a leader-like role in her contemporary time. Together with Talhah and Zubayr (R) she led the army of Muslims in the Battle of the Camel to demand the *qisas* (retaliation) of

[8] *Sahih al-Bukhari*, Kitab ash-Shurut, #2731–2732, available at https://sunnah.com/bukhari/54/19.

[9] *Sahih Muslim*, Kitab as-Salat al-Musafirin, #336, available at https://sunnah.com/muslim/6/99.

the killing of Usman (R). Putting aside the debate, whether she was right in this particular incident to rise against a valid and legitimate Islamic ruler, it undoubtedly establishes the fact that women could also participate in the most sensitive and highest level of political affairs of a state, and even could lead them (Al-Tabari, 2015, pp. 52–164).

Contemporary Turkish theologian, Suleyman Ates has argued that "the hadith discouraging female leadership" contradicts 9:71 in the *Qur'an*, as the *hadith* "was directed at 'Ā'isha's role during the post-Prophetic political conflict. It originated because a group of Muslims felt their own interests in community leadership were in danger." If the *hadith* discouraging women's leadership is really from the Prophet (S), Ates says: "'A'isha's leadership would never have been recognized by Zubayr and Talha." Ates therefore doubts the validity of the *hadith*, which the Qur'an contradicts (Aslan, 2013, p. 39).

3.2.4 Asma bint Abu Bakr (R) voiced her words fearlessly against Al-*Hajjaj* ibn Yusuf

After the murder of Abdullah bin Zubayr (R), Al-*Ḥajjāj* b. Yūsuf Al-*Thaqafī*, the then Governor of Iraq wanted Asma bint Abu Bakr (R), mother of Abdullah, to meet him. She refused. Al-*Hajjāj* threatened that if she resists, he would have her dragged. She said, "I shall not go and meet him even if he drags me." At the end, Al-*Hajjāj* himself came and met her. She said: "I have found you have spoilt his worldly life, and he spoilt your hereafter. You addressed him as 'the son of two sheets of scarf.' I am by Allah the person of two sheets, one of which is used to carry the food for the Prophet and Abu Bakr, and the other that the women need to wear."[10]

These are some incidents which clearly demonstrate that the women in the lifetime of the Prophet (S) and during the era of the companions were not detached from the political arena and pertinent activities. A multi-volume work by Abdul Halim Al-Sukkah documents the freedom women enjoyed and role they played in the full range of life's activities (Al-Sukkah, 1990).

[10] *Sahih Muslim*, Kitab Fadail as-Sahaba, #2545, available at https://sunnah.com/muslim/44/325.

3.3 Key arguments against women's leadership

While there are plenty of and substantive examples for the case of women's active role in the broad range of life, as highlighted earlier, the orthodoxy, in light of the evolution of the general male-dominated political and religious culture, used two key arguments against women's public participation in general, and leadership in particular.

3.3.1 Intelligence deficiency in women

One of the orthodox points against the suitability of women's leadership in general, and the top public office in a society is that women are relatively deficient in intelligence, implying that either they are incapable of assuming any role requiring significant intelligence or that in regard to leadership they are relatively deficient in the requisite level of intelligence. In this regard, a *hadith* is often quoted by these quarters to discredit women for leadership roles.

The Prophet (S) was reported to have visited the women after "Eid" congregation and encouraged them to donate to charity. He apparently reminded them that the majority of the dwellers of hellfire are women, which is due to their frequent cursing of each other, and being ungrateful to their husbands. He is also reported to have said, "I have not seen anyone more deficient in intelligence and religion than you (women), a cautious sensible man could easily be led astray by any of you."[11]

While this *hadith* appears in *Sahih al-Bukhari*, the most highly regarded compendium of *hadith*, it is important to note that *Sahih* (authentic) in collections like Al-Bukhari is based on the validation of *riwayah* (chain of narrations and the narrators). Unfortunately, this validation does not cover examination of *matn* (the narrative) itself. Thus, there could be some authentic *hadith* even in Al-Bukhari that may not be acceptable when the *matn* is examined (Farooq, 2011).

Israr Ahmad Khan deals with the subject of authentication of *hadith* in his book (Khan, 2010, pp. 108–109) where he also examined the *ahadith* pertaining to the intelligence deficiency in women.

> "This tradition unequivocally declares women to be deficient, both intellectually as well as religiously, as compared to men. In order to ascertain that this statement, supposedly made by the Prophet is

[11] *Sahih al-Bukhari*, #304, *Kitab al-Haidh*, available at https://sunnah.com/bukhari/6/9.

> accurate, we need to thoroughly analyse the report.... The Prophet, according to the report, puts women to blame for playing tricks with men and dominating their minds and hearts, thus misleading them. Again, this makes no sense. Is it possible for the less intelligent and the less capable to dominate the more intelligent and the most capable? If women are intellectually deficient, how can they play tricks or outwit men who possess superior intelligence? In fact, if anything the reverse applies, for psychologically, the less intelligent are dominated by the more intelligent. If women really do dominate men and mislead them, then the former should be as strongly intellectually as the latter."

What is even more important is that women being intelligence-deficient is empirically disproven. Even during the time of the Prophet (S) and during the era of the generation of the companions, women like 'Ā'isha (R), Umm Salamah (R) and Fatimah (R) left their marks on the *ummah* for which we continue to refer to them not just as noble and honored women because of their relationship with the Prophet (S) but also for their role as teachers, scholars and jurisprudents of their generation. None ever said from among that generation and none would dare from later generations to say that these women suffered from any intelligence deficiency.

Of course, in modern times with greater participation of women, society empirically negates such notion of intelligence deficiency in women. From this perspective, Khan articulates:

"The Prophet advances, as is claimed, two examples, one to explain intellectual deficiency and the other to prove religious deficiency. The example for intellectual deficiency is a woman's eligibility to be a half witness only. Here it seems intellectual deficiency denotes lack of knowledge. Al-Nawawi mentions three components required of the intellect (*'aql*), (1) knowledge, (2) information about the basic and necessary matters related to life, and (3) the power of discernment. This means that deficiency of mind is actually that of knowledge as well as that of discernment. In this case it is, then, not necessarily only the woman's prerogative to suffer from this, for men may also be victims. *Thus, why should women alone be referred to as intellectually deficient? Many men are also found lacking in knowledge and having less sagacity. There are also women in their millions who are more sagacious, more knowledgeable, and far more intelligent than men*" (Khan, 2010, p. 109).

The same women who are declared in the *Qur'an* to be *awliya'* (guardians) of each other, the same women who are equally tasked for the central role of the believers — *'amr bi al-ma'ruf* and *nahy 'an al-munkar* — how can they fulfill these roles if they are suffering from intelligence-deficiency? For far too long such observations about women have created contexts for a diminutive view of women. Indeed, relying on this specific *hadith* that is contrary to empirical reality, and also contrary to the leadership role played by women in the earliest generation of the era of the Prophet (S), drawing broad and sweeping diminutive view of women stands in opposition to the *Qur'anic* perspective on gender parity.

Indeed, the legacy of women scholars and experts from the time of the Prophet (S) and the generation of the companions was eclipsed by the subsequent marginalizing, and then gradually emptying the domain of the scholarship and jurisprudence of the women. Yet, history records that even by the same *hadith* literature that women are marginalized, women played vital role in the preservation, dissemination and education of the sciences of *hadith*.

Karima al-Marwaziyya (d. 463/1070) is one of many notable female figures whom Muslims should proudly know and remember: "who was considered the best authority on the *Sahih* of al-Bukhari in her own time. Abu Dharr of Herat, one of the leading scholars of the period, attached such great importance to her authority that he advised his students to study the *Sahih* under no one else, because of the quality of her scholarship." Among her students were al-Khatib al-Baghdadi, a noted Islamic scholar and historian (Siddiqui, 1993, p. 119).

3.3.2 Abu Bakrah's (R) famous *hadith*

If one evidence that is used by the orthodoxy as definitive weapon on the issue of women's leadership is the *hadith* by one of the companions, Abu Bakrah (R). This is the only *hadith* of Prophet (S) where he is reported to have condemned the leadership of women, which reads as follows:

> Related Abu Bakrah: Allah benefited me with the word I heard from the Messenger of Allah during the Battle of the Camel[12] after I was about to join the people of the Camel and fight on their side, but then I remembered what I heard from the Messenger of Allah, when he was told that the Persians appointed Kisra's daughter as their Queen. The

[12]It was named as the Battle of Jamal or camel, because 'Ayishah (R.A.), the wife of Prophet (S) led the army on the back of camel.

Prophet said: "a nation that entrusts its affairs to a woman will never prosper".[13]

The *hadith* has other chains of narrators, all of which meet on Abu Bakrah (R).[14] In most cases, it is narrated in the same wording. But Imam Ahmad ibn Hanbal narrated differently than what is narrated in Sahih al-Bukhari and other Sunan Books of *ahadith.*

Imam Hakim authenticated this *hadith* and Imam al-Dhahabi also confirmed it. Imam al-Tirmidhi says: "This is a *hasan* (sound) and *sahih* (authentic) *hadith*". As the *hadith* is reported in Sahih al-Bukhari, it guarantees protection from *sanad* (chain of *transmission*) deficiencies and criticisms. Though some of the narrators of the *hadith* are questioned and debated, it does not affect the authenticity of the *hadith* as a whole. However, that authentication relates to only the *riwayah.* As was mentioned earlier, even a *hadith* is regarded as *sahih* based on its *riwayah,* and it still needs to be scrutinized based on *matn* (text or actual wording). This is where the *hadith* falls apart as an evidence, especially for something as sweeping as prohibiting women from the role of leadership.

The background of the *hadith* is that the Prophet (S) was informed about a political turmoil and unrest in Persia, when its monarch was assassinated by his own son, and the son was also killed by a plot of his father planned before the latter's death. The son was able to hold the reign of power for only six months, after which he was killed by the pre-arranged plot of his father. The elites of the monarchy did not want to be ruled by other than the royal family. Therefore, Buran, the daughter of Daughter of Khosrau II, King of Persia, became the Queen of Persia, the 26th Sassanid Monarch of Persia (Al-'Asqalani, n.d.). Since this is the *hadith* that is used, the only and definitive evidence on this issue, the *hadith* needs to be critically examined and analysed.

The majority of the scholars in the past and the present rejected women's rule over a nation based on this *hadith.* They took it in the literal meaning of legal prohibition for a woman to assume the rule of authority. Though the *hadith* does not literally prohibit assigning women to the rule of authority, the orthodoxy took it as a strict rule of prohibition, as the *hadith* literally declares destruction of a nation that assigns women

---

[13]*Sahih al-Bukhari,* Kitab al-Maghazi, Bab Kitab al-Nabi (PBUH) ila Kisra wa Kaiser, Hadith no. 4073, vol. 13, p. 337.

[14]See Ibn Hanbal *Musnad,* 5/38, *Tirmidhi,* 9/118–119, *Nasa'i,* Hadith No. 4981.

to the leadership position. Going beyond the categorization of this *hadith* as authentic (*sahih*), the textual content (*matn*) analysis reveals rather interesting aspects deserving attention.

Fatimah Mernissi, in her book, *al-Harim al-Siyasi* (The Political Woman), debated extensively on the personality and reliability of Abu Bakrah (R), to whom all reports on the matter converged (Al-Mar'isiy, 1993, pp. 71–79). She points out that Abu Bakrah (R) was punished for false testimony by Umar bin Al-Khattab (R), and hence his testimony is rejected. His reports therefore could not be considered. The "*fisq*" or transgression (i.e., straying from the right path), could be tolerated (*yutahammal*) while learning *hadith*, but not while delivering it to others (*al-ada'*). Abu Bakrah (R) learnt this *hadith* as a companion of the Prophet (S), but while delivering it to others, he lost his trustworthiness. He was involved in a testimony against Mughirah bin Shu'bah (R). He and two others had testified against him, but the fourth withdrew from his testimony as it was not evident to him. Umar ibn al-Khattab (R) rejected all their testimonies and punished them for what was regarded as false testimony.[15] This was the *Qur'anic* verse (24:4) that whoever brings a charge against a person, and does not produce four witnesses, should be flogged with 80 stripes, and his testimonies would be rejected in future.[16] Such individual is regarded *fasiq*[17] (transgressor) unless he repents. Abu Bakrah (R) did not repent and he was insistent that he was right in his testimony.[18]

This issue has other dimensions and the statements of the scholars are diverse on this. The books on legal ruling provided details for it. The most important matter here is that Abu Bakrah (R) was indeed punished by the command of the just Caliph Umar (R). It made him lose acceptability in testimony and narrating *hadith* is like giving testimony. If someone's

---

[15]Imam 'Abd al-Razzaq (d. 211 H) reiterates the fact which connects Abu Bakrah to the verse 24:13. 'Abd al-Razzaq – Ma'mar – al-Zuhri – In al-Musayyab.

[16]*al-Qur'an*, 24:4.

[17]A person who intentionally and constantly transgresses the clearly prescribed boundaries of Allah.

[18]Three people testified against al-Mughirah b. Shu'bah for adultery. But Ziyad recoiled. So, 'Umar punished the three (with lashing), and said to them, "Repent, and your (future) testimonies will be accepted." So, two of the men repented but Abu Bakrah did not repent. Therefore, his testimonies were no longer accepted. Abu Bakrah was a maternal brother of Ziyad. When what happened in the case of Ziyad occurred, Abu Bakrah swore that he would never again speak to Ziyad. As such, he never again spoke to him till his death. The chain is *Sahih*, and has been so declared by the top *muhadithun* of the Ahl al-Sunnah. Imam Muslim (d. 261 H), for instance, has relied upon this chain in his *Sahih*. See Abu Bakr 'Abd al-Razzaq b. Hamam al-Ṣa'nani (n.d.).

testimony is not accepted, his reported *ahadith* would also be rejected, as from religious viewpoint reporting *hadith* is a much greater issue of credibility and trustworthiness of the narrators than regular testimony.

Nevertheless, the scholars of the sciences of *Hadith* and *Fiqh* did not look into this aspect of Abu Bakrah's *hadith*. To them, all companions are just (*'udul*) according to the science of criticism of *hadith* narrators (Ullah, 2015, p. 153). This incident, they argue, did not affect his *iman* (faith), and hence it did not tarnish his image or status as an acceptable narrator of *ahadith* of the Prophet (S). However, once Muslims go beyond this notion of "all companions are just and trustworthy," this *hadith* does not merit the status it has been accorded in drawing such drastic ruling about women's leadership. Furthermore, the aforementioned notion has also appeared in different narrations such as "all companions are assumed to be just (*'udul*) unless they are proven otherwise"; as such it is not believed by Sunni scholars that companions would lie or fabricate *hadith* unless they are proven liars, untrustworthy or opposed to Islam.[19]

3.4 Theological debate on the women's leadership role

The scholars debated over this issue extensively. During the last few centuries, as the modern world evolved, they debated if a woman has any political rights such as voting rights, and being elected as a leader, for example, as a member of parliament and so on. Their debate also continued if she could be elected as the premier of a state.

Contemporary scholars are in general agreement that the women should or could exercise their political rights by selecting their leaders and representatives, though some traditional scholars or groups, such as the Taliban do not even like women's education, let alone political participation (Duderijz, 2011, p. 110).

Mustafa al-Siba'i, a prominent scholar of Islamic Jurisprudence, mentions that women as citizens of a nation should exercise this right in selecting their representatives to voice their concerns. And since there is no prohibition in the Sharī'ah about it, the right should be recognized and implemented. Based on the famous Islamic legal maxim *Al-aslu fi al-ashya'i al-'ibaha* (the norm in regard to things is that of permissibility), he

[19] Companion of the Prophet (n.d.), "World Heritage Encyclopaedia edition", available at: http://webcache.googleusercontent.com/search?q=cache:http://newspaperslibrary.org/articles/eng/Companion_of_the_Prophet.

argues that since there is no text in the *Qur'an* or *Sunnah* that prevents women from exercising this right, Muslims should respect the provision of permissibility. Indeed, the verse 9:71 establishes the fact that the women are also counterparts of men, and are to play their role in *amr bil ma'ruf* and *nahy 'anil munkar* as cited earlier.

The Prophet (S) is also reported to have said: "Women are men's counterparts (*Innama an-nisau shaqaiq ar-rijal*)."[20] This also shows that she should exercise the same rights as men based on her credibility and quality, and not based on gender.

Al-Siba'i believes that though there is no text preventing them from running in the elections, the women in Muslims societies stay out of it due to lack of public interest. According to a leading contemporary Muslim scholar al-Qaradawi, it is against *maslahah* or public interest that the women should stay away from running in the election (Feldman, 2007, p. 64), rather they should run in the election side by side with irreligious women who also run in the elections and get elected. Al-Qaradawi praises the step of Al-Ikhwan Al-Muslimun in Egypt for selecting some women members to run for the election. Of course, during the past century almost all Islamic movements have facilitated and encouraged women's participation in the political process, even though they do hold that women are prohibited from leading even their respective movements, let alone a society or state.

The orthodoxy raises the case of the virtuous wives of the Prophet (S) as they were asked in the *Qur'an* to stay in their homes (33:33) and they generally did. The fact that the *Qur'an* specifically addresses the wives of the Prophet is sufficient and categorical not to extend it beyond the addressed group. If it were to be general, it would not have been addressed to the wives of the Prophet (S).

Some scholars have employed the *sadd al-dhara'i* (blocking the means, i.e., preventive measures) argument: bringing out women in the public space will lead to moral turpitude. However, the counter argument is that barring women from political participation can lead to *sadd ash-Sharaī'* or preventing Sharī'ah itself. If one exceeds the limit in *sadd al-dhara'i*, it will lead to extremism in *fath al-dhara'i* or opening the means to evil acts. Should one avoid cultivating the grapes, lest it may result in producing wine? Should one not study Chemistry, because it may teach

[20]Sunan Abu Dawood, Kitab at-Tahara, #236, available at https://sunnah.com/abudawud/1/236.

him how to produce wine, and may indulge in this? Should one not live in a neighborhood assuming that the neighbors may have daughters, where his sons might get enticed or corrupted?

The position of the scholars and jurists on the issue of what role or position of authority Muslim women can assume is rather divergent. Imam Abu Hanifa allowed women to be judges and *muftis* to issue Islamic legal verdicts except in financial and criminal matters, a position that is somewhat self-contradictory. Imam al-Tabari and Ibn Hazm somewhat more liberally have held that they could be judges in all issues. Ibn Hazm, though known as a *Zahiri* or a person who strictly and literally followed the texts of the *Qur'an* and *Sunnah*, held the view that there is no evidence in the *Qur'an* and the *Sunnah* prohibiting women from being Prophets and that he regarded some special women, such as Maryam, the mother of Isa (Jesus), among the Prophets (Esposito, 1995, p. 365). Had there been any text, Ibn Hazm would be among the first one to accept and defend. So, if they were allowed in principle to be the prophets, they could also be the leaders. Also, allowing women to be judges and *muftis*, but disallowing them as witness in financial and criminal matters on the same level as men does not hold water.

3.5 Women as the heads of state

Generally, Muslim scholars hold that the role of leadership is a challenge and women are exempted from this huge and onerous challenge and responsibility. It is basically expected of men. The nature of job and its quality need men to hold such premiership of a nation. It needs *jihad* (exerted effort) and *ijtihad* (independent interpretation of the legal sources), for which men are regarded as more qualified and capable. It is also required of a Caliph that he should lead them in prayer. And it is unanimous among scholars that women could not lead men in prayers (Jalajel, 2016, p. 85). They could only lead women in prayers as 'Ā'isha and Umm Salamah (R) led women in prayers. In the following section, we present a survey of opinions of major Muslim figures regarding this issue, who prohibit women's leadership, though some of them allowed her to assume the role of chief justice as held by Abu Hanifa and al-Tabari.

Abu Hanifa (d. 767 AD) allowed her to be the chief justice, but not the premier of state (Al-'Asqalani, n.d.). Malik bin Anas (d. 795 AD) also allowed her to hold the position of a judge in one report (Al-'Asqalani, n.d.). Imam al-Baqillani (d. 1013 AD) opposed women's supreme leadership in his book *al-Tamhid* by saying that one of attributes of the position of *imam* is to be experienced about war strategy, management of the army and the administration, protecting the oppressed and who will not be soft and emotional in practicing the *hudud* punishments (Al-Qudah, 1998, pp. 93–97). Al-Mawardi (d. 1058 AD) identified seven necessary qualifications for leadership that include, particularly the ability to do *jihad* and *ijtihad* (Al-Mawardi, 1990, pp. 265–268). Ibn Hazm al-Zahiri (d. 1064 AD) said that women cannot assume the rulership except the ladies of the tribe of Quraysh. He also viewed that she could hold the post of justice (Ibn Hazm, 1988, 8/421–422). Imam al-Ghazali (d. 1111 AD) did not allow woman to hold the post of *khilafah* (caliphate) though she may be more qualified than the man. Like Imam Shafi'i, he did not allow her to hold the post of justice (Al-Ghazali, 1964, p. 180). Al-Kasani (d. 1191 AD) allowed her to issue verdict of justice except *hudud* and *qisas*; her witness was invalid there (Al-Kasani, 1998, 5/439). Ibn al-'Arabi al-Maliki (d. 1240 AD) did not only prohibit woman from holding the topmost public office of a state but he also condemned the authenticity of the reports that are attributed to Abu Hanifa and al-Tabari allowing woman the post of chief justice. To him, these were the fabrications of innovators in *hadith* (Ibn al-'Arabi, n.d, pp. 482–483). Al-Qurtubi (d. 1273) followed the opinion of his mentor Ibn al-'Arabi (Al-Qurtubi, 2013, 13/183/184). Ibn Kathir (d. 1373 AD) presented from historical perspective that women are not qualified to run the state affairs. He also added that she should be barred from holding posts in the court of justice (Ibn Kathir, 1410H, 1/492). Ibn Khaldun (d. 1406 AD) also referred to five important qualities for the office of *imamah* (leadership), where he specifically referred to women leading the congregational prayers (Ibn Khaldun, 1987, pp. 95–98). This also shows that he believed that the post of *imamah* is reserved for male. Al-Shawkani (d. 1834 AD) said that it is not valid for a nation to charge women with the state premiership. For, he said, it is compulsory to avoid things that carry failure and collapse of a nation (Al-Shawkani, 1358H, 7/298). Muhammad Rashid Rida (d. 1935 AD) excluded the premiership from the political posts the women could hold (Rida, 1367H, p. 24). Mustafa Al-Siba'i (d. 1964 AD) believed that the *hadith* is clear in prohibiting women from the post of premiership; and the same ruling should be applied for similar political posts of high significance (Al-Siba'I, n.d., pp. 39–40). Abul A'la Mawdudi (d. 1979 AD) declared manhood as a precondition for rulers based on *hadith*. He viewed that the women's engagement in the political world is a destruction of the family institution. Family is the natural domain for women's activities. Likewise, politics, state affairs and military services, etc. are exclusively meant for men (Al-Mawdudi, 1980, p. 264). Muhammad Hussain Fadlallah (d. 2010 AD), a Shia scholar interpreted the *hadith* of Abu Bakrah (R) as being related to the dictatorial regime of Persia. The rulership then just required general competence, whereas today it requires government machinery, experts and consultative council and so on. He concluded that a woman should not hold the post of top leadership; but she could participate in other activities besides man provided that she is well equipped to protect herself from emotional and sentimental attachments (Fadlallah, 1418AH, p. 542). Hasan al-Turabi (d. 2016 AD) also asserted that women can hold any high position in state including ministers, but not the premiership of a state (Kausar, 1997, pp. 28–29). Many other scholars also prohibited women from assuming leadership role based on this *hadith*. Among these scholars are al-Qaradawi (1996, 1/73), Abu Shiqqah (1990, 2/449-450), al-Bahansawi (1986, p. 108), Zaydan (1993, 4/302) and others. They repeated the similar arguments presented by the scholars mentioned earlier. Though rare, some of the early Muslim scholars of the 19th and early 20th centuries have permitted women to be the top leaders (Shehabuddin, n.d.), for instance Muhammad al-Ghazali (d. 1996 AD) believed that the *hadith* refers to a particular incident in a particular country. It is wrong to generalize it on all Muslim women let alone the women of the world (Al-Ghazali, 1989, pp. 48–49).

In contrast with the orthodox view, these scholars generally related the *hadith* of Abu Bakrah (R) with a political event that occurred in Persia and they refused to generalize it for today's context. There are other contemporary scholars who argued that this *hadith* could not have been stated by the Prophet (S). For example, Mohammed Ali mentions that before considering Abu Bakra's reported Hadith about the qualification of women for the position of head of state, we must note the fundamental test for accepting a Hadith as genuine (Ali, 2004, pp. 124–125). Usmani rejects this reported *hadith* as forged since Abu Bakra (R) did not remember it until the time the Battle of the Camel, long after it was alleged to have been said (Ali, 2004, pp. 124–125). Some other scholars argued based on the analysis of al-Mawardi in his book *al-Ahkam al-Sultaniyyah* that they could be the supreme leaders as al-Mawardi did not mention being male as one of the seven conditions of being Caliph.[21]

[21] http://www.islamtoday.net/nawafeth/artshow-45-2784.htm.

Apart from this *hadith* narrated by Abu Bakrah (R) whose reports are rejected, there is no Islamic prohibition to this effect. Rather *Qur'an*'s acclaimed mentioning of the Queen of Sheba shows that woman can be the leader of a state and in a democratic or representation-based system women have the right to contest election for any office. It is the ability and quality of a particular candidate that matters, and not the gender. Sometimes, women are more qualified than men. Their quality, not gender, should be taken into consideration. Islam is not gender biased. It makes more sense that the *hadith* of Abu Bakrah (R) refers to a particular incident of Persia that the Prophet (S) prophesied about the destruction of that particular nation. This proves his accuracy of prophecy and that he was Allah's Prophet. That disputed *hadith* from a discredited narrator cannot be the basis for such drastic and sweeping prohibition.

3.6 The current socio-political realities

As mentioned already, in the early Islamic history, there exist instances of women's participation in political affairs like 'Ā'isha bint Abu Bakr, Umm Salamah, Umm Waraqah, Samra Bint Wahaib (R) and others. There were other historical female characters in Muslim history, such as Razia Sultana, who ruled Indian sub-continent from 1236 to 1239[22] and Shajarat ad-Durr who ruled Egypt from 1250 to 1257.[23]

In this modern age, the ground reality has moved far ahead of the orthodox position on women's participation in public life in general and their leadership role in particular. Defying the orthodox agreement and the dislike, there are numerous examples of Muslim women's political participation in different countries and societies. Appearance of thousands of Muslim women in the processions and various programs of Hamas in Palestine,[24] Muslim brotherhood in Egypt (Abdel-Latif, 2009), FIS (Islamic Salvation Front) in Algeria (Islamic Salvation Front, 2009) as well as achieving membership of the parliaments by Muslim women in Pakistan, Sudan, Turkey, Malaysia, Kuwait, Qatar, Bangladesh and some other Muslim-majority countries denote Muslim women's increasing participation in general political arena.

[22] http://www.mapsofindia.com/who-is-who/history/razia-sultana.html.
[23] http://www.womeninworldhistory.com/heroine1.html.
[24] http://en.wikipedia.org/wiki/Hamas.

Zeenath Kausar asserts, "A close observation of the student circles of the Islamic revivalist movement in India and its allies, particularly the Students Islamic Movement of India (SIMI) shows that there is a sign of departure from the earliest traditional stance on women" (Kausar, 1997, p. 23). Islamic Society of North America (ISNA), the leading organization for Muslim community in the USA and Canada, took a trailblazing step in electing its first female president, Dr. Ingrid Mattson (CAIR, 2006).

Arab revivalists' position on women had taken shape since the founding of the Muslim Brotherhood movement by Hasan al-Banna (Thameem, 1995). "He established a Muslim sisterhood and mobilized women for the cause of Islam and fully supported women as Zaynab al-Ghazali whose imprisonment, sufferings and brutal torture under Nasser's regime has left a clear impact on Muslim women. The position taken recently by some of the moderate revivalists, for example in Sudan, is a giant step forward in the developments and empowerment of women. The Islamic National Front (INF), under the leadership of Hasan al-Turabi, not only endorsed theoretically the full political participation of women but has also made it an empirical reality. In 1986, two women, Dr. Suad al-Fatih al-Badawi and Hikmat Hasan Syed Ahmed, were included in the parliament under the aegis of INF. Presently, 10% of Sudanese parliament consists of women, three women have been appointed ministers, and one woman judge sits on the supreme court" (Kausar, 1997, p. 24).

Besides the mass participation, some visible and countable epitomes of Muslim women's political role can be seen at the highest level in a number of Muslim-majority countries. In the past several decades, many countries in which Muslims are a majority, including Indonesia, Pakistan, Bangladesh and Turkey, have been led by women. Nearly one-third of the Parliament of Egypt also consists of women. Women in the Islamic World have achieved high political status and have produced more than seven head of states including Benazir Bhutto of Pakistan, Mame Madior Boye of Senegal, Tansu Çiller of Turkey, Kaqusha Jashari of Kosovo, Megawati Sukarnoputri of Indonesia and Bangladesh, probably, was the first country in the world to have election between two female heads-of-state — Khaleda Zia and Sheikh Hasina — each winning two elections since 1990 till today. Other than these women, even in conservative Iran women, like Masoumeh Ebtekar, have held the position of Vice President.[25]

[25]http://en.wikipedia.org/wiki/Women_in_Islam.

There are many contemporary examples of women leading Muslim-majority countries. Remarkably, a majority of all Muslims in the world are living in countries that have, at some time, elected women as their leaders. Indeed, four of the five most populous Muslim-majority countries have had women as leaders: Indonesia, the most populous Muslim-majority country, elected Megawati Sukarnoputri as the President.[26] Pakistan, the second most populous Muslim-majority country, twice (non-consecutively) elected Benazir Bhutto as the Prime Minister.[27] Bangladesh, the third most populous Muslim-majority country, elected Khaleda Zia[28] and Sheikh Hasina[29] as Prime Ministers for almost 20 years. Turkey, the fifth most populous Muslim-majority country, elected Tansu Çiller as Prime Minister.[30]

There are many other politically significant women who have performed their active roles in politics and other responsible offices in different Muslim-majority countries.[31] As mentioned earlier, besides holding the topmost public offices, many women today are playing active roles as ministers, parliamentarians, legislators, judges, rectors, deans, vice chancellors, governors, parliament speakers and other dignified posts with quality and efficiency. Notably, Muslim women are making their marks in arenas beyond

---

[26]Megawati Sukarnoputri (1947–) daughter of Sukarno, the founding President of Indonesia, was the President of Indonesia from 2001 to 2004. Available at https://www.britannica.com/biography/Megawati-Sukarnoputri.

[27]Benazir Bhutto (1953–2007), was a Pakistani political leader who was assassinated in December 2007 as she campaigned for a third term as prime minister. She served as Prime Minister of Pakistan from 1988 to 1990 and from 1993 to 1996. Bhutto was the first democratically elected female prime minister in any modern Islamic country. She was the daughter of Zulfikar Ali Bhutto, who was the Prime Minister of Pakistan from 1971 to 1977. Available at http://www.history.com/topics/womens-history/benazir-bhutto.

[28]Khaleda Zia (1945–) is a politician who served as Prime Minister of Bangladesh in 1991–1996 and 2001-2006. She is the first woman to serve as Prime Minister of Bangladesh, and governed during a period of natural disasters, economic distress and civil unrest. Available at https://www.britannica.com/biography/Khaleda-Zia.

[29]Sheikh Hasina Wazed (1947–) is a politician and the current Prime Minister of Bangladesh. She has been the President of the Awami League, a major political party, since 1981. She is the eldest of five children of Sheikh Mujibur Rahman, the first President of Bangladesh. She has been elected as the Prime Minister of Bangladesh twice in 1996 and in 2008. Available at https://www.britannica.com/biography/Sheikh-Hasina-Wazed.

[30]Tansu Çiller (1946–), is the first female Prime Minister of Turkey (1993–1996). Çiller was re-elected as the DYP's leader in 1999, but, after the party fared poorly in the 2002 elections, she stepped down. See Tansu Çiller (2009). Available at http://www.britannica.com/EBchecked/topic/117856/Tansu-Ciller.

[31]For details, see: http://en.wikipedia.org/wiki/List_of_the_first_female_holders_of_political_offices_in_Africa.

politics. Dr. Zeti Akhtar Aziz served as the Governor of the Bank Negara Malaysia, the central bank of Malaysia, during 2000–2016. Dr. Shamshad Akhtar, a Pakistani development economist, diplomat and intellectual who served as the Under-Secretary General of the United Nations as the head of UNESCAP also served as the 14th Governor of the State Bank of Pakistan, the first Muslim woman to assume this position. She also served as a Senior Adviser to Secretary-General of the United Nations Ban Ki-Moon and the Vice-President at the World Bank.

Not all Muslim-majority countries regard women's leadership as normal, nor do all people accept it without question. Some women leaders faced terrible attack by some fanatics. For example, in February 2007, a Pakistani Minister of Social Welfare in Punjab Province, Zilla Huma Usman, 35, an ally of President Pervez Musharraf, was killed as she was about to deliver a speech to dozens of party activists, by a "fanatic" who believed that she was dressed inappropriately and that women should not be involved in politics, officials said.[32] Similarly, Malala Yousafzai who demanded that girls be allowed to receive an education was shot in the head by a Taliban gunman in 2012, but survived and went on to receive the Nobel Peace Prize.

3.7 Moving beyond male-exclusive Islamic legal/religious discourse

One notable aspect of this analysis of the positions of various scholars throughout history on the issue of women's leadership is that all these scholars are men. It is a reality that needs to be acknowledged that unlike during the era of the Prophet (S) and the generation of his companions, Islamic law and jurisprudence developed and evolved in the hands of men exclusively.

Whether the issues are general or pertaining to women, it is the male scholars who exclusively populated this domain of exegesis, *ijtihad* and *fatwa* (religious edict). Throughout history, women somehow acquiesced and resigned themselves to be marginalized and excluded from the space where Islamic laws were shaped and formulated in the hands of men. In modern times, however, Muslim women are reasserting that they have been denied the rights and dignity that Islam grants them and as exemplified during the era of the Prophet (S) and the generation of the companions. They

[32] Times Online, "Female Pakistani minister shot dead for 'breaking Islamic dress code"', available at http://www.timesonline.co.uk/tol/news/world/asia/article1414137.ece.

further claimed that not only they have no presence in and contribution to the discourse that deals with their rights and position, their concerns and grievances were generally met with utter insensitivity, if not disdain, and that even in the name of Islam.

Muslim women are not willing to take a back seat any more. The quest of Muslim women for their empowerment and leadership has stretched so much beyond the orthodox view that women are rejecting male-exclusive *fatwa* bodies, such as All India Muslim Personal Law Board, and setting up their own all women board since 2005.[33] Voices among Muslim women are also raising the point that "women, because of their experience as *women*, were better equipped to render women-sensitive exegesis" (Badran, 2005; Aslan *et al.*, 2013). In April 2017, a milestone event took place in Indonesia. There was a conference of female Muslim scholars/clerics (*ulama*) (Ramadhani, 2017). From this conference Indonesian Women's Ulama Congress, attended by 570 participants, issued resolutions challenging the orthodox positions on child marriage, polygamy (polygyny, to be specific), marital rape and abuse, and so on (Britton, 2017). *'Ulama* from other Muslim-majority countries also attended this conference and echoed the concerns and grievances highlighted in the conference. Taking a lead beyond their male counterparts, the conference also issued *fatwa* related to the environmental protection. It was also remarkable that they issued *fatwa* for complete ban on child marriage, which of course is considered permissible in male-dominated orthodox Islamic law.

In North America, the Fiqh Council of North America, included a female jurist, Dr. Zainab al-'Alwani.[34] Iran has female *mujtahids*, such as Ayatullah Zuhrah Sifati (Kunkler and Fazaeli, 2012). Strengthened by female Muslim academics throughout the world, the tide against the male-dominated Islamic legal discourse is rising and the same *Qur'an* and *Sunnah* are being referred to for renegotiating the roles, rights and duties of women. This has important implications for how the discourse about women empowerment and their leadership is shaping up at the intellectual level and how that discourse is simply trying to catch up with the evolving ground realities in contemporary time; it raises a critical issue in this context.

---

[33] All India Muslim Women Personal Law Board. Available at http://www.muslimwomenpersonallaw.com/.

[34] http://www.fiqhcouncil.org/node/13.

The *Qur'anic* message in regard to gender relationship is highly egalitarian, and both during the era of the Prophet (S) and the generation of the companions, women's role in and contribution to the society — within the constraint of the time and culture at that time — could not be significantly distinguished from men. Leading women personalities, such as 'Ā'isha (R), served as *mujtahids* of highest stature and were acknowledged and appreciated as highly capable experts in legal and religious matters. Subsequently women's space in this valued field shrunk and their roles were marginalized, except in the field of *hadith* scholarship (Farooq, 2003, pp. 27–33), and the legal discourse became a male-exclusive domain.

The domain of Islamic legal discourse and the body of Islamic law evolved without qualified female input. During the era of the Prophet (S) and the generation of the companions, leading women voices, also jurists of their times, served as both synergistic and countervailing force in correcting any anti-women biases. The same was not possible later as Islamic law took shaped in the male-exclusive domain.

Farooq (2011) makes the relevant case:

> Of course, women should be part of juristic discourse at all levels, including at the very highest level of *ijtihad*. Muslims should find the absence of women a serious violation of the Qur'anic view about women being men's mutual *awliya* (guardians). And any juristic position that deviates from this position should be regarded as deficient. In other words, any juristic view, position, opinion or *fatwa* involving women which emanates solely from an exclusively male club of jurists should be considered deficient by default unless proven otherwise and incontrovertibly. As far as the general juristic discourse occurs in the present, that one half of the mutual *awliya* is absent must be acknowledged. Some effort needs to be effected to remove this imbalance and deficiency gradually but surely, not out of some benevolent generosity to women, but for the benefit and wholeness of society. The revered generation of companions who accompanied the Prophet was not complete without Ayesha, Umm Salamah and other women who acted as mentors, guides, teachers and jurists (Farooq, 2011, p. 73).

As Muslim women are seeking their empowerment within the parameters of the *Qur'an* and the *Sunnah*, their preparation to become qualified *mujtahids* and scholars and broadened participation, especially in the field of Islamic law and jurisprudence, should restore a balance in regard to gender issues as envisioned in Islam and exemplified during the time of the Prophet (S).

3.8 Conclusion

The *Qur'an* honored humankind as a single unity, and as a matter of principle makes no distinction due to blood, color, race or gender. All humans regardless of males or females are equals in the eyes of Allah ("O mankind! Behold, We have created you all out of a male and a female and have made you into nations and tribes, so that you might come to know one another. Indeed, the noblest of you in the sight of Allah is the one who is most deeply conscious of Him..." 49:13). As established in the *Qur'an*, Allah judges people by their *taqwa* (consciousness of Allah), not by gender. The Prophet (S) reportedly proclaimed: "Muslims are one fraternity. No one has any superiority or merit over another, except by piety or consciousness of Allah (*al-Muslimuna ikhwah, la fadla li-ahadin 'ala ahadin illa bi al-taqwa*)" (Al-Suyuti, n.d.).

The *Qur'anic* command of *shura* (consultation) includes both men and women. Women actively participate in enjoining good and forbidding vices. The Prophet Muhammad (S) consulted his wives in making important political decisions. He also upheld the political rights of women by confirming the protection granted by Umm Hani (R) to a polytheist during the victory of Makkah. Some of the female companions also got actively involved in political issues. This establishes the fact that women can play political roles and hold topmost public offices to discharge duties side by side with their male counterparts while observing the Islamic code of life.

Women are parts of human society. Historical experience establishes that women can effectively and capably serve at high and responsible positions, including the position of the head of state. In regard to leadership, capability and experience as part of qualification should be a prime concern to Muslim males and females alike. As Islam grants reciprocal rights between men and women and they can be mutual guardians (*awliya'*) of each other, the *Qur'an* cannot be used to prohibit women's leadership. Also, the specific *hadith* used for prohibition does not carry the credibility to warrant such drastic and sweeping prohibition. Women having full rights to compete with their male counterparts and getting elected with their own abilities would be aligned with the vision of a society from Islamic viewpoint. Leadership should not be determined by gender, but the inherent traits, qualities and gifted attributes to serve the people.

It is facetious to propagate that Islam treats men and women as equal and grants all the rights while not even allowing women to vote and participate in the election process. Some Gulf States have been resisting women's participation in the election process. Of course, most of these states are run by dictatorial regimes, which are incompatible with the *Qur'anic* guidance and the example of the Rightly-Guided Caliphs. While invoking the cover of religion, some of them even prohibit women from driving, which has nothing to do with Islam. It is a great irony that Grand Mufti, the country's most senior religious authority of a Gulf country once declared a *fatwa* against women driving, stating that driving would expose women to "temptation" and lead to "social chaos."[35]

Whether the issue is women's empowerment in general or their leadership in particular, Muslims need to approach the matter from the perspective of the vision and norms identified in the *Qur'an* and that exemplified through the legacy and heritage of the Prophet Muhammad (S), and in this regard one essential step has to be women's presence in the discourse about Islamic law and jurisprudence that determine and shape the framework for permissibility and impermissibility in Islam, and also define the scope of women's participation and empowerment.

References

Abd al-Razzaq b. Hamam al-Ṣa'nani, al-Musannaf [annotator: Habib al-Rahman al-A'zami], Vol. 7, p. 384, # 13564, available at https://www.al-islam.org/bn/node/29005#f_fe99c0ea_15. Retrieved on 12 June 2019.

Abdel-Latif, Omayma (15 April 2009), "Sisters in the Muslim brotherhood", Carnegie Middle East Center, available at http://carnegie-mec.org/2009/04/15/sisters-in-muslim-brotherhood-pub-23002. Retrieved on 12 June 2019.

Abu Shiqqah, Abd al-Halim (1990), *Tahrir al-Mar'ah fi 'Asr al-Risalah* (1st edn.), Kuwait: Dar al-Qalam.

Adnan, Gunawan (2004), *Women and The Glorious Qur'an: An Analytical Study of Women-Related Verses of Sura an-Nisa'*, Göttingen: Universitätsdrucke Göttingen.

Al-'Asqalani (n.d.), Ibn Hajar, in Abdul 'Aziz bin Baz (ed.), (1st ed.), *Fath al-Bari Sharh Sahih al-Bukhari.* Beirut: Dar al-Fikr, 8/482.

Al-Bahansawi, Salim (1986), *Makanat al-Mar'ah bayna al-Islam wa al-Qawanin al-'Alamiyyah* (2nd edn.), Kuwait: Dar al-Qalam.

Al-Ghazali, Abu Hamid Muhammad (1964), *Fada'ih al-Batiniyyah*, Egypt: al-Dar al-Qawmiyyah.

Al-Ghazali, Abu Hamid Muhammad (1989), *Al-Sunnah al-Nabawiyyah bayna Ahl al-Fiqh wa ahl al-Hadith* (1st edn.), Beirut: Dar al-Shuruq.

Al-Hibri, A. (1982), Study of Islamic history or how did we ever get into this mess? *Women Studies International Forum*, 5(2), 207–218.

---

[35] https://www.hrw.org/news/2013/10/24/saudi-arabia-end-driving-ban-women.

Al-Hibri, A. (1997), Islam, law and custom: Redefining Muslim women's rights. *American University International Law Review*, 2(1), 1–44.

Al-Kasani, Abu Bakr (1998), *Bada'i' al-Sana'i' fi Tartib al-Shara'i'* (2nd ed.), Beirut: Dar Ihya' al-Turath al-'Arabi.

Al-Mar'isiy, Fatimah (1993), *Al-Harim al-Siyasi, Al-Nabi wa al-Nisa'* (2nd edn.), Damascus: Dar al-Hisad.

Al-Tabari (2015), *The History of al-Tabari*, Vol. 16, translated by Adrian Brockett, New York: State University of New York Press.

Al-Turabi, Hasan (1991), *Women in Islam and Muslim Society*, London: Milestone.

Al-Mawardi (1990), *al-Ahkam al-Sultaniyyah*, translated by Sajidur Rahman Siddiqi, Lahore: Islamic Publications.

Al-Mawdudi, Abul A'la (1980), *Al-Islam fi Muwajahat al-Tahaddiyyat al-Mu'asirah* (4th edn.), Kuwait: Dar al-Qalam.

Al-Qaradawi, Yusuf (1996), *Fatawa Mu'asirah* (2nd edn.), Cairo: Dar al-Qalam.

Al-Qudah, Muhammad Tu'mah Sulayman (1998), *Al-Wilayah al-'Ammah lil-Mar'ah fi al-Fiqh al-Islami*, Jordan: Dar al-Nafa'is.

Al-Qurtubi (2013), *Ahkam al-Qur'an*, 24 Vols., Beirut: Risalah Publishing.

Al-Shawkani, Muhammad bin Ali bin Muhammad (1358H), *Nayl al-Awtar Sharh Muntaqa al-Akhbar min Ahadith Sayyid al-Akhyar*, Egypt: al-Matba'ah al-Uthmaniyyah al-Misriyyah.

Al-Siba'i, Mustafa (n.d.), *Al-Mar'ah bayna al-Fiqhi wa al-Qanun, Dirasah Shar'iyyah wa Qanuniyyah wa Ijtima'iyyah*, (2nd edn.), Halab: Al-Maktabat al-'Arabiyyah.

Al-Sukkah, Abdul Halim (1990), *Tahrir al-Mar'a fi al-Asr ar-Risalah* (Freedom of Women during the Era of the Messenger), 4 Vols., Kuwait: Dar al-Qalam.

Al-Suyuti, Jalaluddin (n.d.), *Al-Jami' al-masanid wa al-marasil*, Complete Islamic Reference Electronic Database, #23538. Retrieved on 12 June 2019.

Ali, Syed Mohammed (2004), *Position of Women in Islam: A Progressive View* (1st edn.), Albany: SUNY Press.

Ashiq Ilahi, Muhammad (2005), *The Daughters of the Holy Prophet*, New Delhi: Idara Isha'at-e-Diniyat.

Aslan, Ednan (2013), "Early community politics and the marginalization of women in Islamic intellectual history," in Aslan, E., Hermansen, M. and Medeni, E. (eds.). *Muslima Theology: The Voices of Muslim Women Theologians*, Oxford: Peter Lang, p. 39.

Aslan, E., Hermansen, M. and Medeni, E. (2013), *Muslima Theology: The Voices of Muslim Women Theologians*, Oxford: Peter Lang.

Barlas, Asma (2009), *Believing Women in Islam: Unreading Patriarchal Interpretations of the Qur'an*, Texas: University of Texas Press.

Badran, Margot (2005), Between secular and Islamic feminism/s: Reflections on the Middle East and beyond. *Journal of Middle East Women's Studies*, 1(1), 18.

Britton, Jack (2017), "The importance of the world's largest gathering of female Islamic clerics", *Jakarta Globe*, available at http://jakartaglobe.id/opinion/worlds-first-womens-islamic-cleric-congress-hosted-w-java-significant/.

CAIR (23 August 2006), "Islamic society elects first female president", available at http://www.cair.com/press-center/cair-in-the-news/8399-islamic-society-elects-first-female-president.html.

Duderijz, Adis (2011), *Constructing a Religiously Ideal "Believer" and "Woman" in Islam*, New York: Palgrave-Macmillan.

El Fald, Khaled Abou (2014), *Speaking in God's Name: Islamic Law, Authority and Women*, Oxford: Oneworld Publications.

Esposito, John (1995), *The Oxford Encyclopedia of the Modern Islamic World: Libe-Sare*, Oxford: Oxford University Press.

Everson, Stephen (ed.) (1988), *Aristotle, Politics*, Vol. 1, Cambridge: Cambridge University Press.

Fadlallah, Muhammad Husayn (1418AH), *Hiwarat fi al-Fikr wa al-Siyasah wa al-Ijtima'*, Beirut: Matba'ah al-Hadiy.

Farooq, Mohammad Omar (2011), "Islamic law and use and abuse of Hadith" in Farooq, Mohammad Omar (ed.).*Toward Our Reformation: From Legalism to Value-oriented Islamic Law and Jurisprudence*, Herndon: IIIT.

Farooq, Mohammad Omar (2003), Women scholars of Islam: Let them bloom again. *Message International*, 28(8/9), 27–33.

Feldman, Noah (2007), *After Jihad: America and the Struggle for Islamic Democracy*, New York: Farrar, Strauss and Giroux.

Geissinger, Aisha (2015), *Gender and Muslim Construction of Exegetical Authority: A Rereading of the Classical Genre of Qur'an Commentary*, Leiden: Brill.

Ibn al-'Arabi, Abu Bakr (n.d.), *Ahkam al-Qur'an* (1st edn.), Beirut: Dar al-Kutub al-Ilmiyyah.

Ibn Hazm, Ali bin Ahmad al-Andalusi (1988), *Al-Muhalla bi al-Aathar*, Beirut: Dar al-Kutub al-Ilmiyyah.

Ibn Khaldun (1987), *Muqaddimah*, translated by Raghib Rahmani, New Delhi: Ittiqad Publishing House.

Ibn Kathir (1410H), *Al-Bidayah wa al-Nihayah*, Beirut: Dar al-Fikr.

Islamic Salvation Front (2009), "Encyclopædia Britannica," available at http://www.britannica.com/EBchecked/topic/295755/Islamic-Salvation. Retrieved on 12 June 2019.

Jalajel, David (2016), *Women and Leadership in Islamic Law: A Critical Analysis of Classical Legal Texts*, Abingdon: Taylor & Francis.

Jamal, Amina (2013), *Jamaat-e-Islami Women in Pakistan: Vanguard of a New Modernity?* Syracuse: Syracuse University Press.

Kausar, Zeenath (1997), *Political Participation of Women: Contemporary Perspectives of Gender Feminists & Islamic Revivalists*, Kuala Lumpur: A.S. Noordeen.

Khan, Israr Ahmad (2010), *Authentication of Hadith: Redefining the Criteria*, Herndon: IIIT.

Kunkler, Mirjam and Fazaeli, Roja (2012), "The life of two Mujtahids: Female religious authority in Twentieth-century Iran," in Bano, Masooda and Kalmbach, Hillary (eds.). *Women, Leadership and Mosques: Changes in Contemporary Islamic Authority*, Leiden: Brill.

Mejia, Melanie (2007), Gender *Jihad*: Muslim women, Islamic jurisprudence, and women's rights. *Kritike*, 1(1), 1–24.

Qutb, Sayyid (2001), *In the Shade of the Qur'an*, Vol. 3, UK: Islamic Foundation.

Ramadhani, Nurul Fitri (26 April 2017), "Indonesia's first female Muslim clerics congress aims to strengthen women's roles," *Jakarta Post*, April 26.

Rida, Muhammad Rashid (1367H), *Nida' li al-Jins al-Latif fi Huquq al-Nisa' fi al-Islam wa Hazzuhunna min al-Islah al-Muhammadiyy al-'am* (2nd edn.), Cairo: Dar al-Manar.

Sayyid Tantawi (1997), *Tafsir al-Waseet li al-Qur'an al-Kareem*, Cairo: Dar Nahdah.

Shehabuddin, Sarah (n.d.), "Female Leadership in Islam", available at http://www.irfi.org/articles/articles_401_450/female_leadership_in_islam.htm. Retrieved on 12 June 2019.

Siddiqui, Muhammad Zubayr (1993), *Hadith Literature: Its Origin, Development, Special Features and its Criticisms*, Cambridge: The Islamic Texts Society.

Thameem Ushama (1995), *Hasan al-Banna — Vision and Mission*, Kuala Lumpur: A.S. Noordeen.

Ullah, Qazi Fazl (2015), *Science of Hadith*, Lulu.com.

Wadud, Amina (2006), *Inside the Gender Jihad: Women's Reform in Islam*, Oxford: Oneworld Publications.

Zaydan, Abd al-Karim (1993), *Al-Mufassal fi Ahkam al-Mar'ah* (1st edn.), Beirut: Muwassasat al-Risalah.

Chapter 4

The Prophetic Vision of Women Empowerment: Evidence from Prophet Muhammad's (pbuh) Family

Mohammad Abdullah

Abstract

Women empowerment is one of the most crucial factors of a society's overall success story. The determinants of women empowerment are many including both the psychological and material components of rights, power and perception. The term "women empowerment" combines between women's sense of self-worth, control of their choices, their rights to avail the benefits of resources and power to direct their own lives in addition to influencing the social change. The body of Islamic tenets, arguably, contains many indications on the building blocks of women empowerment in Islam, which could be retrieved primarily by exploring the specific aspects of Prophet Muhammad's (pbuh[1]) life. The Prophetic scheme on how and to what extent Islam views the need and significance of empowering women can be illustrated by delving into the pertinent Prophetic traditions on the subject of women's rights. In addition, possibly, the vision of the Prophet on women empowerment can be best analyzed by examining the status of the closest female members of his own family. Among the female family members of Prophet Muhammad (pbuh) with whom he had an opportunity to repeatedly interact for a considerable period of time were his wives, daughters and granddaughters. This chapter aims to critically analyze the treatment of the Prophet to one of these three main categories of his female family members, i.e., his wives, in terms of their empowerment. The chapter is based on a qualitative research approach and primarily examines the literature in Arabic, Urdu and English to explore the Prophetic vision of women empowerment. In order to reach a solid

[1]The abbreviation "pbuh" here denotes "peace be upon him".

conclusion, both the primary and secondary sources such as *Quran*, *Hadith*, *Seerah* (biography of the Prophet) and other academic analyses are referred to in this study.

Keywords: Women rights, Gender equality, Freedom in Islam, Equal opportunity

The subject of gender equality in general and women empowerment in particular has increasingly attracted the interest of international policy-makers since the dawn of the 21st century. In view of this development, academic interest in topics such as gender equality, women rights and the role and relevance of women in socio-economic spheres has been on the rise. To this end, the definition, significance, factors, dimensions and constituents of women empowerment have received special treatment in recent academic discussion (Banu, 2015). What evidences the increasing interest and relevance of women empowerment in the last two decades is the inclusion of gender equality-related key goals in several international developmental schemes and plans (Sachs, 2012). For example, among the Sustainable Development Goals (SDGs), the target of gender equality appears as one of the key goals (Abdullah, 2018). This, along with other related goals aim at achieving women empowerment in various dimensions across the globe. The inclusion of gender equality in the list of SDGs particularly signifies the scope and importance of women empowerment at different levels.

The status of women in a given society determines the level of its development. Arguably, a proper sketch and roadmap of development cannot be schematized in a sustainable manner without affording the rights and provision of due treatment to both the genders in equal manner (Athmar and Mark, 2017). The concept of women empowerment is not a new subject of research among the academia; however, its determinants have evolved over the years. The term "women empowerment" is subject to various definitions depending on society-specific and contextual references (Elhum, 2014; Yusuf, 2005). For instance, what might have been taken as a sign and indication of women empowerment a century ago in a specific society or in a particular context, does not necessarily remain to be understood the same way in the modern context. In other words, it is not necessary that the notions and paradigm of women empowerment as held during the pre-modern times still hold true in the post-enlightenment and modern era.

Contrary to these evolving concepts and notions of women empowerment that are induced based on varying worldviews, the religious rules on the subject need to stand the test of time, at least in principle. To put it in another way, the established principles of religion of Islam on women empowerment, for example, cannot be changed; albeit the related guidelines can be refined within the ambit of the provided rules and regulations of juristic analogy (*Ijtihad*).

The Islamic perspective in this context is worthy of analysis and discussion, primarily due to the fact that Islamic guidelines on women modesty and mobility are generally deemed restrictive. The position and narrative of Islam on women empowerment have been usually portrayed both in academic and non-academic discussion with a pinch of skepticism (Muhammad and Pegram, 2010). Rather, in terms of female equality and empowerment, Islamic approach is considered discriminatory by many feminists (Banu, 2015; Jawad, 2010). There is a contention that, according to the Islamic jurisprudential literature women are disadvantaged compared to their male counterparts. As per the theories which suggest the Islamic discriminatory approach toward women compared to men, the gender biased rulings of Islam are the root cause of under-development of Muslim women. Additionally, it is argued that the problem of gender gap as well as relatively less women participation in economic, social, educational and political spheres in many Muslim Majority Nations (MMNs) are informed by the restrictive Islamic paradigm on this front (Ataul, 2012).

This chapter aims to explore and demystify the Islamic approach on women empowerment by analyzing the Prophetic vision, perspective and practices on this topic. The objective of this chapter is to underline the implications of the Prophetic vision of women empowerment for the modern context. Along with referring to, and dilating on the secondary sources and relevant literature, this chapter examines the primary sources of Islam namely the *Quran* and *Hadith*, to understand the Islamic position on women empowerment and discusses its implications in the modern context.

The chapter argues that the notion of women empowerment as established through the Prophetic vision and practices is, at occasions, consistent with the modern approach, however not without its own limitations. The findings of this chapter suggest that, in principle, under the Prophetic scheme of women empowerment, women acquire a higher status and better means of empowerment than the one envisaged in the modern literature. Nevertheless, the Prophetic vision can be achieved only once the concept and notion of women empowerment are put in a proper perspective and the mechanism and tools of empowerment are applied in the prescribed manner. In other words, the Prophetic vision of women empowerment is better understood once placed and viewed within the Islamic frame of women modesty and the dignified stature which Islam offers to them. However, if misplaced or misapplied, the essence and spirit of Prophetic vision of empowering women is lost; causing the misrepresentation of Islamic position on the issue.

The chapter is structured in the following way; the first part of the chapter, i.e., Section 4.1, attempts to discuss the concept of women empowerment in the modern context followed by exploring the Islamic perspective and paradigm on the subject. The second part of the chapter, i.e., Section 4.2, examines and analyzes the Prophetic vision of women empowerment and its relevance and implications in the modern context. Finally, the chapter concludes with some recommendations on how the proper understanding and application of Prophetic vision of women empowerment can play a crucial role in promoting the notion of empowering women among the Muslim societies.

4.1 Women empowerment: An Islamic perspective

The definition and measurement of women empowerment can vary based on the socio-religious contexts. There may be a great degree of divergence in defining the term "women empowerment" depending on the contextual narrative, religious parameters, the line of academic discourse, methodological preferences and the worldview one adopts. Notwithstanding this, a precise characterization of women empowerment can be carried out by weighing the scope for the availability of opportunities and choices coupled with the respectable socio-economic status to women in a given society (Julie, 2017). The liberty and power to shape one's lifestyle and to influence others as per the set priorities in an esteemed manner can be some of the signs and indication of empowerment (Jouharah, 2017). The power to exercise ones' choices lies in acquisition of various capabilities including protection against socio-economic deprivations, attainment of sufficient education and provision of enough liberty to lead and influence (Kabeer, 2000). Over and above, access to fundamental necessities and other vital resources is key to socio-economic empowerment.

Whether Islamic discourse, specifically related to women empowerment aspects, affords the liberty to women to choose and drive their lives, is the focus of this chapter. This chapter endeavors to examine the status of Prophetic vision of women empowerment against the aforementioned criteria which pave way to empowering women. The availability of the resources, scope of preference and liberty which help enable women to shape and direct their socio-economic priorities with dignity is essentially the point of discussion and analysis.

As a base line, within the Islamic purview, it is obligatory for the leadership of a Muslim society to ensure that there is no gender bias either in treatment or in extending the level-playing field along with provision of social security to both the genders. Similarly, in the religious and spiritual terms, Islam treats the acts and deeds of the two genders equally with the identical scale and parameters (Nadwi, 2004). In addition, though, the roles and responsibilities of men and women may vary in technical terms as per the Islamic texts, the accountabilities of the two are similar in terms of enjoining good and forbidding evil. Within the Islamic purview, male and female are considered as guardian to each other (Nadwi, 2004). In the same way, the Islamic financial levies such as *Zakat* and *Sadaqah al-Fitr* are equally applicable to both the genders (Al-Qardawi, 1985). Additionally, in the Islamic literature, there is neither any evident disparity in the right to claim over the resources between the two genders nor does exist any clue on subordination or subjugation of one at the expense of other in invoking their property rights.

Acquisition and enjoyment of resources such as education, economic independence and health care include among the vital elements of empowerment. The Islamic position in granting access to these resources indiscriminately to both genders is crystal clear. Within the Islamic literature, there is neither gender-specific guidelines on accessing resources nor the prescription of a barrier or restriction on who can avail these in what capacity. In Islamic discourse, while, acquiring education has been prescribed as an obligation equally for both men and women (Ibn al-Maja, 1999), a healthy believer has been preferred over the weak irrespective of his/her gender (Muslim, 1999). In addition to this, the liberty to conduct a business activity and the power to own properties is as much granted to female as to males (Hashmi, 2012). Thus, in terms of these three criteria which make the building blocks of the modern notion of women empowerment, there is scantily any gender-biased rulings which may potentially inhibit the scope of empowering Muslim women compared to their male counterparts (Abbas, 2009). In other words, with reference to acquiring knowledge and education, attainment of economic resources and enjoyment of a healthy life, both male and female are equally treated in Islamic paradigm. A self-reliant and economically independent individual who can participate in economic activities and pursue a dignified lifestyle is something as much desired for a Muslim woman as for a male believer. The active role of women in social and religious financing as well as establishing charitable deeds cannot be envisaged without putting the role and status of women in perspective. Islamic teachings address and engage women on these issues equally with men (Ilahi, 1953).

With this, to what degree the concept of women empowerment as enshrined in the Islamic texts match with the modern notion of empowerment is another question leading to further in-depth analysis of the issue in a comparative manner. Dilating on the points of divergence or dissimilarities between the concept of empowerment as understood within the Islamic and modern paradigms may guide to demystify the level of consistencies and inconsistencies between the two. Nevertheless, this comparison lies outside the scope of this chapter, as the objective of this chapter is to focus on the Prophetic vision of women empowerment without touching on the other theories and practices of empowerment.

The notion of women empowerment as elucidated in the Islamic discourse does not seem to contradict with the feminist aspirations so far as the physical, emotional and mental peculiarities of women is recognized and respected. In other words, what a female can perform compared to a male has its own natural limitations. Islamic purview tends to treat these natural peculiarities of women with diligence. In this sense, delineating the scope of what is termed as "modesty"; Islam prescribes specific guidelines for women to guard this while actively availing the resources (Maududi, 1991). The manifestations of these guidelines appear in the respective prescription of dress codes and other vocal and physical activities of Muslim women compared to men.

An exploration of the Islamic literature reveals that the ambit of women liberty in choosing their career paths as well as in deciding their better halves, to the extent the principles and premises of Shariah are not violated, is flexibly open. In this sense, women are not in any way disadvantaged than the men. Over and above, there are evidences which support the Islamic proposition of women participation in decision-making as well as political and international spheres and affairs (Ilahi, 1953). The following part of this chapter delves into the evidences of women empowerment mechanism and strategies within the house of the Prophet himself. In addition to this, the following part of the chapter analyzes the determinants and key components of women empowerment which are inferred by digging into the tradition and practices of the Prophet particularly with reference to his wives. Thus, the Prophetic vision of women empowerment is deduced through his practical treatment of the issue.

4.2 The Prophetic vision of women empowerment

In the Western academia, a noted amount of literature Islam and women empowerment-related issues attempts to treat the notion of women empowerment within the Islamic jurisprudential discourse as a paradoxical idea (Golnaz and Albert, 2013; Ahmed, 1992). The portrayal of Islamic approach as an adverse and antagonistic toward women advancement and upliftment of their social status is the root cause of all the fallacies which developed in the literature and academic discourse (Ali, 2000; Yamani, 1996). This narrative holds that Islamic rulings and jurisprudential paradigm on the topic are responsible for over-regulating and halting the advancement opportunities for Muslim women (Yusuf, 2005). Rather, there are some radical voices as well which claim a complete mismatch between the Islamic teachings on role of women in the family and the concept of women empowerment (Jawad, 2010; Monica, 2008). The protagonist of this proposition endeavor to substantiate their position by creating an adverse link between the Islamic provisions on women modesty and their empowerment. This spurts the scope for the common fallacy that within the Islamic purview women are considered inferior to men and thus are subject to a set of restrictive impositions (Katlin, 2008). What exacerbates this erroneous belief is the practices of some Muslim societies which impose certain restrictions on the activities of women not due to Islamic but cultural, traditional and contextual reasons (Terrie *et al.*, 2012). Arguably, correlating the cases of least women empowerment among the Muslim Majority Nations (MMNs) or societies with the religious principles or beliefs cannot be justified without touching upon the correct Islamic position on the subject. The Islamic position on the social status of women, scope for their mobility and advancement, their participation in various socio-economic endeavors, liberty to decide their profession and being in a position to influence others can be deduced by examining the traditions and dealing of the Prophet in this context.

For the demystification of the fallacy that the under-development of Muslim women particularly among the Muslim societies has a connection with their religious teachings, it is pertinent to note that, broadly, the edifice of Prophetic vision of social justice and equality started with the call for respect and empowerment of women (Ghaznafar, 2004). The Prophet's advocacy for the treatment of women at equal footing with men has its marks both at the beginning of his Prophethood and at the end of his mission. For instance, strictly prohibiting the tradition of burying baby girls alive, a rampant practice, in some of the Arabian tribes was some of the initial undertakings of the Prophet (Armstrong, 1992). This was complemented with a number of Prophetic traditions which elevate not only the status of women but also the status of those who have been kind and tender to them. The Prophetic strategy to raise the social status of women unfolds in several ways (Azad, 2008). The Prophetic tradition (*hadith*) that the one who rears up a baby girl with care and kindness and inculcate in her good etiquettes — by providing her with quality education — will be ensured a place in the paradise, is one of such examples (Al-Tirmidzi, 1999). In the same vein, at several occasions in the Prophetic traditions, the company of the Prophet is promised in the Hereafter for the one who is blessed with two daughters or more and he treats them well without discrimination between the sons and daughters (Muslim, 1999). Similarly, in his final sermon, the Prophet candidly declared: "O People! Remember you have certain rights with regard to your women ... and do treat your women well and be kind to them for they are your partners" (Azad, 2008).

Interestingly, what collates and confirms the dignified status of a woman from the Islamic viewpoint is the Prophetic observation which terms a dutiful woman as the finest of the creations of this world (Muslim, 1999). That the Prophet recognized the role of women equivalent to men or even greater in supporting the accomplishment of the Prophetic mission is exemplified at the occasion of the first Divine revelation to him. The one in whom the Prophet confided about his first ever revelation experience was a woman rather than a man, i.e., Khadija (R.A.[2]), the wife of the Prophet (Ilahi, 1953). Thus, the journey of the Prophetic mission commences with the entry of a woman at first and not a man in the fold of Islam. This may have various implications for the status of women which Islam and the Prophet of Islam confers on them. Not only that the Prophet showed confidence in his wife Khadija (R.A.) for sharing the first experience of revelation but Khadija (R.A.) was the one who led the Prophet to her

[2]In the context of a companion of the Prophet and his family members the abbreviation "R.A." refers to *"RadhiAllahu Anhu"* (may Allah be pleased with him) with the male companion and *"RadhiAllahu Anha"* (may Allah be pleased with her) with the female.

scholar cousin for the purpose of consulting with him about the experience of the Prophet (Ghaznafar, 2004). This very narration whereby a woman appears to console, cooperate and direct the Prophet on what to do next regarding his own Prophethood makes the women stand at a highly elevated position in the sight of Islam.

Exploring some specific aspects of Khadija's (R.A.) life establishes on how she enjoyed the fundamental elements of women empowerment which includes her sense of self-worth, right to avail the benefits of resources and power to direct her own life along with influencing others (Hashmi, 2012). Khadija (R.A.), in the capacity of a famous business women freely followed her economic interest not only by employing others but by partnering with the Prophet himself for her business undertakings (Ilahi, 1953). Although, narrations indicate that the business activities of the Prophet in partnership with Khadija (R.A.) were undertaken during the pre-Prophetic times, however, there is nothing in the Prophetic traditions to negate or contradict the idea of women's liberty to engage in economic and business activities so long as the principles of Shariah are not compromised. Rather, there is neither a substantial evidence to establish and nor a valid reason to believe that post pronouncement of Prophethood, Khadija (R.A.) stopped engaging in business ventures. Contrary to this, the Prophetic assertion that Khadija (R.A.) always supported the propagation of Islamic cause both morally and financially suggests that she continued her engagement in business activities even afterward, which enabled her to assist the Prophet and his mission financially (Ilahi, 1953). Thus, it can be argued that, in material terms, the economic stability of the Prophet was, by and large, sourced by the wealth of his wife Khadija (R.A.) for a long period of time. This is also substantiated by the interpretation of the Quranic verse "that He (Allah) found you indigent and then He enriched you" which specifically refers to Khadija (R.A.) who dedicated her wealth to the Prophetic mission (Al-Jassas, 1928).

In addition to this, the case of Aisha (R.A.), another wife of the Prophet, helps dispel the misconception that Islam unduly restricts the intellectual development or mobility of women in the name of modesty. Aisha (R.A.), the beloved wife of the Prophet, simultaneously assumes the status of a women's right champion, an embodiment of women empowerment and a typical example of a modest but an active and influential Muslim woman. Aisha (R.A.), later on, became a point of reference for the companions of the Prophet in terms of learning the nuances of Islam (Ghaznafar, 2004). She rose to the stature of a leader for both male and female companions during various expediencies (Ilahi, 1953). Aisha (R.A.) along with other female colleagues at times accompanied Muslim troops and actively engaged in nursing and treating the injured companions at the battle field. At numerous occasions, Aisha (R.A.) appears to freely pose counter-questions to the Prophet on issues which needed further clarification (Hashmi, 2012). One such example refers to the Prophet's observation that in the day of judgment all would be raised in the same state as were born, i.e., without cloths. On this, Aisha (R.A.) reverted with the counter-question that if such is the case, then people would be looking at each other. The Prophet responded that the scene at the day would be much more difficult than one may think, and people would be too scared and nervous to look at each other (Ilahi, 1953). The explanations sought by Aisha (R.A.) in several other similar cases from the Prophet elucidate that under the Prophetic scheme, women were not envisaged to be mute spectators or blind followers of the religious underpinnings. Rather, the ideal Muslim woman was supposed to deploy her intellect and utilize the resources as much as men can do.

During the life time of the Prophet, the role of Aisha (R.A.) in explaining the nuances of particularly women-related Shariah rules was that of an intermediary, i.e., seeking explanation from the Prophet and conveying the same to the fellow women. After the demise of the Prophet, Aisha (R.A.) continued to engage in intellectual discussion to the extent that she was considered as one of the leading scholars of Medina, to whom the companions of the Prophet frequently referred to in the matter of *Deen* (religion) (Nadwi, 2004). In relation to the understanding of certain aspects of Prophetic traditions, the self-confidence of Aisha (R.A.) remained unwavering even in the face of the opinion of the greatest male companions of the Prophet. For instance, on the question of whether Prophet (pbuh) saw the Creator (Allah) at the occasion of his ascendance to the heaven (*al-Meraj*), Aisha (R.A.) fiercely disputed with the opinion of Abdullah Ibn al-Abbas (R.A.) who was one of the most respected scholars among the companions (Azad, 2008).

Arguably, the spirit of self-confidence coupled with the features of leadership as embodied in Aisha (R.A.) and Khadija (R.A.) was not but a reflection of what the Prophetic vision was about an ideal Muslim woman. Perhaps, no one is in a better position than Aisha (R.A.) and Khadija (R.A.) to represent what the Prophet might have envisaged for the ideal Muslim women in terms of recognizing their self-worth, developing their intellectual capacity and enjoying their socio-economic choices along with being an active member of the civil society. The examples of Aisha (R.A.) and Khadija (R.A.) set the stage for the engagement of Muslim women in business, knowledge sharing and discussion on various issues while pursuing their social and educational interests. In a nutshell, to translate the Prophetic vision of women empowerment into practice, perhaps, recalling the accounts of activities of Aisha (R.A.) and Khadija (R.A.) may help the Muslim societies to achieve what the modern theories and framework of empowering women have failed to do.

Though, given some of the biological and physical peculiarities of women, Islam prescribes somewhat a different set of rulings to respect their privacy and modesty. These prescriptions are neither in any way meant to subvert their right to enjoy equal opportunities nor are aimed to hinder the prospects of their empowerment (Maududi, 1999). Nonetheless, since the practices of some Muslim societies seem to contradict the Islamic position of gender equality in terms of avenues of empowerment for women *vis-à-vis* men, at times an artificial link is created between the teachings of Islam on women modesty and underdevelopment of Muslim women to explain this phenomenon (Muhammad and Pegram, 2010; Minai, 1981). To this end, what is essential to underline and appreciate is the point of differences between the true Islamic position on women empowerment and the practices of Muslim societies in treating them. This in turn, may help dispel the doubts and enlighten the blurred lines of correct Islamic paradigm on the status and position of women.

4.3 Recommendations and conclusion

This chapter attempted to analyze the Islamic view of women empowerment by dilating on the Prophetic traditions, treatment and practices on the subject. The objectives of this chapter included the exploration of Islamic position and Prophetic vision of women empowerment and its implications in the modern context. It is argued in this chapter that though the concept of women empowerment, in general, is subject to evolution and open to different interpretations, the Islamic position on the subject has been crystal clear from the very beginning. The chapter found that among the key objectives of the Prophetic mission involved the promotion of equality, social justice and provision of equal opportunities to all in a gender-neutral manner. Women, within the Prophetic vision and Islamic paradigm, are envisaged to freely engage in social, economic and educational spheres so far as the means and mechanism of modesty, civility and dignity, as prescribed in the Islamic texts, is observed. Arguably, the prescription of specific Islamic guidelines on women modesty is meant to recognize their biological, physical and emotional peculiarities, and this shall neither be viewed as a sign of their inferiority nor should hinder their way to equal opportunities and empowerment. The true Islamic position on the status, stature and role of women in the civil society cannot be properly grasped only by referring to the jurisprudential nuances of women modesty in isolation with the Prophetic vision and practices as embodied in his treatment of women.

This chapter underlined that in order to derive a clearer picture and to determine the extent of women empowerment within the Islamic framework, the practical example of the Prophetic treatment toward his wives serves the purpose in the best possible manner.

Some of the key constituents pointing to the vision of empowering women is repeatedly observed within the discourse of Prophetic treatment of his female family members. These include freedom of choice for them, liberty to develop intellectual capabilities, room to voice their concern, scope to follow economic ends, opportunity to freely put counter-questions as well as extending to them the status and stature to lead and influence others. Additionally, the Prophetic practices help guide women on how to avail the freedom of choice, fulfill material needs and develop their own personalities. All these in addition to meeting the requisites of the religion. On the one hand, the Prophetic traditions help women navigate through the paths of attaining a higher moral and spiritual status, on the other, the practices of the Prophet epitomize the role of men in supporting their female family members in realizing their self-worth.

Notwithstanding these, the concept of women empowerment within the Muslim societies remains subject to a plethora of interpretations based on cultural and contextual backgrounds. In view of this phenomena, what is needed in the current scenario is the reform in the approach and perspective of religious leadership in line with the Prophetic vision on the subject of women empowerment. In a nutshell, it can be argued that there is no special need to engage in reinterpretation of Islamic teachings on women empowerment, rather a proper understanding and application of Prophetic vision may suffice to promote the practice of women empowerment among the Muslim societies. Arguably, misapplication of Islamic approach on women empowerment often obstructs Muslim women's potential contribution and participation in the overall developmental process. And, any undue restriction by the Muslim societies on women may be tantamount to infringement of their rights resulting into denial of their dues as enshrined in the primary sources of Shariah. To this end, engagement of various stakeholders and their consolidated efforts with integrated approach can be a catalyst of change. Finally, an active involvement of *Ulama* in promoting the Prophetic vision of women empowerment may play a critical role in achieving the paradigm shift among the Muslim societies. To sum it up, by applying the Prophetic vision of women empowerment in its true sense, the desired outcome of empowering women can be achieved without compromising on the ethos, values and principles of Shariah.

References

Abbas, J. (2009), Islamic perspectives on leadership: A model. *International Journal of Islamic and Middle Eastern Finance and Management*, 2(2), 160–180.

Abdullah, M. (2018), Waqf, Sustainable Development Goals (SDGs) and Maqasid al-shariah. *International Journal of Social Economics*, 45(1), 158–172.

Ahmed, L. (1992), *Women and Gender in Islam: Historical Roots of a Modern Debate*, Yale: New Haven, CT.

Ali, S. (2000), Gender and Human Rights in Islam and International Law: Equal before Allah, Unequal before Men? *Kluwer Law International*, The Hague.

Armstrong, K. (1992), *Muhammad: A Biography of the Prophet*, New York: Harper Collins.

Ataul Huq, P. (2012), Development and democratization from the perspective of Islamic world view: The role of civil society versus state in the Arab world. *Humanomics*, 28(1), 5–25.

Athmar, S. and Mark, S. (2017), Women in leadership in Kuwait: A research agenda. *Gender in Management: An International Journal*, 32(2), 141–162.

Banu, Ö. (2015), Secular and Islamic feminist entrepreneurship in Turkey. *International Journal of Gender and Entrepreneurship*, 7(1), 45–65.

Elhum, H. (2014), Establishing the connection between demographic and economic factors, and gender status in the Middle East: Debunking the perception of Islam's undue influence. *International Journal of Sociology and Social Policy*, 34(7/8), 455–484.

Golnaz, G. and Albert, J. (2013), Unveiling the myth of the Muslim woman: A postcolonial critique. *Equality, Diversity and Inclusion: An International Journal*, 32(2), 157–172.

Jawad, S. (2010), An historical perspective on Islamic modesty and its implications for female employment. *Equality, Diversity and Inclusion: An International Journal*, 29(2), 150–166.

Jouharah M. (2017), Women and leadership: Challenges and opportunities in Saudi higher education. *Career Development International*, 22(2), 165–183.

Julie, H. (2017), Cracking the walls of leadership: Women in Saudi Arabia. *Gender in Management: An International Journal*, 32(1), 34–46.

Kabeer, N. (2000), Resources, agency, achievements: Reflections on the measurement of women's empowerment. *Development and Change*, 30(3), 435–464.

Katlin, O. (2008), Women in management in the Arab context. *Education, Business and Society: Contemporary Middle Eastern Issues*, 1(2), 107–123.

Maududi, A. (1991), *Purdah and the Status of Women in Islam*, Lahore: Islamic Publications.

Minai, N. (1981), *Women in Islam: Tradition and Transition in the Middle East*, London: John Murray.

Monica, G. (2008), The application of feminism in the Arab world: Research perspectives. *Education, Business and Society: Contemporary Middle Eastern Issues*, 1(3), 193–199.

Muhammad, R. and Pegram, H. (2010), Behind the veil: Women-only entrepreneurship training in Pakistan. *International Journal of Gender and Entrepreneurship*, 2(2), 150–172.

Sachs, J. (2012), "From Millennium Development Goals to Sustainable Development Goals", available at www.thelancet.com/journals/a/article/PIIS0140-6736%2812%2960685-0/fulltext. Retrieved on 20 September 2017.

Terrie, C., Arlise, P. and Laila, A. (2012), Muslim women's workplace experiences: Implications for strategic diversity initiatives. *Equality, Diversity and Inclusion: An International Journal*, 32(1), 49–67.

Yamani, M. (ed.) (1996), "Introduction", *Feminism and Islam: Legal and Literary Perspectives*, Reading: Ithaca Press.

Yusuf, S. (2005) Women, work, and Islam in Arab societies. *Women in Management Review*, 20(7), 498–512.

Arabic

Ibn al-Maja (1999), *Mawsuah al-Hadith al-Sharif*, Riyadh: Darussalam.

Al-Jassas, A. (1928), *Ahkam al-Qu_ran*, Cairo: al-Matba'atal-Baha'iyya.

Muslim, Al-sahih (1999), *Mawsuah al-Hadth al-Sharif*, Riyadh: Darussalam.

Al-Qardawi, Y. (1985), *Fiqh al-Zakat*, translated by M. Kahf, London: Dar al-Taqwa Ltd.

Al-Tirmidzi, Jami' (1999), *Mawsuah al-Hadth al-Sharif*, Riyadh: Darussalam.

Urdu

Azad, A. (2008), *Musalman Aurat*, Lahore: Maktaba Jamal.

Ghaznafar, M. (2004), *Sahabiyat Mubasshirat*, Lahore: Maktaba Quddusiyah.

Hashmi, T. (2012), *Tizkar e Suwalihat*, Delhi: Areeb Publications.

Ilahi, A. (1953), *Ummat e Muslima ki Mayen*, Delhi: Irshad Publications.

Nadwi, A. (2004), *Uswa a Sahabiyat*, Azamgarh (Uttar Pradesh): Shibli Academy.

Chapter 5

The Role of Women in Business and the Life of Khadija*

Irum Saba and Khadija Bari

Abstract

Nations where women work side by side with men are considered successful as the manpower is double than the nations where only men work. The role of women in business/workplace is always debated by mankind in all parts of the world. This chapter focusses on the role of women in business in pre-Islam and post-Islam time period. There are several misconceptions about women when it comes to Islam. Whereas in reality Islam gave women a very special place when compared with other religions. The contribution of women in early time of Islam is very crucial as this shows how the light of Islam changed the perception of females. The chapter also focusses on the wonderful exemplary first lady in Islam, that is, Hazrat Khadija. The life and business activities of Hazrat Khadija are discussed in the chapter as she is a role model for many.

Keywords: Muslim women, Business, Khadija, Entrepreneurship, Post- and pre-Islam

The rights of women, and perhaps more fundamentally, the honor, status and value of women in society, in any given time, geography, religion or civilization, is a debate as old as mankind itself.

Islam as a religion, claims to be the complete code for the human life, and the path to obtain *Falah* (the ultimate success), whether for an individual or the community, in this world as well as the Hereafter. A point noteworthy here is that it claims to present the *Shariah* — the Islamic law

*R.A. First Wife of Prophet Muhammad.

and way of life, to all ages, races, nationalities and civilizations, from the time of the Prophet Muhammad (pbuh) in the 7th century AD, till the end of time! This is indeed a monumental claim, a claim made perhaps by no other legal system in the world. For, such a vast time period includes women residing in very different eras. They may be poor women, or even slave women, or females at a time when women right had no global or local recognition whatsoever. They may be those belonging to a simplistic rural life, or a deeply conventional society, a patriarchal community. Or they may be present in a modern world with women facing many new challenges.

Islam accepts women as creations of the Almighty Allah, just as men are. In this respect, it has granted unique honor to women, whatever situations or environments they may belong to, in different roles. Foremost among them, mentioned repeatedly in the *Quran* (Holy Book) and *Hadith* (sayings, actions and approvals of the Prophet Muhammad (pbuh)), are a woman's rank as mother, daughter, wife and sister. Perhaps less mentioned, but equally revered, are her positions as a worshipper, a *Waliya* (friend of Allah), *Taaliba* (student of the sacred knowledge of religion), a teacher, a leader of women, a homemaker, a businesswoman, etc.

Islam has greatly honored the role and value of a woman as a mother. The following verse of the *Quran* and the *Hadith* highlight the position of a mother in Islam.

The popularity of Islam and Prophet Muhammad (pbuh), was seen as threatening by the people of power in Mecca, and Bedouin Tribes of Arab Peninsula. This led to frequent wars and skirmishes between Muslims and Meccan Pagans. Even though, Islam regarded participating in these battles as holy war (*jihad*), and as a duty with the highest reward for men.

However, it was narrated that Mu'awiyah bin Jahimah As-Sulaimi said:

> "I came to the Messenger of Allah (pbuh) and said: 'O Messenger of Allah, I want to go for Jihad with you, seeking thereby the Face of Allah and the Hereafter.' He said: 'Woe to you! Is your mother still alive?' I said: 'Yes.' He said: 'Go back and honor her.' Then I approached him from the other side and said: 'O Messenger of Allah, I want to go for Jihad with you, seeking thereby the Face of Allah and the Hereafter.' He said: 'Woe to you! Is your mother still alive?' I said: 'Yes.' He said: 'Go back and honour her.' Then I approached him from in front and said: 'O Messenger of Allah, I want to go for Jihad with you, seeking thereby the Face of Allah and the Hereafter.' He said: 'Woe to you! Is your mother still alive?' I said: 'Yes.' He said: 'Go back and serve her, for there is Paradise." (Sunan Ibn Majah, *hadith* no. 2781)

Similarly, Abu Hurairah narrated, that a man came to Apostle of Allah (pbuh) and said:

> "O Messenger of Allah, who is most deserving of my good company?" He said: "Your mother." He said: "Then who?" He said: "Your mother." He said: "Then who?" He said: "Your mother." He said: "Then who?" He said: "Then your father." (Al Bukhari, *hadith* no. 5971)

This explains how Islam has protected the right of respect, duty and honor owed to mothers, three times more than fathers.

Moreover, the Holy *Quran* indicates that being dutiful and kind to mother, is a characteristic that is beloved to Allah, and a characteristic shared by His Messengers.

The miraculous speech of Prophet Jesus during his infancy included

وَبَرًّا بِوَالِدَتِي وَلَمْ يَجْعَلْنِي جَبَّارًا شَقِيًّا -

> "... and (He has made me) good to my mother, and he did not make me oppressive (or) ill-fated." (19:32)

One intrinsic beauty of Islam is that Allah, as the creator of both men and women, has not differentiated them in matters that ultimately make a difference in the Hereafter. In the world, we are told to accept that men and women are not identical. Their needs and rights may differ. For instance, men are physically stronger, have a responsibility and authority over their family (which includes women). Women have proven also to be great teachers, better at multi-tasking, etc. A man in a household owes obedience, but Islam also grants a woman the right to physical and financial protection. It grants her the crucial right of knowledge, of choosing her husband, of kindness, safety and provision from her husband and family. Perhaps even more controversially (even in the modern society), in an age when the concept of women owning wealth was foreign, Islam awarded inheritance rights to wives, daughters, mothers and even sisters.

The importance of rank in society, respect, ownership of wealth, degree of choice, etc. tends to differ from person to person in society, what matters at the end (from Islamic perspective) are the *Baaqiyat-us-Salihaat* — the actions and virtues that are everlasting. And here, almost no distinction has been made for the genders: a woman's character, knowledge, prayers, closeness with Allah and His Prophet (pbuh), patience, actions, modesty, etc. are just as valuable as a man's.

It has been highlighted in Quran that the value, status or rank of men and women, particularly regarding their actions and potential of success in the Hereafter, is equal.

إِنَّ الْمُسْلِمِينَ وَالْمُسْلِمَاتِ وَالْمُؤْمِنِينَ وَالْمُؤْمِنَاتِ وَالْقَانِتِينَ وَالْقَانِتَاتِ وَالصَّادِقِينَ
وَالصَّادِقَاتِ وَالصَّابِرِينَ وَالصَّابِرَاتِ وَالْخَاشِعِينَ وَالْخَاشِعَاتِ وَالْمُتَصَدِّقِينَ وَالْمُتَصَدِّقَاتِ
وَالصَّائِمِينَ وَالصَّائِمَاتِ وَالْحَافِظِينَ فُرُوجَهُمْ وَالْحَافِظَاتِ وَالذَّاكِرِينَ اللَّهَ كَثِيرًا
وَالذَّاكِرَاتِ أَعَدَّ اللَّهُ لَهُم مَّغْفِرَةً وَأَجْرًا عَظِيمًا - 33:35

> "Surely, Muslim men and Muslim women, believing men and believing women, devout men and devout women, truthful men and truthful women, patient men and patient women, humble men and humble women, and the men who give Sadaqah (charity) and the women who give Sadaqah, and the men who fast and the women who fast, and the men who guard their private parts (against evil acts) and the women who guard (theirs), and the men who remember Allah much and the women who remember (Him) — for them, Allah has prepared forgiveness and a great reward." (33:35)

It is crucial to have role models or personalities in society that can inspire and motivate individual to be successful in this world and Hereafter. The life of Prophet Muhammad (pbuh) is a role for every person of this world who believes in Allah and Day of Judgment. Moreover, Muslims have been recommended to follow the companions of Prophet Muhammad (pbuh) to be rightly guided.

The female companions of Prophet Muhammad (pbuh) are personalities, that include women who excelled in different walks of life: some were excellent mothers and homemakers, some farmers, some even participated in battles, some became exceptional leaders, some excelled at business and trade, and then there were women who had treasures of knowledge of Islam. It has been acknowledged by scholars that without the contribution by women, a third or a fourth of knowledge of religion would have been lost.

5.1 Pre-Islam status of women in society

Even though the status of women in the society had never been challenged or upraised, before the inception of Islam, through the preaching of Islam, not only the people of Arabia but also the entire world was astonished to see how Islam raised the status of women — the creation of Allah who was previously treated as a low-price commodity or second-class citizens at best.

The inception of Islam eradicated the gender discrimination, which was deeply rooted in customs of Arabian Peninsula prior to the teachings of Islam. It made women stand equal to men in rights and honor. If we look at the pre-Islamic status of a woman, Shaykh Zulfiqar says, "A clear verdict from the history can be taken that pre-Islam, every religion civilization and society treated woman with extremism" (Ahmed, 2000c).

Before Islam dawned upon the world, different societies and religions had various stereotypes and customs regarding women. These stereotypes and customs affected the social well-being of women adversely in these societies.

The Arab Peninsula was however one of the most extremist among them. It was a matter of shame and disgrace for the entire tribe if the news of the birth of a baby girl was given to them.

The most horrendous action which was customary in pre-Islamic Arabia, is narrated in the following verses of *Quran*.

وَإِذَا بُشِّرَ أَحَدُهُم بِالْأُنثَىٰ ظَلَّ وَجْهُهُ مُسْوَدًّا وَهُوَ كَظِيمٌ يَتَوَارَىٰ مِنَ الْقَوْمِ مِن سُوءِ مَا
بُشِّرَ بِهِ ۚ أَيُمْسِكُهُ عَلَىٰ هُونٍ أَمْ يَدُسُّهُ فِي التُّرَابِ ۗ أَلَا سَاءَ مَا يَحْكُمُونَ -

> "When one of them is given the good news of a female child, his face becomes gloomy and he is choked with grief. He hides himself from people because of the (self-presumed) bad news given to him (and wonders): Shall he keep it despite the disgrace (he will face in the society), or put it away into the dust? In fact, evil is what they decide." (16:58–59)

In pre-Islamic Arabia, people were grieved by the birth of a baby girl, whereas, in the *Quran*, Allah, referred to the birth of daughter as "glad tidings".

The Arabs, however, used to keep the news of the birth of a female baby a secret, considered it a disgrace for a father to be raising daughters, loving them or spending on them, and most horrendously, even burying the innocent infant alive in the mud!

The rights of women were so neglected by the society that if a person would die, and as a rule, his wealth was distributed to his decedents, similarly the inheritors would also inherit the wives of the dead person. In other instances, the widows will be locked up in outskirts of Mecca, without the necessities of life, and if a widow resisted against her life, then she was taken out and made a symbol of disgrace (Ahmed, 2000a).

5.2 The light of Islam!

The revelation of Islam shunned the barbaric practice and norms, that were prevalent in the pre-Islamic Arabia, and raised the status of woman in such a way that the world had to accept her.

In a revelation to Prophet Muhammad (pbuh), Allah, warned those involved in barbaric acts against women, regarding Justice to be made on the Day of Judgment, and stated:

وَإِذَا الْمَوْءُودَةُ سُئِلَتْ بِأَيِّ ذَنبٍ قُتِلَتْ -81:9

> "And when the child-girl that was buried alive will be asked. For what sin she was killed." (81:8–9)

Islam did not only reject oppression on women but also categorically told the society that your sister is your honor, your daughter is your respect and matter of pride, and your wife is your life partner.

The following *Hadith* emphasizes on the respect and honor for a woman as a mother, daughter and wife in Islam.

It was narrated from Mu'awiyah bin Jahimah As-Sulami, that Jahimah came to the Prophet (pbuh) and said:

> *"O Messenger of Allah! I want to go out and fight (in Jihad) and I have come to ask your advice." He said: "Do you have a mother?" He said: "Yes." He said: "Then stay with her, for Paradise is beneath her feet."* (Sunan an-Nasai, *hadith* no. 3104).

The Messenger of Allah, Holy Prophet (pbuh) said:

> "He, who brought up two girls properly till they grew up, he and I would come (together) (very closely) on the Day of Resurrection, and he interlaced his fingers (for explaining the point of nearness between him and that person)." (Sahih Muslim, *hadith* no. 2631)

Abu Huraira reported: The Messenger of Allah (pbuh) said,

> "I enjoin you to treat women well, for the woman was created from a rib and the most curved part of the rib is its highest point. If you try to straighten it, you will break it. If you leave it as it is, it will remain bent. Thus, I enjoin you to be good to women." (Ṣaḥīḥ al-Bukhārī, *hadith* no. 3153)

Shaykh Zulfiqar explains, that "Islam has taught the society that woman is created from the rib of man, the rib is not in his feet, this is a clear indication that woman is to be treated with equality. Secondly, ribs in the human body are for the safety of heart, similarly women are the safety ribs of a society" (Ahmed, 2000b).

Furthermore, considering the lack of rights and duties toward mothers and daughters in pre-Islamic Arabia, Prophet Muhammad (pbuh) said:

> "Allah has forbidden you (1) to be undutiful to your mothers, (2) to withhold (what you should give) or (3) demand (what you do not deserve), and (4) to bury your daughters alive. And Allah has disliked that you talk too much about others, ask too many questions (in religion), or waste your property." (Sahih al-Bukhari, *hadith* no. 2408)

This allows us to analyze that, Islam did not only give respect and value to women, but also defined the rights and duties toward her, as a mother, daughter and sister. This in turn, allowed woman to make contributions to religion and society that can never be neglected or overlooked.

5.3 Contribution of women in early era of Islam

The contribution of women in early era of Islam, were commendable, as they were not only involved in daily chores at home but also actively participated in battles, preaching religion, seeking knowledge and doing business.

In the early era of Islam, the popularity of Islam and Prophet Muhammad (pbuh), was see as threatening by people of power in Mecca, which led to frequent battles and skirmishes. The people of power in Mecca, gathered tribes' men from all over Arabian Peninsula with aim to wipe out Muslims and Islam. During these times when Muslims were few against whom armies of thousands gathered, the Muslim women played a vital role, by not only involving directly in battle but also contributing socially.

The bravery and participation of Umm-e-Ammara, in Battle of Trench, of Safya, Battle of Hunain, and Umm-e-Sulaim, have even been acknowledged by the medieval scholar, Ibn Hajar Al Asqalan.

Similarly, Aisha bint Abu Bakr, Rabee bint Muawwiz, Umm-e-Ziyad, Umm-e-Atiya and many more, made significant contributions in battles by, providing first aid to the injured, serving water to the thirsty, cooking and preparing food for the army, arranging arms and weapons for them, and also by financially contributing to the war.

The women also participated by preaching Islam. For example, during a time when Muslims were being persecuted in Mecca and were desperate for help, Hazrat Umar, whose bravery was well known throughout Arabian Peninsula, was invited to Islam by his sister, Fatima Bint Khattab. The acceptance of Islam by Hazrat Umar, gave strength to Muslims, later Hazrat Umar became the second caliph. Similarly, Abu Talha and Ikrama, accepted Islam, on the invitation of Umm-e-Hakeem and Umm-e-Sulaim.

The significant contribution of women regarding seeking, teaching and preserving the religious knowledge cannot be neglected. Umm-e-Salma and Umm-e-Warqa were mostly known memorizers of the *Quran* and Umm-e-Saad used to teach the *Quran.*

Moreover, to preserve religious knowledge, the contribution by Aisha bint Abu Bakr, is so significant that, an entire chapter is written in *Sahih Bukhari* (Book of Hadith), related to interpretation of the *Quran* (Holy Book) from the *Hadith* she narrated. There are more than 2210 narration of the *Hadith* that have been made by Aisha bint Abu Bakr. Other than Aisha bint Abu Bakr, Asma bint Abu Bakr, Umm-e-Hani and Fatima bint-e-Qais are so popular names that are known for narration of the *Hadith* (Ansari, 1995).

The women of early era of Islam, excelled in other areas too, such as, Shafa bint Abdullah was considered to be the authority for decision-making and was appointed as the "Muhtasib" (Ombudsman) of the market by the caliph.

The women, in early era of Islam, were also involved in business and trade. Saeed Ansari writes that first cottage industry of Islam was established by the women — they used to weave and prepare clothes at home and sell them, which was the source of their income. The women in Medina used to practice small-scale farming. Hola, Thaqeefa and Bint-e-Makhraba were well known for their business of perfumes (Ansari, 1995).

Many of them were businesswoman including Khadija tul Kubra. She also had the honor of being the first wife of Prophet Muhammad (pbuh) and first women to accept Islam.

5.4 Syeda Khadija (the first woman of Islam)

There is no doubt that in the history of Islam, numerous women have been mentioned for their struggles and contributions to Islam. The efforts of Muslim women in the upbringing of children, who later became well-known scholars, writers, warriors and righteous leaders, has been praised significantly too.

From these women, who contributed to Islam exceptionally, Syeda Khadija was one of the most significant. The significance of Syeda Khadija, can be emphasized by the fact that she was the first one to know about the revelation on Messenger of Allah, Prophet Muhammad (pbuh). Prophet Muhammad (pbuh) initially narrated the event of first revelation by Allah to Syeda Khadija. Syeda Khadija comforted the Prophet (pbuh) by saying:

> "I swear by Allah! Allah would never humiliate you, for you are good to your relatives, you are true to your word, you help those who are in need, you support the weak, you feed the guest and you answer the call of those who are in distress." (Sahih Bukhari, *hadith* no. 3)

Mujahid writes, "Keeping all virtues of Syeda Khadija aside, this is enough for her greatness and excellency that she is the first woman in Islam to whom Islam was presented and abruptly without any hesitation or question she accepted Islam, believing Muhammad (pbuh), as the last messenger of Allah" (Mujahid, 2008).

He continues to write: "To understand the honor and virtues of the first lady of Islam, it's enough that Syeda Fatima (the Prophet's daughter) — who was declared the leader and the head of (women in) paradise — was the daughter of Syeda Khadija" (Mujahid, 2008).

Khadijah al-Kubra was the daughter of Khuwaylid ibn (son of) Asad ibn Abdul-'Uzza ibn Qusayy and belonged to the clan of Banu Hashim of the tribe of Banu Asad. She was a wife of the Messenger of Allah, Muhammad ibn Abdullah ibn Abdul-Muttalib Ibn Hashim ibn Abd Manaf ibn Qusayy (pbuh).

The Arabs gave her the title of "Tahirah" (the pious one), "the leader of women of Quraish" (Ibn e Asaakir, 1997). And the Quran gave her the title of "Mother of the believers" (*Quran* 33:6). The Prophet of Allah (pbuh) once declared her "the most superior lady of Jannah" (Musnad Ahmed, *hadith* no. 293).

Syeda Khadijah was born 15 years before the "year of elephant" (Abi Sarh, n.d.). Her family and tribe were among the most honorable and pious families of Arab.

Her father was among the noble wealthy businessmen of Makkah, and due to his tremendous skills and business expertise, his business was widespread and was of good reputation in the society. Khadijah's mother

Fatima was daughter of Za'ida ibn al-Asam, she was also from the tribes of Quraish (Al-Jibouri, 2016).

Al-Jibouri writes, "Although the society in which Khadijah was born was terribly male chauvinistic, Khadijah earned two titles: "Ameerat Quraish" (Princess of Quraish), and "At-Tahira", the Pure One, due to her impeccable personality and virtuous character, not to mention her honorable descent. She used to feed and clothe the poor, assist her relatives financially, and even provide for the marriage of those of her kin who could not otherwise have had means to marry.

About her, Mujahid writes, "Khadija was among those noble personalities about which historians have written that she was complete and one of the most perfect ladies, from the angle of pedigree, grace, character, morality, wealth, leadership, sympathy with people, she was the only one of her time. Indeed, whoever titled her with Tahira-The pure one, titled her correctly" (Mujahid, 2008).

On strength of Ibn-e-Ishaq, Mujahid mentions the time when some ladies of Makkah were gathered, one of the Jews said, "O respectable ladies! Soon among you a Nabi (prophet) of Allah will be appearing, anyone of you who could present herself to marry him, do that". Almost all of them accused and abused him considering that he was actually abusing their idols, but Khadija on the other hand kept silent and started pondering over the matter. She had known through her cousin Warqa Bin Nowfil about the arrival of the last Prophet from the ancestry of Prophet Ismail (Mujahid, 2008).

As mentioned earlier, according to historians, the father of Khadija R.A. was a super tycoon businessman and therefore Khadija R.A. inherited not only wealth but also business expertise and skills. Whenever she hired an agent for her business, she gave specific instructions of how to sell the items, the do's and don'ts of the trade.

5.4.1 Trade practices of Arabs

Mujahid mentions, "Busra is 140 km away from Damascus — the capital of Syria near Amman, and Jerusalem, is very near, so due to which it was one of the huge business hubs of that time. The business caravans used to visit it from all around the world and perform great business deals. In winters, the weather conditions of Syria used to become worse, heavy snowfall and extreme low temperature did not allow the traders to enter and therefore the trading caravans used to move in Yemen, where the weather used to be so moderate and pleasant. Business was the backbone of the Arab society and they were brought up in such a way that as a child reached puberty, he was ready for doing business.

Like others, Quraish used to sell their Arabic home products there and purchased the commodities of different countries and sell those things at their homeland" (Mujahid, 2008).

This was the import and export of that time in the free trade economy where no trade barriers were there. And this is the concept which Islam gives; Islamic economics have always highlighted the importance of "no government intervention" and "free trade" and always encouraged them in the normal conditions, where consumer choices and their purchasing power would decide "What to produce" and "For whom to produce". Parallel to that, government and society should always focus on increasing the purchasing power of the "have-nots" by encouraging and imposing *Zakat* and donations. We see that the Arab society was following the same custom of "free trade" at that time.

The businesses in Arab were of two common types:

1. Sole proprietorship.
2. Partnerships (*Mudarabah*).

Small-scale businessmen of that time used the sole proprietorship model. They had small amount of money, they invested it and then ran their business themselves. Unlike these small businessmen, there were some wealthy investors, who had handsome amount of capital, but either lacked business expertise, time or education and hence had to hire agents or sign partnerships agreements.

The great Arab traders normally used the *Mudaraba* model. The *Mudaraba* is an investment by one partner (can be more than one) and the services provision (business expertise) by the second partner. The investor is called Rab-ul-Maal (literally means "owner of wealth") while the other partner (with expertise) is called *Mudarib*. Investor does not serve his expertise at all, Mudarib never invests a single penny. The return would be distributed among them as per the pre-agreed ratio, whatever it is. In the event of loss, all the loss will have to be borne by the investor.

5.4.2 Model of her business — Mudaraba

Many of the successful business tycoons of that time were women. Among them, one was Syeda Khadija R.A., who inherited not only the wealth from his father but also the business expertise, but like others, she always preferred the contract of *Mudaraba*. The reason for acquiring a *Mudarib* to conduct her affairs on her behalf was because she was a single mother and did not want either to leave her children or to take them on long journeys. She evidently managed to make a profit despite the expense of a *Mudarib*.

5.4.3 Searching for a Mudarib

Like every successful businessperson, Khadija always looked for a Mudarib, who is known for honesty and good conducts, and can earn her good and high returns. In 595 A.D., Khadijah needed an agent to trade in her merchandise going to Syria (Al-Jibouri, 2016).

On the other hand, Muhammad (pbuh) entered adulthood, and was well known for his honesty. Due to this quality, he was awarded with the tittle of Sadiq and Al-Ameen.

He started his adulthood by rearing sheep and goats and was 22 years old at that time. His well-disciplined business character soon inspired every person in Arab. His truthfulness and trustworthiness were the talk of the town (Mujahid, 2008). Everybody looked forward for an opportunity to have business dealings with the person having such character of Sadiq and Ameen; therefore, soon he become famous as a trustful trader.

Prophet Muhammad (pbuh), was a man of his words. Abdullah bin Ubai Al-Hamsa was doing some business dealings with the Prophet, when Abdullah remembered of some urgent work and excused the Prophet (pbuh) saying he will be back soon. However, Abdullah forgot that he had promised to return. After 3 days when Abdullah passed from the same place, he was stunned to see that Muhammad (pbuh) was still waiting for him, at the exact same spot. The Prophet did not speak harshly to him, but rather politely remarked, "O Abdullah you put me in great hassle" (Abu Dawood, *hadith* no. 4996).

It was difficult finding trustworthy and truthful partner in the Meccan society, and Khadija wanted to hire someone trustworthy. She discussed her problem with some of her close friends. When the news of the character of the Holy Prophet (pbuh) reached her and she came to know the great qualities about the young orphan of Mecca, she realized that he was the one she needed.

5.4.4 Offer for a business deal

She sent the message for the contract of *Mudaraba*, offering twice the normal market ratio to Muhammad (pbuh). Here the question arises that if we look at this offer from business point of view, why did Khadija R.A. offered double rate to him as this would decrease her portion of return which is not a cost-effective idea as per business point of view? The answer to this query is that Khadija was a very talented woman and she appreciated that whenever a trustworthy person does business with her, he always earns more than the normal return (which we will see in the below paragraphs), so though the ratio of return would be lower for her, the total return could be higher.

The Prophet of Allah (pbuh) (who was not granted the Prophethood at that time), took the advice of his beloved uncle Abu Talib and upon his green signal, accepted the offer.

Muhammad (pbuh) did not have such type of practical business experience, but he had twice accompanied his uncle, Abu Talib, on his trade trips and keenly observed how he traded, bartered and conducted business. After all, the people of Quraish were famous for their involvement in trade more than in any other profession. It was not uncommon to hire an agent who did not have a prior experience.

Abu Saad mentions that some historians have also stated that Abu Talib himself told the Prophet صلى الله عليه وسلم that Khadija wanted the *Mudarib* to take her trade to Syria and that he (the Prophet) should offer his services. He further said that since his nobility, trustworthiness and truthfulness is the talk of the town so she will be accepting his offer happily. Prophet (pbuh) thereupon offered her his services, which she happily accepted, and offered her two times more return than normal (Ansari, 1995).

Khadija did not only send her trade stock with the Prophet of Allah but also her slave Maysera with him for serving the holy Prophet (pbuh). Out of it, the main purpose perhaps was that Khadija was eager to know the key factors behind the success of this young orphan.

One point for us to learn: One of the qualities of successful traders, is that they closely observe the reasons behind the success of others and is always ready to learn from the experiences of others. So was the case with her, she sent him, and I believe she would have asked him to observe this *Mudarib* very closely.

Al-Jibouri mentions, "Before embarking on his first trip as a businessman representing Khadijah, Muhammad (pbuh) met with his uncles for last minute briefings and consultations, then he set out on the desert road passing through Wadi al-Qura, Midian, and Diyar Thamud, places with which he was familiar because of having been there at the age of twelve in the company of his Uncle-Abu Talib, father of his cousin and later son-in-law Ali. He continued the lengthy journey till he reached Busra on the highway to the ancient city of Damascus after about one month. It was then the capital of Hawran, one of the southeastern portions of the province of Damascus situated north of the Balqa"(Al Jibouri, 2016).

He continues to write: "What items did Muhammad (pbuh) carry with him to Busra, and what items did he buy from there? Meccans were not known to be skilled craftsmen, nor did they excel in any profession besides trade, but young Muhammad (pbuh) might have carried with him a cargo of hides, raisins, perfumes, dried dates, light weight woven items, probably silver bars, and most likely some herbs. He bought what he was instructed by his employer to buy: these items may have included manufactured goods, clothes, a few luxury items to sell to wealthy Meccans, and maybe some household goods.

Gold and silver currencies accepted in Mecca included Roman, Persian, and Indian coins, for Arabs during those times, including those who were much more sophisticated than the ones among whom Muhammad (pbuh) grew up, such as the Arabs of the southern part of Arabia did not have a currency of their own; so, barter was more common than cash"(Al-Tibrani & Qasim, 2016).

As discussed earlier, the fruits of trustworthiness and truthfulness came in such a way that Syeda earned profits twice as much as she had anticipated. As a result, Hazrat Khadija, though she had promised twice the market return, earned more than that. Maysera was also inspired by the personality of Muhammad (pbuh) than by anything related to the trip.

Those trade caravans were the only links contemporary Arabs had with their outside world. They brought them the news of what was going on beyond their drought-ridden and famine-stricken desert and sand dunes.

Imam Tabrani, on the strength of Hazrat Jabir says that, in the same caravan of traders, one of Syeda's sister was also there. She had cartelized her business with the Prophet (pbuh) and one other man. Upon returning, and after all calculations, her sister owed some money to him and the other person. The other person demanded her for money two to three times, while the Prophet (pbuh) never asked for it. She asked the Holy Prophet (pbuh) to demand the money too which he refused saying that I feel shy demanding money from someone. When Khadija was told about this, she said that this is the sign of her great nobility (Mujahid, 2008).

Here again we have things to learn. Khadija a successful businesswoman, did not only stick to the promised ratio — rather she doubled the return. She chose to trust in a partner despite his youth and relative inexperience with trading expeditions, based on his character and trustworthiness.

The success of this trip encouraged Khadija for second contract of *Mudaraba* with Muhammad (pbuh) for the winter trip to southern Arabia, i.e., Yemen, the land that introduced the coffee beans to the rest of the world, the land of Saba' and the famous Balqees, the land of natives skilled in gold, silver and other metal handicrafts, not to mention their ingenuity in the textile industry and domestic furniture, and it may even be the land that gave Arabic its first written script.

Yemen, at that time, was being ruled by an Ethiopian regent. This time Khadija offered Muhammad (pbuh) three times the usual. Unfortunately, historians do not tell us much about this second trip except that it was equally profitable to both the employer and the employee. Some historians do not mention this trip at all.

Upon listening to what Maysera told to Khadija, she became astonished. By then she was convinced that she had finally found a man who was worthy of her, so much so that she initiated the marriage proposal herself. When Muhammad (pbuh) sat to provide details of all the business transactions in which he became involved on her behalf, she finally decided to propose him for marriage, which took place when Khadija was 40 years and the Prophet was 25 years old (Al-Jibouri, 2016).

Khadija's successful business life has many lessons for the businessman of today. After-marriage life was too good and happy for all the family members. Mujahid writes: "The wealth of Khadija and her business kept prospering and expanding until it made her the most successful trader of Arabia" (Mujahid, 2008). Perhaps the major reason was her spending of that income to beggars, orphans, widowed and extremely needy one. Not only this, she spent a lot of her wealth for the cause of Islam — and hence we summarize another key insight to the success of her business (the concept of "Barakah" or blessing in Deen): spend the profits or income in the path of Allah. It could be thought of as similar to modern day CSR — Corporate Social Responsibility. Once again, Khadija had practiced all this 1,400 years ago and proved the world the need of CSR and its perfect application such that it has societal impact.

Coming back to the point from where we started our discussion, today unfortunately a misconception in the minds of Muslims is that Islam never encouraged women to participate and contribute in the society. Islam has always given equal if not more importance to her, the business life of this magnificent lady (who is regarded as one of the four most blessed women in the Islamic world) is one standing proof.

It is indeed the need of the hour that our sisters should forgo these myths and come forward, and contribute their part for the welfare of the society.

References

Abi Sarh, Abu Abdullah Muhammad ibn Sa'd (n.d.), *Tabaqat Ibn e Saad*, Karachi: Dar ul Ishaat.

Al-Nasa'i. (214–303 AH; c. 829–915 CE). *Sunan an-Nasa'i*: Darussalam Publishers.

Al-Jibouri, Yasin T. (2016), *Khadija Daughter of Khuwaylid Wife of Prophet Muhammad*, Newington: Yasin Publications.

Al-Tibrani & Qasim, A. (2016), *Al-Mu'jam Al-Kabir*. (G. Dastageer, Trans.). Lahore: Millat Publications.

Ahmed, Zulfiqar (2000a), *Khutbat e Faqeer* (Vol. 2), Faisalabad: Maktabat il Faqeer, p. 205.

Ahmed, Zulfiqar (2000b), *Khawateen ke Liyeh Tarbiyati Bayanat*, Lahore: Dar Ul Mutala, p. 56.

Ahmed, Zulfiqar (2000c), *Sukoon e Dil*, Deoband: Maktaba Soot Al Quran, p 42.

Ansari, Saeed (1995), *Biography of the Women Companions of the Holy Prophet and the Ways of Their Sacred Lives*, Karachi: Darul Ishaat.

Bukhārī, M. I. (1966), *Sahih Bukhari*, Karachi: Muhammad Sarid.

al-Jazri, Abu al-Hasan Ali ibn Muhammad, *Usdul Ghabah Fi Marfat e Sahabah*, Beirut: Darul Marifa.

Ibn e Asaakir, Imam Abu al-Qasim Ali b. al-Hassan (1997), *Tareekh Madinatul Damishq, (History of City, Damascus)*, Beirut: Dar al fikar.

Mãjah, I. (b. 209/824, d. 273/887). *Sunan Ibn Majah*: Darussalam Publishers.

Mujahid, Abdul Malik (2008), *Khatoon e awal, Sayeda Khadija Ke Zindagi Kay Sunehray Waqiyat*, Riyadh, Saudi Arabia: Darussalam Publishers & Distributors.

Mundhirī, A. -A. A.-Q. and Muslim, -H.-Q. (2000), *Mukhtaṣar Sahiḥ Muslim: The Translation of the Meanings of Summarized Sahih Muslim: Arabic-English*, Riyadh, Saudi Arabia: Darussalam Publishers & Distributors.

Chapter 6

Women in the Workplace: *Shari'ah* and Contemporary Perspectives

Mohammad Hashim Kamali

Abstract

An attempt is made in this chapter to expound *Shari'ah* positions on women's right to work and her freedom to choose the work she undertakes, and then also to own its proceeds regardless of her marital status. It is important to explain the Islamic perspective in this regard as it is influential in determining public perceptions among Muslims even if statutory legislation may have ruled on the rights in question. Yet one of the challenges of general concern is also that the *Shari'ah* positions on women's rights are often conflated with patriarchal customs that undermine women's rights. Women's conditions vary widely among Muslim countries and regions which tend to have cultural characteristics of their own, and face similar but also different challenges. Yet perceptions and attitudes prejudicial to gender equality still persist to the effect that women should stay at home and those who try to secure outside employment should obtain their husband or guardian's permission first. With the exception perhaps of educated professional women in urban centers, women who seek employment opportunities, let alone equal status with men, often risk loss of family support, even being ostracized, especially in places where the conditions of women have not changed much in recent decades.

Keywords: *Shari'ah*, Muslim women, Workplace, Women's right, Malaysia

Custom and culture, prevailing economic conditions, education, urbanization and a host of other factors all play a role and need to be taken into account in presenting a holistic picture of women, their role and place in the employment sector, society and government generally. The *Shari'ah* is also cognizant of the role of custom and culture and their liability to change in the course of time, and designates, in turn, a number of formulae under the rubric of *ijtihad*, general custom (*'urf*) and the *maqasid* of *Shari'ah* to integrate necessary and beneficial change. It is inadvisable therefore to draw straight analogies and suggest direct application of some of the rules of *fiqh* that were formulated under different sets of circumstances which differ widely from the conditions prevailing now. This flexibility is also contemplated under the *Shari'ah* principle of permissibility (*iba'hah*), which is applicable to civil transactions and customary matters (*mua'mala't wa ada'at*). New developments in these areas are thus deemed to be permissible barring the existence of a prohibition. This is unlike the sphere of beliefs and devotional matters (*aqa'id wa ibada't*) to which *ibahah* is generally not applied. Work-related matters are generally subsumed under *mua'mala't and ada'at* and unless there be a specific prohibition based on stronger evidence that precludes the application of *iba'hah.*

To address the subject before me, I begin with the definition, scope and value of women's right/freedom of work and then review the basic guidelines of the *Qur'an* and *Sunnah* on the subject. Direct recourse to the source evidence is important, not only in its own right but also due to the medieval social values that crept in overtime and influenced the formulation of *fiqh* rules on women's issues. Even the *Qur'an* commentaries were not spared. Patriarchal customary practices and their reductionist impact of women's right also need attention. As one commentator stated, in most cases, it is the custom rather than religious injunction that hindered women's participation in economic activities. In some communities, working women were deemed to have a lower moral standing (Osman, 1992; al-Khamsah, 1973, p. 22). In the event of a discrepancy between a customary practice and the normative ruling of *Qur'an* and *Sunnah*, the former will not be acceptable. Yet in practice such customary positions gradually influenced the attitudes even of scholars and interpreters by the back door, as it were, to influence *Qur'an* interpretation and *fiqh* (Al-Banna, 1996, p. 197). Whereas the *Qur'an* actually strengthened the position of women *vis-à-vis* the then prevailing customs of pre-Islamic Arabia, medieval interpreters often moved in the opposite direction to weaken it.

Then I review the schools and scholars of *fiqh* and their positions on the continuity of values or otherwise they may have manifested. When there exist more than one interpretation or opinion in the source evidence, I take a selective approach, in accordance with the Islamic jurisprudence principle of selection (*takhayyur*), and take that interpretation or view, whether of earlier or modern scholars, that seems more suitable to the conditions of contemporary Muslims.

In dealing with the subject before us, it is important also to bear in mind, not only the particularities of *fiqh* and contemporary opinion but also the broader principles of *Shari'ah* that provide guidelines for interpretation and enforcement. This is once again a characteristic aspect of *Qur'an* interpretation (*tafsir*) wherein the general provisions (*a'm*) of the *Qur'an* may facilitate a better understanding of its more specific rules so that the general and the specific of the *Qur'an* are not totally separated from one another.

6.1 Definition, scope and value of work or '*amal*

'Amal is basically an economic concept, which is defined as "physical or mental exertion by a human being made for generating economic gain, or for enhancing and developing an existing value." According to another definition "*'amal* consists of self-exertion by a human being either individually or in collaboration with others in order to produce goods or render a particular service."[1]

In modern Arabic writings, expressions such as *a'mil* (worker) and its plural *'umma'l*, the right of work (*haqq al-ama'l*), and *hurriyat al-ama'l* (freedom to choose one's work and profession) refer mainly to work in its legal and economic senses; yet *'amal* also retains its general meaning and it is as such inclusive of religious work that earns one a spiritual reward. *'Amal* is a means of earning a living for the individual and of making a contribution to society, just as it is the principal arena of a person's compliance with, or defiance of, God's injunctions.

Ama'l is a personal duty of every able-bodied Muslim, and a collective obligation (*fard kifa'i*) of the community to build the Earth and develop its resources for the benefit of humanity. References in the *Qur'an* and *Sunnah* that often occur to "work with one's hands" have led some to conclude that agriculture, industry and commerce are the most meritorious of all works as they cater for the basic needs of life, both of humans and other inhabitants of the Earth.

The personal freedom and right of individuals to work is inviolable, unless the work in question partakes in infliction of harm (*darar*) on others, in which case it would fall within the purview of the renowned *hadith*, "Harm may neither be inflicted nor reciprocated in Islam." Work that partakes in harm and corruption is generally unlawful, and so is the revenue that accrues from it. No one may make a business out of defaming

---

[1]See for both these definitions see Kamali (2010) quoting al-Qaradawi, Mushkilat al-Faqr, and al-Dughmi, Nazariyyat al-Amn.

others or profit through acts of oppression. Work that involves prostitution, gambling, sorcery, fraud and immoral behavior is sinful (*ma'siyah*) and must be avoided. The basic rule here is: whatever that leads to *haram*, or used in order to procure *haram* also becomes *haram*. A worker is consequently not entitled to any wages for the unlawful work he or she might have completed, and may even become liable to compensation or punishment (Kamali, 2010, p. 118f).

Work that falls between the two categories of *halal* and *haram* should also be avoided if one can find alternative work which is clear of doubt. This would be to act in conformity with the *hadith* that "One who keeps clear of doubts purifies his faith and his honor."[2] If no other alternative could be found, then one may undertake doubtful work to the extent necessary for the fulfillment of basic needs. Work that is clear of doubt is preferable even if it involves greater hardship (Al-Shishani, 1980, p. 458). Should there arise a conflict between the fulfillment of a personal obligation (*fard a'yn*) and indulgence in unlawful work, the latter is tolerated, according to some *'ulam'a*, including Imam Malik, to the extent necessary. Suppose that someone lives in a place where no other work to support oneself and family is available except through unlawful work, excluding crimes, and one cannot escape to another place either — one may take it but only to the extent of necessity for survival, but no more than that (Al-Shatibi, 1332H, 300; Al-Shishani, 1980, p. 457).[3] This is equivalent to the concession *Shari'ah* has grants to a person who fears death from starvation. According to a legal maxim "necessity (*darur'ah*) makes the unlawful lawful," but the necessity in question must, according to another maxim be "measured according to its true proportions." An accurate assessment of necessity would also indicate when it is no longer the case, at which point one must return to the normal rules of *Shari'ah* (Kamali, 2010, p. 119).

Work which partakes in *fard kifa'i* refers to all beneficial work that promotes public welfare such as working in industry and agriculture, health services, education and the like. If some people in the community undertake it, the duty is fulfilled generally, but works of this kind may never be abandoned altogether. In the event when this happens, the government

[2]Al-Bukhari, Sahih al-Bukhari, kitab al Iman, b. min faal man istabra'a li-dinihi, hadith no. 50; Muslim, Sahih Muslim, k. al-musaqat, b. akhdh al-aalal wa tark alshubhat, hadith no. 2996.

[3]Shatibi wrote that al-Ghazali and Ibn al-'Arabi held similar views.

may compel those who are capable of doing so to work (Abu Zahrah, n.d., p. 51).

The most noble of all professions is intellectual work that involves teaching, writing and research. This is because intellectual development is one of the higher objectives, or *maqasid*, of Islam and bedrock of all other areas of improvement. This is followed by productive and industrial work that meets people's needs, or which brings great benefit, to the people. Those who occupy themselves with such work earn God Almighty's blessing and reward (Al-Qaradawi, 1996/1416, p. 119). The elderly and the child should not be engaged in strenuous work and it is a responsibility partly of the guardians/relatives and the authorities to ensure that this does not occur. Child labor and assignment of paid work to minors is forbidden unless it has educational value and takes place under supervision of the father/guardian (Al-Nawawi, 1975/1395, p. 250; Al-Dughmi, 1988/1408, p. 78). Similarly, women should not be assigned work that is incompatible with their feminine dignity, and this includes work that brings them into contact with doubtful characters and situations. Women are otherwise permitted to work in trades and professions of their choice. They may work in order to earn a living, for career satisfaction, and use the income they earn from work as they wish (Al-Shishani, 1980, p. 535; Badawi, 1980/1400, p. 404).

6.2 Review of the source evidence

Ama'l (lit, work, action, and conduct) is often used in the *Qur'an*, the *Sunnah* and *fiqh* literature in conjunction with *aqida'h* and *'ima'an* (dogma and faith). This juxtaposition of *'aqida'h* and *ama'l* conveys with it the message that the two go hand in hand and that the one is basically deficient without the other. *Ama'l* in this sense has religious and spiritual undertones and it is often viewed in the *Qur'an* and *Sunnah* as the external manifestation of belief. The close relationship of faith and good deeds is also evident in the typical phrase which occurs in over 50 places in the *Qur'an* as "those who believe and do good works — *al-ladhina amanu wa amilu al salihat*. The obvious implication is that *'ima'n* and *ama'l* are intimately related and complement one another. The spiritual content of *'amal* can also be seen in the following *Qur'anic* address to the Prophet Muhammad:

> Tell the believers to work. Then soon will God, His Messenger and the believers will see the work you have done (*Qur'an* chapter al-Tawbah, 9:105).

The Prophet is thus directed to remind the people of the value of work and what it takes to make it a source of pride for the community and a firm basis by which to gain the pleasure of God and His Messenger. It is then declared in another verse that "We shall not cause to waste the recompense of one who excels in *'amal.*" (*Qur'an* chapter al-Kahf, 18:30). The reference to *'amal* in both of these verses is to works, both pertaining to the affairs of this world and those of the next. This is because in Islam lawful *'amal* becomes a dimension of worship (*'ibadah*) when it is done to the best of one's ability. Work that qualifies as service to God must necessarily be of a high caliber wherein attention is paid to quality and the anticipated outcome, and it is free of dishonesty, cheating and negligence. The Prophet has added his voice in *hadith* that "God loves it when a worker undertakes a work that he does it well" (Muhammad Nasir al-Din, 1984/1404H, p. 327, *hadith* no. 1, 201).

And declared in another *hadith* that "No one has ever eaten food purer than what is earned by the toil of one's hands. For the Prophet (cum-King) David (pbuh), used to earn his living by the toil of his hands" (Al-Tabrizi, 1979/1399, p. 759).[4]

These passages are evidently not gender based and apply equally to all. The next verse we quote is explicitly on women's right to work and their exclusive entitlement to what they earn from it. The verse thus declares that "Men are entitled to what they earn and women are entitled to what they earn." (*Qur'an* al-Nisa, 4:32).

The renowned *Qur'an* commentator, al-Tabari (d. 923/310), has considered this to be a clear authority on women's right of work. This conclusion is supported by the words used, in particular, *nasib* (proceeds or result of work), and *iktisab* (acquisition), which mean earning something through work. He disagrees with the view that *iktisab* in this verse refers to a share of inheritance. Al-Tabari explains that inheritance is not earned as such, but received without self-exertion and personal labor. Hence, those who ignore the difference between *iktisb* and *mirath* are taking an unacceptable position (Al-Tabari, 1969, p. 267). Any attempt to equate inheritance with the fruit of personal labor is likely to go against the spirit of the text and the work ethics of Islam that not only entitles everyone but also make it a duty, in certain situations at least, of everyone to work for their living,

---

[4]Al-Tabrizi (1979/1399), *hadith* no. 2. ICR 6.3. Produced and distributed by IAIS Malaysia.

and support his or her family (Othman, 1992, pp. 19–20). According to another observer, this verse also implies that women are entitled to take up all suitable occupations they might be capable of undertaking (Al-'Abudi, 1990/1410H, p. 84). The substance of the foregoing has been endorsed elsewhere in the text where God Most High makes it known that "I will not suffer the work of any worker among you to be lost, whether male or female, the one of you being from the other" (*Qur'an* a'ali-'Imran, 3:195).

The late Rector of al-Azhar, Shaykh Mahmud Shaltut's commentary on this verse draws attention to the phrase (*badukum min ba'ad*) which eliminates the distinction between men and women in respect of religious and all beneficial work, thereby establishing substantive equality between them. This *Qur'anic* language is also indicative of partnership and co-operation between men and women in the work they do within the family and the society at large in the sense that both play equally important roles and there is no superiority of one over the other (Al-Islam, n.d., p. 195).

On the subject of authority, or *wila'yah* (also guardianship, protection), the *Qur'an* clearly entitles men and women equally to its exercise in respect of one another and in respect, by implication, also of participation in the management of public affairs and government. Thus, it is declared that "the believers, men and women, are protectors (*awliya'*, pl. of *wali*) of one another, they command good and they forbid evil." (*Qur'an* al-Tawbah, 9:71).

In addition to validating *wila'yah* for men and women in the sense of cooperation and mutual support, this verse entitles them both to the most comprehensive of all *wilayat*, which is to promote good and to prevent evil, also known as *hisbah*. *Hisbah* is a broad concept of wide-ranging applications, so much so that government itself is a branch of *hisbah*, which means that participation in government and leadership in political affairs is a right equally of men and women. Women are consequently entitled, based naturally on qualification and competence, to hold government positions that may involve the exercise of *wila'yah* in government affairs (Al-Shawiribi 'Abd al-Hamid, 1987, p. 85f). These are further discussed in the following paragraphs.

Work from the *Shari'ah* perspective may be evaluated as either recommendable (*mandub*) or obligatory (*wajib*), just as it may, in the negative sense, be classified as reprehensible (*makruh*) or forbidden (*haram*). Work is recommendable if it is beneficial and prevents the individual from dependency on others, poverty and begging. Work that is obligatory may consist either of a personal obligation (*fard ayn*), or a collective obligation (*fard kifa'i*). To exert oneself in order to earn a lawful living in the face of dependency and degradation is a personal obligation of every capable individual, especially if one's bodily needs and protection against destruction and disease cannot be met in any other way. Work is also obligatory in order to repay a personal debt, if the debt in question cannot be otherwise repaid (Al-Shaybani, 1940/1375, p. 32; Badawi, 1980/1400, p. 381; Al-Shishani, 1980, p. 307). An able-bodied man is also under a duty to support himself and his immediate family, wife and children (cf. *Qur'an* al-talaq: 65:6, *Qur'an* al-Baqarah, 2:133). This is important, especially in male-dominated cultures where employment opportunities for women are scarce to non-existent.

Muhammad al-Ghazali (d.1993) and Sadiq Afifi (Al-Ghazali, 1993/1413, pp. 134–136; Al-Sadiq Afifi, 1980/1400, pp. 209–211) have both concurred with Abu Zahrah (d.1974) to the effect that the *Shari'ah* entitles women to work and to earn their living whenever they need to do so or when they can make a special contribution to society. But they add that it is preferable for women to devote their creative energy and work to motherhood since they can make a unique contribution in this area to the well-being of the family and society. It is then added that women may join the workforce in the following four situations:

(1) When they have abilities and skills that are particularly valuable to the community as a whole. This is when they excel others, including men, and the role they can play here is considered almost as unique as they can play as mothers and managers of households.
(2) When they undertake work to which they are particularly suited such as working in childcare, in health care services and education. Some *ulema*, including Ibn al-Humam al-Hanafi (d.1465 C.E.), have considered this kind of work as a collective obligation (*fard kifai*) that applies particularly to women. As for the question of agreement between the spouses, the husband is advised not to stand in the way of his wife when she wishes to work in any of these capacities.
(3) When women work side by side with their husbands and family and assist them in their work. This is often the case in the countryside where in farming families, small landholders and other low-income families' women assist their men folk in various capacities, often combining their duties as mothers and household managers with these other activities. Their contributions in these capacities deserve special recognition and "these are the exemplary women of our society; they are hardworking,

efficient and compassionate, not like the ones who work as singers and dancers in the night clubs..."

(4) When a woman is in need of earning a living to support herself and her family and there is no one else to support her and her family, in which case she would have to work as a matter of necessity. Having said this al-Ghazali added that in an Islamic welfare state, this last category of women is also entitled to receive support from the public treasury (*bayt almal*) regardless of whether she is a Muslim or a non-Muslim. For this is the purport of the *hadith* in which the Prophet has declared "whoever leaves behind property, it shall belong to his heirs, but if he leaves a debt or dependents in need, they shall be my responsibility."[5]

6.3 Women as a witness, judge and head of state: Issues over *Wilayah*

Commentators from early times have advanced different views concerning on women's eligibility for public office under the rubric of *wilayat*, which are of two kinds, public and private. Some maintain that men and women are equal only in the domain of private authority (*wilayah khassah*), but not in respect of that which involves the exercise of public authority (*wiliyah 'ammah*). *Wilayah* is defined as the authority of one person over another person or persons which renders the latter bound by the decision of the former without any need for prior agreement (Al-Sanhuri, 1989, p. 187). Private *wilayah* refers primarily to guardianship over the person and property of another because of some deficiency in the legal capacity of the latter. It is thus stated by the proponents of this binary division and its application to women, that women can be legal guardians and may be employed as teachers, nurses and supervisors of *waqf* (charitable endowment) but not as ministers, judges and political leaders (Mutawalli, 1974, p. 417).

As for women's eligibility for public office which partakes in *wilayah 'ammah*, such as the office of the head of state, prime minister (*wazir al-tafwid*), judge, governor, officer in charge of market inspection and *hisbah*, the head of public grievances tribunal (*wali al-mazalim*), which partake in both religious and temporal authority, early Muslim scholars have maintained that only the first two are reserved for men but disagree

---

[5] *Hadith* reported by all the major collections of hadith (i.e., muttafaqun 'alayh): al-Bukhari, Sahih al-Bukhari, III, p. 155.

regarding the rest. Abul Hasan al-Mawardi (d.1058/450H) thus precluded women from the top two posts as both involved military leadership for which women were not eligible. The main textual authority quoted for this view is the *Qur'anic* verse, which declared that "men are the maintainers (*qawwamun*) of women for what God has made some of them excel others and for what they spend out of their wealth" (*Qur'an* chapter al-Nisa, 4:35). Also quoted is another verse, which provides that "women have rights similar to those that men have over them in a just manner, and men are a degree above them." *(Qur'an* chapter al-Baqarah, 2:228). And also the *hadith* to the effect that "a nation whose affairs are led by a woman shall not prosper" (Al-Tabrizi, 1979/1399, *hadith* no. 3693).

General consensus (*ijm'a*) is often cited in support of the view that only men are eligible for the offices of head of state and prime minister. There is no explicit consensus (*al-ijma al-sari*) of the learned on record, whether written or verbal, on this, nor is there a clear ruling in the sources to prevent equality even at this level. The most one can say is that it is a practical and a presumptive *ijma*, which has, in any case, been questioned, again in practical terms, by the recent experience of Muslim countries such as Pakistan, Bangladesh and Indonesia, all of which had elected heads of states and prime ministers — some of whom were elected more than once. Hence, the *ijma* in question is not definitive even at the level of practice (i.e., *al-ijma al-fi'li*), which is not a binding form of *ijma* in any case (Kamali, 2003, p. 248f).

Notwithstanding its weaknesses, however, the *ijma* ruling at issue has, in turn, been extended by way of analogy (*qiyas*) to a number of other public offices, as mentioned previously, which are also reserved for men. Imam Abu Hanifah has held, on the other hand, that women may become judges in matters in which they are admissible as witnesses, which means practically all matters except the prescribed penalties (*hudud*) and just retaliation (*qiyas*) (Al-Mawardi, 1966/1386, p. 65). To say that women are not eligible for judicial office or that of the head of state, is thus based on analogical reasoning (*qiyas*), and the original case (*asl*) here is witnesses, not the office of judge, nor that of the head of state. Ibn Hazm al-Zahiri has held, on the other hand, that except for the office of the head of state, women are eligible for all other offices of government. In support of this view, Ibn Hazm has cited the *Qur'anic* text on the very subject of government, which provides that "God commands you to hand over the trusts (*al-amanat*) to whom that they are due, and when you judge between people, you judge with justice" (*Qur'an* chapter al-Nisa, 4:58).

Al-amanat in this text is a reference to public office as a trust and responsibility that may be handed over to the best qualified. Ibn Hazm stated that the verse is perfectly general and draws no distinction between men and women in respect of their eligibility as trustees and repositories of *amanat.* The *Qur'an* basically envisages everyone as qualified, men and women both, and that we follow the general tenor of its ruling as it is (Al-Mawardi, 1966/1386, p. 64).[6]

As for the aforementioned *hadith*, which has been quoted in support of the majority ruling that women are not qualified to become judge or head of state, it is evidently an inference. The *hadith* was, as the records indicate, concerned with a particular situation, that is, when the Prophet was informed that the daughter of the Chosroe of Persia had taken charge of the affairs of that country, and this was the Prophet's response to that particular development. It is also noted that the *hadith* does not contain a ruling but speaks of prosperity and success. Ibn Hazm has commented on this hadith that it refers, in any case, to only one position, namely that of the head of state and does not apply to other public offices (*wilayat*) to which women are generally eligible. More recently, commentators have added the observation that unlike the monarchs or emperors of earlier times, power in a modern state is diffused between its various organs and subjected to a set of constitutional checks and balances in almost all present day Muslim countries. Under these conditions even when a woman becomes the head of state, her powers would be limited by these factors. The rules of war have also drastically changed, and the head of state-cum-commander-in-chief, who was earlier expected to lead the army in the battlefield of *jihad* is no longer expected to play that role. The weapons of war now in use dictate a different logic, which is quite the opposite. It would indeed seem patently inadvisable for the head of state to go into the battlefield under the present conditions.[7] The rules of Islamic jurisprudence also hold that a substantial change in the effective cause and rationale (*'illah*) of a ruling should be followed by a corresponding change and a suitable ruling (*hukm*) to replace it through *ijtihad.*

It may be noted in passing that a group of the Kharijites, namely the Shuhaybiyyah, have held that women are eligible for the office of head of

[6]Muhammad b. 'Ali b. Ahmad b. Sa'id al-Zahiri, *Al-Muhalla* (Vol. X), Hasan Zaydan (ed.), p. 632.

[7]For a discussion of the source evidence on reserving the position of the head of state for men, see Kamali (2002), pp. 63–65.

state (Al-Zahiri, n.d., p. 167). The majority (*jumhur*) have also held it permissible, as a matter of necessity, for a woman to become head of state if she assumes office by military force in order to prevent bloodshed. But this is only tolerated as the caliphate of necessity, which may only last for as long as it has effective power at its disposal (A1-'Abudi, 1990/1410H, p. 228).

A wide spectrum of modern scholars and *ulema*, including Rashid Rida, Mahmud Shaltut, Muhammad Yusuf Musa, 'Abd al-Hamid Mutawalli and others maintains that women are qualified to be representatives (*wakil*) in Parliament, ministers, witnesses and judges, all of which partake in the exercise of public authority (*wilayah ammah*). They have considered the view that sought to confine women's eligibility to the private *wilayat* as weak and less than reliable. The whole debate has come under the scrutiny of the Federal *Shari'ah* Court of Pakistan, which looked into the details and attempted fresh interpretations of *Qur'anic* verses and *hadith*. The FSC came to the conclusion that the two aforesaid verses (i.e., 4:35 and 2:228) basically explain one another and the degree that is granted to men signifies leadership in the family on account of their responsibility for the provision of maintenance. That the general equality of the sexes in respect of rights and duties they enjoy has in the meantime, been confirmed by the second of these two texts. Equality is indeed the principal message of this verse; hence, the exception made in its latter clause should not be taken so far as to suppress its principal theme. This is not a new interpretation, in fact, as some earlier *Qur'an* commentators have also drawn similar conclusions (Kamali, 2002, p. 65f).

6.3.1 Women as witnesses

With regard to women's qualification for appointment to judicial posts, the correct interpretation on this is that of the *Qur'an* commentator Ibn Jarir al Tabari (d.310/923) who held, contrary to the then prevailing majority, that women are fully qualified for employment in judicial posts. The majority of the leading schools, as already noted, passed negative judgments on analogy with the position of the head of state. Al Tabari regarded this to be a discrepant analogy (*qiyas ma al-fariq*) on the analysis that women judges do not lead the *jihad*. The principal task of a judge is to comprehend and implement the *Shari'ah* and attempt *ijtihad*, and men and women stand on the same footing in this regard.[8] Al Tabari thus held that women

[8]See for details on Ibn Jarir al-Tabari's view, Kamali (2002), pp. 66–70.

may become judges in all types of disputes, including the *hudud* and *qisas* (Kamali, 2002).

With regard to women's partial disability to act as witnesses before the courts, my enquiry leads me to the conclusion that there is no clear textual mandate on this in the *Qur'an* or authentic *hadith* (Kamali, 2002, pp. 66–69). The *Qur'anic* provision on this occurs only once (*Qur'an* chapter al-Baqarah, 2:282) and that too in a specific context. The verse thus provides, with reference to money loans and borrowing that it should be clearly documented and testified by "two witnesses from your men. And if two men are not available, then one man and two women of your choice should witness, so that if one forgets, the other woman can remind her. And the witnesses should not refuse when they are called for testimony ..." In their comments on this verse, Ibn Taymiyyah (d. 1328 C.E), his disciple Ibn Qayyim al-Jawziyyah and Mahmud Shaltut observed that the *Qur'anic* text here speaks in a language of persuasion and preference, and not in the manner of laying down an injunction. The text also does not preclude the possibility of one woman acting as a witness, or of women being witnesses in a case without there being a male witness (Al-Jawziyyah, n.d., p. 149). In view of Islam's unwavering commitment to truth and justice, all avenues that vindicate truth and serve the cause of justice must be left open. If allowing women to give credible testimony in the quest for justice, especially in critical cases where a woman may be holding vital testimony, it should undoubtedly be admitted. The verse is confined to commercial transactions and took into account the conditions of women in Arabia at the time, and those have changed since. The context was such that women were easily pressurized by men, often their male relatives, to revoke their testimony due to subsequent change of circumstances/interests. A second female witness was thus needed to remind her about her testimony and be firm on it as any change could prejudice the cause of justice (Wadud-Muhsin, 1992, pp. 85–86).

Furthermore, since the ruling under review is specific to financial contracts, it does not apply to other contracts and transactions. A reference is made in this connection to the *Qur'anic* ruling over witnesses in imprecation in (*Qur'an* chapter al-Nur, 24:6–8) which stipulates that those who accuse their wives and have no witnesses except themselves, let them testify four times, but that the charge will collapse if the wife also testifies four times and rebuts the charge. According to Mahmud Shaltut "four testimonials by a man ... are rebutted by four similar testimonials by a woman, who affirms that she is telling the truth and that the man has lied." Shaltut added that "on matters of human dignity and justice, Islam does not discriminate between the sexes" (Al-Islam, n.d., p. 253). Then also the number specification of two female witnesses equaling one male is not maintained in matters privy to women where one female witness is acceptable. Ibn Qayyim al-Jawziyyah thus stated that the *Shari'ah* credits the testimony of one woman as a full proof in matters in which women's familiarity and understanding are considered to be superior to that of men, such as family matters, pregnancy, child birth and so on.[9] A contemporary commentator adds in confirmation that the present day Muslim countries admit women's testimony in all matters, civil and criminal, without any discrimination and this has now become a matter of general practice (Al-'Ashmawi, 2009/1430H, p. 705).

With reference to *qiwam'ah* in financial matters, women enjoy equal ownership rights over what they earn, or receive by way of gift and inheritance, and are fully qualified also to manage their financial affairs, civil transactions and contracts. The Hanafi school has extended this position also to the contract of marriage, which an adult woman can conclude by herself — although the majority of other schools have considered marriage as an exception and require its solemnization by the legal guardian (*wali*), even if the woman is an adult. But then, since Islamic jurisprudence permits selection (*takhayyur*) among the available rulings of the leading *madhhabs*, the Hanafi view can be adopted by other schools and has, in fact been so adopted, by other Muslim jurisdictions in the course of 20th century family law reforms. Then there is basically no *Shari'ah* issue of concern over an adult women's capacity to conclude her own marriage contract. Yet patriarchal customs among tribal and village populations still present obstacles to women's enjoyment of their financial rights. The problem here is essentially not juridical but one of prejudicial custom and that of male-dominated society.[10] To give an example, the *Qur'an* assigns specified shares in the inheritance to female relatives, which is, however, widely denied to them by their male relatives. Statutory enactments in many Muslim countries that banned such practices on pain of imprisonment and fines have also not succeeded in curbing entrenched customary positions. The lesson one learns here is that prescriptive law reform needs to be followed by wider campaigns on awareness raising, education and supportive

[9]Al-Jawziyyah (n.d.), p. 152. For a fuller discussion of this issue see Kamali (2002), pp. 67–69.
[10]See for details on the role of patriarchal custom in Muslim countries Khan (2007), p. 207f.

policy initiatives. Muslim women in rural Asia and Africa are not well aware of their rights either under the *Shari'ah* or statutory law. Legislation should naturally be encouraged and continue to lead the way in the campaign for economic empowerment of women. In some particularly difficult situations, recourse may be had to affirmative action legislation and or a quota system, for example, in their admission to schools and employment centers, on a temporary basis at least, to promote the objectives of equal rights for all (Kamali, 2008, pp. 271–272).

6.3.2 A historical sketch

Broadly speaking, business activity (*al-tijarah*) was regarded as a respected profession among Arabs, which had also received *Qur'anic* approval (cf. *Qur'an*, chapter Al- Nisa', 4:29). Historical evidence suggests that women were active in business and active in the public space during the lifetime of the Prophet (pbuh), and after his demise during the time of the four Rightly-Guided Caliphs. Lady Zaynab bint Jahsh, the wife of the Prophet, used to work in tanning the hides and gave as charity the income she earned from it. Aishah bint Abu Bakr, also the Prophet's wife, was a learned person who was highly regarded by the Companions, many of whom sought her views on juridical issues, especially after the Prophet's demise, when she also became active in politics. It is further reported that the Cleaner of the Mosque of Madinah, at the time of the Prophet, was a woman by the name of Harqa' (Al-'Asqalani, 1977, p. 221). And then also Ra'itah, the wife of the renowned Companion, 'Abdullah ibn Mas'ud, earned money through handicraft — she had asked the Prophet a question whether it was right for her to spend her earning on her husband and child, for they had no other income than what she earned. She added that she could not spare to give any of it in charity. To this the Prophet replied "you also earn a (spiritual) reward by spending on your family. Spend as you wish" (Ibn Salam, 1991, p. 490).

Reports also indicate that women traders were active in the market of Madinah, a fact which led the second caliph, 'Umar al-Khattab, to appoint, upon assuming office, a Muslim woman, Shifa' bint 'Abdullah, as Controller of the Madinan Market (*Shaykhah Suq al-Madinah*). Some women ran businesses with their husband's participation but many did so on their own, and were as such by no means confined to their home. This they did irrespective of their marital status, with the only condition that they be mature and capable to conduct business activity (Al-'Asqalani, 1977, pp. 4–5). Among the noted businesswomen of that period, mention is made of Umm al-Munzir bint Qays, a date trader in the market of Madinah, and Asma' bint Muhkramah bint Jandal, who was a perfume trader. Note also the report: when Qaylah Umm Bani 'Ammar al-Ansariyyah met the Prophet, she explained to him that she was a businesswoman engaged in buying and selling goods, as she wanted to ensure that what she was doing was permissible (*halal*) (Al-'Asqalani, 1977, p. 106). Many other women of Madinah were engaged in the sale of goods such as cheese, oil and cloth. A second kind of businesswomen of note were those who hired others to run their business, such as Khadijah, Mother of Believers, who engaged Muhammad (later, Prophet Muhammad) to lead her business caravan to Syria (Othman, 1992, p. 28).

Women were also active in agriculture, planting seeds, carrying crops, collecting firewood, fetching drinking water, embroidery and handicraft, whereas herding, raising livestock and warfare were mainly conducted by men.

Women also participated in public services and political affairs. 'Arwah bint 'Abd al-Muttalib, was actively engaged in the propagation of Islam during the Makkan period. She visited her relatives to explain Islam to them. Asma' bint Abu Bakr was instrumental in the Prophet's successful migration from Makkah to Madinah. She kept an eye on enemy movements and informed the Prophet and her father Abu Bakr when they were hiding in the cave of al-Nur (Al-'Asqalani, 1977, p. 114). Umm Ayman was a courageous woman who became well known for walking 270 km all alone when she migrated from Makkah to Madinah, for which the Prophet admired and respected her.

Women also took part in jihad and provided support services such as nursing the wounded and providing food and water, and even fighting occasionally. Thus, it is reported that Nusaybah used a sword when she defended the Prophet in the battle of Uhud, and that Umayyah bint Qays al-Ansariyyah participated in fighting in the battle of Khaybar. The Prophet awarded the latter with a necklace for her bravery, which she always wore and even left a will that it should be buried with her when she dies (Al-Wahid, 1965, p. 45).

Reports further indicate that the women of Makkah and Madinah took part in giving *bay'ah* (pledge of allegiance) to the Prophet, which he received from groups of Muslims. Historical records indicate that *bay'ah* was practiced even before its affirmation in the *Qur'an*. Thus, it is noted that prior to the Prophet's migration to Madinah, two incidents of *bay'ah*, known as the First 'Aqabah and Second 'Aqabah took place (the latter is also known as *Bay'at al-Ridhwan*), the second of which also included women. Also, when the Prophet successfully conquered Makkah in the year 8 Hijrah, many women came to grant him pledge of allegiance. One of them was the legendary Hind bint 'Utbah, wife of Abu Sufyan, a sworn enemy of the Prophet, who had maimed and ripped open Hamzah, the martyred uncle of the Prophet in Uhud. Then when she embraced Islam, the Prophet accepted her *bay'ah* in the presence of his male Companions in al-Safa (Al-'Asqalani, 1977, pp. 165–166). All of this attests to the fact that the women of Arabia during the time of the Prophet were able to arrange their daily lives such that they could cope both with their work as mothers and wives — and their outside activities (Osman, 1992, p. 30).

'Abd al-Halim Abu Shaqqah's encyclopedic work, *Tahrir al-Mar'ah fi 'Asr al-Risilah* (liberation of women during the Prophetic era — in six volumes) (Abu Shaqqah, 1990/1410H), is the most exhaustive and widely acclaimed work on its subject to date. Some of the conclusions he has reached in the second volume of his work may be highlighted as follows. He begins by addressing the question whether it is an Islamic requirement for women to be confined to their homes. To this he responds that "participation of women in public life and her meeting with men is the *Sunnah* of our Prophet, peace be on him." As for the question whether this *Sunnah* is definitive or open to doubt (*qat'i*, or *zanni*), he states that the total number of reports on this subject, which consists of about 300 *hadiths*, including the acts, sayings and tacit approvals of the Prophet, when taken together amount to decisive evidence in the rank of *Mutawatir*. Most of these *hadiths* are also clear beyond interpretation. Participation (*musharakah*) in public life is thus the approved *Sunnah*.

Abu Shaqqah continued: One can hardly find a sphere of life where encounter and participation between men and women did not take place during the time of the Prophet. Available evidence in the *Qur'an* and the *hadith* collections of al-Bukhari and Muslim indicates that women's participation in the life of the community during this time was dignified, and that dignified encounters took place at the initiative of men and women, as and when the occasion required. Women made their own decisions, and they often met with the Prophet accompanied by their men, other Companions, and occasionally on their own. Women met with other women for short times and for longer hours when the occasion so required, within and outside their homes.

On a broader note, one of the reasons many Muslim scholars have attempted fresh interpretation of the source evidence on women's equality is a certain dissonance that exists between the *Qur'anic* directives on human equality and justice, and some of the medieval interpretations thereof. This has motivated, as Sa'diyya Shaikh observed, scholars in Egypt, Kuwait, Turkey and the U.S., including Muslim women, to work on the assumption that much of the unjustified departures from the principles of equality and justice on some aspects of women's rights can be rectified by re-understanding the sacred text. There is a common core of understanding that solutions to the issues concerned must come from the resources of Islam itself. It is further noted that people in different countries and regions, especially Muslims living in the West, tend to relate differently to Islam. Most of the issues relating to women's equality in the workplace, for instance, are not of a great concern for Muslim women residing in the West. They do have other concerns, of course, but this is not a pressing issue to them. For many, it seems, as Shaikh further noted, "Islam is not one among many equally weighted identities but rather a primary source of understanding one's very being in the world" (Shaikh, 2003, p. 156).

6.3.3 Women in the workplace: The Malaysian experience

I begin with recounting an episode over women's rights that gained media attention in Malaysia in the late 1990s. The debate started with a statement of the then Spiritual Leader of Islamic Party of Malaysia (PAS) and Chief Minister of Kelantan, Nik Aziz Nik Mat, who announced (6 March 1999) that the PAS government (PAS was and still is the ruling Party in the state of Kelantan) would conduct a study with a view to prohibit wives from working. Thus, he said: "it was unfair that they should be made to work, which was the responsibility of men." Nik Aziz added that he had no intention of stopping women from work, but that his primary concern was to find ways to ensure that children were not neglected while their mothers were at work. However, he questioned the need for women who worked "*secara seronok atau suka-suka*" — "just for the fun of it" — but were affecting the future of their children. "Islam teaches people to get married so that mothers can look after the children."[11]

Nik Aziz further stated that PAS had adopted a ruling which disallowed its women members to stand as candidates in elections, because "it could not guarantee their safety and dignity," and the ruling would also help to

[11]Reported in *The Star* daily of Kuala Lumpur, 18 March 1999, p. 14.

prevent women from *bergeser* (coming into contact with men), for there were groups out to "disturb" women campaigners during elections.[12] This ruling was said to be temporary and that the party would continue to nominate women Senators. He also stated that PAS already had two women Senators (from Kota Baru and Mekebang), and that the Islamic party had "never prevented its members from supporting women candidates in championing the cause of Islam."[13] He further added that he was not questioning the right of widowed women or orphans to seek employment, but was aiming instead at the well-to-do mothers who "work for the sake of money and enjoyment."[14] One may note here that to say that making an exception for some women, women Senators in this case, appears rather selective and politically expedient. It appears that the women in question were influential and the prohibitive ruling was relaxed in their favor. Nik Aziz's statements were not well received and prompted negative responses from both government leaders and the media. The then Prime Minister, Dr. Mahathir, said in response that women had their roles and responsibilities "but we cannot separate them and tell them to stay at home. Who are the people selling vegetables at the Kota Baru market?" A reference to the fact, as is generally known, that women participate actively in businesses in Kelantan.[15]

The then Human Resources Minister, Lim Ah Lek, in his comment praised women's contribution to the workforce and said that "it was wrong to even think about the idea. Instead of equal opportunities, it is discrimination and regress for the women as well as affecting the livelihood of the family." He added that it would be an offense under the law to disallow women to work, especially when they want to work, and it is their right to do so.[16]

Utusan Malaysia (daily) carried a commentary to say that "Malaysian women were shocked by the statement." That the achievement of several leading women in business and government did not come overnight but came only after "fighting male prejudice" — adding that PAS was unrealistic to have "presented its narrow opinion" to the people of Malaysia.[17]

---

[12]Quoted in *The Star* article "PAS Ruling to 'Protect Women'," 25 March 1999, p. 2.
[13]*Ibid*
[14]"Debate over Nik Aziz's view on working women," *The Star*, Kuala Lumpur, 27 March 1999, p. 20.
[15]Reported in *The Star*, Kuala Lumpur, 22 March 1999, p. 2.
[16]"PAS Proposal Draws Scorn," *The Star*, Kuala Lumpur, 18 March 1999, p. 14.
[17]*Ibid.*

Mingguan Malaysia questioned whether PAS leaders can support single mothers who are jobless. Statistics showed that Kelantan recorded a 13% divorce rate in 1997. Nik Aziz should study the causes, the paper added, and consider the realities that working women were facing.[18]

Pramodini Menon, Vice Chairman of the Malaysian Trade Union Congress's Women's Committee commented that earning money is as important as taking care of the children, teaching them and instilling religious values in them. If the man in the family is unemployed, is the government prepared to provide enough for the family? Besides, the right to work is a basic right of women; to take this away devalues women. In 1997, the Malaysian Government proposed to amend the Employment Act to encourage women to come out and work as the country was facing a labor shortage and did not want to be overly dependent on foreign workers. "What has Nik Aziz to say to this?"

Menon added: We are burdened with the reality that many men are not responsible for their women and children. Many women are being divorced every year without getting their due share of maintenance and matrimonial property. Many more children are abandoned by fathers who ignore court orders to provide for them. The real solution is not denying women the right to work; it is to provide them with the support system needed to exercise their rights. This includes affordable childcare centers in the neighborhood or workplace, flexible working hours and extended maternity leave (Menon, 1999, p. 22).

Representatives from seven women organizations of Malaysia also wrote in a commentary that "Nik Aziz Mat's retrogressive comments on women, work and the family are causing much concern to us in the women's movement" (Shahabudin, 2013, p. 15). This is especially the case in view of the fact that "there is nothing in the *Qur'an* or in the *hadith* which prevents women from working outside the home. In fact the *Qur'an* extols the leadership of Bilqis, the Queen of Sheba, for her capacity to fulfill the requirements of the office, for her political skills, her leadership qualities and her independent judgment ..." (*Qur'an* chapter al-Naml, 27:23–44). Provided a woman is well qualified and best suited to a task, there is no *Qur'anic* injunction to prohibit her from undertaking it because of her sex. The *hadith* literature also records many instances of women leaders, scholars and women who fully participated in public life.

---

[18] *Ibid.*

Women representatives further added that Malaysians live in a society that encourages women to work and excel academically. Malaysian girls outperform boys in almost all areas of education, reflecting similar worldwide trends. A reference was made to the 1998 statistics for Malaysia, which showed that girls formed 65.3% of the enrollment for pre-university education, and that of the 79,014 university students, 54.5% were female. They also showed that 47.1% of the labor force in 1995 were women. A slightly higher ratio of 60:40% of female to male population in Malaysian universities has been maintained ever since.

At the grass roots level, it was added, that women were "daily confronted with the stark reality that many men are not responsible for their women and children, and also that Muslims record the highest divorce rate in Malaysia."[19]

All of this points to the fact that women in Malaysia have been actively campaigning for their rights over many decades, and have made significant progress, partly due to a favorable political environment that obtains in this country. An early piece of legislation, a tangible result perhaps of that campaign, was the Pensions (Amendment) Act 1968, which granted equal pay for equal work to men and women alike. Similarly, married women became entitled to file separate income tax assessments under the Income Tax (Amendment) Act of 1975. In 2001, the Women, Family and Community Development Ministry was set up under the then Prime Minister Mahathir. Then came the landmark amendment to Article 8(2) of the Federal Constitution, which prohibited all discrimination based on gender. This was followed in 2004 by a policy initiative under the then Prime Minister Abdullah Badawi to increase women's participation in government and corporate leadership to 30% (as per UN recommendation). Women are as a result being promoted to leadership positions, a policy which has been

[19] "Denying Women Right to Work Deprives Them of Choice," *New Straits Times*, 20 March 1999. The seven women groups mentioned were: Sisters in Islam, All Women's Action Society, Pusat Khidmat Wanita Pertiwi, Women's Aid Organisation, Women's Crisis Centre, and Women's Development Collective. It was added that the 1997 statistics from the Selangor Syariah Court showed that out of 2,165 registered divorces, only 29 were granted a *mut'ah* (consolation gift), 58 were on division of matrimonial property, 55 of wife maintenance, 63 of child maintenance, and only ten cases of 'iddah maintenance. This "abysmal record from one of the most developed states in Malaysia is a tragic reflection of how far reality is from the Qur'anic ideal of responsible Muslim male." Noted also was the experience of single mothers which showed that their standard of living plunged immediately after divorce or desertion and fell into the poverty trap, while their ex-husbands tended to experience little change in their living standards.

subsequently endorsed, by the incumbent Prime Minister Najib Razak's administration.

6.4 Conclusion and recommendations

This chapter looked into the issues of women's empowerment in the workplace. Our examination of the source evidence of the *Qur'an* and *Sunnah*, historical data, as well as juristic doctrine is generally affirmative of Islam's essentially egalitarian outlook on women's rights. We have also ascertained the scope and size of the challenges that arise from prejudicial customary practices that undermine women's rights — sometimes contrary to Islamic guidelines. This aspect of the challenge tends to be tenacious and difficult to uproot. Some of the more tangible results of past efforts manifested in reformist legislation have also been surveyed, especially in the case of Malaysia. I now conclude with a set of actionable policy recommendations for follow-up reform as follows:

- Women's right of work is part and parcel of the general challenge of gender equality and justice. Hence, it is important that the more particular issues of women's empowerment in the workplace are contextualized into the larger matrix of equality. New solutions to issues should also be related to aspects of equality in matrimonial law, as well as in the economic and social conditions of women in their particular settings.
- Women have always shouldered arduous work as wives and mothers within the family and society, without actually gaining due recognition for it. This should be rectified by due acknowledgment of their contribution as well as grants of material assistance in child benefits and availability of child care facilities, health care and adequate maternity leave for working mothers.
- Countries and regions of the Muslim world differ widely in respect of their capabilities, acceptance or otherwise of major changes in women's rights, notwithstanding also their significant commonalities. Particularities of culture and socio-economic conditions must be duly recognized in one's quest and plan for further improvement.
- Islamic law is cognizant of the differences of custom and culture, in so far as these are recognized as valid bases in law and judgment, provided they do not contravene the basic norms of fair play and justice. The theory of *ijtihad* is also cognizant of the role of custom in so far as it

makes contextualization of custom and culture of society a pre-condition of *ijtihad*.

- Islamic law has stagnated nevertheless and a certain disconnect has developed over time, between the *Shari'ah* and social reality, as well as statutory legislation. The colonial legacy and its inherent bent on secularist modernity ensured that statutory law in the Muslim world is not energized by the guidelines of *Qur'an* and/or the resources of *ijtihid*, but by a wholesale importation of western laws and institutions into their former colonies.
- Gender equality in the workplace still looms large and remains a challenge unmet in the larger part of the Muslim world, not so much because of a lack of statutory law and policy, but that much of what already exists is prescriptive and wanting of effective implementation. A lesson to be learned may be that law and policy making on gender issues need to be action oriented. It is better to be gradual and effective rather than idealistic and ambitious beyond context.
- Our village folks, religious leaders and conservative strata of population have often remained uninvolved or aloof to the issue of women's rights and the efforts to address them at the level of law and policy. These efforts need to be more inclusive and reach out for the people's consultative input. Law and policy should be such that people can relate to and understand. The importance of enlisting the support of imams and religious leaders to the gender justice campaign can hardly be overestimated.
- Muslims need to own the agenda of gender justice themselves. The fact that this has hitherto been largely driven by Western ideas has generated internal resistance among Muslims — sometimes even among those who may otherwise be less than hostile to reform. For Muslims to own that agenda is to anchor it in local culture and Islam. One can still keep an open outlook on beneficial input from other traditions, but only when substantive harmony with indigenous values is carefully ascertained in one's quest for overall improvement.
- Gender justice issues are closely tied to the Muslim perceptions of piety, which adds to religious sensitivities. Even in the *fiqh* tradition, the subject of matrimonial law (*munakahat*) features next, in the order of thematic classification, to devotional matters (*ibadat*), due to the recognition that marriage has a devotional (*ta'abbudi*) aspect and is different in that respect from the rest of civil transactions (*muamalat*). All this

notwithstanding, the fact remains that marriage is a civil contract in Islamic law.

- It is advisable for Western sponsors and advocates of women's equality to recognize in their supportive projects and programs in Muslim countries, or the most conservative among them at least, that an openly assertive stance on gender issues can be counter-productive.
- Gender justice campaigns by the Muslims themselves should approach the outstanding problems according to a carefully graduated approach that takes up the relatively softer issues, such as education, literacy and health care before they move on to the more challenging problems of reform on core issues of local custom, matrimonial law and inheritance. Women's equality in the workplace too is internally diverse. For instance, employment of women in certain professions, such as medical services, teaching, social and family support sectors are not as sensitive as their participation in elected assemblies, police and prison services and the like. Gradualism and pragmatism also avail one of the benefits of self-assessment over time.
- Finally, some Muslim countries, such as Malaysia, Indonesia, Morocco, Turkey and even Egypt can perhaps form a common platform to act in unison in the advancement of gender justice in other parts of the Muslim world. Some of these countries enjoy better prospects of receptivity and cooperation with other Muslim countries. The countries just mentioned may consider participation in projects that seek to strengthen the family unit, local economy and education with the significant participation of women themselves.

References

Arabic

Abu Ishaq Ibrahim al-Shatibi (1332H), *Al-I'tisam*, Cairo: Matba'ah al-Manar, II.

Abu Shaqqah, Abd al-Halim (1990/1410H), *Tahrir al-Mar'ah fi 'Asr al-Risalah 52 Dirasah Jami'ah li-Nusus al-Qur'an al-Karim wa Sahih al-Bukhari wa Muslim* (Vol. II), Kuwait.

Abu Zahrah (n.d.), *Tanzim al-Islam li'l-Mujtama'*, Cairo: Matba'at al-Mukhaymir.

A1-'Abudi, Musin (1990/1410H), *A1-Hurriyyat al-Ijtima'iyyah, bayn al-Nuzum al-Mu'asirah wa'l- Fikr al-Islami al-Siyasi*, Cairo: Dar al-Nahdaha al-'Arabiyyah.

Al-Albani, Muhammad Nasir al-Din, Muslim (1404H), *Mukhtasar Sahih Muslim*, (2nd edn.), Beirut: Dar al-maktab al-Islami.

Al-'Ashmawi, Fawziah (2009/1430H), "Tajdid al-Fikr al-Islami: Manhaj al-Ta'amul ma' Qadaya al-Mar'at al-Muslimah," in Mahmud Hamdi Zaqzuq (ed.). *Tajdid al-Fikr al-Islami: Buhuth wa Fa'aliyyat al-Mu'tamar al-'am al-Wahid wa'l-'Ishrin li'l-Majlis al-A'la li'l-Shu'un al-Islamiyyah*, Cairo.

Al-'Asqalani, Ibn Hajar (1977), *Al-Isabah fi Tamyiz al-Sahabah*, Cairo: Dar al-Azhar.

Al-Banna, Jamal (1996), *Nahw al- Fiqh al- Jadid*, Cairo: Dar al-Fikr al-Islami, p. 197.

Al-Dughmi, Muhammad Rakan (1988/1408), *al-Nazariyyat al- Amn al-Ghaza'I min Manzur al-Islami*, Amman (Jordan): Yutlab min al-Mu'allif.

Al-Ghazali, Muhammad (1993/1413), *Huquq al-Insan bayn Ta'lim al-Islam wa I'lan al-Umam al- Muttahidah*, Alexandriah (Egypt): Dar al-Da'wah li'l-Nashr wa'l-Tawzi'.

Al-Islam, Shaltut (n.d.), *Aqidah wa Shari'ah*, Kuwait: Matabi' Dar al-Qalam.

Al-Jawziyyah, Ibn Qayyim (n.d.), *al-Turuq al-hukmiyyah fi'l-Siyasah al-Shar'iyyah*, Muhammad Jamil Ghazi (ed.), Jeddah: Maktabat al-Madani.

Al-Khamsah, Salwa (1973), *Al-Mar'ah al-'Arabiyyah wa'l-Mujtama' al-Taqlidi al-Mutakhallif*, Beirut: Dar al-Haqiqah.

Al-Mawardi, Abul Hassan (1966/1386), *Kitab al-Ahkam al-Sultaniyyah* (2nd edn.), Cairo: Matba'ah al-Babi al-Halaby.

Al-Nawawi, Yahya ibn Sharaf (1975), Rawdat al-Taliban, Beirut: al-Maktab al-Islami.

Al-Qaradawi, Y. (1996/1416), *fi Fiqh al-Awlawiyat, Dirasah Jadidah fi Daw' al-Qur'an wa'l-Sunnah* (2nd edn.), Cairo: Maktabah Wahbah.

Al-Sadiq Afifi, Muhammad (1980/1400), *Al-Sadiq Afifi, al Mujtamaa al-Islami wa Usul al-hukm*, Cairo: Dar al-I'tisam.

Al-Sanhuri, Abd al-Razzaq (1989), *Fiqh al-Khilifah wa Tatawwuruha*, Nadia al-Sanhuri and Tawfiq Muhammad al-Shawi (eds.), Cairo: al-Hay'ah al-Misriyyah li'l-Kitab.

Al-Shishani, Abd al-Wahhab (1980), *Huquq al-Insan wa Hurriyatuh al-Asasiyyah fi'l-Nizam al-Islami wa'l-Nuzum al-Mu'asirah*, Amman: Matabi' al-Jami'yah al-Malakiyah.

Al-Shawiribi 'Abd al-Hamid (1987), *Al-huquq al-Siyasiyyah li'l-Mar'ah fi'l-Islam*, Alexandria (Egypt): Mansha'at al-Ma'arif.

Al-Shaybani, Muhammad ibn Hassan (1940), *A1-Kitab fi'l-Rizq a1Mustatab*, Muhammad ibn Sama'ah (ed.), Cairo: Maktabah Nashr al-Thaqafah al-Islamiyyah.

Al-Tabari, Muhammad ibn Jarir (1969), *Tafsir al-Tabari* (Vol. VIII), Cairo: Dar al-Ma'arif.

Al-Tabrizi, 'Abd Allah al-Khatib (1965), "Mishkat al-Masabih" (Vol. 2), in Muhammad Nasir al-Din, Beirut: al-Maktab al-Islami.

Al-Wahid, Wafi 'Ali 'Abd (ed.) (1965), *Al-Musawat fi'l-Islam*, Cairo: Dar al-Ma'arif.

Al-Zahiri, Ibn Hazm (n.d.), *A1-Fisal fi'l-Milal wa'l Ahwa' wa'l-Nihal* (Vol. IV), Cairo: Maktabah Salam al-'Alamiyyah, p. 167.

Badawi, Isma'il (1980/1400), *Da'aimim al-Hukm fi'l Shari'ah al-Islamiyyah wa'l-Nuzum al-Dusturiyyah al-Mu'asirah*, Cairo: Dar al-Fikr al-'Arabi.

Ibn Salam, Abu 'Ubay al-Qassim (1991), *Kitab al-Amwal*, translated by Noor Muhammad Ghiffari entitled as *The Book of Finance*, Islamabad: Hijra Council.

Mutawalli, 'Abd al-Hamid (1974), *Mabadi Nizam al-hukm fi'l-Islam*, Alexandriah (Egypt); Mansha'at al-Ma'arif.

English

Kamali, Mohammad Hashim (2010), *The Right to Education, Work and Welfare in Islam*, Cambridge: The Islamic Texts Society.

Kamali, Mohammad Hashim (2003), *Principles of Islamic Jurisprudence*, 3rd edn., Cambridge: Islamic Texts Society.

Kamali, Mohammad Hashim (2002), *Freedom, Equality and Justice in Islam*, Kuala Lumpur: Ilmiah Publishers, and (1999) (2nd revised edn.), Cambridge: The Islamic Texts Society, p. 236.

Kamali, Mohammad Hashim (2008), *Shari'ah Law: An Introduction*, Oxford: Oneworld Publications.

Khan, Maimul Ahsan (2007), *Islamic Jurisprudence and Women's Rights*, Dhaka: The Nahar Light Foundation.

Menon, Pramodini (1999), "Women Have the Right to Choose," *The Star*, 25 March.

Osman, Faisal (1992), Osman, *Women, Islam and Nation Building*, Kuala Lumpur: Penerbit Fajar Bakti, 1992, p. 23.

Othman, Faisal bin Haji (1992), *Women, Islam and Nation Building*, Kuala Lumpur: Penerbit Fajar Bakti.

Shahabudin, Sharifah Hapsa (2013), "Women Have Come a Long Way," *New Straits*, January 29.

Shaikh, Sa'diyya (2003), "Transforming Feminisms: Islam, Woman and Gender Justice," in Omid Safi (ed.). *Progressive Muslims, on Justice, Gender and Pluralism*, Oxford, Oneworld Publications.

Wadud-Muhsin, Amina (1992), *Qur'an and Women*, Kuala Lumpur: Penerbit Fajar Bakti.

Chapter 7

Navigating between Patriarchal Fundamentalism and Islamic Feminism: A Critical Islamic Appraisal

Nabil Yasien Mohamed

Abstract

In this chapter, we discuss the contending notions of patriarchal fundamentalism and feminism, and move toward a moderate discourse on women empowerment, namely, Islamic femininity. In deconstructing patriarchal fundamentalism, we examine literalist and decontextualized readings of the religious tradition which encourages cultural chauvinism and leads to erroneous religious expressions. Navigating the genealogy of Western secular feminism, we note how the term "feminism" has become loaded with the baggage of imperialism, capitalism, homogenization of womanhood and negative incursions on Muslim women.

In rethinking Islamic feminism, we discuss the impasse between egalitarianism and social hierarchy. We show how the verses of social hierarchy and egalitarianism are not mutually exclusive or contradictory, for they admit to functional social differences. Thus, hierarchy is not an institution of oppression and injustice, neither superiority of men over women but a functional hierarchy that governs the family structure. However, the metaphysical reality is that men and women are morally and ontologically equal. Thereafter, we discuss the contending dynamics between essentialism and social constructivism in notions of gender. We discuss that the *essential* attributes of men and women are not just determined by empirical observation, but are metaphysical realities known to us through revelation and our primordial nature. A simplistic socially constructed convention of gender disregards subtle distinctions between men and women that are essential to their being and autonomy.

Lastly, we call toward an Islamic femininity that may produce a cohesive synthesis as opposed to a syncretic formulation such as Islamic feminism. We attempt to establish an organic Islamic model of women empowerment upon the ethical plinth of *Qur'anic* principles rather than the hegemony of patriarchal fundamentalism or the ideologies of feminism. Thus, an Islamic femininity will endorse complementarity and not competition; divine-guided social hierarchy and not a gender eclipse; *essential* female qualities and not dogmatic social constructivism; and dignity and autonomy, not subordination.

Keywords: Patriarchal fundamentalism, Feminism, Egalitarianism, Social hierarchy, Essentialism, Social constructivism, Islamic femininity

Two waves have entered the shores of the Muslim world, the wave of secular modernity with its offshoot of feminism and the wave of dogmatic Islamic literalism with its offshoot of patriarchal fundamentalism. The discourse of women emancipation is blurred by the contending currents of patriarchy and feminism. The stand-off between "patriarchal fundamentalism" and the various feminisms is a dynamic debate in gender discourse. The empowerment of women is rooted in her autonomy, dignity and honor; any ideology or practice potentially averse to such should be interrogated.

The hegemonic tendencies of patriarchal fundamentalism stem from a combination of myopic cultural practices and erroneous interpretations of religious text. However, "patriarchy" itself is not an inherent evil, but perceptible to hegemonic and oppressive tendencies. A benign patriarchy speaks of divine-guided social hierarchy, rather than despotic male behavior. The perpetuation of patriarchal fundamentalism has relegated women to the narrow margins of society, stifles her being and potential for self-actualization. It begs the question, how do we deconstruct patriarchal fundamentalism, understand the place of social hierarchy in the Islamic tradition, and attain women empowerment?

On the other end of the spectrum are the variances of feminism. Secular feminism originates from women activism during the French revolution; first-wave feminism in the 19th and 20th centuries and second-wave feminism in the 1960s and 1970s. The genealogy of Western secular feminism traces back to the enlightenment ideas of rationalism and secularism. Feminism has become laden with the baggage of imperialism, capitalism, homogenization of womanhood and negative incursions on Muslim women. In addition, its secular epistemological underpinnings promote notions of justice and equality void of transcendental wisdom and foreign to the Islamic tradition. Although Islamic feminism is not a clone of secular feminism, can it remove the fetters of its negative baggage?

In our critique of Islamic feminism, we discuss the standoff between egalitarianism and social hierarchy. Thereafter, we discuss the contending dynamics between essentialism and social constructivism in notions of gender. Lastly, we discuss and call toward an Islamic femininity that will endorse complementarity and not competition; divine-guided social order and not a false leveling; *essential* female qualities and not dogmatic constructivism; and dignity and autonomy, not subordination. Thus, we endeavor to carve out an organic Islamic model of women empowerment upon *Qur'anic* ethical principles rather than the hegemony of patriarchal fundamentalism or the ideologies of feminism.

7.1 Deconstructing patriarchal fundamentalism

Understanding patriarchy is fundamental to the discourse of women emancipation and empowerment. Much variance exists in defining patriarchy. Walby defines patriarchy as "a system of social structures and practices in which men dominate, oppress and exploit women" (Walby, 1990, p. 20). The institution of patriarchy is understood in common parlance as hegemonic, unjust and inherently evil. It marginalizes women in the political and economic spheres, and deprives them of educational opportunity. Western secular feminists define patriarchy in this sense. But I prefer to call it *patriarchal fundamentalism*. The secular thrust of Western feminism assumes all religions are patriarchal in this light, adopting an emancipatory and colonialist attitude to women of religious disposition. A classic feature of orientalism is to categorize, homogenize and essentialize entire faiths and people (Sara, 2013, p. 3). It predefines what patriarchy is and assumes Islam is "patriarchal". Traditional Islamic discourse understands the social hierarchy employed by patriarchal tradition as not inherently evil. It understands male leadership in the private sphere as a functional role rather than a bias to privilege men. Therefore, we can say that it is the abuse of the patriarchal social order that has established a system of fanaticism. Patriarchal fundamentalism has led to the marginalization of women, not social hierarchy itself. Due to the erroneous interpretations of Islamic sources and fundamentalist patriarchy, many Muslim women have been relegated to the narrow margins of society.

Western civilization inherited its understanding of gender and morality from the Bible (Lerner, 1986, p. 161). Western patriarchy is rooted in the Judeo-Christian tradition, thus, secular feminism developed as a response to it. The Bible espouses the account of Eve being made of the rib of Adam.[1] It also explains Eve succumbing to the whisperings of Satan, known as the Fall of Man.[2] These biblical traditions have influenced Christian scholars to interpret the Bible in a misogynistic sense, assuming man to be morally superior and dominant to women. Some argue that as Islam expanded to different lands, Islamic scholars were influenced by the Judeo-Christian tradition and interpreted the text in a hyper-patriarchal sense. However, the *rib account* and *the fall* are not in the *Qur'an.*

From the *Qur'anic* verse, "And among His signs is that he created mates for you from among yourselves, that you may find rest in them",[3] some exegetes have implicitly interpreted *from among yourselves* to be understood as the creation of Eve from the rib of Adam. However, other exegetes such as Qurtubi (d. 1273), Muhammad Shafi (d. 1976) and Maududi (d.1979) interpreted *from among yourselves* as from the same species, identical in humanity but different in physical, emotional and psychological dispositions (Shafi, n.d., 6:733; Maududi, 1982, 1:203; Bewley, 2003). The wisdom in the creation of men and women from the same species or from a single soul is to find tranquility in each other. It addresses both men and women to reflect upon the love and mercy among themselves as an extension of God's Love and Mercy (Nasr, 2015, p. 989). In the *hadith* traditions, there are no explicit narrations stating women (Eve) are created from the rib of men (Adam), but rather "they are created from a rib".[4] This was intended as a metaphorical expression implying that women have a particular nature, and attempts to "straighten" her may hurt her.[5] Thus, it is a prescription upon men to understand her nature and take good care of her. Regarding the fall, in the biblical version, Eve alone was beguiled by Satan, which gave men moral superiority over women. By contrast, in the *Qur'an* the dual pronoun is

[1] Genesis (2):22.
[2] Genesis (3):1–6.
[3] *Al-Rum* (30):21. Translation from *The Study Quran.*
[4] *Sahīh al-Bukhari*: *Hadith* 5186. The Prophet (SAW) added: "And I command you to take care of the women in a good manner for they are created from a rib and the most crooked portion of the rib is its upper part; if you try to straighten it, you will break it, and if you leave it, it will remain crooked, so I command you to take care of the women in a good manner."
[5] *Sahīh al-Bukhari*: Hadith 5184. Narrated Abu Hurairah (R.A.), Allah's Messenger said, "The woman is like a rib; if you try to straighten her, you will break her. So if you want to get benefit from her, do so while she still has some crookedness."

used in reference to the notion that *both* Adam and Eve were enticed by Satan.[6]

In addition to the assimilation of the Judeo-Christian tradition, many Islamic scholars interpreted the text through their cultural lens. Influenced by the Persian and Arab culture of their time, they have in some cases drifted from the *Qur'anic* perspective of women. The cultural bias influenced the legal rulings in favor of men in the religious, social and political space. This has perpetuated decontextualized and literalist readings of prophetic traditions. Male-biased interpretations of the tradition led to rulings that were not in keeping with the higher objectives of the law (*maqāsid al-Shari'āh*). In such light, modern scholars call toward a reform of the tradition regarding the role of women, questioning the readings of classical interpretations and judgments. However, a distinction between inherent social hierarchy and fundamentalist patriarchal interpretations should be made to understand the Islamic tradition. Several traditions have been interpreted in a literalist and decontextualized sense such that it yields male hegemony.

The *sahīh* hadith, narrated by Abu Bakra: "Those who entrust their affairs to a woman will never know prosperity",[7] is often cited to justify the isolation and limitation of women in public roles of leadership, i.e., political governance, judicial appointments, organizational leadership, etc. The Egyptian scholar, Muhammad Ghazzali (d. 1996) explains that the context of the *hadith* should be noted to elucidate its true meaning. The Persian Sassanid Empire was on the verge of decline due to internal political strife and military defeat by the Byzantine Empire. During this period, the Persian Sassanid Empire brought a woman to the throne. The Prophet was thus merely remarking that it will not prevent the fall of the empire despite change of leadership (Brown, 2009, p. 163). This *hadith* is thus not a general judgment of women leadership; in fact, during the leadership of the Queen of Sheba, Bilqees, is not looked at in a negative light in the *Qur'an*. Abou El Fadl also puts forward that in light of the eminent downfall of Persia the Prophet was commenting on this *particular* woman and her context and not women in general (Jalajel, 2017, p. 36). David Jalajel makes a pertinent point that the *hadith* is not prescriptive, but rather descriptive,

[6] "Then Satan made them stumble therefrom, and expelled them from that wherein they were". *Al-Baqarah* (2):36. Translation from *The Study Quran*.
[7] *Sahīh al-Bukhari* (4425 and 7099).

thus it cannot be used to justify a command or prohibition on issues of female leadership (Jalajel, 2017, p. 37).

A literalist approach to interpretation breeds an understanding that bolsters male prejudice. A literalist and decontextualized interpretation of the following *hadith* may assume women to lack in moral and intellectual judgment. Abu Said Al-Khudri narrated, according to Bukhari[8]:

> "Once Allah's Apostle went out to the Musalla (to offer the prayer) on 'Id-al-Adha or Al-Fitr prayer. Then he passed by the women and said, 'O women! Give alms, as I have seen that the majority of the dwellers of Hell-fire were you (women).' They asked, 'Why is it so, O Allah's Apostle?' He replied, 'You curse frequently and are ungrateful to your husbands. I have not seen anyone more deficient in intelligence and religion than you. A cautious sensible man could be led astray by some of you.' The women asked, 'O Allah's Apostle! What is deficient in our intelligence and religion?' He said, 'Is not the evidence of two women equal to the witness of one man?' They replied in the affirmative. He said, 'This is the deficiency in her intelligence. Isn't it true that a woman can neither pray nor fast during her menses?' The women replied in the affirmative. He said, 'This is the deficiency in her religion.'

The aforementioned *hadith* does not depict women as inferior to men. Many scholars state from the tone of speech and context of Eid that the Prophet was being jocular in the use of strong terms to convey the teachings. The *hadith* applies the use of hyperbole in the phrase, "a cautious sensible man could be led astray by some of you" to emphasize the point that women hold significant influence over men. The rhetorical trope, synecdoche, in which the whole is made to represent the part, is applied in this *hadith*. Thus, the "deficiency of religion" refers to prayers and fasting during the menstrual period and "deficiency in intelligence" as the difference of legal testimony of women to men. The deficiency in intelligence refers not to her intellectual capacity but particular social circumstances whereby in certain financial transactions the witness of two women is equivalent to one man.[9] Another interpretation is that a woman is deficient in *responsibility*

---

[8] *Sahih al-Bukhari* (304, 1462, 1951 and 2658).

[9] "If one reads this provision for women's testimony in light of the legally established principle upholding women's competence to own property and carry out financial transactions, it suggests that the stipulation regarding women's testimony in the present verse [2:282] is particular to this circumstance [forward sale] and is meant to address certain social or communal difficulties a women might face when witnessing in such a case" (Nasr, 2015, 123).

in matters pertaining to religion and intellect. It is thus more appropriate to translate the word *'aql* (more generally translated as "intelligence") to mean "discriminatory capacity" and *din* (more commonly translated as "religion") as "ritual observance" (Hamid Ali, 2014, p. 2). Hamid Ali observes that "discriminatory capacity" is a "reference to 'alertness and vigilance,' not 'intelligence.' ... men [are] usually more on guard against the threat of treachery, swindle, and fraud in financial agreements" (Hamid Ali, 2014, p. 10). The higher intent of the *hadith* is not to depict women as morally weaker or less intelligent than men, but to encourage the giving of alms and the wisdom and mercy of God in giving them concessions on religious rituals. The phrase "deficient in religion and intellect" is not implied as a universal maxim but in the context of exhortation (Jalajel, 2017, p. 41). Such *hadith* and many others are misinterpreted to portray women as temptresses, morally and spiritually depraved and intellectually deficient. Literalist and decontextualized readings of certain *hadith* encourages cultural chauvinism and leads to erroneous religious edicts limiting women agency in the economic, political and social realms.

The depiction of women's worth, intelligence and social utility should be addressed by contemporary scholars. Such an appraisal should read beyond valuing women solely by their culinary skills, house-keeping duties and child-rearing abilities. A concern of many Muslim women activists is the visibility of Muslim women in society; whether it may be civil participation, political involvement or business undertakings. The faithful adherence and correct understanding of Islamic teachings will grant equal access to women in mosque spaces and Islamic organizations. The public space should not be dictated by gender hierarchy. Women should be given equal status, agency and liberty as men. Their educational and economic self-determination are critical to a healthy socio-political space, and prevents the yoke of masculine hegemony upon the freedoms of women. The question of women leadership in public roles and involvement in religious discourse are frowned upon by those of a hyper-conservative ideological bent. It thus requires critical scholarship and dialogue to question the underlying assumptions of patriarchal fundamentalism that shape hyper-conservative religious expressions.

7.2 Navigating Western secular feminism

Influenced by the political upheavals of the French Revolution (1789–1799) feminist activity began to contest for their legal equality and political rights. The outcomes of the French Revolution saw the establishment of enlightenment principles and secular liberal democracies in Europe. The 19th and 20th centuries witnessed the advent of first-wave feminism; it focused on the exclusion of women from property and voting rights. Between the 1960s and 1970s second-wave feminism widened the scope of feminism to include issues of family, sexuality, the workplace, etc. It brought about a plethora of different feminisms with an array of internal tensions and divergences; however, the genealogy of Western feminism traces back to enlightenment ideas of *rationalism* and *secularism* (Sara, 2013, p. 1).

Hirschkind and Mahmood argue that secular feminist discourse is central to Western imperialism. They recognize that the oppression of women in countries like Afghanistan is not solely religious or cultural, but stems from socio-political issues such as imperialism, civil war or poverty (Hirschkind and Mahmood, 2002, p. 348). In post-9/11 political discourse, U.S. foreign policy took the stance that "the fight against terrorism is a fight for the rights and dignity of women".[10] Secular feminism tends to homogenize the plight of women, assuming a common experience and thus feed into a politically prescriptive project. It assumes its understanding and application of justice is universal, not recognizing that other cultures or faiths may have a different idea of it. In Saba Mahmood's seminal work, *Politics of Piety*, she posits that freedom is a subjective notion, and other cultures may have a different expression of it. She states that Egyptian women activists are not necessarily concerned with dismantling patriarchal structures itself but *any* impediments to achieve higher levels of piety (Mahmood, 2005, p. 15). This she emphasizes is neither a false consciousness nor socialization of patriarchal norms but a strong adherence to Islamic orthodoxy (Mahmood, 2005, p. 6). She thus argues that the notions of freedom and autonomy of secular feminism cannot be applied to all women.

Katherine Bullock argues in her book, *Rethinking Muslim Women and the Veil* that the assumptions that Muslim women receive no agency, are victimized and oppressed due to the head-covering (*hijab*) are steeped in liberal and post-structuralist feminist assumptions (post-colonial variances of feminism) about human nature, the meaning of sexuality, liberation and equality (Bullock, 2002, p. 200). She states that such assumptions of the *hijab* regard human behavior and desire as socially constructed. Thus, the

[10]Abu-Lughod (2002), p. 784 cites a speech of former first lady, Laura Bush, of the U.S.

hijab is looked at as an entrenchment of the structures of male–female difference not religious devotion (Bullock, 2002, p. 200).

In addition to the political thrust behind secular feminist discourse are the materialistic or neo-liberal underpinnings of development. Economic globalization has influenced family structures. Ironically, to emancipate women from the shackles of unpaid domestic duty, Marxist and socialist feminism placed women into the structures of capitalism. The woman is thus compared to the proletariat. The emancipation from the alienation of the household economy is achieved upon her introduction into the wider economy. Economic self-determination of women is a positive stride. However, it is a shortcoming when women are not valued in the qualitative sense (moral, spiritual and social dimensions), but merely as a variable in the labor market. It is the economic determinism of demand and supply that decide her role in society, rather than her personal autonomy or tradition. Progress in the Western and secular world is by virtue of gross domestic profit (GDP) and not moral or spiritual progress. Secular feminism is thus affected by the neo-liberal *status quo* perpetuated by global capitalism.

The homogenizing of women's experience and propagation of a "universal" womanhood promulgated the quest of intersectionality by women of different race, class and religion. Critical theory attempts to challenge the secular and colonial elements in Western feminism. Although Islamic feminism may not be a clone of Western secular feminism, the question arises as to whether it is possible to completely remove the baggage of the Western imperialist project, neo-liberal tendencies and negative assumptions of Muslim women from the term "feminism" or its secular epistemological underpinnings that convey rationalist notions of justice and equality void of transcendental wisdom?

Multiple contributions to integrate feminism and Islam have been attempted.[11] Asma Barlas resists the term feminism in identifying her work, for she rejects feminism's hegemonic conceptions of equality and its negative incursions on Muslim women (Hidayatullah, 2014, p. 41). However, there is much divergence and overlap in Islamic feminism, and it cannot accurately be defined. Barlas asserts that such diversity is open to agendas that are absurdly contradictory and thus rejects the term feminism as it may radically oppose her work (Hidayatullah, 2014, p. 42).

[11] See Ziba Mir-Hosseini, Valentine Moghadam, Miriam Cooke, Sadiyyah Sheikh and Margot Badran.

Two common presuppositions in contemporary feminism that influence Islamic feminism are the absolute equality and constructivism of gender. The primary source of morality in the Islamic tradition is scripture not rationality or the vicissitudes of contemporary moral sentiments. The slippery slope of absorbing feminist paradigms of gender is not only beyond women's liberation but also the deconstruction of normative *Qur'anic* understandings of social structure and notions of womanhood.

7.3 Rethinking Islamic feminism

7.3.1 The impasse between egalitarianism and social hierarchy

To those that advocate for feminist principles of gender justice, an impasse exists between the hierarchical and egalitarian verses of the *Qur'an.* Feminist exegetes of the *Qur'an* argue that the verses of mutuality should subsume a "social equality" of the sexes lest it contradicts moral and ontological equality (Hidayatullah, 2014, p. 160). To traditional exegetes the verses of social hierarchy and egalitarianism are not mutually exclusive or contradictory, for they admit to functional social differences and an ontological equality.

Numerous verses in the *Qur'an* convey a spirit of mutuality or egalitarianism. In verse 30:21, it establishes reciprocity, mutual love and affection between marital partners. In verses 4:124 and 4:40, both men and women are held to the same moral standard of virtuousness and the same guarantee of entry into paradise for their deeds. In verse 9:71, both believing men and women are imbued with the same moral capacity. In verse 4:1, it shows evidence that both men and women originate from the same source or substance. In verse 33:35, it emphasizes no differentiation between men and women in receiving an otherworldly reward for their devotion. This is achieved by the repetition of both the masculine and feminine genders several times in the verse.[12]

Different types of hierarchy exist; spiritual hierarchy between prophets, saints and layman; political hierarchy between kings, governors and the masses; intellectual hierarchy between the scholars, preachers and the public. In a similar sense, the *Qur'an* speaks of functional social hierarchy in the private sphere. Numerous verses advocate social hierarchy. In verse

[12]See also verses 4:32 and 4:19.

4:34, it established the responsibility of husbands to provide for their wives.[13] In verse 2:228, it discusses men's degree over women, understood by exegetes as men's economic advantage and obligations, and ability to engage in armed struggle (*jihad*) (Nasr, 2015, p. 99). Others discuss the financial burden placed upon men, obligatory dowry payment (4:4), financial provision for women they divorce (2:236, 2:237 and 2:241) and alms pay for the family. Other legal differences between men and women govern inheritance and divorce. This does not undermine the social status of women in any sense; in fact, Islam allowed women self-ownership (4:19), and inheritance rights (4:11-13) which were foreign to Arab society before the arrival of the Prophet Muhammad (SAW). Such hierarchy is not an institution of oppression and injustice, or patriarchal fundamentalism, but a functional hierarchy that governs the family structure. Al-Attas lucidly conveys this sentiment:

> In the respect of the human order in society, we do not in the least mean by 'hierarchy' that semblance of it wherein oppression and exploitation and domination are legitimized as if they were an established principle ordained by God. *Any* kind of "hierarchy" and "order" is not necessarily legitimate, for such order is not order at all- it is disorder ... Disorder is the manifestation of the occurrence of injustice. The fact that hierarchical disorders have prevailed in human society does not mean that hierarchy in the human order is not valid, for there is, in point of fact, *legitimate* hierarchy in the order of creation, and this is the Divine Order of creation pervading all Creation and manifesting the occurrence of justice. (Al-Attas, 1985, p. 101)

The advocacy of familial patriarchy is not inherently evil and neither does it imply moral superiority of men over women. In Islam, there is equality before God. Men and women are held equal in moral and legal accountability; however, an absolute equality is not the reality. Thus, women are not superior to men, and neither are men superior to women. Calling toward a false leveling between men and women may incur inequity, not recognizing the biological, psychological and emotional differences between men and women. The feminist discourse calls to dissent against hierarchy, creates a gender eclipse and rejects the divine gender bifurcation. It can be viewed that patriarchy itself is not a case of hatred, bigotry and

---

[13] "Men are the upholders and maintainers of women by virtue of that in which God has favoured some of them above others and by virtue of their spending from their wealth". *Al-Nisa* (4):32. Translation from *The Study Quran.*

oppression (*zulm*) but the natural social order (Hidayatullah, 2014, p. 166). Nasr says that the male–female polarization is a mystery of God that we are to embrace (Nasr, 2010, pp. 62–72). Post-modern feminism has rejected this binary, but instead calls toward fluid gender roles that dislodge the divine social hierarchy. Islam does not call toward a quantitative equality, but a qualitative equality, thus not destroying the complementary nature between male–female relationships. The man's obligation as protector, leader and provider is complementary to the female's responsibility to her family. The social hierarchy in the family structure establishes social equity. However, the metaphysical reality is that men and women are morally and ontologically equal.

A distinction should be drawn between divine-guided social hierarchy and patriarchal fundamentalist interpretations. To interpret the verses that express social hierarchy in an egalitarian light goes beyond the limitations of *Qur'anic* exegesis. Feminists such as Hidayatullah admits that, "feminist exegetical conceptions of gender equality are historically specific to us and thus perhaps not in the end fully reconcilable with the Quranic text" (Hidayatullah, 2014, p. 147). Application of contemporary moral sentiment to interpret the morality of the *Qur'an* yields contradiction. The secularization process is an attempt to morally concede to spatio-temporal domains rather than scripture (Al-Attas, 1985, p. 14). Burdening scripture to popular moral sentiment strains the meaning of the *Qur'an* in time and space, thus yielding anachronistic readings of the *Qur'an*. In light of *both* hierarchical and egalitarian currents that exist in the *Qur'an*; feminist conceptions of justice cannot converge with the *Qur'anic* notions of justice.

7.3.2 Between essentialism and social constructivism

Post-modern approaches to feminism assume masculine and feminine traits as socially constructed, and not a divine-ordained innate disposition. The gender binary of masculine and feminine are dislodged and replaced by a fluid gender conception. Traditionalists advocate a gender binary that is far from an accident (or construct) but a core feature of what constitutes human nature (Nasr, 2010, p. 1).

Seyyed Hossein Nasr propounds that the creation of mankind in pairs is of the Wisdom of God. The *essential* difference between male and female is not just biological but psychological, temperamental and spiritual (Nasr, 2010, p. 2). He recognizes that the entelechy of the two is the same, to participate in virtue and attain spiritual deliverance (Nasr, 2010, p. 2).

He states that these subtle attributes in the nature of men and women are an embodiment of the divine names. The microcosmic qualities, known as the masculine and feminine principles are a reflection of God's names. The masculine principles are a reflection of the attributes of Majesty, Absoluteness and Power (*jalālī*) and the feminine principles are a reflection of the attributes of Beauty and Infinitude (*jamālī*) (Nasr, 2010, p. 2). Nasr states that the predisposed nature of men and women is not just biological (as professed by naturalist), but has metaphysical significance too. He argues that these attributes are manifested at the social and familial level, where men and women are seen as complementary rather than absolutely equal and contending. He says that harmony and union between the two are achieved through embracing these differences and not "reducing both sexes to a kind of "neuter" sex containing each principle in "equal proportions" (Nasr, 1980, p. 6).

In Murata's *Tao of Islam*, she establishes a cosmology based on the theological polarity of similarity (*yin*) such as beauty, mercy and compassion and incomparability (*yang*) such as majesty, justice and wrath as reflected in God's names and attributes. She states that Ibn Arabi "sees a fundamental root of the relationship between husband and wife in the yang/ying relationship between God and the cosmos" (Murata, 1992, p. 9). Ibn Arabi defends this stating that in verse 13:33, God stands over (*qā'im*) creation in the same way that in verse 4:34, men "stand over" (*qawwam*) women.[14] In other cases, she says that Ibn Arabi states that a woman is similar to Nature in her receptive attributes for she is a locus for activity. Whereas, a man "cast the water into the womb", which conveys his active attributes.

Sadiyyah Shaikh critiques Nasr's dichotomization of *jalālī* and *jamālī* attributes to men and women, respectively. She argues that it further entrenches "patriarchy" or unjust hierarchy. She regards the traditional construct of complementarity imbibed in such dichotomization as narrow and simplistic. Instead she calls to a harmonious integration of both *jamālī* and *jalālī* attributes in both men and women (Shaikh, 2012, p. 205). She presents a romanticized, non-hierarchical attribution of these qualities to men and women in equal proportion. Thus, "feminine" qualities are equally imbibed in men, as found in women; and "masculine" qualities are equally imbibed in women, as found in men. Thus, the *jamālī* and *jalālī*

[14]Ibn al- 'Arabi, *Futūḥat* IV 228.3 cited in Murata (1992), p. 9.

qualities are not linked to the polar vision of gender or an innate disposition (*fiṭrah*) distinguishing the inherent differences in men and women. Shaikh commends Murata on her nuanced metaphysical understanding of the spiritual qualities but critiques her understanding of Ibn Arabi, stating that it reinforces social hierarchy and static gender conceptions, and ignores fluid human gendered relationships. Shaikh draws on contemporary notions of equality to establish a *jalālī/jamālī* concentration that is equal in men and women. She ignores the social structures established by the verses of hierarchy that complement the spiritual nuances expiated by Murata. Hidayatullah states that the impasse that exists due to the lack of clear-cut support from the *Qur'an* for feminist principles of equality leads her to instead conceive categories of gender as relative, fluid, evolving, context dependent, historically progressive and constructive instead of fixed innate binaries (Hidayatullah, 2014, p. 189). Thus, to her a deconstruction of binary opposition of sexes, supposedly reconciles equality and difference (Hidayatullah, 2014, p. 189). She gives an example of how this may be explored stating that "contemporary technologies (i.e., formula and breast-milk pumps) now make it possible for men to nurse babies ... here advanced technology alters sex-based roles and thereby changes the relationship between men and women" (Hidayatullah, 2014, pp. 190–191).

In the Islamic tradition, truth, social responsibilities and cosmological realities are not contingent on the spatial-temporal vicissitudes but the guidance of scripture. The *jalālī* and *jamālī* qualities are neither a dichotomy nor an absolute equal concentration in men and women but instead can be viewed as concentrated in different proportion in men and women. Men have an essential capacity for *jamālī* qualities, but their *jalālī* qualities are dominant. Women on the other hand have an essential capacity for *jalālī* qualities, but their *jamālī* qualities are stronger. Surely, when God states in the *Qur'an*, "Oh Mankind! Lo! We have created you male and female ... The noblest among you, in the sight of Allah, is the best in conduct" (49:13). He is not merely referring to the biological differences in men and women, but the psychological, spiritual and temperamental qualities that make up the polarity. The *essential* attributes of men and women are not just determined by empirical observation, as we do in biological science, but are metaphysical realities known to us through revelation and *fiṭrah* (natural innate disposition). A simplistic socially constructed convention of gender disregards subtle distinctions between men and women that are essential to their being and autonomy.

7.3.3 Toward an Islamic femininity

The qualifier "Islamic" to "feminism" yields countless contradictions that stem from the political, economic and secular baggage that the term feminism holds. A commitment to feminist principles of absolute social equality and gender constructivism, and Islamic scripture presents a challenge to convergence. An attempt to rubber stamp or cosmetically Islamize feminism with Islamic elements produces a syncretism rather than a sound synthesis. To argue that the commitments of feminism are indigenous to Islam is to embrace imperialist, neo-liberal and secular elements within the Islamic tradition. "Islamic feminism" has become apologetic in response to secular liberalism, and has compromised social hierarchy and *essential* gender distinctions. A comprehensive gender discourse would speak of oppression and justice in the universal sense and not limit it to the narrow confines of feminism.

Further social problems occur if we ignore the rights and essential nature of women. The centrality of family and responsibility should balance the discussion of rights. The political and economic influence on feminism attempts to masculinize women in order to "liberate" them (Nisar, 2016). Such liberation removes God from the equation, and degrades women from her essence (Nisar, 2016). Furthermore, it regards traditional femininity as weak and submissive. Sumeera Nisar states that historically men have not valued women's femininity beyond their sexual needs, taking care of their progeny and doing menial tasks (Nisar, 2016). Furthermore, she says the world values masculine traits, while feminine traits are to be used and denigrated (Nisar, 2016).

A more sober discourse would call toward an Islamic femininity. This would embrace the natural *fiṭrah* or dominant *jamālī* qualities (mercy, compassion and beauty) of women, rather than betray her being; while still recognizing her potential for *jalālī* qualities. The dignity and honor of women is not in imitating men, or benchmarking men as a standard of liberation but in embracing and cultivating her femininity. An Islamic femininity will promote complementarity and not rivalry; divine-guided social hierarchy and not blind gender neutrality; *essential* female qualities and not dogmatic constructivism; and autonomy, not subordination.

An Islamic femininity embraces the identity of a woman as caring, nurturing, compassionate and kind; yet ensures her autonomy and dignity.

7.4 Conclusion

In the preceding discussion we have navigated between the contending waves of patriarchal fundamentalism and feminism, and moved to the shores of a moderate discourse toward women empowerment, namely, Islamic femininity.

In deconstructing patriarchal fundamentalism, we have interrogated the literalist and decontextualized readings of the religious tradition which encourages cultural chauvinism and leads to erroneous religious expressions. The depiction of women's worth, intelligence and social utility should be addressed by contemporary scholars. The visibility of Muslim women, within civil participation, political involvement or business undertakings should be addressed. The faithful adherence and correct understanding of Islamic teachings will grant equal access to women in mosque spaces and Islamic organizations. The self-actualization of women may be realized through women's educational and economic self-determination. The public space should not be dictated by gender hierarchy, but the achievement of equal status, agency and liberty as men.

Navigating the genealogy of Western secular feminism, we note how the term "feminism" has become loaded with the baggage of imperialism, capitalism, homogenization of womanhood, and negative incursions on Muslim women. In addition, its secular epistemological underpinnings promote notions of justice and equality foreign to the Islamic tradition. This puts into question the juxtaposition of the ideals of feminism and Islam.

In rethinking Islamic feminism, firstly, we have discussed the impasse that exists between social hierarchy and egalitarianism to advocates of feminist notions of equality. The application of contemporary moral sentiment to interpret the morality of the *Qur'an* may yield contradiction. We have shown how the verses of social hierarchy and egalitarianism are not mutually exclusive or contradictory, for they admit to functional social differences. Thus, hierarchy is not an institution of oppression and injustice, neither superiority of men over women but a functional hierarchy that govern the family structure. The social hierarchy in the family structure establishes social equity. However, the metaphysical reality is that men and women are morally and ontologically equal. Secondly, we have discussed that the *essential* attributes of men and women are not just determined by empirical observation, as we do in biological science, but are metaphysical realities known to us through revelation and our *fiṭrah* (primordial nature). A simplistic socially constructed convention of gender disregards subtle distinctions between men and women that are essential to their being and autonomy. The cosmological reality is such that neither the *jalālī* and *jamālī* qualities are bifurcated nor does an absolute equal concentration of it exist in men and women; but instead can be viewed as concentrated in different proportion in men and women. Thus, men have an essential capacity for *jamālī* qualities, but dominant *jalālī* qualities. Conversely, women have an essential capacity for *jalālī* qualities, but a stronger concentration of *jamālī* qualities.

Finally, to develop a body of scholarship and dialogue around the idea of an Islamic femininity we may produce a cohesive synthesis as opposed to a syncretic formulation such as Islamic feminism. It may thus contribute to an indigenously Islamic approach to the gender struggle. An Islamic femininity will endorse complementarity, not competition; and divine-guided social hierarchy, not a gender eclipse. In establishing women empowerment, it will promote dignity and agency, not subordination. The essential female qualities of compassion, love and mercy will be valued and not replaced by a dogmatic social constructivism that betray her being. By the token of an Islamic femininity, Muslim society and civilization may thus loosen the shackles of patriarchal fundamentalism and feminism.

References

Abu-Lughod, Lila (2002), Do Muslim women really need saving? Anthropological reflections on cultural relativism and its others. *American Anthropologist*, 104(3), 783–790.

Al-Attas, Syed Muhammad Naquib a. (1985), *Islam and Secularism*, New York: Mansell Publishing Limited.

Bewley, Aisha, trans. (2003), *Tafsir Al-Qurtubi-Classical Commentary of the Holy Qur'an*, London: Dar Al Taqwa Ltd.

Brown, Jonathan A. C. (2009), *Hadith — Muhammad's Legacy in the Medieval and Modern World*, Oxford: Oneworld.

Bullock, Katherine (2002), *Rethinking Muslim Women and the Veil: Challenging Historical & Modern Stereotypes*, Herndorn: IIIT.

Hamid Ali, Abdullah bin (2014), "Is Intelligence Gender Specific in Islam?" *Lamp Post*, available at http://www.lamppostproductions.com/wp-content/uploads/2011/02/Gender_Intelligence.pdf. Accessed on 21 November 2017.

Hidayatullah, Aysha A. (2014), *Feminist Edges of the Qur'an*, Oxford University Press.

Hirschkind, Charles and Saba Mahmood (2002), Feminism, the Taliban, and politics of counter-insurgency. *Anthropological Quarterly*, 75(2), 339–354.

Jalajel, David Solomon (2017), *Women and Leadership in Islamic Law — A Critical Analysis of Classical Legal Texts*, London and New York: Routledge.

Lerner, Gerna (1986), *Women and History* (Vol. The Creation of Patriarchy, 1). New York, Oxford: Oxford University Press.

Mahmood, Saba (2005), *Politics of Piety: The Islamic Revival and the Feminist Subject*, Princeton and Oxford: Princeton University Press.

Maududi, S. Abul A'la (1982), *The Meaning of the Quran* (6th edn.) (Vol. 1), Lahore: Islamic Publications Ltd.

Murata, Sachiko (1992), *Tao of Islam, The: A Sourcebook on Gender Relationships in Islamic Thought*, Albany, SUNY Press.

Nasr, Seyyed Hossein (1980), The male and female in the Islamic perspective. *Studies in Comparative Religion*, 14(1–2), 67–75.

Nasr, Seyyed Hossein (2010), *Islam in the Modern World*, New York: Harper One.

Nasr, Seyyed Hossein (2015), *The Study Quran*, New York: Harper One.

Nisar, Sumeera (2016), "Contextualizing the Discourse on Feminism." Tariqramadan.com. 2016. https://tariqramadan.com/english/contextualizing-the-discourse-on-feminism-by-sumeera-nisar/. Accessed date: 20/06/2017.

Sara, Salem (2013), Feminist critique and Islamic feminism: The question of intersectionality. *The Postcolonialist*, 1(1).

Shafi, Muhammad (2011), *Ma'riful Quran*. Vol. 6, Maktaba Darul Uloom: Deoband.

Shaikh, Sa'diyya (2012), *Sufi Narratives of Intimacy: Ibn 'Arabī, Gender, and Sexuality*, Cape Town: UCT Press.

Walby, Sylvia (1990), *Theorizing Patriarchy*, Oxford: Basill Blackwell Inc.

Chapter 8

Women's Rights: The *Qur'anic* Ideals and Contemporary Realities

Elmira Akhmetova

Abstract

This chapter is a study of the rights of women in Islam in comparison with the status of women in the contemporary Muslim world. Men and women in Islam, regardless of their age, social class and education, are equal as citizens and individuals, but not identical, in their rights and responsibilities. It suggests that, in the early age of Islam, women were given full confidence, trust and high responsibilities in leadership, educational guidance and decision-making. But this Islamic empowerment of women bears little relation to the real condition of women in modern Muslim societies. Women suffer the most in the MENA and other conflict-ridden regions from insecurity, domestic abuse, low access to education and medical care. The absence of good governance also results in gender inequality and violation of the rights of women. Without good governance, the status of women is not likely to improve. Muslim women have a potential to play a fundamental role in curbing corruption, social ills, violence and crime in the Muslim world. Therefore, in order to achieve stability and prosperity, the government must ensure a platform for women to participate in decision-making and benefit from the rights they are accorded in Islam.

Keywords: Muslim world, Women's right, MENA, Islam, Gender inequality

The status of women in society is neither a new issue nor a completely resolved one. Many studies have been done in this field from different perspectives. They generally suggest that, in ancient civilizations, and even until the late 19th century, a woman was seen as a property of her husband. She did not have any rights to own assets or exercise any civil or public positions; could not be a witness, surety, tutor, curator, could not adopt or be adopted, or make will or contract. In the late

18th century, the question of women's rights became central to political debates in Europe, particularly in France and Britain. Throughout the 19th century, European women were granted the rights of employment, vote and property. Yet, even today, despite the hue cry for equality and human rights for all, violence against women is prevalent. Violence affects the lives of millions of women worldwide, in all socio-economic and educational classes. It cuts across cultural and religious barriers, impeding the right of women to participate fully in society. As the United Nations Human Rights Council reports, violence against women in our days takes a dismaying variety of forms, from domestic abuse and rape to child marriages and female circumcision. All are violations of the most fundamental human rights.

On 18 December 1979, the Convention on the Elimination of All Forms of Discrimination against Women (CEDAW) was adopted by the United Nations General Assembly. The Convention establishes not only an international bill of rights for women but also an agenda for action by countries to guarantee the enjoyment of those rights. It entered into force as an international treaty on 3 September 1981 and its implementation is monitored by the Committee on the Elimination of Discrimination against Women. Yet, discrimination against women continues to grow, particularly in war affected regions. In a statement to the Fourth World Conference on Women in Beijing in September 1995, the United Nations then Secretary-General, Boutros Boutros-Ghali, said that violence against women is a universal problem that must be universally condemned (United Nations Human Rights, 1990).

The main focus of this chapter is in line with these studies. Yet, it gives more emphasis on the comparison between the ideal, presented by the Islamic sources and practiced in the early years of Muslim history, and the current reality of women's rights. Most of the contemporary scholars with a proper knowledge of Islam concur that it was Islam that empowered women for the first time in human history with the most progressive social, legal, economic and political rights since the seventh century. William Montgomery Watt, for example, suggested that Muhammad, the Prophet of Islam (pbuh), "can be seen as a figure who testified on behalf of women's rights" (Maan and McIntosh, 2000). Yet, women in the contemporary Muslim world are suffering most from insecurity, war, domestic and cultural abuses, low access to education and medical care.

8.1 Women in the light of the *Qur'an* and *Sunnah*

The Noble *Qur'an* and the *Sunnah* of the Prophet of Islam, Muhammad (pbuh), indicate equity and parity between men and women although their functions in marriage, family and society are not identical. The *Qur'an* emphasizes that God in His perfect wisdom has created all species in pairs, and so men and women have been created of the same species; as it is stated that: "He created you from a single being; then of the same kind made its mate" (Al-Zumar, 39:6). In the chapter of al-Nisa', Allah Almighty also said that: "O mankind! Fear Allah Who created you from a single person [Adam], and from him [Adam] Allah created his wife [Hawwa], and then from both of them, He created many men and women spread [all over the world]. And fear Allah through Whom you make claims [of your mutual rights]. And do not cut-off the relations with your blood relatives. Indeed, Allah is All-Watching over you" (Al-Nisa' 4:1).

According to Islamic view, men and women complement each other and are a means of mutual fulfillment. Family life is not based on formal hierarchy of rights and responsibilities, but the basis for husband–wife relationship in Islam are: *sakīnah* (peace, restfulness, honor), *muwaddah* (affection), *raḥmah* (forgiveness, grace, mercy, compassion) and *rufq* (gentleness). In his Last Sermon, Muhammad (pbuh) said:

> O People, it is true that you have certain rights with regard to your women, but they also have rights over you. Remember that you have taken them as your wives only under Allah's trust and with His permission. If they abide by your right then to them belongs the right to be fed and clothed in kindness. Do treat your women well and be kind to them for they are your partners and committed helpers. And it is your right that they do not make friends with any one of whom you do not approve, as well never to be unchaste. (McIntire, 2009, p. 79)

The passages from the Noble *Qur'an* confirm that woman is completely equated with man in the sight of God in terms of her rights and responsibilities. It is clearly stated that: "Every soul will be (held) in pledge for its deeds" (al-Muddathir, 74:38). In another occasion, the *Qur'an* articulates that: "Whoso does good, whether male or female, and is a believer, these will enter the Garden; they will be provided therein without measure" (al-Mu'min, 40:40).

Accordingly, men and women are spiritually akin one to another, and are equally the recipients of God's favors and bounties in this life and they will be equally rewarded in the hereafter. On the economic aspect, Islam dictated the right of woman to independent ownership, which she had been completely deprived before the rise of Islam and even after in many societies up to the early 20th century. A woman's right to her money, real estate and other properties, whether she is married or single, is fully acknowledged in Islamic law. She maintains her full rights to buy, sell, mortgage or lease any of her properties. Also, there is no ruling in Islam, which forbids woman from seeking employment although Islam regards her rule in society as a mother and a wife as the most sacred and essential ones. Moreover, there is no restriction on benefiting from woman's skill and knowledge in any field (Badawi, 1971).

There is no textual ruling in the *Qur'an* and in the *Sunnah* of the Prophet (pbuh) and in the consensus of scholars (*ijmā*), to deprive women of public and political rights as well (Ḥasan, 1983). According to Mohammad Hashim Kamali, during the time of the Prophet (pbuh) and the early years of Islam, women were not excluded from public life, and any restrictions that were subsequently imposed on them were partly due to circumstantial developments that did not command normative and undisputed validity in the *Shari'ah* (Kamali, 2002, p. 72). There was a long line of women scholars and activists who attained high positions and were renowned for their excellence as scholars, social workers, public figures, educators during the time of the Prophet (pbuh) and during the next generations, when Islamic civilization was flourishing. Let me bring only a few examples in this occasion.

During the life time of the Prophet Muhammad (pbuh), along with the men, women were assigned to the principal administrative posts. The Prophet appointed a woman, called Samra binti Nuhaik Al-Asadiyyah, as a *muhtasib* (market inspector), to regulate commercial activity and guard public interest; and she was kept at her position during the rule of the first two caliphs (Murtuza, 2004). Caliph Umar ibn Al-Khattab appointed to a position of market inspector and manager another woman, Al-Shifa (Lailah) binti Abdullah, who was well-known and highly respected in the community for her knowledge, piety and morality.

Moreover, Aisha bint Abu Bakr, the beloved wife of the Prophet (pbuh), played a key role in the growth, development and understanding of Islam. She transmitted a great amount of knowledge learned from Muhammad (pbuh) and is considered as the best scholar on the role of women in Islam. Being a role model to a significant number of others added to her attributions as a consultant regarding Muhammad's (pbuh) prayer and practices, soon she introduced herself into a world of politics. In the Battle of the Camel in 656 CE, for instance, Ñóisha participated by giving speeches and led an army on the back of her camel.[1]

The next example of scholarly excellence at the generation of the *tabi'in* (followers) is Amrah bint Abd al-Rahman, the pupil and secretary of Aisha bint Abu Bakr. With her extensive knowledge, 'Amrah was considered an authoritative voice of *hadith* and overrode many other male scholars during that period. The renowned Umayyad caliph Umar Ibn Abd al-Aziz (r.717–720 CE), a great scholar in his own right, said that no one remains alive, who is more learned in the *hadith* of Aisha, than Amrah. Later in her life, she was classified as a judge.

Aisha, the daughter of an eminent *sahaba*, Sa'ad ibn Abi Waqqas, was well learned in Islamic sciences to the point that a number of famous jurists and scholars on hadith, including Imam Malik, Hakim ibn Utaybah and Ayyub al-Sakhtiyani, were her pupils. Imam Sha'fi'i also studied *ilm al-hadith* in Egypt with a woman from the descendent of the Prophet (pbuh), Sayyida Nafisa bint Al-Hassan ibn Ali ibn Abi Talib, one of the leading scholars of that time.

Accordingly, women were actively engaged in public, political, economic and educational spheres of the early Islamic society. Appointment to the influential posts was based on qualifications and skills of the individual, and not on his or her gender. The subsequent sections of the chapter provide a survey of political rights of women throughout Islamic civilization.

8.1.1 Women as citizens of Islamic governance

Respect toward all human beings, regardless of their gender and social status, is the primary rule in Islam. As citizens of Islamic governance, men and women are afforded with equal protection and security. Any fair examination of the teachings of Islam into the sources of the *Shari'ah* and history of Islamic civilization will definitely find clear evidences of women's equality with man on political sphere too, what we call today "political" or "citizenship rights". Along with male citizens, women enjoy at least six basic rights under the Islamic government: the right to vote; the right to nomination for political office; the right of consultation in the affairs of the government; the right to express an opinion on political matters; the

[1]On a detailed account about her political career, see Madelung (1997), pp. 147, 157–176.

citizen's right not to obey a deviant ruler; and, lastly, the right to health, welfare, occupation and education (Kamali, 2013).

Every citizen of an Islamic polity is entitled to participate in the election of the ruler and other representative government bodies. The Prophet (pbuh) received the pledge of alliance (*bay'ah*) from both men and women on at least two or three occasions, the first two of which are known as the First *Aqabah* and the Second *Aqabah*, and the third as *Bayat al-Ridwan* (Kamali, 2002, p. 72).

In addition, the citizen of an Islamic polity enjoys the right to criticize and to express his or her opinion on the conduct of government as well as political matters. This right is manifested in the prominent *Qur'anic* principle of *hisbah*, which means promotion of good and prevention of evil (*amr bi'l-maruf wa-nahy an al-munkar*). Under *hisbah*, no individual in the state, regardless of his or her gender, religious belief or social strata, can be prohibited from promoting a good cause or putting a stop to an evil one (Akhmetova, 2014b).

In the *Qur'an* and *Sunnah* as well as in Islamic history we may find various examples of women who had participated in serious discussions and argued even with the Prophet (pbuh) himself.[2] The same equal treatment of both men and women in regard to the essence of human dignity, accountability, and matters pertaining to property, educational, public and social rights and responsibilities maintained in the early years of Islamic history. During the time of the second caliph, Umar ibn al-Khatab, for example, a woman argued with him in the mosque, proved her point and caused him to declare in the presence of people: "A woman is right and Umar is wrong."

8.1.2 Women as a ruler in Islamic governance

In the previous pages I have suggested that there is no textual ruling in the *Qur'an* and in the *Sunnah* of the Prophet (pbuh) to deprive women of public and political rights. The *fuqaha'* (jurists), however, differed as to whether women enjoy unconditional equality in political rights and participation in government. General consensus (*ijm'a*) is believed to have been reached that only men are eligible for the positions of the head of the state (Kamali, 2002, p. 69), the caliph.

[2]See, the *Qur'an*, al-Mujadilah 58:1–4; and al-Mumtaḥanah 60:10–12.

An Andalusian *faqi'h* (jurist) of the 11th century, Ibn Hazm (994–1064 CE), for example, has held an opinion that, except for the caliphate itself, women are eligible for all other offices of the Islamic government (Kamali, 2002, p. 72). The founder of the Hanafi school of Islamic jurisprudence, Immm Abu Hanifah (699–767 CE), also maintained that women may become judges in matters in which they are admissible as witnesses, which means practically all matters except the prescribed penalties (*hudud*) and retaliation (*qiyas*) (Al-Mawardi, 1386AH).

In running of people's affairs, Islam fully considers inhabitants' public interests (*maÎlaÍah*), which take precedence over individual interests. Therefore, eligibility for leadership in Islam is based on qualifications and skills. In this context, the renowned Maliki jurist of the thirteenth century, Shihab al-Din al-Qarafi (1228–1285) said that:

> In every post or authority, a priority should be given to the one who is the most capable to run it properly. In wars, for example, those who are more experienced in leading armies and fighting plans should take priority in leadership. In judiciary, those who are more aware of legal rules and intelligent enough to deal with people's complaints should be judges. Those who are more capable to take care of the orphans and their money should take the responsibility.[3]

Thus, if a woman or a man possesses the sufficient qualifications to lead his or her community, company or institution, then he or she could be appointed as the leader, the manager or the head of the office. The debarment of women from becoming a caliph by the general consensus of the early *fuqaha'*, therefore, was not due to gender-based discrimination, but mainly related to her competence and fitness for that position.

In the early years of Islamic rule, the caliph occupied the central stage in a four dimensional religious–judicial–military–economic space, which was shared with all members of the community, men and women alike. The caliph had four principal responsibilities. First, he was the religious head of the community and led the congregation in prayer. Second, he was the supreme judge and responsible for the implementation of the *Shari'ah*. Third, he was responsible for the defense of the state and led the army in times of war. Fourth, he was responsible for the economic well-being of

[3]As quoted in "Can Women be Rulers in Islam?" *OnIslam*, available at http://www.onislam.net/english/ask-about-islam/society-and-family/status-of-women/450461-cana-woman-rule.html. Retrieved on 22 December 2014.

the *ummah*; ensured fair taxation, administered public works and arranged for correct and complete documentation of contracts and civil transactions (Ahmed, n.d.).

In the views of the Hanafi, Shafi'i, Hanbali and Ja'fari schools of jurisprudence, a woman may lead a congregational prayer of other women and children only, but not of men. The Maliki school of *fiqh* was even stricter. Since a woman could not lead Friday (*jum'ah*) prayers of the whole community, this automatically barred her from aspiring to be a caliph or imam. This ruling, accordingly, was associated directly with her and the community's religious and spiritual functions and responsibilities, rather than indicating the discrimination of women's political rights in Islam. Soon later, this ruling has been extended by analogy (*qiyas*) to a number of other public offices, which are also reserved exclusively for men (Kamali, 2002, p. 72), contributing largely to the exclusion of women from public sphere. Yet, the spiritual and religious space remained open to women up to the 10th century. All great mosques built in the 8th and 9th centuries, had a separate section for women.

According to Nazeer Ahmed, the exclusion of women from public sphere occurred gradually over centuries and must be understood in the broader context of the fragmentation of the unitary caliphate and the separation of the masses from the rulers (Ahmed, n.d.). In the early years of Islamic rule, there was no distance between the head of the community and the members of the community. The young and the old, the poor and the rich, women and men, immigrants and locals had equal access to the leader. Due to the spread of extremism from the Kharijites, the Umayyad caliph Mua'wiyah ibn Abu Sufyan (r. 661–680) was the first Muslim ruler who surrounded himself with guards as a precaution against possible assassination. This was the first step in the bifurcation of political space between the ruler and the ruled (Ahmed, n.d.).

Very soon, in addition to security matters, the running of a vast empire over three continents required the creation of a new position, the vizier, to organize, manage and provide oversight to the executive functions. The Umayyad dynasty in Andalusia split the office of the vizier into several departments. Coordination between the different viziers and communication between the sovereign and the vizierates led to the creation of a new official, called a *hajib*. The *hajib* functioned as a chief minister, his position was considered higher than that of the viziers. He was the chief representative of the caliph and directed the central secretariat in Cordoba. With the initiation of the *hajib*, thus, the separation of the ruler from the ruled became institutionalized. The caliphs gave up the tradition of leading the congregational prayers. The Abbasid caliph Harun Rashid (r. 786–809) was the first caliph to employ professional *khatibs* to lead prayers. Likewise, the privilege of administering justice and issuing legal opinions (*fatwa*) was also delegated to hired *qadis*.

When the Turks rose in power in the 10th century, they supplanted the institution of the caliphate with a new institution of the sultanate; thus, the separation of temporal rule from religious authority was complete. The Turk sultans became the political and military rulers. Their religious responsibility of dispensing *fatwas* was entirely surrendered by delegating it to professional *qadis*. As the same time, the Ottoman sultans kept the time-honored title "caliph" along with its latest prototype, the "sultan", and remained being the nominal and titular head of the Muslim community. Such separation of political and military authority from religious responsibility, as Nazeer Ahmed suggests, led to the rise of despots (Ahmed, n.d.).

A sultan was not required to lead the congregational prayers as well; and this function was delegated to professional *khatibs*. Women, accordingly, should not be precluded from becoming a sultan anymore. The access of women to political and public space, however, happened rarely, especially among the Arabs.

The Turks, in fact, were more open to the entry of women into the political, judicial and military space. Turkish women rode into battle with men, took part in the affairs of state and sat next to sultans and jurists advising them in the dispensation of justice (Ahmed, n.d.). Ibn Battuta, a Muslim traveler of the 14th century, for example, recorded that the conquered city of Iznik had been ruled by one of the consorts of the sultan (Battuta, 1962, pp. 451–454). In the 16th and 17th centuries, the Ottoman Empire had a period, called the Sultanate of Women. Starting from the reign of Suleyman the Magnificent (r. 1520–1566) for nearly next 130 years, the women of the Imperial Harem of the Sultanate exerted extraordinary political influence over state matters and over the male *de-facto* Ottoman sultans. The majority of the sultans during this time were minors and it was their mothers, the *Valide Sultans*, or their wives, the *Haseki Sultans*, who effectively ruled the sultanate.

The Seljuks, the predecessors of the Ottomans, often had women of nobility playing the prominent role in public policy and affairs too. Such space for women's participation in political and public affairs has been seen by Ann K. S. Lambton, the famous British historian and leading figure on medieval and early modern Persian history and Islamic political theory, as a legacy of the tribal background and cultural traditions of the Turkic nations (Lambton, 1988, p. 258). Nazeer Ahmed also observed that:

> With the introduction of Turkish and African blood into Islam and the later infusion of Mongol, Indian and Indonesian elements, the rigid separation of women from politics and culture was challenged. And it was from among these "newcomers" that the great queens of Islam emerged, women such as Razia Sultana of Delhi, Shajarat al Durr of Cairo and Noor Jehan of the Great Moghuls, who distinguished themselves in the political space and left their indelible mark on Islamic history. (Ahmed, n.d.)

Such cases of women excellence in political and public affairs, however, were exceptional, and the vast majority of common women did not enjoy any political rights. The universal brotherhood and sisterhood that has been created by the Prophet (pbuh) was shattered and, in its place, class distinctions between the ruler and the ruled and sex distinctions between men and women had emerged. The masses were secluded from political life and, among the masses, women were even more secluded (Ahmed, n.d.).

8.2 The status of women in the contemporary Muslim world

I have already emphasized in the previous pages that Islam empowered women since the 7th century. Women took an active part in building what is today called Islamic civilization. But this *Qur'anic* empowerment of women bears too little relation to the real condition of women in many contemporary Muslim societies. Modern Muslim women are mainly marginalized and severely suffering from the consequences of political upheavals, poverty, injustice, corruption and other social ills prevalent in their societies.

The Muslim world today, particularly the Middle Eastern and North African (MENA) region, is experiencing a period of significant political, economic and social transition. It is badly shaken by large-scale bloodshed, political upheavals, poverty and economic depression, particularly following the recent outbreak of the Arab Spring since October 2010 and its aftermaths. For decades, the citizens of these post-colonial nation-states, men and women, suffered from an unending cycle of despotism, economic and political exploitation, poverty and public cruelty. Most of the countries are governed by monarchies, which failed to respond to the needs and opportunities of their own people, or to create a milieu of trust, appreciation and sincerity between the political elite and the people. Within two decades or slightly more, the legitimacy of the ruling families to represent the entire populace became a crucial subject in many Muslim states. Overall, the post-colonial governments in the MENA region failed to ensure the well-being and security of their citizens. Poverty, malnutrition and lack of health security are also among the foremost problems of the MENA countries. The region is home to about seventy million of the world's poor (living on less than $2 per day) and 20 million of the world's extremely poor (living on less than $1.25 per day). Despite possessing 70% of the world's energy resources and 40% of its natural resources, the gross domestic product (GDP) of all member states of the Organisation of Islamic Cooperation (OIC) is less than that of Japan (Akhmetova, 2014a, p. 431).

Furthermore, evils like corruption, nepotism, injustice or chauvinism are widespread in Muslim societies. The results of Corruption Perceptions Index 2013 (CPI), prepared by Transparency International, warn that the abuse of power, secret dealings and bribery wreck the personal and public well-being in the Muslim world, and ranked many Muslim countries as having the highest perceived levels of corruption in the world. The latest Index in 2013 scored 177 countries and territories on a scale from 0 (highly corrupt) to 100 (very clean). In that list, the 10 bottom countries which were ranked as most corrupted, excluding North Korea, are Muslim-majority countries. Somalia and Afghanistan, along with non-Muslim North Korea, made up the worst performers in the year, scoring just 8 points each. It is followed by Sudan (11 points), South Sudan (14 points), Libya (15 points), Iraq (16 points), Uzbekistan, Turkmenistan and Syria (17 points each). Only three Muslim-majority countries score above 50: United Arab Emirates (69 points), Qatar (68 points) and Brunei (60 points) (Akhmetova, 2014b, pp. 273–276).

Such current scenario of the Muslim world suggests that the actual spirit of Islamic principles of governance, i.e., ensuring the welfare and security of the people, and establishing peace and justice in society, is gone. The basic civilian and human rights of the citizens under their authorities, regardless of their gender, age and religious, social or ethnic backgrounds, were ignored as well.

The Arab Spring created more instability, economic depression, insecurity and bloodshed in the entire region. The Middle East got neither democracy nor good governance, but the emergence of the ISIS or the so-called "Islamic State of Iraq and Syria" with its extremely harsh militant principles. As a result, the well-being of women has deteriorated deeply in the recent years, especially in war and conflict zones. Women are the main victims of insecurity, war and radicalization. Gender-based violence, one of the world's most widespread human rights violations, escalates sharply among conflict-related displaced communities. In the case of Syria, gender-based violence predated the crisis and has been singled out as one of the most salient features of the current conflict. According to the United Nations High Commissioner for Refugees (UNHCR), since the outbreak of civil war in Syria in March 2011, over 3 million have fled to the country's immediate neighbors, mainly to Turkey, Lebanon, Jordan and Iraq. Another 6.5 million are internally displaced within Syria;[4] and the majority of them are women and children. In Jordan, as United Nations reports, women, girls and boys, who make up close to 80% of this country's nearly half a million Syrian refugees, are vulnerable to an increased risk of sexual, physical, and psychological abuse, yet have limited opportunities to access safe spaces or social services (UN Women, 2013).

The report prepared by Amnesty International in 2014 indicates serious cases of abuse and offense against the vulnerable young women and children by ISIS militants. In August 2014, ISIS militants abducted hundreds, possibly thousands, of Yazidi minority, mainly women and children, from the Sinjar area in northwestern Iraq, according to the Amnesty report entitled "Escape from Hell." Hundreds of Yazidi women and girls have had their lives shattered by the horrors of sexual violence and sexual slavery in ISIS captivity. The captives, including girls aged 10–12 years, faced torture, rape and forced marriage, and were "sold" or given as "gifts" to ISIS fighters or their supporters in militant-held areas in Iraq and Syria (Amnesty International, 2014). Such cases of war crimes against the vulnerable stratum of the society indicate a direct link between human insecurity and the violation of women's rights. Since women often face cultural, social, economic and political discriminations in their daily lives, they encounter even more oppression, distress and social exclusion in war-ridden societies.

The status of women in relatively peaceful Muslim societies is not encouraging as well. Widespread evils like corruption, nepotism, injustice and chauvinism often inflict the cases of gender discrimination. Since injustice and corruption hits poor, disadvantaged and vulnerable groups the hardest, women are more likely to bear a heavier burden as they are

[4] http://syrianrefugees.eu Retrieved on 31 December 2014.

often marginalized and over-represented among the poorest. According to the United Nations, an estimated 70% of the world's poor are women.[5]

Transparency International also reported that women are more disadvantaged in corrupt systems. Corruption creates additional obstacles for women to access and use public goods, including basic services, as well as to participate in their country's political processes. For instance, as the primary care takers in families, women have a higher likelihood of experiencing corruption, whether enrolling their children in school, seeking medical treatment for their kids or older relatives, or interacting with public officials to access government subsidized programs (Transparency International, 2014; UNDP, 2012).

Besides, in many countries, corrupt judicial procedures and the prevalence of nepotism and gender discrimination makes it in the majority of cases impossible for women to win lawsuits in a transparent and open way. Roslyn G. Hees, Senior Advisor at Transparency International, observed that: "A corrupt legal system reinforces existing gender discrimination in many countries. Women's civil rights are grossly unfair with regard to marriage/divorce, family law, child custody, financial independence and inheritance and property rights. Often they have no ability to make decisions without the consent of a male relative."[6] Therefore, Transparency International strongly recommends that anti-corruption measures need to be gender responsive to facilitate gender equity and women's empowerment.[7]

In sum, the absence of good governance caused many calamities in the Muslim world, including the violation of the basic civilian and human rights of the citizens. As a vulnerable segment of society, women are more likely to be oppressed and discriminated in corrupted and war-ridden societies.

8.3 Encouraging developments across the Muslim world

In spite of many depressing political and social turbulences taking part in the contemporary Muslim world, the awareness about the original status of women in Islam and the potential impact of women empowerment on

[5]See, "A United Nations Objective: Eradicate Poverty," United Nations, available at http://www.un.org/rights/poverty/poverty1.htm. Retrieved on 30 December 2014.
[6]http://www.transparency.org/news/pressrelease/gender_and_corruption_are_women_less_corrupt. Retrieved on 18 October 2014.
[7]http://www.anti-corruption.org/index.php/en/themes/anti-corruption-womens-empowerment. Retrieved on 18 October 2014.

attaining of good governance and a strong society is increasingly common among Muslim-educated circles. In that course, several governments bestow equal rights for education and employment to both genders. The Malaysian government, for example, invests in education without any gender discrimination for a long time. Speaking at the Third Women Deliver 2013 Global Conference, Prime Minister of Malaysia, Datuk Seri Najib Tun Razak, stated that 65% of students in tertiary education institutions in the country are women.[8] Improvement in access to higher learning has helped to empower a larger percentage of Malaysian women, and more are seen moving into higher-paying occupations. According to the statistics from the Mid-term Review of the 8th Malaysian Plan, the proportion of women who are legislators, senior officials and managers has increased from 5% in 2000 to 5.3% in 2002.[9] Currently, Malaysian women represent the workforce at 47%. Such an active participation of women in public and economic spheres is one of the factors for economic and political stability in the country.[10]

Malaysia is a rapidly developing economy in Asia. Since the 1970s, this middle-income country has transformed itself from a producer of raw materials into an emerging multi-sector economy. The GDP in Malaysia expanded 5.60% in the third quarter of 2014 over the same quarter of the previous year. GDP Annual Growth Rate in Malaysia averaged 4.68% from 2000 until 2014, reaching an all-time high of 10.30% in the first quarter of 2010.[11]

Malaysia is perceived as having relatively low corruption levels as well. In the CPI, among ASEAN countries, Malaysia is ranked third, behind Singapore and Brunei; while globally, it managed to position itself better than other developed countries including Italy, Greece and the Czech

[8] "Malaysia to Continue to Empower Women in Education, Work and Maternal Healthcare," *Venus*, available at http://www.venusbuzz.com/archives/45929/malaysiato-continue-to-empower-women-in-education-work-and-maternal-healthcare. Retrieved on 30 December 2014.

[9] "Women's Participation in the Workforce Increasing," UNICEF, available at http://www.unicef.org/malaysia/gift_6068.html. Retrieved on 30 December 2014.

[10] Daud Batchelor in his New Islamic Rating Index of Well-Being for Muslim Countries also considered the substantial role of Muslim women in Malay society as one of the main factors for having a high overall well-being score among other Muslim countries. See Batchelor, Daud (2013), pp. 208–209.

[11] See, "Malaysia GDP Annual Growth Rate," Trading Economics, available at http://www.tradingeconomics.com/malaysia/gdp-growth-annual. Retrieved on 30 December 2014.

Republic.[12] The example of Malaysia once more confirms that gender unfairness and corruption are closely inter-linked. Where countries have made advances in women empowerment and gender fairness, they have witnessed lower levels of corruption over time.

Furthermore, women are an important source for understanding corruption and designing effective strategies to address the problem that affects their everyday lives (Transparency International, 2014). Recent studies have showed that empowered women, who have an opportunity to participate in decision-making, are powerful actors that can contribute to the fight against corruption. A study by the IRIS Centre, University of Maryland, observes that higher levels of women's participation in public life are associated with lower levels of corruption. This cross-country data revealed that corruption is less severe where women comprise a larger share of the labor force, and where women hold a larger share of parliamentary seats (Swamy *et al.*, 1999, p. 19). Another influential study made by the World Bank in 1999, entitled "Are Women Really the 'Fairer' Sex? Corruption and Women in Government," also suggested that higher rates of female participation in government are associated with lower levels of corruption. After studying 150 countries in Europe, Africa and Asia, the research came to the conclusion that women are more trustworthy and less prone to corruption. It consequently suggested that women may have higher standards of ethical behavior and appear to be more concerned with the common good (Dollar *et al.*, 1999).

Hence, some Muslim countries initiated a policy of employing more women in their anti-corruption campaigns. Let me bring the example of Afghanistan, one of the most corrupted and worst hit country by the consequences of the U.S.-led War on Terror since 2001. During his visit to the International Institute of Advanced Islamic Studies (IAIS) Malaysia on 10 December 2013, His Excellency Abdul Salam Azimi, the Chief Justice of Afghanistan and the head of the Afghan Supreme Court, affirmed that women in Afghanistan are less prone to corruption. There are already more than 180 female judges in Afghanistan today, which constitutes approximately 10% of total Afghan judges (5 years ago — 3%). According to Abdul Salam Azimi, there has not been even a single case of corruption

[12] "Malaysia's Rank in Corruption Perceptions Index Improves Slightly," NKRA Against Corruption, available at http://www.nkracorruption.gov.my/index.php/en/component/content/article/19-frontpage-articles/662-malaysia-s-rank-incorruption-perceptions-index-improves-slightly. Retrieved on 30 December 2014.

with these female judges in the face of the high level of corruption in the existing Afghan legislative system overall. Chief Justice Azimi consequently intends to assign more female judges in order to lessen the endemic of corruption in the Afghan society. However, the appointment of female judges in the provinces is still extremely challenging due to safety, economic and customary reasons. At present, 10 female judges are based in Balkh, 5 in Herat, 2 each in Takhar and Baghlan, with the rest based in Kabul. But the presence of female judges in all courtrooms of the country is highly essential for two reasons. Firstly, as has been articulated earlier, female judges are perceived as less corrupt. Secondly, if a female judge is present in a province, a female complainant can share her problems with full confidence while she may not feel easy to share them with a male judge (Akhmetova, 2014b, pp. 274–275).

The similar approach of gender attentive distribution of power is intended to expand to other segments of the Afghan government. The current House of People (Wolesi Jirga), which holds the power to enact, amend and repeal laws, has 69 women members out of total 249 delegates (27.7%), emerging as the 37th country with largest female participation in legislature out of 189 countries in the world. Other countries scored as follows in 2013: Germany (32.9%), France (26.9%), U.K. (22.5%), Turkey (14.2%), Russia (13.6%), Malaysia (10%), Iran (3%) and Egypt (2%) (Akhmetova, 2014b, pp. 274–275). In the long run, it is believed that the engagement of women in the Afghan leadership as decision makers, role models and conflict solvers might bring peace, harmony and betterment to an Afghan society, which is exceedingly suffering from occupation, war and conflicts for several decades.

8.4 Conclusion and recommendations

After a brief evaluation of the status of women and their rights and responsibilities as citizens of Islamic governance in comparison with the contemporary state of women in the Muslim world, the chapter suggests the following conclusions and recommendations.

Firstly, Islam has empowered women with the most progressive rights since the seventh century. In the early years of Islam, women constituted an important portion of their societies with their specific duties and inborn features given by God. They served as full vibrant members of their societies as skillful educators, leading scholars, successful entrepreneurs, and shining public and political figures. Also, along with men, women enjoy full and equal basic civilian and human rights as citizens of an Islamic polity. Respect toward all human beings, regardless of their gender or social status, is the primary rule in Islam.

Secondly, Islamic empowerment of women, as the paper establishes, bears little relation to the real condition of women in modern Muslim societies. Today, the Muslim world is suffering from various political and economic calamities, and social ills, which are directly related to or the reasons of the ignorance of the citizens' rights. The post-colonial governments in the MENA region failed to ensure the well-being and security of their citizens; and women are the stratum that suffered most from insecurity, domestic abuse, cultural influences, and low access to education and medical care. For decades, women remained marginalized, isolated and excluded from decision-making. They were not given any opportunity to amend the unfair systems through peaceful means endorsed by the *Shari'ah*, such as by participation in fair elections, consultation, the assessment of the conducts of the government and freedom of expression.

Thirdly, the chapter establishes a direct relation between good governance and the rights of women. The absence of good governance results in gender inequality and violation of the rights of women. Gender inequalities, in turn, undermine good governance, sustainable growth, development outcomes and poverty alleviation. In addition, gender inequality and corruption are closely interlinked. Since women often face cultural, social, economic and political discriminations in their daily lives, they encounter even more oppression, distress and social exclusion in the corrupt and war-torn societies. Therefore, unless the Muslim states establish good governance, there will be no improvement in the status of women. The chapter accordingly proposes that the status of women is an indicator of good governance.

Lastly, Muslim women have a potential to play fundamental roles in curbing corruption, social ills, violence and crime in the Muslim world; and the active participation of women in legislature, law-making and policy-making processes could be considered as one of the principal keys for the success of the *ummah*. At the end, the chapter proposes the following policy recommendations:

Evils of gender-based discrimination, corruption, nepotism, intolerance, and political and economic injustice should be prevented by the authorities as being extremely harmful for the well-being and security of society, and its stability. Any government must guarantee the rights of every citizen under its authority, regardless of their gender, age, and religious, social and ethnic backgrounds.

The will and rights of women citizens should not be neglected or interfered with by external and internal actors. The governments must ensure a platform for women to participate actively in legislature, law-making and policy-making processes. The promising potential of women in the Muslim world should be recognized and directed in a correct manner through proper education, respect and supervision. The Prophetic (pbuh) model of women empowerment may be considered as the best model on that direction.

Muslim religious leaders, judges, *ulama'*, *muftis* and associations must concentrate on achieving a better understanding of the role of women in Islamic society as individuals and citizens. In order to heal the wounds and negative outcomes of the ill-treatment of women in the Muslim world for a prolonged period, they must condemn publicly all types of gender-based discrimination, domestic violence and abuse, ill-treatment of women in society and the violation of the rights of women.

Appointment to the higher-paying and managing occupations should be based on the qualifications and skills of the candidates rather than on his or her gender. Thus, if a woman or a man possesses the sufficient qualifications to lead his or her community, company or institution, then he or she could be the leader, the manager, or the head of the office; and this is in line with Islamic teachings.

The media and educational system should be actively utilized to raise public awareness about the status of women in Islam under Islamic governance. The Islamic concepts of governance and citizens' rights could be included in university curricula, and textbooks should be prepared to train the Muslim youth to adopt the proper treatment of women and more harmonious ways of life.

Since women in positions of power are perceived as less corrupt and more honest, an active participation of women in law-making and public spheres is highly essential. More researches should be conducted to observe a close correlation between women's active participation in public life and well-being of society. In the Muslim world in particular, which suffers most from the evils of corruption, the rights of women to education and work should not be marginalized. Religious leaders, scholars and judges could play an important role in the betterment of Muslim countries through publicly condemning all types of corruption, cheating and bribery, as well as empowering the status of women in their societies.

References

English

Ahmed, Nazeer (n.d.), "Women Sovereigns in Islam," *History of Islam: An Encyclopedia of Islamic History*, available at http://historyofislam.com/contents/the-post-mongol-period/women-sovereigns-in-Islam. Retrieved on 22 December 2014.

Akhmetova, Elmira (2014a), The Arab Spring, good governance and citizens' rights. *Islam and Civilisational Renewal*, 5(3), 334–350.

Akhmetova, Elmira (2014b), Women and corruption. *Islam and Civilisational Renewal*, 5(2), 273–276.

Amnesty International (2014), *Escape from Hell: Torture and Sexual Slavery in Islamic State Captivity in Iraq*, London: Amnesty International Ltd.

Badawi, Jamal (1971), The status of woman in Islam: Islam's women. *Al-Ittihad*, 8(2), Sha'ban 1391, available at http://www.islamswomen.com/articles/status_of_women_in_islam.php. Retrieved on 19 December 2014.

Batchelor, Daud (2013), A new Islamic rating index of wellbeing for Muslim countries. *Islam and Civilisational Renewal*, 4(2), 208–209.

Battuta, Ibn (1962), *The Travels of the Ibn Battuta*, Cambridge: Cambridge University Press.

Dollar, D., Fisman, R. and Gatti, R. (1999), "Are Women Really the Fairer Sex? Corruption and Women in Government", World Bank Working Paper Series No. 4, Washington DC, World Bank, available at http://www.wds.worldbank.org/servlet/WDSContentServer/WDSP/IB/2000/08/26/000094946_0008120532266/Rendered/PDF/multi_page.pdf. Retrieved on 17 October 2014.

Kamali, Mohammad Hashim (2002), *Freedom, Equality and Justice in Islam*, Malaysia: Ilmiah Publishers.

Kamali, Mohammad Hashim (2013), *Citizenship and Accountability of Government: An Islamic Perspective*, Kuala Lumpur: IAIS & Ilmiah Publishers.

Lambton, Ann K. S. (1988), *Continuity and Change in Medieval Persia*, Albany: The Persian Heritage Foundation.

Maan, Bashir and McIntosh, Alastair (2000), "The Whole House of Islam, and We Christians with Them: An Interview with the 'Last Orientalist' Rev. Prof William Montgomery Watt", available at http://www.alastairmcintosh.com/articles/2000_watt.htm. Retrieved on 31 December 2014.

McIntire, Suzanne (2009), *Speeches in World History*, New York: Facts on File Inc.

Madelung, Wilferd (1997), *The Succession to Muhammad: A Study of the Early Caliphate*, Cambridge: Cambridge University Press.

Murtuza, Athar (2004), "Muhtasib's Role: Safeguarding the Public Interest During the Islamic Middle Ages", *American Accounting Association 2004 Mid-Atlantic Region Meeting Paper*, available at http://ssrn.com/abstract=488882. Retrieved on 20 December 2019.

Swamy, Knack, Lee and Azfar (1999), "Gender and Corruption," IRIS Centre Working Paper No. 232.

Transparency International (2014), "Gender, Equality and Corruption: What Are the Linkages?" Policy Brief 01/2014.

United Nations Human Rights (1990), "Women and Violence," available at http://www.un.org/rights/dpi1772e.htm. Retrieved on 31 December 2014.

United Nations (1997), "A United Nations Objective: Eradicate Poverty", available at http://www.un.org/rights/poverty/poverty1.htm. Retrieved on 30 December 2014.

United Nations Development Program (2012), *Seeing Beyond the State: Grassroots Women's Perspectives on Corruption and Anti-corruption*, New York, NY: UNDP.

UN Women (July 2013), *Gender-Based Violence and Child Protection among Syrian Refugees in Jordan, With a Focus on Early Marriage*, Amman: Peace and Security UN Women, pp. 2, 24–28.

Arabic

Al-Mawardi, Abu al-Ḥasan (1386AH), *Kitab al-Aḥkam al-Sulṭaniyyah* (2nd edn.), Cairo: Muṣṭafa al- Babi al-Ḥalabi, p. 65.

Ḥasan, 'Abd al-Ḥakīm Ḥasan (1983), *Al-'Īlī, al-Ḥurriyāt al-'Ammah*, Cairo: Dār al-Fikr.

PART B
Development Perspectives

Chapter 9

A Relational Well-Being (*Maslaha*) Index of Gender Development in Socio-Economic Development Sustainability

Masudul Alam Choudhury, Ari Pratiwi, Mohammad Shahadat Hossain and Faezy Adenan

Abstract

The inception of *maqasid as-shari'ah al-Tawhid* index of socio-economic development sustainability is presented in its generalized form. This involves a unified relational methodological formalism. The resulting model is that of well-being, which in Islamic context is referred to as *maslaha*. The *maslaha* function is formalized and applied to the specific case of socio-economic development sustainability. This term signifies the importance that moral and ethical values hold in a substantively participatory context of choices of the good things of life, while avoiding the harmful ones. The meaning is linked to and bears on moral, social and economic development perspectives. Sustainability of development as a participatory process yielding well-being is thereby a relational organic continuation in pervasive complementarities between endogenous and circular causation relations of critical variables under the impact of *Tawhid* as law inducing the variables by its ontology of unity of knowledge. A specific example of application is taken as the formulation and relational explanation of the Gender Development Index in terms of its various critical variables of well-being. Statistical analysis and policy conclusions are carried out.

Keywords: Participatory development, Socio-economic development sustainability, Well-being and *maslaha*, Ontology of *Tawhidi* unity of knowledge, Gender Development Index, Methodology, Formalism, Application

Various indexes of human resource development explaining the meaning of ethical sustainability are measured as averages based on subsidiary indicators. For instance, United Nations Development Programme (UNDP) Reports (several reports, 1997–2000) compute Human Development Index

(HDI) as an index of averaged indexes of target income, longevity and educational attainment level. GEM (UNDP) is likewise computed as logarithmic average of basic indexes. In this regard, Table 9.1 lists the various indicators of gender development and inequality. The resulting millennium development indexes are explained as to how they are computed like the UNDP indexes of averages. Here are the various averaging features of the three kinds of indexes, which are HDI, Gender Empowerment Index and the Millennium Index. *Maqasid as-shari'ah* index is included to provide a critical meaning to this indicator contrary to how it is being studied in the literature and looked upon traditionally. The nature of computation of these indexes makes them linearly non-relational, an aspect, which though caused by simplicity, is unable to explain the essential meaning of sustainability as a widening relational concept. This aspect of socio-economic development and well-being as the principal objective criterion of sustainability has been left out from all approaches to the measurement of indexes of sustainable socio-economic development. In the special case of the *maqasid as-shari'ah* context of indexing socio-economic development, great gaps exist in respect of its absence of the essential quiddity of *Tawhidi* law as unity of knowledge between the good things of life and rejection of the bad things of life, and the spanning scope of organic inter-relationship in widening systemic understanding of reality (Choudhury, 2015).

Thus, besides the aforementioned well-known approaches in the UNDP literature to the measurement of indexes of socio-economic development, some authors in the Islamic economic orientation have been developing indexes of socio-economic development using what is termed as *maqasid as-shari'ah* index. This is equivalent to the well-being objective criterion known in Islamic *maqasid* literature as *maslaha*. An example of this is the one proposed by Mohammad and Taib (2016). Similar to other UNDP indexes, the *maqasid* index is linearly expressed as follows:

***Maqasid* Index:** $\text{MI} = \sum_{i=1}^{n} a_i \times X_i$,
where MI denotes *maqasid as-shari'ah* index;
X_i denotes various variables MI is composed of (originally 5);
a_i denotes weights that are thought to be assigned to each X_i; these values are either assumed by the contributing authors or surveyed by a questionnaire to result in Likert ratios;
"i" denotes the "n" — number of variables composition of the MI as viewed by the researchers.

Table 9.1 Quantitative evaluation of well-being.

y		Y	X_1	X_2	X_3	X_4	X_5	X_6	X_7	Employment to population ratio X_8 $X_8/X_9 = X_7$	Labour force participation rate X_9
1	High Income	Qatar	75273.99	70080.77	—	0.991	0.542	—	97.8	84.4	84.6
2		United Arab Emirates	40438.77	40468.51	—	0.972	0.232	—	93.8	77.1	80.1
3		Brunei	30552.66	32823.69	—	0.986	—	—	96.4	62.3	63.5
4		Kuwait	29303.9	30214.46	—	0.972	0.335	—	96.2	66.7	69.2
5		Bahrain	22600.21	21339.75	—	0.970	0.233	—	95.7	68.3	69.2
6		Saudi Arabia	20710.58	21230	—	0.882	0.257	—	94.7	51.6	54.8
7		Oman	15550.85	15035.39	—	0.927	0.281	—	94.8	64.8	69.1
8	Upper Middle Income	Kazakhstan	10359.81	9712.73	0.714	1.006	0.202	0.004	99.8	67.2	71.2
9		Malaysia	9768.37	9494.42	—	—	0.291	—	94.6	61.5	63.3
10		Turkey	9125.79	9100.82	0.645	0.908	0.328	—	95.0	45.1	50.3
11		Suriname	8985.34	8933.56	0.551	0.972	0.448	0.033	95.6	50.2	54.5
12		Lebanon	8571.37	8326.14	0.603	0.893	0.381	—	93.9	43.7	47.0
13		Maldives	8395.84	7517.28	0.529	0.937	0.312	0.008	99.3	59.9	68.0
14		Gabon	7960.72	7484.65	0.531	0.923	0.542	0.073	83.2	38.8	48.8
15		Turkmenistan	6996.74	6683.68	—	—	—	0.011	99.7	55.8	62.0
16		Azerbaijan	5496.54	5870.37	0.659	0.940	0.326	0.009	99.8	61.9	65.0
17		Libya	5488.17	5338.97	—	0.950	0.167	0.005	91.0	42.2	53.2
18		Iran	5038.13	5052.96	0.518	0.862	0.509	—	86.8	39.9	44.5
19		Jordan	4940.05	4882.59	0.619	0.864	0.478	0.004	96.7	34.8	40.0
20		Iraq	4509.02	4495.67	0.505	0.804	0.525	0.052	79.7	35.3	42.4
21		Guyana	4278.81	4268.77	0.518	0.943	0.508	0.031	88.5	52.9	59.5
22		Algeria	4154.12	4050.78	—	0.854	0.429	—	80.2	39.1	43.7

(Continued)

Table 9.1 (*Continued*)

y		Y	X_1	X_2	X_3	X_4	X_5	X_6	X_7	Employment to population ratio X_8 $X_8/X_9 = X_7$	Labour force participation rate X_9
23	Middle Income	Albania	3994.59	3970.93	0.661	0.959	0.267	0.005	97.6	41.6	50.3
24		Tunisia	3708.97	3548.39	0.562	0.904	0.289	0.006	81.8	40.6	47.7
25		Egypt	3452.34	3396.76	0.491	0.884	0.565	0.016	75.2	43.5	49.4
26		Indonesia	3346.49	3234.48	0.563	0.926	0.467	0.024	93.9	63.4	67.4
27		Morocco	2919.32	3179.23	0.456	0.826	0.494	0.069	72.4	44.5	49.2
28		Palestine	2866.8	2866.35	0.581	0.867	—	0.005	96.7	32.4	43.7
29		Nigeria	2714.47	2607.37	0.328	0.847	—	0.279	59.6	53.1	56.3
30		Sudan	2334.6	2431.91	—	0.836	—	0.290	38.4	41.6	48.1
31		Uzbekistan	2204.64	2307.14	0.590	0.946	0.287	0.013	99.6	55.6	61.8
32		Djibouti	1956.31	2088.71	0.310	—	—	0.127	—	24.1	52.3
33		Syria	1534.54	1502.32	0.419	0.851	0.554	0.028	86.4	36.5	41.7
34		Cote d'Ivoire	1412.94	1496.8	0.294	0.814	0.672	0.307	43.1	60.6	67.0
35		Pakistan	1410.39	1309.31	0.380	0.742	0.546	0.290	58.7	51.0	53.9
36		Mauritania	1235	1283.67	0.347	0.818	0.626	0.291	52.1	32.5	47.2
37		Cameroon	1217.26	1199.05	0.348	0.853	0.568	0.260	75.0	72.5	76.0
38		Bangladesh	1207.9	1186.21	0.412	0.927	0.520	0.188	61.5	59.4	62.2
39		Yemen	1106.42	1177.63	0.320	0.737	0.767	0.200	70.1	41.7	49.6
40		Kyrgyzstan	1103.22	1069.5	0.582	0.967	0.394	0.008	99.5	32.5	47.2
41		Tajikistan	925.91	1049.62	0.532	0.930	0.322	0.031	99.8	61.0	68.5

42	Low Income	Senegal	901.07	886.27	0.331	0.886	0.521	0.278	55.7		51.7	57.1
43		Benin	779.07	776.58	0.304	0.858	0.613	0.343	38.4		70.9	71.7
44		Mali	744.35	721.93	0.293	0.786	0.689	0.456	38.7		60.6	66.2
45		Chad	713.05	705.5	0.238	0.765	0.695	0.545	40.2		67.6	71.6
46		Comoros	706.88	691.57	0.270	0.817	—	0.165	77.8		46.2	57.4
47		Guinea	703.87	690.41	0.270	0.784	—	0.425	30.4		80.9	82.3
48		Sierra Leone	694.76	651.81	0.262	0.871	0.650	0.411	48.1		64.5	66.8
49		Uganda	647.72	647.39	0.341	0.878	0.522	0.359	73.9		81.9	85.0
50		Afghanistan	626.62	631.18	0.327	0.609	0.667	0.293	38.2		47.5	52.5
51		Burkina Faso	611.13	602.42	0.267	0.874	0.615	0.508	36.0		81.1	83.5
52		Togo	566.83	528.12	0.332	0.841	0.556	0.242	66.5		74.6	80.9
53		Guinea-Bissau	530.04	521.25	0.257	0.784	—	0.495	59.9		67.2	72.7
54		Mozambique	529.21	507.2	0.280	0.879	0.574	0.390	58.8	1,116	61.5	79.1
55		Gambia	473.16	457.15	—	0.878	0.641	0.289	55.5	1,556	54.0	77.3
56		Niger	358.96	352.72	0.253	0.732	0.695	0.584	19.1	897	62.9	64.7
57		Somalia	123.51	118.53	—	—	—	0.500	—	—	50.2	54.3

Note:
Source: Human Development Report (2016).

Human Development Index (United Nations, 2015, 2016): $\mathrm{HDI}_{\mathrm{male}} = (I^m_{\mathrm{health}} \times I^m_{\mathrm{education}} \times I^m_{\mathrm{income}})^{1/3}$. This converts to log-linear form for computation.
$\mathrm{HDI}_{\mathrm{female}} = (I^f_{\mathrm{health}} \times I^f_{\mathrm{education}} \times I^f_{\mathrm{income}})^{1/3}$. This converts to log-linear form for computation.

Dimension Index: I = [(Actual Value) – (Minimum Value)]/[(Maximum Value) – (Minimum Value)], specified by male and female.

Gender Development Index: GDI = $\mathrm{HDI}_{\mathrm{female}}/\mathrm{HDI}_{\mathrm{male}}$. This converts to log-linear form for computation and the rate of change of GDI.

Indexing Millennium Development Goals (United Nations, 2003): The Millennium Development Goals (MDGs) are calculated independent of each other by averaging data within particular domains that are of interest. These variables are: (1) poverty alleviation, (2) universal primary education, (3) gender equality, (4) reduction in child mortality, (5) improved maternal health, (6) combating diseases, (7) environmental sustainability and (8) developing global partnership. The averaging computational approach in these indicators can be seen in the example of measuring poverty gap (PG) in the following way:

$$\mathrm{PG} = (1/n) \times \sum_{i=1}^{q} [(z - y_i)/z],$$

where z denotes the poverty line of income,

y_i denotes income of the individual i,
q denotes the number of poor people.
n denotes the size of population.

An alternative way for measuring PG is used:

$$\mathrm{PG} = I \times H,$$

where I denotes income ratio calculated as $I = (z - y_q)/z$; with $y_q = (1/q) \times \sum_{i=1}^{q} y_i$;

H denotes head count ratio calculated as $H = q/n$.

It is noted in each of the above-mentioned indexes that the study of socio-economic development by using such averaged indicators does not give the interactive and complex inter-relations between critical variables that together define the idea of sustainability. Relating to such complex inter-relations of the development paradigm, the South Commission Report remarks on the sustainable development worldview. South Commission (1990, p. 13) defines the meaning of socio-economic development in its broad sense encompassing economic, social and human factors as follows: "To sum up: development is a process of self-reliant growth, achieved through participation of the people acting in their own interests as they see them, and under their own control." The central implication and context of the South Commission's definition of socio-economic development is to construct a vastly relational process for determining what human choices are appropriate within a participatory and codetermined perspective of development. Such a principle is particularly prescribed for the developing countries in view of the potential that they can jointly share in, and can be enacted, to realize justice in the global arrangement of ownership and management of resources toward determining self-reliance. This relational view of dynamic complementarities among the various potentials that the developing countries can together render now becomes the premise of a new praxis of development as an organically relational process with respect to the ontology of unity of knowledge. Within this worldview, the interactive and consensual phenomena (integrative) of markets, economies, institutions and policies assume their nature, formalism, objectives and viability.

Objective: The reconstruction of the various development indexes ought to be carried out to answer the question of the relational idea of socio-economic development to address the inter-related issues that together, in complementary ways, establish the simultaneous indicators of socio-economic development. This is an issue that relies upon a particular view of socio-economic development as an endogenous and organic inter-related complementary process of attaining various indicators simultaneously via interactions followed by consensus (integration) and continuing in evolutionary learning processes of the self-same epistemology of unity of knowledge as episteme. The contrary viewpoint is of competition and marginal rates of substitution between the indicators that rejects the principle of pervasively inter-variable relational complementary situations. This is a neoclassical economic idea centering on the so-called economic rationality. This analysis suggests the development of a relational ethical socio-economic development indicator in the context of the substantive meaning of the objective well-being criterion. The resulting index applies the methodology of unity of knowledge denying the neoclassical axiom of economic rationality and marginalism. The socio-economic development implications follow.

The relational approach so undertaken in this chapter reflects the appropriate objective of the *Shari'ah* under the Islamic methodological worldview of unity of knowledge and the world system of sustainable development. The cardinal irreplaceable primal ontology as law of anything in Islamic study and analysis is that of the primal ontology of *Tawhid* as law. In respect of *maqasid as-shari'ah al-Tawhid*, the objective and purpose is to identify the resulting index, the *maslaha* function (well-being objective criterion) that arises from the measurement of impact of various and extended forms of life-sustaining choices of the good things of life at the avoidance of the bad things of life in the framework of a subtle meaning of *Tawhidi* unity of knowledge impacting and constructing the socio-economic development entities and their inter-variable and inter-entity circular causal relations.

The determination of such categories of entities is premised on the *Tawhidi* foundation of the objective and purpose of *Shari'ah*. We term this as *maqasid as-shari'ah al-Tawhid* (Choudhury, 2017). It differentiates itself from the idea of *maqasid as-shari'ah* that has been concocted by human preferences, being different from the primal ontology of *Tawhid* as law. The most pronounced essence and indicator arising from the *Tawhidi* relevance in *maqasid as-shari'ah* is shown in this chapter to rest on the principle of relational organic unity between recommended possibilities and rejection of the morally bad ones. The emergent indicator or index is shown to acquire the nature of the principle of pervasive positive complementarities between good choices and the avoidance of bad choices. A formal methodological and vastly applied model is presented to bring out the objective points.

9.1 The importance of reconstructing sustainable socio-economic development index by inter-causal complementarities between the sub-index and variables

Relating to the multi-dimensional participatory perspectives of sustainable socio-economic development, the World Bank (2000, p. 7) states: "The choice and implementation of public actions that are responsive to the needs of poor people depend on the interaction of political, social, and other institutional processes. Access to market opportunities and to public sector services is often strongly influenced by state and social institutions, which must be responsive and accountable to poor people. Achieving access, responsibility, and accountability is intrinsically political and requires active collaboration among poor people, the middle class, and other groups in society. Active collaboration can be greatly facilitated by changes in governance that make public administration, legal institutions, and public service delivery more efficient and accountable to all citizens — and by strengthening the participation of poor people in political processes and local decision making. Also important is removing the social and institutional barriers that result from distinctions of gender, ethnicity, and social status. Sound and responsive institutions are not only important to benefit the poor but also fundamental to the overall growth."

9.1.1 A brief formalism sustainability as learning system[1]

To formalize, consider the following chain relation comprising the complete phenomenological model of unity of knowledge (Choudhury *et al.*, 2007). From this general form, specific and complex problems can be derived and investigated.

In Figure 9.1, the mapping $\Omega \rightarrow_s$ [initial θ_{new}] is axiomatically premised on the episteme of unity of knowledge in reference to the "universal" open set Ω by a well-defined isomorphic mapping denoted by "s" (Maddox, 1970). (Ω, S) is thus the episteme for morality and ethics, which is denoted here by $E(\theta)$. Such an episteme is also the Moral/Ethical Space or the socio-economic development sustainability space. θ denotes the probability limit of a bundle of knowledge flows derived from (Ω, S). It induces the Moral/Ethical Set, $E(\theta)$.

In Equation (1), θ values represent *quantitatively estimated ranks* that are constructed from actual data and are used to generate estimates followed by simulation of the coefficients of the circular causation system of relations between the morally/ethically induced variables and the ordinal values of ethical determinations in a given state of socio-economic development. The latter are represented by simulated θ values obtained by quantitative ranking (parameterization) and then revised by simulation

{PROCESS 1} {PROCESS 2} $\rightarrow$

$[(\Omega,S)]\rightarrow\{\text{initial } \theta_{\text{new= stage1}}\rightarrow\theta_{\text{weights}}\rightarrow\text{Expression}\rightarrow\}$ $[(\Omega,S)]\rightarrow\{\theta_{\text{new = stage 2}}\rightarrow\}$ continuity (1)

Using θ values as weights — Epistemic Recalling

Figure 9.1 The phenomenological formalism of learning according to the episteme of unity of knowledge.

[1]This section is summarized from Choudhury and Hussain (2011).

in the circular causation relations between the variables and indexes as processes indicated in Figure 9.1 proceed on.

We therefore note that θ_{new} (as opposed to simply θ-value) is *qualitative* in type as a normative indicator for reorganizing participatory and sustainable socio-economic development. θ_{new} represents structural changes required in the direction of attaining unity of knowledge in the learning system of variables and composite indexes by means of targeting desired levels of complementarities between the selected variables of a targeted participatory socio-economic development. A structural change comes about as the consequential organic inter-relationship between state variables and moral/ethical variables of the learning space.

An example of such a social transformation is the market–institution endogenous interaction. Such social transformations yield learnt evolutionary equilibriums. Thus, to be an ethical choice in this structural change, the simulated possibility must represent the bundle of good things of life (e.g., *dynamic* basic-needs regime of socio-economic development). One such choice in socio-economic development comprises HDI and related development indexes — Gender Development Index (GDI) and Human Poverty Index (HPI1 and HPI2). But more extensively, there are also the other development elements such as Entitlement, Empowerment, Poverty Alleviation, Gender Equality, and Environment Sustainability among others.

While θ values may be determined analytically (in accordance with ranking provided by the state-variables), θ_{new} values are set by discourse between the agents of the participatory development system and systemic realities. θ_{new} values do utilize the information provided by the ranked θ values and the resulting θ-induced state variables. But they principally involve selection and assignment by institutional discourse in reference to the episteme, as is (Ω, S) in Figure 9.1.

In this way, the participatory approach to socio-economic development can be understood in a micro socio-economic sense combining the systemic formalism and the institutional endogenous processes of interaction (**I**), integration (**I**) and creative evolution (**E**) (Sztompka, 1991; Choudhury and Korvin, 2001). An example mentioned earlier is the endogenous system of organic relations between learning market variables and institutional policy variables. Such **IIE**-processes of organic learning are premised on the core episteme of unity of knowledge as the epistemic topology, $[(\Omega, S)]$. The organic learning thereafter expands continuously across space, time and knowledge flows as θ values, is continuously derived from $[(\Omega, S)]$, and advances along with the knowledge-induced path of state variables.

Essentially, therefore, "θs" are knowledge parameters reflecting the induced episteme of complementarities and participation as being derived from *Tawhidi* law as primal ontology.

Let the knowledge-induced state and policy variables be denoted by the vector $\mathbf{x}(\theta)$. Creative evolution in **IIE**-processes includes the derived endogenously interactive relations. A complex nexus of sustainable synergy is thus extended in the socio-economic development framework.

The epistemic principle of unity of knowledge is reflected in the principle of pervasive complementarities. Hence, they represent participation by recursive organic linkages of unity of knowledge between the diverse entities and variables of sustainable socio-economic development. This principle is derived across all issues and problems as a universal precept, and uniquely so, because of its specialty to be grounded uniquely on the ontological core (Ω, S). We therefore have a general theory of learnt sustainability in the phenomenological model explained by Figure 9.1.

Figure 9.1 is now deconstructed in terms of knowledge-induced variables and entities in Figure 9.2.

The following legend defines the symbols of Figure 9.2.

L: The Law that determines the Principle of Pervasive Complementarities as the sure sign of unity of knowledge in the learning domain. L also explains the neoclassical Postulate of Marginal Substitution (trade-off, opportunity cost), though this postulate

{PROCESS 1} {PROCESS 2} $\rightarrow$

$[(\Omega,S)]\rightarrow\{$initial $\theta_{new= stage1}\rightarrow\theta_{weights}\rightarrow$Evaluative$\}$ $\rightarrow$ $[(\Omega,S)]\rightarrow\{\theta_{new = stage 2}\}\rightarrow$ continuity

Expression Using θ values as weights — Epistemic Recalling (2)

$\downarrow L$ $\downarrow G$ $\downarrow C$ $\downarrow M$ $\downarrow$EV: Evolutionary processes

Critical Variables and Development instruments To attain participatory Socio-economic development

Model formulation and estimation $\downarrow$ $\downarrow$ $\downarrow$

$\downarrow$Choice of $(\theta,\mathbf{x}(\theta))$ — Simulation of Human Well-being Subject to Circular causation Between $(\theta,\mathbf{x}(\theta))$variables

Figure 9.2 Deconstruction of the learning phenomenological model to its systemic details.

is untenable in the presence of pervasive learning complementarities between requisite variables of socio-economic development sustainability.

G: Guidance on constructing pervasive complementarities is derived from L. Let $\{\theta_{\text{new}}\}$ denote such guidance. Examples are social and economic cooperation and the choice of participatory development financing instruments that promote linkages as organic learning relations in the socio-economic development domain.

C: The guidance derived from the law provides the choice of ranking selected variables and instruments of cooperation, participation and development financing in respect of attaining levels of participatory socio-economic development. At this stage, $\{\theta\text{-values}\}$ along with the selected variables and instruments are determined by institutional discourse in reference to the precepts of L and G emanating from (Ω, S) as the episteme. The properties of interaction (**I**) leading to integration (**I**) are demonstrated at this stage of Process 1 through the medium of social discourse premised on L and G, as derived from (Ω, S). Social Choice is based on complementarities between the good things of life.

$(\theta, \mathbf{x}(\theta))$: It denotes the tuple of consensual knowledge ranking of θ and its knowledge-induced vector of variables, $\mathbf{x}(\theta)$. $\mathbf{x}(\theta)$ includes socio-economic variables, instruments and policies that are selected at the level of C. It can be extended to diverse interactive indexes.

M: This is the stage of model formulation for specific socio-economic problems to analyze. The learning dynamics are used here in reference to circular causation relations between the $(\theta, \mathbf{x}(\theta))$ values. The choice of the model is usually a non-linear product function of the $\mathbf{x}(\theta)$ variables with their respective θ-induced coefficients. We call the non-linear objective criterion to be the Well-being Index because this evaluates the degree of complementarities attained between the $(\theta, \mathbf{x}(\theta))$ variables as good things of life discerned by combining state variables and endogenous policy and guidance development instruments. Because of the methodological implications of *Tawhid* as law in these formalisms, we identify the resulting well-being objective criterion as the *maqasid as-shari'ah al-Tawhid* indicator (*maslaha*).

EV: This evolutionary process emanates from the end of the learning experience in Process 1 as it goes over to Process 2. Such an experience proceeds just after social evaluation is completed by simulating the well-being index, $W(\theta, \mathbf{x}(\theta))$, subject to endogenous circular causation relations between $(\theta, \mathbf{x}(\theta))$ variables. The original episteme of (Ω, S) is *recalled* so as to reformulate a new program of development participation based on heightened understanding of laws, guidance and a combination of socio-economic, institutional and policy variables in reference to the epistemic core, (Ω, S). Thus, all such variables and instruments are endogenously induced by the new flux of knowledge flows θ_{new} arising from the previous process. The emergent learning processes continue. In this way, all the phases of evolutionary processes, namely, the Interactive, Integrative and Evolutionary (**IIE**)-character within and across processes, are completed and continued. **IIE**-processes are inherent in circular causation. They imply continuity between deductive and inductive reasoning in theory formulation while continuously referring to the episteme of unity of knowledge (Ω, S). In this way, a comprehensive model of unity of knowledge in participatory development is established for each phase of the **IIE**-processes. This also conveys the substantive meaning of sustainability attained by pervasive systemic learning.

The total model of human well-being, which is simulated subject to circular causation between the endogenous $(0, \mathbf{x}(\theta))$ variables, is now given in the discussion that follows. This analytical system also yields the complete estimable model of participatory socio-economic model. This is the well-being objective criterion as the *maqasid as-shari'ah al-Tawhid* indicator of socio-economic development; more generally also beyond this special application.

$$\text{Simulate } W(\theta, \mathbf{x}(\theta)); \mathbf{x}(\theta) = \{x_k(\theta)\}_{k=1,2,\dots,n} \tag{3}$$

$$\text{Subject to the circular causation system,}$$

$$x_u = f_u(\{\theta, x_u(\theta)\}_{u=1,2,\dots,n;\ u\neq k}$$

$$\text{and } \theta = g(x_u(\theta)|\theta \text{ values in previous process})$$

$$i, j = 1, 2, \dots, n$$

Equation (3) in its full system form is the well-being (*maslaha*) function, since its properties, form and implications followed by analysis and applications arise from the *Tawhid* primal ontology as law of unity of knowledge between the good things of life to the rejection of the bad and false choices. Equation (3) also forms the complete measured form of the index of *maqasid as-shari'ah al-Tawhid* (Choudhury, 2017). We now proceed to dwell on this formalism in further methodological content followed by empirical estimation.

Note that there are several statistical estimation problems relating to predictors, estimators and the testing of hypothesis that would be taken up here. In order to avoid the strong possibility of multi-collinearity between the variables in reduced equation forms, only structural forms of the equations are estimated (Pindyck and Rubinfeld, 1976). It is recommended that the explanatory variables be taken in their log-linear form, so as to obtain interpretable meanings for their associated coefficients and to identify the simulation possibilities. The entire model is non-linear and complex instead of linear and simple, because as a computerized model its coefficients are all θ induced and estimable.

9.2 Theoretical aspects in the generalized *Tawhidi* model of unity of knowledge

Estimation of the model proceeds in two stages. Firstly, the actual socio-economic state of development is evaluated with the averaging of assigned rankings of the data values, as they actually appear. The estimation results show the degree of complementarities and/or trade-offs between the $\mathbf{x}(\theta)$ variables as they appear in the existing state of socio-economic development. On the basis of this statistical result, the second stage of model estimation corrects the trade-offs, noting though the realistic extent to which such trade-offs can be reduced, and thereby, complementarities can be realized over phases of learning and adjustment. The statistical hypothesis we are testing is the extent to which inter-variable complementarities exist in the actual state of socio-economic development or are constructible into pervasive complementarities by simulation.

In such simulations by correction of the relations between variables and the values of coefficients that emanate from the corrections, it is necessary to keep cognizance of cost, resource availability, budget constraints, development possibilities and possible institutional policy and strategic changes. Thus, the θ values are ranked once again in the light of the degree of complementarities desired and possible. An example here is to replace a neoclassical model of economic growth and development, which is based on marginal rates of substitution, by models of socio-economic development sustainability. These are learning models based on extensive systemic complementarities between good social choices. In the empirical part of this chapter, both the actual estimation and the Spatial Domain Analysis simulation results are provided.

9.2.1 Mathematical properties of the system

We investigate the expression (Choudhury *et al.*, 2007),

$$\partial W(\theta, \mathbf{x}(\theta))/\partial x(\theta)_{\text{each}x(\theta)} = [\partial W(\theta, \mathbf{x}(\theta))/\partial\theta].[\partial\theta/\partial x(\theta)_{\text{each }x(\theta)}] \quad (4)$$

Clearly, $[\partial\theta/\partial x(\theta)_{\text{each }x(\theta)}] > 0$, because of the existence of θ_{new} in continuous **IIE**-processes.

Next, for $[\partial W(\theta, \mathbf{x}(\theta))/\partial\theta] > 0$, with respect to each component of $(\theta, \mathbf{x}(\theta))$ belonging to continuous learning in **IIE**-processes, it is necessary that effective complementarities or a good semblance of these between the $\mathbf{x}(\theta)$ variables be established. This requires the estimation results to be followed by re-setting of the dynamic coefficients (θ induced), and thereby, of the dynamic predictors and estimators.

Now say that, a particular estimated coefficient, α_s of $W(\theta, \mathbf{x}(\theta)) = \Pi_s A(\theta) x_s(\theta)^{\alpha s}$, having no numerical restriction on α_s in the system (3), yields $\alpha_s = \partial \log x(\theta)_{s'}/\partial \log x(\theta)_s < 0$ as an elasticity coefficient of $x(\theta)_{s'}$ relative to $x(\theta)_s$. Such a result will imply the existence of trade-off rather than a complementary relationship between $x(\theta)_{s'}$ and $x(\theta)_s$ in the specific equations of the circular causation system. A θ_{new} value is now required to change the trade-off into a complementary development relationship. An example of complementary choices of $(\theta, \mathbf{x}(\theta))$ variables is dynamic bundles of basic needs. A discursive approach is now combined with the reality of the development system to simulate and thus re-set new α_s-coefficient values. The underlying discursive process on the specific issues of development in the present case re-sets the new $(\theta, \mathbf{x}(\theta))$ values. Through such a process of system-institution discursive relationship to simulate change, α_s too gets θ induced. Likewise, the technology coefficient $A(\theta)$ is θ induced.

The underlying agencies, policies and development instruments are selected to generate the needed complementarities between the social goods. An example is the choice of economic growth complemented with poverty alleviation in a sustainable basic-needs regime of socio-economic development. The well-being function subject to circular causal relations between the development indicators as the variables is explained by the system of relations (3). The quantitative form of the well-being function (*maslaha* function) is evaluated empirically by the θ equation.

9.3 Quantitative evaluation of the well-being model of gender development

The system model given by the expressions in (3) when evaluated by the following data yields the results as analyzed in what follows:

The following variables are modeled according to the system of well-being circular causation relations shown in Equation (3) to test the case for Gender Development in circular causation relations with the explanatory variables (Table 9.1):

Y: denotes countries, which are mostly OIC members;
$x1$: inequality-adjusted HDI;
$x2$: gender development index;
$x3$: gender inequality index;
$x4$: multidimensional poverty index;
$x5$: literacy rate (adult % for 15 and older ages).

We set $\theta = 10$ for highest values (X^*) of $X1$, $X2$, $X3$, $X4$, $X5$, $X6$, $X7$; then prorate for other values by $(10/X^*)^*(X \text{ values}) = \theta_i$, for each columns of $X1, X2, \ldots, X7$. Then average $(\Sigma\theta_i)/7 = \theta$.

The data table for $X1$, $X2$, $X3$, $X4$, $X5$, $X6$, $X7$, θ, with X's in natural logarithmic value is constructed. Data points are for the specific countries taken in the OIC bloc. We take into account only those countries for which the data remain unbroken $\{X1, X2, X3, X4, X5, X6, X7\}$.

Legend: For the current 2017 fiscal year, low-income economies are defined as those with a GNI per capita, calculated using the World Bank Atlas method, of \$1,025 or less in 2015; lower middle-income economies are those with a GNI per capita between \$1,026 and \$4,035; upper middle-income economies are those with a GNI per capita between \$4,036 and \$12,475; high-income economies are those with a GNI per capita of \$12,476 or more.

9.3.1 Calculation of θ values from socio-economic data set

Next we inter-causally relate these variables by estimating the following log-linear equations. We estimate the quantitative form of the log-linear well-being function in respect of "θ" value. The estimated and simulated "θ" equation denotes the quantitative form of the *maslaha* function of *maqasid as-shari'ah al-Tawhid.* The equivalent W(θ) function is the conceptual form, but it alone as it is formulated cannot be evaluated unless converted to the "θ" form. Nonetheless, the formulation of $W(\theta)$ is essential to implicate the Tawhidi ontological methodology in the derivation and analysis of the maslaha function with its conceptual and empirical version and policy-theoretic implications conveyed by the estimated following into simulated coefficients.

Circular causation equations: Note that the same symbols of a's are used in all equations but estimated results are different.

$$\ln X1 = a0 + a1 \times \ln X2 + a2 \times \ln X3 + a3 \times \ln X4 + a4 \times \ln X5 + a5 \times \ln X6 + a6 \times \ln X7 + a \times \theta \quad (1)$$

$$\ln X2 = a0 + a1 \times \ln X1 + a2 \times \ln X3 + a3 \times \ln X4 + a4 \times \ln X5 + a5 \times \ln X6 + a6 \times \ln X7 + a \times \theta \quad (2)$$

$$\ln X3 = a0 + a1 \times \ln X1 + a2 \times \ln X2 + a3 \times \ln X4 + a4 \times \ln X5 + a5 \times \ln X6 + a6 \times \ln X7 + a \times \theta \quad (3)$$

$$\ln X4 = a0 + a1 \times \ln X1 + a2 \times \ln X2 + a3 \times \ln X3 + a4 \times \ln X5 + a5 \times \ln X6 + a6 \times \ln X7 + a \times \theta \quad (4)$$

$$\ln X5 = a0 + a1 \times \ln X1 + a2 \times \ln X2 + a3 \times \ln X3 + a4 \times \ln X4 + a5 \times \ln X6 + a6 \times \ln X7 + a \times \theta \quad (5)$$

$$\ln X6 = a0 + a1 \times \ln X1 + a2 \times \ln X2 + a3 \times \ln X3 + a4 \times \ln X4 + a5 \times \ln X5 + a6 \times \ln X7 + a \times \theta \quad (6)$$

$$\ln X7 = a0 + a1 \times \ln X1 + a2 \times \ln X2 + a3 \times \ln X3 + a4 \times \ln X4 + a5 \times \ln X5 + a6 \times \ln X6 + a \times \theta \quad (7)$$

$$\theta = b0 + a1 \times \ln X1 + a2 \times \ln X2 + a3 \times \ln X3 + a4 \times \ln X4 + a5 \times \ln X5 + a6 \times \ln X6 + a \times \ln X7 \quad (10)$$

9.3.2 Statistical results

Circular causal variables "AS IS":

LNX1 = 10.62477 + 1.799076 LNX2 − 0.410032 LNX3 + 1.945767 LNX4 + 0.274892 LN1X5
3.897872 2.105590 −0.350944 −3.419761 −1.693265
−0.216612 LNX6 − 0.859712 LNX7 + 0.894641 × θ
−0.558479 −1.812600 4.377644

R-squared 0.843918
Adjusted R-squared 0.801896
Durbin–Watson stat 1.465304

LNX2 = −2.206726 + 0.080974 LNX1 − 0.038359 LNX3 − 0.244143 LNX4 − 0.071206 LN1X5
+0.187197 LNX6
−3.7704792. 105590 −0.154459 −1.779068 −2.125757
2.523170
−0.096710 LNX7 − 0.008669 × θ
−0.920222 −0.151780

R-squared 0.943671
Adjusted R-squared 0.922410
Durbin–Watson stat 2.192338

LNX3 = −0.012692 LNX4 + 0.012686 LNX5 + 0.106575 LNX6 + 0.043057 LNX7
−0.110660 0.444525 1.721565 0.513380
+0.050999 × θ − 0.011498 LNX1 − 0.023899 LNX2 − 0.950887
1.159552 −0.350944 −0.154459 −1.749751

R-squared 0.621636
Adjusted R-squared 0.519769
Durbin–Watson stat 2.691600

LNX4 = −0.020243 LN1X5 − 0.096836 LNX6 + 0.021804 LNX7 − 0.235152 × θ
−0.414759 0.879791 0.151384 −3.805492
+ 0.159448 LNX1 − 0.444505 LNX2 − 0.037090 LNX3 − 1.585829
3.419761 −1.779068 −0.110660 −1.702224

R-squared 0.887974
Adjusted R-squared 0.857813
Durbin–Watson stat 1.994172

LNX5 = 0.116221 LNX6 + 1.651078 LNX7 − 0.900484 × θ + 0.361314 LNX1 − 2.079422
LNX2
0.260148 3.456304 −3.554743 1.693265
−2.125757
+ 0.594593 LNX3 − 0.324694 LNX4 − 9.511717
0.444525 −0.414759 −2.746621

R-squared 0.934504
Adjusted R-squared 0.916870
Durbin–Watson stat 1.640053

LNX6 = −0.100088 LNX7 + 0.068230 × θ −0.054724 LNX1 + 1.050750 LNX2
−0.396784 0.506453 −0.558479 2.523170
+ 0.960146 LNX3 + 0.298543 LNX4 + 0.022339 LNX5 + 5.977946
1.721565 0.879791 0.260148 4.726716

R-squared 0.776934
Adjusted R-squared 0.716878
Durbin–Watson stat 2.056577

LNX7 = 0.317871 × θ − 0.130496 LNX1 − 0.326152 LNX2 + 0.233065 LNX3 + 0.040389 LNX4
3.765512 −1.812600 −0.920222 0.513380
0.151384
+ 0.190673 LNX5 − 0.060135 LNX6 + 3.769981
3.456304 −0.396784 3.385289

R-squared 0.694411
Adjusted R-squared 0.612137
Durbin–Watson stat 2.252034

θ = 0.474288 LNX1 − 0.102114 LNX2 + 0.964149 LNX3 − 1.521293 LNX4 − 0.363200 LNX5
4.377644 −0.151780 1.159552 −3.805492
−3.554743
+ 0.143175 LNX6 + 1.110191 LNX7 − 5.175182
0.506453 3.765512 −2.267165

R-squared 0.965227
Adjusted R-squared 0.955864
Durbin–Watson stat 1.314262

9.3.3 Simulation by spatial domain analysis

Simulated (AS IT) ought to be:

We simulate the following estimated equation in order to improve the *maqasid as-shari'ah al-Tawhid* index of *maslaha* into an acceptable form of positive complementarities.

$$\theta = -5.175182 + 0.474288\ \text{LNX1} + 0.102114\ \text{LNX2} + 0.964149\ \text{LNX3} + 1.521293\ \text{LNX4} + 0.363200\ \text{LNX5} + 0.143175\ \text{LNX6} + 1.110191\ \text{LNX7}$$

The SDA method of Geographical Information System is applied here as a socio-economic adaptation to simulate the socio-economic development well-being topography. Figure 9.3 translates the estimated statistical model into spatial domain in a two-dimensional way. It can be observed that the level of intensity of the interactions between "θ" and the other variables has been demonstrated by using the intensity of the colors. The interaction between the "θ" and the variable "$X4$" is the highest since its coefficient value is 1.521293 and this is demonstrated by the highly intense color. In

Table 9.2 Descriptive statistics.

	LNX_1	LNX_2	LNX_3	LNX_4	LNX_5	LNX_6	LNX_7	TETHA
Mean	7.462581	−0.881365	−0.148544	−0.711022	−2.616295	4.197903	3.970032	5.351450
Median	7.185224	−0.878308	−0.132392	−0.628423	−2.144305	4.310100	4.051239	4.955535
Maximum	9.245689	−0.336872	0.005982	0.265268	−0.537854	4.603168	4.405499	9.743590
Minimum	5.883211	−1.435485	−0.495937	−1.599488	−5.521461	2.949688	3.481240	3.390735
Std. Dev.	0.958078	0.324783	0.103046	0.323730	1.695632	0.402819	0.266767	1.477918
Skewness	0.340814	−0.045405	−1.241098	−1.029557	−0.381669	−1.072319	−0.321606	0.900102
Kurtosis	1.865256	1.652392	5.025362	3.255234	1.633781	3.803723	2.019955	3.449192
Jarque Bera	2.482367	2.584415	14.53980	6.098890	3.469754	7.431038	1.946799	4.876887
Probability	0.289042	0.274664	0.000696	0.47385	0.176422	0.024343	0.377797	0.087297
Sum	253.7278	−29.96641	−5.050500	−24.17475	−88.95402	142.7287	134.9811	181.9493
Sum Sq. Dev.	30.29117	3.480980	0.350408	3.458438	94.88049	5.354684	2.348427	72.07999
Observations	34	34	34	34	34	34	34	34

Table 9.3 Inter-variable correlation matrix.

	LNX1	LNX2	LNX3	LNX4	LNX5	LNX6	LNX7	TETHA
LNX1	1.000000	0.839768	0.543215	−0.617568	−0.786675	0.720567	−0.371743	0.812363
LNX2	0.839768	1.000000	0.637250	−0.820403	−0.938276	0.860506	−0.415799	0.893220
LNX3	0.543215	0.637250	1.000000	−0.688425	−0.615070	0.674238	0.047904	0.741559
LNX4	−0.617568	−0.820403	−0.688425	1.000000	0.824688	−0.698083	0.064396	−0.908966
LNX5	−0.786675	−0.938276	−0.615070	0.824688	1.000000	−0.805175	0.427426	−0.899449
LNX6	0.720567	0.860506	0.674238	−0.698083	−0.805175	1.000000	−0.331252	0.788348
LNX7	−0.371743	−0.415799	0.047904	0.064396	0.427426	−0.331252	1.000000	−0.113850
TETHA	0.812363	0.893220	0.741559	−0.908966	−0.899449	0.788348	−0.113850	1.000000

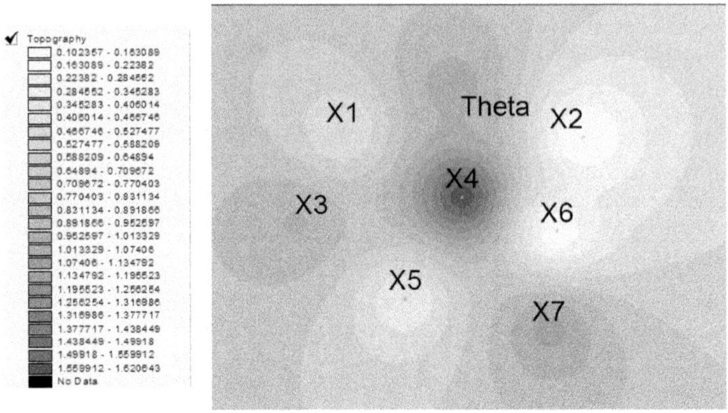

Figure 9.3 SDA Illustration of interactions among estimated θ variable (quantitative *maslaha*) and other variables.

this way, the interaction of other variables with the "θ" can be perceived in the SDA domain which is more interactive and user friendly. In addition, the two-dimensional surface consists of infinite number of points and the level of interactions can be demonstrated at each point in the SDA domain, which is not the case with statistical approach. In the statistical approach, only the interaction at a point can be calculated.

9.4 Policy conclusion of statistical results

Firstly, we note from the quantitative θ form of well-being function (*maslaha* function) that there is a loss of economy of scale in the learning system underlying the *Tawhidi* formulation of *maslaha* function. Hence, also there is a loss of economy of scope. The implication of this result is that, in the inter-variable equation of the well-being function large degrees of marginal rates of substitutions, and thereby, presence of the neoclassical economic trace of *marginalism* are found in the negative contribution of the variables, namely, inequality-adjusted HDI (X_2), Gender Inequality Index (X_4), and Multiple-dimensional Poverty Index (X_5). In respect of GDI, a 1% change in GDI (X_3) causes a significant 0.964149 of 1% change of well-being (up or down together in the same direction) of GDI. Gender Development is thereby a most important target to focus on in respect of world sustainable development using the formulated version of the well-being function as the *maslaha* function of *maqasid as-shari'ah al-Tawhid*.

The aforementioned result is further reinforced by the circular causation statistical estimation of ln$X3$ (GDI). Economy of scale between the complementary variables is shown by the positive coefficients of the specific variables in this estimated equation. The policy conclusion derived from the earlier statistical results is the much-required inter-causal relations that ought to be built in the sustainable development focus between GDI and well-being (*maslaha*) in the presence of the other inter-variable causality of the circular causation relations. Along this line of evidence and explanation, the negative coefficient relations between GDI (X_3) and Inequality-Adjusted HDI (X_2) (elasticity coefficient $= -0.023899$) can be further noted. Negative relationship between Gender Inequality Index (X_4) and Multiple-dimensional Poverty Index (X_5) (elasticity coefficient $= -0.020243$) signifies the need to intensify the socio-economic development efforts to increase GDI by reducing its adverse relationship with X_4, X_5, and thus improving the complementarity between GDI (X_3) and X_2.

References

Choudhury, M. A. (2015), Res extensa et res cogitans de maqasid as-shari'ah. *International Journal of Law and Management*, 57(6), 662–693.

Choudhury, M. A. (2017), *A Phenomenological Theory of Islamic Economics*, Kuala Lumpur: University of Malaya Press.

Choudhury, M. A. and Hussain, Z. (2011), Estimating an ethical index of human wellbeing. *Journal of Developing Areas*, 45(fall), 375–409.

Choudhury, M. A. and Korvin, G. (2002), Simulation versus optimization in knowledge-induced fields. *Kybernetes: International Journal of Systems and Cybernetics*, 31(1), 44–60.

Choudhury, M. A., Zaman, S. I. and Harahap, S. S. (2007), An evolutionary topological theory of participatory socioeconomic development. *World Futures: Journal of General Evolutionary Systems*, 63(8), 584–598.

Choudhury, M. A., Zaman, S. I. and Nassar, Y. (2007), A knowledge-induced operator model. *Journal for Science*, 12(1), 19–40.

Maddox, I. J. (1970), *Elements of Functional Analysis*, Cambridge: Cambridge University Press.

Mohammad, M. O. and Taib, F. M. (2016), The performance measures of Islamic banking based on the *maqasid* framework (Chapter 5), in Choudhury, M. A. (ed.). *Islamic Financial Economy and Islamic Banking*, London: Routledge.

Pindyck, R. S. and Rubinfeld, D. L. (2001), The degree of economies of scope, in *Microeconomics* (5th edn.). Upper Saddle River, New Jersey: Prentice-Hall Inc., p. 231.

South Commission (1990), *The Challenge to the South*, Oxford: Oxford University Press.

Sztompka, P. (1991), *Society in Action, The Theory of Social Becoming*, Chicago, IL: The University of Chicago Press.

United Nations (2003), *Indicators for Monitoring the Millennium Development Goals*, New York.

United Nations (2015), *Millennium Development Goals Report*, New York.

United Nations (2016), *Millennium Development Goals Report*, New York.

United Nations Development Programme (UNDP) (1997, 1998, 1999, 2000 issues), *Human Development Report*, New York: Oxford University Press.

World Bank (2000), *World Development Report*, New York: Oxford University Press.

Chapter 10

Women Empowerment and Globalization Evidence from the Organisation of Islamic Cooperation (OIC) Countries

Muhammad Tariq Majeed

Abstract

How do rising levels of international interconnectedness affect social, economic and political conditions for women? Research on gender and international relations frequently offers clear propositions but seldom submits them to broad, quantitative testing. This chapter attempts to fill that gap. We attempt to answer the question: Do increasing cross-national exchange and communication lead to improvements in the status and equality of women in the Organisation of Islamic Cooperation (OIC) countries? We have measured women empowerment with the economic, political and social rights of women. The empirical analysis is based on Order Logit model. The results show that globalization in the form of trade improves the economic, political and social rights of women while in the form of foreign direct investment (FDI) its favorable impact is limited to only political rights of women.

Keywords: Women rights, Globalization, FDI, Trade, OIC countries

How do rising levels of international economic integration influence the social, economic, and political conditions for women? Research on gender and international interactions offers theoretical links and propositions but rarely submits them to quantitative testing. This chapter aims to fill that lacuna.

Economic aspects of globalization bring new opportunities and resources to women. Moreover, globalization promotes the diffusion of ideas and norms of equality for women; although some societies resist such notions, others gradually abandon rules and practices that have functioned to subordinate and constrain women.

The contribution of women in the socio-economic activities of the state is an important factor to increase the living standard of a society. However, women have been subjugated by the male-dominant society since the existence of this world. Women's opinions are still ignored while taking important decisions at the family, regional or country levels. In the developed countries, women are equally equipped with higher education, skills and knowledge to participate in the important decision-making process of the country.

In effect, the developed countries are exploiting the true potential of their available talents in the country without taking into account the gender differences. However, the situation in the developing countries is just the opposite because women are facing discrimination in every field of life on the basis of the gender differences. Women empowerment differentials are perhaps one of the main reasons for the differences in economic prosperity across the developed and the developing countries. Women's rights have been secured over time, but still the world is tolerating significant discrimination against women in the political, social and economic aspects of life.

The available literature on women empowerment generally focuses on the effects of globalization on gender wage differentials (Becker, 1971; Berik *et al.*, 2004; Busse and Spielmann, 2006; Villarreal and Yu, 2007; Oostendorp, 2009). Another strand of the literature focuses on female labor force participation as a consequence of globalization (Wood, 1991; Tejani and Millberg, 2010; Wacker *et al.*, 2017). However, gender wage differentials and female labor force participation are narrow dimensions of women empowerment.

In effect, women empowerment is a multi-dimensional concept that covers the economic, social and political rights of women. The economic rights cover the different aspects of women's professional life such as choice of profession, job environment, wages, unemployment benefits and share in labor force. The social rights comprise the rights of marriage, rights of divorce, participation in the decision of children and religious freedom. The political rights include the rights to vote, rights to hold election, rights to sit in the parliament and rights to participate in the political decisions of country.

The available literature on globalization and the status of women provides mixed evidence. For instance, one strand of the literature predicts unfavorable effects of globalization on the conditions of women (Ward, 1984; Chafetz, 1984; Shiva, 2005; Enloe, 2007; Klein, 2007;

Van Staveren *et al.*, 2007). While, on the contrary, another strand of the literature predicts favorable effects of globalization on the conditions of women (Bhagwati, 2004; Spar, 1998; Spar and Yoffie, 1999).

The extant literature ignores different dimensions of women's rights in relation to economic globalization. Particularly, empirical research ignores an exclusive empirical analysis for the Organisation of Islamic Cooperation (OIC) countries. Why is it important to estimate the consequences of globalization only for the OIC countries? Majeed (2015) concludes that Islamic countries differ from non-Islamic countries in terms of their exposure to globalization. In a recent study, Estes and Tiliouine (2016) conclude that economic and social progress in OIC countries is substantially different from other organizations of countries such as Association of Southeast Asian Nations (ASEAN), Commonwealth of Independent States (CIS) and the South Asian Association for Regional Cooperation (SAARC). Therefore, a generalized analysis for all countries may yield a biased analysis.

That said, this chapter attempts to provide an empirical analysis of globalization and women's rights in the case of the OIC countries by addressing the following questions: Does economic globalization improve the economic, social and political rights of women? Does economic globalization cause similar effects on different forms of rights of women?

The remaining chapter is structured as follows: Section 10.2 provides a brief literature review of the relevant literature. Section 10.3 describes methodology. Section 10.4 explains the data description and sources. Section 10.5 comprises the discussion of empirical results. Section 10.6 concludes the chapter.

10.1 Women empowerment

Women empowerment plays an important role in the socio-economic, ethical, educational and cultural progress of a society. Some religious, traditional and cultural extremists are still skeptical about the freedom and empowerment of women. There are many feminists who are skeptic about the positive effects of globalization on women empowerment (see Ward, 1984; Chafetz, 1984; Shiva, 2005; Enloe, 2007; Klein, 2007; Van Staveren *et al.*, 2007). They argue that globalization exacerbates the prevailing gender inequality in developing countries due to the exploitive nature of multinational and transnational corporations.

Wichterich (2000) and Parpart *et al.* (2002) argued that globalized women are the price-taker workers in the trade industry, who take up the shocks of structural adjustment and social cutbacks. Globalization has malignant and pernicious effects on the family and the socio-economic, financial and political lives of women because the profit-seeking and selfish international corporations are exploiting the weak and vulnerable women instead of empowering them. There are gender differences in job market, and usually, women are recruited for the low-paid, unstable and the poor positions (Pearson and Mitter, 1993; Cagatay and Ozler, 1995; Howes and Singh, 1995).

On the contrary, some studies argued that trade and foreign direct investment (FDI) are playing a positive and efficient role in empowering the women by providing them the chance to participate in global economic activities. Studies by Spar (1998), Spar and Yoffie (1999) and Bhagwati (2004) proposed that women are the winners of globalization because FDI inflows and trade openness create economic opportunities for women. They argued that multinational corporations seek talent irrespective of gender differences. They further stressed that the improved quality of life and women's rights in the developed countries spillover to the laggard developing countries through global interactions.

Htun and Weldon (2010) highlighted that the lower cost of entering in the international market, trade liberalization and modern technology have increased job outcomes for women. On the basis of his survey, Duflo (2012) proposed that there is a consensus that trade liberalization assured significant status to women in the society.

Gray *et al.* (2006) studied the effect of trade and FDI on the political, social and economic rights of women using the data of 180 countries from 1975 to 2000. They argued that economic integration can improve the financial aspects of women's lives by providing them economic opportunities. Moreover, economic integration also causes the diffusion and spillover effects of norms that secure women's rights. They conclude that globalization in the form of trade and FDI improves the outcomes for women.

The modernist theory asserts that globalization increases women empowerment because in the present world of technology and knowledge it is quite difficult to exploit women's rights. Using a global sample over the period 1981–2007, Neumayer and Soysa (2011) found favorable effects of trade and FDI on women's rights.

Neumayer and Soysa (2011) found out favorable effects of FDI and trade on women empowerment using the data of 152 countries over the period 1981–2007. Cho (2011) empirically studied the effect of globalization on women's rights using the data of 150 countries over the period 1981–2008. He found out that economic and social globalizations have a positive effect on women's economic rights in the OECD (Organisation for Economic Co-operation and Development) countries while social globalization increases women trafficking. Majeed and Malik (2017) also found evidence of increasing women trafficking as a result of globalization.

Another strand of the literature predicts mixed effects of globalization on wages provided to women. Neoclassical trade theories suggest that trade increases the demand and wages of low-skilled and abundant resources like female labor, which decreases the gender wage differentials. Becker (1971) illustrated that competition due to trade decreases the marginal profits of the company and, consequently, wage discrimination against women becomes less likely.

In a case study of East Asia, Berik *et al.* (2004) exhibited that the international trade concentrated in import industry curtails the wages of women due to increased competition and their rights remain unsafe. Using the data of manufacturing firms in Mexico from 1992 to 2001, Villarreal and Yu (2007) found that foreign firms significantly employ more women as compared to domestic firms, and foreign firms discriminate less in terms of wages. In contrast, Busse and Spielmann (2006), in a sample of 92 developed and developing countries showed that trade widens the gender wage gap. Oostendorp (2009) showed that trade and FDI decrease the gender wage gap in the developed countries but increase gender wage gap in the developing countries.

Another strand of the literature proxies women empowerment with "women participation in labor force" and finds inconclusive evidence. Wood (1991) employed the panel data of 35 countries from South and North over the period 1960–1985 and found out the positive effects of trade liberalization on women labor demand. On the contrary Wacker *et al.* (2017) revealed the negative impacts of FDI and trade on female labor force participation in a sample of 80 developing economies from 1980 to 2005. Using the panel data of 65 countries from 1985 to 2007, Tejani and Millberg (2010) showed that female employment rate in the developing countries has increased but decreased in the developed countries as a result of trade liberalization.

Thus, the extant literature on women empowerment and globalization provides mixed evidence. Moreover, women empowerment is simply measured with wage rates and labor force participation ignoring the other social and political dimensions of women empowerment. The available empirical literature did not focus on the OIC countries. This chapter, therefore, conducts an empirical analysis of the OIC countries using comprehensive measures of women rights.

10.2 Methodology

Following the empirical literature on women empowerment, three different equations have been specified to estimate the economic, social and political rights of women. The equation for the economic rights of women is specified as follows:

$$\text{WER} = \beta 1_i + \beta 2Y_{it} + \beta 3\text{Dem}_{it} + \beta 4\text{Trade}_{it} + \theta 1Z_{it} + \theta 2X_{it} + e_{it}. \quad (1)$$

WER shows the economic rights of women, Y is the real per capita GDP, Dem shows democracy level in the country, and Z incorporates regional dummies to control the effect of regional heterogeneity. The term X represents a row vector of control variables such as female fertility, female share in labor force participation and female share in total population. The term e shows the error term and subscripts i and t indicate country and time, respectively.

Equation 2 includes the social rights of women as a dependent variable:

$$\text{WSR}_{it} = \beta 1_i + \beta 2Y_{it} + \beta 3\text{Dem}_{it} + \beta 4\text{Trade}_{it} + \theta 1Z_{it} + \theta 2X_{it} + v_{it}. \quad (2)$$

WSR shows the social rights of women. The term v_{it} is the error term. The definition of women empowerment is incomplete without the political rights of women. Finally, Equation (3) includes the political rights of women as a dependent variable:

$$\text{WPR}_{it} = \beta 1_i + \beta 2Y_{it} + \beta 3\text{Dem}_{it} + \beta 4\text{Trade}_{it} + \theta 1Z_{it} + \theta 2X_{it} + u_{it}. \quad (3)$$

WPR shows the political rights of women. u_{it} is the error term of Equation (3). Since FDI and trade can have diverse effects on women's rights, we estimate the same equations separately for FDI.

10.2.1 Data description

The data on the economic, political and social rights of women are taken from Cingranelli and Richards (2010). Initially, we had selected all the OIC countries, but due to data limitations, the final sample includes 52 countries. The time period of the study (1996–2011) is limited due to the availability of series. The data on the economic, social and political rights of women are ordinal comprising four categories (0–3). A complete description of categories is given in Tables 10.1 and 10.2.

Economic globalization is measured with trade and FDI. Trade is measured as the sum of export and import as ratio of GDP and FDI is also ratio of GDP. GDP per capita is taken at constant 2005($). Fertility rate refers to the number of children born to a woman at the end of her childbearing years of life. Female population refers to the share of female population in the total population. The data on trade, FDI, GDP per capita, fertility rate, female population and female labor force have been taken from World Development Indicators. The data on democracy are taken from the polity IV. The data of polity index range from −10 to 10, where 10 shows complete democracy and −10 shows complete autocracy in the country.

We have also introduced the following regional dummies based on the World Bank regional classification to control the heterogeneity in the countries: East Asia and Pacific countries (EAP), Middle East and North African countries (MENA), European and Central Asian countries (ECA), South Asian (SA) countries, Sub-Saharan African countries (SSA) and Latin American and Caribbean countries (LAC). Table 10.3 reports descriptive statistics of the variables used.

Table 10.4 shows that the measures of globalization (trade and FDI) are positively correlated with all dimensions of women's rights. The correlation between women's fertility and women's rights is negative.

Table 10.1 The description of the ordinal ranking of the index.

Ranking	Women's economic/social/political rights
0	There are no economic/social/political rights for women under law, and systematic discrimination based on sex may be built into the law. The government tolerates a high level of discrimination against women.
1	There are some economic/social/political rights for women under law. However, in practice, the government does not enforce the laws effectively. The government tolerates a moderate level of discrimination against women.
2	There are some economic/social/political rights for women under law. In practice, the government does enforce these laws effectively. However, the government still tolerates a low level of discrimination against women.
3	All or nearly all of women's economic/social/political rights are guaranteed by law. In practice, the government fully and vigorously enforces these laws. The government tolerates none or almost no discrimination against women.

Table 10.2 Description of index.

Women's economic rights index includes
- ☐ Equal pay for equal work
- ☐ Free choice of profession or employment without the need to obtain the consent from husband or a male relative
- ☐ The right to gainful employment without the need to obtain consent from husband or a male relative
- ☐ Equality in hiring and promotion practices
- ☐ Job security (maternity leave, unemployment benefits, no arbitrary firing or layoffs, etc.)
- ☐ Non-discrimination by employers
- ☐ The right to be free from sexual harassment in the workplace
- ☐ The right to work at night
- ☐ The right to work in occupations classified as dangerous
- ☐ The right to work in the military and police force

Women political rights index includes
- ☐ The right to vote
- ☐ The right to run office
- ☐ The right to hold election and appointed government positions
- ☐ The right to join political parties
- ☐ The right of petition of government parties

Women social rights index includes
- ☐ The right to equal inheritance
- ☐ The right to enter into marriage on a basis of equality with men
- ☐ The right to travel abroad
- ☐ The right to obtain a passport
- ☐ The right to confer citizenship to children or a husband
- ☐ The right to initiate a divorce
- ☐ The right to own, acquire, manage and retain property brought into marriage
- ☐ The right to participate in social, cultural and community activities
- ☐ The right to an education
- ☐ The freedom to choose a residence/domicile
- ☐ Freedom from female genital mutilation of children and of adults without their consent
- ☐ Freedom from forced sterilization

Figure 10.1 shows the regional time trends of globalization (trade) in the Muslim world. Muslim countries located in South Asia are the least integrated while Muslim countries located in the East Asian and Latin American regions are the most integrated. Economic integration over time is very slow in all regions of the Muslim world. Figure 10.2 indicates that Muslim countries located in Central Asia receive high FDI inflows while countries in the South Asian and Latin American regions receive low flows of FDI over time. Moreover, FDI inflows are highly volatile. In particular,

Table 10.3 Descriptive statistics.

Variable	Observations	Mean	Std. Dev.	Min.	Max.
Women's economic rights	770	0.9116883	0.5925357	0	3
Women's political rights	777	1.700129	0.6104017	0	3
Women's social rights	469	0.673774	0.6081488	0	2
Per capita income	789	4289.04	9744.411	196.1729	60874.38
Trade	770	75.91614	35.67458	17.85861	220.4074
FDI	782	3.470384	5.37922	−16.58887	46.4937
Democracy	832	−3.43149	20.60207	−88	9
Fertility	832	4.222184	1.720554	1.502	7.869
Female labor	832	34.81875	17.07253	6.8	81.4
Female population	832	48.84381	3.976484	23.77579	52.21949

Table 10.4 Correlation matrix.

Variables	1	2	3	4	5	6	7	8	9	10
Women's economic rights	1.00	—	—	—	—	—	—	—	—	—
Women's political rights	0.18	1.00	—	—	—	—	—	—	—	—
Women's social rights	0.46	0.397	1.00	—	—	—	—	—	—	—
Per capita income	0.04	−0.51	−0.18	1.00	—	—	—	—	—	—
Trade	0.32	0.08	0.31	0.15	1.00	—	—	—	—	—
FDI	0.07	0.14	0.12	−0.07	0.26	1.00	—	—	—	—
Democracy	0.04	0.02	0.05	0.01	0.01	−0.03	1.00	—	—	—
Fertility	−0.22	0.05	−0.24	−0.30	−0.32	−0.09	−0.06	1.00	—	—
Female labor	0.07	0.47	0.16	−0.25	−0.13	0.13	0.09	0.34	1.00	—
Female population	0.00	0.57	0.24	−0.92	−0.12	0.10	0.04	0.21	0.35	1.00

FDI in Latin America exhibits the highest volatility. Figures (10.1A–10.3A) reported in the Appendix also show that trade volatility across countries within a region is low while FDI volatility is high.

Figure 10.3 shows time trends of women empowerment, which is constructed taking simple average of women's economic, social and political

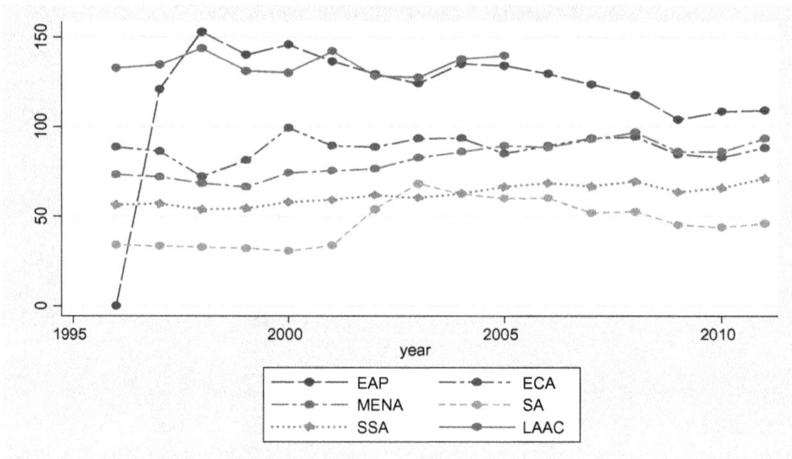

Figure 10.1 Time trend of globalization (trade).

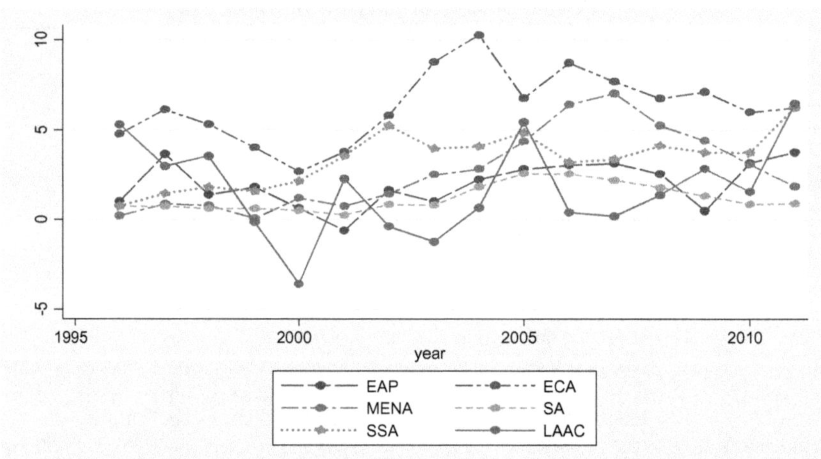

Figure 10.2 Time trend of globalization (FDI).

rights. Muslim countries located in MENA and SA regions have been showing upward trend since 2000 while ECA, EAP and SSA regions have a stagnant trend. Latin American countries have been showing a declining trend since 2000. Overall, women empowerment is indicating convergence over time across regions.

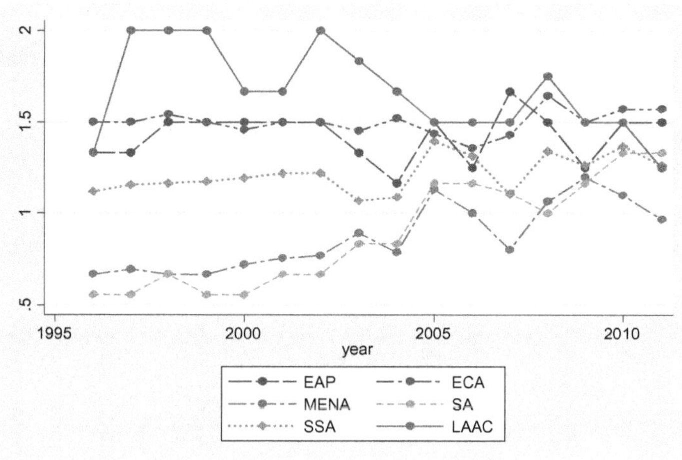

Figure 10.3 Trend of women empowerment.

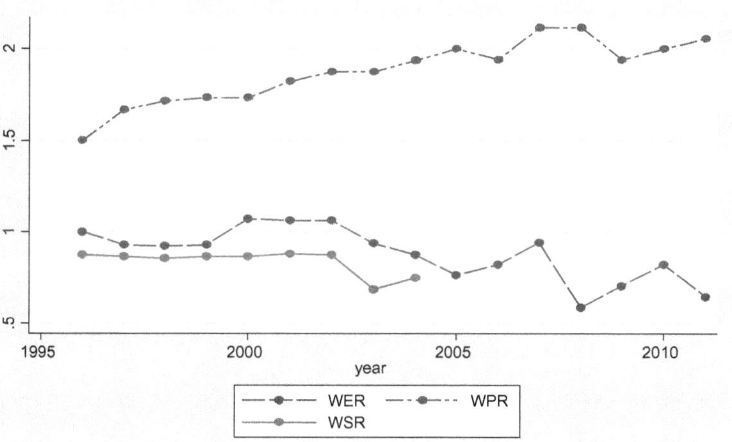

Figure 10.4 Time trend of women's rights in LICs.

Figure 10.4 demonstrates that women's political rights are the highest while social rights are the lowest in low-income countries (LICs). In the case of middle-income countries (MICs), Figure 10.5 exhibits that women's economic rights are declining, political rights are increasing and social rights are stagnant. For high-income countries (HICs), Figure 10.6 shows that, in 1990s political and social rights were lowest while economic rights

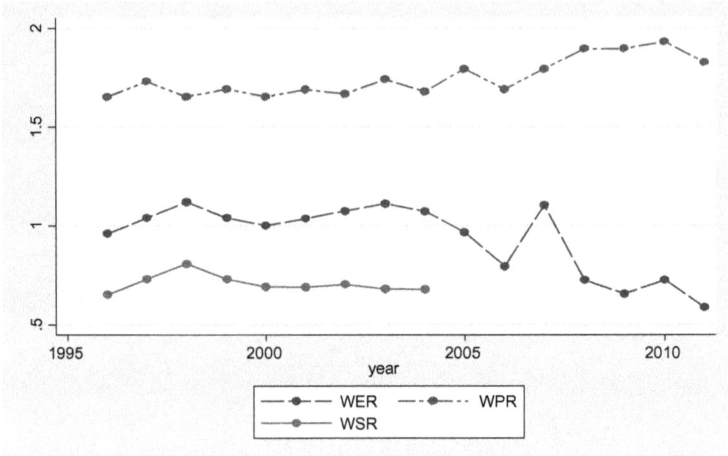

Figure 10.5 Time trend of women's rights in MICs.

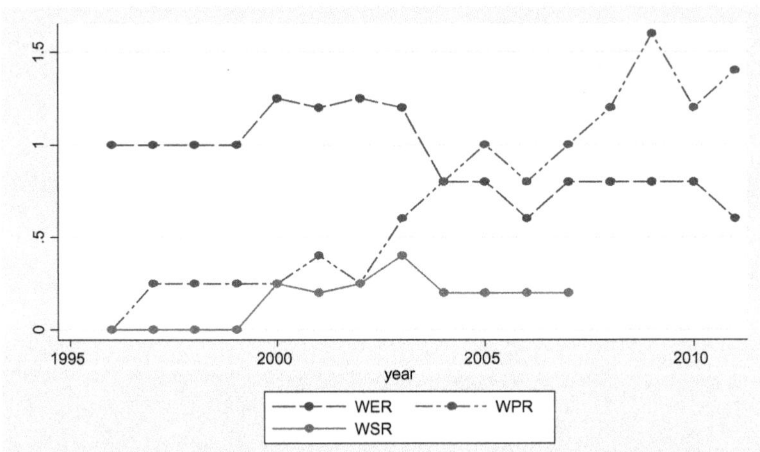

Figure 10.6 Time trend of women's rights in HICs.

were highest; however, over time political rights increased, economic rights fell and social rights remained stagnant. Thus, the picture of women empowerment in relation to the development stage is not promising.

Figure 10.7 shows that economic integration is increasing at a slower pace. LICs and HICs are showing an increasing trend while MICs are showing stagnant trend. Figure 10.8 shows that FDI inflows are high in

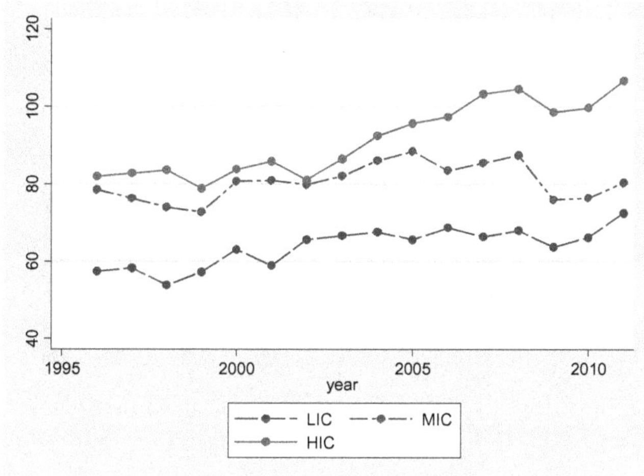

Figure 10.7 Time trend of globalization (trade).

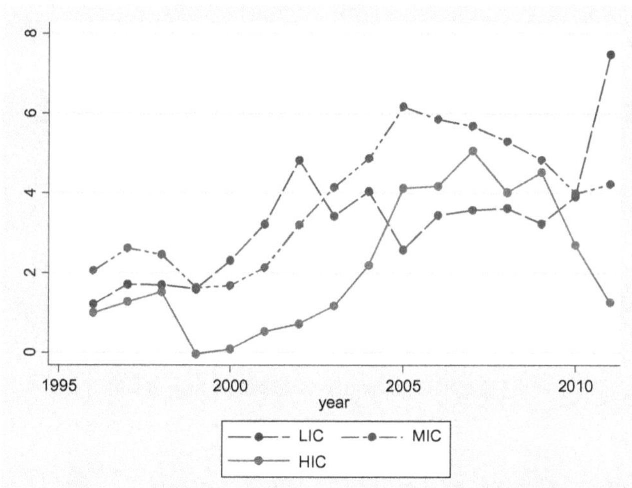

Figure 10.8 Time trend of globalization (FDI).

LICs, whereas the FDI inflows are low in HICs. Moreover, FDI inflows are highly volatile irrespective of the development level.

Figures 10.9–10.12 depict a cross-sectional comparison of women's rights in selected regions. Muslim countries in Central Asia show similar

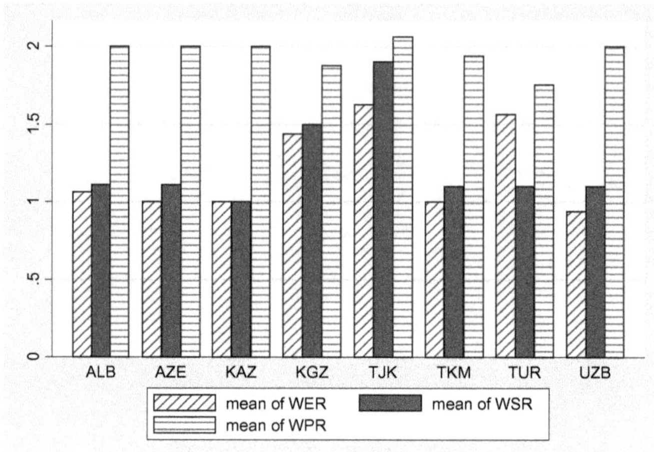

Figure 10.9 Central Asia.

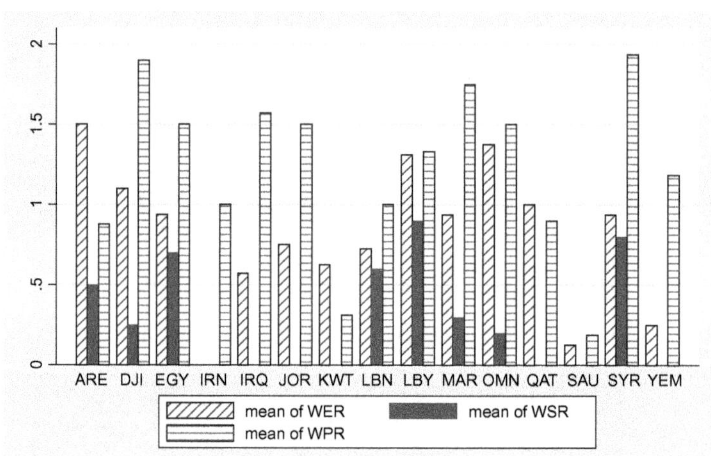

Figure 10.10 Middle East and North Africa.

pattern of women's rights. However, in other regions, women's rights show dissimilarity within a region.

Figures 10.13 and 10.14 indicate a regional comparison of globalization across different regions of the Muslim world. Economic globalization is lowest in the OIC countries located in South Asia, whereas globalization in other regions varies depending upon the measure of globalization. For

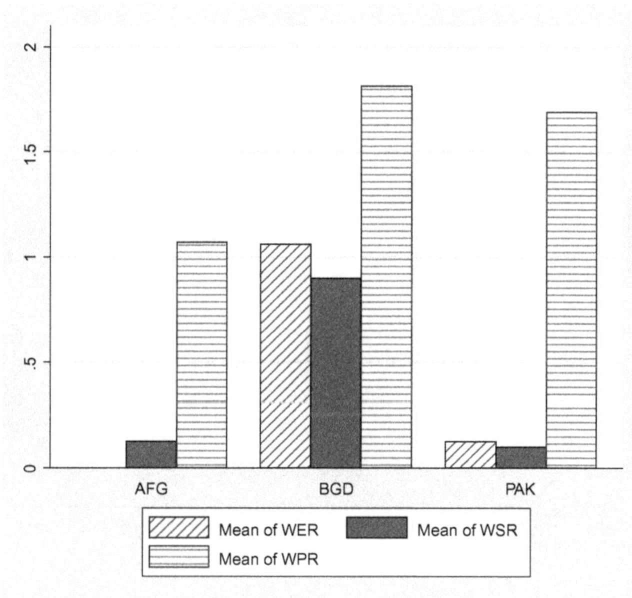

Figure 10.11 South Asia.

instance, FDI is highest in Central Asian countries while trade is highest in Latin American countries.

Finally, Figure 10.14 demonstrates a regional comparison of women's rights. It is evident that no region of the Muslim world falls in the highest category of women empowerment. South Asia comprises the lowest position in women's rights. It is noteworthy that South Asia is also the lowest in terms of economic integration.

10.2.2 The results

Column (1) of Table 10.5 shows that trade has a positive effect on women's economic rights. The coefficient of trade indicates that one unit increase in trade causes 0.01 unit increase in the higher order log-odds of women's economic rights. Column (2) includes an additional control of fertility that turns out to be negative and significant at the 1% significance level implying that one unit increase in the fertility of women causes 0.3 unit decreases in the higher-order log-odds of women's economic rights. The opportunity cost of working due to increase in the number of children causes negative effect on economic aspects of women life.

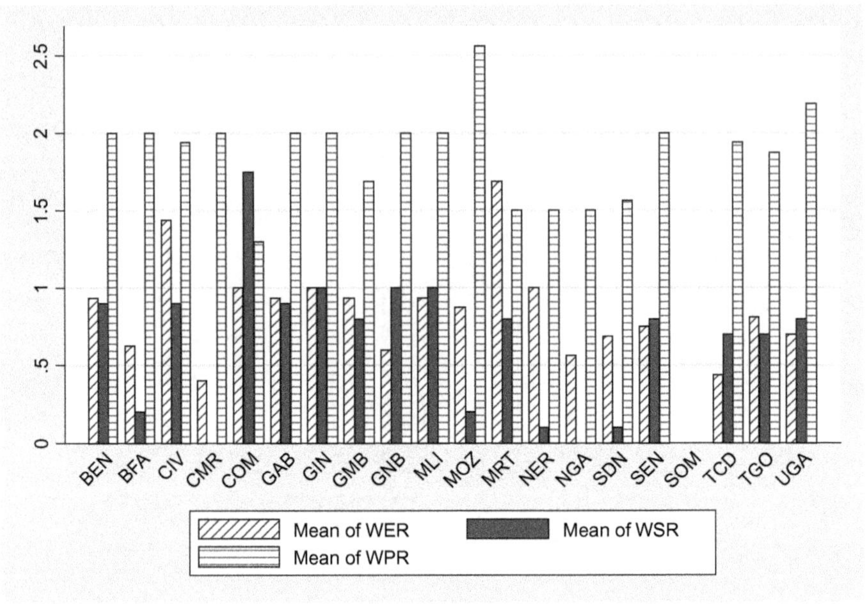

Figure 10.12 Sub-Saharan Africa.

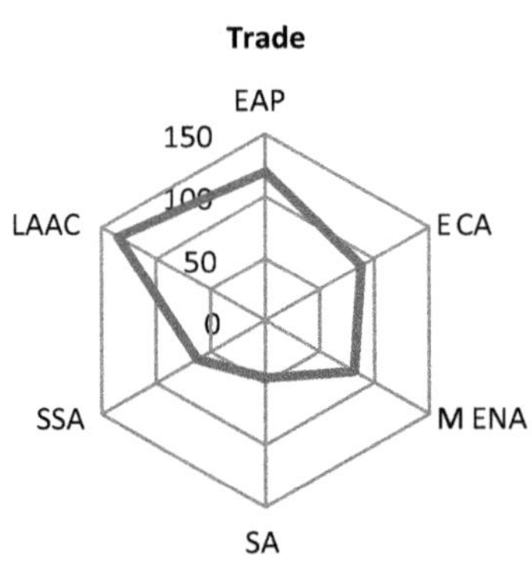

Figure 10.13 Regional classification of trade.

Columns 3 and 4 include additional controls of female labor force participation and female population, respectively. The increase in participation of women in labor force protects women's economic rights. The coefficient of female labor force participation is positive while the coefficient of female

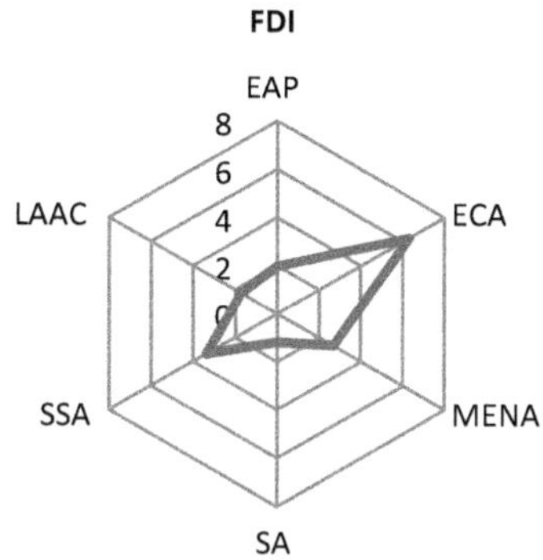

Figure 10.14 Regional classification of FDI.

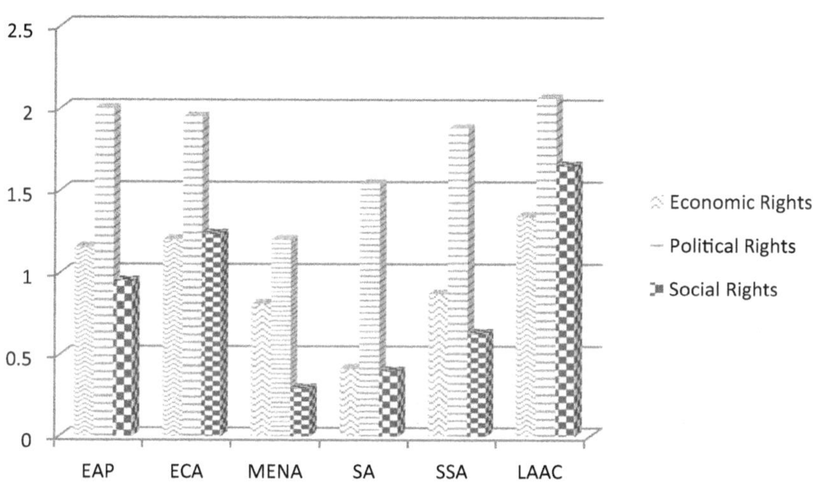

Figure 10.15 A regional comparison of women's rights.

population is negative. The coefficient of trade remains significant and positive.

All models include regional dummy variables to control for the regional heterogeneity. The dummy of MENA countries is a base category to evade the dummy trap. The dummy of South Asia is negative and significant at the 1% significance level, implying that the higher order log-odds of getting women's economic rights in the SA countries is about 0.7 unit less than those of the MENA countries. The dummy of all other regions is positive,

Table 10.5 Women's economic rights and globalization.

Variables	(1)	(2)	(3)	(4)
Per capita GDP	0.0901	−0.113	−0.103	−0.308**
	(0.0818)	(0.0982)	(0.101)	(0.128)
Democracy	0.0191	0.0151	0.0142	0.0155
	(0.0247)	(0.0251)	(0.0252)	(0.0253)
Trade	0.0106***	0.0118***	0.0118***	0.0111***
	(0.00276)	(0.00282)	(0.00282)	(0.00283)
Fertility	—	−0.381***	−0.374***	−0.433***
	—	(0.100)	(0.101)	(0.104)
Labor force (female)	—	—	0.00254	−0.00256
	—	—	(0.00639)	(0.00669)
Female population	—	—	—	−0.0857***
	—	—	—	(0.0320)
EAP	0.905**	0.472	0.436	0.784
	(0.448)	(0.467)	(0.476)	(0.498)
ECA	1.683***	1.167***	1.139***	1.365***
	(0.280)	(0.314)	(0.322)	(0.335)
LAAC	1.856***	1.320**	1.321**	1.516**
	(0.638)	(0.662)	(0.662)	(0.668)
SA	−0.602	−0.764*	−0.772*	−0.931**
	(0.404)	(0.413)	(0.414)	(0.418)
SSA	0.674**	1.245***	1.182***	1.412***
	(0.263)	(0.304)	(0.343)	(0.355)
Others	1.588***	1.421***	1.400***	1.604***
	(0.465)	(0.454)	(0.458)	(0.468)
Constant cut1	0.703	−2.189**	−2.034*	−8.039***
	(0.696)	(1.038)	(1.109)	(2.517)
Constant cut2	4.370***	1.528	1.682	−4.287*
	(0.726)	(1.042)	(1.112)	(2.497)
Constant cut3	8.479***	5.645***	5.799***	−0.165
	(1.012)	(1.256)	(1.315)	(2.591)
LR chi-squared (13)	113.73	128.43	128.58	135.70
P-value	0.000	0.000	0.000	0.000
Observations	721	721	721	721

Note: Standard errors are provided in parentheses (***$p < 0.01$, **$p < 0.05$, *$p < 0.1$).

implying that women's economic rights are least protected in the MENA countries.

Table 10.6 reports results for women's social rights. Column (1) shows that trade has a consistently positive and significant effect on women's social rights, implying that one unit increase in trade will cause 0.01 unit increase in higher order log-odds of getting women's social rights. The cuts show the intercepts of the categories of women's social rights and the cuts

Table 10.6 Women's social rights and globalization.

Variables	(1)	(2)	(3)	(4)
Per capita GDP	−0.262**	−0.547***	−0.521***	−0.626***
	(0.112)	(0.141)	(0.146)	(0.178)
Democracy	−0.000891	0.00737	0.00512	0.00733
	(0.0349)	(0.0350)	(0.0352)	(0.0355)
Trade	0.0113***	0.0137***	0.0138***	0.0136***
	(0.00356)	(0.00369)	(0.00370)	(0.00372)
Fertility	—	−0.511***	−0.499***	−0.539***
	—	(0.140)	(0.141)	(0.147)
Labor force (female)	—	—	0.00507	0.00357
	—	—	(0.00814)	(0.00825)
Female population	—	—	—	−0.0577
	—	—	—	(0.0549)
EAP	2.355***	1.658**	1.573**	1.698**
	(0.641)	(0.677)	(0.691)	(0.707)
ECA	4.212***	3.439***	3.384***	3.474***
	(0.490)	(0.525)	(0.533)	(0.540)
LAAC	5.203***	4.339***	4.342***	4.423***
	(0.860)	(0.918)	(0.923)	(0.930)
SA	0.885	0.630	0.624	0.525
	(0.541)	(0.553)	(0.557)	(0.568)
SSA	1.176***	1.948***	1.827***	1.959***
	(0.336)	(0.410)	(0.453)	(0.474)
Others	2.339***	2.151***	2.102***	2.191***
	(0.684)	(0.688)	(0.694)	(0.701)
Constant cut1	−0.263	−4.197***	−3.833**	−7.578*
	(0.938)	(1.427)	(1.538)	(3.914)
Constant cut2	4.451***	0.597	0.962	−2.765
	(1.010)	(1.447)	(1.558)	(3.900)
LR chi-squared	207.79	221.89	222.28	223.35
P-value	0.000	0.000	0.000	0.000
Observations	449	449	449	449

Note: Standard errors are provided in parentheses ($^{***}p < 0.01$, $^{**}p < 0.05$, $^{*}p < 0.1$)

are significant, implying that regressions are parallel. Table 10.7 reports the results for women's political rights. The effect of trade on political rights is consistently positive and significant in all models.

Finally, the impact of FDI is estimated, which is another measure of economic globalization. The empirical results are reported in the Appendix. The role of FDI is not promising as its effect turns out to be negative but insignificant in the case of economic and social rights of women. However, its effects on political rights are consistently positive and significant in all models (see Table 10.3A).

Table 10.7 Women's political rights and globalization.

Variables	(1)	(2)	(3)	(4)
Per capita GDP	−0.618***	−0.911***	−0.849***	−0.545***
	(0.0914)	(0.113)	(0.115)	(0.151)
Democracy	−0.0291	−0.0354	−0.0502	−0.0538*
	(0.0307)	(0.0310)	(0.0321)	(0.0321)
Trade	0.0133***	0.0159***	0.0179***	0.0201***
	(0.00349)	(0.00358)	(0.00369)	(0.00380)
Fertility	—	−0.529***	−0.476***	−0.395***
	—	(0.114)	(0.116)	(0.119)
Labor force (Female)	—	—	0.0681***	0.0799***
	—	—	(0.00955)	(0.0105)
Female population	—	—	—	0.107***
	—	—	—	(0.0341)
EAP	2.856***	2.315***	1.432*	0.960
	(0.636)	(0.663)	(0.772)	(0.758)
ECA	2.502***	1.938***	1.291***	0.981**
	(0.331)	(0.354)	(0.385)	(0.403)
LAAC	2.634***	1.910**	2.065**	1.859**
	(0.839)	(0.817)	(0.803)	(0.802)
SA	1.163**	1.035**	1.072**	1.434***
	(0.462)	(0.467)	(0.486)	(0.504)
SSA	1.621***	2.516***	1.155***	0.916**
	(0.277)	(0.346)	(0.376)	(0.382)
Others	2.643***	2.483***	1.938***	1.735**
	(0.641)	(0.665)	(0.748)	(0.773)
Constant cut1	−6.185***	−10.25***	−8.081***	−0.00296
	(0.812)	(1.230)	(1.250)	(2.858)
Constant cut2	−3.458***	−7.393***	−5.215***	2.917
	(0.746)	(1.148)	(1.188)	(2.852)
Constant cut3	2.511***	−1.265	1.771	10.02***
	(0.769)	(1.125)	(1.196)	(2.913)
LR chi2	258.02	279.92	339.88	349.87
P-value	0.000	0.000	0.000	0.000
Observations	728	728	728	728

Note: Standard errors are provided in parentheses (***$p < 0.01$, **$p < 0.05$, *$p < 0.1$).

10.3 Conclusion

Does globalization increase women empowerment across Muslim states? To answer this question, we have assembled a panel data of 52 OIC countries and applied the Order Logit method of estimation in this analysis. The results show that the effect of trade on all forms of women's rights is consistently positive and significant in all models. However, the effect of FDI on women's economic and social rights is not significant while FDI significantly improves the political rights of women.

We can conclude that globalization in terms of trade is an effective way to empower women in the Muslim world while the favorable effects of FDI are limited. Thus, OIC countries need to support economic integration in terms of trade, and simultaneously, they need to improve domestic conditions to attract stable flows of FDI. This chapter just focuses on economic globalization, whereas future research can focus on other dimensions of globalization such as social and political globalization.

Appendix

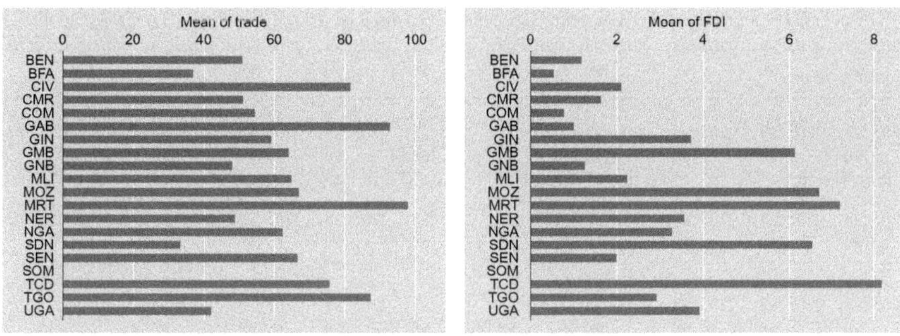

Figure 10.1A Trade and FDI in Sub-Saharan Africa.

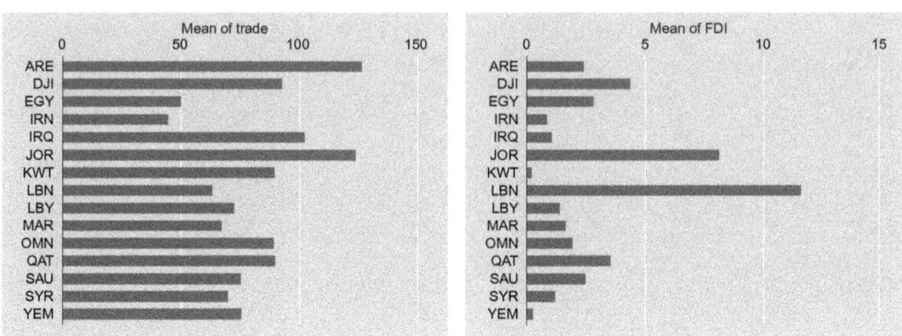

Figure 10.2A Trade and FDI in Middle East and North Africa.

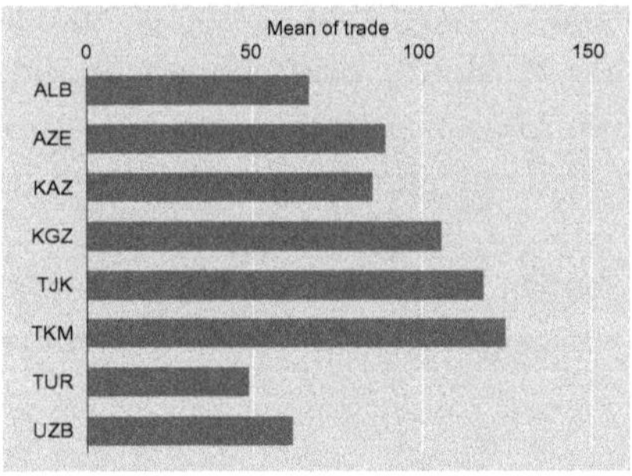

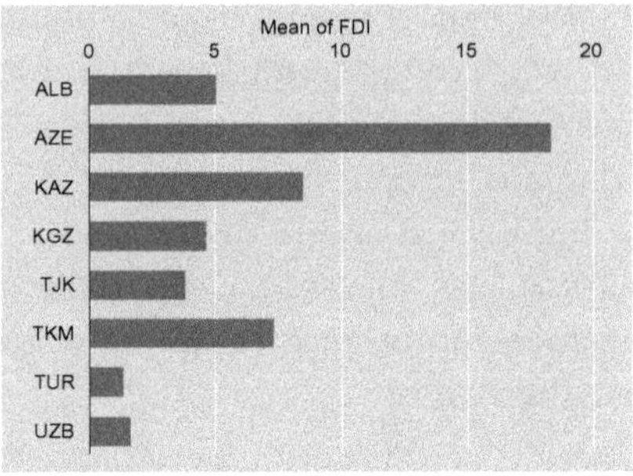

Figure 10.3A Trade and FDI in Central Asia.

Table 10.1A Women's economic rights and globalization (FDI).

Variables	(1)	(2)	(3)	(4)
Per capita GDP	0.211***	0.0759	0.101	−0.210*
	(0.0782)	(0.0928)	(0.0960)	(0.123)
Democracy	−0.00358	−0.00719	−0.00954	−0.00331
	(0.0232)	(0.0235)	(0.0237)	(0.0240)
FDI	−0.00716	−0.0122	−0.0131	−0.0127
	(0.0146)	(0.0146)	(0.0147)	(0.0147)
Fertility	—	−0.267***	−0.253**	−0.347***
	—	(0.0982)	(0.0992)	(0.102)
Labor force (female)	—	—	0.00645	−0.00146
	—	—	(0.00633)	(0.00666)
Female population	—	—	—	−0.123***
	—	—	—	(0.0305)
EAP	1.440***	1.170***	1.080**	1.524***
	(0.421)	(0.437)	(0.446)	(0.466)
ECA	1.827***	1.501***	1.435***	1.774***
	(0.273)	(0.300)	(0.306)	(0.322)
LAAC	2.013***	1.734***	1.750***	1.969***
	(0.456)	(0.469)	(0.469)	(0.474)
SA	−0.713*	−0.841**	−0.865**	−1.071***
	(0.397)	(0.404)	(0.406)	(0.409)
SSA	0.705***	1.113***	0.958***	1.326***
	(0.256)	(0.298)	(0.334)	(0.349)
Others	1.570***	1.467***	1.416***	1.728***
	(0.453)	(0.446)	(0.451)	(0.464)
Constant cut1	0.818	−1.221	−0.840	−9.553***
	(0.672)	(1.010)	(1.076)	(2.427)
Constant cut2	4.311***	2.291**	2.673**	−5.962**
	(0.699)	(1.019)	(1.086)	(2.403)
Constant cut3	8.426***	6.406***	6.786***	−1.836
	(0.992)	(1.237)	(1.293)	(2.499)
Observations	738	738	738	738

Note: Standard errors are provided in parentheses (***$p < 0.01$, **$p < 0.05$, *$p < 0.1$).

Table 10.2A Women's social rights and globalization (FDI).

Variables	(1)	(2)	(3)	(4)
Per capita GDP	−0.211**	−0.408***	−0.397***	−0.546***
	(0.107)	(0.129)	(0.135)	(0.173)
Democracy	−0.00741	−0.00364	−0.00480	−0.000291
	(0.0342)	(0.0344)	(0.0347)	(0.0352)
FDI	0.00352	−0.00206	−0.00255	−0.00216
	(0.0206)	(0.0205)	(0.0206)	(0.0206)
Fertility	—	−0.395***	−0.390***	−0.448***
	—	(0.135)	(0.136)	(0.144)
Labor force (Female)	—	—	0.00203	−0.000140
	—	—	(0.00810)	(0.00825)
Female population	—	—	—	−0.0707
	—	—	—	(0.0501)
EAP	2.951***	2.543***	2.512***	2.679***
	(0.620)	(0.633)	(0.645)	(0.657)
ECA	4.297***	3.759***	3.738***	3.858***
	(0.489)	(0.519)	(0.526)	(0.533)
LAAC	5.727***	5.233***	5.238***	5.323***
	(0.718)	(0.736)	(0.737)	(0.742)
SA	0.546	0.327	0.323	0.200
	(0.531)	(0.545)	(0.547)	(0.558)
SSA	1.009***	1.625***	1.580***	1.763***
	(0.335)	(0.407)	(0.446)	(0.471)
Others	2.269***	2.090***	2.073***	2.197***
	(0.674)	(0.678)	(0.681)	(0.690)
Constant cut1	−0.741	−3.732***	−3.596**	−8.337**
	(0.912)	(1.371)	(1.473)	(3.716)
Constant cut2	3.847***	0.893	1.028	−3.679
	(0.969)	(1.393)	(1.493)	(3.695)
Observations	447	447	447	447

Note: Standard errors are provided in parentheses (***$p < 0.01$, **$p < 0.05$, *$p < 0.1$).

Table 10.3A Women's political rights and globalization (FDI).

Variables	(1)	(2)	(3)	(4)
Per capita GDP	−0.577***	−0.774***	−0.713***	−0.351**
	(0.0867)	(0.105)	(0.106)	(0.150)
Democracy	−0.0582*	−0.0669**	−0.0898***	−0.0971***
	(0.0301)	(0.0303)	(0.0315)	(0.0317)
FDI	0.0566***	0.0459**	0.0501**	0.0550***
	(0.0181)	(0.0187)	(0.0194)	(0.0195)
Fertility	—	−0.398***	−0.356***	−0.249**
	—	(0.112)	(0.114)	(0.118)
Labor force (Female)	—	—	0.0713***	0.0835***
	—	—	(0.00961)	(0.0105)
Female population	—	—	—	0.114***
	—	—	—	(0.0340)
EAP	3.675***	3.342***	2.587***	2.233***
	(0.626)	(0.626)	(0.735)	(0.782)
ECA	2.496***	2.104***	1.433***	1.114***
	(0.331)	(0.348)	(0.382)	(0.397)
LAAC	4.114***	3.762***	4.219***	4.250***
	(0.652)	(0.660)	(0.699)	(0.720)
SA	0.905**	0.756*	0.680	1.028**
	(0.453)	(0.456)	(0.476)	(0.490)
SSA	1.614***	2.290***	0.934**	0.651*
	(0.274)	(0.339)	(0.374)	(0.380)
Others	2.598***	2.467***	1.999***	1.804***
	(0.613)	(0.642)	(0.674)	(0.695)
Constant cut1	−6.637***	−9.689***	−7.621***	1.172
	(0.800)	(1.199)	(1.218)	(2.875)
Constant cut2	−4.012***	−6.965***	−4.900***	3.959
	(0.731)	(1.121)	(1.158)	(2.875)
Constant cut3	1.912**	−1.018	2.017*	10.97***
	(0.744)	(1.113)	(1.189)	(2.937)
Observations	745	745	745	745

Note: Standard errors are provided in parentheses (***$p < 0.01$, **$p < 0.05$, *$p < 0.1$).

References

Becker, G. S. (1971), *The Economics of Discrimination* (2nd ed.), Chicago: University of Chicago.

Berik, G., Rodgers, Y. V. D. M. and Zveglich, J. E. (2004), International trade and gender wage discrimination: Evidence from East Asia. *Review of Development Economics*, 8(2), 237–254.

Bhagwati, J. (2004), *In Defence of Globalization*, Princeton: Princeton University.

Busse, M. and Spielmann, C. (2006), Gender inequality and trade. *Review of International Economics*, 14(3), 362–379.

Cagatay, N. and Ozler, S. (1995), Feminization of the labor force: The effects of long-term development and structural adjustment. *World Development*, 23(11), 1883–1894.

Chafetz, J. S. (1984), *Sex and Advantage — A Comparative, Macro-Structural Theory of Sex Stratification*, New Jersey: Rowman & Allanheld.

Cho, S. Y. (2011), Integrating Equality-Globalization, Women's Rights, Son Preference and Human Trafficking (No. 73). Courant Research Centre: Poverty, Equity and Growth-Discussion Papers.

Cingranelli, D. L. and Richards, D. L. (2010), The Cingranelli-Richards (CIRI) Human Rights Dataset. Available at http://www.humanrightsdata.org/. Accessed on 30 September 2017.

Duflo, E. (2012), Women empowerment and economic development. *Journal of Economic Literature*, 50(4), 1051–1079.

Enloe, C. H. (2007), *Globalization and Militarism: Feminists Make the Link*, Lanham, MD: Rowman & Littlefield.

Estes, R. J. and Tiliouine, H. (2016), Social progress in Islamic Societies: Achievements and challenges. In Bent Jesper Christensen and Carsten Kowalczyk (eds.), *The State of Social Progress of Islamic Societies*. Berlin: Springer International Publishing, pp. 69–106.

Gray, M. M., Kittilson, M. C. and Sandholtz, W. (2006), Women and globalization: A study of 180 countries, 1975–2000. *International Organization*, 60(2), 293–333.

Howes, C. and Singh, A. (1995), Long-term trends in the world economy: The gender dimension. *World Development*, 23(11), 1895–1911.

Htun, M. and Weldon, S. L. (2010), When do governments promote women's rights? A framework for the comparative analysis of sex equality policy. *Perspectives on Politics*, 8(1), 207–216.

Klein, N. (2007), *The Shock Doctrine: The Rise of Disaster Capitalism*, London: Penguin Books.

Majeed, M. T. (2015), Distributional consequences of globalization: Is Organization of the Islamic Conference countries different? *The International Trade Journal*, 29(3), 1–20.

Majeed, M. T. and Malik, A. (2017), Selling souls: An empirical analysis of human trafficking and globalization. *Pakistan Journal of Commerce & Social Sciences*, 11(1), 452–487.

Neumayer, E. and De Soysa, I. (2011), Globalization and the empowerment of women: An analysis of spatial dependence via trade and foreign direct investment. *World Development*, 39(7), 1065–1075.

Oostendorp, R. H. (2009), Globalization and the gender wage gap. *The World Bank Economic Review*, 23(1), 141–161.

Parpart, J. L., Rai, S. M. and Staudt, K. (eds.) (2002), *Rethinking Empowerment: Gender and Development in a Global/Local World*, London: Routledge.

Pearson, R. and Mitter, S. (1993), Employment and working conditions of low-skilled information-processing workers in less developed countries. *International Labour Review*, 132, 49.

Shiva, V. (2005), *The Polarized World of Globalization*, New York: Global Policy Forum.

Spar, D. (1998), The spotlight and the Bottom Line: How multinationals export human rights. *Foreign Affairs*, 77, 7–12.

Spar, D. and Yoffie, D. (1999), Multinational enterprises and the prospects for justice. *Journal of International Affairs*, 52(2), 557–581.

Tejani, S. and Milberg, W. (2010), Global defeminization? Industrial upgrading, occupational segmentation and manufacturing employment in middle-income countries. Schwartz Center for Economic Policy Analysis Working Paper, Schwartz Center for Economic Policy Analysis, New York.

Van Staveren, I., Elson, D., Grown, C. and Çağatay, N. (2007), *The Feminist Economics of Trade*, Oxon: Routledge.

Villarreal, A. and Yu, W. H. (2007), Economic globalization and women's employment: The case of manufacturing in Mexico. *American Sociological Review*, 72(3), 365–389.

Wacker, K. M., Cooray, A. and Gaddis, I. (2017), Globalization and Female Labor Force Participation in Developing Countries: An Empirical (Re-) Assessment. In Bent Jesper Christensen and Carsten Kowalczyk (eds.), *Globalization*. Springer Berlin Heidelberg, pp. 545–583.

Ward, K. B. (1984), *Women in the World-System*, New York: Praeger.

Wichterich, C. (2000), *The Globalized Woman: Reports from a Future of Inequality*, London: Zed Books.

Wood, A. (1991), North–South trade and female labour in manufacturing: An asymmetry. *The Journal of Development Studies*, 27(2), 168–189.

Chapter 11

Islamic Paradigm of Women's Socio-Economic Empowerment: Ideals and Realities

Muhammad Iqbal Anjum

Abstract

This chapter highlights the truth that Islam aims at ensuring equal rights for men and women as well as equal valuation of the work of women and men. It asserts that Islam itself does not generate inequality and low levels of women's development and empowerment.

Historically, the advent and implementation of the Islamic paradigm ensured the restoration and protection of the women's fundamental individual and socio-economic rights,[1] which were mercilessly denied in the pre-Islamic times of ignorance called *Jahiliyyah* — the era of pagan Arabs. Therefore, the Islamic paradigm ensured the socio-economic empowerment of women in both transcendental and mundane realms in the Golden Age of Islam.

Keywords: Islam, Women's empowerment, Socio-economic Rights, Ideals, Realities

"No economy can grow to its full potential unless both women and men participate fully. As half the world's population, women have an equal role in driving economic growth."

"If women have equal opportunities to reach their full potential, the world would not only be fairer, it would be more prosperous as well."

Kristalina Georgieva, interim President, World Bank

[1]For example, right of dignified physical survival/development/empowerment, right to get education, right of ownership, right to conduct business and right to inherit.

11.1 Prologue

After the Golden Age of Islam, the socio-economic progress of women has been continuously compromised in the regions of the Islamic world in frameworks of capitalist and communist imperial regimes institutionalized earlier in the guise of colonialism and later in the guise of neocolonialism and the post-colonialism.

This chapter's discourse on the Islamic paradigm of women's socio-economic empowerment is warranted by facts that women are poorer than men in general, and, therefore, even the secular development economists have acknowledged the central role of the women in development of nations.[2] According to development economists, investment in women has numerous progressive effects on individuals, families, national labor force, national income and national standard of living. Therefore, they have been advocating acceleration of women's socio-economic empowerment and development. Their pro-women empowerment discourses have eventually culminated in universal acknowledgment of women's socio-economic empowerment as a highly prioritized Millennium Development (Policy) Goal (MDG) — a reflection of the universal consensus of all nations of the world on the empowerment of women. Because this MDG was only partially achieved by the end of 2015 and currently it is one of the United Nations Organization's Sustainable Development Goals (SDGs) targeted to be achieved by the year 2030, now it is high time to present a pertinent Islamic paradigm of women's socio-economic empowerment as an alternative to the secular paradigm of women empowerment along with an overview of the contemporary ground realities and the recent progress made in the arena of women's socio-economic development as well as political empowerment.

Against the aforementioned background, Section 11.2 contributes the literature review on the subject. Section 11.3 presents an overview of the contemporary socio-economic disempowerment in the world. Section 11.4 contributes the Islamic paradigm of women empowerment as an embodiment of original Islamic ideals of women empowerment. Subsection (a) identifies causes of women disempowerment in the contemporary Islamic countries. Subsection (b) portrays two stages of the feminist movement.

[2]Development economists especially highlight the "role of women as mothers, who are embodiment of altruism for developing personalities of their children and, thereby, building a robust national labor force. They argue, mothers tend to spend a significantly higher fraction of income under their control for the benefit of their children than fathers" (Todaro and Smith 2012, p. 22).

Finally, Section 11.5 presents conclusions and pertinent policy recommendations for accelerating the process of socio-economic empowerment of women in the Islamic world in particular and in the world as a whole in general.

11.2 Literature review

There is a large volume of diverse literature on women empowerment throughout the world. This literature points to the universal consensus on the socio-economic imperatives of women development and empowerment. It deplores the contemporary as well as the past widespread regressive global phenomena of socio-economic and political disempowerment of masses of women in the human history and, in this context, it generally acknowledges as well as appreciates the uniquely matchless revolutionary practical contributions of Islam toward emancipation, empowerment and development of women since the advent of the Islamic world's Golden Age, when generally the rest of the world and especially the Western world were experiencing the problems of trivialization, humiliation, harassment, criminalization, victimization, enslavement, expropriation, exploitation, impoverishment, underdevelopment and disempowerment of women in the ancient Dark Civilizations — Greek civilization, Hindu civilization, Chinese civilization and the Western civilization in their Dark Ages. An overview of certain pertinent pieces of literature on women empowerment is being presented in the following paragraphs.

There is consensus of the Islamic scholars that theoretically Islam guarantees equal rights of education to both men and women without any discrimination (for example, Yamani (1997), Ghazi (2008), Hamid (2011), Nasir and Akhtar (2016) and Omar (2018)).

Mutahhari (1981) highlights the fact that movement for women's rights originated from the 17th century movement for human rights, which identifies and emphasizes a series of natural, undeniable and inalienable human rights and freedoms such as human freedoms and equality of all humans. He identifies culmination of the movement for human rights in emergence of both the revolutionary movements of socialism in the 19th century and the feminist movements for women's rights, which raised the slogan of women freedoms and equal human rights in the 20th century and generated a global consensus on the United Nations' Universal Declaration of Human Rights. This declaration emphasizes freedom — liberty — and equality of women with men such that the human rights are incomplete and meaningless without ensuring women rights of liberty and equality of women with men (Mutahhari, 1981). It asserts that women, as humans, are entitled to all rights of men (Mutahhari, 1981). While incisively criticizing the feminist movement for ignoring the significance of the system of family rights, he also identifies the feminist movement's wrong approach of defining gender equality as similarity and uniformity of men and women realized through imperfect and deficient women's practices of imitating the perfect and ideal personalities of men in spite of their inherent natural dissimilarities and different positions necessitating their different capabilities, roles, rights and responsibilities, emphasizing only the identity of woman as a human being, and deemphasizing the fact that she is indeed a women as well. He criticizes as well as laments the capitalist industrialists' business tactics of using the feminist slogans of women empowerment, women's freedoms and women's equality with men through practices of luring them to come out of their homes for working in industries at lower wages than wages demanded by male workers for increasing their industrial profits by exploiting the vulnerable female workers and, thereby, weakening and eventually corrupting as well as destroying their families in the Europe. He paraphrases a genuine critique of the aforementioned wrong feminist approach of emancipation and empowerment of woman based on egalitarianism and woman's freedoms, "They intended to beautify her eyebrows, but deprived her of her eyesight ... " He advocates the validity of the Islamic approach to human rights according to which men and women are Islamically blessed with their respective natural human rights exactly according to the complementary nature of their personalities as men and women. In this context, he argues:

> Man and women are two stars with their distinct orbits within which they should move.
>
> "It is not given to the sun to overtake the moon, nor can the night outpace the day ... Each in its orbit floats." (The Holy Quran Surah Yasin: 36, 40)
>
> Their happiness, as well as the happiness of the whole human society, depends on the condition that they move in their respective orbits. Liberty and equality can be useful only if both the sexes follow their normal and natural courses.

For ensuring growth and development in the contemporary Muslim world, Timmer and McClelland (2008) highlight the developmental role of women to be realized through socio-economic and political empowerment of women and the corresponding policy imperatives of increasing the participation of women in the labor force, increasing the integration of women in society, and increasing the facilities of both microfinance for women and access of women to credit. In the context of low level of the women empowerment in the contemporary Muslim world, they lament the empirical facts of generally low status of women in the societies, low female literacy rates, low female labor force participation rates, low proportion of women borrowers to total borrowers having actual access to the facility of microfinance, low female life expectancy and low proportion of female seats in the parliament. In light of the empirical evidence, they find that women do not generally have economic or political parity with men in most Muslim countries.

Hamid (2011) asserts that Islamic *Shari'ah* acknowledges woman as a completely independent personality and, accordingly, highlights numerous pertinent dimensions of the revolutionary empowerment of women accomplished by Islam as reflections of facts that the *Shari'ah* views women as the spiritual and intellectual equals of men. He asserts, "If a Muslim is engaged seriously with his religion, his conscience would never be at ease if there is gender injustice in his society or country ... In Islamic law, all persons are equal before the law and are entitled to equal protection of the law. It prohibits any kind of discrimination and guarantees equal and effective protection to all against any discrimination on the grounds of race, color, sex, religion etc. When it states that all are equal it implies that no distinction should be made between male and female and between the ruler and the ruled." (Hamid, 2011, pp. 146–147). Especially, he asserts that Islam has conferred equal political rights on both men and women and has, thereby politically empowered the women as well along with the Islamic accomplishment of socio-economic empowerment of women particularly through the Islamic right of individual freedom of a woman, the Islamic right of women to get education, the Islamic right of women to own and trade — buy, sell and transfer — the property, the Islamic law of marriage requiring consent of spouses, the Islamic law of inheritance guaranteeing rights of women to inherit the property of their relatives and the Islamic law of evidence according to which generally the testimony of a woman is equal to that of a man. In the context of actual Islamic accomplishment of socio-economic empowerment/development of woman, he concludes, "In Islam a woman is a completely independent personality. She can contract or bequest in her own name. She has perfect liberty to choose her husband subject to the restriction imposed by religion regarding the choice of spouse.

This was a revolutionary step keeping in view the prejudices the pagan society of pre-Islamic Arabia had against their female children, whom it is said, they used to bury alive. The Messenger of Allah was totally opposed to this practice" (Hamid 2011, p. 162).

Nasir and Akhtar (2016) document an incisive critique and rebuttal of the secularists'/feminists' claim that Islam has been regressive in its approach applied for addressing the issue of role of women. They illustrate the glorious contribution of the Islamic movement of human empowerment and development especially toward academic, social, economic and administrative empowerment of women in the early Islamic era by means of practically acknowledging as well as guaranteeing the rights of life and education of women for their academic development through emancipation of women from ignorance and professional development as well as their right of earning livelihood. They also highlight the so-called Western Cradle of civilization, Greece's unjust treatment of women (for example, ancient Greeks considered women as child-bearing slaves, deprived them of their education, kept them (as wives) secluded in homes and gave them few rights) and Rome's legal perception regarding women as imbeciles, which culminated in paralysis of the feminine section of society. They pointed to the Western clergy's dogmatic perception of woman and devils being the same two sides of the same image — the belief that the women caused the human expulsion from paradise — and its culmination in severe victimization, punishment, imprisonment and executions of women. Similarly, they alluded to Hinduism's characterization of women acts of remarrying as crimes and denial of property rights to women until the passage of Hindu Code Bill in 1956. In light of a verse of the Holy *Qur'an*, they argue that the Final Holy Prophet Muhammad (Peace Be Upon Him) and earlier Prophets (Peace Be Upon Them) of Islam did not discriminate on the basis of gender because they were aware of the justice-based rights of humans and that later the behavior of the followers of the earlier Holy Prophets (Peace Be Upon Them) toward women deteriorated to baser levels. They highlight the progressive and egalitarian Islamic approach of liberally granting property rights to women. They document the fact that there were only five literate women in Mecca before the advent of Islam. While highlighting the glorious contribution of Islam toward the emancipation of the then enslaved women from slavery to both ignorance and humans, they refer to the inspiring Saying of the Holy Prophet Muhammad (Peace Be Upon Him), "Whosoever possessed a female servant (slave girl), and brought her up well and educated her well, then set her free and arranged her marriage would get twice the reward" (Hanbal). In the context of illustrating the fact of the Islamic significance of education of women, they mention the fact that the Holy Prophet Muhammad (Peace Be Upon Him) dedicated one of seven days in the weeks for imparting knowledge to women in response to their request and that some of his (Peace Be Upon Him) wives[3] [Allah Pleased With Them All] became authority in scholarship and knowledge, imparted knowledge to a large number women as well as men, and issued Islamic legal judgments — for example, one-fourth of orders of the Islamic *Shari'ah* (law) were narrated by Hazrat Ayesha (Allah Pleased With Her).

Abdul Mannan (1986) argues that the full implementation of the Islamic law of inheritance in its letter and spirit enriches women and enables them to have their greater participation in the economic activity in the three possible ways; (a) Islamic law of inheritance will increase the probability of greater participation of women in economic activity as they can own, possess, enter a profession, join an industry and enter into contracts in their own name while following the Islamic laws. (b) Islamic law of inheritance will increase possibilities of participation of women in education and training by women. (c) Islamic law of inheritance would increase the probability of better start in life by the women and will have a multiplier effect in augmenting level of income of society. According to his opinion, women are not only equally entitled to benefit from the Islamic social security measure of *Zakat* but are also free to invest their resources through partnership arrangements of *Musharikah* and *Mudharabah*.

Omar (2018) presents a concise objective critique of the socio-economic status, rights, roles and practical experiences of women in realms of different ideologies, religions, civilizations, societies and economic systems prevalent in the different phases of the entire history of humanity. She identifies the derogatory status of women being salable, who were treated as salable slaves and were generally denied their rights of education, ownership, trading and civil rights in the Greek Empire. She points to various civilizations' general derogatory treatment of women as imbeciles, inferiors and completely subordinate to the absolute authority of men, who had the right to kill the women.[4] She mentions religious views of Judaism and Christianity

[3]For example, Hazrat Ayesha (Allah Pleased with Her) and Hazrat Um-e-Salma (Allah Pleased with Her).

[4]For example, Roman civilization, Chinese civilization, Hindu civilization, Persian civilization and pre-Islamic pagan Arab civilization.

according to which women are sinful, devoid of right of inheritance in presence of male inheritors, a source of original sin, and occasionally filthy, impure and /untouchable. Against this historical background, she highlights the revolutionary emancipation and empowerment of women by Islam, which legally guarantees and protects numerous sanctified personal and civil rights of her life, survival, honor, property, trading, investment, inheritance, education, work/employment for livelihood, marriage, separation from husband, custody of children, etc.

11.3 An overview of contemporary realities of socio-economic disempowerment in the world

Empirical analysis of a total number of 189 national economies generated the following pertinent empirical findings on the subject documented in the International Bank for Reconstruction and Development's Annual Report entitled *Women, Business and the Law 2018*:

(a) Over 2.7 billion women in the world are restricted from having same choice of jobs as men.
(b) A total of 104 national economies continue to place restrictions on women's employment.
(c) About 60% of the national economies do not mandate equal pay for work of equal value.
(d) The Middle Eastern and North African women had fewer than half of the rights of men — a reflection of serious problem of socio-economic disempowerment of women in the certain contemporary Muslim countries of the Middle East and North Africa.

The aforementioned facts being the indicators of widespread socio-economic disempowerment of women in the world point to the imperative of launching a revolutionary proactive global pro-women program of social economic and political reforms for accelerating women's socio-economic empowerment and development.

11.4 Islamic paradigm of women empowerment as an embodiment of original Islamic ideals of women empowerment

In light of the Islamic worldview originating from the Holy *Qur'an*, Allah (*Subhanuhu Wa Ta'ala*) — The Only One Creator and Master of the entire universe including humanity — miraculously created the first man and the

Holy Prophet Adam (Peace Be Upon Him) from clay and breathed soul in him (Peace Be Upon Him) as well as appointed him (Peace Be Upon Him) and his children (Women as well as Men) as His vicegerents on the Earth for worshiping Him (*Subhanuhu Wa Ta'ala*):

> "Verily, I am going to place mankind generations after generations on earth.' They said: 'Will You place therein those who will make mischief therein and shed blood, while we glorify You with praises and thanks and sanctify You.' God said: 'I know that which you do not know." (The Holy *Qur'an*: 2:30)
>
> "Truly, I am going to create man from clay. So when I have fashioned him and breathed into him (his) soul created by Me. Then you fall down prostrate to him." (The Holy *Qur'an* 38:71–72)
>
> "And (remember) when your Lord said to the angels: 'I am going to create a human (Adam) from sounding clay of altered black smooth mud. So when I have fashioned him and breathed into him (his) soul created by Me, then you fall down prostrate to him." (The Holy *Qur'an*: 71–72)
>
> "...Prostrate to Adam and they prostrated except *Iblees* (Satan)...." (The Holy *Qur'an*: 7:11)
>
> "O Mankind fear your Lord, Who created you from a single person, and from him He created his mate and from the twain He spread abroad many men and women. So fear Allah by Whom you demand (your rights) of one another, and fear (breaking) kinship of wombs.. Surely Allah is ever watchful ever over you." (The Holy *Qur'an*: 4:1)
>
> "Indeed, the example of Jesus [his creation] to Allah is like that of Adam. He created him from dust; then He said to him, 'Be', and he came into being." (The Holy *Qur'an*: 3:59)

Then Allah (*Subhanuhu Wa Ta'ala*) created the first women Eve (Peace Be Upon Her) from Adam (Peace Be Upon Him) as well as created other men and women [first from Eve (Peace Be Upon Her) and later from other women] as highly esteemed and privileged personalities as mothers having paradise positioned beneath their feet for their children and, therefore, commanding the unconditional/indisputable respect of all humans — of all generations and times as implied by the following *Ahadith* (Sayings) of the Holy Prophet Muhammad (Peace Be Upon Him):

> The Prophet Muhammad said, may Allah's peace and blessings be upon him: Your Heaven lies under the feet of your mother (Ahmad, Nasai).
>
> A man came to the Prophet and said, 'O Messenger of God! Who among the people is the most worthy of my good companionship? The Prophet said: Your mother. The man said, 'Then who?' The Prophet said: Then

> your mother. The man further asked, 'Then who?' The Prophet said: Then your mother. The man asked again, 'Then who?' The Prophet said: Then your father." (Bukhari, Muslim)

Therefore, both men and women are not only equally sacred, dignified and exalted spiritual personalities but also guardians, protectors, allies and supporters — complements — of one another in their numerous roles at micro level of family as a basic unit of the Islamic human society and at macro levels of the Islamic global human family, tribe, society, social system, *Ummah*, polity and economy as the Holy *Qur'an* mentions the whole mankind as a tribe of the Holy Prophet Adam (Peace Be Upon Him) and highlights believing men as well as believing women as allies and supporters of one another:

> "The believing men and believing women are allies of one another. They enjoin what is right and forbid what is wrong and establish prayer and give *zakah* and obey Allah and His Messenger. Those — Allah will have mercy upon them. Indeed, Allah is Exalted in Might and Wise." (The Holy *Qur'an*: 9, 71)

For ensuring just rewards of works of both men and women and, thereby, guaranteeing all-encompassing justice — including comprehensive socio-economic justice for both men and women, Allah (*Subhanuhu Wa Ta'ala*) never allows the socio-economic exploitation of women by men and the socio-economic exploitation of men by women.

> "And their Lord responded to them, "Never will I allow to be lost the work of [any] worker among you, whether male or female; you are of one another." (The Holy *Qur'an*: 3, 195)

Islam ensures security of all men and women by ensuring peace on Earth and, thereby, guaranteeing their security in light of the following prediction of the Holy Prophet (Peace Be Upon), which was made in the very initial phase of spread of Islam and which proved true in the later period of dominance of Islam, mentioned in the authentic Collections of His (Peace Be Upon Him) *Ahadith* (Sayings) documented by Imam Bukhari and Imam Abu Daud:

> The Holy Prophet (Peace Be Upon Him) addressed Adi Ibn Hatim, "O Adi you are reluctant to accept the truthful Deen because Muslim nation is poor and no one takes care of it. But you will see that Muslims will assume the control of treasuries of Kisra Ibn HurMuz. Yes, Kisra Ibn HurMuz, and there will be such a great abundance of wealth that

> when wealth will be given to people, they will refuse to take it, and Muslims will be using the white palace of Kisra Ibn HurMuz ... O Adi, have you seen Herah ... O Adi, (I) swear in the name of that Who is controller of my life. That time is about to come when a lonely women rider will come from Herah and will walk around the Ka'ba and no one will raise eye to look at her. After a number of years Adi (May Allah be Pleased With Him) reported and confirmed that a women rider walked around Ka'ba and similarly returned to her territory/ region."
>
> Once, during the days of trouble and torture in Makkah, I went to God's Messenger, who was sitting in the shade of the Ka'ba. I was still a slave in the hands of the Makkans then. They inflicted on me severe tortures. Unable to endure those tortures any more, I requested God's Messenger to pray to God for help and salvation. But he turned towards me and said: By God, previous communities had to endure more pitiless tortures. Some of them were made to lie in ditches and cut in two with saws but this did not make them forsake their faith. They were skinned alive but they never became weak against the enemy. Surely God will perfect this religion, but you display undue haste. A day will come when a woman will travel alone by herself from San'a to Hadramawt fearing nothing but wild beasts. However, you show impatience. Khubab concluded: By God, what God's Messenger predicted that day, have all come true. I have personally witnessed it all."

In the humanitarian framework of the fundamental objectives of Islam (*Al-Maqasid Al-Shari'ah*) emphasizing the sacred imperative of ensuring protection, defense and development of life — human personality — religion, intellect, wealth and children of all humans (both men and women of all ages), Islam effectively and constructively integrates women with the mainstream of overall universal human society, social system and economy not only by unifying them on the plane of their social existence in the ideally peaceful as well as absolutely tension-free framework of their perpetual common practice of worshiping Allah (*Subhanuhu Wa Ta'ala*) in accordance with its holistic approach of treating all Muslims as living parts of a living human body which do not harm one another, truly feel as well as share their individual pain as well as pleasure, and genuinely mutually support one another to relieve each other of their individual socio-economic pains and hardships in light of the following universal teachings of the Holy Prophet Muhammad (Peace be Upon Him) included in his (Peace Be Upon Him) farewell address:

> "O People, just as you regard this month, this day, this city as sacred, so regard the life and property of every Muslim as sacred trust ... Return

> the goods entrusted to you to their rightful owners. Remember you have taken them as your wives only under Allah's trust and with His permission. If they abide by your right then to them belongs the right to be fed and clothed in kindness. Do treat your women well and be kind to them for they are your partners and committed helpers and it is your right that they do not make friends with any of whom you do not approve, as well as never to be unchaste."

In this manner, Islam precludes any possibility of discrimination, exploitation, harm and damage of both women by men and men by women by conferring relatively greater personal as well as spiritual privileges and esteem on women than the personal as well as spiritual esteem and privileges conferred on men while generally bestowing, protecting and promoting equal human socio-economic, educational and political rights side by side with the assignment of their respective Islamic individual as well as joint responsibilities of both men and women in the framework of the universal Islamic system.

Here it is pertinent to acknowledge that migration and mobility is regarded as investment in human capital having practical returns. After being guaranteed the individual and collective security of both men and women by the Islamic state and its system as this security is warranted by women's socio-economic vulnerabilities and imperative, women can safely journey and migrate from the point of view of fulfilling their Islamic socio-economic responsibilities related to the alleviation of their socio-economic hardships in light of the insight emanating from the following verse of the Holy *Qur'an*:

> "Indeed, those whom the angels take [in death] while wronging themselves — [the angels] will say, 'In what [condition] were you?' They will say, 'We were oppressed in the land.' The angels will say, 'Was not the earth of Allah spacious [enough] for you to emigrate therein?' For those, their refuge is Hell — and evil it is as a destination." (The Holy *Qur'an*: 4, 97)

Their Islamically sanctified, protected and advanced individual lives, Islamic religion/intellect/marriage (*Nikah*)-based prerogative of having children and future generations in the framework of family and wealth as well as economic rights, ownership rights, inheritance rights, educational rights, entrepreneurial rights, working rights as well as their Islamically warranted and guaranteed and secured freedom of mobility, movement, travel, migration within the borderless jurisdiction of the peaceful universal

Islamic state are potential vehicles of their religious and socio-economic success, development and empowerment in light of the following relevant verses of the Holy *Qur'an*:

> "For men is a share of what the parents and close relatives leave, and for women is a share of what the parents and close relatives leave, be it little or much — an obligatory share." (The Holy *Qur'an*: 4, 7)
>
> And their Lord responded to them, "Never will I allow to be lost the work of [any] worker among you, whether male or female; you are of one another. So those who emigrated or were evicted from their homes or were harmed in My cause or fought or were killed — I will surely remove from them their misdeeds, and I will surely admit them to gardens beneath which rivers flow as reward from Allah, and Allah has with Him the best reward." (The Holy *Qur'an*: 3, 195)
>
> "And whoever emigrates for the cause of Allah will find on the earth many [alternative] locations and abundance. And whoever leaves his home as an emigrant to Allah and His Messenger and then death overtakes him — his reward has already become incumbent upon Allah. And Allah is ever Forgiving and Merciful." (The Holy *Qur'an*: 4, 100)

This scenario culminates in perfect harmony, cohesion and solidarity among all humans in all walks of multi-dimensional life of all humans (men and women) of all ages in their perpetual blissful simultaneous submission to Allah (*Subhanuhu Wa Ta'ala*) and their life-long worship of Allah (*Subhanuhu Wa Ta'ala*). Its enviable dazzling living illustration is the perfectly peaceful coexistence of millions of men and women of all ages, colors, languages, tribes, regions and countries during a long foreign journey for accomplishing the sacred Islamic duty of Hajj, which is indeed a glorious practical long-term refresher course for peaceful coexistence and spiritual development of all Muslim men and women throughout their entire lives in all parts of the world. This ideally peaceful scenario eventually culminates in preclusion and nonexistence of all types of gender-based socio-economic stereotypes, injustice, discrimination, exploitation, tensions, exploitation, tensions, conflicts, violence and feminism.

In sharp contrast to both the practical denial of the fundamental rights of women to even physically live and survive in the pre-Islamic times of widespread darkness of old ignorance (*Jahiliyyah*) and in times of the modern ignorance,[5] Islam's Final Holy Prophet Muhammad (Peace

[5] *Jahiliyyah* was observed in the era before the advent of the final message of Islam when even innocent infant daughters used to be buried alive as they were regarded

be Upon Him) institutionalized guarantee of sanctity, inviolability and security of life/honor/property of women, which eventually culminated in the practical fulfillment of his (Peace Be Upon Him) prediction about the actual safe voyage of a women in the jurisdiction of the Islamic state without the fear of being harmed by any human on her way to the destination in light of the following prophecy of the Holy Prophet Muhammad (Peace be Upon Him):

> Bukhari and Abu Dawud quote Khabbab IbnArat, who said: Once, during the days of trouble and torture in Makka, I went to God's Messenger, who was sitting in the shade of the Ka'ba. I was still a slave in the hands of the Makkans then. They inflicted on me severe tortures. Unable to endure those tortures any more, I requested God's Messenger to pray to God for help and salvation. But he turned towards me and said: By God, previous communities had to endure more pitiless tortures.... Surely God will perfect this religion, but you display undue haste. A day will come when a woman will travel alone by herself from San'a to Hadramawt fearing nothing but wild beasts. However, you show impatience. Khubbab concluded, "By God, what God's Messenger predicted that day, have all come true. I have personally witnessed it all."

The aforementioned factual scenario was the practical manifestation of his (Peace Be Upon Him) final Islamic pilgrimage's universal farewell address including the following universally progressive and egalitarian Islamic humanitarian teachings:

> "O People! just as you regard this month, this day, this city as Sacred, so regard the life and property of every Muslim as a sacred trust. Return the goods entrusted to you to their rightful owners. Hurt no one so that no one may hurt you. Remember that you will indeed meet your LORD, and that he will reckon your deeds."
>
> "O People! it is true that you have certain rights with regard to your women but they also have rights over you. Remember that you have taken them as your wives only under Allah's trust and with His permission. If they abide by your right then to them belongs the right to be fed and clothed in kindness. Do treat your women well and be kind to them for they are your partners and committed helpers. And it is your

by the then ignorant people as shame and disgrace (Nasir and Akhtar, 2016). Modern ignorance is characterized by the ever-escalating misogyny, women disempowerment, anti-women discrimination, conflict, exploitation. inequality. injustice, tension, violence and the reactionary Western feminism in the framework of the greed-based self-interest and selfishness-driven secular, amoral, materialist and predatory capitalist system.

> right that they do not make friends with anyone of whom you do not approve, as well as never to be unchaste."
>
> "All mankind is from Adam and Eve, an Arab has no superiority over a non-Arab nor a non-Arab has any superiority over an Arab; also a white has no superiority over black nor a black has any superiority over white except by piety and good action. Learn that every Muslim is a brother to every Muslim and that the Muslims constitute one brotherhood. Nothing shall be legitimate to a Muslim which belongs to a fellow Muslim unless it was given freely and willingly."
>
> "Do not therefore do injustice to yourselves. Remember one day you will meet Allah and answer your deeds. So beware, do not astray from the path of righteousness after I am gone."

This is how the universal and inclusive Islamic human development and empowerment program leads to the development of a peaceful and harmonious global society — society consisting of the Islamized and truly civilized humans — wherein everyone whole-heartedly respects, protects and promotes not only the rights and interests of other humans (for example, rights of their lives, property and honor), considering them as his/her brothers and sisters but also the rights and interests of animals, trees and plants and the environment as a whole.[6]

This Islamic human empowerment program culminates in an optimal level of social capital, which ensures Ummah-level development and empowerment of all spiritually and socially integrated humans — men and women having reciprocal rights as well as responsibilities such that one individual's rights are responsibilities of other individual and the rights of the later are the responsibilities of former. By placing more emphasis on the simultaneous practical fulfillment of responsibilities by everyone than the emphasis on individuals' demands of fulfillment of their rights by other individuals, Islam ensures fulfillment of rights of all individuals — all men/women (Akhtar, 1992).

In this Islamic framework, all men and women protect and promote their developmental interests on the basis of the Islamic principle of "right is might", thereby enabling the global society to realize sustainable

---

[6]For example, in light of the Islamic ethics elders respect and protect rights of youngsters affectionately, youngsters honor and protect the rights of elders respectfully, men respect and protect the rights of women in their respective positions as mothers and sisters, women respect and protect the personality and rights of men, students respect their teachers and teachers teach their students affectionately, employer and employee enjoy a pleasant working relationship based on the universal human brotherhood. (Anjum 1998).

economic development from the individual, social, environmental and universal points of view without ever exploiting and victimizing the weaker economic agents and without prejudice to the global environmental interests in the framework of a harmonious global society.[7] This Islamic human empowerment program culminates in an optimal level of social capital, which ensures Ummah-level development, empowerment and bliss of all spiritually and socially integrated humans — men and women.

Acknowledgment, protection and promotion of the Islamically inviolable universal women's privileged inviolable universal rights of life/ownership/education/inheritance/migration/marriage are indeed the matchless revolutionary contributions of Islam toward universal women empowerment and development at par with the inviolable universal men's inviolable universal rights of life, worship, education, inheritance, business, travel, migration and marriage.

In sharp contrast with the Western civilized world's oldest documented Roman Law determining the women's permanent subordination to men as permanent guardians and monitors of women — Roman law did not allow the women to acquire property and exercise their control on the property without securing the permission of their male guardians throughout their lives, Islamic jurisprudence (*Fiqh*) acknowledges and ensures equal civil and citizenry rights of both adult men and adult women citizens of the Islamic state (Ghazi, 2008). Islamic jurisprudence acknowledged and ensured the personal freedom of women in personal matters of acquiring and exercising their ownership rights with respect to their objects of ownership (Ghazi, 2008). In contrast to bride's obligation of paying dowry to their husband in Roman Law, the Islamic jurisprudence makes it obligatory for the husband to pay dowry to the bride as well as to finance her living expenditures, thereby ensuring women's socio-economic security (Ghazi, 2008).

In fact, the beauty of the Islamic universal sustainable development program lies in its unique agenda of eliminating all types of hardships encountered by individuals and society, thereby emphasizing that its agenda transcends the elimination of merely a limited number of economically undesirable phenomena such as poverty, malnutrition, ill health, homelessness, unemployment, debt, inflation and environment.

---

[7]A harmonious global Islamic society consists of the Islamically oriented and truly civilized humans — wherein everyone whole-heartedly respects, protects and promotes not only the rights and interests of other humans (for example, rights of life, property and honor) by considering them as his/her brothers and sisters, but also the rights and interests of animals, trees and plants, and the environment as a whole.

Ummah consists of the entire humanity in general and all Muslims in particular — Muslim Ummah. Both Ummah in general and Muslim Ummah, which envelope all the equally privileged dignified humans (men, women, old, young and children) as the best of all creation of Allah (*Subhanuhu Wa Ta'ala*), are the audience of the most progressive humanitarian and egalitarian Islamic program of universal human development and empowerment. This progressive Islamic program ensures protection and promotion of human rights of all the aforementioned constituents of humanity without any discrimination based on gender, age, color, language, region, generation, caste and class in the divine Islamic institutional framework of social, educational, economic, political, strategic, legal, environmental justice and benevolence on the global platform of universal family of all humans in general and all Muslims in particular. Islam integrates them through the sacred spiritual as well as blood relationship of universal human brotherhood and sisterhood, which peacefully guarantees mutual respect, affection, love, care, protection, harmony, coexistence, cooperation, help, development and empowerment of all humans.

Islam, as the most progressive, inclusive, perfect and universal system of life for the humanity, develops, empowers, elevates the entire social system of Ummah of humanity in general and Muslim Ummah in particular to the zenith of personality and character of all humans, including women, men, children, young and old through their integration instead of artificially disintegrating them into mutually hostile rival groups of rival men, women, children, young, old, workers, capitalists, feminists, misogynists and environmentalists in the framework of Muslim Ummah. In this setting, Islam presents the most progressive universal paradigm of sustainable human empowerment and development, which is based on the Islamic concept of *Tawhid* — Oneness and Unity of Allah, Who guarantees the need fulfillment of everything in this universe on the basis of His unique attribute of *Rububiyyah* (Allah's Divine scheme for nourishment, sustenance, and directing things toward their perfection) through the Divine arrangement of *Tazkiyah* — purification and growth of human personalities as well as material wealth and global environmental assets (Anjum, 1998). *Tawhid* asserts that Allah (*Subhanuhu Wa Ta'ala*) purposefully created this universe (including humans, who are the best of all His creation) for the service of the humanity — all men and all women — according to His pre-planned scheme.

For precluding the clash of mutually challenging progressive forces and regressive forces, this paradigm activates and promotes the pro-human development progressive forces (for example, progress of scientific as well as technological knowledge, sizes of populations of both men and women, etc.) and deactivates and precludes the regressive forces (for example, depreciation of physical and human capital, decline of human values, discrimination and exploitation of humans by humans, class conflicts, warfare, and deterioration of environment), and, thereby, ensures simultaneous holistic sustainable development and empowerment of both men and women — quantitative as well as qualitative development of human and nonhuman universal resources — through strict implementation of the Islamic universal laws, which are primarily concerned with the establishment of the authentic Islamic social/politico-economic and environmental justice, which is flavored with the Islamic spirit of benevolence (Anjum, 1998). By imbibing all humans with the noblest quality of *Taqwa* (God-consciousness/fearingness) in *Ibadaat*[8] (diverse forms of worship of Allah *Subhanuhu Wa Ta'ala*) and *Mua'amalaat* (human interactions among them and with the universe) and making them educated, honest, civilized, and simple lifestyled, altruist, benevolent, dutiful, punctual, efficient, it completely harmonizes all human activities with the course of perfect discipline that is prevailing in the entire universe and, thereby, culminates in the simultaneous spiritual and material ascent, development and empowerment of men as well as women to the heights of ideally developed humans by means of compulsory Islamic (religious-cum-scientific) education for all humans (men and women).

This Islamic universal program of all-inclusive Islamic program of development and empowerment of both men and women culminates in a matchless paradigm of empowerment of women in the framework of Muslim Ummah in which neither women are inferior to men nor men are inferior to women. Therefore, from the Islamic point of view, both men and women are equally privileged as being the equally important constituents of the Islamically exalted Muslim Ummah.

11.4.1 Causes of women disempowerment in the contemporary Islamic countries

Practically, the Zenith of the Islamic paradigm of women development and empowerment as an integral part of the Islamic human development

[8]In Islam, *Ibadaat* refer to all the *Shari'ah*-based Islamic activities of humans — for example, Islamic rituals, politico-economic activities, family life.

and empowerment program occurred in the blessed Golden Age of Islam. Afterward, human development and empowerment in general and women development and empowerment in particular have been compromised in the regressive global regimes of the Western imperialism and colonialism. Fortunately, now the achievement of gender equality and empowerment of all women as well as girls is listed among the SDGs. Here it is pertinent to note that the continuous systemic failures of a whole gamut of the contemporary Western as well as Eastern secular civilizations and their defective paradigms of development have warranted the culmination of the universally acknowledged imperatives of ensuring gender equality and women empowerment in universal SDGs, which command universal consensus on their achievement in narrow nationalistic framework instead of a universal framework of the global humanity. Therefore, the Islamic paradigm of universal development and empowerment of all humans (both men and women) has assumed vital significance in the universal framework of SDGs.

Islam acknowledges the women's rights of ownership and their entitlement to own their own share of earned income in proportion to their contribution in the production process.

Certain religions (for example, Hinduism, which precluded the possibility of inheritance of wealth of their deceased husbands by burning them alive) and certain economic systems like capitalism with system of primogeniture, have caused economic and social impoverishment of women in both the East and the West of world. In contrast, Islam has economically and socially empowered the women by giving them a share in inheritance according to the Islamic law of inheritance.

Women disempowerment in the world in general and in the Islamic world in particular has been a highly influential legacy of Bentham. Bentham advocated that rights are not natural rights. He asserted that all rights are created by the state and that these rights can be taken back or suspended by the state in case of an actual or perceived emergency. He rejected natural rights by regarding both natural law and humans' natural rights as two kinds of fictions. His aforementioned views had widespread influence in Britain for almost 150 years. His influence spilled into British colonies such as British India, which included regions of the post-colonial era nation states called Bangladesh, India and Pakistan. These views indirectly paved the way for idea of governmental interference in the arena of basic rights. These views have been occasionally practically enforced in Pakistan as implied the following observation of Nyazee:

> "The "benefit" is that some of these colonies still suspend basic rights for the flimsiest of reasons and imaginary emergencies. Apparently, we have to thank Britain and Bentham for this."

Apparently due to the roles of Britain and Bentham, there have been the practices of denial of females rights and males' rights to develop and empower themselves in the Muslim countries. Hence, Islam is not the cause of denial of women's rights to develop and empower themselves. In contrast, *Shari'ah* — the Islamic law — grants the human rights, which can be neither taken away nor suspended by any governments.

It is a red herring and logical fallacy to regard Islam as the cause of underdevelopment and disempowerment of women and men in the contemporary Muslim World. In fact, underdevelopment and disempowerment of women as well as men in the contemporary Muslim World has been directly caused by the colonial legacies of the still persisting anti-Islamic as well as inhumane colonial political, economic, legal, social, educational systems and their regressive socio-economic outcomes. This fact is illustrated by Nyazee (2003) in his following statement (Nyazee, 2003):

> "Most of the laws provided by Islam are not implemented in Muslim countries. The primary reason is that the Islamic legal systems prevalent in the Muslim countries were dismantled by the dominant colonial powers leaving a fragmented structure of Islamic laws that could not blend in with the Western model — a model which is alien for its masses and does not make any contact with the life and the spirit of Muslims. Brutal colonial exploitation also left the economies of the Muslim countries in shambles and the residents in abject poverty, disoriented and disorganized having lost their Islamic moorings. The colonial powers often encouraged a feudal system that helped them amass as much wealth as possible and facilitated the optimum exploitation of resources. The colonial systems and structures continue to haunt many of the Muslim countries, half a century after independence, and they are yet to realize their full potential in accordance with their Islamic heritage. The state in which we find Muslim countries, is often mistaken for Islam, but the truth is that most of the problems are due to the colonial legacy that severed the natural bond between Islam and Muslims and between the rulers and the ruled."

Against this background, the disempowerment of women in the world in general and in the Muslim world in particular and the resulting proactive feminist movements are inevitable outcome of the actual implementation of the so-called "modern" Western secular political, administrative, legislative, economic, social, educational, and civilizational systems in both the world as a whole in general and the Muslim world in particular.

11.4.2 Two stages of the feminist movement

While ideologically, the origin of modern feminist movement can be traced in egalitarian Platonic theory, which acknowledges and assigns the same equal socio-economic, political and strategic roles of both men and women, practical dynamics of the egalitarian feminist movement highlight its two stages:

Stage 1: Era of Pre-Industrial Agricultural/Domestic Production Systems Characterized by Socio-economic Security, Development and Empowerment of All Humans — Men and Women

Pre-industrial agricultural/domestic production systems ensured protection, stability and development of both family and all individuals — men and women — as constituent members of families in the religious (for example, Christian)/agricultural/household production society of times before the Industrial Revolution amidst the then increasingly widespread powerful influence and proliferation of religious values of Christianity, which culminated in increases in levels of defense, stability, development and empowerment of all families and their male/female members within both the agricultural code of life and the domestic/household production.

Stage 2: Era of Culmination of the Atheist Enlightenment Movement Against Religion in Secularization of Humans — Men and Women — as well as Their Individualization, Industrialization, Alienation, and Degeneration of Their Families and Societies amidst the Scientific and Technological Revolution, Industrial Revolution and International Wars/Regional Wars/World Wars Leading to Ever-increasing Exploitation, Degradation and Disempowerment of Women.

In this second stage, feudalism/enlightenment/secularism/Protestantism/anarchism/factory systems/industrial revolution/conservativism/capitalism/communism/socialism/dictatorships/democracy/aristocracy/capitalist/globalization/colonialism/anarchism/neocolonialism/regional and global wars — World Wars (I and II) — culminated in women's socio-economic and political disempowerment/ exploitation/stagnation/stasis based on the generally increasing gender-based political/socio-economic/legal/academic discrimination against women in particular. This scenario resulted in emergence of reactionary movement of feminism, disintegrated families, disrupted societies and urban chaos-oriented shattered cities.

These facts warrant the policy of the simultaneous implementation of the Islamic political/administrative/social/economic/educational/civilizational systems for ensuring equal opportunities for the development and empowerment of all men and women as natural complements for one another instead of being rivals of one another in sharp contrast to feminism, which is an embodiment as well as practical outcome of a long history of mutual antagonism between men and women in the West.

Practically, Islam has been the matchless protector and guarantor of the rights of the life of girls and boys in contrast to the inhuman un-Islamic practices of infanticide in general and the killing of the girls in particular, which has been continued since the pre-Islamic period of ignorance, called *Jahiliysah* until today (for example, in India) due to the so-called problems of ignorance, fear of want, poverty, misfortune, grief, shame, sufferance, contempt, and population control. The aforementioned crimes against children/girls/humanity have been condemned and attacked by the Holy *Qur'an* as following:

> "Lost are those who slay their children, from folly, without knowledge, and forbid food which Allah hath provided for them, forging (lies) against Allah. They have indeed gone astray and heeded no guidance." (The Holy *Qur'an*: 6, 40)
>
> "Kill not your children on a plea of want; We provide sustenance for you and for them."(The Holy Qur'an: 6, 151)
>
> "Kill not your children for fear of want; We shall provide sustenance for them as well as for you. Verily killing of them is a great sin." (The Holy *Qur'an*: 17, 31)
>
> "When the female (infant), buried alive, is questioned for what crime she was killed." (The Holy *Qur'an*: 81, 8–9)
>
> "When news is brought to one of them, of (the birth of) a female (child), his face darkens, and he is filled with inward grief. With shame does he hide himself from his people, because of the bad news he has had. Shall he retain it on (sufferance and) contempt, or bury it in the dust? Ah! What an evil (choice) they decide on?" (The Holy *Qur'an*: 16, 58–59)

In this setting, Islam has uniquely ensured the survival of girls as well as guaranteed all the Islamic socio-economic and educational human rights of all women and thereby secured/enriched/developed their lives and personalities in the framework of the Islamic legal system, which simultaneously ensures the protection, preservation, promotion and development of the Islamic institution of family as a primary goal of the Islamic law (*Shari'ah*) through implementation of Islamic family values, Islamic family system, the Islamic socio-economic system and the Islamic governmental system.

11.5 Conclusions and policy recommendations for women empowerment

Islam has been developing and empowering both women and men by integrating them in the framework of family, relatives, neighborhood, society, economy on local, regional, global and universal levels by precluding the possibilities of their personal alienation, factionalism, rivalry, clash of interests, misogyny and feminism since the time of its origin.

After the Golden Age of Islam, disempowerment of humans in general and women in particular is the inevitable outcome of feudalism, capitalism, socialism, communism/and secularization of human societies all over the world. Especially, secularization of the Western society, rise of capitalism, the Industrial Revolution and the World Wars culminated in individualization of human society of the West, weakening and destruction of families, alienation of women, economic exploitation as well as industrialization of women, gender-based discrimination/humiliation/exploitation/disempowerment of women, and the reactionary rise of feminism.

The capitalism has disempowered women by alienating and disintegrating them from family, relatives, neighborhood and society. More specifically, the disempowerment of women in the Western capitalist system was a product of industrialization of economy, which was accompanied by secularization, individualization of society, breakdown of family, and alienation of both men and women in society. Against this background, feminism emerged as a reactionary movement for defending women as well as ensuring their individual, social, economic and political empowerment.

Islam has contributed a matchless universal paradigm of women's socio-economic empowerment. This paradigm is premised in the original divine Islamic humanitarian mission of unifying the entire global human race consisting of all men as well as women of all places and times on the basis of their mutually respectful/beneficial/peaceful coherence on the plane of egalitarian social existence, where all of them are spiritually and physically united (as children of Adam and Eve — both created by Allah — in their submission to Allah (Only and Only One God) in the intertwined transcendental and mundane realms. This progressive universal paradigm guarantees discrimination-free socio-economic justice and equality of opportunities for all men and women for ensuring successful spiritual as well as material development of their personalities in a highly dignified manner in the progressive Islamic ethical environment characterized by the universal fraternity of men and women, which is conditioned by the Islamic values such as the inherent sanctity of the life/honor/property of all humans — men and women — as well as the mutual respect/trust/sympathy/rights/responsibilities. In this setting, the universal Islamic paradigm precludes scenarios of adversarial/exploitative/regressive socio-economic relationships among men and women, which have culminated in both the actual socio-economic disempowerment of women and rise of Western feminist movement. Implementation of the universal Islamic paradigm of human development and empowerment will ensure the socio-economic empowerment of women in both transcendental and mundane realms in the dynamic framework of the eternal Golden Civilization of Islam.

The promotion and achievement of the women empowerment in letter and spirit warrants the policy recommendation of ensuring the implementation of Islamic policy of defense, enforcement, development and dominance of Islam as a complete code of life and its all academic/familial/social/political/legal/political/judicial/economic/banking/financial institutions for effectively educating all humans about their mutual Islamic rights and responsibilities and instituting/protecting/promoting their Islamic religious/political/legal/judicial/administrative/monetary/financial/banking/inheritance sub-systems in letter and spirit. All these institutional as well as all the available human and other economic resources must be proactively harnessed by the Islamic countries' governments and societies for bringing about a whole gamut of effective Islamic socio-economic/political/legislative/judicial/educational/institutional reforms especially for guaranteeing empowerment and development of women according to the Islamic ideals.

Especially for women empowerment, it is recommended for the Governments of the Islamic countries to ensure perfect security of all women and perfect defense of their individual Islamic rights of life/worship/honor/family/socio-economic as well as political freedom/ protection of clean environment/education/children/ownership of property/inheritance/healthy/participation in labor force/employment/choice of spouse/divorce through the Islamic courts/migration/in case of necessity and proactive participation in Islamic polity/politics.

Finally, the Islamic socio-economic and political justice warrants the perfect enforcement of a proactive policy of ensuring the presence of the number of women representation of all women of the society in parliament, cabinets, ministerial bureaucracies, judicial system, political parties and public/private sectors' economic institutions exactly in proportion to their national population shares in national societies.

References

Al-Husain, A. F. (2010), *Paani Aur Hufzaan-e-Sehat*, International Islamic University Islamabad: Da'wah Academy.

Anjum, M. I. (1998), Human capital formation as the locomotive of economic development in the Islamic world in the twenty first century. *Hawaliyah (Annual Journal of International Islamic University Islamabad)*, 6, 1418A.H, available at http://irigs.iiu.edu.pk:64447/gsdl/collect/hwaliyya/index/assoc/HASH576a.dir/doc.pdf. Retrieved on 1 January 2020.

Akhtar, M. R. (1992), An Islamic framework for employer employee relationship. *The American Journal of Islamic Social Sciences*, 9(2), 202–218.

Aslam, S. (2017), *From Stasis to Mobility: Arab Muslim Feminists and Travelling Theory* (1st edn.). Karachi, Pakistan: Ameena Saiyed, Oxford University Press.

Bonine, M. E. (1997), "Population growth: The labor market and Gulf security", in Long, E.D. and Koch, C. (eds.), The Gulf Security in the Twenty-First Century, Abu Dhabi: The Emirates Center for Strategic Studies and Research, pp. 226–264.

Durant, W. (1953), *The Pleasures of Philosophy: A Survey of Human Life and Destiny*, New York: Simon and Schuster, Inc.

Ghazi, M. A. (2008), *Muhazrat-e-Fiqh*, Lahore: Al-Faisal. Nahsiran.

Hamid, J. A. (2011), *Human Rights in Islam and Contemporary International Law* (1st edn.), Islamabad: Shari'ah Academy, International Islamic University.

Mannan, M. A. (1986), "The economics of poverty in Islam with special reference to Muslim countries", in Iqbal, M. (ed.). *Distributive Justice and Need Fulfilment in an Islamic Economy*, Leicester: Islamic Foundation, pp. 303–347.

Motahhari, A. M. (1981), *Women and Her Rights in Islam*. Translated by M. A. Ansari. Qom (Iran): The Islamic Seminary Publications. Available at: http://www.iranchamber.com/personalities/mmotahari/works/woman_rights_islam.pdf. Retrieved on 1 January 2020.

Nasir, M and Saeed Akhtar, M. (2016), Scholarly and economic empowerment of women in early Islamic era. *Journal of Research (Humanities)*, 52, 195–207.

Nyazee, I. A. (2003), Islamic Law and the CRC (Convention on the Rights of the Child). *Islamabad Law Review*, 1, 65–121.

Omar, S. (2018), *Rights and Role of Women in Contemporary Muslim Society*, International Islamic University, Islamabad: Da'wah Academy.

Permanik, A. H. (1997), *Human Development with Dignity: Role of Human Capital, Human Rights and Ethico-moral Values*, Kuala Lumpur: Cahaya Pantai (M) SDN. BHD.

Qurashi, M. M. (1998), *Introduction to Muslim Contributions to Science & Technology*, Islamabad: International Islamic University.

Rafi, M. S. and Tariq, Z. (2010, 6), *Rahmat-al-lil-Aalameen*, International Islamic University, Islamabad: Dawah Academy.

Rahman, K., Khan, K. and Shahzad, I. (2007), *Conference Proceedings Pakistan Economy: An Assessment with Special Reference to Quality of Life*, Islamabad: Institute of Policy Studies.

Selected Papers on Science and Islam (Vol. 1) (1994), Pakistan Council for Science and Technology.

Timmer, P. and McClelland, D. (2008), *Economic Growth in the Muslim World: How Can USAID Help*, Bureau for Policy and Program Coordination, available at https://www.cgdev.org/sites/default/files/archive/doc/commentary/timmer_USAIDw.pdf. Retrieved on 1 January 2020.

Todaro, M. P. and Smith, S. C. (2012), *Economic Development* (11th edn.), New York: Addison-Wesley.

Ullah, M. K. (2011a), *Ta'leem-ul-Islam: Eemaaniyaat, Hissa Awwal.* International Islamic University Islamabad: Da'wah Academy.

Ullah, M. K. (2011b), *Ta'leem-ul-Islam: Tahaarat, Hissa Doam.* International Islamic University Islamabad: Da'wah Academy.

World Bank (2018), *Women, Business and Law 2018 Report*, Washington: The World Bank.

Yamani, M. (1997), "Health, education, gender and the security of the Gulf in the twenty-first century", in Long, E.D. and Koch, C. (eds.). *The Gulf Security in the Twenty-First Century*, Abu Dhabi: The Emirates Center for Strategic Studies and Research, pp. 266–279.

Chapter 12

Is Press Freedom an Effective Tool to Empower Women? Empirical Evidence from Organisation of Islamic Cooperation (OIC) Countries

Muhammad Tariq Majeed

Abstract

Feminists are concerned about the role of media in protecting rights of women. The available empirical studies are largely based on narrow case studies or anecdotal stories. This study empirically investigates the relationship of press freedom with women empowerment using a panel data of 52 Organisation of Islamic Cooperation (OIC) countries from 1996 to 2011. Ordered Logit method is applied to estimate the empirical model. The empirical findings show that press freedom is an effective tool to empower women. The role of press freedom matters more for political rights of women. Women are becoming more politically strong in all regions of the Muslim world. However, social empowerment of women is weak across the OIC countries. A comparative regional analysis indicates that women rights in Middle East and North African countries are rather weak.

Keywords: Women empowerment, Press freedom, Panel data

Women empowerment is referred to participation of women in economic, social and political sphere of life. The fundamental goal behind empowering women is to assure that women's rights are discriminated in a society. In practice, developed countries provide more rights to women as compared to developing nations. This is perhaps one reason of economic performance differences between the developed and the developing nations.

An empowered woman plays a critical role in improving health, education and living standards of her family. The betterment of families contributed favorably in the improvement of the society. Thus, women empowerment contributes significantly in improving economic performance of a country. Empowering the women develops talented workers, best mothers and responsible house mangers (King and Mason, 2001; Sen, 1999; UNIFEM, 2008).

One of the factors that play a key role in protecting women's rights is press freedom. Media covers various human rights violation in the world and forces national and international organizations to take step against tyranny against human. If media has full freedom then it can easily report any misconduct against society or an individual (Apodaca, 2007). Crocco (2007) points out that media helps in protecting the rights of women by diffusion of information and providing knowledge in a society. Moreover, media plays a significant role in assuring social rights to women by reporting physical torture and abuses against women.

Dahal (2013) also emphasized that media plays an important role in spreading voice of any group, individual or sects if they are threatened regarding their due rights. He showed that media in Nepal is contributing in development of women. Many experiments have been done on poor women, low caste groups and uneducated people to empower them by delivering their message to the policymakers and parliament. These experiments went successful, which means the right of expression in an important factor in empowering weak and subjugated creatures (Kramer, 2008; Nepal South Asia Centre, 1999; Vishwakarma, 2002).

Research on gender and press freedom frequently offers clear propositions but rarely submits them to broad, quantitative testing. This study attempts to fill this gap. This study contributes into the empirical literature on gender studies using a panel data of 52 Organisation of Islamic Cooperation (OIC) countries over the period 1196–2011. This single study explores diverse dimensions of women empowerment. To the best of my knowledge, this is the first empirical study of its kind that provides firm empirical evidence on the relationship of press freedom with women empowerment.

12.1 Women and freedom of press

Freedom of press is an important tool that protects women's socio-economic rights. It reports discrimination against the subjugated creatures of nature. It brings awareness among women to flourish their talents in order to participate in socio-economic decisions of life. Rostow (1963) emphasizes that mass media assists development of societies. Media contributes in assuring human rights. Media promotes women empowerment and narrows the socio-economic gap between genders by disseminating information.

Ceulemans and Fauconnier (1979) pointed out that female participation in labor force has increased since 1947. In 1973, half of the women in the U.S. were employed and had the significant share in total labor force of America. The contribution of women in professional occupation has also increased significantly due to mass media that was bringing awareness among women about their abilities. They also proposed that women's earning above $10,000 increased about seven-fold during the 1960s because media was empowering women by advocating their rights of education and rights of job, though the participation of women in the profession of media did not increase.

Prabhash (2005) proposed in his study that the strategic purpose of media is to report and critique all illegitimate practices in a country. It is a liability of media to protect human rights. However, in reality it flops in protecting the rights of women. Gallagher (2005) also verified in his study that in the early stages of international women movement, press had given secondary status to the problems related to women's rights. Now the conferences on women's development emphasize on contribution of media in promoting women empowerment.

Okello-Orlale (2006) analyzed the role that media has played in promoting gender equality, peace and development which was spelt out by the Nairobi International Women's Conference in 1985. He emphasized that media has contributed significantly in in achieving the goals in Nairobi Conference. He underscored that media has reinforced women empowerment in Africa.

Mourtada *et al.* (2011) illustrated that social media such as "Twitter and Facebook" has brought historical change in the status of women of Arab countries. Social media is driving the campaign of Arab swing and awaking awareness in women about their rights. Women in Arab countries are now relatively in a better state of knowledge regarding their capabilities, abilities, opportunities and talents.

Media is also contributing in political and social empowerment of women. Eslen-Ziya (2013) pointed out that new wave of political activism in the Middle East called "Arab swing" is actually fostered by social media. Social media has provoked political activism among women of the Middle East. The women who got education in secular system have played an important role in rejecting male dominant society and led the new wave of feminism.

Harish (2014) highlighted that right of expression is an important tool to protect the rights of the submissive group of gender. There is no other important strategy to empower women than providing them equal access to education and economic opportunity. Free media is a platform through which women can express their thoughts and ideas. Women had been considered as a subjugated creature of nature by male dominant society and some orthodox traditions and culture. Now free media has empowered women in different aspects of life and they are occupying top positions in international corporations and organizations by the dint of their talent and the role of media.

Thus, media and press freedom is considered as an important tool that protects the rights of women. It plays a significant role in empowering women economically, politically and socially. However, the investigation of women empowerment and press freedom relationship is based on anecdotal stories and case studies. To the best of our knowledge, no one has empirically explored the impacts of press freedom on women empowerment. In particular, the empirical analysis for women's rights in the OIC countries is not available.

12.2 Methodology

To empirically explore the relationship between press freedom and women empowerment we have employed the data of 52 OIC countries from 1996 to 2011. We have followed empirical studies of the literature that have also employed women's rights, gender equality or gender discrimination as dependent variables (Kucera and Milberg, 2000; Neumayer and de Soysa, 2007 and 2011; Oostendorp, 2009).

$$\mathrm{WR}_{\mathrm{it}} = \gamma_1 + \gamma_2 Y_{\mathrm{it}} + \gamma_3 \mathrm{Dem}_{\mathrm{it}} + \gamma_4 \mathrm{PF}_{\mathrm{it}} + \gamma_4 \mathrm{FF}_{\mathrm{it}} + \gamma_5 \mathrm{FF}_{\mathrm{it}} + \gamma_6 X_{\mathrm{it}} + e_{\mathrm{it}}. \tag{1}$$

In Equation (1), dependent variable is women's rights (WR) while independent variables are per capita GDP (Y), democracy (Dem) and press freedom (PF). The control variables are female fertility (FF) and female labor force (FL). The term X stands for a row matrix of regional dummy variables which is introduced to capture heterogeneity in the panel data and e is an error term.

According to modernization theory, high economic development mitigates the probability of discriminated attitude of employers against women (Forsythe *et al.*, 2000). The relationship between economic opportunities for women and per capita GDP is likely to be nonlinear. The reason is that in initial stage of economic development men will be preferred to women but after threshold level of economic development, women will also be employed as paid worker. On the other hand few feminist proposed that high economic development may reinforce discrimination against women (Charlton, 1997). To test it empirically, we have taken into account of per capita GDP as a cause of women empowerment.

Democracy is also a main determinant of women empowerment. In full democratic country there will be less chance of poor economic, political and social rights provided to women. Although in parliament most of the policymakers are men, yet there is low chance of discrimination against women in democratic regimes than dictatorial regimes. Democratic country protects human rights and has low prevalence of forced labor (Poe *et al.*, 1999; Majeed and Malik, 2017). Press freedom is a variable of our main concern in this study. The available case studies, hearsay stories and scholarly arguments propose positive linkage between press freedom and women empowerment. This study advances the current state of knowledge by providing firm empirical evidence.

According to Morrisson and Jütting (2005), different geographical regions of the world bear sharp differences in long-standing norms such as religion, tradition, culture, dress code, movement rights, marriages, genital mutilation, inheritance rights and ownership rights. To take into account such dissimilarities we have employed regional dummies for East Asian Pacific (EAP), European and Central Asian (ECA), Middle East and North Africa (MENA), Latin America and Caribbean (LAAC), South Asian (SA), and Sub-Saharan African (SSA) countries. The regional dummies are based on World Bank regional classification.

Fertility and female labor force participation can also influence the deliverance of women rights. The high fertility of women increases the chance of discrimination against women while participation of female in labor force assists to protect women's rights. We employed three dimensions of women's rights, which are women's economic rights, women's political rights and women's social rights. The empirical model to measure theses

Table 12.1 The description of the ordinal ranking of the indexes.

Index ranking	Women's rights
0	No rights are provided to women in relevant dimension. There is no law that assures women's rights and women endure high level of discrimination.
1	Women's rights are assured in law but it is not enforced in a country. They tolerate significant level of discrimination in relevant dimensions (economic, political and social).
2	Women's rights are assured in law and also enforced in a country but still women tolerate some discrimination in relevant dimensions.
3	Women's rights are guaranteed in law and also enforced effectively in a country. There is no discrimination against women and they enjoy full economic, political and social rights.

dimensions of women's rights are:

$$\mathrm{WER}_{\mathrm{it}} = \gamma_1 + \gamma_2 Y_{\mathrm{it}} + \gamma_3 \mathrm{Dem}_{\mathrm{it}} + \gamma_4 \mathrm{PF}_{\mathrm{it}} + \gamma_4 \mathrm{FF}_{\mathrm{it}} + \gamma_5 \mathrm{FF}_{\mathrm{it}} + \gamma_6 X_{\mathrm{it}} + e_{\mathrm{it}}. \tag{2}$$

$$\mathrm{WPR}_{\mathrm{it}} = \partial_1 + \partial_2 Y_{\mathrm{it}} + \partial_3 \mathrm{Dem}_{\mathrm{it}} + \partial_4 \mathrm{PF}_{\mathrm{it}} + \partial_4 \mathrm{FF}_{\mathrm{it}} + \partial_5 \mathrm{FF}_{\mathrm{it}} + \partial_6 X_{\mathrm{it}} + e_{\mathrm{it}}. \tag{3}$$

$$\begin{aligned}\mathrm{WSR}_{\mathrm{it}} &= \emptyset_1 + \emptyset_2 Y_{\mathrm{it}} + \emptyset_3 \mathrm{Dem}_{\mathrm{it}} + \emptyset_4 \mathrm{PF}_{\mathrm{it}} + \emptyset_4 \mathrm{FF}_{\mathrm{it}} \\ &\quad + \emptyset_5 \mathrm{FF}_{\mathrm{it}} + \emptyset_6 X_{\mathrm{it}} + e_{\mathrm{it}}.\end{aligned} \tag{4}$$

WER stands for women's economic rights, WPR stands for women's political rights and WSR stands for women's social rights.

12.2.1 Data description

The data of women's economic, political and social right is taken from Cingranelli and Richards (2011). The data for women's rights indexes are available from 1981 to 2011 while the data for press freedom are available from 1996 to 2014. Given these data constraints the analysis is limited for the years from 1996 to 2011. Women's rights indexes are based on discrete data and have ordinal ordering ranges from 0 to 3. The complete description of ranking of women rights is given in Table 12.1. The description of items used to construct the indexes is given in Table 12.2.

The Index of democracy lies in the range of −10 and 10. Where 10 refers to complete democracy and −10 refers to complete autocracy in a country. The data of democracy are taken from the polity IV (2014). The

Table 12.2 Full description of the women rights index.

Women's economic rights index
Equal pay for equal work, equality in hiring and promotion practices and no discrimination by employers.
Free choice of profession or employment without the need to obtain a husband or male relative's consent.
The right to gainful employment without the need to obtain a husband or male relative's consent.
Job security (maternity leave, unemployment benefits, no arbitrary firing or layoffs, etc.).
The right to be free from sexual harassment in the workplace and to work at night.
The right to work in occupations classified as dangerous such as military and police force.
Women's social rights index
The right to equal inheritance and education.
The right to enter into marriage on a basis of equality with men.
The right to travel abroad and obtain a passport.
The right to confer citizenship to children or a husband.
The right to initiate a divorce and own, acquire, manage, and retain property brought into marriage.
The right to participate in social, cultural, and community activities.
The freedom to choose a residence/domicile.
Freedom from female genital mutilation of children and of adults without their consent.
Freedom from forced sterilization.
Women's political rights index
The right to vote, run office, hold election and appointed government position.
The right to join political parties.
The right of petition of government parties.

data of press freedom are extracted from Freedom House (2014). It ranges from 0 to 100 where values between 1 and 30 indicate press freedom, values between 30 and 60 indicate partial press freedom, and values between 61 and 100 indicate no press freedom. To arrange press freedom in ascending order we have transformed index by subtracting it from 100. Now values between 0 and 40 denote no press freedom, 41–70 indicate partial press freedom and 71–100 show press freedom. The data of Freedom House cover the dimensions shown in Table 12.3.

The data of per capita GDP (constant 2005 $), female education, Total Fertility Rate (TFR) and female participation in labor force is extracted from World Development Indicators (2014). Table 12.4 indicates that women's economic rights have positive correlation with per capita income,

Table 12.3 Description of press freedom dataset.

Dimensions covered in press freedom dataset
Data of press freedom from 1994 to 2001 cover following aspects:
A. Law and principles which affect media content
B. Political influence on media
C. Economic impact on media
D. Oppressive action on journalists (killing, physical violence, harassments, facilities and censorship of journalists)
Data of press freedom from 2001 to 2013 cover following aspects:
A. Law and principles which effect media content
B. Political influence on media
C. Economic impact on media

Table 12.4 Correlation matrix.

Variables	1	2	3	4	5	6	7	8	9
1. Women's economic rights	1.00	—	—	—	—	—	—	—	—
2. Women's political rights	0.12	1.00	—	—	—	—	—	—	—
3. Women's social rights	0.44	0.40	1.00	—	—	—	—	—	—
4. Per capita income	0.12	−0.56	−0.21	1.00	—	—	—	—	—
5. Press freedom	0.04	0.21	0.08	−0.07	1.00	—	—	—	—
6. Democracy	0.03	0.001	0.03	−0.003	0.18	1.00	—	—	—
7. Fertility	−0.23	0.08	−0.22	−0.31	0.22	−0.02	1.00	—	—
8. Female labor	0.05	0.46	0.18	−0.26	0.27	0.09	0.36	1.00	—
9. Female population	−0.08	0.61	0.25	−0.94	0.11	0.03	0.23	0.34	1.00

press freedom, democracy and female participation in labor force. Women's economic and political rights have negative relationship with fertility of women while women social rights have positive relationship with fertility of women.

Table 12.5 reports descriptive statistics of the data used for empirical analysis. The data show that on average women's political rights are the highest while the women's social rights are the lowest in the Muslim world. Press freedom on average is very low in Muslim countries. Moreover, high dispersion of press freedom indicates that it varies considerably across Islamic countries.

Figure 12.1 indicates that Latin America is the only region where media is free while in Sub-Saharan Africa and East Asia Pacific media is just

Table 12.5 Descriptive statistics.

Variables	Observations	Mean	Std. Dev.	Min.	Max.
1. Women's economic rights	770	0.9116883	0.5925357	0	3
2. Women's political rights	777	1.700129	0.6104017	0	3
3. Women's social rights	469	0.673774	0.6081488	0	2
4. Per Capita income	789	4289.04	9744.411	196.1729	60874.4
5. Press Freedom	831	36.16606	17.53554	0	82
6. Democracy	832	1.6478	3.8525	−8.8	9
7. Fertility	832	4.222184	1.720554	1.502	7.869
8. Female labor	832	34.81875	17.07253	6.8	81.4
9. Female population	832	48.84381	3.976484	23.7758	52.2195

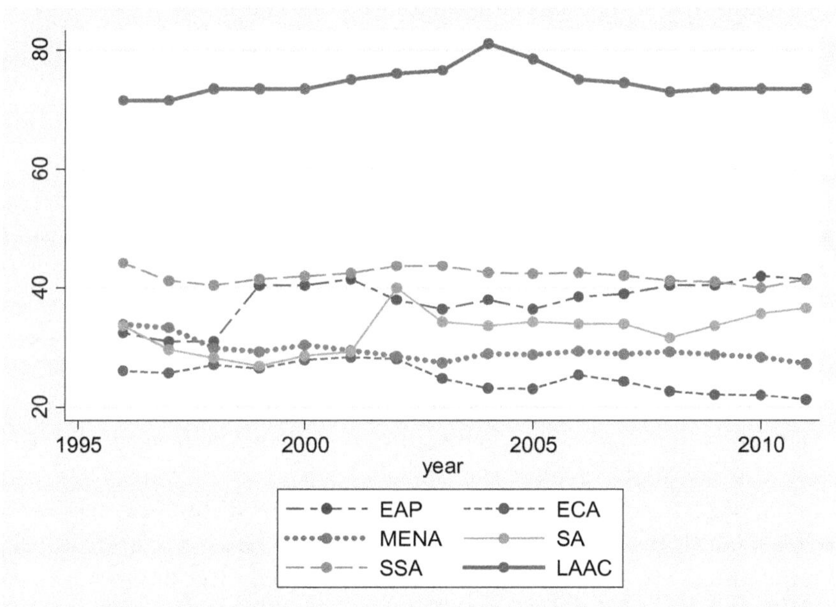

Figure 12.1 Time trend of press freedom.

partially free. In remaining regions media is not free. Press is lowest in the case of Europe and Central Asian countries. Figure 12.2 denotes that women's economic rights are the highest in the Latin American countries but they are not showing a stable trend over time. On the contrary,

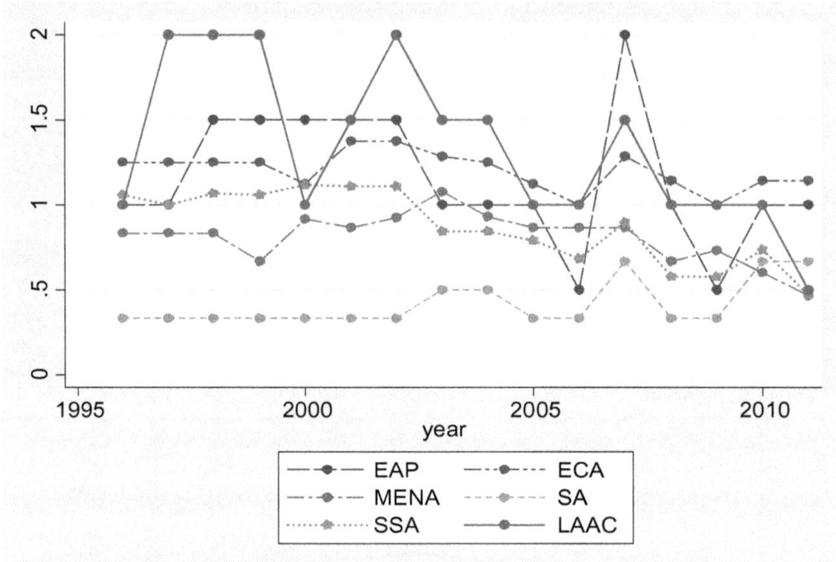

Figure 12.2 Time trend of women's economic rights.

economic rights are lowest in South Asian countries. Since 2003 women's rights in Middle East and North African countries are showing a declining trend. Figure 12.3 presents that women's social rights are most protected in Latin America and least protected in MENA regions.

Figure 12.4 indicates that there is an upward trend in the provision of political rights to women all over the Muslim world. The women enjoy more political rights in Latin American countries and least in MENA countries. Nevertheless, political rights for women have been increasing in MENA countries since 2000. In 1995, there was a law to protect women's political rights in MENA countries but that was not enforced. In 2011, the law for women's political rights was enforced, yet women have to tolerate political discrimination. In South Asian countries, the law to protect women's political rights was not enforced in 1995 but law has been enforced since 2000 and women endures only minor level of political discrimination in South Asian countries.

Figure 12.5 presents that 0% economic rights provided to women are fully protected and assured, whereas 22% regions of the Muslim world provide no economic rights to women. Figure 12.6 presents that in 70% regions of the Muslim world women enjoy satisfactory political rights which

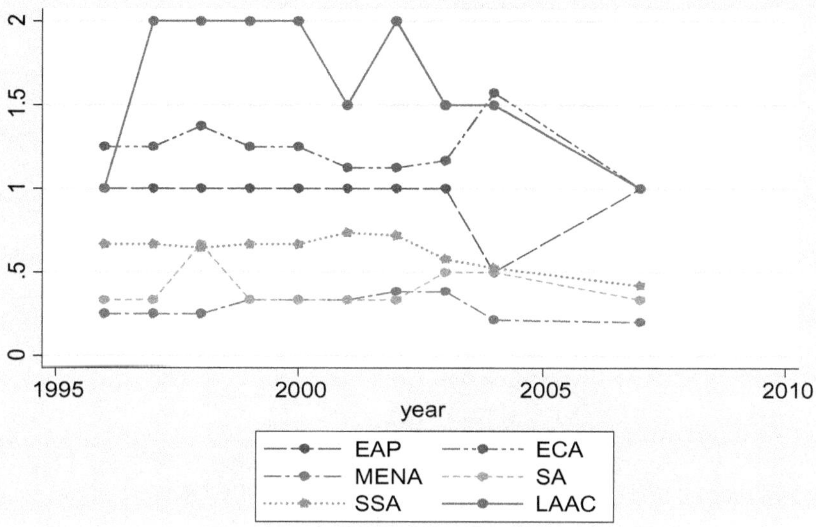

Figure 12.3 Time trend of women's social rights.

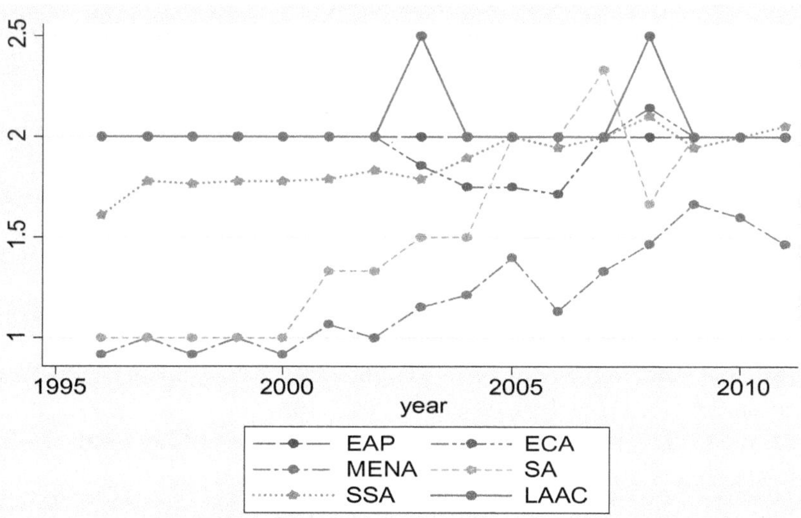

Figure 12.4 Time trend of women's political rights.

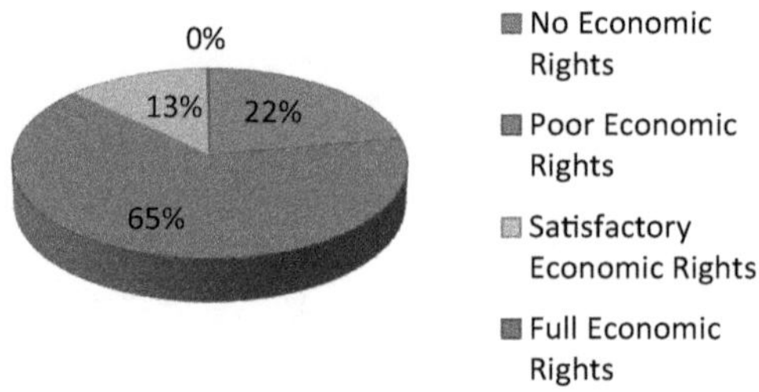

Figure 12.5 Women's economic social rights in the Muslim World.

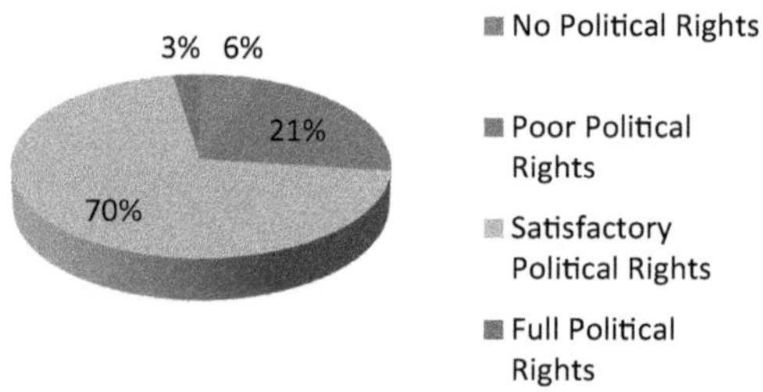

Figure 12.6 Women's political rights in the Muslim World.

implies that the law that protects women's political rights is enforced and women endures only minor level of political discrimination. While 0% women's political rights are fully protected implying that political discrimination exists to varying degrees all over the Muslim world. Finally, 6% regions of the Muslim world do not provide any political rights to women.

Figure 12.7 denotes that women do not have full social rights. While in 40% regions of the world women have no social rights, and they have no right to take any decision about their social life. Women in 52% regions of the Muslim world tolerate high levels of discrimination and have poor social rights for women. In only 8% regions of the Muslim world women enjoy satisfactory social rights.

Figure 12.8 indicates that in the low-income OIC countries 67% of the economic rights are poor. In 23% of the low-income countries there are no economic rights for women. Women of low-income countries also endure high level of discrimination in social life. Only 11% of the low-income countries protect women's economic rights up to satisfactory level. The picture of women's political rights is better than women's economic and

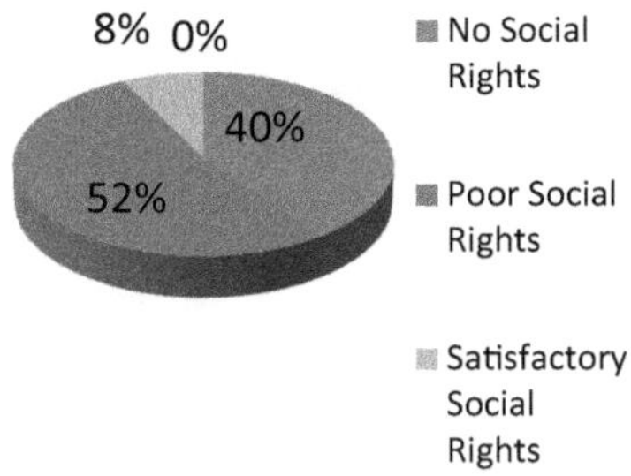

Figure 12.7 Woman's social rights in the Muslim world.

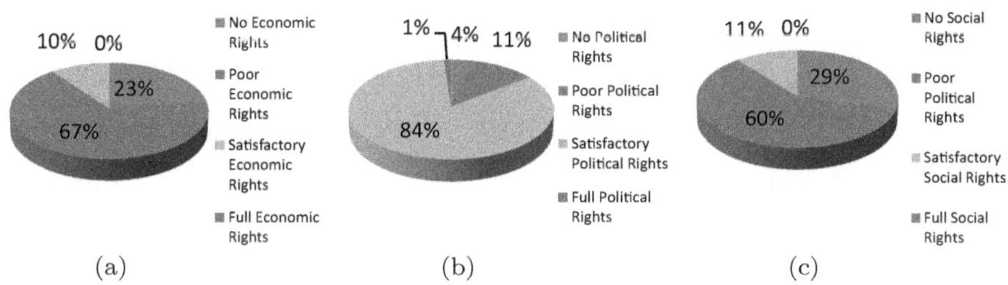

Figure 12.8 Women's economic, political and social right in low-income countries.

social rights. In low-income countries, 80% of women's political rights are satisfactory. However, women still tolerate political discrimination in low-income countries. Only in 1% regions of the low-income countries women's political rights are fully protected.

Figure 12.9 shows that economic and social rights of women are highly discriminated even in middle-income countries. In the middle-income countries, 66% of women's economic rights are poor and 55% of women's social rights are poor. This implies that there are economic and social rights for women in law but these are not enforced. Only 1% of women's political rights in the middle-income countries are fully assured and protected while 0% of women's economic and social rights are protected. Women's political rights are relatively more protected than women's economic and social rights. The 73% of political rights are satisfactory and 1% are fully assured and protected in the middle-income countries.

The picture of women's political, economic and social rights is quite unsatisfactory in high-income countries. Figure 12.10 presents that 20% of women's economic rights are quite satisfactory while 0% of economic rights provide full freedom to women to participate in any economic activities in

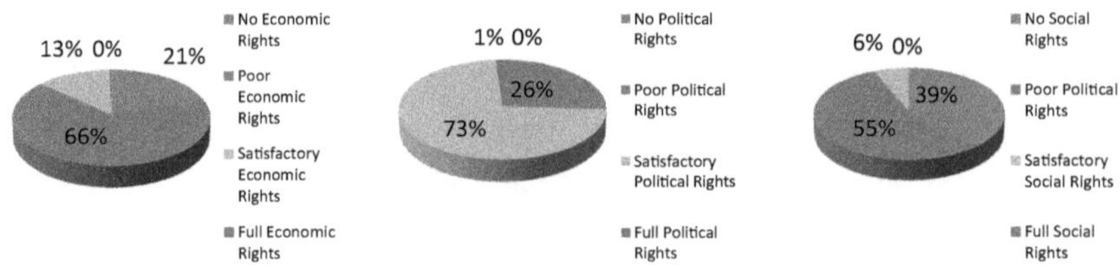

(a) (b) (c)

Figure 12.9 Women's economic, political and social right in middle-income countries.

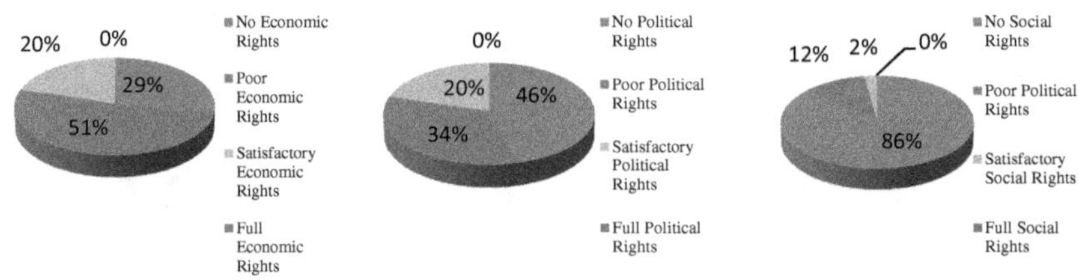

(a) (b) (c)

Figure 12.10 Women economic, political and social right in high-income countries.

a country. In high-income countries, 0% of women's social rights are fully protected and there is no evidence of zero discrimination against women. The political rights of women are more protected in low-income and middle-income countries as compared to high-income countries. In high-income countries, only 20% of women's political rights are satisfactory while in low and middle-income countries 80% and 73%, respectively, of the political rights are satisfactory.

12.2.2 Empirical results

The data of women's rights are not continuous; it has ordinal ordering from 0 to 3 that ranks women's rights from no rights to full rights. Since our dependent variable is a categorical variable, we have applied Ordered Logit method of estimation. We have individually explored the impact of press freedom on women's economic, political and social rights for the OIC countries. The empirical results of Table 12.6 indicate that freedom of press has positive and significant impact on women's economic rights. The coefficients of Ordered Logit model are the log odds of getting full economic

Table 12.6 Women economic rights: Empirical results of ordered logit models.

Variables	(1) WER	(2) WER	(3) WER
Per capita GDP	0.206***	0.0722	0.0941
	(0.0787)	(0.0933)	(0.0972)
Democracy	−0.0217	−0.0270	−0.0264
	(0.0275)	(0.0279)	(0.0279)
Press freedom	0.00669	0.00809	0.00708
	(0.0066)***	(0.0066)***	(0.0067)**
Fertility	—	−0.262***	−0.248**
	—	(0.0978)	(0.0992)
Labor force (female)	—	—	0.00514
	—	—	(0.00640)
EAP	1.496***	1.232***	1.156***
	(0.423)	(0.439)	(0.448)
ECA	1.870***	1.536***	1.475***
	(0.272)	(0.301)	(0.310)
LAAC	1.828***	1.500***	1.545***
	(0.504)	(0.519)	(0.522)
SA	−0.688*	−0.830**	−0.843**
	(0.399)	(0.405)	(0.406)
SSA	0.655**	1.033***	0.913***
	(0.263)	(0.299)	(0.334)
Others	1.614***	1.512***	1.466***
	(0.456)	(0.450)	(0.455)
Constant cut1	0.984	−0.966	−0.667
	(0.685)	(1.004)	(1.070)
Constant cut2	4.505***	2.575**	2.874***
	(0.713)	(1.015)	(1.081)
Constant cut3	8.616***	6.685***	6.983***
	(1.001)	(1.234)	(1.289)
LR chi2(13)	93.11	100.33	11.98
P-value	0.000	0.000	0.000
Observations	746	746	746

Note: $^{***}p < 0.01$, $^{**}p < 0.05$, $^{*}p < 0.1$ (Standard errors in parentheses)

rights vs. the combined number of poor and satisfactory women's economic rights.

The coefficient of press freedom in the 1st column of Table 12.6 implies that one unit increase in press freedom increases the log odd of getting full women's economic rights up to 0.007 units. It indicates that press freedom plays a significant role in protecting women's economic rights. The coefficient of democracy denotes that one unit increase in democracy will decrease the log odd of assuring full economic rights to women about 0.02;

however, the impact of democracy is insignificant. The coefficient of per capita income implies that one unit increase in per capita income, the log odd of full economic right to women increases about 0.20 units.

We have also introduced regional dummies to capture socio-economic differences in the OIC countries. MENA region is an omitted dummy in order to avoid dummy variable trap. The empirical findings infer that women's economic rights in all geographical regions are greater than women's economic rights in the MENA countries. The Latin America and Central Asia countries provided highest level of economic rights to women.

In the 2nd and 3rd column of Table 12.6, fertility and female participation in labor force are successively incorporated as control variables to check the robustness of our results. The coefficient of press freedom remains positive and significant which implies that increase in press freedom will increase the log odds full economic rights to women. The P-value of likelihood ratios indicates that model is better than empty model which implies our model is correct. The cuts are also significant in all the specification of Equation (2) implying that Ordered Logit is more efficient than OLS because there is significant difference in the intercept of different categories of women's rights.

Table 12.7 presents empirical findings of Equation (3). The empirical results in the 1st column of Table 12.7 indicate that press freedom contributes in assuring political rights to women. The coefficient of press freedom implies that one unit increase in press freedom increases log odds of being in full women's political rights category about 0.03 units. The coefficients of per capita income in the 1st column of Table 12.7 depicts that a unit increase in per capita income decreases the order log odds of high political rights about 0.6. It indicates that in low-income Muslim countries women enjoy more political rights. The coefficient of democracy is negative and significant. The literature on democracy and women empowerment is not conclusive. Richards and Gelleny (2007), for example, found a positive relationship between gender equality and democracy, whereas Bego (2014) found no relationship, and Paxton (1997) and Yoon (2001) a negative one.

Högström (2015) argues that the overall positive correlation between democracy and gender equality disappears when one looks at nations at different income levels separately. The most significant improvement in gender equality is observed at the margin between weak democracies and fully consolidated democracies.

The most significant improvements regarding gender equality are achieved when countries fully transition into strong, consolidated

Table 12.7 Women political rights: Empirical results of ordered logit models.

Variables	(1) WPR	(2) WPR	(3) WPR
Per capita GDP	−0.617***	−0.848***	−0.776***
	(0.0888)	(0.107)	(0.108)
Democracy	−0.125***	−0.139***	−0.137***
	(0.0346)	(0.0349)	(0.0353)
Press freedom	0.0315***	0.0341***	0.0248***
	(0.00791)	(0.00797)	(0.00819)
Fertility	—	−0.450***	−0.413***
	—	(0.110)	(0.112)
Labor force (female)	—	—	0.0578***
EAP	3.734***	3.368***	2.664***
	(0.613)	(0.611)	(0.682)
ECA	2.882***	2.406***	1.755***
	(0.335)	(0.352)	(0.380)
LAAC	3.120***	2.623***	3.253***
	(0.709)	(0.721)	(0.758)
SA	0.840*	0.637	0.572
	(0.467)	(0.474)	(0.488)
SSA	1.274***	1.993***	0.931**
	(0.277)	(0.333)	(0.364)
Others	2.798***	2.636***	2.193***
	(0.599)	(0.636)	(0.660)
Constant cut1	−6.289***	−9.700***	−8.115***
	(0.817)	(1.193)	(1.207)
Constant cut2	−3.552***	−6.848***	−5.280***
	(0.750)	(1.115)	(1.143)
Constant cut3	2.371***	−0.869	1.369
	(0.764)	(1.103)	(1.155)
LR chi2(13)	294.16	311.22	355.78
P-value	0.000	0.000	0.000
Observations	753	753	753

Note: $^{***}p < 0.01$, $^{**}p < 0.05$, $^{*}p < 0.1$ (standard errors in parentheses).

democracies. Most of the OIC countries belong to low-income group countries. Some of them are experiencing hybrid regimes. The strength of democracy on average for the OIC countries is very weak. The score of democracy for the OIC countries on average is just 1.64 (Table 12.5). The regional dummies are also introduced to control the differences in norms, cultures, traditions and religions in countries. We have treated MENA as a base category and women's political rights in all the regions of the world is higher than MENA regions. Women's political rights are highest in EA countries and lowest in SA countries.

Table 12.8 Women social rights: Empirical results of ordered logit models.

Variables	(1) WSR	(2) WSR	(3) WSR
Per capita GDP	−0.222**	−0.425***	−0.417***
	(0.107)	(0.129)	(0.136)
Democracy	−0.0484	−0.0403	−0.0401
	(0.0396)	(0.0395)	(0.0395)
Press freedom	0.00991	0.0108	0.0105
	(0.00807)	(0.00811)	(0.00838)
Fertility	—	−0.415***	−0.411***
	—	(0.137)	(0.139)
Labor force (female)	—	—	0.00142
	—	—	(0.00827)
EAP	3.082***	2.629***	2.605***
	(0.626)	(0.639)	(0.653)
ECA	4.450***	3.856***	3.839***
	(0.490)	(0.522)	(0.532)
LAAC	5.553***	4.959***	4.975***
	(0.763)	(0.786)	(0.791)
SA	0.665	0.367	0.365
	(0.540)	(0.553)	(0.554)
SSA	0.985***	1.609***	1.578***
	(0.340)	(0.411)	(0.447)
Others	2.353***	2.159***	2.146***
	(0.675)	(0.680)	(0.685)
Constant cut1	−0.538	−3.613***	−3.522**
	(0.926)	(1.377)	(1.475)
Constant cut2	4.098***	1.060	1.151
	(0.982)	(1.400)	(1.495)
LR chi2(13)	201.40	210.85	210.88
P-value	0.000	0.000	0.000
Observations	455	455	455

Note: $^{***}p < 0.01$, $^{**}p < 0.05$, $^{*}p < 0.1$ (standard errors in parentheses).

In order to test the robustness of results we incorporate fertility and female participation in labor force as control variables in the 2nd and 3rd columns of Table 12.6. Our results remained intact. The impact of fertility on women political rights is negative and significant while the impact of female labor force is positive. It implies that if fertility rate in a country will increase then women will be less politically empowered. The p-value of likelihood ratio is less than 0.05 that implies our model is better than an empty model.

Table 12.8 presents the empirical results of women's social rights and press freedom nexus. In the 1st column of Table 12.8 the coefficient of press freedom indicates that one unit increase in press freedom will increase the order log odds of being in category of full women's social rights about 0.01 units, however the coefficients are not significant. Women of Latin American countries enjoy highest social rights than other regions of the Muslim world wherein SA region women's social rights are lowest across the world.

12.3 Conclusion

Does press freedom empower women across the OIC countries? To answer this question, this study assembles panel data of 52 OIC countries from 1996 to 2011. The empirical results of Ordered Logit model suggest that press freedom is an efficient tool that helps in protecting due economic, political and social rights of women. The increase in freedom of press will enhance the log odds of getting full rights for women vs. zero, poor and satisfactory women's rights. The women of Latin America enjoy more economic, social and political rights because media is comparatively free in Latin America. On the other hand in MENA region women are discriminated because press is not free. The graphical and statistical analysis also supports the positive relationship between press freedom and women rights.

Policymakers, who want to extract the full potential of human capital of a country, should take positive steps in making favorable policies for women through which they can flourish their channels. Freedom of press is an important tool that helps women to fight for their economic, political and social rights. Free media protects the rights of women by reporting biased attitudes of society against women. It assists in proving respectful social status to women by informing people about the due rights of women. It is recommended by our study that press freedom is pre-requisite to abolish discrimination against women.

Appendix 12.A

Table 12.1A Women empowerment index: Empirical results of ordered logit models.

Variables	(1) WEI	(2) WEI	(3) WEI
Per capita GDP	-0.121^{*}	-0.370^{***}	-0.315^{***}
	(0.0669)	(0.0809)	(0.0833)
Democracy	-0.0108^{***}	-0.0128^{***}	-0.0141^{***}
	(0.00415)	(0.00416)	(0.00421)

(*Continued*)

Table 12.1A (*Continued*)

Variables	(1) WEI	(2) WEI	(3) WEI
Press Freedom	0.00870*	0.0112**	0.00916**
	(0.00475)	(0.00482)	(0.00488)
Fertility	—	−0.481***	−0.456***
	—	(0.0865)	(0.0867)
Labor Force (female)	—	—	0.0146***
	—	—	(0.00542)
Female Population			
EAP	2.703***	2.213***	2.021***
	(0.347)	(0.363)	(0.370)
ECA	3.022***	2.424***	2.268***
	(0.242)	(0.266)	(0.272)
LAAC	3.435***	2.835***	2.959***
	(0.450)	(0.461)	(0.462)
SA	0.448	0.205	0.161
	(0.361)	(0.354)	(0.350)
SSA	1.354***	2.046***	1.734***
	(0.235)	(0.265)	(0.290)
Others	2.330***	2.157***	2.030***
	(0.399)	(0.388)	(0.394)
Observations	754	754	754

References

Apodaca, C. (2007), The whole world could be watching: Human rights and the media. *Journal of Human Rights*, 6(2), 147–164.

Bego, I. (2014), Accessing power in new democracies: The appointment of female ministers in post-communist Europe. *Political Research Quarterly*, 67(2), 347–360.

Ceulemans, M. and Fauconnier, G. (1979), *Mass Media: The Image, Role, and Social Conditions of Women. Report No. 84*. Paris: UNESCO.

Charlton, S. E. (1997), "Development as history and process", in N. Visvanathan, L. Duggan and L. Nisonoff (eds.). *The Women, Gender, and Development Reader*, London: Zed Books.

Cingranelli, D. L. and Richards, D. L. (2011), *Cingranelli and Richards Human Rights Dataset*, available at http://www.humanrightsdata.com. Accessed on 30 September 2017.

Crocco, M. S. (2007), Speaking truth to power: Women's rights as human rights. *The Social Studies*, 98(6), 257–269.

Dahal, S. (2013), Power, empowerment and community radio: Media by and for women in Nepal. *Women's Studies International Forum*, 40, 44–55.

Eslen-Ziya, H. (2013), Social media and Turkish feminism: New resources for social activism. *Feminist Media Studies*, 13(5), 860–870.

Forsythe, N., Korzeniewicz, R. P. and Durrant, V. (2000), Gender inequalities and economic growth: A longitudinal evaluation. *Economic Development and Cultural Change*, 48(3), 573–617.

Freedom House (2014), *Freedom in the World* (New York: Freedom House).

Gallagher, M. (2005), "Who Makes the News?", *The Global Media Monitoring Project, WACC, London*, available at http://www.whomakesthenews.org/. Retrieved on 4 July 2006.

Harish, R. (2014), "Role of Mass Media in Women Empowerment", *Social Media*, available at http://www.slideshare.net/harishhari58760608/role-of-mass-media-in-women-empowerment. Accessed on 30 September 2017.

Högström, J. (2015), Do development and democracy positively affect gender equality in cabinets? *Japanese Journal of Political Science*, 16(3), 332–356.

King, E. M. and Mason, A. D. (2001), *Engendering Development: Through Gender Equality in Rights, Resources, and Voice*, Oxford and Washington, DC: Oxford University Press and World Bank.

Kramer, K.-H. (2008), "How representative is the Nepali state?" in Gellner, David N. (ed.). *Resistance and the State: Nepalese Experiences*, New Delhi: Social Science Press, pp. 179–198.

Kucera, D. and Milberg, W. (2000), Gender segregation and gender bias in manufacturing trade expansion: Revisiting the "wood asymmetry". *World Development*, 28(7), 1191–1210.

Majeed, M. T. and Malik, A. (2017), Selling souls: An empirical analysis of human trafficking and globalization. *Pakistan Journal of Commerce and Social Sciences*, 11(1), 353–388.

Morrisson, C. and Jütting, J. P. (2005), Women's discrimination in developing countries: A new data set for better policies. *World Development*, 33(7), 1065–1081.

Mourtada, R., Salem, F., Al-Dabbagh, M. and Gargani, G. (2011), The Role of Social Media in Arab Women's Empowerment. *The Arab Social Media Report.*

Nepal South Asia Centre (1999), *Nepal Human Development Report 1998: Report Submitted to the United Nations Development Programme.* Kathmandu: Nepal South Asia Centre.

Neumayer, Eric and Soysa, Indra de (2007), Globalization, women's economic rights and forced labour. *World Economy*, 30(10), 1510–1535.

Neumayer, E. and Indra de Soysa (2011), Globalization and the empowerment of women: An analysis of spatial dependence via trade and foreign direct investment. *World Development*, Forthcoming.

Okello-Orlale, R. (2006), Looking back and ahead: The media and the struggle for gender equality after the Nairobi UN women's conference. *Agenda*, 20(69), 48–56.

Oostendorp, R. H. (2009), *Globalization and the Gender Wage Gap, World Bank Economic Review*, Oxford: Oxford University Press, 23, 141–161.

Paxton, P. (1997), Women in national legislatures: A cross-national analysis. *Social Science Research*, 26(4), 442–464.

Poe, S., Tate, N. and Keith, L. (1999), Repression of the human right to personal integrity revisited: A global cross-national study covering the years 1976–1993. *International Studies Quarterly*, 43(2), 291–313.

Prabhash, J. (2005), Mediated rights: Media, women and human rights in India. *The Indian Journal of Political Science*, 66(1), 53–74.

Richards, D. L. and Gelleny, R. (2007), Women's status and economic globalization. *International Studies Quarterly*, 51(4), 855–876.

Rostow, W. W. (1963), *The Stages of Economic Growth: A Non-Communist Theory*, Cambridge: Cambridge University Press.

Sen, A. (1999), *Development as Freedom*, New York: Alfred A. Knopf.

UNIFEM (2008), *Who Answers to Women: Gender and Accountability. In Progress of the Worlds Women 2008/2009*, New York: United Nations Development Fund for Women.

Vishwakarma, H. (2002), The dalits of Nepal and their struggle for social justice. *Development*, 45(3), 90–92.

World Bank (2014), *World Development Indicators on CD-Rom*, Washington, DC: World Bank.

Yoon, M. Y. (2001), Democratization and women's legislative representation in Sub-Saharan Africa. *Democratization*, 8(2), 169–190.

Chapter 13

Islamic Nano-Finance for the Very Poor by Women: Hopes for Addressing the Islamic Microfinance Gap

Khairunnisa Musari

Abstract

Poverty is the fruit of unequal distribution and has become a market for loan sharks. Financial inclusion for all is the key for creating a distributive justice. Islamic finance should be a solution to eradicate poverty. Inability of the Islamic financial institutions to complete the missions of the Islamic finance to bridge the financial and real sectors, to distribute the wealth and to manage the lack and excess of liquidity may also create distributive injustice. This chapter believes that Islamic nano-finance can be an answer to cope with the Islamic microfinance gap in financing the very poor. The existence of conventional microfinance institutions in some countries that focus on nano-finance should be a reflection for Islamic finance to engage in this society. Microfinance actually helps poor households by empowering women to contribute to the economic growth and sustainable livelihoods of their families and communities. Some studies also confirm that women in general are a better credit risk for microfinance institutions throughout the world. But, in the absence of banking facility, the very poor frequently borrow money from the loan sharks and microfinance institutions that come to help these people by charging an interest rate. So, this chapter is intended to: (1) Describe the profile of microfinance for women in some countries; (2) Compile a working model of nano-finance activities in the world; (3) Propose a model of Islamic nano-finance for women by integrating the Islamic finance and Islamic philanthropy to finance the poor in meeting their immediate needs, especially to avoid them from the trap of loan shark.

Keywords: Poverty, Microfinance, Nano-finance, Women, Indonesia

Poverty is a dynamic phenomenon. It has a lot of dimensions with respect to time and region. Many studies confirm that microfinance[1] is a useful tool and makes significant contribution for fighting the poverty. ADB (1997, 2000), Robinson (2001), Morduch and Haley (2002), Segrado (2005), Obaidullah (2008), Obaidullah and Khan (2008), Dusuki (2008), Rosenberg (2010), Ali (2011), BWTP (2011), Leikem (2012) and Macchiavello (2016) see microfinance as a powerful poverty alleviation tool. It implies provision of financial services to poor and low-income people whose low economic standing excludes them from formal financial systems. These people are traditionally considered non-bankable, mainly because they lack the guarantees that can protect a financial institution against a loss risk.

Further, women and microfinance have been identified as strategic developmental tools, especially in emerging countries, to alleviate poverty among women. Women are a critical part of society. From the beginning of its operation in Bangladesh, Rahman (1999) mentions that the Grameen Bank has maintained a mandate to alleviate rural poverty in the country which not just preferred to lend to women borrowers.[2] According to ILO (2008), 70% of the world's poor are women. Yet traditionally women have been disadvantaged in access to credit and other financial services. Commercial banks often focus on men and formal businesses, neglecting the women who make up a large and growing segment of the informal economy. Although microfinance institutions (MFIs) cannot empower women directly, Addai (2017) claims MFIs can help them through training and awareness-raising to challenge the existing norms, cultures and values which place them at a disadvantage in relation to men, and to help them have greater control over resources and their lives. Addae (2015) argues that empowering women would escalate their participation in the labor force and in the decision-making processes, reduce poverty, and would significantly enhance their contribution to national income and the development of their countries as a whole. By using a large global dataset covering 350 MFIs in 70 countries, D'Espallier *et al.* (2009) discover that more women clients are associated with lower portfolio-at-risk, lower write-offs and lower credit-loss provisions, *ceteris paribus.* These findings confirm common believes that women in general are a better credit-risk for MFIs.

However, although the positive impact of microfinance on women's empowerment is evident, ILO (2008) reminds that microfinance providers

[1]Otherwise known as microcredit, micro-lending, microloan or micro-capital.
[2]But, since the mid-1980s it has focused primarily on women.

must also be cautious to avoid possible negative outcomes. Studies have shown that women sometimes have little or no control over their loan, with the husband or male family member making all decisions. Moreover, differences in literacy, property rights and social attitudes about women may limit the impact outside of the immediate household. Residents of rural areas specifically continue to have difficulties in accessing microfinance. Women may also struggle with the heavier workload created by the responsibility for loan repayment. Kato and Kratzer (2013) notice MFIs are extorting money from poor women through high interest rates, causing higher social pressure and in some cases lead to domestic violence.

This chapter believes that nano-finance can be a true help for the poor, including the poor women. Microfinance actually helps poor households by empowering women to contribute to the economic growth and sustainable livelihoods of their families and communities. But, microfinance in practice also has weaknesses. Microfinance faces some serious challenges, especially for helping the very poor. In the fact, microfinance is not enough as a tool of financing for them. Musari (2017a, 2017b, 2016a, 2016b, 2016c) and Musari and Simanjuntak (2016) assert that nanofinance can be addressed to the microfinance gap as well as Islamic microfinance gap. Nowadays, some of MFIs are concerning to the very poor and they introduce a new term "nano-finance" to provide opportunities for the very poor, very low income, and very micro enterprises to access financial services. The existence of conventional MFIs which focus on nano-finance should be a reflection for Islamic finance to engage this concept. Islamic finance should be a solution for alleviating the very poor. Inability of the Islamic financial institutions (IFIs) to complete the missions of Islamic finance to bridge the financial and real sector, to distribute the wealth, and to manage the lack and excess of liquidity may also create distributive injustice. Overall this chapter is intended to: (1) Describe the profile of microfinance for women in some countries; (2) Compile a working model of nano-finance activities in the world; (3) Propose a model of Islamic nano-finance for women by integrating the Islamic finance and Islamic philanthropy to finance the poor in meeting their immediate needs, especially to avoid them from the trap of loan shark.

13.1 Women and microfinance in some selected countries

Does microfinance really help the poor? Rahman (2007) argues that this question cannot be answered in a single sentence. The impact that microcredit programs have had on the rural economy has produced mixed results. Sample (2011) states that the microfinance movement is, indeed, at a crossroads. After many years of learning and growth, the field is now confronted with unprecedented problems and criticism. MFIs are faced with the choice of two directions, one where the microfinance industry splits into two warring camps and the other where the industry works together and takes leadership in the movement to end severe poverty. Rahman (1999) claims that micro-lending to the poor is focused on the achievement of equitable (women as equal partners) and sustainable gain (in regard to livelihoods for beneficiaries and financial viability for service-providing institutions). All is the key element for the 21 century's economic and social development.

So, are women good for microfinance? Is microfinance good for women? In Ghana, the government has developed several policies to enhance microfinance to simultaneously empower women and alleviate poverty. For women who had no access to credit from the banking system, Lott (2009) explains that the women may borrow the money from an MFI. This MFI will be able to lend her money by using a group lending system, in which groups of women are jointly responsible for the repayment of the loan. The loans allow her to make her business more profitable and to spend the extra income on her children's education and her family's medical expenses. In addition to the loan, she received training in business and leadership to get elected in public offices to represent her community. However, Addai (2017) mentions that there has been a debate on the potency of microfinance to empower the Ghanaian women because loan given to women is controlled by men. MFIs are also exploiting money from poor women through very high interest rates just like the loan shark. Owusu *et al.* (2013) found out that MFIs give credits with conditions that are not favorable to the needs of the women. The dependency burdens on women coupled with the low credit which the women access from the MFIs for productive activities lead the women to exploit the credit to meet the business and household needs. Research of Dzisi and Obeng (2013) suggest that the women's enterprises have expanded and their socio-economic status has improved highly after taking the loans. It is, however, recommended that MFIs provide education[3] in finance management for their clients, since only few of them undertake such an exercise.

[3]Norwood (2014) encounters that microcredit membership of women in Ghana with greater education and less wealth are likely to have higher levels of autonomy.

In Bangladesh, Girón (2015) notes that there are 86 MFIs controlled by nongovernment organizations (NGOs), and most of their credit is intended for rural women. Very clearly, MFIs have a close relationship with banks and institutional investors. They are a part of structured finance and guarantee profitability from collateral and make profits from loaning money to the marginalized people. They manage large investment through granting small credits to small businesses. Banks and institutional investors dominate loans and their profits exceed 100%. Thesis of Rahman (1998) of Grameen Bank lending finds that women become the primary target of the microcredit program because of their sociocultural vulnerability. The program extends credit to women, but at the domestic front women often "pass on" their loans to men, or men take control over women's loans, or loans are used to meet the emergency consumption needs of the household. In this system, women borrower often lose control over their loans but bear the consequences of the debt burden in their households and loan centers.

In Egypt, referring to Hadidi (2016), microfinance can trace its origin back to the early 1970s when the Self-Employed Women's Association formed an urban cooperative bank with the objective of providing banking services to poor women employed in the unorganized sector in rural areas. His study shows that the women empowerment in rural Egypt can be improved if certain microfinance services such as socio-economic status upgradation, autonomy for life choices and women position in the family/society increases. Thus, it has positively developed their contribution in running their families. Given the importance of accompanying women in the process, and the difficulty for individual women to meet their strategic needs given the structural economic and social realities, study of Drolet (2010) argues that microcredit has a potentially important role to play. In Nepal, study of Sharma (2007) comes across the consistent results with the view that women's participation in microcredit programs helps to increase women's empowerment. Credit program participation leads to women taking a greater role in household decision-making, having greater access to financial and economic resources, having greater social networks, having greater bargaining power compared with their husbands, and having greater freedom of mobility.

In Botswana, Okurut *et al.* (2014) found that microfinance had no significant effect on household welfare. However, women's access to microfinance has led to their empowerment through participation in household expenditure decisions-making, being respected by family members and the community and participation in local leadership activities which addresses the strategic needs of women. In Philippines, by replicating The Grameen Bank, Center for Agriculture and Rural Development (CARD) has been targeting women from the low-income households as the clientele since 1990 to deliver microcredit for the alleviation of poverty. Study of Hossain and Diaz (1997) locate that the microcredit contributed to 25% of increase in household incomes. However, the institution is not yet financially viable, as the cost of operation is about 54% of the amount of the outstanding loan. Without high rates of interest, the microcredit operations will not be able to expand their operations on a large enough scale to have a significant impact on poverty alleviation.

In Indonesia, Yaumidin (2015) finds that microfinance has no great impact to improve the preference of Muslim women empowerment in urban area of Bandung City. Study of Srimulyani (2013) in Aceh suggests that the microfinance program for women should tackle the problem of existing gender ideals in the community carefully, or otherwise it will add to the burden of women instead of empowering them. In Tanzania, microfinance programs have significantly increased. According to Kato and Kratzer (2013), empowerment of women is one of the main issues in Tanzania and microfinance services are considered as an entry point or a vehicle toward empowering women. Based on the study result from three regions of Tanzania, they found that women members of MFIs have more control over savings and income generated from the business, greater role in decision-making, greater self-efficacy and self-esteem, and greater freedom of mobility and increased activities outside home.

In Sri Lanka, Rathiranee and Semasinghe (2016) affirm that microfinance is considered as an important tool to enlarge the women's living condition and lead income opportunity. However, it is found out that women entrepreneurs do not have easy access to microfinance factors for their entrepreneurial activity and as such have low business performance due to lack of infrastructure facilities. By utilizing two leading MFIs, study of Herath *et al.* (2015) obtain that if the woman owned the loan and acted as a canal of credit, it had a positive and significant impact on her competence to make decisions at home. The empirical evidence indicates the importance of concentrating on women's empowerment as a part of the socio-economic mission of microfinance.

Microfinance actually has the power to alleviate poverty. Unfortunately, the needy people usually repay the loans at extremely high rates. Duvall (2004) claims interest rate ceilings are found in many countries throughout the world and small loans to poor people generally cost more than normal commercial bank rates. Though meant to protect consumers, interest rate ceilings almost always hurt the poor. Rosenberg (2010) believe microcredit is a tool of extraordinary power to lift poor people, especially women, out of poverty. There is a strong proof that microcredit is very valuable for poor people in helping to deal with their circumstances. But, most of them come back for additional loans. They usually repay those loans at extremely high rates year after year. Rosenberg (2002), Rosenberg *et al.* (2009), Mitra (2009), Levin (2012), Rosenberg *et al.* (2013) also confirm some of the problems associated with the practice of MFIs, particularly about high interest rates by MFIs which have been criticized. Rahman (1999) during his fieldwork found that the Grameen Bank, the pioneer of microfinance, also charge annual interest rate on most of microloans to the poor at 20%. It was at least 8% higher than the commercial market rate in the country. Groen (2002) elucidates the costs of making a small loan are higher in percentage terms than the costs of making a larger loan. The financial institutions must set interest rates that cover all administrative costs, plus the cost of capital (including inflation), loan losses and a provision for increasing equity. Meyer (2002) confirms that transaction costs have a large fixed cost component so the unit costs for smaller savings deposits or smaller loans are higher than for larger financial transactions. MFIs can survive if they charge high enough interest rates or achieve high levels of efficiency. Bateman (2011) also sees that MFIs charge lower interest rates than loan sharks, but interest rates have not fallen as much as predicted, and in some countries have remained very high. Addai (2017) mentions that exorbitant interest rates of MFIs lead to many women running away from their homes and villages after failing to repay the loan installments and avoiding their properties to be taken by MFIs.

13.2 Nano-finance: The new paradigm of microfinance

As the provision of a wide range of financial services, particularly credit, to low-income people or financially excluded people, Macchiavello (2016) mentions that a true microfinance combines a business structure with social inspiration, often resorts to technological innovations to lower costs (through financial technology) and merges with traditional local experiences (such as financial cooperatives and also Islamic finance). Ahmed (2002) regrets that most of the MFIs have non-Islamic characteristics because the financing is based on interest. How about Islamic MFIs?

UN HABITAT (2005) appraises that the contemporary Islamic MFIs are still a recent phenomenon and have not yet fully evolved. They have also experienced generous growth. While diverse models and practices are inherent in the option and sociability Islamic microfinance proposes that these services need to be regulated in order to serve transparency, embed consumer confidence and avoid fraud on beneficiaries due to the unfamiliarity with the products. Rahman and Dean (2013) summary the challenges of Islamic MFIs into four main categories: market penetration, sustainability of Islamic MFIs, high transaction costs and the effectiveness of Islamic MFIs in alleviating poverty. Similar to conventional MFIs, Islamic MFIs have experiences in high transaction costs. Small loans are expensive because of high overhead costs, which usually have a great fixed cost attached.

Further, access of the poor to financial services is indeed important for the success of sustainable poverty alleviation programs. In this regard, microfinance has been recognized worldwide as an important policy instrument. Almost all the literatures examine about microfinance but not many discuss about nano-finance. The coexistence of nano-finance has not garnered as much concern as microfinance theoretical work. However, Musari (2017a, 2017b, 2016a, 2016b, 2016c), Musari and Simanjuntak (2016), Chonlaworn and Pakanee (2015), Parpart (2014), Mahanti (2008), Deb *et al.* (eds.) (2008), and Pathak and Sriram (2004) show that nanofinance are being practiced in some Asian countries. There are MFIs, nanofinance institutions (NFIs) and local/rural banks that provide nano-finance to serve the poor, especially to the poorest of the poor.

In India, as the country with the largest Hindu majority in the world,[4] there is Sarvodaya Nano Finance Limited (SNFL).[5] SNFL found that in actual practice it is very difficult for the poor to access loans without security. The only sustainable long-term solution was to have in place a financial institution, which is not only oriented to the needs of the

[4]But, Deny (2017) mentions that India is predicted to overtake Indonesia as the world's largest Muslim population. Despite Indonesia has the largest Muslim population in the world, the population in Indonesia is only 1/5 of the total Indian population of 1.2 billion inhabitants. By 2045, the Muslim population of minority India is expected to surpass the number of Muslim Indonesians. Today, there are even areas in India where the population is predominantly Muslim. Geubrina (2017) describes that in Uttar Pradesh provinces, 130 km southeast of New Delhi, North India, there is a Muslim-majority city with 800,000 inhabitants.

[5]See http://www.sarvodayanano.org/; Pathak and Sriram (2004).

poor but is also fully owned by the rural communities. SNFL took the role of such a financial institution and was registered with the Reserve Bank of India as a Non-Banking Financial Company (NBFC) in 1996 with a mission to promote a large number of sustainable livelihoods for the rural poor, especially women and rural artisans, through the provision of financial services and technical assistance in an integrated manner. SNFL was established as a part of the BASIX group of companies in Hyderabad. The initial design of BASIX was to use Sarvodaya to make very small loans to individuals, addressing the microfinance needs of the poor — landless, marginal and small farmers and women, while a related company Bhartiya Samruddhi Finance Limited would make larger loans to micro-entrepreneurs and commercial farmers, who in turn generated livelihood opportunities to the poor. However, at the end of the 2 years of operation, BASIX group found that it was better to carry out all the lending operations through a single company and SNFL became neglected since 1999.

Other than SNFL, there are Aamara Biswas[6] and Our Biswas,[7] which are official NFIs. NFIs are established to truly help the poorest of the poor women in the society. Mahanti (2008) explains that women who fall into this category constantly struggle for their daily livelihood. One of the root causes of their helpless situation is the emergency needs for small amounts of money. They cannot go to the government, commercial banks or MFIs for their emergency needs. The procedures in those institutions are impractical and unhelpful to the poorest of the poor. The only choice they have is going to the moneylender. The women will get the loan with a minimum interest rate of 120% per year. Most of the time, they cannot pay back the entire principal in a lump sum which is required by the moneylender, and therefore, continue to pay interest for the rest of their lives. Sometimes, the fettle forces them to take another loan from other moneylender to pay back their previous loan or take another emergency loan. As a small interest free loan, nano-finance could be given to women for their emergency needs. NFIs are not meant to compete with MFIs. Instead, NFIs are an outgrowth of MFIs. The women who are not able to get loan from MFIs will benefit through NFIs. The concept of nano-finance is very simple and the operational method is not complicated. Everyone can understand its

---

[6]See http://www.aamarabiswas.org.

[7]Our Biswas is an acronym which stands for Our Belief in Services for Women of All Societies. See https://www.ourbiswasusa.org/.

basic structure without going through training and explanation. The main objective of nano-finance is to give small and interest-free loan (up to Rs 2,000[8]) to women for their needs and which they can return in a year. They have a choice of not going to the money lenders to borrow money with high interest rate.

In Uganda, global initiative Our Biswas[9] spread the spirit through Clover Foundation[10] in Kampala and Bliss Femme in Kasese District to introduce the innovative, economic empowerment concept of nano-finance to ultra-poor women in developing countries around the world. As a nano-finance program, The Kisoboka Initiative in Kampala is the first effort to realize the concept of nano-finance beyond India. The systems and processes were developed by Mahanti of Aamara Biswas with more than 10,000 women. The approach is a finely tuned method for loan distribution and collection, along with clearly established rules of engagement for women in a process that fosters the importance that the participants own the program. Trust is essential.

In Indonesia, there is an MFI for Society which is usually called as the Bank for Poor Family or Bank *Keluarga Miskin* (Gakin).[11] It was initiated by the Department of Cooperative & Micro Small Medium Enterprises (MSMEs) since 2005 for nano-finance[12] in Jember. Study of Musari and Simanjuntak (2015, 2016) describe this institution as a good alternative financing for the very poor, very low income, and very micro enterprises rather than formal banks or loan shark. Its main target is productive women. Each Bank Gakin consists of a maximum of 200 poor people with predominantly 90% of women, who are administrators and 46% of them are elementary school graduates and 5% had never undergone

---

[8]Equal to Rp 417,179 ~ USD 30.9 (Rs 1 ~ Rp 208.6 ~ $0.0154528) on 20 October 2017.
[9]See https://www.ourbiswasusa.org/global-initiative.
[10]The Clover Foundation is a non-profit organization in the United States (U.S.) and an NGO in Uganda that enables young children living in the urban slums to have the health, confidence and ability to be the change in their community. Programmatically, Clover is an early childhood learning center and pre-school for young children who live in the slums of Busega, Kampala District, and who without free quality education would not be able to access their right to be educated.
[11]The term "Bank Gakin" is given by poor people who became its members and is used by the administrators and other people in Jember. Bank Gakin is an alternative financing for the very poor, very low income, and very micro enterprises rather than formal banks or moneylenders.
[12]This financial institution does not use the term "nanofinance", but according to the amount of loan can be categorized as nano-finance than microfinance.

a formal school education[13] Bank Gakin serves about 30 groups with more than 150 households. They use the principle of joint responsibility among its members. Business group consisting of 5–10 people can apply for business loans between Rp 50,000 and Rp 1 million.[14] People who apply for credit does not have to submit business proposals, especially through a convolution survey. Proposals can be submitted orally. Funds can be directly treated as liquid funds after a survey of the business is conducted with credit disbursement period of 10 weeks paid in installments every week with a rate 0.5% per week. This mechanism is very helpful for the group of microenterprises.

Other than Bank Gakin, there is the Koperasi Wanita (Kopwan) Setia Bhakti Wanita (SBW)[15] in Surabaya. SBW was established and developed by women in 1978. It started as *arisan* which was motivated by Mursia Zaafril Ilyas with 35 women members The first loan was Rp. 2,000. In 1975, this *arisan* had implemented a savings and loan business and got a venture capital. In 1977, Mrs. Zaafril started to introduce cooperative concepts in order to expand the group's business of *arisan*. The members of the *arisan* group were able to get a loan of Rp. 5,000 in five installments. In May 1978, this *arisan* group became an organization which was called Koperasi Wanita Setia Bhakti Wanita that was inaugurated by the Department of Cooperative Surabaya City.

Today, SBW has become a famous women's cooperative in Indonesia. Based on history, Supriyanto (2017) clarifies that SBW actually is the pioneer of microfinance because it existed before the Grameen Bank. Muhammad Yunus was inspired by Mrs. Zaafril from SBW after sharing joint responsibility system of SBW and its unique all female members concept. Through the joint responsibility system, the non-performing loan (NPL) of SBW can be reduced to 0%. The capital of this cooperative is derived from its own capital, namely the savings of members and external

---

[13]However, they show a good performance for Bank Gakin. In 2008 and 2009, Jember obtained Autonomy Award from the Jawa Pos Institute of Pro-Autonomy (JPIP) due to Bank Gakin which showed impressive financial performance: performing loan 90%, non-performing loan 8% and loss only 2%. Referring to Sukarno and Damayanti (2012), Bank Gakin indicated a financial performance that continued to improve from year to year. This was reflected by positive financial ratio from period to period. The ratio of Bank Gakin had also been able to meet the performance standards of MFIs issued by the International Fund for Agricultural Development (IFAD).

[14]Equal to \$3.704 – 74.082 (\$1 ≈ Rp 13,498.50) on 20 October 2017.

[15]See http://setiabhaktiwanita.com.

capital derived from loans from banks by using the office as collateral. The composition of capital until 2002 was 45% of its own capital and 55% of external capital.

In Thailand, Musari (2017a, 2017b, 2016a, 2016b, 2016c), Musari and Simanjuntak (2016) describe the phenomenon of bank and non-bank businesses that shift to nano-finance, and provide small loans without any collateral requirements. To support many small entrepreneurs or people at the grassroots who have no access to capital and who require it to use out of system debt service known as loan sharks, the Thai Government has implemented the Nano-finance Project. Bank of Thailand (BOT) has been also authorized to issue nano-finance regulations and approved the nano-finance scheme that aims to reduce the loan shark problem and promote better access to capital that would expand occupational chance of the borrowers. Chonlaworn and Pongpirodom (2015), Parpart (2014) explain that nano-finance is different from informal loans and personal loans. In nano-finance, each borrower will get a loan not more than Bt 100,000 at an interest rate up to 36% p.a. without any collateral. Loan targets are to promote better access to capital, increase occupational opportunities and alleviate illegal lending. Target group includes new business owners who may not have a constant income, monthly paycheck or have limited financial history and low-income groups/individuals that do not meet financial institutions' borrowing criterion. The requirements for borrowers are individuals capable of repaying debts. For debt collection method, a lender issues an invoice to notify the borrower the amount and time the repayment is due, or directly credits monthly payments from a bank account according to the agreement term between the lender and the borrower. Debt collection method, however, must comply with BOT regulations and related legislations.

Further, The BOT has also introduced pico-finance. Pico-finance is viewed as a final solution to the longstanding problem of moneylenders, in addition to earlier suggested nano-finance. The Thai Government implement pico-finance and nano-finance to handle loans at rural level. Pico-finance will handle smaller funds and with loans not exceeding Bt 50,000 whereas nano-finance handle larger loans up to Bt 100,000.

13.3 Nano-finance for the poor (Islamic)

In the perspective of Islamic finance, some of the MFIs/NFIs practices still do not meet the *sharia* compliance due to the rate of interest charged on loans despite it being relatively low, and not being considered as a burden to the borrower compared to loan shark. In the name of humanity, interest rate hurts the poor and nano-finance must avoid the usury. As a new paradigm of microfinance, nano-finance can be also addressed as the (Islamic) microfinance gap in order to alleviate the poverty. Poverty alleviation is the principal goal in such way that the financing for the poor should negate the interest rate. The finance provision and accessibility for the poor are inevitably relevant to IFIs in order to achieve the Islamic economic objectives, including social justice, equitable distribution of income and wealth and promotion of economic development. Musari (2017a) claims that nano-finance can be a meeting point between conventional microfinance and Islamic microfinance for financing the poor through *qardhul hassan*[16] as the contract.

According to Deb *et al.* (eds.) (2008), nano-finance is different from microfinance as it aims to cope with the severe problems of the destitute within the community. In nano-finance, very small grants, credit, savings and other welfare services are offered to the poorest. Through subsidized funding, nano-finance is addressing the harsh poverty by integrating NGOs, social security funds, grants, interest-free loans, etc. with special government investment in health, education and infrastructure development that can help raise the level of the extremely poor. Musari (2016b, 2017a, 2017b) propose a generic concept of nano-finance whose major assumptions can be summarized as follows in Table 13.1.

It is clear that microfinance has a prominent potential for contributing to women's empowerment. McCarter (2006), Mayoux (2002), Vonderlack and Schreiner (2002) confirm that microfinance has enabled thousands of women to use small sums in creative and effective ways to expand their livelihoods, remedy their families' well-being and construct savings. Microfinance encourages the empowerment of women in economic, social and political levels. Informal savings mechanisms throughout the world indicate that poor women save and that they value low transaction costs and external support for deposit discipline. In emerging countries, women play a crucial role as risk managers and drivers of development, particularly for alleviating poverty.

[16] *Qardhul hassan* (also written as *qard hasan; qard-ul-hassan*) is an example of a unique instrument recommended by Islamic economics and finance. *Qardhul hassan* is often referred to as a zero-return loan, benevolent loan, voluntary loan, soft loan, charitable loan or beautiful loan.

Table 13.1 The proposed generic concept of Islamic nano-finance.

Aspect	Description
Definition	A new paradigm of microfinance, namely a small financing that operates with simple processing system for the poor, particularly the very poor, for their emergency needs (for food, health care, education, death, wedding, daily livelihood, small trading or very micro enterprises).
The concept of financial institution	Flexibility in financing issuance. The borrower does not need to have a steady income, payroll, financial history or collateral.
Mission	1. To avoid the very poor to go to the loan shark. 2. To fill the (Islamic) microfinance gap; 3. To encourage the very poor to be independent and have the minimum necessities to live a decent life; 4. To build sufficient internal financial and human resources and to use them to leverage resources from external sources; 5. To reduce the humanitarian cases as impact of the extremely poverty and loan shark.
Funding source	NFIs/MFIs must get low cost fund to finance the very poor to avoid interest rate. Funding source may be obtained mostly from grants, donations, corporate social responsibility (CSR), philanthropy institutions, crowdfunding, *infaq, shadaqa, waqf, waqf-sukuk*, etc.
Market target	1. Very poor people. 2. Very micro enterprises that may not have a constant income, monthly paycheck, or have limited financial history. 3. Very low-income groups/individuals that do not meet financial institutions' borrowing criterion.

Table 13.1 (*Continued*)

Aspect	Description
Credit needs	Emergency needs
Loan size	\$1–100[a]
Interest rate	0%[b] (using *qardhul hassan* contract for the emergency needs (for food, health care, education, death, wedding, daily livelihood, small trading or very micro enterprises))
Lending procedures	People do not have to go through paper work and/or rigid rules and regulations for getting small financing for their emergency needs. For business, people can be submitted orally. Funds can be directly treated as liquid funds after a survey conducted at a glance toward the business.
Disbursement process duration	1 day.
Repayment periods	Time agreed together, but must <1 year.
Collateral/guarantees	—

Source: Musari (2017a, 2016a), modify and improve.
Notes: [a]This number is an approximate figure. Each country may have different levels for the amount span of nano-finance.
[b]This contract should be used by nano-finance or pico-finance. When the people have increased their income, capacity and capability, they have to use microfinance. Because of that, the nano-finance (and also pico-finance) must be submitted to the hierarchy of Islamic finance.

However, there are some of the problems associated with microfinance. Levin (2012) argues the complex socioeconomic factors may cause loan programs to flop. She highlights these problems stem from the basic tenet of microfinance: the need for lending programs to be managed locally in order to understand the needs of a community and assess the sustainability of each project. Lending programs vary a great deal around the world due to cultural differences, and the success of each must be evaluated in a geographic context. The industry of microfinance cannot be standardized due to these vitally important differences, and there are few organizations which have the ability to watch over the practices of individual lenders. Musari (2017a) mentions that people in poverty contains many anomalies. The treatment for them should be distinguished in the planning and implementation of effective financial inclusion strategies. Then, implementing usury for the poor is fighting the humanity and hurting the poor. Arzayeva and Dochshanova (2016) believe that one of the main causes of these crises is the existing financial system, based on usurious credit interest.

Thus, nano-finance should not extort money from poor women through high interest rates. Nanofinance, with or without "Islamic" label, may help women by integrating the Islamic finance and Islamic philanthropy to finance the poor in meeting their immediate needs, especially to avoid them from the trap of loan sharks. Therefore, the NFIs/MFIs must get low cost fund to finance the poor to avoid interest rate. The source of funding may be acquired mostly from grants, donations, CSR, philanthropy institutions, crowdfunding, *infaq, shadaqa, waqf, waqf-sukuk*, etc.

13.4 Conclusion

There is a close relation between women and microfinance. The influence that microfinance had on the women's empowerment has produced mingled results. On one side, microfinance leads to women's empowerment, especially to the poor women, by positively influencing women's decision-making power and enhancing their overall socio-economic status and also their households. But, on the other side, microfinance also has other faces, which some studies have also detected as a negative impact on women's income and employment and also higher social pressure to ensure loan repayment.

Nano-finance can be an answer to reduce the weaknesses of microfinance for women. The coexistence of nano-finance has not gained as much attention as microfinance. However, nano-finance activities are prevalent in some countries such as in India, Thailand and Indonesia. In order to avoid the loan sharks, microfinance is not enough a tool of financing. In order to alleviate poverty, microfinance in practice also has infirmity.

However, some of the MFIs/NFIs practices are not in accordance with the *sharia* compliance. In the name of humanity, interest rate hurts the poor and nano-finance must avoid the usury. Nano-finance based *qardhul hassan* can be an expectation for helping the poor without interest rate. Nano-finance organize small financing that operates with simple processing system to the very poor for the emergency needs, particularly to keep away from the loan sharks. Nano-finance also can be a meeting point between conventional and Islamic finance for financing the poor without interest rates. By integrating the Islamic finance and Islamic philanthropy to finance the poor in meeting their immediate needs, nanofinance should be promoted in the hierarchy of Islamic finance, especially for financing the very poor and for averting them from the loan sharks.

References

ADB (1997), *Microenterprise Development: Not By Credit Alone*, The Philippines: Asian Development Bank.

ADB (2000), *Finance for the Poor: Microfinance Development Strategy*, The Philippines: Asian Development Bank.

Addae, J. A. (2015), Effect of microfinance on women's empowerment: A review of the literature. *Africa Development and Resources Research Institute (ADRRI) Journal of Arts and Social Sciences*, 13(8-2), 1–15.

Addai, Bismark (2017), Women empowerment through microfinance: Empirical evidence from Ghana. *Journal of Finance and Accounting*, 5(1), 1–11.

Amin, Md. A. L. and Chowdhury, Tayub (2008), Women, poverty and empowerment: An investigation into the dark side of microfinance. *Asian Affairs*, 30(2), 16–29.

Ahmed, Habib (2002), Financing microenterprises: An analytical study of Islamic microfinance institution. *Islamic Economic Studies*, 2(2), 27–64.

Arzayeva, Maiya and Dochshanova, Assel (2016), Problems of development of Islamic financing in Kazakhstan: Financial and legal aspects. *Indian Journal of Science and Technology*, 9(S1), 1–5.

BWTP (2011), *A History of Asia's Regional Microfinance Network (20 Years of Working for Greater Financial Inclusion in Asia 1990–2010)*, Singapore: The Banking with the Poor (BWTP) Network Ltd. & The Foundation for Development Cooperation.

Deb, Bimal J., Sengupta, Keya and Ray, B. Datta (eds.) (2008), *Globalization and North East India*, New Delhi: Ashok Kumar Mittal.

D'Espallier, Bert, Isabelle Guérin and Roy Mersland (2009), Women and Repayment in Microfinance. Rural Microfinance and Employment (RUME) Working Paper Series. March. Marseille.

Drolet, Julie (2010), Women, micro credit and empowerment in Cairo, Egypt. *International Social Work*, 54(5), 629–645.

Dzisi, Smile and Obeng, Francis (2013), Microfinance and the socio-economic wellbeing of women entrepreneurs in Ghana. *International Journal of Business and Social Research* (IJBSR), 3(11), 45–62.

Duval, Ann (2004), *The Impact of Interest Rate Ceilings on Microfinance*. Donor Brief No. 18, May. The Consultative Group to Assist the Poor (CGAP) Donor Information Resource Centre (DIRECT).

Dusuki, Asyraf Wajdi (2008), Banking for the poor: The role of Islamic banking in microfinance initiatives. *Humanomics*, 24(1), 49–66.

Girón, Alicia (2015), Women and financialization: Microcredit, institutional investors, and MFIs. *Journal of Economic Issues*, XLIX(2), 373–396.

Groen, Ruth P. Goodwin (2002), *Making Sense of Microcredit Interest Rates.* Donor Brief No. 6. September. The Consultative Group to Assist the Poor (CGAP) Donor Information Resource Centre (DIRECT).

Hadidi, Hala El (2016), Impact of microfinance services on rural Egyptian women empowerment: An empirical study. *American Scientific Research Journal for Engineering, Technology, and Sciences (ASRJETS)*, 22(1), 109–125.

Herath, H. M. W. A., Guneratne, L. H. P. and Sanderatne, N. (2015), Impact of microfinance on women's empowerment: A case study on two microfinance institutions in Sri Lanka. *Sri Lanka Journal of Social Sciences*, 38(1), 51–61.

Hossain, Mahabub and Diaz, Catalina P. (1997), Reaching The poor with effective microcredit: Evaluation of a Grameen Bank replication in the Philippines. *Journal of Philippines Development*, XXIV(2), 275–308.

ILO (2008). *Small Change, Big Changes: Women and Microfinance.* Geneva: International Labour Organization (ILO).

Kato, M. P. and Kratzer, Jan (2013), Empowering women through microfinance: Evidence from Tanzania. *The Academic Collaboration and Research Network, Austria, Cambridge UK (ACRN) Journal of Entrepreneurship Perspectives*, 2(1), 31–59.

Leikem, Kirsten (2012), Microfinance: A Tool for Poverty Reduction? *Senior Honors Projects. Paper 300.* Retrieved from http://digitalcommons.uri.edu/srhonorsprog/300, be accessed 28 December 2019.

Levin, Grace (2012), Critique of microcredit as a development model. *Pursuit — The Journal of Undergraduate Research at the University of Tennessee*, 4(1), 9.

Macchiavello, E. (2016), Microfinance and Financial Inclusion: The Challenge of Regulating Alternative Forms of Finance (Introduction) (December 20) excerpt from Macchiavello, E. (2017). *Microfinance and Financial Inclusion: The Challenge of Regulating Alternative Forms of Finance.* Oxon & New York: Routledge.

Machogu, Clifford, Jairus Amayi and Dharit Desai (2011), The contribution of micro-finance on the growth of micro-enterprises in Ukerewe District, Mwanza, Tanzania. *International Journal Of Micro Finance*, 1(1), 1–13.

Mayoux, L. (2002), Microfinance and women's empowerment: Rethinking 'best practice'. *Development Bulletin*, 57, 76–81.

McCarter, Elissa (2006), Women and microfinance: Why we should do more. *U. Md. L.J. Race Relig. Gender & Class*, 6(353), 353–366.

Meyer, Richard L. (2002), *Track Record of Financial Institutions in Assisting the Poor in Asia.* Asian Development Bank (ADB) Institute Research Paper 49, December, Tokyo: ADB.

Mitra, Subrata Kumar (2009), Exploitative microfinance interest rates. *Asian Social Sciences*, 5(5), 87–93.

Morduch, Jonathan and Haley, Barbara (2002), Analysis of the Effects of Microfinance on Poverty Reduction. NYU Wagner Working Paper No. 1014, 28 June.

Musari, Khairunnisa (2016a), *Redefining the Islamic Nanofinance and Its Institutional Strengthening: Lesson Learned from Asian Countries.* A paper was presented at 11th International Conference on Islamic Economics and Finance (ICIEF) "Rethinking Islamic Economics and Finance: Paving The Way Forward for Inclusive and Sustainable Development" with Organizer and Host Institution Kulliyyah of Economics and Management Sciences International Islamic University Malaysia (IIUM) and Co-Organizers Islamic Research and Training Institute (IRTI), Islamic Development Bank (IDB) & International Association of Islamic Economics (IAIE), Kuala Lumpur, 11–13 October.

Musari, Khairunnisa (2016b), Economic sustainability for Islamic nanofinance through *sukuk–waqf* linkage program (case study in Indonesia). *International Journal of Islamic Economics and Finance Studies* (*IJISEF*), 2(3), 83–94.

Musari, Khairunnisa (2016c), *Nanofinance, Redefine the Microfinance for the Very Micro Society*. A poster was presented at the 13th Indonesian Regional Science Association International Institute (IRSA) and was hosted by the Department of Economics, Faculty of Economics and Business, Brawijaya University, at Atria Hotel, Malang, 25–26 July.

Musari, Khairunnisa (2017a), *Promoting Qardhul Hassan in Nanofinance to Against the Moneylender* (*Case Study Indonesia, Cambodia, Brunei, Vietnam, and Thailand*). A paper presented at the 2nd Studia Islamika International Conference 2017 "Southeast Asian Islam: Religious Radicalism, Democracy, and Global Trends" at Post-Graduate School of State Islamic University Syarif Hidayatullah, Jakarta, 8–10 August.

Musari, Khairunnisa (2017b), *Nanofinance, Addressing the Islamic Microfinance Gap Through Global Islamic Humanitarian Institution*. A paper for Conference on Philanthropy for Humanitarian Aid 2017 held by International Research Centre of Islamic Economics and Finance (IRCIEF) International Islamic University College Selangor (KUIS) in collaboration with Islamic Research & Training Institute (IRTI) International Islamic Development Bank (IDB) and Sultan Sharif Ali Islamic University (UNISSA) at UNISSA, Brunei Darussalam, 23–24 May.

Musari, Khairunnisa and Simanjuntak, Rusli (2015), *Reconstruction the Bank for Poor Family Through Islamic Linkage Program*: (*Case Study in Indonesia*). A paper to be presented at 4th International Conference on Inclusive Islamic Financial Sector Development 2015 held by Islamic Research and Training Institute-Islamic Development Bank (IRTI-IDB) and International Islamic University, Islamabad, Pakistan, 17–18 November.

Musari, Khairunnisa and Simanjuntak, Rusli (2016), Nanofinance, Redefinition of Microfinance for the Very Micro Society Through Philanthropy Linkage Program (Case Study in Indonesia, Cambodia, Thailand, India). *Asian Academic Research Journal of Social Science & Humanities (AARJSH)*, 3(4), 455–463.

Norwood, Carolette (2014), Women's empowerment and microcredit: A case study from rural Ghana. *Journal of International Studies and Development*, 4, 1–22.

Obaidullah, Mohammed (2008), *Introduction to Islamic Microfinance*, New Delhi: The Islamic Business and Finance Network (IBF Net) and Islamic Relief Worldwide.

Obaidullah, Mohammed and Khan, Tariqullah (2008), Islamic Microfinance Development: Challenges and Initiatives. Policy Dialogue Paper No. 2, Jeddah: Islamic Research and Training Institute (IRTI).

Okurut, F. N., Kagiso, M., Ama, N. O. and Okurut, M. L. (2014), The impact of microfinance on household welfare in Botswana. *Botswana Journal of Economics*, 12(1), 45–58.

Owusu Joseph, Akanbasiam, A. C. and Anyesepari, A. A. (2013), Microfinance schemes and poverty reduction among women in the northern region of Ghana. *International Journal of Humanities and Social Science*, 3(19), 99–108.

Pathak, Akhileshwar and Mankal S. Sriram (2004), *Community at the Core: A Study of Sarvodaya Nano Finance Limited.* Indian Institute of Management Ahmedabad (IIMA) Working Paper No. 2004-10-04. Ahmedabad: IIMA, Research and Publication Department.

Rahman, Aminur (1998), *Rhetoric and Realites of Micro-credit for Women in Rural Bangladesh: A Village Study of Grameen Bank Lending.* A Thesis/Practicum submitted to the Faculty of Graduate Studies of The University of Manitoba in partial fulfillment of the requirements of the degree of Doctor of Philosophy.

Rahman, Aminur (1999), Micro-credit initiatives for equitable and sustainable development: Who pays? *World Development*, 27(1), 67–82.

Rahman, R. A. and Dean, Faisal (2013), Challenges and solutions in Islamic microfinance. *Humanomics*, 29(4), 293–306.

Rahman, Sayma (2007), *The Impact of Microcredit on Poverty and Women's Empowerment: A Case Study of Bangladesh.* A thesis submitted in fulfilment of the requirements for the award of the degree of Doctor of Philosophy, School of Economics and Finance, College of Law and Business, University of Western Sydney, Sydney, Australia. March.

Randleman, Rae M. (2013), Women as leaders in differing microfinance models. *Journal of Interdisciplinary Feminist Thought*, 7(1), 3.

Rathiranee, Y. and Semasinghe, S. D. (2016), The impact of micro finance factors on women entrepreneurs' performance in northern Sri Lanka. *International Journal of Social Science Studies*, 4(3), 94–99.

Robinson, Marguerite S. (2001), *The Microfinance Revolution: Sustainable Finance for the Poor*, Washington: International Bank for Reconstruction and Development (IBRD)/World Bank.

Rosenberg, Richard (2002), *Microcredit Interest Rates.* Revised Occasional Paper The Consultative Group to Assist the Poor (CGAP). No. 1. November, Washington: CGAP.

Rosenberg, Richard (2010), *Does Microcredit Really Help Poor People*? Focus Note 59, Washington: The Consultative Group to Assist the Poor (CGAP).

Rosenberg, Richard, Gonzalez, Adrian and Narain, Sushma (2009), The New Moneylenders: Are the Poor Being Exploited by High Microcredit Interest

Rates? Occasional Paper, The Consultative Group to Assist the Poor (CGAP) No. 15. February, Washington: CGAP.

Richard Rosenberg, Gaul, Scott, Ford, William and Tomilova, Olga (2013), *Microcredit Interest Rates and their Determinants 2004–2011.* Access to Finance Forum Reports by The Consultative Group to Assist the Poor (CGAP) and Its Partners No. 7, June. Washington: CGAP.

Sample, Bob (2011), *Moving 100 Million Families Out of Severe Poverty: How Can We Do It?* 2011 Global Microcredit Summit, Auxiliary Session Paper, 14–17 November, Valladolid, Spain.

Segrado, Chiara (2005), *Islamic Microfinance and Socially Responsible Investments*, Torino: Meda Project, University of Torino.

Sharma, Puspa Raj (2007), Micro-finance and women empowerment. *The Journal of Nepalese Business Studies*, IV(1), 16–27.

Srimulyani, Eka (2013), Women, Micro-finance and income generation after the political conflict and the tsunami in Aceh. *Asian Journal of Women's Studies*, 19(1), 93–112.

Sukarno, Hari and Damayanti, Dila (2012), Bank Gakin: Telaah Kinerja Lembaga Keuangan Mikro di Jember, Proceeding of Seminar & Konferensi Nasional Manajemen Bisnis. 26 May, pp. 73–79.

UN-HABITAT (2005), *Islam, Land & Property Research Series: Paper 8* (*Islamic Credit and Microfinance*), Nairobi: United Nations Human Settlements Programme (UN-HABITAT).

Vonderlack Rebecca M. and Schreiner, Mark (2002), Women, microfinance, and savings: Lessons and proposals. *Development in Practice*, 12(5), 602–612.

Yaumidin, Umi, (2015), *Financial Inclusion for Women: The Impact of Islamic Microfinance on Women's Empowerment in Indonesia.* A paper was presented at the 10th International Conference on Islamic Economics and Finance (ICIEF) held by Islamic Research and Training Institute (IRTI) Islamic Development Bank (IDB), International Association of Islamic Economics (IAIE), and Qatar Foundation. Doha, Qatar, 23–23 March.

Newspaper/Magazines

Ali, Suleman Muhammad (2011), "Islamic Microfinance Securitization: Structuring a Sukuk Musharakah", *Islamic Finance News*, 7 September, pp. 20–22.

Parpart, Erich (2014), BOT Considers 'Nano-Financing' for Grass-Roots People. *The Nation*, October 25. Retrieved from http://www.nationmultimedia.com/business/BOT-considers-nano-financing-for-grass-roots-peopl-30246202.html, be accessed 28 December 2019.

Internet

Bateman, Milfrod (2011), *Microfinance As A Development and Poverty Reduction Policy: Is It Everything It's Cracked Up To Be?* Background Note of Overseas Development Institute (ODI), March. Retrieved from https://www.odi.

org/sites/odi.org.uk/files/odi-assets/publications-opinion-files/6291.pdf, be accessed 28 December 2019.

Chonlaworn, Piyakorn and Pakanee Pongpirodom (2015), Can Nano Finance unleash The Grassroots From Loan Shark Problems? *EIC Analysis*, April 1st. Retrieved from https://www.scbeic.com/en/detail/product/1255, be accessed 28 December 2019.

Deny, Septian (2017), India Bakal Susul RI Jadi Negara Muslim Terbesar di Dunia. Retrieved from http://global.liputan6.com/read/3070827/india-bakal-susul-ri-jadi-negara-muslim-terbesar-di-dunia, be accessed 28 December 2019.

Geubrina, Cut Anggi Dwi (2017), Kampung Muslim di India. *Serambi Indonesia, Citizen Reporter*, Januari 7th. Retrieved from http://aceh.tribunnews.com/2017/01/07/kampung-muslim-di-india, be accessed 28 December 2019.

Mahanti, Joyasree (2009), Women Helping Women Through Nano Finance Institution. Retrieved from https://www.aamarabiswas.org/pdf1/2007-2008_Annual_Report.pdf, https://www.aamarabiswas.org/about.html, and http://www.ourbiswasusa.org/our_biswas/about_us/our_founder_note.php, be accessed 28 December 2019.

Supriyanto, Gatot (2017), SBW dan Grameen Bank. Retrieved from http://setiabhaktiwanita.com/seputar-sbw/sbw-dan-grameen-bank/, be accessed 28 December 2019.

PART C
Country Studies

Chapter 14

The "Islamic Women's" Movement: Transition from the Private Domain to the Public Sphere

Ömer Çaha

Abstract

This article emphasizes the development of the Muslim women's movement in Turkey. It traces the historical roots of this movement as well as its evolution toward two different understandings of women. It is clearly seen that there exist two main approaches to the role of women among Islamic groups: while the traditional Islamic understanding strives to maintain women's traditional roles notwithstanding that it advocates the right to benefit from modern education, another understanding challenges this and tries to ensure women's existence on a "womanly" base in the public life. The author attempts also to depict the story of how Muslim women have attempted to be articulated in the public sphere, their 50-year struggle to achieve that goal, as well as the discourses, values and symbols that have generally been centered on the "headscarf debates".

Keywords: Muslim women, Movement, Turkey, Headscarf, Women's role

This chapter emphasizes the development of the Muslim women's movement in Turkey. It traces the historical roots of this movement as well as its evolution toward two different understandings of women. It is clearly seen that there exist two main approaches to the role of women among Islamic groups: while the traditional Islamic understanding strives to maintain women's traditional role notwithstanding that it advocates the right to benefit from modern education, another understanding challenges this and tries to ensure women's existence on a "womanly" base in the public life. In this chapter, I depict how "Islamic women" attempted to express themselves in the public sphere, over 50 years, as well as the discourses, values and symbols that have generally been centered on the headscarf debates, and how the "women's movement" developed on the basis of this issue.

14.1 The rise of democratic public life and "Islamic women"

It is generally accepted that in the early decades of the Turkish republican regime, established after 1923, women started to serve the regime not only in public institutions individually but also through various organizations. During the single party regime, which continued until 1950, women were directed to serve the regime mostly under the banner of the Republican People's Party (CHP). In the 1950s, when multi-party life started, we observe that the political and ideological separation which emerged in Turkey also triggered women. Islamic groups that got rid of oppression through liberal policies pursued by the Democratic Party gradually started to be a part of public life and interested in politics. The attendance in modern educational institutions and their interest in politics would lay the foundations of the separation between the "cultural" Islam and the "political" Islam in the following years. The importance of "science", or "wisdom" as it is used in the Islamic literature, has been emphasized in both groups and the idea that "science is a religious obligation for men and women" has rapidly become popular among them.[1] In particular, the translation of Islamic sources like the *Qur'an*, the *aḥadith* of the Prophet (saw), and works on Islamic jurisprudence (*fiqh*) into Turkish has enabled Muslim groups to get acquainted with the essential religious resources, and to further comprehend the importance of science and education by benefiting more from Islamic resources. The religious atmosphere ascending in the country has expectedly found some women in the public sphere and modern institutions. The headscarf was first seen at university in the early 1950s (Barbarosoğlu, 2001). Fevziye Nuroğlu, who started to wear the headscarf at university in the early 1960s, recounts that in total there were four students with headscarves attending Turkish educational institutions in those days (Kutluoğlu, 2005, p. 72). Nuroğlu states that modern educational institutions and the well-developed districts of modern

[1]The duties that must be fulfilled in Islam are divided into two: *farḍ al-'ayn* and *farḍ al-kifayah*. While *farḍ al-'ayn* is the individual duty of everybody, *farḍ al-kifayah* is not incumbent upon everybody and is deemed to be fulfilled if some people perform it in a neighborhood. Studying science is accepted as *farḍ al-'ayn* for men and women.

cities like Istanbul were not yet familiar, at that time, with the headscarf and did not show tolerance toward students like her. Until then, headscarf and traditional dress had been considered as symbols identified with peasantry, backwardness and ignorance. Although no regulation was made about women's dress during the single-party period, the struggle against the traditional veil such as *çarşaf* (a traditional dress covering a woman's whole body) laid the foundations of an elitist attitude and perspective. Women in schools and public institutions and even those working in the tobacco, soap and textile industries were "modern looking" women freed from traditional dress. While women employed in public institutions as officials were required to dress up "modern", other women working as cleaners or tea servants were asked to cover their heads.[2] The message delivered through this policy was that the women working in white-collar jobs had been modernized by getting rid of their veils while women doing errands remained traditional. Veiled female students in modern institutions were perceived to be a challenge to the elitist official policy of the state and were punished harshly. For instance, Gülsen Ataseven graduated from a faculty of medicine as the top student in 1964. However, because she was wearing a headscarf, her degree was taken away and given to the second best student. Although there was a big difference between the two students' scores, the university management did not deem Gülsen Ataseven to be the "appropriate" top student. Later, veiled women in various institutions came to be punished in similar ways. The punitive attitude of the state toward the headscarf naturally created a reaction among traditional conservative groups.

The incident that made this reaction visible in the public sphere took place in Ankara University Faculty of Divinity. In 1968, the dismissal of Hatice Babacan, a student in the Faculty of Divinity, brought a strong reaction from Islamic groups. Hatice Babacan immediately became the symbol of Islamic groups. The issue was covered by the publications of these groups, a boycott campaign started in front of the Faculty of Divinity and the boycott became a current issue in parliament. The dean, Neşat Çağatay, was obliged to resign from his office as a result of the slogans "resign, dean" (Berberoğlu, 1999). The next case involved the lawyer Emine Aykenar in 1972. After she declared that she would not uncover her head

---

[2]For example, İş Bank pursued this policy in its employment decisions; see Özdemir (n.d.).

as a "requirement of her faith" in a trial in the Council of State she was dismissed from her profession by the Head of the Ankara Bar Association. In brief, the harsh punishment for religious veiling among individuals during the 1960s by the state created a social interest in — and even a resistance to — such politics.

The 1960s were the years when Şule Yüksel Şenler occupied the stage among Islamic circles and initiated the process of a radical break from the "official" way of dressing. Şenler, who had been a modern townswoman and a columnist for the *Yeni İstiklal* newspaper since the mid-1960s, started to wear the veil by developing a "stylish" and "elegant" dressing style. She began a struggle to popularize veiling through 5 years of nationwide conferences in which she spoke of her cause and the importance of veiling to women. The headscarf, which Şenler tried to popularize, created a strong reaction in the ruling elite and the secular media. The "stylish" and "elegant" style of headscarf, to be distinguished from the traditional style, was talked down by being named as *şulebaşı* (head of Şule). This naming would be transformed into *turban* by the same groups in the 1980s.

Şenler's beliefs left an indelible impression on young girls and religious women, and the headscarf rapidly became popular in the streets. This trend became so notable that the then President of the Republic, Cevdet Sunay, stated that "the pioneers of veiled women in the streets will get their deserts."[3] Şenler tried to popularize her cause through her book *The Tranquil Street* (*Huzur sokağı*) which has become one of the most-read novels not only by women but also by men after the 1970s. Şenler is a notable figure whose achievement was to put the "issue of the woman" on the agenda of Islamic groups in the 1960s and 70s (Tezcan, 2007). In addition, interest in the "issue of the woman" has increased among theologians since the mid-1960s and various publications have appeared on the subject. Hayrettin Karaman's book *Woman and Family in Islam* (*İslam'da kadın ve aile*) and Bekir Topaloğlu's *Woman in Islam* (*İslam'da kadın*) were intended as a response to the West and other civilizations and to prove how "perfect" Islam is supposed to be and what "rights"

[3]Following President Sunay's statement, Şule Yüksel Şenler sent him a letter stating that "the President should apologise to God and society!" As a result, she was sentenced to nine months in prison. Despite Sunay remitting her after two months, she did not accept it and stayed in prison for the full nine months; see Aköz and Atal (2004). This event made Şule Yüksel Şenler a hero in the eyes of Islamic circles. UD_OBJS/IH%20Efsaneler-Gercekler.pdf (accessed on 23 June 2011).

it provides women with. These books cover the necessity of women to be "protected" through values such as veil, modesty, chastity and morality, and the importance of this protection for the social order.[4]

In the 1970s, the issues of veiled woman and woman's education became of interest to ordinary citizens of various religious communities and political Islamic groups. Şule Yüksel Şenler set a significant example on this issue with her identity of "educated woman". On the other hand, conservative fathers acquired the opportunity to school their daughters when girls' classrooms were launched in *imam hatip* schools (government-run religious schools). The *Qur'an* classes and *imam hatip* schools were important instruments for the schooling of daughters of conservative families in the 1970s.[5]

It was after the 1980s that real momentum was experienced among Islamic circles about the "issue" of women. The mentality-change experienced by Turkey after 1980 in many fields was naturally reflected in the social values. As a consequence of liberal politics initiated by then Prime Minister Turgut Özal, Turkish society made a rapid transition toward modernization. The blasting point of the social modernization was and still is observed in the rising interest in getting modern education. After the 1980s, education started to be perceived as an important necessity by all parts of society. The policy to spread English-based education opportunities to the remotest corners of Anatolia through Anatolian High Schools (*Anadolu Liseleri*) naturally created the consequence that the demand for modern education took rural people into its circle. Conservative fathers, who had sent their daughters to *Qur'an* classes and *imam hatip* schools in the 1970s, started to send their daughters to high schools and universities offering modern education. Especially with the dissemination of university preparatory courses throughout the country, it has become possible for students from small towns to get into universities. In this respect, it can be argued that university preparatory courses served for a very important social mobilization. As a consequence of all these factors, a hitherto unobserved number of veiled young women started to appear in educational institutions, streets, and workplaces. The modernization policies in the country, on the other hand, paved the way for what has been

[4]These two books are still read in Islamic circles; see Karaman (1995) and Topaloğlu (2001).

[5]Despite all barriers, *imam hatip* schools still have a significant function in the schooling of girls. For the report prepared by TESEV see Çakır *et al.* (2004).

referred to as "Islamic Calvinism."[6] The flow of capital to the periphery and to the grassroots, the opening of Turkey to the world markets, Özal's encouragement of Anatolian businessmen to enter the global markets, and the emerging business opportunities due to the collapse of the Soviet Union all played important roles in the emergence of an Islamic *bourgeoisie* or a Muslim middle class. Religious values and symbols, which had been popular among the lower classes until the 1960s, were increasingly embraced by people from middle and even high classes. The "headscarf" as a religious symbol used by women started to be visible in modern cities, modern neighborhoods, holiday resorts and even on podiums. Veiling fashion shows, staged in Turkey from time to time, demonstrate that an economic market had emerged on headscarf and veiling.[7]

While the conservative-religious woman tries to be involved in modern institutions, she pursues the goal of preserving her veil as a traditional religious value. She carries out the modern practice of life oriented toward education, trade, holiday and entertainment in traditional dresses with modern patterns. In other words, the religious woman experiences modern values *within* traditional forms. The *turban*, which is more stylish compared to *çarşaf* and the traditional headscarf, has become a symbol of the synthesis of "the traditional and the modern" (Göle, 2004). Similarly, she carries out swimming and vacationing, which are parts of a modern lifestyle, with *haşema* (a full body suit designed to let women and men swim without having to uncover the parts of their bodies which are religiously prohibited from being seen by strangers). In this respect, it would not be wrong to argue that the understanding of modernization through "Western values", which has been prevalent in Turkey for about 200 years, has undergone a transformation in terms of form and content through "Islamic women."[8]

From the mid-1980s, Islamic groups started to attach special importance to the issue of woman. After the feminist women's movement took to the streets, the "issue of woman" left its mark on the country's agenda

[6]European Stability Initiative (ESI) in Berlin published its report on Kayseri in 2005 under the title Islamic Calvinists: Challenge and Conservatism in Central Anatolia and pointed to how a city in Anatolia was included in the process of modernization through religious-conservative values. The report is available online at http://www.esiweb.org/index.php?lang=en&id=156&document_ID=69. Retrieved on 23 June 2011.

[7]Some Islamic writers go against veiling fashion shows by arguing that privacy becomes a show material. For a discussion on the issue see Barbarosoğlu (2001), pp. 125–130.

[8]Nilüfer Göle views the "Islamic women's" movement as a quest for a modernization alternative to the standardizing understanding of modernization based on assimilation; see Göle (1998), 53–70.

and became the hottest discussion topic in Turkey. The religious woman, who started to take a greater part in social life, naturally started to constitute a new problem area in the Islamic part of society, beyond the headscarf problem in universities. In order to deal with this problem, various magazines were published by Islamic groups. Among the first were *Mektup* (Letter), which started in 1985, and then *Kadın ve aile* (Woman and Family), and they reached circulation levels of hundreds of thousands. It is estimated that there were a total of 27 magazines published by Muslim women in the 1990s (Eraslan, 2002, p. 252). Through these magazines, each Islamic group developed its own understanding of womanhood. Based on the themes covered in these magazines it could be argued that mainly two stances have been developed on the role of women among Islamic groups. The first one attempts to limit women to familial roles, does not lean toward their employment, and considers the quests for women's rights to be unnecessary and even harmful. The other one, on the other hand, tries to present a political and somehow existentialist understanding of women, believing in the self-realization of women through participation in public life.

14.2 The transformation of the 'Islamic woman's' role

It is correct to state that the headscarf is a tool to participate in public life and a way of "existence" for "Islamic women". The Kemalist reaction against the headscarf has caused religious groups to unite and to gain dynamism. This dynamism has also brought about several women and groups in the "Islamic women's" movement to question the *traditional* role of the Muslim woman. The Muslim woman in the traditional understanding of Islam is a woman whose prominent characteristics are her commitment to her house, her obedience to her husband and her maternity. The woman, in a sense, is surrounded and protected by the man. However, the process of taking part in public life has brought about the chance for women to cease being the passive object beneath or behind a man. The headscarf struggle has rendered the woman the comrade of the man and given her a new role that is embodied in the concept of "political sister". It can be argued that the political sisterhood, which denotes positioning beside — not behind — men, constitutes the first step of the path leading to the "individual woman."

The individualization process for "Islamic women" developed within the struggle against the prohibitive attitude of the state toward the headscarf in the 1980s. Individual cases in the 1960s and 1970s had not yet been able to render the issue a "nationwide" problem that the state would be interested in. The headscarf issue gained real prominence in the eyes of Islamic groups and the state at the national level following the decision of the Council of Higher Education (*Yüksek Öğretim Kurumu*, YÖK) in 1982 that prohibited veiled students from attending classes. The headscarf, which then turned into the *turban* with this decision, started to occupy the agenda of both politics and the media. Although the severity of the decision was moderated following the reactions of students, student demonstrations erupted after entrance to universities was banned in 1984. These demonstrations started in Ankara University's Faculty of Divinity, as was the case in 1968. As the headscarf ban spread to other universities, protests naturally became widespread. Attempts by the political authorities under Turgut Özal to solve the problem through laws were halted by the Council of State, the Constitutional Court, the President or central left parties of the time and the issue became vague. On the other hand, in parallel with the liberalization in the 1980s, approval and tolerance toward the headscarf became widespread throughout the country. The ambiguous situation on the issue of *turban* and attitudes differing from one university to another continued until the "28 February period."[9]

The "28 February process" became a serious starting point, and in some sense the breakaway point, for this issue. The "28 February period" rendered the headscarf a national problem toward which the state developed a singular attitude. The total war started by the state against the headscarf under the leadership of the YÖK administration paved the way for "Islamic women" to form a movement around this symbol. One of the epicenters of this movement was Istanbul University, which was selected as a model by YÖK. The headscarf ban came to be applied in all departments of Istanbul University in 1998 and female students were enjoined to shed their headscarves through the "persuasion rooms" set up at the entrance of the university campus. The reaction was swift. The Beyazit Campus of Istanbul University became the center of the "headscarf demonstrations". Female students were at the forefront of most of these demonstrations. However,

[9]The "28 February" process refers to the intervention of the military into civilian politics through a National Security Council composed of civilian politicians and militaries in 1997. Since its military members were dominant in this structure they mostly pressed their stamp on the decisions taken by the Council. A clear example of this was the decision it took against the *imam hatip* schools and the headscarf in universities, a decision which eventually gave way to the resignation of the religious conservative government under Necmettin Erbakan.

as with other protest demonstrations, male students, some feminist women, leftist student unions and a number of politicians were present. Support for the demonstrations, which lasted for months with concerts and other activities, increased daily and the attention of the entire country was attracted to the issue. Headscarf demonstrations were not limited to the Beyazit Campus of Istanbul University. Similar protests erupted in almost all cities with universities. 1998, when the "28 February" decisions came into effect, is the year in which "headscarf demonstrations" took place throughout the country. The protests in some cities were considered by the state as an "uprising" against the political order and were harshly quelled.[10] One of the demonstrations initiated at the national level which attracted the attention of the entire country, was launched by medical faculty students in June 1998. About 60 veiled medical students initiated a march from the Cerrahpaşa Faculty of Medicine toward Ankara under the name of the "White March", with the aim of traveling through the entire country. The demonstrators walked up to Ankara with enormous support from the people living *en route*.[11] Following this demonstration, another large-scale protest was staged which attracted the highest popular support throughout the history of the republic. On 11 October 1998, pioneered by various NGOs, the protest aimed at forming a countrywide human chain under the motto "hand-in-hand for freedom of belief and thought" (*inanca saygı, düşünceye özgürlük için el ele*). The human chain started in front of the Cerrahpaşa Faculty of Medicine and continued up to the town of Bolu — stretching over nearly 250 km! Although the chain was blocked in Bolu by a military unit, it succeeded in reaching up to Van in the east and Hopa in the north of the country. It was the first time in Turkey that millions of people from different locations were gathered simultaneously and formed a human chain of more than 1,000 km without causing any disorder.[12] This demonstration created a shocking impact on the government, especially on

[10] One of such protests was made in Malatya but it was harshly penalized and many people were jailed. Çakır (2000), p. 84.

[11] One of the protesters, a student of the Cerrahpaşa Faculty of Medicine named M.A., told how the local people greeted them with enthusiasm as follows: "We came to Gebze from Tuzla. Again, an enthusiastic crowd welcomed us. They were asking 'Can we hug you?' This time, I was ashamed. I did not think how Anatolia would greet us when I set off. We were heroes in their eyes. I later noticed this and then I was proud of them" (quoted from Sişman (2004), pp. 120–121.

[12] According to estimates, around 3 million people supported the demonstration. For detailed information on the demonstration, see Ak-der bülten. Beyaz yürüyüş (Istanbul: Ak-Der, n.d.).

YÖK, and participating officials have subsequently been subjected to legal investigations and prosecutions.[13]

However, despite these large-scale demonstrations and increasing social awareness, the headscarf issue continued to be a critical problem occupying the country's agenda. After the 28 February period, the application initiated in Istanbul University was disseminated into all universities in Turkey and transformed into a national politics controlled by YÖK. Students, unable to get the results they expected from street demonstrations and the judicial authorities in Turkey, resorted to the European Court of Human Rights at Strasbourg. Leyla Şahin, who was expelled from Istanbul University Faculty of Medicine due to her headscarf in 1998, also took the issue to Strasbourg. However, the Court decided to justify the practice. While this decision created a shock among Islamic groups, it strengthened the hand of Turkey's Kemalist elites. It can be said that the headscarf constituted the main focus of the struggle during the "28 February" period. The obdurate stance of the state against the headscarf did not remain limited to universities and was exported to other fields. Schools controlled by the Ministry of National Education have been among the places where the ban was executed harshly. Numerous veiled teachers working in schools were eventually dismissed from their jobs. The ban was even attempted to be disseminated into private training centers (*dersane*). The actors of "28 February" have rendered the veil of women an existential issue for the regime. Merve Kavakci who was elected as a member of parliament (wearing a headscarf) stepped on the toe of this hyper-active group. As a result, a "hunt" was organized. The most dramatic scene of this "hunt" was the midnight bust by the Chief Public Prosecutor Nusret Demiral, accompanied by a police group and an army of reporters to her house. Kavakci's membership in the parliament was soon terminated and the Virtue Party (*Fazilet Partisi*, FP), mediating her election as deputy, was closed down by the Constitutional Court.[14] The constitutional amendment of 2008 made by the currently ruling Justice and Development Party (*Adalet ve Kalkınma Partisi*, AKP) to make the wearing of the headscarf

[13]One of them was Professor Dursun Odabaş, the Dean of the Faculty of Medicine at Van Yüzüncü Yıl University. He was both dismissed from his job at the university and his professor title was taken away for participating in the demonstration. The court later reversed this decision.

[14]Merve Kavakci tells her experiences in detail in her book *Başörtüsüz demokrasi: Tarih içinde tarih*, Istanbul: Timaş Yayınları, 2004.

permissible in universities has made this political party even more popular. The constitutional amendment was invalidated by the Constitutional Court. The Court also punished AKP by ruling to deprive the party of financial assistance from the Treasury. What kind of impacts does the headscarf issue — occupying the country's agenda for about 50 years, resulting in the hardline stance of the state — have on Muslim women? Undoubtedly, these impacts have psychological, sociological and political dimensions. It would not be wrong to argue that the political atmosphere that emerged around the headscarf has paved the way for a significant transformation among Muslim women as well as creating traumas. The most significant dimension of this transformation is the fact that women have developed a "women's movement around the headscarf" While this women's movement formed by Muslim women strives to overcome the state and its uniform modernization policy on the one hand, it continuously questions the traditional roles of women, on the other. It should be noted that there exist various lines within the "Islamic women's" movement, and the end of one of these lines reaches up to feminism. "Islamic women" who strive to take part in public life turn upside down the traditional religious roles expected of them. As Sibel Eraslan puts it, "whereas men want to seclude them and demand from them to be beautiful wives and mothers, they dare to poke their noses into the life" (Eraslan, 2002, p. 260). The awareness and the feelings of self-reliance in women stirred by the struggle to take part in public life have eventually directed them to question their traditional roles. It is noteworthy to claim that street demonstrations have had multi-dimensional consequences on Muslim women who tried to be insistent followers of their own decisions. Above all, young girls have been politicized through street protests and built political identities on this foundation. As Sibel Eraslan, who became prominent when she was the head of the Welfare Party's (*Refah Partisi*, RP) Istanbul Women's Branches, stated: "the organisational daring of the 'Islamic women' in the 90s has become a journey from being sisters and wives to being citizens" (Eraslan, 2002, pp. 255–256). Considering that the "headscarf demonstrations" required not only a multi-dimensional background preparation but also courage, it becomes clear how transformative this was for women. This, indeed, points to a revolutionary transformation for the religious women who were expected to become socialized with such characteristics as "solemnity", "silence" and "obedience to men". Women who took part in the headscarf struggle have directed their interests from housework, obedience to the husband and childcare to the state, political participation, demonstrations, protests, knowledge, information and so forth. Some have likened this interest to the 1968 generation of leftist movements. Sibel Eraslan stunningly depicts how a new generation, which can be called the "98 Generation", has emerged among Muslim women in Turkey: March 1998: Thousands of youths were protesting in front of the university behind a large red banner on which, written in yellow, were the words "students arm-in-arm, to a general boycott" (*oğrenciler kol kola genel boykota*). These were the colors not hitherto used in "Islamic women's" protests. Some metal and rock bands accompanied them with music. Environmentalist youths were also among the groups supporting the girls. Headscarf demonstrations would go down in the history of the Republic as the women's demonstrations, which attracted large and different groups but remained inconclusive. Veiled women were shouting a slogan, which we had been used to hearing from leftists; "don't be silent! If you do, you will be the next!" (*susma sıra sana gelecek*).

What has changed from 1968 to 1998? How come these proper little girls (*hanım hanımıck*) continuously resembled to the image of other militant women? (Eraslan, 2002, p. 261). Street demonstrations have at the same time provided young girls with a personality and a sense of self-realization. Young girls, who had matured in such protests, have become able to show the courage and self-reliance to continue their educations in various universities in Europe and America alone. It would not be wrong to claim that women who entered into an intense struggle on the headscarf issue have fought for an "identity", "personality" and "existence" (Göle, 2002, pp. 173–190). It would not be an exaggeration to say that the Muslim woman, by maturing in this struggle, has realized the role of the woman (as characterized in Atif Yilmaz movies), a woman who is able to exist and pursue her own choices without needing her husband or father or another man's support. The following expressions strikingly demonstrate how the headscarf ban has rendered an ordinary young girl a militant: "I was unable to associate myself with shouting at the top of my voice in protests. Moreover, I used not to consider marching on streets to be wise. Yet, I no longer had a class to go, or a course to study for [...]. I was at loose end, feeling quite empty, I felt myself dwindling. So dwindled that I fell prey to the wind and suddenly found myself among my friends in Beyazit. At that very moment, little Ayşe began to grow up. Her tears were not sorrowful anymore, they were the tears scattering lights of hope. I was both shouting slogans and marching towards the school I had been expelled from."[15]

The struggle over the headscarf has provided women with maturity, change and transformation; as well as paving the way for great feelings of defeat, disappointment, hatred and anger.[16] There are many groups toward which such feelings are directed. The most prominent of them is undoubtedly those people acting under the name of Kemalism. It is thought-provoking that Kemalism, which had developed as a modernizing and civilizing project in the first half of the 20th century, turned against some women at the end of the second half of it with a narrowed vision and mind. This vision has also become the source of a strong hatred among women involved in Turkey's Islamic movements. The following expressions strikingly reveal what Kemalism is identified with in the eyes of these women: "January 1998: Female students attending universities with headscarves started to be blacklisted by secretaries at doors. The letter 'T' was put in the place of or near the names of these students. [...] Women were marked only, simply and shortly with the letter 'T'. I liken the letter 'T' attached to my name to the Zion badge that Anne Frank was obliged to carry. And of course I liken those who attached it to the Nazis [...]" (Eraslan, 2002, p. 261).

We can say that the feeling of aversion and hatred found in these sentences contains multi-dimensional and deep traumas. The "Nazi" is a figure that constitutes the indelible subconscious of Jewish people today. Kemalism, on the other hand, has become an entity which is considered equal to Nazism at least in the eyes of some people living in Turkey (a group of substantial size, however, when considering the size of the social base) — a comparison which is certainly a bit too farfetched. Nevertheless, it is unfortunate for a society moving toward modernization that Kemalism, which had constituted an important reference to the salvation and emancipation of women in the first quarter of the 20th century, has turned into an ideology, an oppressive policy, which is identified

[15] A.Y., a junior student at Cerrahpaşa Faculty of Medicine; quoted by Şişman (2004), pp. 67–68.

[16] For a book that angrily and execrably tells of the treatment that the author was subjected to when she was a student at Middle East Technical University due to her headscarf, see Demir (1998).

with Nazism in the eyes of some other women at the extremist fringe. It is observed that many Muslim women involved in Islamic movements are largely disappointed with secular women. Although some feminist women and leftist groups supported them, the deafness of most secular women to the issue has created a deep resentment among them. The feelings expressed by a medical student who had been expelled from the Hacettepe Faculty of Medicine are thought provoking in this sense: "My elder sisters are not veiled and all of us have acquaintances who are not veiled. Due to the prejudiced attitude I experienced in the school, I became timid with all people who are not veiled. I still feel uneasy when I meet somebody. We took up new phobias due to their discriminatory attitudes towards us" (Şahin, 1998, pp. 226–227). It would not be inaccurate to argue that this attitude has paved the way among "Islamic women" for a common trauma. Mualla Gülnaz, known as a "Muslim feminist", states it in the following way: "the women who fought the headscarf struggle feel that they are left alone. They no longer trust the state, nor politicians, nor their families and nor the men they share the same faiths with" (Çakır, 2000, p. 52). Many women who really suffered from the headscarf issue bear these feelings.

The struggle over the headscarf ban has functioned as a bridge between women from the Islamic movements and some women from other sectors of Turkish society. Some feminist and leftist groups have taken sides from the very beginning with the women who were fighting against the headscarf ban. It would not be wrong to argue that a mutual empathy and an interaction emerged in this process. While some feminists and leftist women supported the headscarf by considering it to be a right and a different way of existence, it can be argued that a sympathy and an interest in their ideas, and a feminist discourse, have gradually emerged among "Islamic women". Sibel Eraslan depicts this change and transformation: "The opportunity to know and talk to other women means a more feminine colour and voice among 'Islamic women'" (Eraslan, 2002, p. 256). One can thus argue that the movement called "Islamic feminism" has flourished on the ground created by this interaction.

14.3 Flirting with feminism or the advent of "Islamic feminism"?

The concept of "Islamic feminism" was developed in the 1990s by various Iranian and Arabic academics and writers.[17] Academics and writers like

[17] For a study on the issue see Moghadam (2002).

Asaneh Najmabadeh, Haleh Afshar and Mai Yamani have used this concept in their studies, but the concept eventually started to be used by other academics and writers in various countries. One of them is the Egyptian author Aziza M. Karam. According to her, everyone who thinks that women occupy a secondary position due to their sex/gender and who make efforts to develop egalitarian and fair gender relationships are feminists. Karam, departing from this common feminist definition, draws attention to the difference between "secular feminism" and "Islamic feminism" in Egypt.[18] Those who advocate "Islamic feminism" center all of their claims on the *Qur'an*. Their main thesis is as follows: the *Qur'an* used the symbols and language of the patriarchal Arabic culture. The messages in the *Qur'an* are naturally expressed within the form of this language. Only the Prophet can grasp the *real* spirit of the *Qur'an*, which is a universal and eternal source. If the message and cause of the *Qur'an* is universal, then we should not read it as a given text with a uniform definition. Naturally, the *Qur'an* could be perceived differently in different historical circumstances, different social environments and different languages and cultures. In this respect, the spirit and message of the *Qur'ān* can be interpreted in different ways within a certain context.[19] Does "Islamic feminism" have an equivalent in Turkey? Or how do the groups of women who drive the women's movement in Turkey approach "Islamic feminism"? Prominent researchers and writers in the "Islamic women's" movement like Cihan Aktaş, Yıldız Ramazanoğlu, Nazife Şişman, Mualla Gülnaz, Hidayet Ş. Tuksal, Fatma K. Barbarosoğlu, Sibel Eraslan, Ayşe Böhürler and Nihal Bengisu Karaca prefer to stand aloof from the identity of "feminism."[20] It can be argued that the main reason lying behind the distant stance of "Islamic women" from the feminist identity is the belief that feminism is identified with enmity against man, unlimited sexual freedom and a movement that attacks the family. A woman, in an article for *Aksiyon* magazine wrote the following, articulating the common concern of numerous "Islamic women": The author of the following sentences is very anxious while writing that they would contain the word "feminism" abundantly; "worst than the nightmares in dark nights having being labeled with a feminist identity [...]." Who can say that we are possessed by an unjustifiable anxiety while feminism means

---

[18]Karam (1998). Another similar classification was made by Badran (2005).

[19]For an original and detailed study on how the *Qur'ān* shapes the image of women through the language it uses, see Fidan (2006).

[20]Along with these names appearing frequently in the media, numerous other female researchers and writers have emerged in Islamic circles.

enmity to man, deviation, shrewdness, spinsterhood and even ugliness? Today, most veiled bluestocking women who define themselves as "pious" approach the word "feminism" with the same hesitation. While some get all tuckered out trying to get rid of this intrusive trouble, some others challenge the use of the term as a method of punishment; "I am a feminist, so what!" (Akagündüz, 2006, p. 24). The perception of women in the Islamic movements of feminism is not limited to this. The fact that the majority of women in the feminist movement did *not* support "headscarf victims" and that they even did not support the headscarf as a women's right has paved the way for the feminist movement to be viewed by "Islamic women" as a Kemalist/elitist movement. *Yenişafak* newspaper columnist Özlem Albayrak labeled feminism as "a movement in the monopoly of a few modern and brand-loyal women of *Nisantaşı*."[21] Albayrak, in the same interview, stated "if I believed in the objectivity and truthfulness of the feminism in Turkey, I'd become a feminist" (Sever, 2004, p. 37). The number of those women who are sympathetic to feminism but avoid being identified with it is very high among "Islamic women".

The reason lying behind this is not only the aforementioned image of feminism but also the fact that "Islamic women" see the problems of women from a perspective different from that of feminists. Ayşe Böhürler articulates the common opinion of many "Islamic women" writers as follows: "I define myself as a person who advocates women's rights but who is not a feminist" (Sever, 2004, p. 37).

Some Muslim women are of the opinion that the concept of Islamic feminism is intentionally imposed from outside and it is a part of the project of creating a moderate understanding of Islam. Nazife Şişman, who translated Amina Wadud Muhsin's book *Qur'an and Woman* (Vedud-Muhsin, 1997) and who became notorious for the mixed-gender Friday prayers she led, indicates that she considers the idea of 'reinterpretation' that she used to appreciate to be dangerous for today. Şişman states that she views the re-interpretation of Islam "both as an outcome of an imposition and as an attempt to destroy the religious base that is the basic foundation of the Islamic world" (Şişman, 2005, p. 94).

Based on this understanding, Şişman wrote a book entitled *Globalisation's Grip, Islam's Veil* and argues that orientalism imposes a

[21]Nişantaşi is known as the center of upper-class and high-society Istanbul.

new understanding on the Islamic world through women. According to Şişman, the modernization or reformation in religion that includes the reinterpretation of Islam from the perspective of women has occurred within a hegemonic relationship with the West from its very beginning (Şişman, 2005, pp. 93–94). In a similar fashion, Sibel Eraslan, who argues that the terms Islam and feminism are in contradiction with each other, asserts that the conception of "Islamic feminism" is a part of the attempts to modernize the third world countries through women's bodies (Akagündüz, 2006, p. 25). Yıldız Ramazanoğlu, who is notable among "Islamic women" with her works in literature, shares this opinion but she points to another problem that the attempts of the West to reconcile Islam and feminism will generate: the risk of Muslims to avoid advancing toward the problems experienced by Muslim women so as not to be subjected to accusations of "they serve the purposes of the West". It seems that most "Islamic women" pay special attention to stay away from feminism due to the fear of appearing to be serving for the West. When one considers the facts that the Islamic subconscious in Turkey is anti-Western in character, then one sees how difficult it is for these women to be identified with a feminism originated in the West.

The group that has frequently been shown as an authority in debates on Islamic feminism in Turkey is Ankara Capital City Women's Platform. One of the founders of the Platform, Zehra Reçber, gives the message that they do not fully reject feminism by stating "our feminism is a self-appointed feminism, we do not believe that we have to accept the entire feminist discourse" (Özkan, n.d.). Similarly, the Safiye Özdemir says, "we criticise the male-dominated discourse and structure, we question gender roles. But religion is important for us. Our view of family and sexuality is different from that of feminism. I define myself as a pious defender of women's rights" (Özkan, n.d.). As is seen in these expressions, the point that detaches both the Capital City Women's Platform and many "Islamic women" from feminism is centered on the issue of the view of family and sexuality. Although they defend women's rights on the basis of equality by criticizing the traditional religious values, women who are defined as "Islamic feminists" attach a great deal of importance to the family and they advocate the idea that women should experience their sexuality within the limits defined by Islam. Hidayet Ş. Tuksal, whose name has been identified with "Islamic feminism" *per se*, explains the distance between them and feminism in an interview as follows:

> *I have a feminine perspective when considered in terms of the basics of feminism; because I have read a lot, and once you get that perspective it becomes very difficult to unlearn it. However, there emerged a discourse within feminism that is discriminatory, that excludes and ignores men, and even aims to create a separate world free from men. I do not consider this attitude reasonable. We have to live with our fathers, husbands and sons anyway. But I believe that it is necessary to have a feminine perspective in order to be able to correctly understand the existing systems, practices and the religion. In brief, I am a person who aims to interpret what is going on from the point of view of a woman* (Çakır, 2000, p. 28).

It would not be wrong to assert that "Islamic women" could not resist the gravitational field of feminism, even though they carefully point to their distance from feminism and to points of differentiation. It is observed that they ever increasingly use the jargon, language, concepts and even the perspectives used by feminists. It should not be forgotten that the "interpretation from the point of view of a woman" underlined above by Tuksal is a feminist jargon. This jargon is today used by many "Islamic women". The use of the feminist jargon by "Islamic women" is not limited only to female writers whose names have been identified with feminism. Numerous Islamic organizations use the language brought by feminism to Turkey in either this or that way. The slogan "we are women, we exist and we are strong" (*kadınız, varız, güçlüyüz*) used in a booklet prepared by the Women's Branch of FP can be given as a clear example of this (Şişman, 2005, p. 162). The name *Woman's Identity* (*Kadın Kimliği*) given to a magazine by Islamic groups is also meaningful in that sense. It is noteworthy to state that many concepts increasingly being used among "Islamic women", such as woman's identity, consciousness-raising, the woman problem, women's rights, women's human rights, women's point of view, the oppression of women and womanly existence, have been borrowed from feminists. Fatma K. Barbarosoğlu, who is notable amongst "Islamic women" writers for her successful works in the field of story writing and novels, states that this is a "conscious/deliberate borrowing" (Şişman, 2005, p. 151). In fact, the meanings attributed to these concepts by "Islamic women" suggest that this is not a simple borrowing but it points to much deeper ties of influence. "Islamic women", in truth, were timid of feminism when it first appeared. This stemmed mainly from the aforementioned widespread prejudices/stereotypes about feminism. However, as feminist concern has turned toward the real problems experienced in Turkish society, the walls between these two groups are pulled down and "Islamic women" have become more familiar with the women's studies literature. One can say that this eventually paves the way for "Islamic women" to comprehend feminism and even develop deep interactions with it.

14.4 Conclusion

As a concluding remark, it may be observed that the understanding of modernization through "Western values", which has been prevalent in Turkey since the establishment of the republican regime in 1923, has undergone a transformation in terms of form and content through "Islamic women" who started to be visible in the public sphere.

- The "Islamic women's" movement not only undermined the culture and social pillars of centuries-old tradition but also caused Kemalism, which had been one of the most modernizing movements at the turn of the 20th century, to increasingly assume a conservative and reactionary character based on the idea of a single truth.
- The "Islamic women's" movement continues to develop an alternative manner of existence and self-realization through a different and subjective identity and a system of values, against a standardizing, assimilative understanding of Kemalist modernization.

References

Turkish

Akagündüz, Ülkü Özel (March 2006), "İslami feminizm: Adı var kendi yok", *Aksiyon*, 587, 24.

Aköz, Emre and Atal, Nevzat (December 2004), "Said Nursi'den Fethullah Gülen'e Nur Cemaati", *Sabah*, p. 22.

Barbarosoğlu, Fatma Karabıyık (February 2001), "Başörtülülerin Tarihine Küçük Bir Katki", *Yenişafak*, p. 9.

Barbarosoğlu, Fatma Karabıyık (2006), *Şov ve Mahram* (2nd edn.), Istanbul: Timaş.

Berberoğlu, Enis (10 May 1999), "Türbanın 30 Yıllık Yükselişi" *Hürriyet*.

Çakır, Ruşen, Bozan, İrfan and Talu, Balkan (June 2004), "İmam Hatip Liseleri: Efsaneler ve Gerçekler", *TESEV*, available at http://www.tesev.org.tr/ (accessed on 17 July 2011).

Çakır, Ruşen (2000), *Direniş ve Itaat: İki Iktidar Arasında Islamcı Kadın*, Istanbul: Metis, p. 84.

Demir, Zekiye Oğuzhan (1998), *Bir Başörtüsü Günlüğü*, Istanbul: İz Yayıncılık.

Eraslan, Sibel (2002), "Uğultular... Silüetler", in Aksu Bora and Asena Güldal (eds.). *90'larda Türkiye'de Feminizm*, Istanbul: İletişim.
Fidan, Hafsa (2006), *Kur'anda Kadın Imgesi*, Ankara: Vadi Yayınları.
Göle, Nilüfer (2004), *Modern Mahrem: Medeniyet ve Örtünme* (8th edn.), Istanbul: Metis.
Karaman, Hayrettin (1995), *İslam'da Kadın ve Aile*, Istanbul: Ensar Neşriyat.
Kavakci, Merve (2004), *Başörtüsüz Demokrasi: Tarih Içinde Tarih*, Istanbul: Timaş Yayınları.
Kutluoğlu, Fatma (2005), "Fevziye Nuroğlu 'Yürüyen Hayrat"' (Interview Fatma Kutluoğlu), *Umran*, p. 129.
Özdemir, Ufuk (n.d.), "Türkiye'de Kadın Kıyafetinde Modernleşme Süreci Ve Medyanın Etkisi", available online at http://www.enfal.de/tes17.htm (accessed on 23 June 2011).
Özkan, Fadime (n.d.), "Muhafazakar Kesimde Kadınlar Artık Hareketli" (interview).
Şahin, Yeter (1998), *Bütün Yönleriyle Başörtüsü Sorunu* (extended 2nd edn.), Istanbul: Mazlum-Der.
Sever, Metin (2004), *Türban ve Kariyer*, Istanbul: Timaş, (interview).
Şişman, Nazife (2004), *Başörtüsü Mağdurlarından Anlatılmamış Öyküler* (4th edn.), Istanbul: İz Yayıncılık.
Şişman, Nazife (2005), *Küreselleşmenin Pençesi Islam'ın Peçesi*, Istanbul: Küre Yayınları.
Şişman, Nazife (2004), *Kamusal Alanda Başörtülüler*, Istanbul: Timaş.
Tezcan, Demet (2007), *Bir Çığır Öyküsü: Şule Yüksel Şenler*, Istanbul: Timaş.
Topaloğlu, Bekir (2001), *İslam'da Kadın*, Istanbul: Rağbet Yayınları.
Vedud-Muhsin, Amine (1997), *Kur'an ve Kadın* (2nd edn.), translated by Nazife Şişman, İstanbul: İz Yayıncılık.

English

Badran, Margot (Winter 2005), Between secular and islamic feminism/s: Reflections on the Middle East and beyond. *Journal of Middle East Women's Studies*, 1(1), 6–28.
European Stability Initiative (ESI) (2005), "Islamic Calvinists: Challenge and Conservatism in Central Anatolia" available online at http://www.esiweb.org/index.php?lang=en&id=156&document_ID=69 (accessed on 23 June 2011).
Göle, Nilüfer (1998), Islamism, feminism and post-modernism: Women's movements in Islamic countries. *New Perspectives on Turkey*, 19(Fall), 53–70.
Göle, Nilüfer (2002), Islam in public: New visibilities and new imaginaries. *Public Culture* 14(1), 173–190.
Karam, Aziza M (1998), *Women, Islamisms, and the State: Contemporary Feminisms in Egypt*, London: Macmillan Press; New York: St Martin's Press.
Moghadam, Valentine M. (2002), Islamic feminism and its discontent: Toward a resolution of the debate. *Journal of Women in Culture and Society*, 27(4), 1135–1171.

Chapter 15

Women of Aceh: The Struggle for Peace and Justice

Asna Husin

Abstract

We explore the concept of peace from a broader sense than merely the absence of war, through the eyes of Acehnese women who continue to strive for better political representation and social justice utilizing Islam as their foundational point. The study analyses Islamic principles of peace, cultural beliefs and practices, as well as the political environment, which engulfed Aceh. Historical accounts and academic research form a theoretical base for our analysis, while interviews with influential women, Ulama leaders, political figures as well as community activists provide integral content for our survey. This inquiry concludes that in spite of widespread political conservatism being promoted by the GAM political party of *Partai Aceh* and parochial religious fanaticism being advocated by certain transnational groupings, women themselves provide hope for gender equality and empowerment. Women of the *dayah* (Islamic boarding school) and NGO activists may work together to pursue their Islamic endowment of peace and accomplish pragmatic actualization of equality and justice.

Keywords: Acehnese, *Shari'ah*, Women empowerment, Peace, Justice

Gender is regarded by many as a secular value infiltrated into Acehnese and other Muslim societies through Western influence. Though there is some truth in this perception, especially with the use of the terms "gender equality" or "human rights" for women and the discursive debates employed in promoting them, Muslim women's efforts for representation and arguments for equity are as old as Islam itself. Umm Salamah, the wife of the Prophet Muhammad, once asked him: "What is with us (women) that we are not mentioned [by God] in the *Qur'an* as men are mentioned?" God heard her complaint and then the verse[1] (*Qur'an*, chapter al-Ahzab 33:35): "*Surely the Muslim men and women and the faithful men and women...*" was revealed (Al-Zuhayli, 1411/1991). Similarly, Arwah or Umm Musa, wife of the second 'Abbasid Caliph al-Mansur, requested a written marriage stipulation from her husband that he would neither marry a second wife nor take a concubine while she was still alive.[2] When the Caliph subsequently regretted his agreement and sought it annulled, Arwah appealed to the chief justice whose verdict ruled in her favor. Both Umm Salamah's advocacy for equal treatment of men and women in Allah's revelation, and Arwah's attempt to not share her husband with other women, were gender-oriented advances advocating women's rights and equity. These examples demonstrate that while these two great ladies of Islam may never have recognized the term gender nor promoted explicit gender discourse, yet gender was acted upon as second nature to them. Understanding gender as an act rather than a discursive idea is very important in our discussion of women's rights and responsibilities in an Islamic context, for this same attitude is being repeated in Aceh and was found in many other Islamic societies throughout history.

This chapter explores women's active participation in public life in Indonesia's westernmost province of Aceh, as a form of peacemaking in which women mediate paths to active peace in their community providing a sense of orientation and objective in the activities of their family and society. We begin with a brief survey of the role of Islam in women's understanding of peace, their search for individual and collective rights as well as for public responsibilities. Then we focus on the challenges facing women within the constraints of a traditional Islamic society such as Aceh, as they evolve toward their own specific form of modernity, highlighting their religious and cultural possibilities and limits in their engagement. The last section explores the new reality that may fuel the further advancement of women or hinder them in moving forward, recognizing the essential contribution of female religious authorities in their work to educate youth and to uplift their society, as well as those conservative political elements which manipulate religious aspirations and seek to mitigate peace building efforts.

---

[1]Those unfamiliar with the "causes of revelation" of the *Qur'an* (the exegetical genre known as *asbab al-nuzul*) should be mindful that among the many occasions of *Qur'anic* revelation were events provoking answers and responses to requests by the Muslim community of the time — including prominent women. The complaints and veiled protests by the Prophet's wife Umm Salamah fall within this category.
[2]See narratives of courageous women in Islam recounted in Walther (1995).

15.1 Islam and Acehnese women's participation in public life

The name *Islam*, or the Arabic term "*al-Islam*", derives from the notion of *salm*, *silm*, and *salamah* meaning security, peace-making, resignation and conciliation, and is also associated with the term *salam* "salutations of peace and security". Sincere resignation to Allah's revealed guidance is the essential connotation of the word "*Islam*", and as a conventional technical term it serves as the name for the Muslim faith: "*I have chosen Islam as your religion*" (*Qur'an* chapter al-Ma'idah 5:3).[3] Another important spiritual foundation for peace in Islam is the belief that God is the ultimate source of Peace: "*He is God; there is no god save He; the King; the Holy and the Peace [al-Salam]*" (*Qur'an* chapter al-Hashr 59:23). The notion of God being named *al-Salam* is repeated in the supplication (*du'a'*) recited by Muslims at the conclusion of the five daily obligatory prayers (*salat*): "*O God, You are Peace, the Source of Peace, and to You Peace returns...*" This understanding that God is the origin of Peace is traditionally attributed to Khadijah, the beloved first wife of the Prophet, when she responded to "the salutations of peace from [her] Lord" by saying: "*Allahu l-Salam wa minhu l-Salam* [God is Peace and from Him Peace derives]".[4] The *Qur'anic* testimony and Khadijah's recognition of God being *al-Salam*, as well as the divine naming of the Muslim faith *al-islam*, highlight that peace is an intrinsic part of Islam. Therefore, peace from an Islamic perspective embodies both a vertical spiritual dimension as well as horizontal practical aspects, for God *al-Salam* reveals *al-islam* as a religion enjoining human beings to experience lives of peace and security in the best sense of the word.

Peaceable living in the real sense of the word is reflected in the notion that peace in Islam is neither merely the absence of war nor the elimination of discrimination and injustice in the community. It is holistic peace implanted in the essence of the human constitution (*fitrah* — innate recognition of monotheist reality) radiated into their hearts as a manifestation of their sincere resignation to God *al-Salam* as true Source of Peace, and translated into healthy thinking and positive attitudes extended to peaceful treatment of fellow men and women, as well as the flora and fauna or their natural surroundings. Such a comprehensive approach to

---

[3]For the semantic scope of these terms see Crow (2013).

[4]Cited by Ibn Hisham in his al-Sirah al-Nabawiyah on an unknown authority; also cited by al-Bukhiri, Sahih, vol. IV, 136.

peace is a fundamental principle in the Muslim activation of peace and security throughout ages. However, the complexity of Muslim cultural life and recent history, the nature of relations within their own communities and with their fellow humans and other nations, and the level of Muslim spiritual and intellectual astuteness as well as their collective political stability, has led many Muslims to overemphasize one dimension of Islamic teachings at the expense of other aspects. When it comes to the issue of the role of women, cultural dimensions guided by intellectual discrepancies now clenching Muslim communities worldwide often overrule the spiritual inclusiveness and foundational openness of Islam. These challenges actually provide women either an opportunity to engage in social activities and peace building, or pose an obstacle preventing their progress. Deciphering the situation from the reality of contemporary cultural constraints: women may be both victims of societal incompetency as well as advocates for communal advancement.

Women in Aceh, like many other areas in Indonesia and Southeast Asian nations, have historically lived in a women-friendly environment. The form of Islam, which penetrated Aceh from the 9th to 12th centuries CE by means of traders and Sufi fraternities, contributed to and encouraged the free movement and social engagement of women. Commonly engaged in the market place and within Sufi groupings, women were as active as men in commerce and the *tariqah.* In the political arena, Acehnese have romanticized their experience of women leaders, especially the famous four *Sultanahs* who ruled over Aceh for 59 consecutive years (1641–1699), and the woman admiral Keumala Hayati who controlled the Sultanate's sea security, as well as female revolutionary leaders fighting the Dutch colonials.[5]

The women leaders of traditional Islamic learning institutions called *dayah* (from Arabic *zawiyah* "study lodge") were also celebrated. However, prolonged conflicts during Suharto's centralization and unification policy (1967–1997) limited women's active role as religious preachers (*penceramah*) and as community leaders, which had been common phenomena up to 1970s. While traditional religious openness enabling the public role of women evaporated, a new kind of women social activism emerged. Conflict,

[5]For further information about these women refer to Hasjmy (1977); Khan (2007); Pamenan (1959); also refer to the prominent Acehnese women during the wars against the Dutch in Zentgraaff (1983).

violence and political limitations (to evoke Michel Foucault's "docile body") brought a new energy to the people of Aceh. Many students and young men and women reacted to their political limitations by establishing new non-governmental organizations (NGOs), and this fresh civic energy mushroomed in Aceh and all over Indonesia. This was made possible as Indonesia opened up during the peaceful political and social revolution of *reformasi* in the late 1990s that led to the fall of Suharto, and encouraged political openness and democracy.[6]

Sympathy and support from national and international NGOs further strengthened the civic movement in Aceh. Even though this new activism was initially religiously neutral or even secular in its nature, many students from Islamic universities such as the Ar-Raniry State Islamic University were among the most active advocates of this new energy. Many women activists, including victims of conflict, emerged during this period and were as actively engaged as their male counterparts. While religious conservatism steadily gained support and its advocates became more organized, the religiously neutral and secular activists became more comprehensive in their outlook, realizing they could not antagonize traditional Islamic groups and religious convictions while operating in Aceh. Interestingly enough, women were among the leading advocates of this convergence, and to overcome religious conservatism they had to work both with the political establishment and with the existing Islamic institutions utilizing religious language and aspirations. Conflict and violence in Aceh for nearly three decades led to the victimization of numerous men, women and children, with the latter two suffering the most. As conflicts intensified in the last decade of Suharto's iron grip over Indonesia, Aceh was put under the "Operasi Darurat Militer" (DOM — Military Emergency Operation).

During this period, certain pockets of Aceh underwent great intimidation and brutality with many hundreds of Acehnese killed without this being known by the rest of the citizens of Indonesia. As *reformasi* erupted and DOM was finally lifted in 1998, the numerous military atrocities in Aceh were unveiled to the public eye. Aceh received sympathy from the across the nation and internationally — which strengthened Acehnese civil society. Initially, while the situation in Indonesia progressed, Aceh suffered even further. The information about military atrocities during the DOM period

[6]For a comprehensive description of the Indonesian new revolution, refer to O'Rourke (2002).

fueled Acehnese support for independence (*merdeka*). For the first time ever a large majority of the population in this province would have selected the *merdeka* option had they been given a chance to hold a referendum, which became the popular demand at the time. To contain the political unrest, thousands of non-organic troops were inserted into Aceh, and in May 2003 during the era of President Megawati Sukarnoputri the province was once again put under military emergency law (a while later a civil emergency was imposed), which was only lifted in 2005 after the convulsive disaster of the Tsunami inundation. Consequently, the bloodbath of torture, killings and sexual abuse of women became a daily reality. The Indonesian military victimized many women during this period, and burnt numerous villages and towns, while gangs of *orang tidak dikenal* ("unknowns") burnt over 1,000 local schools during this emergency era. Although most of the schools were rebuilt and victims were rehabilitated after the signing of the 2005 peace agreement in Helsinki in the aftermath of the Tsunami, the pervasive fear, intimidations, extortions and the severe limitations of movement during that era could not be easily forgotten or forgiven.

In the midst of the high civilian contentions and referendum demands, a group of Aceh women convened in February 2000 the first All Acehnese Women Congress of *Duek Pakat Inong Aceh* attended by 437 women from across this province. Women activists led by Naimah Hasan walked a fine line,[7] taking a neutral position between the demands for referendum (inviting independence) or for re-integration with Indonesia. They also had to convince both the military and the rebel leaders of their neutrality and the importance of their *Duek Pakat.* Several women leaders, for example, had to sneak into the jungle to meet the late GAM military commander Tengku Abdullah Syafi'i in his hide-out in order to solicit his blessing for their congress and to request the participation of the GAM female combat wing known as the *inong balee* (*lit.* "female widowers"), even while the military was circling the area in order to capture him dead or alive.[8] Intimidation, terror and coercion for or against the existing options of plebiscite and re-integration were among the challenges faced by the organizers and participants of this congress. Some participants even walked out during the deliberations accusing the *Duek Pakat* of having

[7]For a brief biography of Hasan refer to Husin (2015a).
[8]Tengku Abdullah Syafi'i was killed by the Indonesian military while still in hiding in January 2002.

been hijacked by the reintegration camp, while one outsider told a student participant: "you are dead if the congress recommends a referendum."[9] What was interesting about this congress is the fact that women in Aceh were among the first to demand that "the Aceh conflict be resolved through dialogue and nonviolent means."[10] They were also the first to request the quota of 30% women representation in politics and decision-making, long before the issue was debated at the national level in Indonesia. The *Duek Pakat* also publicly registered women's support for the implementation of *Shari'ah* law, requesting a form of Islamic juristic practice friendly toward women.[11]

Praise for this deliberative council of women was great. The late Acehnese historian M. Gade Ismail was quoted by the *Jakarta Post*: "The most valuable thing to come out of the *Duek Pakat* ... is that women are showing us men and the students how to solve differing points of view in a democratic manner."[12] Another person spoke of the *Duek Pakat* in the context of "Acehnese women map the future." Indeed, at the time when the voices of moderation were absent, these women filled the gap. When the Acehnese were polarized between the rival camps of referendum and that of re-integration, women initiated a middle way by concentrating on the process rather than the result. They insisted that whether it be *merdeka* through referendum, or reaffirmation of Aceh's connection with Jakarta, the issue had to be debated in a non-violent manner. Women's capacity to negotiate their presumed victimhood by turning it into strength, guided the path of their society and country. The voices of women in this *Duek Pakat* became a turning point, for since then many have followed the example set by these courageous women in their demands for negotiation and for seeking a peaceful means to resolve the Aceh conflict.

Women's demand for compromise to solve the conflict became increasingly adopted in the province, for despite a few failures at the end of the road in 2005 the peace agreement between GAM and Jakarta was achieved through nonviolent means. But their call for women political representation in public life has been a continuing struggle. Even though women have succeeded in putting in place regulations for their 30% representation in

[9] *The Jakarta Post* (27 February 2000).
[10] Interview with Naimah Hasan (December 2013).
[11] For an excellent study on the *Shari'ah* as a potential tool for social transformation in contemporary Aceh, consult Feener (2014).
[12] *The Jakarta Post* (27 February 2000).

the political process and decision-making activities at both the national Indonesian and provincial Acehnese levels, such laws have never been properly implemented. Loopholes in the laws and lack of will among the political authorities are some of the obstacles preventing women from achieving due representation in different dimensions of public life. The following example explains both the ambiguity of the law and the absence of good will among the political elites. The Indonesian election law of 2003 requires every political party to register 30% women representation in their party leadership structure and on their candidacy list. To meet this requirement the party enlisted female relatives or friends of the party leadership who often had no experience, and registered them on the "shoe number [*nomor sepatu*]" on their candidacy list. Since the law followed a vertical voting system accumulating all votes onto the first and the next candidates on these lists, very few women received enough votes in Aceh in the 2004 nationwide elections.

Similar experiences occurred across the country. Though the law was improved, the women's struggle continued. The 2009 election law required political parties to crisscross one woman for every two male candidates on their candidacy list, but this slight improvement of the status of women in the law from the previous "shoe number" did not increase women's election to the parliament. At the national level, out of the 560 members of the 2014 parliament there were only 79 female representatives, or 14% – lower than the 2009 parliament when 103 women, or 18%, became national law makers. Although further improved from both the 2009 and 2014 elections, the 2019 representation of women has not reached the required 30% benchmark, since only 118 women (20.5%) won parliamentary seats out of the total 575 members. The situation in Aceh is the same: of the 81 parliamentary seats in 2014, women gained 12 places or 14%, compared to the 2009 elections when only 5 women or 7%, assumed parliamentary positions of 69 members.[13] In 2019 female representation in the provincial parliament was again reduced to 11% as women obtained only nine seats of the total 81 parliamentary posts. When the representation of women at both Aceh's provincial and district levels is assessed jointly, a similar digit of 11% is found. Eighty three women secured the parliamentary positions out of the total 731 members. Furthermore, representation of Acehnese women in the national

[13]For detailed analysis refer to "Sulitnya Wanita ke Parlemen" in local daily *Serambi Indonesia*, 28 April 2014.

parliament in Jakarta is even weaker, for with 13 representatives there is only one woman. Numerous reasons contributed to women's inability to gain access to the "male world arena." Among the many factors that put barriers on women are the high elections costs and the prevalence of money politics in which women are inexperienced players. The placement of women's candidacy on the zigzag numbers 3, 6 and 9; the lack of a political network; and the lack of logistical support from the party leadership are other obstacles preventing women from gaining equal representation in this political field. In other words, in spite of improvements in the law, many political parties continue to regard women as only fulfilling regulatory requirements without whose participation their own election registration would be void. This shortsighted political culture remains strong in Aceh and across the country.

15.2 Challenges and cultural possibilities

Women have always been active in public life in Aceh. Traditional Acehnese society centered around villages never explicitly talked about gender equity and women's public engagement, yet women were involved in every aspect of village activity. It is true that very few women had assumed the position of village heads, but until as recently as 1995 when the law on local government was enacted the position of the village head was more symbolic. Village activities were run by the most influential members of society, namely the Ulama and enlightened leading individuals, the wealthy and the most generous. A few of these persons were women who were the most influential in their village, including during the elections of village heads.[14] This was the era when politics, intrigues and hope for financial gains were remote from village experience. Although the 1979 and 1995 laws on village governance do contain a positive statement on the role of women and require a female representative in the village council, yet in practice that very same position actually mitigates the traditional collective voluntarism of influential women in village affairs. Coupled with financial gains for village leadership promised by these laws, collective responsibility slowly subsided

[14]As a young girl I observed that my female religious teacher, my mother and a few other local ladies were consulted about every move of our village. Nothing could happen in the village without their support, and these great women always acted in the best interests of their village and community, and were among the wisest and most generous leaders. These ladies also worked together as a group in support of their male counterparts and the village head.

in many Acehnese villages. For the same reasons, united female engagement in their village life became minimal. Politics and selfish intrigues have further damaged the situation, and now most village activities and women involvement in community affairs is decided from the top. Ironically, such is the price of modernity and legal reform.

This relapse or regression of the strength of women in village leadership does not mean that women's participation in public life in traditional Acehnese society disappeared completely. The traditional form of income generation should reflect a positive reality. The most important rural income production in Aceh is farming and selling produce in the traditional markets. The two are connected for each supports the other. The involvement of women as vendors in markets remains overwhelming, and they continue to control a great number of small and medium size operations. This commercial activity allows women to contribute to their family income and to be financially independent to some extent. Although these informal business actors may not play a very important role in the country's economic growth, since very few of these women could make a decent income, they indeed contribute greatly to the well-being of their family and the fair upbringing of children — and thereby to the health and vigor of society. These petty-trader women often possess bargaining power and are very independent. In addition to the market, women in Aceh are also active in agriculture. In this arena women share more than half the work of planting, caring and harvesting of agricultural products (especially, rice and vegetables), thereby controlling their family finances. They often decide either to sell the produce or to retain them for family consumption. Such economic independence is a reflection of their strong character manifested in their overall role as equal partners in both the household and society.

Cooperation between men and women in traditional society has to some extent influenced daily life in urban centers. Medium-size enterprises and petty trade in Aceh's cities and towns still depends on a partnership between men and women. However, the real challenges occur in the areas of modern urban occupations, such as employees in government offices, in political parties, the police force, academic institutions, major local and national companies, international corporations, important social organizations and the Ulama body. All these institutions are important because they control most of the resources, decide policies and shape public opinion. When the 2000 *Duek Pakat* requested 30% female representation in politics and in decision-making bodies, the women participants had in mind all these institutions. Although over recent years they have succeeded in incorporating the 30% quota into laws and regulations at both local and national levels, women continue to face great obstacles in putting those laws into practice. Similarly, they have been able to persuade the Ulama Consultative Council (MPU) since 2007 to accommodate female representation in its leadership structure, but again such singular women have not been allowed to play a key role in this important organization's decision-making. The police force has also been accommodating women, but female officers are still far below quota.

Finally, major business enterprises are still beyond women's reach, given that few women are truly large entrepreneurs. The challenge to implement the 30% quota remains a constant exertion and the following two examples reflect this reality. After the 2006 provincial elections women in Aceh worked to transform the tiny Women Empowerment Bureau in the provincial government system into the Women Empowerment and Child Protection Body (*Badan*) with a major profile and sizable budget. They worked hard and negotiated the issue with Aceh's Governor, Vice Governor, members of parliament, and political parties. Although they experienced a number of setbacks along the way, the government and the parliament finally accepted the proposal and transformed the Bureau into the *Badan*. However, this was not the end of their struggle, for a new challenge of selecting the right person to lead this Body emerged. Since its inauguration in 2008 the Governor has appointed four different women to lead the *Badan*, the profile of which has now been further raised to the provincial cabinet level (or *Dinas*). Unfortunately, the quality of its activities and vision has not matched its cabinet status. Also, the selection of the second one was regrettable for she had little interest in women empowerment and gender equity. When the then Governor Irwandi Yusuf was questioned about placing the wrong individual to head this institution, sadly his response reflected his indifference to women's concerns: "I cannot resist, she keeps asking."[15] The third leader of the *Badan* was slightly better, but her political and cultural conservatism, coupled by her attachment to the

[15]His response in Acehnese: "*han ek kudeungoe dingeng-ngen sabe*", was reported by the former Dean of the Law School at Syiah Kuala University, who was an advisor to the Governor.

See "Berdalil Syariat, Irwandi Tolak Copot Camat Perempuan", *The Globe Journal* (8 October 2010). Among the national newspapers discussing this case, see "Opposition to Woman's Leadership of District Wanes", *The Jakarta Post* (October 12 2010).

ruling party prevented her from viewing women issues from a wider more comprehensive scope.

The aforementioned Irwandi episode and the current practice show the nature of political culture in contemporary Aceh, and women's continuing need to struggle in order to gain political rights and their legal share in decision-making. The second example is more telling of the unproductive environment for women's engagement in public life. The issue emerged in April 2010 when Anisah was sworn in as *camat* (head of sub-district) in Plimbang in North Aceh. While Anisah was not the only female *camat* in Aceh, her position became very controversial when the head of the local parliament in that district — Ridwan Muhammad, of Partai Aceh — argued for her removal on the basis that in a province such as Aceh ruled by the *Shari'ah*, a women could not be a legitimate political leader.[16] His conservative judgment led to heated debates on the role of women in decision-making with ongoing media coverage, and many counter arguments expressed both locally and at the national level.[17] The Governor, who is also of the Partai Aceh, registered his support for Anisah,[18] invoking Aceh's history when the four *Sultanahs* had ruled over Aceh for 59 consecutive years with the full support of the Ulama of that era. Anisah's fate was decided by the enormous support she received from both men and women across the province as well as from community leaders, yet the controversy reveals the growing strength of a deeply embedded conservative political culture being promoted in certain areas of Aceh. The appeal to *Shari'ah* is being used and abused by ill-educated "illiterate" politicians in order to gain political traction, while the silence of major Ulama leaders over this issue of legitimate female political leadership further complicates the situation.

These debates did indeed lead to some positive outcomes. They have encouraged people to think seriously about this issue, and many have gone beyond their normal capacity and conventional knowledge to learn more about the range of Islamic legal positions on the issue of women leadership.

---

[16]Rejection of women *camats* in other parts of Indonesia occurred in 2001 when the selection of five female *camats* by the Bupati of Tasikmalaya was refused by the community on religious grounds.

[17]For a good overview of the debates refer to the article in Modus Aceh (24 November 2010) and provincial daily *Serambi Indonesia* (October 2010).

[18]See "Berdalil Syariat, Irwandi Tolak Copot Camat Perempuan", *The Globe Journal* (8 October 2010). Among the national newspapers discussing this case, see "Opposition to Woman's Leadership of District Wanes", *The Jakarta Post* (12 October 2010).

While arguing for women participation in politics is a difficult undertaking, women could have gained more success in academic institutions such as schools and universities. However, no Acehnese major universities have had women Rectors or even candidates running for the office of Rector. There are several female Deans of academic departments, but their number is insignificant. Similarly, a few women have assumed positions as school principals, especially at the high school level, even though the majority of teachers in such schools are women. The lack of women leadership in Aceh's academic institutions may best be explained in relation to both internal factors concerning women, and those of external public reality. Externally, society and academic institutions have not awarded affirmative action any priority, and although women are normally given the same opportunity they don't have any enthusiasm to run for high office. Secondly, since running for important positions involves "chopping off the heads of other candidates" when garnering supporters and denigrating rival candidates, most women are not prepared for such unhealthy distasteful competition. Internally, a few women who meet the requirements for such positions are prevented from running due to their personal situations including family responsibilities or the attitude of their husbands. Another internal factor placing obstacles on women is the concern that they would not receive proper support even from other women, and therefore it is better not to run. Thus, family pressures and lack of self-confidence are two chief internal factors preventing women from moving forward in this arena. In order for them to climb this ladder they should not be faced with a choice of family or career. Rather, women should receive support in their efforts both to raise family and to advance their career. This undoubtedly requires unfailing assistance and cooperation from their husbands and other family members, for only with their corporation may women progress in both domains. The lesson here is that women's empowerment is not just about educating women — but about enlightening husbands and young men as well.

15.3 Contemporary conditions for or against women empowerment

In addition to these issues, the following two contemporary conditions may further hinder women's advancement in Aceh. One is the dominant political conservatism widespread in society, and the other is parochial religious fanaticism. The Acehnese government, like the rest of Indonesia, has never been very willing to accommodate gender concerns without effective pressure exerted from women and by international bodies like the United Nations. True: the forces acting from within and from without have gradually changed the political discourse in Aceh and throughout Indonesia, leading to the reform of laws and public regulations. Nevertheless, the implementation of those legal requirements continues to be problematic, even though government rhetoric on gender has often been accommodating. The situation is even less constructive in Aceh. Although Aceh has a long history of women leadership and the general positive attitude toward women social involvement, their experience in politics is not very encouraging. Since the 2009 elections of GAM leaders through their *Partai Aceh* to govern the province, women met a more conservative political environment. The controversy over a female *camat* described earlier reflects the recent spread of political conservatism. Even Irwandi, who supported the legitimacy of the female *camat*, is conservative on many other gender issues.

The reason for his selection of the Head of the *Women Empowerment Body* mentioned previously, the budget he assigned for gender concerns and his views on certain cultural–religious practices such as polygamy are just a few examples of his conservatism. The next Governor Zaini Abdullah was not very different either. He was not known for supporting women's agenda and his silent attitude was overtaken by his more flamboyant Vice Governor famous for his love of women and enthusiasm for polygamous marriage.[19] The latter was also known for his religious conservatism. As one activist commented: "We cannot confirm his support for women since the issue of equality is the lowest of his agenda. Unfortunately, neither he nor the Governor has promoted a constructive policy for women after more than 2 years in the office."[20] The local parliaments both at the provincial and district levels were then controlled by the *Partai Aceh*, whose many members were quite insensitive about women's issues.[21] The current parliaments selected in 2014 and 2019 has reduced the Partai Aceh membership, yet the provincial government's gender concerns remain lower in priority. The *Partai Aceh* not only tolerates but promotes polygamy, and many of its leaders, including the current Vice Governor, are polygamous

[19]These two Partai Aceh members were elected as Governor and Vice Governor of Aceh on 9 April 2012.
[20]Interview with Syarifah Rahmatillah of MISPI (August 2014).
[21]Interview with T. Husein Banta (14 October 2010).

husbands.[22] In fact, since their rise to power, polygamy has become a statement of status among political elites.[23] Conservative political culture is also reflected in the policy and programs of the provincial government, and therefore "gender mainstreaming efforts are not moving anywhere."[24] In short, the political culture and religious conservatism promoted by the Partai Aceh, and supported by certain religious establishment figures, have created a low intellectual and social atmosphere that is unhealthy for future women equity projects.[25]

In addition to parochial political conservatism, religious fanaticism is also on the rise in this province. While Aceh has always been a very devout Muslim region and the Acehnese are proud of their Islamic roots,[26] many are quite concerned with the ways Islam is now being applied. Women do support the implementation of the *Shari'ah*,[27] as they clearly expressed during the *Duek Pakat*, because they believe strongly in the Islamic principles of justice and equity. "*Shari'ah* is about justice and the protection of the weak, but the version of the *Shari'ah* being implemented in Aceh is about punishment and exposing the wrong doing of others.[28]" The problem with the Acehnese version of the *Shari'ah* is that "everyone claims it is God's law while in reality it is the interpretation of God's law

---

[22]No serious study has been made on the practice of polygamy among PA leaders or among the contemporary Acehnese, but judges at the religious courts and female lawyers who defend divorce cases clearly suggest that polygamy is on the rise in Aceh, and GAM leaders are among the faithful practitioners of polygamy.

[23]Just recently Aceh's parliament debated a *qanun* (legal penal code) to regulate family affairs, allowing men including public servants to engage in polygamy. Islam permits polygamy for specific reasons. Yet this law is deemed highly controversial by many, in view of the fact that the government of Aceh is now encouraging polygamy. 'Religiously permissible' is not quite the same as being encouraged by the provincial government and political elites. Due to this controversy, the debate over this *qanun* has ceased, leaving it to the 2019 new parliament.

[24]Statement by a former member of parliament during the discussion on gender sensitive budgeting (9 December 2013).

[25]One example of this low culture occurred on 10 March 2015 when the then Rector of Ar-Raniry Islamic University met with a group of 30 women activists under the program "Meet the Rector." This professor spent the first half hour of his two hour speaking session dwelling on the importance of polygamy which generated protests from some members of the audience.

[26]Aceh is credited for the historical spread of Islam in the Archipelago and for the development of Islamic intellectual scholarship throughout Indonesia and the entire Malay speaking region in South East Asia.

[27]For an excellent concise discussion of the *Shari'ah*, consult Kamali (2008); also Hallaq (2009).

[28]Interview with Nurjannah Ismail (March 2010).

by the Ulama and politicians. Our inability to distinguish between human interpretations and divine injunctions is a serious matter."[29] Another criticism regarding the application of *Shari'ah* law has to do with the target of legal enforcement. The critics observe that the *Shari'ah* has only punished women and the weak, while the politicians and the powerful have not been touched by it.[30] In spite of all these criticisms, many women continue to expect that the *Shari'ah* can truly promote the spirit of justice and equality[31] — and thus the problem is not with the *Shari'ah* as such, but with the manner it is being interpreted and applied. Other women feel that the *Shari'ah* can never be just toward women, but they have no choice except to work within the existing legal framework. Despite the differences of opinion, these two groups of women often work together in order to accomplish common objectives. In addition, there are others who always view the *Shari'ah* or its implementation very positively, and these represent the most conservative among Acehnese women. According to them, the problem is not with "God's law and its application" but with the people who are not following divine commands.[32] Aligned with each of these three main orientations one finds men who share their respective views, and thus the discourse on *Shari'ah* in Aceh is dominated by these three differing views, with the first two often found supporting each other.

These debates among lay women and men are also reflected in discourse among the Ulama. While all of the Ulama in Aceh unequivocally support the *Shari'ah* and have worked hard to get it adopted by the government, it is the Acehnese traditional Ulama heading the *dayahs* (religious boarding schools) represented by the MPU who are truly the core of Acehnese religious authority. They are generally open to criticisms concerning the implementation of the *Shari'ah* as long as these views are expressed in a proper venue and in a dignified manner. As a matter of practical distinction, I may refer to them as the *sarung* Ulama (i.e., who wear traditional clothing). In addition to this traditional or *salafi* religious establishment, there are university Ulama who are largely professors and

[29]Interview with Fuad Mardhatillah (September 2010).
[30]For a balance of views on the application of the *Shari'ah* in Aceh see Husin (2015b).
[31]For details see Feener (2014).
[32]Global groups such as Hizbut Tahrir Indonesia (HTI) fall under this category. It is one of the most active groups advocating the implementation of Islamic law through its utopian idea of *khilafah* (Islamic caliphate).

graduates of Ar-Raniry Islamic University, being the most open to pluralist views and social-religious criticisms. These "white collar" Ulama are also well represented in the MPU. The two groups share a great deal of commonalities, but are not always in agreement. The third type is the most conservative group and is a new comer in Aceh. This group may be identified as the *jubbah* religious authority (wearing the white Arab-style shirt or *jubbah*), and comprises several groups of outside origin: *Hizbu t-Tahrir*,[33] *Jama'ah Tabligh*,[34] *Wahhabism*,[35] as well as several national groups that all arrived in Aceh recently to assist during the 2004 Tsunami, and have grown roots in the province. The *jubbah* Ulama are very active in promoting their views and, despite being outside imports, they are gaining ground in Aceh. The most conservative women group mentioned above belongs to this new *jubbah* religious establishment.

Although all of these Ulama groups and their women supporters share the same enthusiasm for the *Shari'ah*, the Ar-Raniry Ulama are more understanding of women's predicament in the context of the unintended abuses of *Shari'ah*. The *sarung* Ulama are also listening to criticisms and complaints, but they are more careful and limited in their accommodations and responses. In contrast, the *jubbah* leaders see nothing wrong in the *Shari'ah* implementation, suggesting that problems have arisen due to the lack of positive responses from the public and therefore, more severe forced implementation is necessary. Although the *sarung* Ulama share very little in common with the *jubbah* group regarding Islamic viewpoints, when it comes to *Shari'ah* discourse the *sarung* Ulama are in alignment with this ultra-conservative group. A prominent leader of MPU Tengku Ismail Yacob stated about the *jubbah* leaders: Even though the (*dayah*) Ulama disagree with the ways in which they express their views, they help promote greater support for the *Shari'ah*. Their opinions on certain aspects of Islam in the

---

[33]For an Introduction to Hizbut-Tahrir consult Ahmed and Stuart (2009).

[34]For a brief exposition of the Tablighi, see "Jamaah Tabligh di Tengah Kritisi Positif dan Negatif," in Era Muslim: Media Muslim Rujukan, available at http://www.eramuslim.com/umum/jamaah-tabligh-di-tengah-kritisi-positif-dan-negatif.htm. Retrieved on September 2014.

[35]Wahhabism had arrived in Aceh prior to the Tsunami largely through the Acehnese graduates of Saudi universities who promoted the puritanical type of Islam upon their return to Aceh. Some of them have even established *dayahs* in some areas of Aceh. However, in spite of their initial puritanical views, the pre-Tsunami Wahhabi leaders worked within the Ulama system by making necessary adjustments and cultural changes. The post-Tsunami Wahhabism arrived in Aceh with Gulf money supported by Indonesian promoters predominantly from Java. Unlike the Acehnese Wahhabis, the new comers are outside the mainstream of Aceh's Ulama leadership and culture.

manners of just *halal* and *haram* are problematic because Islamic norms consist of more than halal and haram options.[36]

Since the *salafi Ulama* rarely express their opinions on controversial issues in public, the general masses are left vulnerable to the conservative views of the *jubbah* groups, or those of the Ar-Raniry scholars. When asked the reasons for their silence, the *dayah Ulama*'s typical response: "these are minor issues". One wonders what are their major concerns? Proselytizing is certainly one.[37] Another explanation for their silence is that the *Ulama* generally dislike to contradict one another in public, and therefore when they disagree on issues they discuss them behind closed doors. Solidarity and consensus is a chief characteristic of *Ulama* culture in Aceh, as elsewhere in Muslim societies. However, the new more radical jubbah *Ulama* do not appear to exhibit this characteristic, and therefore they are outside the mainstream. The real concern is that such radical well-organized groups may assume the lead in providing public guidance, which in turn puts them on better terms with the masses. Too much attention to obstacles may distort reality.

Among the conditions that provide hope for women empowerment are women factors. Two of the three groups of women described earlier are active members of society and are well aware of the obstacles which hinder gender equity. These women groups work in different arenas to improve their own condition and those of their families and society. Similarly, the conservative group is also providing services, but its activity falls outside the purview of this study. Two examples may explain the nature of activism by women groups in promoting gender empowerment. One is the effort by the *dayah* women who seek to shine within their cultural limits. Women presently consist of about 1.5–2% of the *dayah* leadership in Aceh, for there are only 10–15 women among the 700 *dayah* leaders. Therefore, *dayah* culture is overwhelmingly male in nature.[38] However, a few women who are leading *dayahs* work systematically to break barriers and to act within the constraints of the dominant *dayah* environment.

Their mission is significant on a number of grounds. First, internally they are reclaiming the role and the position of women in the predominantly male world of the *dayah* and *Ulama*, highlighting the veritable Islamic

---

[36]Interview with Tengku Ismail Yacob (November 2010).
[37]In early 2010, the Ulama were speaking against conversion of Acehnese to Christianity by some NGO workers assisting in Aceh after the *Tsunami*.
[38]For the role of women in Aceh's *dayahs*, see Husin (2014).

position on equal rights and shared responsibilities between men and women in seeking and disseminating knowledge. Second, they are also providing religious leadership in the community which is otherwise dominated by male *Ulama* — demonstrating that females can also exercise Islamic intellectual and spiritual authority. Third, they offer themselves as religious role models not only for young women but for young men as well, since their students in the *dayahs* are both male and female. Lastly, *dayah* women leaders and teachers may enrich debates on the role of women in public life not only for the consumption of the general public but also, more especially, for the enlightenment of the *dayah* community. Ummi Rahimun, one of the *dayah* leaders in Aceh Besar, expressed her view that "the involvement of women in politics is necessary since women like their male counterparts are given the responsibility to bring benevolence (*rahmah*) and goodness (*kebaikan*) to others." She contended that many *Hadīths* (narrated traditions from the Prophet) support women's social engagement, and that dissenting views are in contradiction with "the spirit of Islam and Prophetic practice."[39] This type of discourse by a noted female Ulama such as Rahimun is sorely needed in the social and religious context of contemporary Aceh.

The second group of women who are laying the groundwork for women empowerment are the general social activists. As mentioned earlier, they are of two types: the religious and the liberal.[40] These two groups view the role of Islam in public life differently, yet they share the view about the need for active engagement of women in society. They argue that this cannot be achieved without hard work by women themselves. Therefore, some concentrate on improving the legal foundations for the empowerment of women,[41] while others provide assistance to inexperienced female members of parliament and policy makers in order to help them improve their capacity and be aware of gender concerns.[42]

Furthermore, they represent women assisting other females and their families to improve their quality of life, and by so doing they hope

[39]Rahimun referred to the widely reported recent controversy and debates over women's political leadership in Aceh in her response to the right of a woman to be a sub-district head (*camat*) and other political appointments (see Husin, 2014).
[40]The term "liberal" does not imply their being irreligious, since with respect to personal devotions they may be as devout as the more conservative religious.
[41]Jaringan Perempuan untuk Kebijakan (Women Network for Policy Improvement) is one of the significant groups created by women to negotiate legal and policy issues.
[42]Mitra Sejati Perempuan Indonenesia (The True Partnership of Indonesian Women) and Balai Syura Ureng Inong Aceh (The Consultative Council of Acehnese Women) are two major women organizations focusing on capacity-building of female policymakers.

to make these women aware of their rights and responsibilities in their respective surroundings. Finally, there remains a large number of women who constantly try to improve their own qualifications through both formal and non-formal education in order to become better members of family and society and to improve their material conditions, so that they may compete for political appointment and important public offices. All these women are indeed true agents of change in contemporary Aceh.

15.4 Conclusion

The present study demonstrates that peace building forms an Islamic core value manifested in the inner provision of human capacity (*fitrah*), in human relations with the divine, in their horizontal connections as community members, and in their treatment of nature. Women as part of the human family are endowed with rights and responsibilities to enjoy and fulfill their earthly obligation of maintaining and promoting peace. However, in reality this remains a luxury for most women who continue to struggle to overcome difficult conservative religious, cultural and political battles in order to claim the very provisions bestowed upon them by God *al-Salam*. Understanding these Islamic core values provides Acehnese women genuine hope to pursue their striving for their Islamic endowment of equality and justice.

15.4.1 Policy recommendations

Our study on the role of Acehnese women in advocating peace and justice invites reflection on broader efforts for women equity across communities and cultures. Government ministries, planners and civic actors must heed and apply the following insights.

- Women empowerment and social justice are essential Islamic principles that should be embraced by all Muslim communities and cultures for they are important milestones for reviving civilizational Islam.
- Women empowerment is not only about educating women about their rights and responsibilities, but also, more significantly, about enlightening husbands and young men in society to uphold essential principles.
- Women empowerment always works against cultural conservatism and religious fanaticism, since these two often impose a low intellectual and

social atmosphere dangerous for both women agenda and civilizational renewal.

- Muslim women including the Acehnese sincerely believe and continue to expect that the *Shari'ah* can truly promote the spirit of justice and equality.

References

English

Ahmed, Houriya and Stuart, Hannah (2009), *Hizb ut-Tahrir Ideology and Strategy*, Center for Social Cohesion, London, UK, available at http://henryjacksonsociety.org/wp-content/uploads/2013/01/HIZB.pdf. Retrieved on August 2015.

Crow, Karim Douglas (2013), "The concept of peace-security (Salm) in Islam: Uncovering the basis of Islamic peace," in HRH Prince Ghazi bin Muhammad *et al.* (eds.). *War and Peace in Islam: The Uses and Abuses of Jihad*, Cambridge: The Islamic Text Society, pp. 250–268.

Feener, R. Michael (2014), *Shari'a and Social Engineering: The Implementation of Islamic Law in Contemporary Aceh, Indonesia*, Oxford: Oxford University Press.

Hallaq, Wael E. (2009), *An Introduction to Islamic Law*, Cambridge: Cambridge University Press.

Husin, Asna (2014), "Leadership and authority: Women leading Dayah in Aceh", in Bianca J. Smith and Mark Woodward (eds.). *Gender and Power in Indonesian Islam: Leaders, Feminists, Sufis and Pesantren Selves*, London: Routledge, pp. 49–65.

Husin, Asna (2015a), "An exploration of three contemporary Acehnese peace leaders," in Yasmin Saikia and Chad Haines (eds.). *Women and Peace in the Islamic World: Gender, Agency and Influence*, London and New York: I.B. Tauris, pp. 136–168.

Husin, Asna (2015b), Women and *Shari'ah* law: Lessons from Aceh. *Journalar-raniry.com*, 2(2), pp. 165–186.

Kamali, Mohammad Hashim (2008), *Shari'ah Law: An Introduction*, Oxford, UK: Oneworld Publications.

Khan, Banu A. L. (2007), "The Jewel Affair: The Sultana, Her Orangkaya, and the Dutch Foreign Envoys," paper presented at *the Conference on Aceh and Indian Ocean Studies*, organised by the Rehabilitation and Recontruction Agency of Aceh (BRR) and the Asia Research Institute, Singapore, Banda Aceh, 24–27 February.

O'Rourke, Kevin (2002), *Reformasi: The Struggle for Power in Post-Suharto Indonesia*, Crows Nest, New South Wales: Allen & Unwin.

Walther, Wiebke (1995), *Women in Islam: From Medieval to Modern Times*, Princeton: Markus Wiener Publishers.

Arabic

Al-Zuhayli, Wahbah (1411/1991), *Al-Tafsir al-Munir fi l-Aqidah wa al-Shari'ah wa l-Manhaj* (Vol. 22), Beirut: Dar al-Fikr al-Mu'asir, p. 17.

Indonesian Bhasa

Hasjmy, A. (1977), 59 *Tahun Aceh Merdeka di Bawah Pemerintahan Ratu*, Jakarta: Bulan Bintang.

Pamenan, Iljas Sutan (1959), *Rentjong Atjeh di Tangan Wanita: Zaman Pemerintahan Radja Putri Atjeh, 1641–1699*, Jakarta: self-published.

Zentgraaff, H. C. (1983), *Atjeh*, translated by Aboe Bakar Aceh, Jakarta: Penerbit Beuna, pp. 77–147.

Chapter 16

Social Values and the Female Labor Force Participation in Turkey: A Historical Evaluation from Ottoman Empire to the Present

Kadir Yildirim

Abstract

"A nation's women are the measure of its modernity."[1]
Working life refers to the process by which employees using mental or physical labor are used to produce goods and services. When the development of this process is analyzed with regard to Turkey, it can be seen that the economic structure and relations of production that were taken over from the Ottoman Empire were a key determinant for the working life during the Turkish Republic. The key determinant of the economic structure was agriculture in the early Republican era. Apart from the manufacturing workers in a few cities where the industry was relatively advanced, 90% of the workers were employed in the agricultural sector. The adventure of the working life of Republican era is actually a story of immigration from the countryside to the city in a sense. Having started with the 1950s and accelerated after the 1980s, migration to cities from agricultural regions has deeply affected not only Turkey's political and social structure but also its labor markets.

Keywords: Female labor force, Social values, Ottoman Empire, Turkey, Urbanization

The fact that the basic unit of production in the agricultural sector is the family and almost every family that owns land have provided sufficient work space for the male and female members of the family. However, the second half of the 20th century has also unearthed a significant problem in terms

[1] A slogan from *Kadin* (woman) magazine which was published in Thessaloniki in 1908–1909 (*Kadin*, 26 October 1908, p. 1).

of Turkish women along with the wave of migration to urban areas. Women working in the fields while living in rural areas were pushed into a position where they felt rather like strangers in the cities and remained out of social and economic life. Significant decreases in female labor force participation (FLFP) with urbanization have kept women away from working life and in a way, they became housebound.

Statistical data related to the last 50 years' development about the amount of women labor in rural and urban Turkey can easily make us imagine the aforementioned data. This reading might allow us to diagnose the problem; however, it will not suffice to make us understand the reasons for the problem. The factors causing Turkish women to remain outside the labor market cannot be only explained by the unplanned urbanization or insufficient employment opportunities in urban areas. In fact, these are the developments helping a much radical problem to become visible, rather than being the main reasons for the quite low FLFP rate. As a matter of fact, a long-termed view on the history of the subject will show that current discussions have been ongoing on the same platforms and with the same datum for almost 100 years. The social values and sensibilities taking place right in the middle of the discussions also play a decisive role in the status of women. By the 19th century, women who tried to make their presence felt more in social and economic life faced an invisible barrier, almost a kind of public opposition. The fact that her invisible barrier's presence can be still strongly felt illustrates how deeply rooted it is.

In this chapter, I will try to make a reverse chronological evaluation in order to examine the past and present state of social values in question. First, I will present current data on the FLFP in Turkey. I will evaluate the causes and the effects of the data in order to elaborate the table that these data reveal. Through international reports, I will try to show that the problem is not only related to the labor market but it also brings forth influences designating the women's positions in the overall social, political and economic fields. The most important factor in determining the FLFP in Turkey is the informal institutions rather than the formal institutions. These informal institutions, negatively affecting the women's participation in the social and economic life, originate from the social values that have emerged and strengthened in a long historical process. Besides making the study unique, Ottoman archival resources and other historical records will not only allow clarifying the history of the subject but will also help to shed light to present.

16.1 Women in Turkey's working life: Current status

"I was doing workshops about the problems women faced in working life and I was suggesting solutions. However, I received a lot of criticisms from the men, or even from the managers few and far between ... 'There are so many problems in Turkey, is "women" the only remaining issue in Turkey? Is this the only issue?' they would say."[2]

Agricultural sector ranked first in the sectoral distribution of employment in Turkey until 1990s. As a result of the accelerated migration wave since 1980s and the developments in the economy, the share of the agricultural sector in employment has begun to decrease. This decrease has led to a variety of problems concerning Turkey's labor market to come to light. The problems women generally facing in social and economic life and privately in working life have been long ignored due to the agricultural cover that has covered them. However, developments in domestic migration, urbanization, communication technologies and developments such as international expansion in order to integrate with the world brought this issue to the surface in full clarity.

When assessed the labor force participation rate in Turkey in terms of men with an international comparison, we do not see any significant difference today as it was in the past. For example, in 2000 the labor force participation rate for men over 15 was 72%; however, in 2015, it was 71%. The world average for the same years was 78% and 76%. When we make the same comparison for women, we see a rather different picture. The FLFP rate for women was 26% in 2000 and 30% in 2015. The world average was 52% and 49% for the same years (World Bank, 2018, http://wdi.worldbank.org/table/2.2). Therefore, when compared with other women in the world, it can be seen that women in Turkey fall considerably behind in terms of labor force participation in regard to men. Table 16.1, dealing with basic indicators of Turkey's labor market, shows that FLFP rate is 34% in 2017.[3]

[2]A statement of a female instructor who gave seminars on occupational health and safety to union members and managers (Topgül, 2016, p. 2361).

[3]Although this figure is too low, there are arguments that this figure is actually much lower. This rate, which was 23% in 2004, was 26% in 2009. However, since 2010, there has been a rapid increase (Turkstat, 2017b). A significant part of the increase after 2010 is due to the statistical changes. A similar situation is also related to the unemployment rates. The unofficial unemployment rate for women is 15%. However, due to the method of calculation, it is claimed that this ratio is actually well below the real unemployment figures. Hence, an alternative method of calculation claims the real unemployment rate for women to be 30% (KSGM, 2004, p. 57).

Table 16.1 Main labor force indicators (August 2017).

	Total	Male	Female
15+ age		Million	
Population 15 years and over	60.0	29.7	30.3
Labor force	32.2	21.8	10.4
Employed	28.8	20.0	8.8
Unemployed	3.4	1.84	1.56
Not in labor force	27.7	7.8	19.9
		%	
Labor force participation rate	53.7	73.5	34.3
Employment rate	48	67.3	29.1
Unemployment rate	10.6	8.4	15
Non-agricultural unemployment rate	12.8	9.7	20.3
Unemployment rate for youth (15–24 age group)	20.6	16.8	27.7
Neither in employment nor in education or training*	28	17.7	38.6

Note: *The rate of young people (15–24 age group) neither in employment nor in education in total youth population.
Source: Turkstat (2017a).

This rate was 34% in 1988 as well. The ratio shows that the past 30 years have shown no progress (KEFEK, 2013, p. 3).

During the era when Turkey's economy was an agrarian economy, FLFP rate was also high. For example, this rate which was 70% in the mid-1950s, dropped down to 30% with internal migration wave and urbanization. While the 60% of Turkey's population was generally living in cities in 1993, 77% of working women were living and working in rural areas. This important impact of agriculture in the female labor force shows that a significant proportion of women migrating to the city is withdrawn from the working life. A World Bank report prepared on the situation of women in Turkey in 1993, likened Turkey's situation at that time in terms of FLFP to the OECD countries in the 1960s. In OECD countries, before the 1960s, the rate ranging between 15% and 30% has exceeded 50% over the next 30 years since that date (World Bank, 1993, pp. 9–11). However, even though the same amount of time has passed from the 1990s to present day, the fact that FLFP in Turkey has stayed at the same level indicates an experience that is different from the Organisation for Economic Co-operation and Development (OECD) countries and that cannot be understood only by numbers.

It can be seen from Table 16.1 that women are in a more disadvantageous position than men for almost every entry. Employment rates for women are less than half of the male employment rate; however, the unemployment rate is almost double. When the agricultural sector is not factored in, the female unemployment rate exceeds 20% (Turkstat, 2017b). The last two lines Table 16.1 which show the situation concerning the young women between the ages of 15–24 years indicates that new generations suffer from the problems such as unemployment more heavily. The unemployment rate for young women is almost twice as large as the overall unemployment rate for women. The fact that approximately 4 out of every 10 females in the same age group have neither education nor employment is an important question that should be dealt not only with its economic results but also with its social and psychological effects. About 47% of women in the 20–24 age group and 57% of women in the 25–29 age group are neither educated nor employed (Turkstat, 2017b). These rates mean that half of the women in the 20–29 age group are in some way trapped at home.

There are a number of problems generating from not being involved in the workforce for women. However, treating women as a single mass can cause other women groups who are affected more severely to be overlooked. For example, the FLFP rate throughout Turkey is 34%; however, this rate decreases to 24% for the 50–54 age group and 17% for the 55–64 age group. Rates for these age groups in OECD countries are 66% and 49%, respectively (Öğütoğulları and Kılıç, 2016, p. 92). Therefore, while it is difficult to find a work for women in Turkey, it is observed that the problem gets more challenging as they grow older. Another point that we should pay attention to is the regional differences. The 10-year average data show that there are differences nearly up to five times between the regions in terms of FLFP (Güçlü, 2017, p. 89). Especially, in the southeast of the country, it seems as if women have been ignored in labor markets as well as in other fields.

While two-thirds of women remain out of the working life, working and being able to find a job does not mean the end of the problems for women. HAK-IS, which is the second biggest trade union confederation in Turkey together with its 440,000 members, indicates that discrimination against women in working life is a primary problem (Topgül, 2016, p. 2359). Also, one in every four employed females has a temporary status and works part-time. This type of work does not originate from a voluntary choice but from the difficulty in finding a permanent job. The rate of women working informally is 96% in the agricultural sector and 35% in the industrial sector. Especially, almost all of the female agricultural workers lack social security (KSGM, 2014, pp. 37–52). Around 60% of the female workers are employed in jobs that do not require qualification; such as an agricultural worker or a salesperson. About 84 of every 100 women in rural areas work in agriculture. Approximately 77% of them are family members of the workers who are not paid any wages. A recent study about the city of Kars, one of the country's leading livestock region, reveals that the majority of women in this area who want to move into big cities work for 4.5 hours in agricultural work in a day and they do almost everything from milking to making cow dung. (Demir *et al.*, 2017, pp. 81–82). Because the average level of education in rural areas is low, the conditions are tougher for women.

16.2 Education and FLFP

A significant reason for the low FLFP is the low education level. As can be seen from the Table 16.2, the higher the level of education gets, the higher the workforce participation rates get.

As the level of education increases, so do the wages of women workers. A woman with a higher education degree gets paid almost three times more than a woman with a primary education degree (Turkstat, 2015). However, we should also add that women with all different education degrees earn lower wages than men who do the same job. The fact that the women's wage earned by participating in working life is regarded only as a contribution to the family budget and the idea of male being the only family member providing the house having been generally accepted by the society, play an important role in women getting lower wages in the labor market compared to men (Gökkaya, 2014, p. 376).

It is a fact that as the level of education in the country increases, so does FLFP. However, a comparison to be held only between different groups of women within the country will not help us to fully understand the issue. For example, a comparison made between Turkey and Greece, Italy, Portugal and Spain which are countries from Europe's relatively less developed

Table 16.2 Labor force participation and unemployment rates of women by educational background (August 2017 — %).

Educational level	Labor force participation rate	Unemployment rate
Illiterate	16.5	3.6
Below high school	28.6	10.2
High school	34.2	20.8
Vocational high school	41.9	21.8
Higher education	73.1	21.9

Source: Turkstat (2017b).

regions, clearly shows that education is not the sole determinant for FLFP in Turkey. As a matter of fact, FLFP rates are lower in almost all education levels, from elementary to higher education when compared to those in the aforementioned countries. Gürsel, Acar and Uysal, in their unique study relating to the subject, seek the answer to the question "How would FLFP rates be if the level of education in aforementioned countries were as low as in Turkey?" The results they reached reveal that if the education levels of these countries were to be the same as Turkey's, FLFP rates would still be much higher. A large part of differences between Turkey and Southern European countries is not because of the differences in education levels but because of lower participation rates for each education level. Even if the education level increases in Turkey as FLFP improves, it still falls behind the rates in these countries at all levels of education. The share of non-educational factors in the total difference is over 70%. These non-educational factors taking place at the heart of cultural factors constitute obstacles difficult to overcome for the women in Turkey in participating labor force (Gürsel, Uysal and Acar, 2011, pp. 197–200).

16.3 Woman of the house, mother of the child: Being a Woman in a patriarchal society

"I was in the Women's Employment Monitoring Board within the Ministry of Labor. When I expressed the subject, all the senior representatives were male and said that child care was a woman's job. If the high-level managers utter these words, what will the workers say?"[4]

The traditional social structure regarding the men–women relationships continues its strong presence in Turkey. The role which this structure assigns for women leads to an unequal situation in terms of access to opportunities and distribution of resources. This structure, makes the society's general point of view a determinant while specifying the social or economic status of individuals rather than the qualifications or educational status. The fact that the division of domestic labor has been thrown on women's shoulders due to social gender perception and pressure is the most important factor that causes women to withdraw from the working life.

Among the reasons why women are not included in the workforce, being engaged in household affairs is by far the first reason by 57% (The General

[4]The statement of a woman who participated in the law-making process about having lactation rooms in companies (Topgül, 2016, p. 2359).

Directorate on Status of Woman, 2016, p. 5). About 98.4% of those showing housework as the reason for not participating in the workforce are women, whereas men who do the same thing is only 1.5% (Öztürk and Coşar, 2017, p. 534). While the FLFP among women without children aged 25–49 years is 40%, that rate decreases to 29% among women with children (KSGM, 2014, p. 34). Surveys show that the employers believe that if female workers get married or have children, they will quit work and therefore they do not want to employ women (KEİG, 2013, p. 29). Data show that child care in Turkey is largely determined by social gender inequality. This situation does not change for women who are employed and who work full time. Parenting is generally taken as motherhood and the role of the father is usually ignored. It is inevitable that a child care model determined by such social gender inequality will be an obstacle to FLFP (Paker and Uysal, 2016, pp. 2–5).

This dominant understanding of society has even affected the thoughts of the women. A survey in 2008 shows that 49% of the women between the ages of 15 and 19 years state that the place of a woman was at home. The percentage of women who favored the idea that women should have their economic independence remained at 45% (Acar and Fraker, 2016, p. 908). This view of society toward married women or women with children decreases the rate of FLFP in Turkey down to 26% while this rate navigates between 50% and 60% among the women having children aged 0–6 years in Southern European countries; such as Spain, Italy and Greece (Gümüş and Türkyılmaz, 2017, p. 73).

In fact, the low rate of FLFP is not a situation which can merely be explained by the dynamics of the labor market. Global Gender Gap data evaluating the situation of women in the world over four criteria (economic participation and opportunity, educational attainment, health and survival, political empowerment) clearly show this situation. According to the results of 2017 report, Turkey was at 131 in a list consisted of 144 countries (World Economic Forum, 2017, p. 11). In the year 2006, when the report was first published, Turkey stood at 106 in a list of 115 countries (World Economic Forum, 2006, p. 9). According to Gender, Institutions and Development Database prepared by OECD, unpaid care work ration is 6,22 for Turkey. That is to say, women spend 6.2 times more time on free care for their family members than men (OECD.Stat, 2014). As a conclusion, women in Turkey are faced with a significant social opposition when they want to get outside from their home, when they want to participate more in public and economic life. This established social understanding has not emerged all of a sudden and it has a long historical background. Hereinafter, we will focus on the developments and discussions that have occurred since the 19th century when the Ottoman social and economic life underwent fundamental transformations which we can interpret as the beginning of this adventure.

16.4 Social resistance and historical roots against the women in working life: Ottoman era

In the Ottoman Empire, a patriarchal society, very few records were kept about women for social and economic purposes. Just like all other areas, women were even only included in population censuses relatively late (Faroqhi, 2000, p. 12). This problem, encountered in particular in early periods, diminished in the late 19th century and more data can be reached about their participation in working life and their problems.[5]

The 19th century, which is considered the most eventful century of the Ottoman Empire, was a period when the conditions of the state and society changed and became harder. The Ottoman government, which was trying to find a solution to economic backwardness, started a period of reform that imitated the European countries that had experienced industrial revolution. The state, considering industrialization to be one of its main targets, began to open factories in markets such as textiles, silk, tobacco and food. Private entrepreneurs also started to open factories once international commercial and financial relations had strengthened. The emergence of factory-type production, rather than guilds, which were based on small producers, led to an increase in waged labor.

In this new period, when the roles of employee and employer became clear and their benefits changed, a novelty seen in industrial life was the rise of women workers. In parallel with the breakdown of the economic structure, negations such as inflation gained strength and they reduced people's purchasing power, which meant that, for women, working became an obligation rather than a choice. However, this choice encountered some obstacles because of the patriarchal-conservative structure of the society and state administrators. The Ottoman state tried to prevent women from

[5] A recent study shows that the number and the proportion of the female members are not fully known in Türk-iş, which is the oldest and biggest labor trade unions confederation in Turkey. An answer to a question related to this issue was also interesting: "inferentially around 10%" (Topgül, 2016, p. 2358).

working with male workers in industrial life and, where it could not do this, it tried at least to enforce physical control in production centers in line with religious criteria.

One of the main obstacles for women to attend working life as waged laborers was that Ottoman society had a structure based on agriculture and that the industry sector and industrial life in cities were not developed. Thus, *Büyük Duygu* magazine even stated in 1913 that "in the country the underdeveloped structure of industrial and economic life causes even men not to exist in this field; so it must be taken naturally that women cannot get a foot-hold in industry" (Haydar, 1913, p. 118). *Büyük Duygu*, in which this article was published, was a women's magazine. The magazine, which regards "women's not being able to work when even men do not find work" normal, shows that the patriarchal mentality is also strong among women. Obviously, it is interesting to see a similar understanding among women over the past 100 years. According to the results of the World Values Survey, two-thirds of women living in Turkey, believes that, men have the right to work primarily in a situation where the job opportunities are limited (Acar and Fraker, 2016, p. 908).

The negative view for women's working was not because the industry was not widespread. Social values and cultural reasons were more significant than this. In fact, developments in Kastamonu in 1909 are a good example for this situation. After the number of women working on weaving looms in the region increased, some men reacted and a dangerous event took place: armed groups tried to prevent women from working. Those people established an armed community (BOA, 1909).[6] In the report from Kastamonu Prosecution Office, local state administration was stated to support these groups. The oppression of local state institutions and this community, said to be founded with the aim of preventing women in Muslim society from working for religious reasons, went so far as imposing a ban on women going outside (BOA, 1909).

There were some similar cases in other regions of the empire. The government considered women working in the same environments as men to be an unfavorable situation under religious rules. In this way, the Ministry of Internal Affairs requested an investigation from local administration about the disobedience of Islamic rules among Muslim women and girls working in tobacco shops in Aydin Province in 1912. The governorship tried to ease

[6]Prime Ministry Ottoman Archives, hereafter BOA.

the reaction of Istanbul by stating that Muslim women were working in environments completely separate from male workers (BOA, 1911).

According to the *Şark* newspaper, dated 14 May 1874, men and women in silk factories in Mount Lebanon were working together and it was obscene. Some physical arrangements took place in factories, aiming to construct a workplace in which women and men worked separately without seeing each other, following a warning from regional administrator to factory owners. By this arrangement, male workers could not enter the women workers' departments and *vice versa* (*Şark*, 1874, p. 2). Another reaction to female-waged labor was against women working in non-Muslims' businesses. The state tried to prevent Muslim women from working in houses or small workshop units belonging to non Muslims. In a command sent from Istanbul in 1898, it was put forward that Muslim women worked as maids or carpet weavers in the shops and houses of Christians in Isparta, but that this was not suitable in Islam; local governorship was asked to prevent this situation (BOA, 1898).

To see how women's work was viewed negatively due to religious sensibilities and social values, especially in industrial life, we can read from the views of Islamist thinkers. Musa Kazim, one of these thinkers stated his negative thoughts, saying: "the duty of the women is inside the house, but the man's is outside; changing this is like changing the nature, like trying to change men into women and women into men." Additionally, Galip Bahtiyar reacts to those who assert that women in Ottoman society live under captivity: "which of these two lives is captivity? Being the worker of capitalists, or being the owner of her house?" (Kurnaz, 1996, pp. 65–69).

The comment of *Vakit*, one of the Islamist newspapers, "factory life will destroy family life in our country" (*Vakit*, 1918, p. 1) on women working at the factories has shown the source of fear. Women leaving their homes to go to work would hinder their tasks such as motherhood and domestic work and that would harm the family structure. Ahmed Midhat, one of the most important names in the history of Turkish literature, expressed similar expressions in his writings. After criticizing the women in Europe for being obliged to work, he would portrait the woman, who waits for her husband to come home after she finishes the housework during the day, as a happy and ideal woman (Ahmed Midhat, 1315/1899).

Contradiction criteria to religious beliefs and general morality were important criteria in the Ottomans in terms of FLFP. However, this criterion was not exclusive to the Muslims only. The same feelings could have been valid for the Christians living in various parts of the country.

In Lebanon, where the silk industry was developed, factory owners tried to persuade the families by going to the villages in order to employ their girls and women when there was a worker deficit. Many of the people living in the villages reacted and responded negatively to the idea of sending women to work. The reason behind this decision was not the fact that the working places were boring, dark or stuffy, but rather cultural and religious values. The families reacted to the fact that their daughters were to work full time next to stranger men or in the same environment with the stranger men. Moreover, people called these silk factories "*karakana*" which means "brothel". Factory owners consulted to the archbishops in 1869 to persuade the people to send women to work. The clergy inspected the factories and stated that women could be allowed to work after having taken the necessary measures. In 1845, a silk factory was opened in Bursa by foreign investors. In the region where Christian Greek population was intense, employers had similar troubles about finding workers. The solution to the problem was found only after the bishop of the region sanctioned the factory, just like in Lebanon (Aktar, 1990, pp. 164, 168–169).

This approach, which hinders the entry of women into working life freely, also created various negative effects for working women. In almost every work sector, the wages of female workers are lower than those of male workers. This difference, which is 100% in industrial sector (Yazgan, 1982, p. 25), was much higher in the agricultural sector (BOA, 1914).

The last period of the Ottomans, which started by the declaration of the Constitution and shaped by the Balkans and World War I, was a different era for the women workers both in opinion and practical terms. The feeling of freedom that arose with constitutionalism affected Ottoman women; people began to speak up about women becoming included in both social and economic life. Wars that later began in the Balkans and penetrated into the entire country with World War I differentiated priorities for the state and society, and also caused women to participate in the labor market more as waged labor.

In this period, the women's movement was led by media organs for women and voluntary associations founded for women. In magazines and newspapers for women, many publications supported women joining working life and promoted vocational trainings. These articles were critical that women fell behind men in economic life and they endeavored to create public opinion and to give self-confidence to women about working. In this direction, an article by Ulviye Mevlan published in the magazine *Kadinlar Dünyasi* (January 1915) against the dominant idea criticizing women's joining working life is remarkable:

> Another excuse of those who prevent women from earning their living is the illiteracy and clumsiness of women. For God sake! I wonder if men dealing with trade are graduates of a commercial school or had higher education? It's clear that 80 percent of them are illiterate. It has been understood well with some experiences that the potential of women in commerce is not lower than men. In fact, the truth is that the women who are deemed worthy of sitting on the ground and selling handkerchiefs or begging with their children were not considered worthy of dealing with trade in a clear shop. (Oktar, 1998, p. 55)

The issue has not been discussed only through the press. After the needs increased along the wars, various women's associations have started to provide vocational education for women and girls in order to help them to be an income-generating business owner. For example, Mamulat-i Dahiliye İstihlak-i Milli Kadinlar Cemiyet-i Hayriyesi (A Philanthropic Association of Women for Domestic Goods and National Production) (1912) aimed to train poor girls in the country as tailors, so as to help them into jobs (*Ikdam*, 1914, p. 1). Osmanlı Hilal-i Ahmer Hanımlar Merkezi (1912) (The Women's Section of the Red Crescent Society), created employment for more than 1,000 women right after it was established (Torun, 2016, p. 83). Türk Kadinlari Biçki Yurdu Derneği (Turkish Women Tailoring School Association) (1913) aimed at teaching tailoring to Muslim women. In this direction, by 1923 the association had enabled 1,380 women to be trained as tailors (Kurnaz, 1996, pp. 214–218). Osmanli ve Türk Hanimlari Esirgeme Derneği (The Association of Protection of Ottoman and Turkish Women) (1913), stated its aims "to enlighten and awaken Ottoman women for occupation and commerce" (Osmanli ve Türk Hanimlari Esirgeme Derneğinin Nizamnamesi, n.d., pp. 2–3).

The most effective and strongest associations targeting the employment and economic development of women in the Ottoman period was Kadinlari Çalistirma Cemiyet-i Islamiyesi (Islamic Society for the Employment of Ottoman Women), established in 1916. In its regulations, it stated its target as helping women to find jobs and gain income in a moral way (BOA, 1916). Society, which placed advertisements on the newspapers immediately after the establishment, asked women to apply if they wanted to work. As 14,000 women applied for jobs in the four months after it was established, it is seen that the association functioned to meet a significant need (BOA, January 1923; Ahmed Emin, 1918, p. 1; *Ikdam*, 1916, p. 4). The association helped

24,254 women to find jobs at the end of its first year and played a great role in including women in working life (Sümer, 1968, pp. 59–61).

These associations, which received the state and society's support suggest that there was a change in mentality about women working. However, the policies carried out after the war show that this thought is not correct at all; we see many examples of women, whose employment was encouraged during the war, being fired when men returned. For instance, in the state record of the discharge of women working in the Censorship Committee after the war finished, women were mentioned as "female civil servants who were formerly accepted to service and then whose duties finished by the end of the military mobilization," and the connection between war and women's employment in the state was put forward (BOA, 1919). In an article in *İnci* magazine dated 1 March 1919, it was recorded that after the war, female employees were being removed from their work as civil servants with some reasons, noting that;

> when the disbanding began, many female servants who did not show any laziness in their work and who would provide the food of family with her salary were fired. First, Kadiköy Sultanisi [Kadiköy High School] discharged women in school stating men and women could not work in the same place. After a while the Ministry of Postal imitated it. We also learn in the last periods female servants in Ziraat Bank were discharged. Above all, the reason for the removal of these women from the bank is rather strange.... But we can't see it true that the rights of our women are being extorted with meaningless reasons. (Oktar 1998, p. 66)

Just like in Kadiköy High School, in other public institutions there had been no problem with women working with men in the war period, but they had afterward been discharged on the grounds that it was not suitable for them to work together with men. Sometimes savings measures were put forward as the reason for discharging women. Nevertheless, as in the case with Sehremaneti (Istanbul Municipal), some female servants were dismissed and then male civil servants received raises! (BOA, 1920).

The fact that women were discharged in this way after the war shows that the old sensibilities of the state and society related to women's employment continued. War was an extraordinary period when all the formal and informal institutions lost their importance. As soon as this period ends, we can see that social opposition has come to the forefront again in terms of women's social and economic existence. After a short break, the understanding of restricting the women to the care of their houses and children was again on the scene.

This understanding, which has strong roots in the Ottoman society, has maintained its importance in the Republican era, which was claimed to be a modernization project that liberated women. The common feature of both periods is that the most important determinant of women's social and economic viability is the informal institutions situated at the center of social values. These informal institutions, which became visible through industrialization attempts in the 19th century and afterward, were the factors that always existed but were largely undetectable in an agrarian-oriented and closed economy. Despite all the attempts to increase FLFP, the inability to level up the rate to the desired levels demonstrates that the resistance of social traditions toward the change is quite challenging.

16.5 Conclusion

> "Social womanlessness is a two-fold terrible harm and waste for a nation, a vital and civil danger. Because the nation who is seized by this firstly loses its economy, in other words, its life and power, reduces its producers' elements, breaks its moving arms and wastes educational and administrative minds..." (Salahaddin Asım, 1910)

Mainstream economics describes the decision of men and women to join the workforce as a choice between leisure and work determined by wage. However, even a single-handed study conducted on the Ottomans and Turkey clearly demonstrates how effective social values and informal institutions are on the economic life. With the increasing FLFP in Ottoman Empire, considerable debates started between different social groups. The general approach which confines the women's place to the domestic sphere and restricts her role as a housewife and motherhood has been recognized by the vast majority of society, state and public opinion. This acceptance idealizes the motherhood or housewifery and regards working women as a threat to family life, which is the core of the society. This understanding does not object to the women working intensively in the rural areas since they regard working in the fields belonging to the family as domestic work; however, they strongly resist women working especially in cities, industrial sectors or in a foreign environment that cannot be controlled by the family. While this resistance was broken during extraordinary periods such as war, the women's work was put forward as a social duty or as a virtue. When the extraordinary periods were over, the general acceptance that the place of a woman is at home has been interestingly re-established.

While this understanding continues as a vicious circle, the initiatives which aim the empowerment of women in social and economic life cannot go beyond hope. The consequence of this situation results for the women with the lower employment and FLFP rates and higher unemployment rates when compared to the rates for men in the country or to women in the world.

This problem is clearly known by policymakers today as it has been in the past. For example, in the 10th Development Plan (2014–2018), which is Turkey's top policy document, goals such as enabling of employment incentives for women, the widespread adoption of childcare services, which are the most important obstacles to the women's employment, support for female entrepreneurs and alignment between work and family life were set. Also, in the government programs, it is stated that measures such as strengthening the socio-economic status of women, increasing their participation in the working life, preventing any discrimination in the workplace and providing equality of opportunity will be taken (KSGM, 2014, p. 3). These statements and targets are the wishes that are often found in almost every government program in the Republican era. The fact that the very same topic, having been debated in the 19th century onward by the Ottoman intellectuals, is still being discussed with similar perspectives shows that the measures stay on paper and are not implemented in real life. When it meets the streets where the social values dominate, namely when it is faced with the facts, any kind of law or report prepared for the subject with a dazzling language is condemned to silence like its previous counterparts. The role that the society provides for women is the most important reason why women's social and economic existence is weak today as it was in the past. This fact not only causes the FLFP to remain at lower rates but also causes all kinds of wishes or precautions related to the subject to be largely inconclusive.

References

Turkish

Acar, E. and Fraker, A. (2016), Kadınların işgücüne katilim oraninin belirleyicileri: Türkiye örneği *Ataturk University İİBF Dergisi*, 30(4), 907–919.
Ahmed Emin (1918), Kadınlarıçaliştirmak teşebbüsü *Vakit,* 111, 1334.
Ahmed Midhat (1315/1899), Bend-i mahsus: Feminizm *Tercüman-ı Hakikat,* 8 August 1315/20 August 1899.

Aktar, A. (1990), *Kapitalizm, Az Gelişmişlik ve Türkiye'de Küçük Sanayi*, İstanbul: Afa Yayınları.
BOA (19 September 1898), *DH. MKT.* 2107/141. 3 Cemaziyelevvel 1316.
BOA (1 April 1909), *DH. MKT.* 2783/5. 10 Rebiülevvel 1327.
BOA (7 February 1909), *DH. MKT.* 2733/57. 16 Muharrem 1327.
BOA (10 July 1911), *DH. İD.* 107/29. 13 Receb 1329.
BOA (12 July 1914), *DH. MB. HPS. M.* 14/51. 18 Ş 1332.
BOA (13 November 1916), *DH. KMS.* 42/10. 17 Muharrem 1335.
BOA (29 September 1919), *DH. İ. UM.* 16–2/1–02. 4 Muharrem 1338.
BOA (6 April 1920), *DH. UMVM.* 90/69. 17 Receb 1338.
BOA (January 1923), *DH. EUM. 6. SB.* 53/78. Kanunusani 1338.
Demir, P. A., Elmalı, D. A. and Işık, S. A. (2017), Kırsal alanda kadinlarin tarim ve hayvancilik faaliyetlerine ilişkin sosyo-ekonomik katkısı. *Journal of the Faculty of Veterinary Medicine Istanbul University*, 43(2), 81–88.
Faroqhi, S. (2000), "18. Yüzyıl Anadolu Kırsalında Suç, Kadınlar ve Servet," translated by N. Alpay, M. C. Zilfi (ed.). *Modernleşmenin Eşiğinde OsmanlıKadınları*, İstanbul: Tarih Vakfı Yurt Yayınları, pp. 7–26.
Gökkaya, V. B. (2014), Cam tavan, kadin ve ekonomik sjddet. *International Journal of Social Science*, 26, 371–383.
Güçlü, M. (2017), Türkiye'de kadinlarin bölgesel işgücüne katiliminin belirleyicileri. *Hacettepe University Journal of Economics and Administrative Sciences*, 35(3), 83–101.
Gümüş, İ. and Türkyılmaz, B. (2017), Güney avrupa ve Türkiye'de iş-yaşam dengesi: karşilaştirmali bir analiz. *Kırklareli Üniversitesi İİBF Dergisi*, 6(1), 64–88.
Gürsel, S., Uysal, G. and Acar, A. (2011), "Toplumsal değerler kadinlarin işgücüne katilmalarina engel", in Gürsel S. (ed.). *Türkiye Ekonomisinde Büyüme ve Yapısal Sorunlar*, İstanbul: Bahcesehir Uni. Yayınları, pp. 196–201.
Haydar, Hakkı (1913), "Kadınlığa Dair". *Büyük Duygu*, Y. 1, 8(14) Receb 1331, pp. 118–120.
Ikdam (12 April 1914), No: 6156, 30 March 1330.
Ikdam (9 August 1916), No: 7001, 27 July 1332.
Kadin (26 October 1908), 13 Teşrinievvel 1324, Vol. 15.
KEFEK (2013), *Her Alandaki Kadın İStihdamının Artırılması ve Çözüm Önerileri Komisyon Raporu*, Ankara: KEFEK Yayınları.
KEİG (2013), *Türkiye'de Kadın Emeği ve İstihdamına Yönelik Politikalar*, İstanbul, KEİG Yayınları.
KSGM (2014), *Türkiye'de Kadin İşgücü Profili ve İstatistiklerinin Analizi*, Ankara.
Kurnaz, Ş. (1996), *II. Meşrutiyet Döneminde Türk Kadini*, Istanbul: Milli Eğitim BakanlığıYayını.
Öğütoğulları, E. and Kılıç, C. (2016), Türkiye işgücü piyasasında yeni bir problem alanı: 40 yaş ve üstü işsizler. *Çalışma İlişkileri Dergisi*, 7(1), 85–97.
Oktar, T. (1998), *Osmanlı Toplumunda Kadının Çalışma Yaşamı Osmanlı Kadınları Çalıştırma Cemiyet-i İslamiyesi*, Eskişehir: Bilim Teknik Yayınevi.

Osmanli ve Türk Hanimlari Esirgeme Derneğinin Nizamnamesi (n.d.), Istanbul: Nefaset Matbaası.

Öztürk, S. and Coşar, K. (2017), İşgücüne katılmama kararında toplumsal cinsiyetin rolü. *GU İİBF Dergisi*, 19(2), 527–543.

Paker, H. and Uysal, G. (2016), Çocuklara kim bakiyor? Kadın işgücüne katilimi ve toplumsal cinsiyet. *Betam Araştırma Notu*, 16(202), 1–5.

Salahaddin, A. (1989), *Osmanlıda Kadınlığın Durumu*, Martı M. (ed.), İstanbul: Arba Yayınları.

Şark (14.05.1874), No: 128, 2 May 1290.

Sümer, T. (1968), Türkiye'de ilk defa kurulan kadinlari çaliştirma cemiyeti. *Belgelerle Türk Tarihi Dergisi*, 10, 59–63.

Topgül, S. (2016), Sendika içi kadin örgütlenmeleri Türk-iş ve hak-iş için bir değerlendirme. *International Journal of Human Sciences*, 13(1), 2349–2367.

Torun, S. (2016), Türkiye Hilal-i Ahmer cemiyeti hanımlar merkezi Dâr-üs-Sanâ'sı1920 raporu. *Lokman Hekim Tıp Dergisi*, 6(2), 81–93.

Turkstat (2015), "Kazanç Yapısı Araştırması, 2014", available at http://www.tuik.gov.tr/PreHaberBultenleri.do?id=18861. Retrieved on 07 December 2017.

Turkstat (2017b), Available at http://tuik.gov.tr/PreTablo.do?alt_id=1007. Retrieved on 4 December 2017.

Vakit (1918), Kadınlarıçalı ştırma cemiyet-i islamiyesi vasıtasıyla akd edilen ilk izdivaç. *Vakit*, 146, 1.

Yazgan, T. (1982), Türkiye'de sendikal hareketler-kısa bir tarihçe. *Türk Dünyası Araştırmaları*, 20, 17–43.

English

OECD.Stat (2014), "Gender, Institutions and Development Database 2014", available at http://stats.oecd.org/viewhtml.aspx?datasetcode=GIDDB2014&lang=en. Retrieved on 9 December 2017.

The General Directorate on Status of Woman. (2016), *Women's Participation in Labour Force and Employment in Turkey*, Ankara.

Turkstat (2017a), "Labor Force Statistics, Agustos 2017", available at http://tuik.gov.tr/PreHaberBultenleri.do?id=24633. Retrieved on 4 December 2017.

World Bank (2018), "World Development Indicators: Labor Force Structure", available at http://wdi.worldbank.org/table/2.2. Retrieved on 27 November 2017.

World Bank (1993), *Turkey: Women in Development*, Washington.

World Economic Forum (2006), *The Global Gender Gap Report 2006*, available at http://www3.weforum.org/docs/WEF_GenderGap_Report_2006.pdf. Retrieved on 9 December 2017.

World Economic Forum (2017), *The Global Gender Gap Report 2017*, available at http://www3.weforum.org/docs/WEF_GGGR_2017.pdf. Retrieved on 9 December 2017.

Chapter 17

The Socio-Economic Conditions of Women in Iran

Mohammad Soleimani and Hasan Kiaee

Abstract

Women's increasing presence in the economic and social activities is one of the main pillars of the economic development. In Iran, especially after the Islamic Revolution, special efforts were made to increase the role of women in the society. As a result, the fields of health and education enjoyed a significant improvement. However, despite the fact that the development of all the predisposing factors has contributed to the greater participation of women in the economy and society in previous years, a large proportion of the population of Iranian women, especially women with academic achievements, are not actively engaged in social activities. The non-economic attitude toward education, lack of success in finding suitable jobs, the inconsistency of education with the needs of the market and low wages seem to be among the barriers in this area. Nevertheless, it is expected that Iranian women's participation in economic and social activities will be enhanced by taking appropriate measures in the area of entrepreneurship development and empowerment of women.

Keywords: Women empowerment, Socio-economic Status, Iran, Gender inequality

In the context of development economics, women's problems are considered as one of the causes of underdevelopment in the developing countries. If women are excluded from social activities, do not have adequate education and good health, the next generations will certainly face many problems. This is why women are considered as key factors for economic development (World Bank, 1994). Women can contribute to economic growth as labor forces and their lack of participation in economic activities is considered as neglecting a large portion of the society's potential. On the other hand, as mothers and wives, women can play a major role in the economic development of countries by playing the role of consumer managers and educators of future generations.

The dramatic increase in women's employment in the world since the second half of the 20th century is considered as the most important feature of the "sex role revolution" (Davis, 1984; Cotter *et al.*, 2001). Women's employment is always measured and evaluated as one of the components of economic development. Sociologists believe that by increasing job opportunities for women, the level of culture and education of the society will be enhanced. Improvement in women's independence, income, education and health would lead to better family nutrition and health, lesser oppression and discrimination against women, and practically higher social and economic status for them (Cowling and Taylor, 2001).

It should be noted that, from the Islamic point of view, while men and women are equal in terms of humanity, they have natural and social differences (Hosseini, 2010, 23–27); therefore, they have equal but not similar rights. God stated this equilibrium of duties and rights in the Holy *Qur'an*, "for women is the same rights as they hold for men" (2:228). Justice requires setting the same rights and duties for men and women in the area of their similarities, and setting different rights and duties according to their talents and capacities, in the area that they are different. Islam never attributes superior rights and privileges to men over women; it respects the principle of equal rights for men and women and does not disagree with their equality; what Islam opposes to, is the similarity of their rights (Motahhari, 1991).

Iran, as a developing country, has faced a revolution in 1979 which aimed at implementation of Islamic teachings and the realization of the Islamic society. Therefore, after the revolution, we have witnessed fundamental changes in the attitudes, policies and executive programs in line with the implementation of Islamic rulings.[1] After the Islamic Revolution of Iran (1979), the approach toward women also changed raising the issues of women's equal rights (not similarity) and dignity. During this period, efforts were made to provide women with the opportunity to enter the social and political arena while maintaining their chastity and modesty.

[1]Preamble to the constitution of the Islamic Republic of Iran stipulates the recognition of the rights of women, non-discrimination between women and men in determining their political, economic, social and cultural fate (Article 8, para 3), the elimination of undue discrimination and the creation of just opportunities for all (Article 9, para 3), the provision of fair and just judicial justice (Articles 14, 3 and 20), the right to work (Article 28), the right to social security (Article 29), and the right to free and public education (Article 31) for all members of the society.

As will be seen in the following paragraphs, despite significant capabilities of women and tangible changes that has recently occurred regarding the predisposing factors which could contribute to increasing women's participation in the labor market such as an increase in women's level of education, especially academic education, an increase in the average age of marriage, a decline in fertility and the growing trend of women-employment acceptance, women's participation still remains low in the labor market. In fact, it can be said that while many social factors of the modern lifestyle for women, especially the attitude toward their social and economic role and the norms of marriage and fertility, are in place in the Iranian society, the economic effects of these factors including increased employment and economic growth are not achieved.

This report continues as follows: In Section 17.2, the status of women in Iran's active and employed population is examined. In Section 17.3, the factors behind increasing the participation of women in Iran's economic activities are explained. In Section 17.4, the barriers to the presence of women in the active population are reviewed. In Section 17.5, some of the measures taken to increase women's participation in Iran's economic activities are introduced. And finally, in Section 17.6, summary and conclusion are provided.

17.1 Women's status in Iran's active population and employment

According to the latest statistics released by the Statistical Center of Iran,[2] there was a huge difference between the active population of Iranian men and women in 2016 and also, there was an increasing trend regarding this gap during 2005–2016. Although the survey of the economic participation rate of the population showed that in the last 20 years the rate of economic activity of women has increased from 8.1 in 1986 to 14.9 by late 2016, the participation rate for women has always been less than men. The active population of men aged 10 years or more consisted of 18,803,000 individuals in 2016, while the active population of women was 6,987,000 individuals. As shown in the Table 17.1, about 64% of men are active members of the population, while only 14% of women are included in this population. In

[2]Statistical Center of Iran, Labor Force Statistic Program, 2016.

Table 17.1 Relative distribution of the Iranian population aged 10 years or more (economically active and inactive) in terms of activity and gender — 2016.

Percentage	Economically active population	Employed	Unemployed
Male and female	38.9	34.0	12.5
Male	63.7	56.8	10.8
Female	14.2	11.4	20.1

Source: Statistical Center of Iran, Labor Force Statistic Program, 2016.

other words, more than 85% of women over the age of 10 years are not considered as the active population of the country.

It should be noted that a large portion of the economically inactive population of Iranian women are "housewives". In 2012, more than 64.3% of Iranian women (equivalent to 32.3% of the total population of Iran and about three quarters of the inactive female population) were housewives, while the second place was held by female students with 17.4% of all Iranian female population (20% of the non-active female population) who did not participate in active economic activities due to their studies.

A report by the International Monetary Fund (IMF) on the role of women in economic growth in 40 countries of the world showed that women's lack of participation in the economy leads to a 15–40% reduction in Gross Domestic Product (GDP). According to this study, Iran is among the three countries with the most economic losses due to women's lack of participation (Vice Presidency for Women and Family Affairs, 2016). Therefore, examination of the factors that reduce the participation of women in economic activities and making policies to improve this situation will lead to the economic exploitation of the potential of the female population (for further discussion in this regard, see IMF, 2013).

17.2 Predisposing Factors for the Presence of Women in the Iran's Active Population

Considering the fact that the presence of women in social and economic arenas is dependent on certain conditions and factors, in this section the most important predisposing factors that can enhance women's activities in economic roles such as education, health and age of marriage are studied. It seems that when women's level of education and health status improves and age of marriage increases, they will have more opportunities to participate in social and economic activities.

17.2.1 Women's position in literacy and academic education

In recent decades, Iran has achieved significant success in reducing women's illiteracy. Since the Islamic Revolution (1979), huge efforts were made for education and education equality. In 1976, the literacy rate of women over 6 years of age was 36%, and men's literacy rate was 64%. Women's literacy rate then increased to reach 44% in 1991, 77% in 2001 and 81.1% in 2011. According to the latest Census of Population and Housing in 2016, the literacy rate in the entire country is 87.64%, with the literacy rate for men being 91.1% and for women 84.2%. Evidently, the literacy rate among men has always been higher than that of women, but this difference is rapidly declining.

Attention to gender equality in the access to secondary education and reduction of girl's dropout rates, especially in deprived areas of the country, were among the key priorities of Iran's Ministry of Education. Accordingly, significant measures were taken including making secondary education compulsory, increasing educational facilities and establishing boarding secondary schools, especially in rural areas as well as remote training for girls who could not continue their education. These measures led to an increase in secondary school attendance rates for girls. Table 17.2 indicates the ratio of girls to boys in terms of school years.

Moreover, statistical data showed that the percentage of female students in higher education levels has doubled over the past 20 years indicating that the programs for increasing the access of both sexes to higher education were enforced equally. According to the Ministry of Science, Research, and Technology (2015), during the academic years of 2012–2013 more than 45% of the universities and higher education institutions graduates were women. In the academic year of 2015–2016,

Table 17.2 Ratio of girls to boys in different grades (%) during 2011–2015.

Grade \ Year	2011	2012	2013	2014	2015
Elementary	0.994	0.990	1	0.995	0.998
Junior high school	0.947	0.890	0.930	0.950	0.950
Senior high school	97.6	92.9	88.4	84.55	NA

Source: Management and Planning Organization of Iran, Indices of the Article 68 of Iran's Fifth Development Plan Act (2016), Publication of Statistical Center of Iran.

more than 48,000 female students were enrolled in specialty doctoral programs in Iran, which accounted for more than 41% of all doctoral students (Statistical Yearbooks, 2015 and 2016). Therefore, it seems that education was considerably improved in recent years as one of the most important predisposing factors of the presence of women in the social and economic arenas.

17.2.2 Women's health and fertility

Among other factors that affect women's participation in social and economic activities are their health and fertility rate, in a way that health has a positive effect and higher fertility rate has a negative effect on the presence of women in the social and economic arenas (Keshavarz and Baqeri, 2011; Sheikh Ansari, 2006). In recent decades, significant advances were made in various areas related to women's health. Iran has included the right to access appropriate health programs and facilities for preventing and treating illnesses and mental disorders of women in national documents and policies.

Life expectancy is one of the important indices of the outcomes of health services and improvements due to the promotion of society's overall health. Examination of life expectancy in Iran showed that while the life expectancy of both men and women has increased significantly during 2006–2015, it has always been higher in women than in men. As showed in Table 17.3, the life expectancy of women was 74.6 years in 2006 which reached 75.6 years in 2015. For men, this index increased from 72.1 years in 2006 years to 72.8 years in 2015. The main reasons for the increase in life expectancy were improving health services, especially in rural and deprived areas, improving livelihoods, and reducing child mortality.

The maternal mortality ratio[3] is another important index of health, social and economic development which is included in the Millennium

Table 17.3 Life expectancy during 2006–2015.

Gender \ Year	2006–2011	2013	2014	2015
Female	74.6	74.5	75	75.6
Male	72.1	71.7	72.2	72.8

Source: Vice Presidency for Women and Family Affairs, 2016.

[3]Maternal Mortality Ratio is the number of women who die, per 100,000 live births, during pregnancy or within 42 days after the childbirth due to pregnancy or delivery complications.

Development Goals. Decrease or increase in the maternal mortality depends on various factors such as the level of women's education, the development of rural roads, the existence of telecommunication networks, household income, access to urgent obstetrics and childbirth emergency services, the quality of health services, awareness of reproductive health issues and the cost of health care. The maternal mortality rate in Iran has dropped dramatically, that is to say, it has decreased from 91 per 100,000 in 1989 to 21.8 per 100,000 live births in 2006 and 19.5 in 2012. This decrease reflects the effectiveness of the implementation of the health system and other development programs in Iran. The development of the health and treatment network, especially by establishing health care homes in urban and rural areas, is one of the main reasons for the decline of maternal mortality throughout Iran (Mansourian *et al.*, 2014).

On the other hand, pregnancy is one of the factors restricting women in social and economic activities. Following an increase in the 1970s and 1980s (reaching its highest, 7.2, in 1986), the fertility rate showed a gradual decline (Abbasi-Shavazi and McDonald, 2006). The Iranian overall fertility rate was 5 and 2.9 children per woman in 1991 and 1996, respectively. This has significantly decreased in the 5-year period between 2006 and 2011. The total fertility rate in 2006 was estimated to be 1.9 children per woman while in 2011 this figure was 1.8 for the entire country. In 2016, the fertility rate has slightly raised reaching 1.9 children per woman (Statistical Center of Iran, Census of Population and Housing, 2016). Factors such as access to family planning services, decline of child mortality, the increase of urbanization, the development of healthcare network system, increase in literacy and education especially among girls play a significant role in reducing fertility (Abbasi–Shavazi, 2000, 2002; Aghajanian and Mehriar 1999; Mirzaei, 2005).

Unfortunately, fertility has reached a low level in Iran, in a way that real fertility rate is under the replacement level, and the ideal fertility of couples is close to the replacement level. In a long-term view, this can be very dangerous for the development of the country. But, this decline in fertility should have led to more participation of women in the social and economic areas regardless of its reasons or its future risks for the development of Iran.

17.2.3 Marriage and divorce

Marriage is important in an Islamic country because of its role in the mental health of individuals and the consolidation of the family foundation.

Therefore, the decline in registration rate of marriage is considered a serious risk despite the effects it can have on more female participation in economic and social activities. According to Iranian National Organization for Civil Registration, the number of registered marriages dropped by 21% during 2011–2015. In addition to the cultural, economic and social factors, this decline could also be attributed to the size and structural changes of the population at the age of marriage.

Based on civil registration data, in 2015, the average age of marriage for Iranian men and women was 27.9 and 23.3 years, respectively. The trend of changes in the average age of marriage during 1986–2015 indicated that the average age of marriage had an increasing rate. Although the average age at the first marriage for women is still lower than that of men, the marriage age for women is increasing at a higher speed compared to men. In recent years, women's age of marriage has risen six times faster than men's. It seems that the increasing access to education, especially higher education throughout the country, and the tendency of young people to continue their education played a role in delaying the marriage (Population Statistics Report, 2017).

Moreover, according to the Iranian National Organization for Civil Registration, the number of registered divorces had a 14.6% increase during 2011–2015. The divorce to marriage ratio shows the number of divorces per 100 marriages. Examination of the trend of changes in the aforementioned index during 1986–2015 indicated an increase in the registered divorce compared to registered marriages. This index was 22.9% in 2015 and 25.3% in the first nine months of 2016. In other words, in the first nine months of 2016, 25 per 100 registered marriages in Iran ended up in divorce. It is important to pay attention to the statistics and take certain measures considering the economic, social and psychological damage caused by divorce, especially in the mentioned age groups. It should be noted that increasing social participation should not result in the collapse of the family and lack of attention to the physical and psychological development of children.

17.3 Obstacles to the presence of women in Iran's active population

As previously discussed, the changes in women's education, health and age of marriage in the recent years should have increased their participation in the social and economic arenas. However, the statistics for the active population, examined in the second section, showed that the female presence has been much less than expected. In this regard, the following barriers should be studied.

17.3.1 Education as a social status creating factor

One of the social reasons for the lack of adequate female participation in the active population is that a significant proportion of women consider education as a means of reaching higher social status and thus do not attempt to enter the labor market. Consequently, primary and academic education for these women only costs the economy while its benefits are not absorbed. This issue would be more evident in examining the status of university graduates in Iran. In 2015, the active population of female graduates was 2.1 million with a 75% increase compared to 2005. However, according to the data from the Statistical Center of Iran, the share of educated girls entering the labor market (employed + unemployed and in search of work), or in other words, the supply of labor force with higher education had a declining trend during the last decade (the Statistical Center of Iran, Labor Force Statistic Program, various years). While in 2005, about 48% of women entered the labor market after graduation, and in 2013 this share decreased to 37%.

The result indicated an increase in the inactive population of graduated women in Iran. According to the statistics, 52.5% of female graduates were inactive in 2005 which increased to 62.8% in 2015. In other words, in the present situation, many female graduates are reluctant to enter the labor market. This suggests that, despite the significant improvement in women's educational status and their access to educational facilities in recent years, women's education failed to bring about more participation in economic activities and entry into the labor market. This group of women generally pursues university entry and higher education in order to obtain a higher social status. Table 17.4 presents the ratio of inactive graduates to all university graduates by gender.

17.3.2 Unsuccessful attempts at finding a suitable job

Another factor that can be considered for the lack of adequate female participation in the active population of Iran is the frustration and discouragement that is experienced by graduates in unsuccessful attempts at finding a suitable job and people, particularly women, sharing these feelings. Therefore, even if women seek to participate in economic activities

Table 17.4 The ratio of inactive graduates to all university graduates.

Year	Male	Female
2005	28.2	52.6
2006	33.2	56.1
2007	35.8	59.2
2008	40.8	63.2
2009	38.2	64.4
2010	39.9	61.3
2011	44.3	64.6
2012	41.6	63.0
2013	39.0	65.7
2014	38.4	65.5
2015	35.2	62.8

Source: Statistical Center of Iran, Labor Force Statistic Program (2016).

by continuing their education and getting academic degrees, they feel frustrated and discouraged when they encounter unemployment for a long time, and these feelings are shared with other students and graduates in a way that not seeking employment and entering the active population becomes a common practice among women.

In the same vein, Pahlavan and Safa-manesh (2012) showed that an increase in the unemployment rate of women in the society leads to their discouragement from searching and trying to find suitable jobs, which greatly reduces their economic participation. Some other studies suggested that low quality of the jobs found by the female graduates is the main source of frustration and discouragement preventing them and others from entering economic activities. For example, Amini (2004), Fakouhi (2005) and Pahlavan and Safa-manesh (2012) believed that women's focus on a limited number of economic activities, which are generally counted as low job levels and their lack of entry into many occupational groups are counted as demotivating factors causing the reduction of female participation in social and economic activities.

Table 17.5 compared the unemployment rate of graduates to the total unemployment rate by gender. According to the table, the unemployment rate for female graduates was higher than that of men, both in 2005 and 2015. The important point is that the difference between the unemployment rate of graduates and total unemployment in women is higher than that of men which indicates women's lack of success in finding jobs resulting in a relatively higher frequency of unemployed female graduates.

Table 17.5 Unemployment rate of people with academic education by gender in 2005 and 2015.

	Total unemployment rate		Unemployment rate of academic education	
Year	Female	Male	Female	Male
2005	17.1	10	25.4	10.4
2015	19.4	9.3	29.5	12.9

Source: Statistical Center of Iran.

17.3.3 Inconsistency between education and labor market demand

Another factor that has reduced the presence of women in the social and economic arenas in recent years is the inconsistency between education and labor market demand in areas related to women. Inconsistency between demands of the labor market and educational settings surely exists in areas related to men as well; however, it is more evident in women's. Given the inherent differences between men and women, their abilities to perform social tasks are different, and as a result, they can only participate in different areas of society. These differences are often neglected in academic disciplines, creating a gap between the needs of the society and the skills of the labor market applicants.

An examination of the existing economic statistics on the share of women workers in the industrial sector[4] shows that the largest share of economic activities for women in the said field is related to manufacturing activities and handicrafts industry. Handicrafts can be very productive and generate employment, especially in rural areas. Unfortunately, this industry was not sufficiently developed due to the shortage, or in some regions, lack of educational, specialized and supporting resources (Pahlavan and Safamanesh, 2012).

Furthermore, according to statistics released by the Ministry of Cooperatives, Labor, and Social Welfare as well as the Statistical Center of Iran, while women have a fewer share in all the major occupational groups, they are given almost equal share as men in the specialized fields for which they are trained. Table 17.6 presents the ratio of male and female working in various occupational groups. According to the table, in 2013, only in the

[4]Yearbooks of Labor Statistics, various years.

Table 17.6 Ratio of employment of 10 and more years by major occupational groups.

Description		Lawmakers, senior officials, managers	Specialists	Technicians, assistance	Office clerks	Service workers, store and market salespeople	Skilled workers, farmers, foresters, fishermen	Craftsmen and related employees	Machine operators, assemblers, drivers	Workers
Female	1996	12.8	39.1	15.9	16.9	5.2	8.4	19.0	1.1	4.3
	2006	15.4	42.8	19.5	26.3	9.0	10.0	13.8	1.5	6.0
	2011	16.9	44.9	21.0	28.6	9.9	13.8	8.3	1.6	4.2
	2013	15.2	41.3	17.7	25.5	11.3	19.1	14.6	16.0	6
Male	1996	87.2	60.9	84.1	83.1	94.8	91.6	81.0	98.9	95.7
	2006	84.6	57.2	80.5	73.7	91.0	90.0	86.2	98.5	94.0
	2011	83.1	55.1	79.0	71.4	90.1	86.2	92.0	98.4	95.8
	2013	84.8	58.7	82.3	74.5	88.7	80.9	85.4	84	94

Source: Statistical Center of Iran (1996, 2006, and 2011); Ministry of Cooperatives, Labor, and Social Welfare (2013).

field of "specialists" women's share was 41.3, almost the same as men's. In other fields such as "technicians and assistance," "farmers and foresters," "craftsmen," or "machinery managers," women's share was generally much lower than that of men due to unsuitability. However, in many cases, both male and female students were equally admitted and trained in the universities in the related fields of education.

17.3.4 Low and unequal wages compared to men

Another reason leading to lower participation of women in the economic arena is the wage inequality. Given the high unemployment rate among women and the fact that in many cases women are not the breadwinner of the household, they are willing to enter the labor market with lower wages which over the years turned into a common belief. In addition, women's wages are lower than men, especially in private-sector occupations with lower supervision. This makes women feel dissatisfied with their work, and in some cases, they lose their interest to do economic activities for the same reason.

Another factor for women's presence, especially in the private sector, is to help their family members without payment. According to the latest available statistics, 60.1% of women employed in the private sector were unpaid family workers, 16.9% were paid workers, and 14% were independent employees (Center for Strategic Information and Statistics of the Ministry of Cooperatives, Labor and Social Welfare, 2013). Meanwhile, many Iranian women worked in unofficial sectors which are not included in the statistics (Mahboobi-manesh and Habibzadeh Maleki, 2011). The high number of unpaid female family workers reflects the traditional labor market structure in many parts of the country that limits the positive and active role of women in Iran's socio-economic development.

17.4 Measures for increasing the participation of women in the economy

Serious policies and measures should be taken so that the country's economy can benefit from the potential of the female population considering the obstacles and problems mentioned in the previous section. The most important measures taken in this regard in the recent years are summarized and reviewed in the *entrepreneurship development* and the *empowerment of vulnerable women* sections.

17.4.1 Leading women to entrepreneurship

Women's entrepreneurship can be considered as one of the factors contributing to the increasing participation of women in the active population. Today, individual and corporate entrepreneurship is one of the important factors for growth and economic development which is considered as the main source of development in most developed and developing countries (McCline *et al.*, 2004). Women's tendency toward entrepreneurship, especially educated women, leads them to decent jobs and favorable social situations on the one hand, and gain an acceptable income for their presence in the social and economic arenas, on the other hand. These would contribute to motivating other women of the society and provide the basis for their greater presence in the economy.

As was mentioned earlier, women's enrollment in higher education had a significant growth in recent years. In this context, encouraging and promoting entrepreneurship among Iranian female graduates for creating independent businesses can play an important role in the economic and social activities of the society (Rabiee and Nazarian, 2013). Although research shows that women's incentive to enter a business in countries with low income is to earn a living for themselves and their families (GEM, 2006), achieving independence, providing better living conditions, avoiding poverty, gaining power and credibility in the community, providing the ideal conditions for personal life at old age, being useful to society and other individuals, identifying and developing personal abilities can also be considered as other incentives (Ylinenpää and Chechurina, 2002).

Entrepreneurship is increasing among Iranian women; however, considering that Iran has the largest population of women with higher education in the Middle East (IMF, 2017), there is a long way to go. Nevertheless, Iran is witnessing a significant number of women entering professions previously performed by men. According to recent statistics, the number of female entrepreneurs in 2016 was 98,001 among which 40,534 women were board members, and 21,627 inspector women were involved in the management of entrepreneurship companies. There were also 119 entrepreneurial women in more than 28 active sectors in the field of entrepreneurship. The largest female presence was in the fields of the Communication and Information Technology (Vice Presidency for Women and Family Affairs, 2016).

A quick inspection of the growing number of women entrepreneurs in recent year reveals the rise of Iranian women in business startups. The share of female employers has increased from 3.2% of all employers in

2009 (equivalent to 32,427) to nearly 5% (approximately 40,000) in 2015 (statistics and data from the Statistics and Strategic Information Center of the Ministry of Cooperatives, Labor and Social Welfare, 2016). According to the Vice President of Technology, 20% of the board members of knowledge-based companies consisted of women among which approximately 18% were executives, and 22% were head of the board of directors. Moreover, 55 companies of the top knowledge-based companies had female CEOs (Reports of Vice President of Technology, 2016). Iran also has a National Women's Entrepreneurs Association with 100 members, of which 70 are entrepreneurs, and 30 are business owners.

According to a study by Arasti and Akbari Jokar (2008) women were more prone to starting their own business due to the following reasons; an increase in the number of university-educated women, the possibility of greater autonomy and more flexible working hours in a personal business which helped them balance work and family life, and the inability of the public and the existing private sectors to hire them given their limited capacity. However, the small number of female employers is indicative of the many obstacles and problems that Iranian woman face in starting a business.

17.4.2 Empowering vulnerable women

In the human development process, women should be provided with an enabling environment to develop their capabilities as individuals and in groups. It should be noted that, due to physical weaknesses and specific biological, psychological and social characteristics, women are more likely to fall prey to crimes; hence, empowerment of poor women also has a high priority from a social and religious point of view. Various institutions are active in the empowerment of women in the economy which will be presented briefly:

(1) State Welfare Organization: The State Welfare Organization of Iran was formed to lay the grounds for independence, and economic, social, cultural, and educational self-sufficiency and, ultimately, the rehabilitation and empowerment of underprivileged families. The most important measures of this organization in supporting female-headed households include providing pension and occasional funds for medical treatments, marriage, child education, basic goods, housing, and nutrition improvement for family members. Paying monthly pensions to female heads of households and providing different empowerment plans are also among other services of this organization.[5]

(2) Imam Khomeini Relief Foundation: Imam Khomeini Relief Foundation is one of the institutions that support the underprivileged people including female heads of households. This Foundation is one of the largest custodians to support and empower female heads of households in Iran. The support of the Relief Foundation is provided in four areas: empowerment, employment, specialized services and social insurance. However, the Foundation's priority in recent years has been the empowerment measures. In this context, female heads of households are trained and supported in two ways: firstly, the trainees are introduced to the labor office and helped to find a job suitable to their expertise, and secondly, they are paid employment loans to help them set up a business according to the expertise they have acquired.[6]

(3) Special Microfinance Institutions: Several special microfinance projects have been observed in Iran in the recent years, the most important of which are as follows:

(A) Women's Microfinance Funds: The Rural and Nomadic Women's Affairs Office of the Ministry of Agricultural Jihad launched a rural women's microfinance project aiming to improve the economic status of rural areas, decrease unemployment rate, increase social justice, and decrease poverty in these areas. The rural women's microfinance project, which runs in all provinces of Iran, is based on the "Village Bank" model at the Finca Microfinance Bank. The official website of the Rural and Nomadic Women's Affairs office of the Ministry of Agricultural Jihad states the general goals of these funds as, "easy access of rural women to financial resources for the creation and expansion of domestic jobs in the agricultural sector". Indeed, given that one of the important obstacles to the development of rural women's activities is their limited funds, microfinance funds were created to make easy and quick financial resources available.[7]

(B) Non-governmental Funds Supporting the Development of Agricultural Activities of Rural and Nomadic Women: The "Non-governmental Funds Supporting the Development of Agricultural Activities of Rural

[5]For more information see the official site of the State Welfare Organization of Iran at www.behzisti.ir.

[6]See portal.emdad.ir.

[7]For more information see nrw.areeo.ac.ir.

and Nomadic Women" project was launched in 2010 with the collaboration of the Rural and Nomadic Women's Affairs Office of the Ministry of Agricultural Jihad and the "Fund for the Promotion of Investment in Agricultural Sector Development", aiming at organizing and consolidating micro-financing funds of rural and nomadic women in each county.[8]

(C) Microfinance Plan. Joint Program of State Welfare Organization, Agriculture Bank, and TAK Institute: One of Iran's comprehensive and well-implemented microfinance initiatives in micro-financing was introduced by the International Fund for Agricultural Development (IFAD) to Iran in the early 2000s as "Microfinance Plan". The project was sponsored by the International Fund for Agricultural Development (IFAD), the Agricultural Bank of Iran and the TAK Institute.[9] The statistics for the latest program portfolio indicated that the female participation rate increased to 95%. Field observations showed that the design of the program was consistent with the needs of this group of women.

17.5 Conclusion

In the context of development economics, women's problems are counted as one of the causes of underdevelopment in developing countries. Women can contribute to economic growth as labor forces and their lack of participation in economic activities is considered as neglecting a large portion of the society's potential. Unfortunately, studies show that Iran is among the countries that have suffered losses in social and economic activities due to women's low rate of participation. Iranian women's share of the active population is very low, and any action and policymaking in this regard can have beneficial effects on the economy.

It is important to note that in recent years there has been a change in predisposing factors of increasing women's participation in the labor market, which unlike the evidence, should have increased the participation of women in the active population. Significant measures have been taken in recent years to reduce the illiteracy of women in a way that women's literacy rate has reached 84.2%. Furthermore, more than 45% of the graduates from the university and higher education institutions are women. Developments in the fields of health and fertility were also in favor of women's participation in the economy. Women's life expectancy increased, and the maternal

[8] http://nrw.areo.ir/HomePage.aspx?TabID=21824&Site=nrw.areo&Lang=fa-IR.
[9] http://www.tak-int.org/Fa/TAKPosition.aspx#.

mortality rate decreased indicating a health promotion among Iranian women. On the other hand, women's fertility rate decreased which should have led to an increase in women's participation in the economy, despite the problems it will cause in the development of the country in the coming years. The rapid increase in the age of marriage among girls, along with the decrease in marriage and the increase in divorce should have led to an increase in the participation of women in economic activities, despite the adverse social effects. However, at present, a significant proportion of women's populations is inactive and has no tendency to participate in social and economic arenas.

The factors that appear to have the most significant effects on women's unwillingness to appear in an active economic population include regarding university education as a means for gaining a better social status, unsuccessful attempts at finding a suitable job, especially among graduates, inconsistency of trainings in educational centers with the demands of the labor market, and low and unequal wages. On this basis, many women, especially women with a university education, have no tendency to participate in active population and play roles in economic areas, and therefore, the economy of the country is practically deprived of the services of a large portion of production agents.

Nevertheless, it is hoped that more female participation in economic activities is achieved by focusing more on the measures that were taken in recent years. The promotion of entrepreneurship among women is one of these activities. Women's tendency toward entrepreneurship, especially educated women, would lead them to decent jobs and favorable social situations on the one hand, and bring about an acceptable income for them due to their presence in social and economic arenas, on the other hand. These two factors would contribute to motivating other women of the society and providing the basis for their greater presence in the economy. The empowerment of vulnerable women is another step that was taken to promote the role of women and their greater presence in the economy. Institutions such as the State Welfare Organization of Iran, the Imam Khomeini Relief Foundation, and the institutions specifically designed to provide microfinance for women are engaged in women's empowerment plans regarding creation and facilitation of employment. It is expected that with the completion and development of the abovementioned projects as well as by enforcing specialized policies in the field of education, culture, and employment of women in the upcoming years, more Iranian women would participate in the economic and social arenas.

References

Abbasi-Shavazi, M. J. (2000), National trend and social inclusion: Fertility trends and differentials in the Islamic republic of Iran, presented at the conference on fertility and family planning in the 21st century, 17–21 January, Dhaka.

Abbasi-Shavazi, M. J. (2002), Recent change in the future of fertility in Iran, presented at the expert group meeting on continuing fertility transition, population division of the United Nation, 13 March 2018, New York.

Abbasi-Shavazi, M. J. and McDonald, P. (2006), Fertility decline in the Islamic Republic of Iran: 1972–2000. *Asian Population Studies*, 2(3), 217–237.

Aghajanian, A. and Mehryar, A. H. (1999), Fertility transition in the Islamic Republic of Iran: 1967–1996. *Asia-Pacific journal*, 14(1), 21–42.

Amini, Alireza (2004), Gender approach to labor market imbalance. *Women's Research*, 2(1), 133–146.

Arasti, Zahra, and Akbari Jokar, Mohammadreza (2008), Investigating the characteristics of business owned by entrepreneurial women with academic education and their problems in launching a business. *Daneshvar Raftaraf*, 15(32), 48–37.

Center for Strategic Information and Statistics of the Ministry of Cooperatives, Labor and Social Welfare (2013), *Quantitative and Qualitative Changes in Women's Employment*, Tehran, Ministry of Labor and Social Affairs.

Cotter, D. A. *et al.* (2001), Women's work and working women: The demand for female labor. *Gender and Society*, 15(3), 429–445.

Cowling, M. and Taylor, M. (2001), Entrepreneurial women and men: Two different species? *Small Business Economics*, 16(3), 167–175.

Davis, K. (1984), Wives and work: The sex role revolution and its consequences. *Population and Development Review*, 10(3), 397–417.

Diane E. Eynon (auth.) (2017), *Women, Economic Development, and Higher Education Tools in the Reconstruction and Transformation of Post-Apartheid South Africa*, London: Macmillan, Palgrave Publication.

Fakouhi, Naser (2005), Positive discrimination mechanism as a poverty-eradication tool. *Quarterly Journal of Women's Studies*, 3(3), autumn, 115–141.

GEM (2006), *Report on women and entrepreneurship: Global entrepreneurship monitor.* Available at: https://www.gemconsortium.org/report/gem-2006-report-on-women-and-entrepreneurship.

Hosseini, Seyyed Ebrahim (2010), *Women's Personality and Rights, Qom*, Office of Educational Publishing.

IMF (2013), *Women, Work, and the Economy: Macroeconomic Gains from Gender Equity, International Monetary Fund Strategy*, Policy, and Review Department and Fiscal Affairs Department, Washington: International Monetary Fund.

IMF (2017), *Islamic Republic of Iran Selected Issues*, Washington: International Monetary Fund.

Keshavarz Haddad, Gholamreza and Bagheri Ghanbarabadi, Morteza (2011), Analysis of the participation likelihood of Iranian urban and rural women in the labor market using the parametric and non-parametric econometric methods. *Journal of Economic Research*, 97, 151–174.

Mahboobi-manesh, Hossein and Habibzadeh Maleki, Ashab (2011), Women's status in the development process. *Biannual Journal Women's Policy*, 5(15), Autumn and Winter.

Mansourian, M., Rastegari B., Kalantari Z., and Mahram M. (2014), The effect of family physician program on health indicators in rural population. *Razi Journal of Medical Sciences*, 21(1256), 27–32.

McCline, R. L., Bhat, S. and Baj, P. (2004), Opportunity recognition: An exploratory investigation of a component of the entrepreneurial process in the context of the health care industry. *Entrepreneurship theory and practice*, 25(2), 81–94.

Mirzaei, M. (2005), Swing in fertility imitation in Iran. *Critique, Critical Middle Eastern Studies*, 14(1), 25–33.

Motahhari, Morteza (1991), System of Women Right in Islam, Sadra publication.

Pahlavan, Mossayeb and Safa-manesh, Haniyeh (2012), Estimation of women's labor force model in Iran. *Quarterly Journal of Economic Modeling Research*, 8(summer issue), 159–174.

Population Statistics Report (2017), *Iranian National Civil Registration Organization*. Available at: https://www.sabteahval.ir/Upload/Modules/Contents/asset99/talagh.96.pdf.

Rabiee, Ali and Nazarian, Zahra (2013), Study of Entrepreneurship Barriers for Academic Educated Women in Iran. *Innovation, and Creativity in Liberal Arts*, 2(4), spring, 1–26.

Sheikh Ansari, Sahar (2004), Influential Factors of Iranian Women's Participation in the Labor Market, Master's thesis of Sharif University of Technology, Iran (unpublished).

The Statistical Center of Iran (2016), *Labor Force Statistic Program, Tehran*, available at https://www.amar.org.ir/Portals/0/Files/abstract/1395/ch_ntank_95-4.pdf.

The Statistical Center of Iran (2016), *Population and Housing Census Report*, Tehran.

Vice Presideny for Women and Family Affairs (2016), *Report on the Statistical Status of Women and Family during 2011–2016*, Deputy Strategic Review. Available at: http://women.gov.ir/uploads/images/gallery/%DA%AF%D8%B2%D8%A7%D8%B1%D8%B4%20%D8%AD%D9%88%D8%B2%D9%87%20%D8%B2%D9%86%D8%A7%D9%86%20%D9%88%20%D8%AE%D8%A7%D9%86%D9%88%D8%A7%D8%AF%D9%87/zanan.pdf.

Vice President of Technology (2016), Vice President of Technology, Report of Vice President of Science and Technology (2016), available at http://www.isti.ir/uploads/zistboom-daneshbonyan-kh96-site.pdf.

World Bank (1994), *Enhancing Women's Participation in Economic Development*, New York: World Bank Publications.

Ylienenpää, H. and Chechurina, M. (2000), Perceptions of female entrepreneurship in RUSSIA, paper presented at 30 Euroupean Small Business Seminar in Ghent, 1–40.

Chapter 18

Women's Involvement in Developing *Waqf* in Malaysia

Farhana Mohamad Suhaimi and Asmak Ab Rahman

Abstract

Women's involvement as income seekers has been accepted in the Muslim community, especially in Malaysia. Besides recognizing the need for women to work, Islam also recognizes women's rights to property ownership. Women are obliged to fulfill the same requirements as men in sharing their wealth with others as a religious duty. For example, those who are wealthy are required to give *zakat* and alms. Based on history, many female figures from other countries have shared their wealth with the community through *waqf* (pious endowment), which funds various infrastructures and public facilities. Thus, this chapter analyses women's involvement in the development of *waqf* in Malaysia. This was a qualitative study in which the methods of data collection were interviews and documentation. The findings of this research showed that women's participation in *waqf* exists in Malaysia. Property donated by women is in the form of land, houses, buildings and cash. The *waqf* property has value and can generate revenue either through rent or leases. It can also boost economic activities in an area as in the case of Seetee Aishah and Toh Puan Chah *waqfs*. Moreover, in Malaysia, there is vast potential for women in developing *waqf*. It was found that *waqf* funding obtained either through money, land or even buildings could contribute to socio-economic development in Malaysia.

Keywords: *Waqf* fund, *Waqf* management, Public financing

Islam encourages wealthy people to be socially responsible by helping those who are less fortunate. *Waqf* (pious endowment) is one of the most highly recommended deeds in Islam. The practice of *waqf* is done not only to benefit contributors of *waqf* by purifying their hearts and showing closeness to God (Allah) but also to provide benefits to the community. *Waqf* resources consist of land, buildings and cash used for charitable activities in the religious, educational and health fields. *Waqf* traditionally provides significant financial support for public education, religious institutions, health facilities and public works. For example, when Al-Azhar University was established, it wholly depended on private donations, grants and *waqf*.

In education, for example, *waqf* is used to defray the maintenance and expenditures of mosques which acted as the educational institutions in the past, paid the teachers' allowances and provided living allowances for students (Ibrahim, 2009; Janan, 2008; Kuran, 2001, pp. 841–897). In the context of health, the cost of construction and the maintenance of hospitals come from *waqf* resources; *waqf* resources even fund scholarships for medical students. There are also *waqf* hospitals that provide complete medical services by charging less or providing free services to patients who are less fortunate (Sulaiman and Manaf, 2009, pp. 2–30; Yalawae and Tahir, 2008; Toraman and Tuncsiper, 2007, pp. 1–19; Sunny, 2007, pp. 33–44). Regarding welfare, soup kitchens (provide free meals), for example, are set up and operated using *waqf* resources. These soup kitchens provide nutritious meals to the less fortunate, students who live near the *waqf* property and wayfarers. *Waqf* is also used to fund, create and maintain other public facilities for the community, including libraries, public baths, roads, housing, and watersheds and water fountains. Normally, large *waqf* project financiers are the wives and families of rulers, royal families and the upper classes while the remaining *waqf* contribution comes from lower classes (Amedoski, 2009, pp. 43–56).

Thus, the objective of this chapter is to show women's involvement in *waqf* development in Malaysia. First, this chapter will explain women's position in Islamic context and women's rights in their wealth management. The chapter also will identify women's involvement in *waqf* through history and reveal some remarkable *waqf* which has benefited many people. Then, the chapter will discuss Malaysian women's involvement in *waqf* development, especially in their respective states.

18.1 Women in Islam

The status of women in Islam has been lifted by granting them the legal right to be involved in contracts, run a business and possess property independently from their husbands or any kinsmen. Islam allows women to participate and serve the community by working and building a career as long as they maintain their dignity and responsibilities to their families.

Furthermore, women's right to property ownership is now recognized, whether it has been acquired through their efforts or a legacy from kin, or *hibah* (gift) to women from others. Once a woman owns a property, she is allowed to manage it. This ownership is based on *Qur'an* verses as mentioned in Surah an-Nisa' verses 7 and 32:

> Verse 7 Meanings: "There is a share for men and a share for women from what is left by parents and those nearest related, whether, the property be small or large, a legal share."
> Verse 32 Meanings: "For men, there is reward for what they have earned, (and likewise) for women there is reward for what they have earned, and ask Allah of His Bounty. Surely, Allah is Ever All-Knower of everything."

Women are given the same right as men to own and manage property. Even if a woman is married, she has the right to manage her own property; a husband cannot take his wife's property unless it is given by his wife willingly, as stated in Surah an-Nisa' verse 4:

> Meanings: "And give to the women (whom you marry) their Mahr (obligatory bridal money given by the husband to his wife at the time of marriage) with a good heart, but if they, of their own good pleasure, remit any part of it to you, take it, and enjoy it without fear of any harm (as Allah has made it lawful)." (al-Hilali and Khan, 2000, p. 106)

A wife controls her property and income completely since family maintenance is the husband's responsibility. However, she can help her husband support the family, and this is considered charity if done sincerely for Allah. While Islam recognizes the right of ownership of any individual, it also teaches its followers not to spend wastefully and for those who are wealthy not to be greedy or selfish. This is explained through the words of Allah in the Surah al-Isra' verses 27 and 29 and Surah Adh Dhariyat verse 19:

> Meanings: "And let not your hand be tied (like a miser) to your neck" (al-Hilali and Khan, 2000, 372).
>
> Meanings: "And in their properties, there was the right of the beggar, and the Mahrum (the poor who does not ask the others)." (al-Hilali and Khan, 2000, p. 708)

Thus, wealthy women are required to give *zakat* and alms to carry out their responsibilities as members of society. *Zakat* is one of the pillars of Islam. There are two types of *zakat:* obligatory and recommended. Women can make their own decisions about the management of their property, such as giving to charity and endowing their wealth, without their husbands' permission. The act of charity, including *waqf,* is a sign of devotion to God in Islamic views (Afzal-Ur-Rahman, 1994, pp. 68–76; Ismail, 2000, p. 14).

18.2 Women's historical involvement in *waqf* practice

According to Ziauddin Ahmad, in early Islamic history, Muslims were enthusiastic about performing the *Fard Al-Kifayah.* Typically, they used part of their property for public welfare, and one of the ways was through *waqf.* This property was channeled to finance infrastructure and public facilities, such as hospital buildings, boarding houses and educational centers (Ahmad, 1989). Çizakça discovered that of more than 300 *waqf* in the 15th and the 16th centuries in Edirne, 20% of them were from women donors. While in Istanbul and Aleppo, about 40% of women have been *waqf* contributors (Çizakça, 2000). Amedoski also mentioned that in the mid-16th century, 37% of the *waqf* in Istanbul was contributed by women. Some women endowed their properties to finance large- and small-scale projects for public facilities in their countries or other places. Typically, the financiers of large-scale *waqf* projects are the wives and families of the rulers, royal families and upper classes. Even large-scale projects such as mosques, palaces and summer houses on the Bosporus were donated by women from the upper classes; most of them were the ruler's wives and women involved in the judiciary (ladies court), but there were also small-scale *waqf* projects such as water fountains. Most women of the Ottoman ruling family funded the public facilities through *waqf* to improve the public facilities available in the complex including mosques, schools, libraries, public kitchens, public baths and guest rooms. Hasseki Hürrem and her daughter, Mihrimah Sultan, funded the construction of two *kulliyes* in Istanbul located in Uskudar and Edirnekap. Also, some women's *waqf* contributors in Krusevac and Leskovac in the 16th century endowed their properties in various forms of *waqf* assets, including cash, business premises and agricultural land. Some also used their revenue from the *waqf* for the management of the *waqf* (Amedoski, 2009). According to the Kuwait Awqaf Public Foundation (KAPF), Iman found that women contributed 47% of the *waqf* in Kuwait and 80% came from the women's *waqf* contributions for charitable purposes (al Humaidan, 2007).

Since a mosque was one of the places for early education in the past besides being used as a place of worship, most mosques were funded by *waqf* contributors. *Waqf* resources funded the development and maintenance of mosques, *imam* and *muezzin's* salaries and teaching classes. One of the famous women *waqf* contributors was Fatima al-Fihri, who funded the development of the Qarawiyyin Mosque in Fez, Morocco, which was later developed into a university. Qarawiyyin University is one of the oldest universities in the world. Fatima al-Fihri's sister, Maryam al-Fihri, also funded al-Andalus Mosque construction (Dar al-Nicosia, 2011). Fatima al-Fihri was a young, well-educated princess who received a significant amount from her father, a successful businessman. She vowed to spend her entire inheritance on building a mosque and learning center for her Qarawiyyin community, which was completed in 859. Qarawiyyin University was a remarkable *waqf* and became Morocco's number-one university (Woodcock and Saoud (eds.), 318). Zumurrud Khatoon, the wife of the Abbasid Caliph al-Mustadhi'e, established a mosque known as the Mosque of Khafafin on the Tigris River banks in Baghdad, and Mrs. Khatoon, the daughter of Muhammad Bey, built Fatima Khatoon al-Kabeer Mosque (al Humaidan, 2007). In the 16th century, women *waqf* contributors in Krusevac and Leskovac, such as Şâhmânî Hatun, Fatima Hatun, Şâhbola Hatun and Âyişe Hatun endowed their property to finance mosque expenses as a place of spiritual and cultural activity, and *imam* and *muezzin*'s salaries (Amedoski, 2009).

In the field of education, *waqf* resources were used to build and fund the management of schools, libraries and orphan's uniforms. Among women involved in building and funding schools through *waqf* were Hasseki Hürrem, the wife of Sultan Sulayman I, Zeynep Hatun in Eyup, Sitti Hatun, Gulfam in Uskudar, and Okumus Hatun Hatice Kadin at Fener (Amedoski, 2009). Most of them funded complexes which also included a school, or *madrasa,* for educational purposes. In Baghdad, women involved in these educational *waqf* were the wife of Caliph al-Musta'sem, who built Al-Bashiria School; Zumurrud Khatoon and Shams el Dhuha, who established al-Mutasamia School. In Damascus, al-Barraniyya and al-Juwainiyya School were established by Sitt al Sham bint Ayobub el Shadi. In Yemen, al-Shamsia School in Taez was built by al-Dar al-Shamsi, and Merriem built al-Sabeqia School. In Mecca, Sawlat el Nisa'a Begum built al-Sawlattia School, and Princess Iffat al-Thunayyan al-Saud built Dar al-Hanan School for orphaned girls (al Humaidan, 2007). Meanwhile, Zubaidah, the wife of Caliph Harun al-Rashid, funded the development of Bayt al-Hikmah, a library and a leading center for education and research for translation in Baghdad (Sadeq, 2002, pp. 135–151; Saifuddeen and Salleh, 2003; White, 2006). Other women dedicated their books to students, such as Fatima al-Hadhena and Fatima bint Hamad. According to Moststafa, Fatima al-Hadhena dedicated her books and works to Oqba Ibn Nafie Mosque in al-Qairawan (al Humaidan, 2007). Moreover, Zeyni Hatun endowed new clothes for students at Mustafa Celebi School in Uskudar on religious celebrations (Amedoski, 2009). Riham mentioned that in Egypt, Princess Fatima Ismail donated her land to support the University of Cairo's finances and provided scholarships for talented students inside and outside Egypt. Meanwhile, Princess Zeinab allocated her property for charitable purposes, allowances and food for the Hanafi scholars (al Humaidan, 2007).

In financing infrastructures and other public facilities through *waqf*, Zubaidah also funded road facilities and rest houses on a route from Baghdad to Mecca (Sadeq, 2002; Saifuddeen and Salleh, 2003; White, 2006). In addition, she gave a substantial contribution for a watershed route, known as "Ain Zubaida", between Mecca and Mina for the convenience of travelers who wanted to perform pilgrimages. The project cost 1,700,000 dinars (Man and Abdulwaheed, 2011). Hasseki Hürrem funded mosque construction in Istanbul and residential houses with 55 rooms for pilgrims in Jerusalem (Peri, 1989; Singer, 2006). She also funded public bath facilities in the complex. Meanwhile, Mihrimah Sultan provided a row of shops that generated rental revenue, which in turn was used to finance a complex. Besides that, a soup kitchen was among the facilities provided from *waqf* resources.

The soup kitchens provided free meals for people in need. The soup kitchen that was donated by Hasseki Hürrem was placed near her *waqf* complex buildings in Jerusalem, Istanbul, Ankara, Edirne and Mecca (Isin and Üstündağ, 2008). According to Amy Singer, an estimated 450 people enjoy meals twice a day at a soup kitchen in Jerusalem (Singer, 2006). Meanwhile, the soup kitchen donated by Mihrisah Valide Sultan supported more than 1,500 people who dined there.

There was also a complex equipped with a public hospital, such as Atik Valide kulliye in Uskudar, which was funded by Nurbanu's *waqf*, and a hospital for women funded by Hasseki Hürrem's *waqf* (Isin and Üstündağ, 2008). Another woman, Qut el Qulub al-Demardashia, cooperated with her father to establish the Demardash Hospital in Egypt. Princess Aziza Ahmad also established Al-Sadeqi Bimaristan polyclinic from her property as *waqf* (al Humaidan, 2007).

In terms of welfare financing, Hasseki Hürrem, for example, gave a significant amount of money as *waqf* for poor girls, pilgrims and servants.

Ayanoglu stated that Zeyni Hatun donated 1000 akçes for the poor and people in need, especially poor women and widows (Isin and Üstündağ, 2008). As for financing economic development, Fay found documents in the Egyptian Ministry of Awqaf showing how Shawikar Qadin, a woman in Egypt, endowed two houses, agricultural land, some shops, apartment buildings and shares for a complex. The complex consisted of a storage room, shops, workshops and accommodation units that were the home of transit trade contributing to the commercial economy of the Ottoman Empire in Egypt (Fay, 1998).

Overall, there is evidence showing how women are involved in *waqf* around Muslim countries. Women's contributions to national development through *waqf* comprises a range of infrastructures and public facilities for the community. Contributions include mosques, schools, universities, libraries, research centers, translation centers, rest homes, residential homes, public baths, soup kitchens, hospitals, water catchments, water fountains, roads, bridges, shops and workshops. Further, the *waqf* contribution was used to finance the needs of the poor, orphans and widows.

Although the number of women who have been involved in *waqf* is a little lower than that of men. Fay cites in the 15th and 16th centuries, women made 36.8% of the new *waqf* in Istanbul. In the 18th century, women made 36.3% of *waqf* in Aleppo and 24% in Jerusalem (Fay, 1998), detailed information is limited. However, from the information obtained, it can be seen that women's participation in *waqf* includes various forms of property such as lands, buildings, business premises and cash. Their involvement in *waqf* is not limited in certain aspects but comprehensive, including education, spiritual development, economy, health and public facilities, as well as welfare. Public facilities provided by *waqf* resources are diverse and include roads, rest houses, waterways and so on as shown in Figure 18.1. In fact, the effects of some facilities funded by *waqf* have been substantial and benefit society, such as public soup kitchens that give free meals to up to 500 people twice a day, as well as universities and hospitals (Singer, 2006).

The author relied on the historical records, so the above are the only figures available. However, women who endowed their property for national development in that century demonstrate that women are conscious about contributing to society and participating in national development.

Moreover, Islam allows women as *waqf* contributors to become trustees or managers in *waqf* management. Thus, there are also women who manage their own *waqf* property, which is usually *waqf* for a family member who

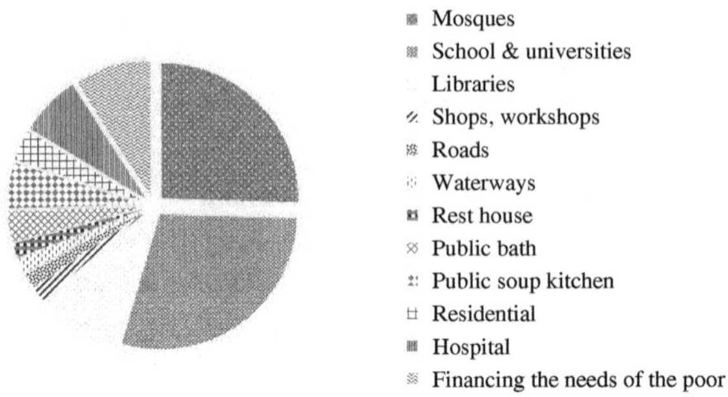

Figure 18.1 Women's contribution to *waqf* funding based on history.
Source: Singer (2006); Amedoski (2009); Fay (1998); al Humaidan (2007); Isin and Üstündağ (2008); Peri (1989); Man and Abdulwaheed (2011).

owns a commercial estate, such as flour mills, weaving workshops and shop buildings (Reilly, 1995, pp. 79–106). *Waqf* trustees are permitted to use or even take the benefits of the *waqf* property prudently and not in an extravagant way and can allow others to use benefits of the *waqf* property if not intended for personal gain (Bukhārī, 2012, p. 308). Usually, women contribute through cash *waqf*. However, various types of *waqf* properties have been endowed by women including residential, agricultural and commercial. These include homes, shops, factories, gardens and agricultural land. Briefly, women also owned and endowed properties that generate income (Fay, 1997, pp. 35–36).

18.3 Factors in women's involvement in *waqf* practice

Early literature also discusses factors that motivated women to become involved in *waqf*. For example, Bozorgmehr and Baron described how women often endow their properties for the safety of their property and income to keep it from being compromised or confiscated by the husband or the husband's family. This is because the continuity of benefits from a *waqf* property is assured and can be used by *waqf* recipients only; even the government cannot take that property arbitrarily (Bozorgmehr and Baron, 2001). Dallal stated that during the Ottoman Empire, nearly 40% of the endowment assets were contributed by women. Most of those who made endowments wanted to protect their property from the intervention and control of their husbands or male relatives (Dallal, 2004). In fact, the study found that they also participated in their *waqf* management (UN-Habitat, 2005). In addition, Alterman and Hunter concluded that, with *waqf*, women have an advantage in managing and protecting their property as well as the power to give the benefits of their property solely to their relatives (Alterman and Hunter, 2004). Doumani also suggested that women endowed their properties with the intention to protect those who are weak (Doumani, 1998, pp. 3–41).

Based on the opinions of the writers regarding factors that have motivated women to do *waqf*, the author argues that one driving factor is the religion. Islam promotes *waqf* as a practice that gives a continuous reward, as the Prophet Muhammad SAW stated:

> Meanings: "When a man dies, his deeds come to an end except for three things: Sadaqah Jariyah (ceaseless charity); a knowledge which is beneficial, or a virtuous descendant who prays for him (for the deceased)." (Muslim, 1998, p. 670)

Sadaqah jariyah is a kind of charity with a continuous reward, and within the meaning of this hadith, it is a way of endowing wealth in Allah's way, as the benefits continue for public use even after the death of its contributors (al-Sharbini, p. 162; al-Husni, n.d). This is because what is endowed will not be owned again; it will be property for the use of *waqf's* recipients. In other words, when women do *waqf*, they forfeit their ownership of the property, and the property will no longer be owned by them or their family, other than for the *waqf's* recipients or public use. Therefore, a reason for women to do *waqf* is their belief that they will be rewarded hereafter.

18.3.1 Purpose of study

The objective of this article is to analyze the role of women's involvement in the development of *waqf* in Malaysia. The contribution of women through *waqf* has not been very well explained and explored in the Malaysian context. Although *waqf* is developing worldwide, especially in Malaysia, the involvement of Malaysian women, especially Muslim women in Malaysia, in *waqf* practice is slightly known. There is a significant gap in understanding Malaysian Muslim women's contribution to the development of *waqf*, its importance, and relationship with economic development. Therefore, the present study addresses this gap by exploring Malaysian Muslim women's involvement in the development of *waqf* as a source of funding for public infrastructures and needs.

18.3.2 Research methodology

Qualitative research was conducted to achieve the objective of this study. Methods of data collection used were from the primary and secondary sources. The primary source of data was obtained through interviews conducted by the researcher with nine Islamic Religious Council officers from eight states in Malaysia: Selangor, Perak, Melaka, Negeri Sembilan, Kelantan, Penang, Federal Territory and Johor. In Malaysia, the State Islamic Religious Council (SIRC) has a role as a trustee of the *waqf* in their respective states. According to List II, List of State of the Ninth Schedule of the Federal Constitution (FC), states as follows:

> *Waqf* and the definition and regulation of charitable and religious trusts, the appointment of trustees and the incorporation of persons in respect of Islamic religious and charitable endowments, institutions, trusts, charities and charitable institutions operating wholly within the State...

As stated in the Federal Constitution, Islamic affairs are under the jurisdiction of the Sultan in every state. *Waqf* is one of the Islamic properties. Hence, *waqf* is included in matters of Islamic affairs and considered under the supervision of SIRC which represents Muslim affairs at the state level.

The open-ended interviews were conducted using a checklist of questions to serve as a guide. Altogether, eight interviews were conducted with SIRC officers. The interviews, which took place in the Islamic Religious Council officer's offices, respectively, lasted from one to two hours, with an average of an hour and a half. Interviews were tape-recorded and transcribed verbatim.

The method of data collection from secondary sources was from journals, conference papers and seminars, books and websites related to women's participation in *waqf*. This research only focused on women's involvement in *waqf* in Malaysia. However, due to confidential data from other states, the research only presents evidence of women's involvement in *waqf* practice in Malaysia from three states: Selangor, Perak and Penang. These data were obtained from the Selangor *Waqf* Corporation (PWS), the Islamic Religious Council and Malay Customs Perak (MAIAMP), Islamic Religious Council of Penang (MAINPP) and Federal Territory Religious Department (JAWI).

18.3.3 Discussion

In Malaysia, women represent almost half of the population. As such, they are significant in contributing to national development. According to the Minister of Women, Family and Community Development in Malaysia, in 2013, 48.6% of Malaysia's population (14.44 million of the 29.71 million population) are women. The female population increased at an average rate of 2.5% in 2012, and 68% (9.8 million) of the total female population is 15–64 years old. This is a productive age group that might be working optimally and receiving pay for employment.

Statistics also showed an increase in the percentage of employed women in Malaysia, from 44.7% in 1995 to 46.1% in 2010 (Portal Berita Universiti Sains Islam Malaysia (USIM), 2014; Yusof, 2012). The Malaysian government set a goal of achieving a 55% female workforce by 2015. The World Bank Economic Report 2012 stated that eliminating the gap in market participation employment will increase the Gross Domestic Product (GDP) per capita (World Bank Economic Report, 2012). According to Dr. Jorah Ramlan, senior analyst at Institute of Strategic and International Studies (ISIS) Malaysia, in the Asia-Pacific Human Development report of 2010 (AHDR), if women's labor participation rate increases to 70%, Malaysia would enjoy an increase in Gross Domestic Product (GDP) between 2% and 4% (Yusof, 2012) (Figure 18.2).

A study conducted by the Department of Statistics Malaysia 2014 obtained information from 9.3 million wage and salary earners in Malaysia, of which 5,913.5 million were males, and 3,380.1 million were females. This study found the mean (Malaysian ringgit [MYR] 2,185) and median (MYR 1,700) of monthly salaries and wages for Malaysia in 2013. Mean monthly salaries and wages of Malaysian females (MYR 1,992) was lower than that of Malaysian males (MYR 2,086). However, mean monthly salaries and wages of females increased 7% from MYR 1,861 in 2012 to MYR 1,992 in 2013. Median salaries and wages for Malaysian males and females were recorded at the same value (MYR 1,500). The Malaysian gender wage gap increased by 0.1 percentage (4.5%) in 2013 compared to the previous year (4.4%).

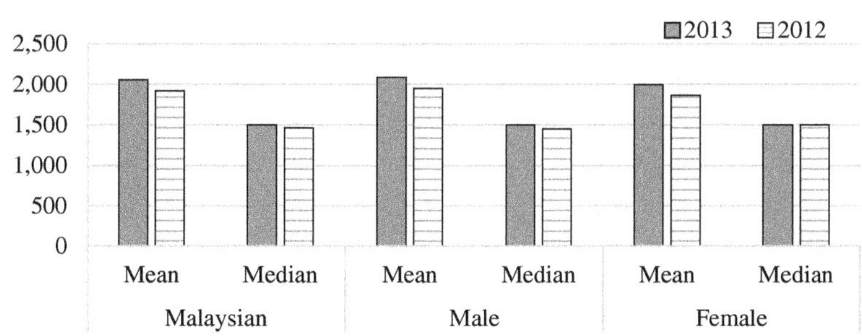

Figure 18.2 Monthly salaries and wages by gender, Malaysia, 2012–2013.
Source: Department of Statistics, Malaysia (2014).

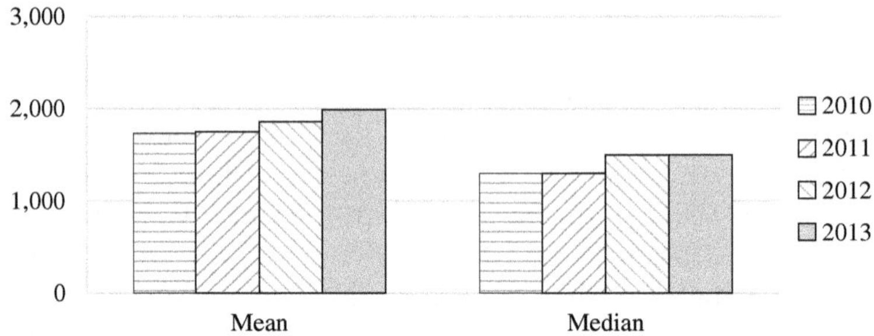

Figure 18.3 Monthly salaries and wages for Malaysian females, 2012–2013.
Source: Department of Statistics (2014).

Mean monthly salaries and wages for females increased by 15% compared to 2010 (MYR 1,734). Median monthly salaries and wages for females in 2010 and 2011 were MYR 1,300, while in 2012 and 2013 were MYR 1,500, an increase of 15%, as illustrated in Figure 18.3 (Department of Women Development, Malaysia, 2014).

The statistics from 2012 showed the percentage of female registered professionals was high, such as accountants (50.3% women), dentists (64.3%), medical doctors (47.8%) and lawyers (50.5%). In terms of industry, the following percentages of women employees were recorded: in accommodation, food and beverage services, 49.4% of the total employees are women; finance and insurance industry, 54.3%; and professional industries, scientific and technical, 48.9% (Department of Women Development, Malaysia, 2014).

Apart from the positive impact on the country's GDP, women's participation in the workforce, even in professional fields, allows them to have their own income and helps increase household income, indirectly, by allowing a more equitable increase in per capita income distribution (Yusof, 2012). One factor that encourages Malaysian women's participation in the employment sector is the rising cost of living, especially in cities, which leads women to work to increase their family income (Lembaga Zakat Selangor, 2014; Marican *et al.*, 2011, pp. 4883–4890).

In 2012 and 2013, participation in Malaysia's employment sector by Malay women who were mainly Muslims increased to a total of 1.94 million and 1.96 million, respectively. Among the major ethnic groups of Malaysian citizens, the Malay recorded the smallest gender wage gap at 5.7% (Department of Statistics, Malaysia, 2014). This means Malay women, who are primarily Muslim, have the smallest income gap compared to Malay men than the wage gap for other ethnicities.

In the current context, since the number of Malay women employed in Malaysia has increased, there is a huge potential for *waqf* contributions from Muslim women in Malaysia to increase. Muslim women's participation in the workforce allows them to have their own income, which means they can help those who are less fortunate through charitable activities such as *waqf* (Afzal-Ur-Rahman, 1994, pp. 68–76; Ismail, 2000, p. 14).

18.3.4 Waqf in Malaysia

In Malaysia, *waqf* has long been practiced by the Muslim community. This is proven by the presence of many buildings such as mosques, religious schools or cemeteries built on *waqf* land (Ahmad, 2008, pp. 87–98; Mahamood, 2007, pp. 61–83). It is estimated that there are over 35,727 hectares of *waqf* land in Malaysia. Johor represents the widest-registered *waqf* land, while *waqf* land in Federal Territories only covers 27.54 acres. According to Hasan, in terms of value, *waqf* lands in Penang, Federal Territory and certain parts of Johor, particularly within the area of Johor Bahru, are considered more strategic and valuable than other areas (Hasan, 2008).

In Malaysian law, *waqf* is mentioned as an Islamic matter which is considered under the supervision of the States Islamic Religious Council, which represents Muslim affairs at the state level. Thus, *waqf* matters are conducted with different methods by States Islamic Religious Councils. To overcome issues of differences in *waqf* management, the Malaysian Federal Government established the Ministry of *Awqaf*, Zakat and Hajj (JAWHAR) by to help State Islamic Religious Council (SIRC) in developing *awqaf* properties in Malaysia. JAWHAR functions to generate systematic, synchronized and effective *awqaf* institutions in Malaysia with the cooperation of the States Islamic Religious Council. Through JAWHAR, the federal government has distributed about MYR 366 million to develop *awqaf* properties throughout Malaysia.

18.4 Women's involvement in developing *waqf* in Malaysia

Generally, even though women have less wealth than do men, they are more likely to endow their property than men are (Doumani, 1998). In the Malaysian state of Selangor, for example, even though the amount of property donated by women is less than men in Malaysia, women in

Selangor are more likely to endow their property than are men. Statistics show that nearly 80% of *waqf* contributors in Selangor are women (Che Ahmad, 2013; Hamdan and Jamaludin, 2013). Similarly, in Penang, *Waqf* Fund Scheme, which was established by the Islamic Religious Council of Penang (MAINPP), showed that women contributors (52%) are greater than men (48%) (Firafizal, 2010; Suhaimi *et al.*, 2014, pp. 227–254). For other states, the gender gap for *waqf* contributors is small and presents almost no differences between men and women contributors (Abdul Karim, 2014; Halim, 2013; Mauludin, 2014; Mohamad, 2013). This means Muslim women in Malaysia still participate and contribute in *waqf* as Muslim men in Malaysia do. The trend of women dedicating their wealth to *waqf* must be welcomed. Muslim women in Malaysia have been involved in *waqf* for a long time based on several records that can be found as proof.

18.4.1 Women have been involved in developing *waqf* funding in Malaysia as *waqf* contributors and have endowed some properties in the form of land, houses, buildings and cash

Regarding land, there is one *waqf* by Mrs. Rahmah Said in Federal Territory of Kuala Lumpur and one by Seetee Aishah in Penang. The land donated by Hjh Rahmah Hj Said at Lot 2056, Batu 3/4, Jalan Gombak is a *waqf* land for general purposes. Originally, the land was suitable for agriculture, with a total area of 111,623 square feet, while 15,777 square feet of it was endowed and managed by the state treasury (*Bayt al-Mal*), and the Federal Territory Religious Department (JAWI) (Jaafar, 1999, pp. 43–64; Ismail, 2014). The land *waqf* by Seetee Aishah in Penang was donated by Seetee Aishah Mahmood in September 1901. Meanwhile, regarding houses, there is *waqf* by Datin Hjh Habibah Abdul Malik and Datin Zabedah Osman located in the Federal Territory. The rental house that was endowed was also managed by the treasury, the Federal Territory Religious Department (JAWI) (Ismail, 2014; Jaafar, 1999).

Other than land and houses, women contributors have endowed some buildings, such as Toh Puan Cha's *waqf* building located at 52 Clare Street, Ipoh, Perak. Based on Mohd Yusop's studies, the building is listed by the Islamic Religious Council and Malay Customs of Perak (MAIAMP) as a *waqf* property that has the potential to be developed as shop houses or offices (Padli, 2014; Yahya, 1999, pp. 65–104). Besides *waqf* buildings, there is also *waqf* in terms of cash contributed by Muslim women. For example, in the *Waqf* Fund Scheme implemented by the Islamic Religious Council of Penang (MAINPP) through the Salary Deduction Scheme, contributions made by Muslim women in Penang are more than the cash *waqf* contributions made by men. Statistics show that out of 712 people who contributed, 52% of them were women (Suhaimi *et al.*, 2014, pp. 227–254).

18.4.2 The involvement of women in developing *waqf* funding in Malaysia has also benefited the community

Land endowed by Mrs. Rahmah Said, located in Federal Territory of Kuala Lumpur, has been developed to build 14 units of longhouses. The houses are used to accommodate abused wives and those with domestic problems. The endowed land also helps the Federal Territory Islamic Religious Council (MAIWP) provide welfare homes and reduce the cost of buying other lands to develop (Ismail, 2014; Jaafar, 1999).

18.5 Property donated by women has also generated revenue through rental or lease

Some *waqf* buildings have been leased to generate income, namely Toh Puan Chah *waqf* buildings in Perak located in different locations. At 137, 137A Jalan Sultan Idris, the rent price is MYR 500 per month, and at 130, 130A, Jln Sultan Yusof, the rent price is MYR 700 per month. Rental income from the buildings is managed fully by the Islamic Religious Council of Perak (MAIAMP). Of the remainder of Toh Puan Chah *waqf* buildings, 40% is distributed to MAIAMP and 60% to the committee. Among them are Toh Puan Chah *waqf* buildings located at No. 1, No. 2, No. 3, 1, 2 and 11 Jalan Raja Muda, Kuala Kangsar as mentioned in Table 18.1. MAIAMP's total revenue from Toh Puan Chah *waqf* buildings is MYR 17,712. Other than that, there is also a *waqf* building donated by Raja Salamah located at 22 Laluan Taman Jati with a rental rate of MYR 150 per month; the total rental income managed by MAIAMP is MYR 1,800 per annum (Yahya, 1999; Padli, 2014). Revenue from the development of *waqf* properties either through rental or lease managed by MAIAMP will be used to build or to buy other *waqf* properties (Padli, 2014).

In Penang, *waqf* Seetee Aishah was initially rented as agricultural land with a rental rate of MYR 400 (approximately $95). The Islamic Religious Council of Penang (MAINPP) has taken the initiative as trustees to collaborate with a developer, Uda Land North, and a housing project

Table 18.1 Revenue from Toh Puan Chah *waqf* buildings.

	Revenue (MYR)		Managed by	
Location	Monthly	Yearly	MAIAMP	Committee
137, 137A Jalan Sultan Idris	500	6,000	100%: MYR 6,000	—
130, 130A Jalan Sultan Yusof	700	8,400	100%: MYR 8,400	—
1 JLN Raja Muda, Kuala Kangsar	30	360	40%: MYR 144	60%: MYR 216
2 JLN Raja Muda, Kuala Kangsar	30	360	40%: MYR 144	60%: MYR 216
11 JLN Raja Muda, Kuala Kangsar	40	480	40%: MYR 192	60%: MYR 288
No. 1	200	2,400	40%: MYR 960	60%: MYR 1,440
No. 2	190	2,280	40%: MYR 912	60%: MYR 1,368
No. 3	200	2,400	40%: MYR 960	60%: MYR 1,440
Total Revenue	1,890	22,680	MYR 17,712	

Source: Yahya (1999), pp. 65–104.

carried out on the *waqf* land was successfully developed; 76 units of double-storey terrace houses priced at MYR 281,000 to MYR 439,000 were sold. The project is also a business center which contains 27 shop units (nine units of three-story shops), rented by MAINPP at MYR 2 per square foot per month. From the housing project's revenue, MAINPP can generate about MYR 1.2 million a year. Furthermore, MAINPP will get a 30% gain from the terraced house's sale (Hashim and Ab. Rahman, 2012, pp. 103–123; *MyMetro*, 2012).

Waqf's property development projects, such as the construction of business centers and residential areas, will ensure the land is utilized optimally rather than it being left and disused. Utilization of *waqf* land will reduce project cost due to no land cost. Thus, more *waqf* projects will assist the government in allocating places to build houses at affordable prices, which represents a fundamental need for the community. These houses and business centers can create economic activity in a particular area, and that economic activity can create employment and business opportunities. Hence, the *waqf* will indirectly modify economic and social development in these areas (Hamdan and Jamaludin, 2013).

In response to the overwhelming response from women in Malaysia, especially in Selangor, PWS has launched a product of *waqf* specifically for women called Gold *Waqf*, and "The Month of *Waqf* with Women" to promote this product (Hamdan and Jamaludin, 2013). Before the launch of Gold *Waqf*, contributions totaling MYR 27,000 had been received from women (Che Ahmad, 2013). *Waqf* Gold makes it more convenient for women to do *waqf* since women usually are gifted jewelry such as wedding gifts, anniversary gifts, or by inheritance from their mothers and grandmothers (Hamdan and Jamaludin, 2013). Sometimes, this jewelry is not used and only placed in a safe box.

18.5.1 Factors related to women's involvement in *waqf* practice in Malaysia

Muslims believe that *waqf* contributors will be rewarded in the Hereafter. Compared to alms, *waqf* as a kind of charity with a continuous reward even after the death of its contributors, has motivated Muslim women in Malaysia to do *waqf*. Also, seminars and talks regarding *waqf* matters carried out by the States Islamic Religious Council (SIRC) have increased awareness and understanding of *waqf* among Muslims in Malaysia, including women. *Waqf* promotional campaigns through mass media such as radio, television, billboard advertising and *waqf* booths help disseminate information related to *waqf* to the public and increase *waqf* collection funds in Malaysia (Hamdan and Jamaludin, 2013; Abd Halim, 2013; Mohamad, 2013; Firafizal, 2010). For example, the Johor Islamic Religious Council (MAIJ) launched radio advertising regarding *waqf*, and consequently Muslims public throughout Malaysia contributed to MAIJ's *waqf* collection (Abd Halim, 2013). Other factors that have encouraged Muslim women in Malaysia to be involved in giving *waqf* are their sense of responsibility to help others in their community and their willingness to improve society for (Hamdan and Jamaludin, 2013; Abd Halim, 2013; Mohamad, 2013; Firafizal, 2010).

18.6 Conclusion

Indeed, there is no doubt about the involvement of women in *waqf*. Historically, women have served as *waqf* contributors, trustees and even *waqf* managers. Women's contributions in endowing land, buildings, cash and other properties are also used to finance infrastructure projects and public facilities for the community including mosques, schools, universities, libraries, research and translation centers, rest homes, residences, public baths, soup kitchens, hospitals, water catchment, fountains, roads, bridges, shops and workshops. Further, *waqf* contributions have also been used to assist the poor, orphans and widows.

Similarly, in Malaysia, women have been involved in *waqf* too. Properties donated by women not only have their own value and can generate income, either through rent or lease and have potential for development, they can also promote economic activities in their states such as the *waqf* of Seetee Aishah and Toh Puan Chah. Furthermore, based on women's involvement women in *waqf*, the *Waqf* Fund Schemes and PWS have a significant increase in their *waqf* collection. Thus, *waqf* products for women should be further intensified in Malaysia.

References

Malay

Afzal-Ur-Rahman (1994), *Doktrin ekonomi Islam* (Vol. 1), translated by Mustafa Kasim, Kuala Lumpur: Dewan Bahasa dan Pustaka.

Ahmad, Azri (2008), Pelaksanaan skim wakaf tunai oleh yayasan waqaf Malaysia. *Journal Pengurusan JAWHAR, Yayasan Waqaf Malaysia, Putrajaya*, 2(4), 87–98.

Alterman, Jon B. and Hunter, Shireen (2004), *The Idea of Philanthropy in Muslim Contexts*, Washington, DC: The Center for Strategic and International Studies.

Che Ahmad, Mohd. Shah (2013), "PWS Perluas Konsep Wakaf", *Utusan Malaysia Online*, 12 April 2013, available at http://ww1.utusan.com.my/utusan/Bicara_Agama/20130412/ba_02/PWS-perluas-konsep-wakafwakaf. Retrieved on 20 March 2014.

Hashim, Hydzulkifli and Ab. Rahman, Asmak (2012), Pengurusan pembangunan harta wakaf: Pengalaman Majlis Agama Islam Negeri Pulau Pinang (MAINPP) terhadap wakaf Seetee Aishah. *International Journal of Management Studies*, 19(2), 103–123.

Ismail, Faizah (2000), *Asas-asas Muamalat Dalam Islam*, Kuala Lumpur: Dewan Bahasa dan Pustaka.

Jaafar, Zainal Abidin (1999), "Pengurusan wakaf di Wilayah Persekutuan: Amalan dan perancangan", in Nik Mustapha Nik Hassan (ed.), *Konsep dan Pelaksanaan Wakaf di Malaysia* (Vol. 4), Kuala Lumpur: Institut Kefahaman Islam Malaysia (IKIM), pp. 43–64.

Janan, M. Jandra Moh (2008), "Memproduktifkan *wakaf*: Pengalaman di Indonesia", paper presented at Prosiding Konvensyen Kebangsaan Pengurusan Harta Pusaka, Wasiat and Wakaf, 18–19 October 2008, Universiti Kebangsaan Malaysia (UKM), Bangi.

Lembaga Zakat Selangor (2014), "Menjana Peranan Wanita Dalam Zakat", available at http://www.e-zakat.com.my/artikel/3135/. Retrieved on 20 March 2014.

Mahamood, Siti Mashitoh (2007), Pembentukan dana wakaf menurut perspektif Syariah dan undang-undang serta aplikasinya di Malaysia. *Jurnal Syariah*, 15(2) 61–83.

MyMetro (2012), "Bisnes: Wakaf Setee Aishah jana RM1.2j setahun", *Harian Metro Online,* 24 October 2012, available at http://www2.hmetro.com.my/articles/WakafSeteeAishahjanaRM1_2jsetahun/Article/. Retrieved on 20 March 2014.

Portal Berita Universiti Sains Islam Malaysia (USIM) (2014), "Wanita Malaysia mampu seimbang keluarga dan kerjaya — Dr. Rafidah", available at http://news.usim.edu.my/ms/berita-penyelidikan-penerbitan/item/374-wanita-malaysia-mampu-seimbang-keluarga-dan-kerjaya-dr-rafidah. Retrieved on 20 March 2014.

Sulaiman, Norsiah and Manaf, Farahdina Abdul (2009), Peranan harta wakaf dalam bidang pembangunan dan pendidikan ummah: Fokus dalam bidang perubatan. *Journal Pengurusan JAWHAR*, 3(1), 2–30.

Sunny, Abdul Halim (2007), Dana wakaf pendidikan: Satu tinjauan awal. *Journal Pengurusan JAWHAR*, Putrajaya: Yayasan Waqaf Malaysia, 2(1), 33–44.

Yahya, Mohd Yusof (1999), "Pengurusan wakaf di Perak: Amalan dan perancangan" in Nik Mustapha Nik Hassan (ed.), *Konsep dan Pelaksanaan Wakaf di Malaysia*, Kuala Lumpur: Institut Kefahaman Islam Malaysia (IKIM), 5, 65–104.

Yusof, Nor Afzan Mohamad (2012), "Kemelut pekerja wanita", *Berita Harian Online*, 1 Mei 2012, available at http://www2.bharian.com.my/articles/Kemelutpekerjawanita/Article/. Retrieved on 20 March 2014.

English

Ahmad, Ziauddin (1989), *Public Finance in Islam*, IMF Working Paper International Monetary Fund.

Al Humaidan, Iman Mohammad (2007), *Women and Waqf: A Series of Translations on Philanthropic and Voluntary Work (12)*, Kuwait: Kuwait Awqaf Public Foundation.

al-Hilali, Muhammad Taqi-ud-Din and Khan, Muhammad Muhsin (2000), *Translation of the Meanings of the Noble Qur'an in the English Language*, Madinah: King Fahd Complex for the Printing of the Holy *Qur'an*.

Amedoski, Dragana (2009), *Women waqfs in the Sixteenth-century Sanjak of Kruševac (Alaca Hisâr)*, Belgrade: Institute of History, pp. 43–56.

Bozorgmehr, Mehdi and Baron, Beth (2001), *Philanthropy among Middle Eastern Americans and their Historical Traditions of Giving*, New York: Middle East and Middle Eastern American Centre, The City University of New York.

Çizakça, Murat (2000), *A History of Philanthropic Foundations: The Islamic World from the Seventh Century to the Present*, Eighth draft, Kuala Lumpur: International Institute of Islamic Thought and Civilization (ISTAC).

Dallal, Ahmad (2004), "The Islamic institution of *waqf*: A historical overview", in Stephen P. Heyneman (ed.), *Islam and Social Policy*, Nashville: Vanderbilt University Press.

Dar al-Nicosia (2011), "Fatima al-Fihri Founder of the Qarawiyyin", available at daralnicosia.wordpress.com/2011/06/19/fatima-al-fihri-founder-of-the-qarawiyyin/. Retrieved on 20 March 2014.

Department of Statistics, Malaysia (2014), "Malaysia Salaries & Wages Survey Report 2012", available at http://www.statistics.gov.my/portal/download_Labour/download.php?file=BPTMS/Salaries_and_Wages_Survey_Report_2012_11092013.pdf. Retrieved on 1 December 2014.

Department of Women Development, Malaysia (2014), Draft speech text by the Minister of Women, Family and Community Development at Perdana NUR Hall, Ministry of Women, Family And Community Development, Putrajaya on 7 March 2014, available at: http://www.jpw.gov.my/web/home/article_view/0/157/. Retrieved on 20 March 2014.

Doumani, Beshara (1998), Endowing family: *Waqf*, property devolution, and gender in greater Syria, 1800 to 1860. *Comparative Studies in Society and History*, 40(1), 3–41.

Elizabeth Woodcock and Rabah Saoud (eds.) (2007), *1001 Inventions: Muslim Heritage in Our World*, United Kingdom: Foundation for Science, Technology and Civilization (FSTC).

Fay, M. A. (1998), From concubines to capitalists: Women, property, and power in eighteenth-century Cairo. *Journal of Women's History*, 10(3), 118–140.

Fay, M. A. (1997), "Women and *waqf*: Property, power and the domain of the gender in eighteenth-century Egypt", in M. Zilfi (ed.), *Women in the Ottoman Empire: Middle Eastern Women in the Early Modern Period*, Leiden: E. J. Brill, pp. 35–36.

Hasan, Zulkifli (2008), An Overview of the Effectiveness of the Administration of Waqf Land in Malaysia, *Shariah Law Report, Current Law Journal,* 2008. Available at SSRN: http://ssrn.com/abstract=2234208.

Ibrahim, Ahmad Zaki (2009), *Institusi al-Azhar: Keunggulan pengurusan dana wakaf dalam sejarah tamadun Islam*, paper presented at Seminar Wakaf Melestarikan Hadharah Ummah, Putrajaya, 22 December 2009.

Isin, E. and Üstündağ, E. (2008), Wills, deeds, acts: Women's civic gift-giving in Ottoman Istanbul. *Gender, Place and Culture*, 15(5), 519–532.

Kuran, Timur (2001), The provision of public goods under Islamic law: Origin, contribution and limitation of the *waqf* system. *Law & Society Review*, 35(4), 841–897.

Man, Zakariya and Abdulwaheed, Salihu (2011), New dimension in the mobilization of *waqf* funds for educational development. *Kuwait Chapter of Arabian Journal of Business and Management Review*, 1(1), 155–175.

Marican, S., Sabil, S., Zakaria, R.H. and Ab Rahman, A. (2011), Can supportive management contribute to the wellbeing of Muslim working women in Malaysia? *African Journal Of Business Management*,

5(12), 4883–4890, available at http://www.academicjournals.org/ajbm/PDF/pdf2011/18June/Marican%20et%20al.pdf. Retrieved on 20 March 2014.

Peri, Oded (1989), Waqf and Ottoman welfare policy — The poor kitchen of Hasseki Sultan in eighteenth-century Jerusalem. *Journal of the Economic and Social History of the Orient*, XXXV, 167–186.

Reilly, James A. (1995), Women in the economic life of late-Ottoman Damascus. *Arabica*, 42(1), 79–106.

Sadeq, Abdul Hasan M. (2002), *Waqf*, perpetual charity and poverty alleviation. *International Journal of Social Economics*, 29(1/2), 135–151.

Saifuddeen, S. M. and Salleh, S. M. (2003), "Extending Role of *Waqf* to Spur R&D. IKIM View" *New Straits Times* (21 June), available at http://e-kiosk.ikim.gov.my/downloadarticle.asp?id=660. Retrieved on 20 March 2014.

Singer, Amy (2006), Soup and *sadaqa*: Charity in Islamic societies. *Historical Research*, 79(205), 306–324.

Suhaimi, F. M., Ab Rahman, A. and Marican, S. (2014), The role of share *waqf* in the socio-economic development of the Muslim community: The Malaysian experience. *Humanomics*, 30(3), 3–3, available at: http://dx.doi.org/10.1108/H-12-2012-0025. Retrieved on 20 March 2014.

Toraman, Cengiz and Tuncsiper, Berdiye (2007), "Cash *awqaf* in the Ottoman as philanthropic foundations and their accounting practices", paper presented at The Fifth Accounting History International Conference, 9–11 August 2007, Banff, Alberta, Canada, pp. 1–19.

UN-Habitat (2005), *Waqf (Endowment) and Islamic Philanthropy*, Islam, Land & Property Research Series, UN Habitat.

White, Andrew (2006), The role of the Islamic *waqf* in strengthening South Asian Civil Society: Pakistan as case study. *International Journal of Civil Society Law*, IV(2), 7–36.

World Bank Economic Report (2012), "Gender Equality and Development 2012", Washington, DC: The World Bank, available at http://siteresources.worldbank.org/INTWDR2012/Resources/7778105-1299699968583/7786210-1315936222006/Complete-Report.pdf. Retrieved on 20 March 2014.

Yalawae, A. and Tahir, I. M. (2008), "The Role of Islamic Institution in Achieving Equality and Human Development: Waqf or Endowment", available at http://www.capabilityapproach.com/pubs/Asming%20Yalawae,%20and%20Izah%20TahirWaqfAsmeng.pdf. Retrieved on 20 March 2014.

Arabic

al-Ḥuṣnī, Taqī al-Dīn Abī Bakr Muḥammad al-Husainī (n.d.), *Kifāyah al-Akhyār fi Hil Ghāyah al-Ikhtiṣār*, Dimashq: Dar al-Khair.

al-Sharbīnī, al-Khaṭīb (n.d.), *al-Iqnā' fī Ḥil al-Alfāẓ Abī Shujā'* (Vol. 2), Beirut: Dar al-Kutub al-'Ilmīyyah.

Bukhārī, Muḥammad bin Ismā'il (2012), *Ṣaḥīḥ Bukhārī*, Beirut: Bayt al-Afkār al-Dauliyyah.
Muslim, Abū al-Ḥusīn Muslim al-Ḥujjāj al-Qushaīrī al-Nisāburī (1998), *Ṣaḥīḥ Muslim*, 'Ammān: Bayt al-Afkār al-Dauliyyah.

Interviews

Abd Halim, Mustafayuddin (Assistance Director, Awqaf Division, Islamic Religious Council of (MAIJ)), in interview with author on 7 November 2013.
Abdul Karim, Mohd Khabir (Assistant, Department of Waqf and General Resources, Islamic Religious Council of Melaka (MAIM)), in interview with author on 4 February 2014.
Firafizal, Ahmad Syah (Waqf Fund Scheme Manager, Waqf Division, Islamic Religious Council of Penang (MAINPP)), in interview with author on 18 March 2010.
Hamdan, Mohd Huzairi (Assistant Executive of Assessment, Selangor Waqf Corporation (PWS)), in interview with author on 5 November 2013; Jamaludin, Shahrul Ashraf (Assistant Executive of Marketing, Selangor Waqf Corporation (PWS)), in interview with author on 25 November 2013.
Ismail, Mohd Azrul (Assistant Manager of Zakat, Waqf, Wasiat and General Resources Management Unit, Majlis Agama Islam Wilayah Persekutuan (MAIWP) or Islamic Religious Affairs Council of Federal States), in interview with author on 28 January 2014.
Mauludin, Ali Mazri (Executive, Negeri Sembilan Waqf Corporation (Perbadanan Wakaf Negeri Sembilan)), in interview with author on 4 February 2014.
Mohamad, Shakirah (Assistance Manager, Baitulmal Unit, or Islamic Religious Council of Kelantan (MAIK)), in interview with author on 27 October 2013.
Padli, Mohd Khairul Adli Ahmad (Assisstance Manager, Property and Investment Division, Islamic Religious Council of Perak (MAIAMP)), in interview with author on 3 March 2014.

Glossary

bayt al-mal House of money. Historically, a financial institution responsible for the administration of taxes. Acted as a royal treasury for caliphs and sultans, managing personal finances and government expenditures. Administered distribution of *zakat* (obligatory alms) revenues for public works. Modern Islamic economists deem the institutional framework appropriate for Islamic society.

fard al-kifayah — Defines a communal obligation in Muslim legal doctrine. In juxtaposition to *fard al-ayn*, *fard al-kifayah* is a legal obligation that must be discharged by the Muslim community as a whole; if enough members in the Muslim community discharge the obligation, the remaining Muslims are freed from the responsibility before God. However, if a communal obligation is not sufficiently discharged, then every individual Muslim must act to address the deficiency. In recent Islamic literature, this terminology is used to discuss social responsibility, such as feeding the hungry, commanding good and forbidding evil.

hibah — Gift, bequest, donation, grant.

imam — A leader of congregational prayer in a mosque.

kulliye — A complex of buildings associated with Ottoman architecture cantered on a mosque and managed within a single institution, often based on a *waqf* (pious endowment) and composed of a school, a clinic, kitchens, bakery, Turkish bath other buildings for various charitable services for the community and further annexes. The term is derived from the Arabic word kull "all".

mahr — Dowry paid by a husband to his wife. Can be either money or property. Required for the marriage contract and the marriage itself to be valid.

mawlid — Birth. Commemoration of Muhammad's birthday, believed to be the twelfth day of *Rabi al-Awwal.* Celebrated as a holiday marked by popular festivities and state ceremonies in most Muslim countries except Saudi Arabia.

muezzin — The official of a mosque who calls the faithful to prayer five times a day from the minaret.

pilgrim — A person who undertakes a journey to a sacred place as an act of religious devotion.

sadaqah jariyah — Ceaseless charity.

waqf — An Islamic endowment of property to be held in trust and used for a charitable or religious purpose.

Chapter 19

State of Women in Pakistan

Irum Saba and Khadija Bari

Abstract

Pakistan came into existence in 1947 on the name of Islam. The idea behind the creation of Islamic Republic of Pakistan was to develop/lay foundation of a state where people can practice the laws prescribed by Allah SWT. The founder of Pakistan, Quaid-e-Azam Muhammad Ali Jinnah said that women are third power after sword and pen for the development of nations. The Islamic viewpoint about the importance and respect of females is discussed. This chapter focuses on the current status of women in Pakistan in terms of their number, age bracket, issues and growth opportunities. Few names of currently leading women in Pakistan are also included in the chapter. Pakistan, the land of pure, has very strong women who are making all of us proud.

Keywords: Muslim women, Pakistan, Issues of women, Islamic law, Women participation

19.1 Vision of the founder of Pakistan Mohammad Ali Jinnah (*Quaid-e-Azam*)

Pakistan — named "the Land of Pure", was founded with the primary objective of having a separate state from India that would be free of social menace and would ensure equitable opportunities to all sections of the society, including religious minorities and women.

Our beloved Father of the Nation, Muhammad Ali Jinnah, proclaimed his clear stance on the issue of women's rights, in a speech at Islamia College, on 25 January 1940;

> "I have always maintained that no nation can ever be worthy of its existence that cannot take its women along with men. No struggle can ever succeed without women participating side by side with men. There are two powers in the world. One is the sword and the other

the pen. However, there is a third power stronger than both, that of the women." (World Bank Pakistan Celebrates Pakistani Women's Achievements, 2013)

In another speech, at Aligarh University, on 10 March 1944, Muhammad Ali Jinnah, highlighted the importance of women in a society and his dissent about the current state of women in subcontinent.

> "Another very important matter which I want to impress upon you, is that no nation can rise to the height of glory, unless women are side by side with you. We are victims of evil customs. It is a crime against humanity to shut up women within the four walls of houses as prisoners. Let us try to raise the status of women according to Islamic ideals and standards. There is no sanction anywhere for the deplorable conditions in which our women have to live. We should take the women along with us as comrades in every sphere of life. We cannot expect a woman who is ignorant herself to bring up our children properly. Women have the power to bring up children on the right lines. Let us not throw away this asset." (Quaid-e-Azam on Women, 2010)

Similarly, in another speech, Muhammad Ali Jinnah, emphasized on woman being a man's equal, his friend and a comrade.

> "It is woman and woman alone who can teach men how and when to wield the sword or pen when the occasion arises... You, young women, are more fortunate than your mothers are. You are being emancipated. I do not mean that you must copy the west. But I do mean that man must be made to understand that a woman is his equal and that woman is his friend and comrade and they together can build up homes, families and nations." (Quaid-e-Azam on Women, 2010)

19.2 Position of Women in sources of Islamic Law (*Qur'an* and *Sunnah*)

Islam has dawned upon the world as a complete code of life, underpinning basic human rights for women, which they were deprived of in the "Ages of Ignorance".[1] Islam has laid down a strong foundation for women's well-being and has elevated their status in society over time, dispelling the wrong customs, disallowing the social practices that undermined the gender as a

[1] A term used to denote pre-Islamic Arabia, or the conditions and evil practices of the times before the advent of Prophet Muhammad S.A.W in the early 7th century A.D.

whole and restored its dignity. Islamic sources of law, both primary (*Qur'an* and *Hadith*) and secondary (*Ijma* (Consensus) and *Qiyas* (Analogy)) have put forth strong advocacy for women in social aspects. The fourth chapter of the *Qur'an* (Holy Book) is dedicated to highlight the rights of women; therefore, it is named "An Nisa" — The Women.

Gender roles in Islam are simultaneously explained by two of the *Qur'anic* commandments:

(i) spiritual equality between women and men; and
(ii) The idea that women are meant to exemplify femininity, and men masculinity (Eaton, 2000, p. 91).

The following verse is a beautiful and comprehensive proof that in the eyes of God, the value, status or rank of men and women, particularly regarding their actions and potential of success in the hereafter, is equal.

إِنَّ الْمُسْلِمِينَ وَالْمُسْلِمَاتِ وَالْمُؤْمِنِينَ وَالْمُؤْمِنَاتِ وَالْقَانِتِينَ وَالْقَانِتَاتِ وَالصَّادِقِينَ
وَالصَّادِقَاتِ وَالصَّابِرِينَ وَالصَّابِرَاتِ وَالْخَاشِعِينَ وَالْخَاشِعَاتِ وَالْمُتَصَدِّقِينَ
وَالْمُتَصَدِّقَاتِ وَالصَّائِمِينَ وَالصَّائِمَاتِ وَالْحَافِظِينَ فُرُوجَهُمْ وَالْحَافِظَاتِ وَالذَّاكِرِينَ اللَّهَ
كَثِيرًا وَالذَّاكِرَاتِ أَعَدَّ اللَّهُ لَهُم مَّغْفِرَةً وَأَجْرًا عَظِيمًا - 33:35

"Surely, Muslim men and Muslim women, believing men and believing women, devout men and devout women, truthful men and truthful women, patient men and patient women, humble men and humble women, and the men who give Sadaqah (charity) and the women who give Sadaqah, and the men who fast and the women who fast, and the men who guard their private parts (against evil acts) and the women who guard (theirs), and the men who remember Allah much and the women who remember (Him) — for them, Allah has prepared forgiveness and a great reward." (33:35)

In another verse in the *Qur'an*, it is narrated:

وَمِن كُلِّ شَيْءٍ خَلَقْنَا زَوْجَيْنِ لَعَلَّكُمْ تَذَكَّرُونَ -

And of all things We created two mates; perhaps you will remember. (51:49)

This verse indicates Islam's basic view of women and men is that both women and men postulate a complementarity of functions: like everything else in the universe, that humanity has been created in a pair — neither can be complete without the other (Murata, 1992, p. 14).

The emphasis which Islam places upon the feminine/masculine polarity (and therefore complementarity) results, quite logically, in a separation of social functions. In other words, the emphasis in Islam is not that men and women are *identical* in their rights, responsibilities and characteristics, but rather that they both have rights and status, but are *different.* In general, a woman's sphere of operation is the home in which she is the dominant figure — and a man's corresponding sphere is the outside world. However, this separation is not, in practice, as rigid as it appears.

There are many examples — both in the early history of Islam and in the contemporary world — of Muslim women who have played prominent roles in public life, including being, qualified narrators of hadith, religious scholars, leaders, elected heads of state and wealthy businesswomen. Moreover, it is important to recognize that in Islam, home and family are firmly situated at the center of life in this world and of society: a man's work cannot take precedence over the private realm (Eaton, 2000, p. 93).

Both the *Qur'an* — Islam's sacred text — and *Hadith* — the spoken or acted examples (or tacit approvals) of the Prophet Muhammad (pbuh), advocate the rights of women and men equally to seek knowledge. The *Qur'an* commands all Muslims to exert effort in the pursuit of knowledge (and particularly in religions knowledge, or knowledge termed in Sunnah as *"ilmun Nafi'an"* "knowledge that is beneficial"), irrespective of their biological sex: it constantly encourages Muslims to read, think, contemplate and learn from the signs of God in nature.

Moreover, Holy Prophet (pbuh), encouraged education for both males and females: he declared that seeking knowledge was a religious duty binding upon every Muslim man and woman. Like her male counterpart, each woman is under a moral and religious obligation to seek knowledge, develop her intellect, broaden her outlook, cultivate her talents and then utilize her potential to the benefit of her soul and her society. The interest of the Prophet Muhammad (SAW) in female education was manifest in the fact that he himself used to teach women along with men. Muhammad's S.A.W. teachings were widely sought by both genders, and accordingly at the time of his death it was reported that there were many female scholars of Islam. Additionally, the wives of the Prophet Muhammad (pbuh) — particularly Aisha (R.A.: May God be pleased with her) — also taught both women and men; many of Holy Prophet's (pbuh) companions and followers learned the *Qur'an*, *ḥadīth* and Islamic jurisprudence (principles of Fiqh) from Aisha R.A. Notably, there was no restriction placed on the type of knowledge acquired: a woman was free to choose any field of knowledge that interested her. Because Islam recognizes that women are in principle wives and mothers, the acquisition of knowledge in fields which are complementary to these social roles was specially emphasized (Jawad, 1998, p. 21).

Jabir ibn Abdullah R.A reported: The Messenger of Allah, Holy Prophet (pbuh) said:

> "Whoever has three daughters and he care for them, he is merciful to them, and he clothes them, then Paradise is certainly required for him." A companion inquired, 'O Messenger of Allah, what if he has only two?' The Prophet said, 'Even two.' (Musnad Ahmed, *Hadith* no. 13835)

It is the opinion of some companions that if they would have asked Prophet Muhammad (pbuh) about one, the Prophet would have said even one.

The Messenger of Allah, Holy Prophet (pbuh) said:

> "He, who brought up two girls properly till they grew up, he and I would come (together) (very closely) on the Day of Resurrection, and he interlaced his fingers (for explaining the point of nearness between him and that person)." (Sahih Muslim, *Hadith* no. 2631)

Hazrat Ayesha — Mother of Believers, narrated a beautiful story:

> "A woman came to me along with her two daughters. She asked me for (charity) but she found nothing with me except one date, so I gave her that. She accepted it and then divided it between her two daughters and herself ate nothing out of that. She then got up and went out, and so did her two daughters. (In the meanwhile) Allah's Apostle (pbuh) visited me and I narrated to him her story. Thereupon Allah's Apostle (pbuh) said: He who is involved (in the responsibility) of (bringing up) daughters, and he accords benevolent treatment towards them, there would be protection for him against Hell-Fire." (Sahih Muslim, Book 45, *Hadith* 190)

For parents raising sons is also considered very important in Islam, but nevertheless, in the society having sons has material and/or social benefits as well. Parents may feel respected in the society for having so many sons, or "male heir", or for carrying on the father's name, looking after the parents in old age, financially helping the family, etc.

Raising daughters well (according to the *fitrah* of Deen) is considered more precious — for the Prophet Muhammad (pbuh) described them as a "barricade to Hell fire":

The Holy Prophet (pbuh) said:

> *"If a person has troubles due to her daughters but takes care of them, her daughters will be barricades that will save him from the fire of Hell."* (Sahih Bukhari)

The Messenger of Allah, Holy Prophet (pbuh) said;

> "Whichever (people) are tried by any of them (girls/daughters), and he treats them kindly, they will screen him from the fire (of Hell)." (Al-Bukhari and Muslim)

19.3 Cultural sediments from pre-partition era

The people of Pakistan, each year on 14 August, celebrate Independence Day, to commemorate the immense sacrifices by Muslims of the Subcontinent, to achieve the ideology of Two Nation Theory, a homeland of their own for ordering their lives in accordance with their religion, culture and traditions.

Even-though the Two-Nation Theory was instrumental in staging of the partition of Indo-Pak, the fact is that the culture that has been inherited has left deeply ingrained impressions on even our modern day's Pakistani social norms and cultural values. Having pre-partition shared experiences of living together for ages has brought together ethos that are strongly influenced by typical Hindu belief system (or simply from the subcontinent customs of the 17th, 18th and 19th centuries), and that may have no clear credence from Islamic injunctions and traditions of *Hadith* from the Holy Prophet S.A.W. (may Allah's blessings and peace be on him).

A profound look in the retrospect unravels the events that shape our customs, norms and social practices that were never uprooted from the original essence of Islam but was a resultant of social mix that the society was in sub-continent prior to independence. As effectively explained in the following paragraph:

> "In patriarchal and feudal societies, women are almost always seen as the bearers of culture and "honor". Traditional, conservative South Asian culture fetishizes women to such an extent that, while the official line says they are held in high esteem and regard, in actual fact, they are treated simply as vessels of that honor, and their lives are forced to be

> structured around preserving that. They are not allowed to do anything that compromises those ideals, while men have much freer rein without the same burden." (Hundal, 2007)

The perception of women as an emblem of honor, women fell prey to the anguish of either side during partition in 1947. During the riots of 1947, to avenge misery caused by one and another, the rioters would be on a team look-out for the other side's women to devour on their prized "honor", or simply abduct them, implying the same distress to inflict pain to the religious and political opponents, all in the name of shared sense of misogyny, which was much rife at the time.

Both countries, after partition promised each other that they would try to restore women abducted and raped during the riots. The Indian government claimed that 33,000 Hindu and Sikh women were abducted, and the Pakistani government claimed that 50,000 Muslim women were abducted during riots. By 1949, there were governmental claims that 12,000 women had been recovered in India and 6,000 in Pakistan (Visweswaran, 2011). By 1954, there were 20,728 Muslim women recovered from India and 9,032 Hindu and Sikh women recovered from Pakistan (Menon and Bhasin, 1998). Most of the Hindu and Sikh women refused to go back to India, fearing that they would never be accepted by their family, a fear mirrored by Muslim women (Jayawardena and de Alwi, 1996).

Honor associated with women is often still used as a pressure point to unleash full potential cropped up in South Eastern youthful minds to incite inter-faith riots or to cause social upheavals. However, education has contributed substantially to the evolution of the social values and capacitated the inter-faith harmony, but political beneficiaries highlight such issues to cash in on the sentiments of the oppressed. The traditions and the customs in Asia are so rigid that they do not allow a woman to seek justice even when she has the legal right. Reports from the South Asian countries demonstrate a phenomenon of injustice, suppression and helplessness due to traditional attitudes faced by women, in order to obtain the rights given to them by the local legislation.

Throughout South Asian countries, there are two historical factors that affect the women in South Asia adversely.

Agriculture-based economies: The tribal feudal system and patriarchal structures accord a secondary role at best to women. For instance, women may not have access to education, may be unpaid workers on the farms and be deprived of their inheritance.

Industrialization: Having missed out on the industrial revolution, South Asian countries are now being pushed into post-industrial society. Therefore, radically different levels of development are found in the different areas of these countries. Due to widespread unemployment, women were pushed out of the lucrative job market and forced to return to traditionally unpaid labor in agriculture and family business.

These factors make women weak and subservient. Marriages were arranged by parents — this in itself is not necessarily against the bride and bridegroom's interest, but sometimes women have no choice in the matter (whereas Islamic law puts the bride's acceptance as a prerequisite for the marriage); they lose their identity as an individual or as a member of community and became almost like a commodity which could be bought and sold (Niaz, 2003).

19.4 Background and history of atrocities on women in Pakistan

The status of women in Islam was much higher than the one granted by Hinduism and Buddhism. Islam gave women the legal right to own property, to marry and seek divorce (*khula*) (Nasr, 2004). Her status in the community was similar to a man and determined by her deeds and character. In early Islam, women excelled in scholarship, medicine, farming and even warfare. However, with the passage of time and with its basic teachings of tolerance and respect for other religions, Islam as practiced in the subcontinent absorbed much from the local cultures in India, and people changed their view of women's status according to the culture of the host country. Thus, one finds blend of Muslim and Hindu culture during the Mughal era, which lasted for more than 600 years in the Indian subcontinent. During this time there were many women rulers.

Muslims in Indian subcontinent have absorbed some of the customs and values from the Indian subcontinent culture of patriarchal values. The indigenous Indian cultures present sometimes supported female inferiority and these values were transmitted to the younger generations, resulting in family violence, which was tolerated simply as a male's right to control those who were dependent. Hence, the practice of Islamic personal law in some areas (e.g., inheritance, education of women, marriage and divorce) in many countries of the world today is the male interpretation of uneducated or semi-educated men. This interpretation came to include all the negative implications of other religions such as the inequality and subjugation of women, denying women's rights of inheritance, divorce and marriage, etc.

Today, the culture prevalent in the South Asian Muslim countries is contrary to many elements of Islamic religious teachings. In Afghanistan, for example, under the Taliban rule, women were often deprived of the right to education, work, health care, legal recourse and recreation.

In Pakistan and other South Asian countries, the situation of women varies considerably depending upon the geographical location and class. For instance, in the less-populated frontier provinces of Pakistan, life for women is restricted, and women are expected to comply with tribal beliefs and traditions. Any woman who deviates from these traditions, such as being seen with a man to whom she is not related or married can suffer penalties, sometimes even death. The women are rarely seen outside their homes. However, in the more heavily populated Sindh and Punjab provinces (accounting for well over half of Pakistan's population) women may have relatively greater social mobility. Even in some educated families of Sindh or Punjab, for example, in matters of inheritance distribution of fathers' property, sometimes sons are regarded as "sole heirs".[2] They are visible working in village areas and in the fields, and they have access to education and health care. In urban areas of Pakistan, a small minority of the total female population have the greatest mobility, with greater access to jobs, education and greater freedom in marriage and divorce.

Since the founding of Pakistan, a continuing controversy over the role of Islam in the nation's political life has had a direct bearing on the trajectory of women's advancement. Following partition, the constitutional debates and arguments ensuing between the religious scholars and politicians produced a constitution that "demonstrated [an] unwillingness to articulate and implement an Islamic ideology" in that the "relationship of modern constitutional concepts of Islamic principles was asserted but not delineated" (Esposito, 1986).

The collapse of the political institutions paved the way for the military to assume a dominant role in Pakistani politics. In the late 1970s and 1980s, for example, under General Zia ul Haq's rule, fundamental rights

[2]This is against Islamic teachings, as under Islamic law of inheritance, although (depending on the case) a particular female inheritor may have a smaller share than her brother or husband, nevertheless wives, mothers, daughters, grand-daughters, sisters etc. have assigned shares. In fact, mothers, daughters and wives of the diseased (if alive) are never deprived of inheritance.

guaranteed in the 1973 Constitution were suspended, including the right to be free of discrimination on the basis of gender. A series of laws were introduced that gave legal sanctions to women's subordinate status, including the Hudood Ordinance (which changed the law of rape and adultery), the Qanun-e-Shahadat Order (Law of Evidence Order which sometimes renders the testimony of a women equal to half that of a man's) and the Qisas and Diyat Ordinance (Islamic penal laws governing compensation and retribution in crimes involving bodily harm).

The general elections, which were held on 16 November 1988, led to Benazir Bhutto, becoming Pakistan's and Muslim world's first female head of the government. The civilian government heralded a new era which promised an unprecedented alignment of state power with an apparently progressive woman's rights policy. But soon after the election, it became evident that, once again, the protection of women's rights had been subordinated, to maintain a delicate balance between various political forces, including those representing conservative religious values. Although the campaign pledged to resurrect the women's rights and to repeal the Hudood laws, the other discriminatory statutes had great appeal during terms in office, and not a single Islamization law was repealed. In 1997, the new government which assumed the prime ministerial office adopted policies which appeared to have blocked many opportunities for the advancement of women's rights. The government of the time in parliament enacted the Qisas and Diyat Ordinance which instituted *Shariah*-based changes in Pakistan's criminal law, making it a permanent part of the Pakistan Penal Code, rather than an ordinance subject to periodic renewal.

The continuing so-called "Islamization" efforts not only reinforced the legitimacy of perhaps somewhat discriminatory laws but, in effect, also bestowed greater discretion and authority on judges to invoke the so-called Islamic precedents and references at random.

Under General Pervaiz Musharaf's government, women were encouraged to participate in the national politics. The discriminatory laws against women's rights were being looked into for repeal of the old ordinances. The then Minister of State, Rtd. Justice Majida Rizvi of the Women's Commission organized a workshop on Hudood Ordinance and other discriminatory laws.

The prevailing trends in the health and education sectors are encouraging. Three federal ministers pertaining to the Departments of Education, Law and Population were women. Moreover, the participation of women in the national assembly is encouraged; currently 8 women have been elected

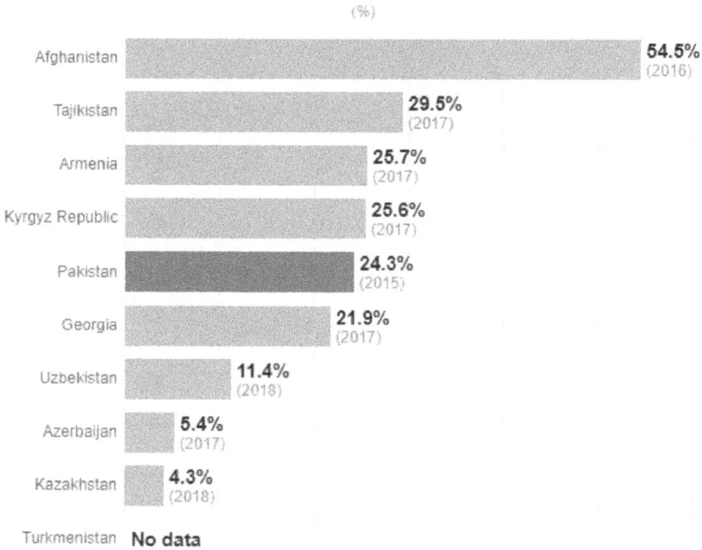

Figure 19.1 Share of Pakistani population below the poverty line.
Source: Asian Development Bank (2019).

for general seats, 60 seats are reserved for women in national assembly, and one non-Muslim seat. This allows 20% of the seats in national assembly being represented by women.

Women's awareness of their rights has increased, undoubtedly due to the relentless endeavors of Pakistani Women's Rights groups. However, most women still remain ignorant of even their most basic rights. But still clear violations of International Law in the Rights of Women occur daily in Pakistan and other South Asian countries. Laws that discriminate against women remain on the books and are actively enforced, discrimination in access to government resources and services continues unchecked, and discriminatory practices go unpunished (Niaz, 2003).

19.5 Social dilemmas, menaces and stigmas in Pakistan

The major culprit tends to be the poverty and lack of education that is stemmed from the former. As per the figures by Asian Development Bank, almost 24.3% of the Pakistani population were below the poverty line in 2015. Figure 19.1 shows the comparison of Pakistan with some developing nations of the region.

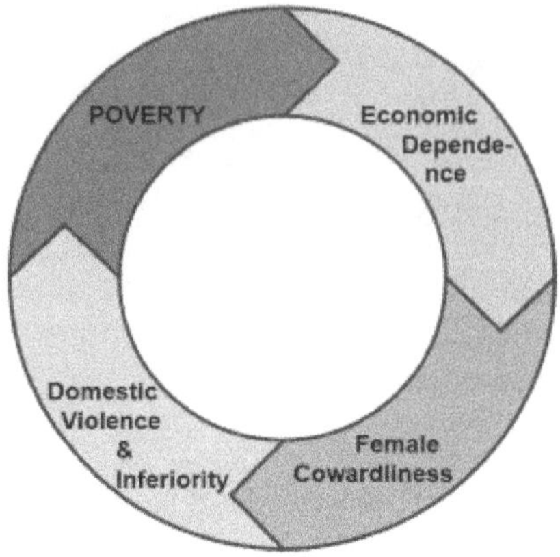

Figure 19.2 The vicious cycle for women.

Poverty happens to be the driver of a vicious cycle that entraps women of a developing society. Being members of a patriarchal social structure, the lower-class ends up prioritizing educational and social development of male children over the female ones, and restrains the latter to four walls of a house for domestic learning only. If school education is expensive, and not freely provided by the government, the poor families tend to spend only on son's education, considering that they would then support their family, whereas the daughters would be married off, and therefore responsibility of their husbands.

Whereas male children are naturally deemed to be the financial support system for the family, this however is not the case in the upper-middle, upper or even in middle class. It occurs that the role of women is an exact opposite in the elite class, their women are quite functional and proactive in social and professional activities, either adding their bit to home finances or being total financially self-sufficient. In a long run, this would eventually have a trickle-down effect but for now, progression is lagged and meddled by severity of economic conditions, as mentioned afore. Consequently, the psychological barriers do not seem to evolve and pose a greater challenge in the much-needed shift in the collective thought process, then there would be a way forward and our ever-growing human capital of women could be capitalized upon to reap socio-economic benefits.

Figure 19.2 depicts the social vicious cycle that encapsulates women and hinders their fateful evolution.

As the social bounds limit their prospects, their ancestral influence impresses them to be compliant of the system rather accept it in inheritance in their formative years and this has been passed on as a generational norm. Mothers preaching their daughters of patience, imprinting the significance of tolerance on their receptive minds and leaving them in a limbo of monotony with remote chances of any counter-narratives to ever pop up on self-discovery or purely miraculous basis.

The product of this kind of child-rearing leads to a stereotypical girl, ready to be wed-locked and be subservient to her husband for the rest of her days. Lack of awareness comes from her perception from early days; had her first institute, her mother, been an educated woman, the life of the poor child could be quite different. She could have developed an instinct of learning, would have pursued formal education and may have become an informed individual, who would do a better job at bringing up her children, be aware of her civil rights, be more involved in the economy and much relevant to the modern society.

Yet another challenge that casted a shadow for women to deliberate any promising efforts in early days of Pakistan, was the absence of social security and no old age benefits. A dilemma is that educated woman today are not career-oriented — they would outperform their male counterparts academically by miles and that too consistently, but later in career would retract from the leading positions, often due to social pressures or family responsibilities. This has been observed largely, as soon as they are done with universities and professional education, they would engage in a job or alike activity as per a transition phase till the time they are officially married to a *financially sound* suitor of the opposite gender, pertaining to the lackluster on their own part and taking them back in the fold of economic dependence, all over again, this time may be for good. This is an established fact that only features a few exceptions from the female population of the country. Perhaps one factor partially responsible for this is that from early childhood, boys are not groomed to help out in even the most basic chores at home — this is considered the exclusive domain of girls. So, when a married wife decides to focus on her career and double her efforts at her work and qualifications, she is still held responsible for the every-day care-taking of her husband and home.

19.6 Women demographics and their participation

At the moment, females in Pakistan is almost an equivalent part of the Pakistan's 207 million population which is about 101 million (Pakistan Bureau of Statistics, 2017a). On the other hand, the female labor force participation rate is only 25%, though it is increasing by more than half over the past two decades (Asian Development Bank, 2016). In 1998, the female participation rate was at abysmal low, making just 2.23% of the total labor participation, despite all the socio-cultural and socio-political challenges the growth recorded has been steady and double digit in the last 20 years (Pakistan Bureau of Statistics, 2017b).

In Figure 19.3, comparative statistics shed light on how numbers have evolved in a span of 11 years, just above a decade period. On a brighter note, from 2002 to 2013, a prominent upward shift is observed, based upon fairer exposure to education, social awareness and the resultant overall employment status through the distinguished age groups in each respective year. Interestingly, each group has performed better than its former self and working-age bracket, from 15 years all the way to (around) 60 years (retirement age), all nine groups have shown noticeable growth in participation rates. Once again, education has emerged as a critical success factor here, as it has paved way for the rise in the female labor participation rate, from 36.9% in 2002 to 48.1% in 2013 (Women's Employment, 2014), recording almost a percentage increase on average each year.

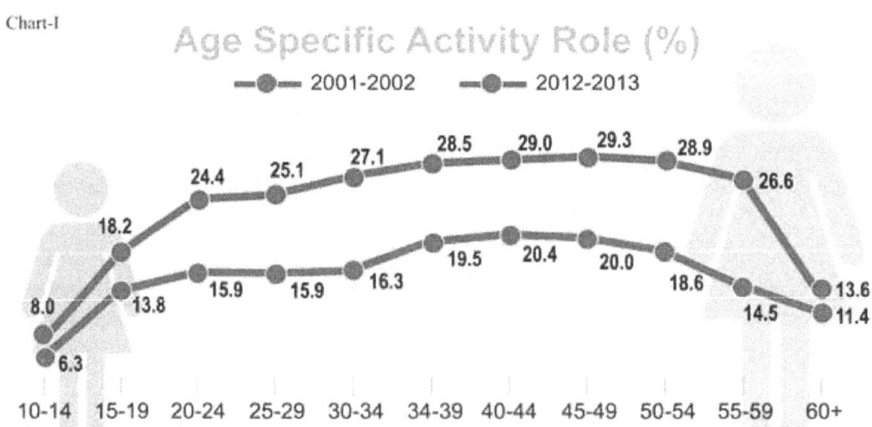

Figure 19.3 Female age group labor participation percentage.
Source: https://www.pakistangendernews.org/womens-employment/.

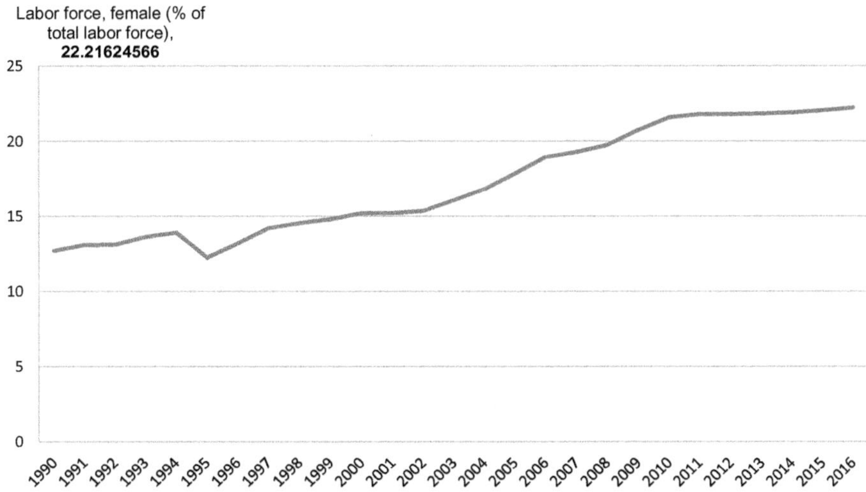

Figure 19.4 Female labor participation in Pakistan.[3]
Source: World Development Indicator, World Bank.

Figure 19.4 reflects the increasing trend of women in labor force of Pakistan (1990–2016).[4] Apart from that, women economic cooperation and integration in terms of ranking is very low. The Global Gender Gap Report 2018, by World Economic Forum, ranked Pakistan 148th in Global Index, 146th in Economic Participation and Opportunity, 139th in Educational Attainment, 145th in Health and Survival, and 97th in Political Empowerment.

The vitality and the potential of women in Pakistan has never been fully realized in the past 70 years regardless of having their male counterpart in every field of life. Pakistan's conservative patriarchal society is primarily held responsible for the relatively low female labor force participation rate. Although there are other complimenting factors that cause friction in female economic activation, as discussed earlier.

Figure 19.5 depicts the percentage participation of women in labor force, provincially segregated in the labor survey of 2014–2015. As it is evident from the illustration that the infrastructural development featuring

[3]Data on female labor force participation rate are taken from World Development Indicators (WDI) of the World Bank.
[4]Data from 1947 to 1989 are not available for the case of Pakistan.

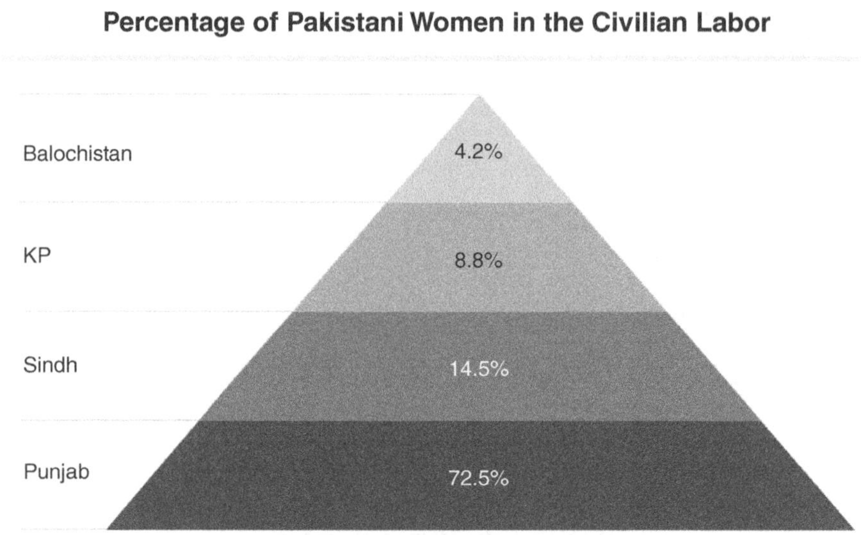

Figure 19.5 Women in civil labor by percentage.
Source: Pakistan Bureau of Statistic's Labor Force Survey 2014–2015.

relatively efficient education system, better social security, comparatively better off health care and living standard could have a major impact on the female population of the area. Thereby, Baluchistan being the least developed and lowest in population has formed tip of the pyramid with negligible women participation, KPK has slightly better result with almost twice the rate of labor share. Sindh, chiefly due to Karachi, biggest metropolis of Pakistan and the only commercial port-city has helped the province secure a second position with a little less than two-fold female activation to KPK. Whereas, Punjab is head and shoulders above all three provinces, even combined figure for Sindh, KPK and Baluchistan sit behind Punjab alone for women engagement in the economic activity.

Furthermore, for the period in question, 14.66 million women (only 24%) in contrast to 46.38 million of their male counterparts were part of the workforce of Pakistan (Rehman *et al.*, 2017).

19.7 Governmental endeavors to escalate presence of women in economy

The constitution of Pakistan is very inclusive of women, attempts to safeguards their equitable human rights and empowers the state to go an extra mile for children and women to make a special provision, in case a need arises to ensure their protection.

The **Article 25** states: **Equality of citizens.**

(1) All citizens are equal before law and are entitled to equal protection of law.
(2) There shall be no discrimination on the basis of sex.
(3) Nothing in this Article shall prevent the State from making any special provision for the protection of women and children.

A complimentary **Article 27 provides Safeguard against discrimination in services.**

(1) No citizen otherwise qualified for appointment in the service of Pakistan shall be discriminated against in respect of any such appointment on the ground only of race, religion, caste, **sex**, residence or place of birth, it enabled women to enter the esteemed civil service of Pakistan on equal opportunity basis in all cadres that fall under the umbrella of the CSS. It was further substantiated in 2006, when women were granted 10% reserve seat quota to enhance the women participation in the Central Superior Services (Fatima, 2017).

Similarly, **Article 32** mandates the state to designate representation of women in local Government institutions, as follows:

Promotion of local Government institutions. The State shall encourage local Government institutions composed of elected representatives of the areas concerned, and in such institutions special representation will be given to peasants, workers and women.

To supplement the effect, the constitution of Pakistan emphasizes the participation of women in all walks of life in the motherland, **Article 34** emboldens the guiding principle in the following text:

Full participation of women in national life. Steps shall be taken to ensure full participation of women in all spheres of national life.

Moreover, **Article 37(e)** obligates the employer to assure workplace safety, healthy, secure and conducive environment for women to perform their duties effectively. The directions given in the Article are as such:

Promotion of social justice and eradication of social evils. Make provision for securing just and humane conditions of work, ensuring that children and women are not employed in vocations unsuited to their age or sex, and for maternity benefits for women in employment.

In addition, **Article 51, National Assembly** categorically mentions reservation of seats for women on national level public representation, as per the article out of total 342 seats, some 60 seats are specified for women from all four provinces, FATA and the Federal Capital, i.e., Islamabad.

Article 59, the Senate, lays down clear guidance in **59(c)** that a woman is to be selected in the Upper-house from the Federal Capital out of the 4 seats restricted for the city. Secondly, **59(d)** assigns members of each provincial assembly to elect 4 women.

Likewise, **Article 106 Constitution of Provincial assemblies** embodies 132 seats for women in all four provinces combined out of the total 728 seats (The Constitution of Islamic Republic of Pakistan).

Therefore, women of Pakistan have clairvoyant rights, dedicated and essential presence alongside dignified status in the political system of the state.

In order to promote gender equality and women empowerment, the federal government of Pakistan has agreed upon many international and nationwide commitments like Convention on Elimination of all Forms of Discrimination Against Women (CEDAW), National Plan of Action (NPA) and Millennium Development Goals (MDGs).

19.8 How far our women have come?

Seventy years after the hard-earned independence, and after relentless struggles to develop as a nation on a rather sluggish pace, we are still able to foresee promising times ahead, our women have proved to be tenacious and persistent and now the world acknowledges that. Pakistani women have been challenging stereotypes lately and making the difference in every field of the modern-day world, from Tech startups, Banking and Finance, Fashion, Visual and Performing arts, Education, Social entrepreneurship and as motivational ideals. To mention a few and their inspiring journeys, a business forum that has listed out Top CEOs of Pakistan for last 3 years, had stepped up their screening criteria due to increased competition and even then among the list of 13 top CEOs of 2017, there were 3 remarkable women with their distinguished names in one of the demanding and most challenging industries, namely investment banking and Fin-Tech (Mohammad, 2017).

Kalsoom Lakhani — CEO/Founder of Invest2Innovate (i2i): she set that up in 2011 to catalyze potential startups through their incubation phase to lead them to a sustainable business model. She has successfully led 25 startups ever since. She has trained and spoken at several international events, and was also nominated among Top 99 Foreign policy leaders under 33 in 2012. She is a U.S. graduate with masters in conflict resolution from George Washington University.

Ayesha Aziz — She is the CEO of Pak Brunei Investment Company; MBA alumnus from the prestigious IBA Karachi and retained the spot in the list for the second time. Her authority in investment banking, asset management and portfolio management has earned her the rightful place.

Maheen Rahman — She is an LUMS graduate who topped with Master's in Economics and Finance from Warwick Business School: she hauled IGI funds asset base in 2009 by an exponential growth of 200%. The company was later acquired by Alfalah GHP investment management, where she continues to be in the top office.

Maleeha Lodhi — She is currently a representative of Pakistan at the UN and a permanent ambassador, first female to be in the position, seasoned diplomat and a doctorate from London School of Economics. She was named in *Time* magazine as one of the hundred people who would shape the 21st century. She has also authored two books and edited another. Lodhi is an aspiration among the young women in Pakistan and beyond (Harvard Kennedy School, n.d.).

Malala Yousafzai — She is a young educationist and a philanthropist with special focus on female education, child activist and most notably the youngest Nobel laureate. She comes from very humble beginnings from Sawat, KPK in Pakistan, and her surge to prominence came after she was brought to limelight for her fondness for education in a documentary shot by Adam B. Ellick. She was also nominated for International Children's Peace Prize. In October 2012, she survived an assassination attempted by the Taliban, and that lead to a global uproar, which brought her to the mainstream media and she emerged as an inspiration for women across the globe for her persistence toward women's education (The Noble Prize, n.d.).

Muniba Mazari — She is a painter, motivational speaker, activist, model, TV anchor and a singer. Muniba is a symbol of resilience and firm belief. She hails from a Baloch background with rigid and strict family system, yet she has charted her own course and people are in her awe for her exhilarating optimism. Mazari is the ambassador to UN Women Pakistan and has been featured in *Forbes' 30* under 30 in 2016. She has been on wheelchair since 2007 after meeting a tragic road accident but that takes nothing away from her goodwill for all to absorb and prosper (Haider, 2019).

All the aforementioned women are only the highlight of what is to follow in forthcoming years; there are many in the pipeline, only to be launched in due time and pursued by even more aspirants to make it to the pinnacle of success. Pakistan continues with its mission to align itself with the vision of its founder, Muhammad Ali Jinnah, the message of our beloved Holy Prophet (pbuh) and to evolve as a balanced society that stands firm on the support system powered by both genders in harmony.

References

Asian Development Bank (2016), *Policy Brief on Female Labor Force Participation in Pakistan.*

Asian Development Bank (2019), "Poverty in Pakistan", available at https://www.adb.org/countries/pakistan/poverty accessed on 6 May 2019.

Eaton, G. (2000), *Remembering God: Reflections on Islam*, Cambridge, England: The Islamic Texts Society, p. 91, 93.

Esposito, J. (1986), Islam: Ideology and politics in Pakistan, in Ali Banuazizi and Myron Weiner (eds.). *The State, Religion and Ethnic Politics*, Syracuse, NY: Syracuse University Press, p. 336.

Fatima, Q. (2017). "Substantive Female Representation in Civil Service [Op-ed]", *Daily Times*, available at https://dailytimes.com.pk/120574/substantive-female-representation-in-civil-service/.

Harvard Kennedy School (n.d.), Dr. Maleeha Lodhi, available at https://iop.harvard.edu/fellows/dr-maleeha-lodhi.

Haider, M. (2019), "Muniba Mazari: A Picture of Fortitude", *Dawn*, available at https://www.dawn.com/news/1470533.

Hundal. S. (2007), "The Sexual Politics of Partition", *The Guardian*, available at https://www.theguardian.com/commentisfree/2007/aug/17/thesexualpoliticsofpartition.

Jawad, Haifaa A. (1998), *The Rights of Women in Islam: An Authentic Approach*, London, England: Palgrave Macmillan, p. 21.

Jayawardena, K. and de Alwi, M. (1996), *Embodied Violence: Communalizing Women's Sexuality in South Asia*, London: Zed Books.

Menon, R. and Bhasin, K. (1998). *Borders & Beyond Women in India's Partition*, New Brunswick, New Jersey: Rutgers University Press.

Mohammad, W. (2017), "Top CEOs in Pakistan — 2017", available at https://pakwired.com/pakistans-top-ceos-2017/ accessed date 30 August 2017.
Murata, S. (1992), *The Tao of Islam: A Sourcebook on Gender Relationships in Islamic Thought*, Albany: State University of New York Press, p. 14.
Niaz, U. (2003), Violence against women in South Asian countries. *Archives of Women's Mental Health*, 6(3), 173–184.
Nasr, S. H. (2004). *The Heart of Islam: Enduring Values for Humanity.* New York: HarperOne, p. 400.
Pakistan Bureau of Statistics (2017a), "Provisional Province Wise Population by Sex and Urban/Rural [Data file]", available at http://www.pbs.gov.pk/sites/default/files/DISTRICT_WISE_CENSUS_RESULTS_CENSUS_2017.pdf.
Pakistan Bureau of Statistics (2017b), "Labour Force Participation Rates [Data file]", available at http://www.pbs.gov.pk/sites/default/files//tables/LABOUR%20FORCE%20PARTICIPATION%20RATES.pdf.
Quaid-e-Azam on Women (2010), available at http://m-a-jinnah.blogspot.com/2010/12/quaid-e-azam-on-women.html.
Rehman, A., Naveed, F. and Raza, M. (2017), "A Pakistani Woman's Workplace Dilemma", *Dawn*, available at https://www.dawn.com/news/1318989.
The Noble Prize. (n.d.), "Malala Yousafzai — Biographical", available at https://www.nobelprize.org/prizes/peace/2014/yousafzai/biographical/.
Visweswaran, K. (2011), *Perspectives on Modern South Asia: A Reader in Culture, History, and Representation*, Hoboken: Wiley-Blackwell.
World Economic Forum (2018), *The Global Gender Gap Report 2018.*
Women's Employment (18 August 2014), "Pakistan Gender News", available at https://www.pakistangendernews.org/womens-employment/.
World Bank Pakistan Celebrates Pakistani Women's Achievements (2013), available at http://www.worldbank.org/en/news/feature/2013/04/05/world-bank-pakistan-celebrates-pakistani-womens-achievements.

Chapter 20

Gender Relations in Singapore Malay (Muslims) Dual-Income Households: (Un)changing Views and Practices

Suriani Suratman

Abstract

Over the last four decades the labor force participation rate of women in Southeast Asia has been steadily increasing. While gender relations are changing in the public sphere as more women play dominant roles in the employment sector, whether gender relations in the domestic sphere are changing is rather ambiguous. In this chapter, the author looks at gender relations in Singapore Malay dual-income households. She shows that there are existing cultural perceptions of Malays regarding the roles of women and men in the family, i.e., women see to care-giving and men see to bread-winning. She also argues that parallels of this perception can be found at the state level as well. The Singapore government too is of the view that the primary caregiver in the family is the woman. The author illustrates this by using the example of the discourse on the "supermom" in Singapore to show the government's expectations of women's role as mother. There is external support which makes Malay women affirm their maternal role. In conclusion, the author suggests that Malay women and men's decisions around the division of labor must be conceived within the wider framework of society. Explanations for persistence of unequal division of labor in Malay dual-income households must take into account state views of gender roles.

Keywords: Gender relations, Singapore, Malay Muslims, Dual-income households, Maternal role

For quite some time, the labor force participation rate of women in Southeast Asia including Singapore, has been steadily increasing. Women are making the choice to stay employed after marriage and childbirth

(Stivens, 2007; Roces and Edwards, 2009). Malay women in Singapore too are making the choice to be employed. Consequently, the labor force participation rate of Malay women is steadily increasing. While there are Malay women who are leaving the work force after getting married, about 46% (Singapore Department of Statistics, 2006) continue to stay employed. Studies on employed women in the United States, Australia and Europe show that apart from having to fulfill demands at their workplace, women are also responsible for work at home (Hochschild, 1989; Shelton, 1992; Goodnow and Bowes, 1994; Brannen and Moss, 1991; van der Vinne and Brink, 1997; Walper and Galambos, 1997). Furthermore, findings from these studies show that women see to the bulk of the household work. The view that women are the primary caregiver remains. Findings from my study show that Malay women in Singapore are seeing to the bulk of household work (Suratman, 2002a). Nevertheless, Malay men are assisting their wives in carrying out household work. There seems to be some change in practices of sharing out work in Malay households. This change however depends on three factors: women's time constraints, notions of skills in carrying out tasks and availability of partners to carry out tasks (Eadem, 2003). I also found that the women in my study are the ones who decide what tasks can be transferred and to whom these tasks can be delegated to (Eadem, 2009). As such Malay women's notions of women and men's work matter in defining what her husband can or cannot do. It appears that Malay women's maternal gate-keeping is inhibiting Malay men's involvement in household tasks and therefore determining more equal household division of labor.

In this chapter, I show that there are existing cultural perceptions of Malays regarding the roles of women and men in the family, i.e., women see to care-giving and men see to breadwinning. Malay women who are employed do not relinquish care-giving tasks. More importantly I argue that parallels of this perception can be found at the state level. The Singapore government too is of the view that the primary caregiver in the family is the woman. I illustrate this by using the example of the discourse on the "supermom" in Singapore to show the government's expectations of women's role as mother. Indeed, as Allen and Hawkins (1999) also point out, there is external support which makes Malay women affirm their maternal role. In conclusion, I suggest that Malay women and men's decisions around division of labor must be conceived in a wider framework of society. Explanations for persistence of unequal division of labor in Malay dual-income households must take into account the state's views of gender roles.

20.1 Malay women's participation in the labor force

20.1.1 Industrialization and female labor force participation

When the Singapore government embarked on its industrialization journey soon after independence in 1965, women were highly encouraged to participate in its labor force. Rapid industrialization in this period had caused a labor shortage to the extent that foreign workers had to be employed (Wong, 1975). The concern of the government then was how to increase the country's supply of labor. The focus was directed at young women who were described by the then Prime Minister Lee Kwan Yew as "underutilized".[1]

Women were drawn into the labor force — albeit in the low-income jobs. The female work force was predominantly in the labor-intensive manufacturing industries such as electronics and textiles (Eng and Keong, 1984; Lee *et al.*, 1999). This was followed by commerce and trade sector where women worked as secretaries, clerks, saleswomen or service personnel and finally in the professional and technical sector as teachers and nurses (Eng and Keong, 1984; Lee *et al.*, 1999, p. 14).

Judging from the statistical data, the Singapore government's policies regarding the increase of the female labor force participation was a success. Since the 1970s the rate has been steadily increasing. Not only is there an increase in female labor force participation but the participation rate of married women in the labor force is also rising. This can be seen in Table 20.1. The General Household Survey 2005 reported that the growth rate of labor force participation was higher for females than males (Singapore Department of Statistics, 2006, p. 21).

A breakdown according to the ethnic groups shows that even though the Malay female labor force participation rate is lower than for other groups, nevertheless, Malay female labor force participation has been steadily increasing since 1970 (see Table 20.2). The 2000 figures show a decrease in the participation rate of both Malay and Indian women. However, the General Household Survey 2005 shows that while there are Malay women who are leaving the labor force after getting married, 46% continue to stay employed.

[1]See Wong (1975), for the Prime Minister's remark in his appeal to the Singapore Employer's Federation.

Table 20.1 Labor force participation rate in Singapore.

	1970	1980	1990	2000	2010
Total labor force participation	55.3	63.2	63.2	63.2	66.2
Female labor force participation	**28.2**	**44.3**	**48.8**	**50.2**	**56.5**
Married women participation rate	14.7	29.8	45.6	49.2	58.4

Source: Department of Statistics Singapore (2011), Time Series on Labour Force Participation Rate, available at http://www.singstat.gov.sg/stats/themes/economy/hist/labour.html; Report on Labour Force in Singapore (2010), Department of Statistics Singapore — Singapore Population (2001), Singapore Census of Population 1990 Economic Characteristics, Census of Population Singapore 1980 Economic Characteristics.

Table 20.2 Female labor force participation rates, by ethnic group.

	1970	1980	1990	2000
Malay	14.3	44.6	45.0	40.8
Chinese	27.0	44.5	49.4	52.0
Indian	16.0	44.1	50.9	46.9
Others	23.9	34.7	42.0	45.7

Source: Statistics Singapore — Key stats, available at http://www.singstat.gov.sg. Census of Population 1980 Singapore Release No. 4 Economic Characteristics, Singapore Census of Population 1990 Economic Characteristics.

20.2 Trend toward dual-income couples

The increase in the participation rate of married women in the labor force contributed to the trend toward dual-income couples.[2] Over the last two decades the number of dual income couples in Singapore has been gradually increasing. Indeed by 1990 the number of dual career couples was 40% of the total married couples compared to 27% in 1980 (Singapore Department of Statistics, 1994, p. 3). In a labor force survey in Singapore, it was found that the number of dual-income households was 45% among married couples in 2001 (Ministry of Manpower, 2001, p. 3). Taking a closer look at women's participation in the labor force, the rate of participation

[2]I use the term dual-income couples and not dual-career couples in a similar manner as Lewis *et al.* have used the term dual-earner family. Dual-earner family applies to all families in which both spouses are employed. Dual-career families refer to "more elite groups of middle-class couples in high-status occupations with an opportunity structure, who may or may not be more highly committed to their jobs than the dual-earners" (Lewis *et al.*, 1992, p. 3).

corresponds with the level of educational attainment of women. Women with tertiary education are the majority of female labor force in Singapore (Ministry of Manpower, 2001, p. 3). There is a close relation between women's educational qualification and their participation in the labor force.

The increasing number of women in the labor force must also be seen in terms of occupational opportunities for women. The government's development strategy of import-substitution industrialization since Singapore's independence in 1965 has indeed created opportunities for women to work. In its efforts to restructure Singapore's economy in the late 1970s the government's emphasis on human resource development has increased its demand for labor even more. Singapore's Economic Development Plan for the 1980s, announced in Parliament, conveyed the government's commitment to "optimise scarce manpower by encouraging more women [...] to work" (Goldberg, 1987, p. 26).

The trend toward dual-income couples is also tied to rising standards of living. In a report of the national survey on married women in 1983, it was found that "about half of the married women indicated income as their main motive for working" (Ministry of Social Affairs, 1983). Furthermore, as pointed out by Yuen and Lim (1991), the extra income from working women allows families "to afford the many 'luxuries' which have become part and parcel of 'modern living'." This has also been highlighted by Lee *et al.* (1999). Data from the Department of Statistics show that the income of working women "has boosted the financial situation of married couples" (Singapore Department of Statistics, 1994, p. 9). In addition, the average percentage of a woman's earnings to the dual-income has increased from 36% in 1980 to 41% in 1990 (Singapore Department of Statistics, 1994, p. 10). Women's contribution to the household income has become increasingly significant.[3] It is thus important to note the combination of factors that explain the trend toward dual-income couples. Together with the push from the government for women to participate in the labor force and the increasing need for an extra income this new form of family structure comprising working parents is increasingly familiar in the lives of Singaporeans.

[3]Such a case is also found in other Asian countries, for example, India where "two incomes are essential for the vast majority of the middle class wishing to maintain a comfortable standard of living (Sekaran, 1991, p. 47). In other cases, such as in Sweden, the contribution of a woman's income is crucial where "two incomes are necessary to remain above the poverty line" (Sandqvist, 1991, p. 83).

20.3 Division of labor in dual-income households

20.3.1 Division of household labor and gender equality

Studies have shown that household work is women's work.[4] As such when women have paid work through employment, they are doubly burdened in having to do their "second shift" of having to see to household work (Hochschild, 1989; Bianchi, 2000, pp. 13–24). While studies show that men do carry out household and child-caring work, women still see to the bulk of household work (Hochschild, 1989; Brannen and Moss, 1991). In this body of literature on household division of labor, there are also those who argue that there are couples who "shared it all", i.e., housework, childcare and financial responsibility (Haas, 1982, pp. 747–760; Kimball, 1988). Goodnow and Bowes (1994) in their study of 50 couples from different socio-economic backgrounds in Sydney, Australia, elaborated on how "sharing" is worked out. The findings of their study show that couples moved away from the conventional distinctions between "men's work" and "women's work" by dividing work on the basis of fairness, practicality or likes and dislikes. These studies very often show that household and child-caring work is divided between wives and husbands (and sometimes children). There can be another solution, i.e., allocating tasks to yet another person such as a live-in helper. This option is available to couples in Singapore. This opens up questions as to whether such households are more or less equal.

20.4 Division of labor in Malay households in Singapore

In her ethnographic work on Malay households in Singapore in the late 1950s, Djamour (1959) described the clear division of responsibilities between women and men in Malay households. The head of the household is the chief wage earner and is usually a man. Women see to housework and caring small children. Because of the lack of other studies on Malay households at that time, Djamour's ethnography is indeed valuable and important in providing details of practices in Malay households. It nevertheless is vital to take note, as I have pointed out elsewhere, that Djamour's work tends "to subscribe to the notion of the ideal-type family or household" (Suratman, 2002b).

Studying Malays in Singapore, Li (1989) outlined the principle by which a Malay household is managed. She pointed out that the husband's

[4]For example, Oakley (1974) and Hochschild (1989).

obligation is "to provide adequate food, housing and clothing for his wife" (Li, 1989, p. 18) and the wife's obligation is to "provide domestic services for her husband and children" (Li, 1989, p. 19). Li, however, argued that there are internal negotiations. Nevertheless, her findings indicated the persistence of the principle that the Malay man has to provide financially for his wife and children and the Malay wife provides domestic services for her husband and children. Therefore, in cases where women are employed, they are seen to be going beyond their obligation. Furthermore, the idea of the husband's role to provide can be seen to operate in the household's budget where the husband's wage is used for "essentials" and the wife's income is used for items perceived as "supplementary" (Li, 1989, p. 18). In her study, Li emphasized what she thought was the common situation, i.e., one in which the wife was not working and the husband was the sole wage earner (Li, 1989, p. 20). Given that Li herself noted that Malay women were not forgoing the opportunity to have employed work, there is a need to take into account what the practices of management in Malay dual-income households are and to ask if the principle which Li cited continues to operate in such households.

20.5 Practices of division of labor in Malay dual-income households

My research on Malay dual-income households carried out between 2002 and 2006 looked at how young Malay couples manage child-caring as working parents. The use of the term "young" here is derived from the study by Wong (1992), which divides family according to its life cycles — that is, beginning family, young family, mature family and aging family. A young family is a nuclear family with young pre-primary and primary school children. Couples whose family life cycle is at the young stage face the need for childcare management and would need to work out the different tasks in child caring. A total of 10 dual-income couples who are professionals were interviewed (see Appendix 20.1A for profile of couples). I conducted in-depth semi-structured interviews. Each interview lasted between two and three hours. There were cases when follow-up interviews had to be conducted. While the focus was on child caring, the research also encompassed how working couples combine family and work in general. In the research, household tasks include both caring for children and seeing to housework. The delineation between child caring and household tasks is crucial especially to discern Malay men's contribution to household tasks.

The biggest challenge in the research was the time factor. It was not easy to accommodate the work schedules and family time of both informants and me. Some of the interviews had to be conducted within sandwiched time during lunch hours or after work before returning home. The time constraints faced by dual-income couples because of their work hours and family commitments is very evident.

Already at the beginning of my research I sensed that informants, both female and male, assume that women are responsible for child caring. This was reflected by an unwillingness of some male informants to be interviewed. These men explicitly said that their wives deal with anything to do with their children. Some of them agreed when I pressed to interview them while others were not keen to be interviewed. Five out of the 10 men agreed to be interviewed (Couples E, F, H, I and J). Out of the five who did not want to be interviewed, one (Couple G) could not fit in time because of his tight work schedule. The wife of another (Couple B) decided that it would not be necessary for me to interview her husband. It was not possible to persuade the husbands of the remaining three (Couples A, C and D) for an interview.

20.6 Distribution of child caring by young Malay dual-income couples in Singapore

The concern for working parents is how to combine family and work responsibilities. The most immediate dilemma for young dual-income couples is how to see to the caring of their young children while they are at work. I have dealt with the kinds of childcare arrangement options which young Malay dual-income couples decide on (Suratman, 2002c). In this chapter, I emphasize how Malay working parents handle child caring. Child caring involves many tasks. The child has to be bathed, dressed and fed for the babysitter, kindergarten or school. The child has to be brought to and from the child minder be it a member of the family or a childcare center. There is a need to put aside time for leisure with the child and for helping her/him to adjust and deal with kindergarten or school. When the child is sick, special attention and care must be given. In a family context of working mothers and fathers the caring for children has to be carefully thought over; requiring working out and carrying out tasks and always being prepared for the unexpected. One of my concerns in my research is how child-caring tasks are divided in Malay dual-income households.

20.6.1 Allocating daily child-caring tasks

In my interviews, informants were given a list of childcare tasks, which they could expand on. They were asked to indicate who carries out these daily tasks (see Appendix 20.2A). The tasks include bathing, dressing, changing diapers, meal preparation, feeding, ferrying children, playing, reading, supervising homework and putting children to sleep.

The kinds of tasks depend on the ages of the children. Thus, for example, babies and toddlers would need to be bathed, dressed, fed, have their diapers changed and put to sleep whereas schoolchildren would need supervision for their homework. Similarly, the need to see to particular tasks varies with age. For couples with schoolchildren the frequency of ferrying their children to school and other school-related activities is very high. Some couples send their children to special classes or tuition and therefore ferrying children is again high. Child-caring tasks in Malay dual-income households are divided between the couples sometimes shared out with their parents and in several cases allocated to live-in helpers (Eadem, 2009).

From the findings it is clear that in Malay dual-income households, wives carry out the bulk of the daily child-caring tasks particularly the preparation of meals. They rely on grandmothers and helpers to carry out some tasks such as bathing, dressing, changing diapers, meal preparation, feeding and playing. Other than ferrying the children, men do not predominate in any of the other child-caring tasks. For these other tasks, men share the workload with women.

20.6.2 Seeing to unpredictable childcare demands and other special requirements

Apart from the daily childcare tasks there are also childcare demands that are unpredictable (Eadem, 2003). In particular when children are sick special attention and care may be required. The task demarcations include taking the child to the doctor, caring for the sick child and administering medication. Who takes the child to the doctor depends on the seriousness of the child's illness.

If the child's situation does not require the attention of doctors immediately, most couples would take their sick child to the doctor together. This is often after their working hours, i.e., in the evenings or on a weekend. In a situation where the child is very sick and needs to be seen by the doctor immediately, who takes the child to the doctor would depend on who has the most flexible work hours. "It is easier for me to call my office and tell them I have an emergency and need to take my daughter to the clinic. It is not so easy for my husband because of his class schedule" (wife of Couple C). Similarly, in the case of Couple H where the husband has more flexibility at work: "It is easier for me to take off from work than my wife. Besides, I have the car" (husband of Couple H). Only one couple (Couple B) occasionally turns to the grandparents to take their sick child to the clinic. In this case the grandparents take care of the two children while the couple is at work. Couples do not usually take leave from work to be with the sick child. They rely on their respective child minders to look after the sick child, i.e., grandmothers or maids. However, in situations where the child is seriously ill, some of the women took leave from work to be at home with the sick child (Couples C and G). These women take advantage of the five days unrecorded leave per year granted to female civil servants for each child below 6 years old. Only one man (Couple E) took leave from work to take his sick child to the clinic and stayed home with his child. In this case, his wife is not a civil servant. Both parents and child minders, depending on who is available at the time the child needs to take her/his medicine, share administering of medication to the sick child. School holidays create a situation where schoolchildren will need to be taken care of during the time they would otherwise be in school. In my study, there are six couples with schoolchildren. Very often the children will be taken care of by the respective child minders. However, couples do make special arrangements for children to have activities during the school holidays. These special arrangements would involve extra ferrying of children or taking leave from work. As one woman relates: "My children get bored and that is when they start irritating each other. They will call me or my husband and start complaining. My husband and I will tell them what they can do for the day [...] but it is boring for them to be at home the whole day. Sometimes we take them to their cousins' house for them to spend the day or my sister will send her children over to our place [...] or they'll spend the day with their grandparents. This means that one of us will have to send them and pick them up. We take leave to go for a holiday together. The school holidays are long but I don't have that many leave days. Sometimes my husband takes the afternoon off from work when he doesn't have too much work. I try and make sure I come home early" (wife of Couple G). Two other couples (Couples F and J) arrange for their children to take part in holiday programs offered by private organizations or by schools. No ferrying is involved, as the children are old enough to take public transport: "My son is in the school band. The school has extra music practices during the school holidays because they are preparing for a music tour. We let him participate because he likes music and he has something to do during the holidays. Otherwise he will just be at home [...]. He goes to school by bus with a friend who lives nearby. It's not far [...] just a few bus stops" (wife of Couple J). Since the husband of Couple C is a school teacher, he is able to spend time with their two daughters during the school holidays. On the days when he has to be in school for a meeting, the live-in helper will look after the children. The wife will also take leave from work to spend time with the children during the school holidays. Three out of four of the children of Couple D are old enough to organize their own program during the school holidays. Nevertheless, both husband and wife do take leave to go for a holiday with the children.

There appears to be more sharing out between husbands and wives for unpredictable childcare demands and special requirements during school holidays. The common point in the narrations of informants, both women and men, are the time constraints because work conditions require them to be present at the workplace and, therefore, they are prevented from being present at home when their children are sick or when they have school holidays.

20.7 Division of housework in Singapore Malay dual-income households

Six of the 10 couples in my study have live-in helpers.[5] The main reason for these couples to have a live-in helper is to have someone mind their young children while they are at work. The added advantage of having a live-in helper is that housework can be transferred to the helper. Except for cooking, all couples who have live-in helpers transfer most housework tasks to their live-in helpers. In the case of two couples (Couples C, F) the women do the cooking for dinner although the helpers will be asked to prepare the ingredients for the dishes. For these women, the reason is because they prefer their own cooking to the cooking of the helper. The wife of Couple G occasionally cooks and the wife of Couple C sometimes cooks on weekends. There are differences in the practices of couples who do not have

[5]Eadem (2009). Couples C, D, E, F, G and H have live-in helpers (see Appendix 20.1).

live-in helpers. The wife of Couple A sees to all the household tasks: "I do everything. It's manageable — we don't have a big flat. I get up early to do the washing and hanging up of the clothes. And mopping I do before I go to bed. And ironing, when I am back from work. He will look after our daughter when I am doing the housework. He helps [...] like changing the cushions and curtains for Hari Raya" (wife of Couple A). For Couples B, I and J there is some sharing of household tasks although the bulk is seen to by the women. The tasks which men tend to see to include vacuuming, cleaning the bathroom and toilet. The housework task allocation in Couple I is based on whether the house space is seen to "belong" to either of them. For example, the kitchen is the wife's space so she sees to the cleaning of the kitchen. There are two toilets in the apartment; one claimed by the wife, the other by the husband. They clean their respective toilets. Similarly, they have their own work spaces and each is responsible to clean her/his space. The cleaning of the shared spaces like the bedroom and living room is however the responsibility of the wife: "That's because she wants it in a certain way" (husband of Couple I) [...] Yah, I like it cleaned in a certain way [...] we just do it differently and I like it my way" (wife of Couple I). Going to market is one task which most couples share irrespective of whether they have live-in helpers or not. The sharing varies from couples going to the market together (Couple B, C and H) or the husband driving the wife to the market and waiting for her to complete the purchases (Couple A), or the wife sees to shopping in the wet market and the husband going to the supermarket (Couple G) or, the market shopping is done by whoever has the time (Couple E, F and I). The wife of Couple D sees to the shopping and the husband of Couple J sees to the shopping. "I have always done it [...]. I like to go to the market. Anyway she [wife] doesn't like to go to the market" (husband of Couple J). Housework is clearly a woman's responsibility in the Malay dual-income households of my study. In accordance with the findings of other studies on the contributions of women and men to household tasks, Malay women continue to do the bulk of the work even when they are employed (Brannen and Moss, 1996). Living in Singapore allows for the hiring of live-in helpers — an option that is not always available in other countries. With a live-in helper household tasks which would have been done by women are transferred to another woman, i.e., the live-in helper. However, Malay women also see to training the live-in helper when they are newly employed. Those women in my study who have live-in helpers take charge in supervising their respective helpers with regards to the housework. If the work is not done satisfactorily, it is the woman who sees to it that the helper is told. As such, even when women are not directly carrying out housework tasks, they take full responsibility in ensuring that the tasks are carried out well by the respective helpers.

20.8 Task-sharing in Malay dual-income households changing practices

From the preceding section we can notice some changes in the division of labor in Malay dual-income households. While Malay women are managers of the household and continue to be responsible for the bulk of household work, there are changes in Malay women's practices of managing household work. This is especially so for women who have live-in helpers. Although some women had reservations about transferring the task of cooking to their helpers, most no longer directly perform the housework tasks. Clearly, the women in my study with live-in helpers have no problems transferring housework tasks to live-in helpers despite some women's occasional dissatisfaction with the quality of performance of their helpers. This is somewhat contrary to the findings of Inserto who found that even though the majority of the women in her study had live-in helpers, they relied on the helpers only to see to the cleaning of the house, doing the laundry and minimal cooking (Inserto, 1977, p. 116). Inserto also pointed out that the women in her study had anxieties about losing their spouses because of "perceived role changes" (Inserto, 1977, p. 136). The women in my study were more selective when transferring child-caring tasks to helpers. Women rarely transfer child-caring tasks to helpers when they are at home. They would rather do these tasks themselves while the live-in helpers are made to carry out housework tasks. Some of the women feel that transferring tasks to live-in helpers gives them "quality time" with the children: "My maid prepares dinner so when I come home, I have some time with my children before dinner. I take them to the playground or the swimming pool at our place" (Wife of Couple G). There are specific tasks which the women think their helpers are not capable of. This includes spending playtime with children or reading to children. Live-in helpers are delegated all other child-caring tasks. As such, the women in my study do not have uncertainties about transferring most of the child-caring tasks to their helpers unlike the women in Inserto's study (Inserto, 1977, p. 135).

Women are turning to their husbands to assist them. As pointed out, the delegation of housework tasks to men depends on whether or not couples have live-in helpers. In the absence of live-in helpers, women rely on husbands to see to some housework tasks. However, even with helpers they do depend on their husbands for assistance in some child-caring tasks. Malay fathers, like their counterparts in America (Coltrane, 1996) and Britain (Brannen and Moss, 1991), do carry out some child-caring tasks. Nevertheless, the Malay men in my study mostly perform these tasks as helpers, i.e., taking instructions from their wives. This applies even to the task of ferrying children which the Malay men in my study predominantly carry out. Brannen and Moss, in their study on constraints that women in Britain face in combining employed work and motherhood, found that the men also carry out tasks "in the role of assistant, helping out with children [...] rather than the role of equal participant" (Brannen and Moss, 1991, p. 191). In his study on American men's involvement in family work, Coltrane also found that men are generally "helper husbands" (Coltrane, 1996, p. 74). There are differences in the amount of Malay men's contributions to housework. Men in households with live-in helpers do less housework tasks than those men in households without live-in helpers. While the decision to hire live-in helpers is to mind young children while parents are at work, helpers are made to do the bulk of housework tasks. There is therefore no change for the men in such households where housework division of labor is concerned. However, men in households without live-in helpers are helping out in some housework tasks. Indeed, findings from my study show that there are small changes taking place in Malay dual-income households. There is some sharing of child-caring and housework tasks between husbands and wives of the households. All men in my study do carry out some household work. This echoes the study by Coltrane and Adams (2001) who found that men in dual-income households in America participate in both child-caring and housework tasks. Like Sullivan (2006) I stress the importance of recognizing such small changes. There has indeed been a transformation within Malay households when we look back to earlier studies on household division of labor which show that there was hardly sharing of household work between Malay women and men (Djamour, 1959).

20.9 Determinants for sharing household work

The sharing of household work, however, cannot be assumed. Taking a closer look at the nuances of the sharing of household work, there are factors which determine when sharing occurs between husbands and wives. Here, it is significant to note that Malay women are managers of the household. As managers they are the ones who decide what tasks are to be delegated to someone else as well as to whom the tasks should be delegated to.

20.9.1 Women's time constraints

Clearly employed women cannot fully see to all household tasks because of their work responsibilities. The normal eight working hours, not inclusive of travel time to and from work, means that mothers need to manage their time. Not having enough time is a concern shared by the mothers in my study. They say that they "do not have enough time" (*tak ada masa*) for the tasks they have to do. But it is only when the time constraint is acute that women will transfer tasks. Prior to having a live-in helper Couple E had to share out the housework task:

"Both of us had to do the housework [...] we come home late. I can't do everything on my own. I clean the house. He ironed the clothes. (Wife of Couple E) Weekends [...], sometimes at night [...]" (husband of Couple E).

Women also transfer child-caring tasks to their husband:

"It's always a rush in the mornings. The maid will see to breakfast. The children will have to be woken up. I will wake the older children. My husband will wake our youngest up and get him ready. I can't do everything. I need help. The children won't be ready on time for the school bus [...]" (wife of Couple G).

"Sometimes I ask my husband to take them to the doctor when they are sick especially when I have to work on Saturday and he doesn't. I tell him [...] how can I go? I have to work so he has to take them" (wife of Couple D).

Time constraints faced by women are clearly a result of work demands where women have very little space to negotiate their time. Their concern here is that someone else other than them has to see to the task.

20.9.2 Notions of skills in carrying out tasks

Women say that they transfer tasks according to the ability (or inability) of the husband:

"I prepare the dinner while my husband minds the children. It's not that he can't cook. He can cook [...] simple dishes. But he takes too long. I can cook better and faster than him" (wife of Couple C).

"My husband doesn't bathe her [daughter] or change nappies. He cannot do these things [...], he doesn't know [...], he's not used to doing this [*tak biasa*]. So I do everything" (wife of Couple A).

This also applies to housework tasks:

"I don't expect my husband to do housework. It's not saying anything bad about him. He can do other things but housework [...]. I don't think he can" (wife of Couple D).

Goodnow and Bowes (1994) highlighted competence of partners as a contributing but not a decisive factor for sharing out household work. The couples in their study say that competence is not a "real reason" and may be challenged (Goodnow and Bowes, 1994, 144). The aforementioned narrations show some women excusing their husband for incompetence or setting their standards to judge their respective husbands' level of competence. However, not all women in my study excuse or judge their husband's skills in carrying out household work. Interestingly husbands of those who do, tend to refuse to be interviewed.

20.9.3 Availability of partners to carry out tasks

Some couples declared that their particular allocation of child-caring tasks is for practical reasons. The partner's work schedules or other responsibilities either make them available or not available to carry out child-caring tasks. The husband of a couple did say that he actually could cook better than his wife. His wife agrees but he still does not see to daily meal preparation:

"He [husband] can cook very well [...] better than me. If we invite family and friends he will cook but he doesn't cook every day. No time [...] he's so busy. He has to visit his sick father every evening after work. So I cook" (wife of Couple E). In the case of Couple J, for example, the wife sees to the caring needs of their son because she works from home whereas her husband is away at work. Differing as well as flexible working hours of couples also means that a task has to be assigned to the partner who is available.

"He [husband] starts work very early and his working hours are fixed whereas mine are flexible and erratic sometimes. I can go in late but I also get back home late. So I get the children ready, give them breakfast and take them to the childcare center by taxi. He has the car and picks them up from the center and sees to their dinner. Sometimes he will pick me up from work and we'll go out for dinner" (wife of Couple I). Similarly, when a partner is not available because of long working hours then the other has to see to the child-caring tasks. There were two couples (F, G) where the male partners have longer working hours and therefore their wives carry out child-caring tasks or allocate them to live-in helpers:

"He [husband] comes home late because he has meetings with clients. So, most of the time I spend the evenings with the children. He is just not there" (wife of Couple G). That men are less available for child-caring and housework tasks because they work longer hours is familiar in the literature.[6] Availability as a factor affecting the way in which household tasks are arranged has also been pointed out by Goodnow and Bowes (1994).

20.10 Malay women and maternal gate-keeping

In their study of women from dual-income households in America, Allen and Hawkins (1999) argue that "maternal gate-keeping", i.e., the idea that only women can see to certain tasks in the household, inhibits greater involvement of men in household and child-caring work. Allen and Hawkins (1999) outlined three dimensions of maternal gate-keeping: "mother's reluctance to relinquish responsibility over family matters by setting rigid standards, external validation of a mothering identity, and differentiated conceptions of family roles."

My study provides findings that there are Malay women who "gate-keep". This is exemplified in the way that Malay women as managers of households, decide what tasks husbands can or cannot do. To this extent, very much depends on what she defines as women's work and men's work. Women in my study determine the ability or inability, efficiency or inefficiency of their husbands in performing household and child-caring tasks and decide whether or not a task should be assigned to their respective husbands. While all the women with live-in helpers express the need to train their helpers (especially the new ones), none have expressed the need to teach their husbands skills to carry out tasks. It is also important to note that the men, who were willing to be interviewed, do not refuse the tasks that are allocated to them by their wives. It appears that Malay women's maternal gate-keeping is excluding more opportunities for collaborative arrangements for family work. I would however exercise some caution in that gate-keeping is not restricted to mothers. Fathers too can carry out

[6] For example, Brannen and Moss (1991) and Shelton, (1992).

paternal gate-keeping in various domains pertaining to roles within family life. One indication of this is the way that most of the men in my study very often initially questioned the necessity to be interviewed in this study because "child-caring is my wife's department". As pointed out by Coltrane (1996), the belief of separate spheres and distinct roles for mothers and fathers are not confined to women alone. He argues that men's willingness to be involved in family work is very much tied with their view about women and men's roles.

20.11 Views on gendered roles — beyond households

Views about gendered roles are not confined to the households. In this section, I show the prevalence of the view of gendered roles outside of the households. My concern here is with regards to "maternal identity confirmation" which Allen and Hawkins (1999) delineate as a dimension of gate-keeping. They emphasize "the impact that the internalization of cultural expectations of mothering has on attitudes about maternal and paternal involvement in family work" (Coltrane, 1996, p. 204). In this regard, I demonstrate the occurrence of such external validation in the Singapore context. I first of all look at Malay cultural expectations of "the ideal Malay woman". I then present the discourse of the "supermom" to show the Singapore government's expectations of woman's role as mother.

20.12 Singapore Malay cultural perceptions of roles of women and men

To reiterate, studies by Li (1989), Zarinah (1990) and Inserto (1977) indicate that there are prevailing Malay cultural perceptions regarding roles of women and men. In her study on how Malay women manage their multiple roles as worker, mother and wife Inserto points out that while the preference of the women in her study is for an egalitarian relationship whereby husbands will help out, there is nevertheless an underlying view that "the husband's main responsibility is to provide for the family, and the wife's duty is to take care of the family" (Inserto, 1977, p. 137).

Such perceptions are reproduced in different sites. Nurhaizatul, for example, critically analyzed portrayals of Malay women in the *Berita Harian*, the local Malay newspaper. Covering the period between the 1970s and 2009 she uncovered the constructions of "the ideal Malay woman" that among others include articles which reminded Malay women of her "important duty" to "organize the household effectively" (Jamil, 2009, pp. 20–21).

Indeed, within the context of Malay women's increasing involvement in the labor market, their roles as mothers and wives become crucial elements in which these perceptions of gendered roles surface. This is visible is public talks on topics pertaining to the family organized by Malay organizations and mosques[7] The emphasis in these talks is always on the gendered role of men and women, i.e., the responsibility of the father is to provide and the responsibility of the mother is to take care of children. An example can be seen in a public forum organized by the Malay Activity Executive Community (MAEC) of the Clementi Community Centre on the theme of "Harmonious Family" (*Keluarga Harmoni*) in September 2003. Local and regional religious experts were invited to talk at the forum. In this forum both speakers are of the opinion that a harmonious family is achieved when all family members perform their respective roles accordingly. The role of the father is to provide and lead while the role of the mother is expressed in terms of the mother's responsibility to give love and care (*beri kasih sayang*). Citing verses from the *Qur'ān* these religious experts reiterate that such roles are backed by the tenets of Islam. In a Friday prayers sermon,[8] the Muslim congregation is reminded that "[h]usbands have a heavy responsibility. He is a leader. He is responsible for leading the family, for controlling it and for protecting each member in it. [...] Wives also have a role to play. They give birth to a new generation of Muslims. They raise children who contribute to the community." That expectations of Malay women's role are very much informed by religion is clearly illustrated by Nurhaizatul's study on Singapore Malay women's embodied agency. She showed how duties of a mother and wife are perceived as religious contributions (Arab. *'ibadah*). As such, all household tasks are acts of piety (Jamil, 2009, p. 50).

Malay organizations also repeat the perceptions of gendered roles of Malay women and men. This is discernible in the efforts of Majlis Ugama Islam Singapura (MUIS) or the Islamic Religious Council of Singapore to remind Muslim parents of their responsibilities. In August 2000, MUIS launched its Family Development Department TAQWA Family Values

[7]As part of my study, I attended talks organized by Malay organizations as well as mosques on topics related to the family.
[8]MUIS, 27 July 2001.

campaign following the recommendations made by the Muslim Divorce Committee to look into rising divorce rates. Focusing on the need to build "strong and cohesive families", the campaign carried out talks promoting the idea of TAQWA family. An aspect of such a family is the need for parents to fulfill their responsibilities (*tanggung jawab*) as fathers and mothers, i.e., to see to the provisions to children and to see to caring for children, respectively. Such views recur in marriage preparation courses which Malay couples have to attend prior to solemnizing their marriage. These courses are offered by private companies that are endorsed by the Registry of Muslim Marriages in Singapore. Stretching over two days the course prepares couples with "the knowledge and skills for marriage, financial management, relation communication skills and managing the responsibilities, pressures and expectations of married life".[9] *Bersama Mu* (Together with you) Marriage Preparation Course for example offers couples an interactive 14-hour session designed by marriage counselors. A range of topics are covered including roles and responsibilities of husband and wife. Shared responsibilities are discussed. However, the underlying understanding remains of the provider role of the men and the care giver role of the women. It can be seen that existing Malay cultural expectations of women's role predominantly stress appropriate behavior of mothers as care givers. Indeed, from the narrations of the women in my study, Malay women who are employed do not willingly relinquish care-giving tasks. These women refer to these normative guidelines that spell how they should behave. It can be inferred that while the Malay women in my study are increasingly pursuing education and career their role as mothers remain vital to them.

20.13 The discourse on the "supermom": the government's perceptions on the woman's role as mother

In the earlier efforts to promote women to participate in the work force, it was assumed that women would continue to fulfill their role as wives and mothers. How this role is to be fulfilled was very much left to individual women to work out. So, while the government wants a change of attitude

[9]Registry of Muslim Marriages 2011.

and to "break barriers that keep women at home" it has left it to the woman "to choose her role."[10]

The kinds of answers that women gave when they chose to work reflected the tie between the roles of women as mothers. Wong points out that women turned to "the services of close kin and relatives living in the same household" but when these services were not available women "schedule their work activities in such a manner as to enable them to shoulder the burden of childcare and other household duties at the same time" (Wong, 1981, p. 42). Women were expected to take up the dual roles of mother and employee and see to mothering and work responsibilities. It was not until trends showing that women stopped work when they married and had children that the government began to concern itself with provisions for child-caring services.[11] In this section, I present the discourse on the "supermom" and thereby tease out the Singapore government's perceptions on woman's role as mother.

The attempts by the government to entice women to join and stay in the work force via a number of incentives and provisions since the early 1980s opened up debates in various directions pertaining to employment conditions and gender inequalities at work, woman's employment and child development as well as the suitable minding arrangements for children. These debates unveil the very notion of woman's role as mother. As such, when she is employed she therefore has to somehow juggle responsibilities at work and in the family.

In line with its need for female labor force participation the image of the "working mother" became a prominent feature. The positive outcome of employment for women and children became an argument and that "a woman can be a better mother if she is also a good worker."[12] Anticipating guilt conscience and concern about the mother–child relationship, experts in the form of psychologists, educationists and family counselors provided

[10] *The Straits Times* [Singapore] (2 March 1980), "Break Barriers that Keep Women at Home, Says Mattar".

[11] Quah (1998, p. 128) too points out that "[a]s the evidence on withdrawal from the labour force underscores the importance of motivating women to get a job and to remain working, policy planners felt that the most 'important issue is the availability of childcare facilities' ".

[12] *The Straits Times* [Singapore] (26 February 1984), "Good Worker = Better Mum. Eight Women Say Career Does not Mar Role as Mothers".

assurance that "the ill effects of maternal employment are not always evident".[13] Advice to women who were feeling guilty came from female readers of the local newspaper. The letters pointed to quality childcare in terms of time management: "efficiently using whatever time she is able to spend with the child" or "The mother can indeed organize her time efficiently, in accordance to the maturity of the child".[14]

Indeed, to be good mothers, women must "know how to divide your time".[15] In the local newspaper, stories of how women juggle family and work are presented. The answers range from having a husband who cooperates and does his share of housework to making child-minding arrangements, to juggling a full-time career and managing family with a live-in helper.[16] These stories end with a note of how "career and motherhood need not be mutually exclusive" (Ministry of Social Affairs, 1983, p. 9) and that women must learn how to do a "balancing act".[17] Being a mother therefore is the ability to balance family and work. When women are able to do this, they become "quality mums" or "supermoms".[18]

The government is not unaware that married women who decide to continue to work are facing problems in managing this "balancing act". Part of the problem is in the home. As a study by the Singapore Council of Women's Organizations found, "there was hardly any difference in the amount of housework done by the woman who goes out to work and one who stays at home".[19] That a coordinated national policy was needed to

[13] *The Straits Times* [Singapore] (3 July 1985), "When Mothers Go to Work ..."
[14] *The Straits Times* [Singapore] (8 October 1984), "Working Mothers Can Get Rid of Feeling of Guilt"; and *The Straits Times* [Singapore] (23 October 1984), "Working Women and Bringing up Children. Part-Time Work is the Real Answer".
[15] *The Straits Times* [Singapore] (26 February 1984), "Good Worker".
[16] *The Straits Times* [Singapore] (5 April 1982), "Fostering"; *The Straits Times* [Singapore] (22 February 1982), "A Quiet Revolution"; and *The Straits Times* [Singapore] (19 April 1982), "Time Tussle".
[17] *The Straits Times* [Singapore] (30 March 1984), "Balancing Work", *The Straits Times* [Singapore] (7 November 1987), "Mum Who Wants to Carry on Working: Fitting in Job and Family is a Fine Balancing Act"; and *The Straits Times* [Singapore] (30 September 1996), "Women Urged to 'Strike Balance'".
[18] *The Straits Times* [Singapore] (12 May 1985), "Dhana Supports 'Quality Time' Mums"; *The Straits Times* [Singapore] (9 May 1986), "'Supermom' Who's Working Smart"; *The Straits Times* [Singapore] (18 September 2000), "Supermoms"; *The Sunday Times* [Singapore] (18 January 2004), "Supermom".
[19] *The Straits Times* [Singapore] (8 March 1989), "'Housewives Cannot Be Nudged Back into Job Market'. Survey: Hardly Any Incentive for Them to Return to Work".

help women play "dual roles of being a mother and a working person" was spelled out.[20] This need was later reiterated at a United Nations forum on women in terms of improving women's lives.[21] The answers are formulated in terms of subsidy provisions and increasing numbers of childcare centers as well as improving their quality. This reinforces the government's push for women to be employed and for childcare centers as substitutes while mothers are at work.

Voices that called for men to change their attitudes and contribute to domestic chores and child-caring did surface in the parliament, in letters from the public, as well as through support of a woman's non-government organization, AWARE.[22]

This call was reiterated as a national survey and it found that "husbands are chief cause of problem".[23]

Over the following decades the government's stand continued to push women to balance family and work but while the emphasis in the 1970s and 1980s was to shift the weight from the family to employment, the emphasis from the 1990s was to push the weight to family:

Working women need to strike a balance between their career goals and family responsibilities so as not to neglect their children, especially when they are young, said Labour Minister Lee Boon Yang yesterday.[24]

While the idea of "part-time motherhood" of the 1980s lingers on, women are now asked to spend more time with their children.[25] There

[20] *The Straits Times* [Singapore] (2 January 1988), "Help Career Mums Play Dual Role — Coordinated National Policy Needed, Says MP".

[21] *The Sunday Times* [Singapore] (11 June 2000), "More Help for Working Mum Says Yu-Foo".

[22] *The Straits Times* [Singapore] (24 November 1983), "From Mum to Dad: Help Do the Chores"; *The Straits Times* [Singapore] (17 January 1989), "Call to Help the Working Mum in Other Ways"; *The Straits Times* [Singapore] (12 January 1980), "Sharing Domestic Chores 'Can Ease Burden on Wives' "; *The Straits Times* [Singapore] (2 October 1984), "It's About Time the Men did Something..."; *The Straits Times* [Singapore] (2 January 1988), "Working Mothers Torn between the Demands of Home and Workplace"; *The Straits Times* [Singapore] (14 November 1987), "Making Life a Little Easier for Our Working Mothers"; *The Straits Times* [Singapore] (30 January 1989), "Aware Backs Lobby by Working Mothers. Childcare Facilities Inadequate, Says Women's Group".

[23] *The Straits Times* [Singapore] (2 October 1996), "Stressed Out? It's Worst for Working Women".

[24] *The Straits Times* [Singapore] (30 September 1996), "Women Urged to 'Strike Balance' ".

[25] *The Straits Times* [Singapore] (3–4 February 1996), "Mums Who Work from Home".

were calls that more help is needed for "working mums".[26] Nevertheless, what prevails is the image of the "supermom" who succeeds in climbing up the career ladder and being 'number one person' to her children.[27]

Even as the government recognizes the need to help parents have a "work–life balance"[28] through its Marriage and Parenthood Packages of 2001, 2004 and 2008, these packages are based on the assumption that child-caring remains to be the responsibility of women. This can be seen, for example, in the number of leave days apportioned to mothers and fathers. Women have 16 weeks as compared to three to six days of paternity leave. Official responses to questions as to why paternity leave is still minimal were quick to cite studies from Scandinavian countries which show that "most men don't take paternity leave".[29] Interestingly, findings from a survey conducted by AWARE on parenting leave in Singapore show that when paternity leave is available 75% of the men in their study utilize it. More recently, in his Chinese New Year Message in February 2010 Prime Minister Lee Hsien Loong expressed his hopes that fathers will help working women to balance work and family:

"Husbands can do many things to help their wives look after the children, including changing the nappies [...]."[30]

Here, while the dual roles of women are taken for granted the dual roles of men as employees and fathers did not surface. Statements pertain to men having to assist. To this extent, what is being re-produced is women's role as mothers despite being involved in employed work and men's primary role remains as economic provider.

[26] *The Straits Times* [Singapore] (11 June 2000), "More Help for Working Mums, says Yu-Foo", and *The Straits Times* [Singapore] (15 November 2000), "Make Bold Moves for the Family, Urge MPs".
[27] *The Straits Times* [Singapore] (23 September 2000), "Fine Balance to Have It All — Kids and Career".
[28] Prime Minister National Day Rally Speech 2008.
[29] *The Straits Times* [Singapore] (3 September 2004), "Bringing Up Baby: Why Dads Can't Be Left Out", and *The Straits Times* [Singapore] (20 August 2008), "More Tax Breaks, Parental Leave to Boost Singapore's Birth Rate".
[30] *The Straits Times* [Singapore] (15 February 2010).

20.14 Conclusions and recommendations

What emerges from the findings of my study is as follows:

- There are changing practices in contemporary Malay dual-income households in Singapore in terms of household and child-caring tasks.
- However, there are unchanging perceptions pertaining to notions of women and men's work such that there is unequal distribution of labor. It seems that Malay women's maternal gate-keeping limits the Malay men's involvement in household and child-caring work.
- As I have also indicated, men's paternal "gate-keeping", although not the focus of my study, can also act as barriers toward a more equal division of household labor. These gendered notions of family work, however, are not confined to Malay women and men in the household.
- I have demonstrated that there are existing Malay cultural expectations as well as the Singapore government's perceptions that validate gendered division of labor in the household.
- It is therefore imperative to take into account these normative guidelines of appropriate gender behavior in an attempt to explain the persistence of an unequal division of labor.

Appendix 20.1A: Profile of couples.

Couples	Educational qualifications	Occupation	Combined household (approx)	Number of children	Ages of children	Current childcare arrangement	Cost
A	Sec.4 (wife) Sec.4 (husband)	Management officer Foreman	S$3,400	1	2	Grandparents	S$500
B	MA (wife) PSLE/VITB (husband)	Legal officer Storekeeper	S$7,200	2	8, 2	Grandparents	S$600
C	BA (wife) College (husband)	Admin. officer teacher (primary)	S$5,000	2	7, 3	Live-in helper	S$575*
D	Sec. 4 (wife) Sec.4/Malay stream (husband)	Management officer technician	S$4,600	4	19, 15, 11, 7	Live-in helper	S$605*
E	Sec. 4 (wife) Sec.2/VITB (husband)	Clerical officer Security officer	S$3,700	2	$1^{1/2}$, 6 months	Live-in helper	S$575*
F	PhD (wife) MSc (husband)	Lecturer librarian	S$11,500	2	10, 2	Live-in helper	S$645*
G	MEd (wife) MSc (husband)	Lecturer engineer	S$10,500	4	12, 10, 8, 6	Live-in helper	S$595*
H	MA (wife) PhD (husband)	Teacher (primary) Lecturer	S$10,000	3	7, 5, 3	Live-in helper/ Childcare center	S$595*/S$710†
I	BA (wife) MA (husband)	Feature writer Teacher (college)	S$8,000	2	5, 3	Live-in helper/ Childcare center	S$500/S$475†
J	Sec. 4 (wife)	Own business	S$4,500	1	13	Own	—

Note: *Includes Foreign Maid Levy of S$345. This amount however does not include the half yearly medical expenses required by the government and any other extra expenses such as food consumption, clothing etc.

†This is the total amount for all children after the subsidy of S$150 (full-day care) or S$75 (half-day care).

Appendix 20.2A: Division of daily childcare tasks.

	Bathing	Dressing	Changing diapers	Meal preparation	Feeding	Ferrying children	Playing	Reading	Homework	Putting children to sleep
A Wife	X	X	X	X	X	X	X	X	NA	X
Husband	—	—	—	—	—	X	X	—	—	—
Others (grandparents)	X	X	X	X	X	—	X	—	—	—
B Wife	X	X	X	X	X	—	X	X	X	X
Husband	X	X	X	—	X	X	X	—	—	X
Others (grandparents)	X	X		X	X	—	X	—	—	—
C Wife	X	X	—	X	X	—	X	X	X	X
Husband	X	X	NA	—	—	X	X	X	X	X
Others (maid)	X	X	—	—	X	—	—	—	—	—
D Wife	—	—	—	—	—	—	—	—	X	—
Husband	NA	NA	NA	—	NA	NA	—	NA	—	NA
Others (maid)	—	—	—	X	—	—	X	—	—	—
E Wife	—	—	X	X	—	—	X	—	—	X
Husband	—	—	X	—	—	NA	X	X	NA	—
Others (maid)	X	X	X	—	X	—	X	—	—	X
F Wife	X	X	X	X	X	—	X	X	X	X
Husband	—	—	X	—	—	NA	X	—	X	X
Others (maid)	X	X	X	X	X	—	X	—	—	—
G Wife	X	X	—	X	X	—	X	X	X	X
Husband	X	—	NA	—	—	X	—	X	X	X
Others (maid)	—	X	—	X	X	—	—	—	—	—
H Wife	—	—	—	—	—	—	X	X	—	—
Husband	—	—	NA	—	—	X	X	X	—	X
Others (maid)	X	X	—	X	X	—	—	—	NA	X
I Wife	X	X	—	X	X	X	X	X	—	X
Husband	—	—	NA	—	X	X	X	X	—	X
Others (grandparents)	X	X	—	X	X	—	—	—	—	—
J Wife	NA	NA	NA	X	NA	X	NA	NA	X	NA
Husband	—	—	—	—	—	—	—	—	—	—
Others (none)	—	—	—	—	—	—	—	—	—	—

References

Allen, S. M. and Hawkins, A. J. (1999), Maternal gatekeeping: Mothers' beliefs and behaviours that inhibit greater father involvement in family work. *Journal of Marriage and Family*, 61(1), 199–212.

Bianchi, S. M. (2000), "Setting the Stage: Work and family lives of Americans", in Eileen Appelbaum (ed.). *Balancing Acts: Easing the Burdens and Improving the Options for Working Families. A Conference Volume*, Washington DC: Economic Policy Institute, pp. 13–24.

Brannen, J. and Moss, P. (1991), *Managing Mothers: Dual Earner Households after Maternity Leave*, London: Unwin Hyman.

Brannen, J. and Moss, P. (1996), *Managing Mothers; Scott Coltrane, Family Man: Fatherhood, Housework and Gender Equity*, New York, Oxford: Oxford University Press.

Djamour, J. (1959), *Malay Kinship and Marriage in Singapore*, London: Athlone Press.

Eadem (2003), "Looking for Help: Organising Childcaring by Employed Women in Singapore", paper presented at the "Workshop on Women as Workers, Mothers and Caregivers: Coping with Changes, Challenges and Commitments", Singapore, 18 January.

Eadem (2009), "He Has a Career — So Does She! Changing Gender Relations in Singapore Malay Dual Income Households?" paper presented at the International Conference on Malay Culture and Society, Universiti Brunei Darussalam, Brunei, 3–6 November.

Eng, L. A. and Keong, Y. L. (1984), *Economic Restructuring, Female Labour Participation and Female Skills Formation in Singapore: 1976–1984*, Singapore: Asian Pacific Development Centre.

Gayle, K. (1988), *50–50 Parenting: Sharing Family Rewards and Responsibilities*, Toronto: Lexington Books.

Goldberg, S. (1987), Mixed messages: Public policy and women in Singapore: Commentary. *Journal of the National University of Singapore Society*, 7(2–3), 25–37.

Goodnow, Jacqueline, J. and Jennifer, M. Bowes (1994), *Men, Women and Household Work*, Melbourne: Oxford University Press.

Haas, L. (1982), Determinants of role-sharing behaviour: A study of egalitarian couples. *Sex Roles*, 8, 747–760.

Hochschild, A. (1989), *The Second Shift: Working Parents and the Revolution at Home*, New York: Viking Penguin Inc.

Idem and Adams, M. (2011), "Men's family work: Child-centered fathering and the sharing of domestic labour", in Rosanna Hertz and Nancy L. Marshall (eds.). *Working Families: The Transformation of the American Home*, Berkeley CA: University of California Press.

Inserto, F. E. (1977), *Choice, Social Structure and Serendipity: A Study of Multiple Roles Among 20 Malay Women in Singapore*, Ann Arbor MI: University Microfilms International.

Jamil, N. J. (2009), "Perempuan, Isteri, dan ... Embodied Agency and the Malay Women of Contemporary Singapore", MA thesis, National University of Singapore, Department of Sociology.

Lee, J., Campbell, K. and Chia, A. (1999), T*he Three Paradoxes: Working Women in Singapore*, Singapore: Association of Women for Action and Research.

Lewis, S., Izraeli, Dafna N. and Hootsmans, Helen (1992), *Dual-Earner Families: International Perspectives.* London: Sage Publications.

Li, T. (1989), *Malays in Singapore: Culture. Economy and Ideology*, New York and Singapore: Oxford University Press.

Ministry of Social Affairs (1983), Public Forum 'Married Women in the Workforce', Organised by the Ministry of Social Affairs on 25 November 1983, Regional English Language Centre, Singapore, Singapore: Ministry of Social Affairs.

Ministry of Manpower (2001), *Report on Labour Force in Singapore*, Singapore: Manpower Research and Statistics Department.

Mohamed, Z. (1990), "Parenting in Singapore: Father's Attitudes Towards Involvement in Childcare", academic exercise, National University of Singapore, Department of Sociology.

Oakley, A. (1974), *Housewife*, London: Allen Lane.

Quah, Stella R. (1998), *Family in Singapore: Sociological Perspectives* (2nd edn.), Singapore: Times Academic Press.

Races, M. and Edwards, L. (2009), *Women in Asia (Critical Concepts in Asian Studies)* (Vol. 1), London: Routledge.

Sandqvist, K. (1991), "Sweden's sex-role scheme and commitment to gender equality", in Lewis, S, Izraeli, D. N. and Hootsmans, H. M. (eds.). *Dual-Earner Families: International Perspectives*, London: Sage Publications.

Sekaran, U. (1991), "Middle-Class Dual-Earner Families and their Support Systems in Urban India", in: Lewis, S; Izraeli, D. N. and Hootsmans, H. M. *Dual-Earner Families: International Perspectives*, London: Sage Publications.

Shelton, B. A. (1992), *Women, Men and Time: Gender Differences in Paid Work, Housework and Leisure*, New York: Greenwood Press.

Singapore Department of Statistics (1994), "Dual-Career Couples in Singapore", Occasional Paper on Social Statistics, Singapore: Department of Statistics.3.

Singapore Department of Statistics (2006), *General Household Survey 2005*, Singapore: Department of Statistics.

Stivens. (2007). "Post-Modern motherhoods and cultural contest in Malaysia and Singapore", in Theresa Devasahayam and Brenda S.A. Yeoh (eds.). *Working and Mothering in Asia: Images, Ideologies and Identities*, Singapore: National University of Singapore Press, pp. 29–50.

Sullivan, O. (2006), *Changing Gender Relations, Changing Families: Tracing the Pace of Change over Time*, Oxford: Rowman and Littlefield Publishers Inc.

Suratman, S. (2002a), "Old Problems, New Strategies? Childcare Management in Malay Dual-Income Families in Singapore", paper presented at the Southeast Asian Association for Gender Studies, Malaysia Branch (SAMA) Conference on "Women and Men in Changing Societies", Bangi (Malaysia), 14–15 September.

Suratman, S. (2002b), "Studies on Malay Families and Households in Singapore: A Critical Assessment", NUS Seminar Papers No. 35, National University of Singapore, Department of Malay Studies.

Suratman, S. (2002c), "Working Out Child Care Arrangements: Case Studies on Malay Dual Income Couples in Singapore", paper presented at the 5th Asia Pacific Sociological Association Conference "Asia Pacific Societies: Contrasts, Challenges and Crises", Queensland University of Technology, Brisbane, Australia, 4–7 July.

Vinne, H. van der and Brink, M. M. (1997), "Dilemma or compromise: The Division of housework and child care among dual earners", in Gerard Frinking and Tineke Willemsen (eds.). *Dilemmas of Modern Family Life*, Amsterdam: Thesis Publishers, pp. 91–111.

Walper, S. and Galambos, N. L. (1997), "Employed mothers in Germany", in Judith Frankel (ed.), *Families of Employed Mothers: An International Perspective*, New York and London: Garlan Publishing Inc., pp. 35–65.

Wong, A. and Wong, K. (1975), *Women in Modern Singapore*, Singapore: University Education Press.

Wong, A. (1992). "Sex roles, lifecycle stages, social networks and community development in Singapore", in Shirley Ardener (ed.). *Persons and Powers of Women in Diverse Cultures: Essays in Commemoration of Audrey I. Richards, Phyllis Kaberry and Barbara E. Ward*, New York: Berg Publishers Limited.

Wong, A. (1981), *Working Mother and the Care of Pre-School Children in Singapore: A Research Report for the Singapore Girl Guides Association*, Singapore: The Singapore Girl Guides Association.

Yuen, E., Yuen, C. and Lim, V. (1991), "Dual-earner families in Singapore: Issues and challenges", in Lewis, S, Izraeli, D. N. and Hootsmans, H. M. (eds.). *Dual-Earner Families: International Perspectives*, London: Sage Publications.

Chapter 21

Does the Dower Equate to Economic Security for Muslim Women in Malaysia?

Raihanah Azahari, Zalina Zakaria, Asmak Ab Rahman and Hasbi Muh Ali

Abstract

Dower-giving symbolizes the love that a husband holds for a wife, and in Islamic teaching it is also a type of socio-economic guarantee for the wife. This chapter investigates the practice of dower-giving among Muslims in Malaysia. The interview method was used to collect data that could be used to identify dower practices among Muslims in Sabah, a state in Malaysia. It was found that, notwithstanding the fact that a dower, according to the religion of Islam, should be a form of economic security for women in their marriage contract, this is not the case in practice in Malaysia.

Keywords: Dower, Economic security, Muslim, Women

Dower-giving (or the Islamic term *mahr*) has been practiced since pre-Islamic times when it was based on the concept of the "bride-price" for a woman. This would be determined by the parent or guardian who was the closest male relative, and was usually owned by the woman's guardian (Rapoport, 2000, pp. 1–2; Coulson, 1964, p. 14; Kumar, 2010, p. 58). In pre-Islamic practice, a dower was a necessary condition for a lawful marriage because only after it was paid was the marriage was considered valid (Azahari, 2006, p. 316). The payment of a dower was also considered a payment to the guardian, known as *wali*, who had raised the daughter. It was a customary practice that when a baby girl was born, the community would congratulate the father of the baby by saying, "Safe, may it be a source of wealth for you". "Congratulations, may she be a source of wealth for you". This was an allusion to the fact that the father would receive the dower after his daughter's marriage. This is a symbol of ownership for the father because the dower would become his property (Mutahhari, 1980, p. 204). This practice in pre-Islamic times shows that women were regarded as merchandise or commodities, with a dower paid to the custodian or trustee for the woman a man wanted to marry. The stipulation of a specific dower provision in the *Qur'an* changed the concept of the pre-Islamic dower system that degraded women (Rapoport, 2000, p. 1). The *Qur'anic* verse in question describes the honor and advantages that flow from the gift of a dower to a bride compared to other types of gifts, such as wedding presents based on local customs and culture. It should be emphasized that the dower provision as stated in the *Qur'an* has been seen as a form of appreciation toward women (Kumar, 2010, p. 58), conferring dignity and protection to them (Mir-Hosseini, 1993, p. 80), and it was never intended to identify women as commodities. In Malaysia, there are guidelines that set the minimum rate for a dower payment in some states in order to facilitate marriage and so that men do not pay the dower that they wish to as this could be very low. Although there are differences between the 14 Malaysian states in the rates set by the guidelines, states that do not implement such guidelines are not breaking Islamic law because they are simply following the guidelines rather than mandatory fixed rates.

In addition to a dower, there exists the practice, known as *hantaran* or *belanja hangus*, of making optional gifts to the bride which takes the form of money given to the bride's parents for personal and wedding expenses, such as food preparation, entertainment of guests, arrangements for the wedding dais; in other words, all the things that would normally be borne by the bride's parents (Rahman, 2007, pp. 1–18). However, there is confusion over the difference between dower and *belanja hangus* in Malaysian society (Rahman, 2007, pp. 1–18). While *belanja hangus* is fixed by the bride's family (Sharifah and Sven, 1997, p. 253; Kasimin, 1989, p. 24), and is usually in the form of cash amounting to tens of thousands of ringgit (Azahari *et al.*, 2009, pp. 107–124), the dower payment is much lower and is calculated according to the rate in the guidelines. This chapter investigates the dower that must be provided as a condition of a valid marriage contract, as well as highlighting its wisdom and objectives as stipulated in the *Qur'an* by focusing on the dower practices in Malaysia, particularly in Sabah.

21.1 Islamic perspective on dower

In pre-Islamic practice, when a father married off his daughter the dower would be given to him and would be his property. It was also considered to represent the price of a woman (Rapoport, 2000, p. 1) as she was considered an asset and a source of family wealth. This is evident from the fact that, when a daughter was born, the community at large would congratulate the father of the baby because the dower received would become his property (Mutahhari, 1980, p. 204) and a source of his wealth. They considered a dower as payment and wages or compensation for the cost of bringing up their daughter (Mutahhari, 1980, p. 204), much like the concept of the bride-price.

It should be reiterated that a dower is a mandatory provision in the form of property or benefit given by the husband to the wife under a marriage contract (Zaydan, 1993, p. 79) or intercourse (Al-Zuhayli, 1989, p. 64). In addition, dower is a symbol of honesty with which the husband signifies his willingness to commit and be responsible financially during the marriage. The dower provision shows that Islam implemented a fairer and more transparent system, in contrast to the system and practice in place before Islam. Islam recognizes that a dower is an exclusive right of women which allows no interference from the government or from a guardian. Thus, a dower wisely accords importance to women's interests. The dower obligation has been stipulated (Zaydan, 1993, p. 50) in certain verses in the *Qur'an*. For example, verse 24 of Sura al-Nisa' states that:

> "Therefore, have you enjoyed (associated with) your wives (after they became your wives), give them their dowries (perfect) as a duty."

The aforementioned text does not mention the amount of dower that should be given by the husband to the wife. This is because Islam recognizes the fact that every individual has a different socio-economic status and different financial capacity (Sabiq, 2000, p. 102). In practice, the payment of a dower has also been influenced by local customs and traditional practices which constantly grow and change (Sabiq, 2000, p. 102). It is said that this is why Islam does not prescribe any minimum and maximum rates of dower (Al-Sabuni, 2007, p. 324) but leaves it to the community to determine (Khan, 2000, p. 59). However, there are some Islamic jurists who are of the opinion that payment of a dower must be at a certain minimum rate. Abu Hanifah, a classical Islamic jurist, has fixed a minimum rate of

10 dirhams of dower (equivalent to $300) (Zaydan, 1993, p. 59). Another classical jurist, Malik, set the rate at a quarter dinar or 3 dirhams ($32.9) (Zaydan, 1993, p. 59). Meanwhile, Shafi'i and Hanbali jurists do not set any minimum rate (Zaydan, 1993, p. 59), which is also the consensus among many other Muslim jurists (Qudamah, 1997, p. 99). Another verse from the *Qur'an* states that a dower is a gift of a substantial amount, mentioned as *qintar*, which can be given to the wife during marriage. Therefore, in this context, women are entitled to ask for a dower at a rate derived from their requirements and needs because Islam does not set a specific rate. However, Islam encourages its followers to adopt rates which do not exceed the wedding costs (Qudamah, 1997, p. 101).

Among the objectives of the dower provision, in Islam it is the right of ownership of property for women (Sabiq, 2000, p. 301; Moors, 1994, p. 301). It is a right that they have by virtue of marriage. In pre-Islamic times, the carer or guardian did not give women the right to manage property, let alone own it. Dower provision in Islam has demonstrated the opposite principle. This is a better system and more transparent than the pre-Islamic community practices (Haddad and Esposito, 1998, p. 149). The dower system as practiced in pre-Islamic times did not offer women much security in marriage as the husband was entitled to claim back the dower given, either wholly or partly, by asking for a divorce from his wife (Mutahhari, 1980, p. 207). When a divorce took place, the wife had to return the dower as required by the husband (Glassé and Smith, 2001, p. 60).

As explained earlier, the position of women since the advent of Islam has become more secure than it was during pre-Islamic times. Dower provision has not only changed the concept and the practice of dower-giving which previously exploited and diminished the status of women but it also symbolizes honor, showing that Islam honors women highly (Mutahhari, 1980, p. 210; Kumar, 2010, p. 4). The groom's responsibility of paying the dower shows that women have been liberated and are esteemed in Islam. This philosophy distinguishes the practice of giving dower from other wedding gifts, such as dowry (a payment from bride to the groom), which can be burdensome to women as it requires them to provide money or other assets and wealth as the cost of marriage (Umar, 1998, p. 68).

21.1.1 Dower as economic security for wives

The dower provision is not only a symbol of love between a husband and a wife but also a form of economic guarantee for the wife (Qaisi, 2000,

p. 70; Kumar, 2010, p. 59). As explained earlier, a dower has also been described as *qintar*, i.e., a substantial gift. This is mentioned in the Quran in Chapter 3, al-Nisa' verse 20:

> "And if you want to replace your wife with another, and you have given one of them a sum of money (qintar), so do not take the least of it."

In the aforesaid verse, the large amount of property implied by the pronouncement of *qintar* (Al-Tabari, 2000, p. 123) indicates that the dower can be given at a high rate, and can also be in form of valuable property that can be beneficial to the wife (Qaisi, 2000, p. 70). The majority of Islamic jurists are of the opinion that dower can also be in the form of valuable property (Al-Zuhayli, 1989, p. 260) which can benefit the owner, such as gold, silver, land and the like (Al-Zuhayli, 1989, p. 257). They agree that if the dower given is not beneficial or useful then it is not acceptable (Al-Bassam, 2003, p. 257; Hussain, 2004, p. 83).

Although the primary purpose of dower provision is not to give women economic security, it could help in this respect (Mutahhari, 1980, p. 214; Qaisi, 2000, p. 70), in particular, in the event of divorce or the death of the husband. Looking at the dower practice of Muslim communities in the Middle East, Europe and Africa, it can be seen that dower is a gift of great importance not only as a symbol of the love that the husband has for his wife but also as a form of economic security (Korson, 1967, p. 527; Mir-Hosseini, 1993, p. 75). However, the substantial amount of dower demanded by the bride is generally beyond the economic capacity of the groom (Rapoport, 2000, p. 8) so that they usually pay on a deferred basis (Løvdal, 2009, p. 116; Korson, 1967, p. 523). It must be highlighted that deferred dower, either wholly or partially (Zilfi, 1997, p. 98), must be paid within a period that has been agreed upon or when a divorce takes place or one spouse dies (Kumar, 2010, p. 64; Welchman, 2004, p. 189). Through payment of even part of the dower, the wife gains a right to the assets, and the right still exists if there is a divorce in the sense that the whole agreed amount (Løvdal, 2009, p. 40) can be claimed from the husband (Korson, 1967, p. 529). A deferred dower is seen as security (payment for release from the marriage through divorce) in the event of harm, such as abuse or family violence (Mir-Hosseini, 1993, p. 80).

Korson (1967, p. 527), Agnes (1996, p. 2835), Fournier (2010, p. 21), Moon (2008, p. 148), Hussain (2004, p. 83) and Welchman (2004, p. 189) explain that dower is not only a symbol of love and of the ability of a man to marry but it also gives the woman security in the marriage as it can potentially prevent easy divorce since the husband is obliged to pay the whole dower as agreed (Zaydan, 1993, p. 84).

When discussing the history of the emergence of the dower in pre-Islamic and post-Islamic times and how it is now practiced by the Muslims, Kumar (2010, pp. 58–73) argues that such development has evidently secured the rights and interests of women in some social and economic respects. Dower-giving is often identified as providing security and protection against economic insufficiency, for example, in case of the husband's death, violence during the marriage or divorce. He claims that dower paid on this basis can give some economic security to women as the deferred payment is of bigger/greater value than the one-off payment.

Rapoport (2000, pp. 15–16) mentions that the deferred amount of the dower could be equal to the value of the house for that particular family. As the deferred portion of the dower is a substantial sum, some husbands have undoubtedly been deterred from fully exercising the right of unilateral divorce and other legal privileges that they formally enjoyed under Islamic matrimonial law. According to Rapoport, by practicing deferred dower, wives can exercise the right to claim their deferred portion of the dower as a penalty imposed on the husband in case of unilateral divorce. Alternatively, wives can forfeit this right if they themselves initiate a separation. After termination of the contract, the deferred portion might provide the woman with some economic security.

A study by Korson (1967, pp. 527–533) found that even if the dower paid was not a substantial amount, it surely had the role of providing economic security to women, especially those from a lower social class. In his case study on Pakistan, he observed that due to the difficulties in finding jobs, women would rely on the dower payment, which is also considered one of their economic bases. The allegedly lower status of women in Pakistan at least affords them the protection of a system of dower which, even though it may indeed be a small sum, provides a temporary financial buffer. Korson also explains that, according to many Pakistani observers, the system of dower contributes heavily to keeping couples together, especially when the husband is confronted with his obligation to pay the amount of dower that he is committed to.

In another study of dower among Palestinian women living in Israel, Moors (1994, pp. 301–331) described that their socio-economic status had changed as an effect of dower practices. As women's rights there are very limited, the women are totally dependent on the provision of dower to secure their economic position in the event of any problems in the marriage. Mehdi (2003, pp. 115–129), who identified the impact of dower on Pakistani Muslim women in Denmark, explains that the dower given to them must be at least a potential asset to the wife in the event of unforeseen circumstances, such as the death of the husband or divorce.

Engineer (pp. 297–300), Agnes (1996, pp. 21–23), Mutahhari (1980, p. 194), Esposito and De Long-Bas (2001, p. 97) agree that the system of dower in Islam benefits women as it is considered a form of exclusive or absolute property rights for women, which allows no interference from the husband, the guardian or the government. This contrasts with the system of dowry and bride-price given to the woman's parents or guardian. Other researchers, such as Qaisi (2000, pp. 67–81), Mir-Hosseini (1993, pp. 72–79) and Freeland (2011), find that dower has increased the status and socio-economic position of women in addition to the potential economic security it provides in the event of divorce or widowhood.

Having considered the aforementioned text, it must be emphasized that the practice of paying a higher dower in many countries to prevent divorce from taking place easily does not necessarily constitute security in the marriage itself. In certain circumstances, it can even become a burden on the wife in the sense that it might be difficult for her to ask for divorce in such situations if she is abused by the husband during marriage or where he can no longer carry out his responsibilities as a husband, for example, due to drug addiction or disease. In such situations, many husbands may hesitate or delay the payment of dower to the wife. This defeats the purpose of stipulating the provisioning of dower in the Quran.

21.1.2 Dower as early assurance to women in marriage

The dower is the initial payment for a wife, whereas maintenance must be given by the husband to the wife during the marriage. It has been argued that it is better for a woman to ask for a dower that has a high value, such as gold, land, homes, vehicles, shares or other valuable assets, since dower represents the exclusive right of a woman and serves as an early guarantee (Agnes, 1996, p. 2833) at the start of a new life with a husband. Usually, after marriage a woman will start life in a new place with her husband (Zilfi, 1997, p. 101). Therefore, a form of economic security is needed to help her start the new life after her marriage. Furthermore, not all women have the opportunity to achieve economic independence. With such a right, the dower not only acts as a guarantee of economic security in a new place but can also be used as capital for investment (Haddad and Esposito, 1998, p. 131) in a business or elsewhere. It has the potential to improve a woman's economic status, regardless of whether she has a job.

21.1.3 Dower as economic security in the event of death or divorce

In addition to the wives' right to inheritance, it has been argued that the dower can become the socio-economic security of a woman if she becomes a single mother (Mehdi, 2003, p. 120). If a wife is left without any property, the payment of a high amount of dower or dower with a high value can sometimes enable her to carry on with her life and maintain herself. Similarly, the dower can help when a wife who has become a single mother falls sick and is not capable of earning.

Moreover, the wife who completely depends on her husband for living expenses can continue with her life when divorce occurs (Abd Manan, 2010, p. 95). Although Islam has placed the responsibility for maintenance on the husband during the marriage, there is no guarantee that the wife will receive a monthly maintenance payment from the husband, as well as the other rights that she should receive after the occurrence of divorce (Mehdi, 2003, p. 120).

In conclusion, despite the potential for a dower to become economic security in a marriage, there are many cases in which wives do not claim or fail to get their dower back after a divorce (Moors, 1994, p. 146). When divorce or death occurs, claiming the dower is not straightforward (Moors, 1994, p. 142) but involves a long process which is not without hurdles. For example, the woman may have to travel to court to claim the dower (Moors, 1994, p. 127). This makes it difficult and burdensome for women to obtain their rights. Refusal and failure of the husband or the heirs to assist in resolving the debt portion of the dower have also contributed to women being unable to claim their rights.

21.2 Dower in Malaysia

Malaysia is located in Southeast Asia and is divided into West Malaysia and East Malaysia. East Malaysia, also known as Peninsular Malaysia, consists of 12 states while East Malaysia has two. The population of Malaysia includes various communities: Malays, Chinese and Indians, as well as the ethnic groups of East Malaysia which comprise the Kadazans and Dusuns. In terms of marriage, the Muslim community in Malaysia is governed by Islamic law enforced through the enactment of Islamic family law and it is also influenced by local customs. Muslims practice two types of marriage payments in Malaysia: the dower and wedding gifts. It must be noted that the practice of these two types of payments differs among states in Malaysia and local customs dictate their unique character.

The dower is usually given in the form of money and is typically paid promptly and in full. Even though early Islamic tradition established that the state may not interfere and impose a specific amount of dower, the *Qur'an* reveals that a woman has the right to receive a dower it is the right of the woman (Al-Hibri and El Habti, 2006, pp. 150–225). However, all states in Malaysia, through the Islamic Religious Department, have issued guidelines or regulations on the amount of dower that should be paid.

The amount is stipulated on the basis of current gold values and ranges from between RM25 and RM100, approximately $7 and $21. It should be emphasized that the guidelines also distinguish between the amounts of dower for virgins and for widows.[1] Although these amounts are only guidelines and compliance is not mandatory, typically the community at large complies with these policies in the practice of dower-giving. Pressure within the community has led individuals to stipulate a low amount based on the assumption that the guidelines are consistent with the Prophet's hadith: "The most blessed marriage is the one with the least dower". It can be reiterated that according to Islamic jurists the term "the least dower" here does not denote a low amount of dower but an amount that is within the groom's means.

There are states that have no guidelines on the subject. In these states, the amount of dower is decided in advance by the girl's father and the father of the groom. A comparison between the states that have guidelines with those without guidelines reveals significant differences in the amount of dower. A bride from these states receives a dower as high as RM1000–RM5000 (approximately $300–$1,500), while a bride from the other states receives a dower in the range of RM25–RM100 ($7–$30). For brides from states with guidelines, they receive a lower amount of dower as there are also additional monetary wedding payments known as *hantaran*.

21.2.1 The history of dower in the Malay community

In Malaysia, Malay is the largest ethnic group. According to Malay custom, a dower is known as *mahr*. It represents a gift from a man to a woman whom

[1] http://www.islam.gov.my/sites/default/files/6.maskahwin.pdf.

he will marry. The dower must come from the groom himself. In the earlier practice of the Malay community, since gold was the medium of exchange, the dower had to be in the form of gold and weigh *sabahara*. According to the Islamic family law, dower is defined as a payment that is due to be paid under the *Shari'ah* by the husband to the wife within the marriage contract, whether in the form of cash, of debt with or without security, or of something valued by the *Shari'ah* that can be measured in money as according to Islamic Family Law Act of Malaysia (Federal Territories, 1984). However, the *Shari'ah* does not fix the amount of dower that must be paid. This is why, in Malaysia, not every state has specific guidelines on how much dower is to be paid. Three states out of the 14, namely Terengganu, Kelantan and Kedah, do not specify a particular rate for the payment of *mahr*. On some occasions in the three states, the rate is determined by the community on the basis of financial ability and agreement between the parties, as well as the traditions in their families.

Azahari examined the influence of local traditions or customs on the determination of the rate of dower, and found that the specified rates differed from state to state (Pengaruh Budaya Dalam Penentuan Kadar Mahar, 2006, pp. 315–323). The study also ascertained that, although Islam does not prescribe a specific rate, social customs have certainly influenced the dower rates in Malay communities, especially in some aspects such as time, place and the person's financial capacity or the social position of the family. Rahman attempts to address the question of whether or not the amount of *mahr* in Malaysia is reasonable today. She suggests that the rate needs to be reviewed due to economic and social changes that have occurred. According to her, the old rates are no longer reasonable or practical given the rise in the price of goods. Everyone would agree that RM22.50 ($6.8) or RM100 ($30) was too low a sum to purchase anything worth giving to a bride as a gift.

Abdul Hak (2012, pp. 215–229) states that the concept of *mahr* in Islam is neither an actual nor a symbolic price for a woman, as is the case in certain cultures, but rather is a gift offered to the wife. Abdul Hak links dower with the woman's modesty and chastity. In her view, a woman should know that she should not give herself freely to a man as she is worth more. Abdul Hak also states that the amount of *mahr* in Malaysia should be reviewed as at present the rate in most states is relatively low compared to the cost of living, especially in the big cities such as Kuala Lumpur, Shah Alam, Petaling Jaya and Johor Bahru. Abd. Rahman and Musa (2006, pp. 1–13) studied the effects of dower on the welfare of the household. They found that dower rates were too low and, in the context of current conditions, did not appear to attach any value to women when compared with dower practices in other countries where the dower was paid at a higher rate.

21.3 Research setting

We studied the practice of *mahr* in Tawau, located in Sabah, a state in Malaysia. Tawau is the third largest town of Sabah after Kota Kinabalu and Sandakan. According to the census, in 2010 Tawau's population was estimated to be 381,736 (Population Distribution by Local Authority Areas and Mukims). We chose Sabah as the study area, especially Tawau District, because it contains various tribes, including Tidung, Bajau, Bolongan, Visaya, Bugis, Banjar, Butun and Java. The district is unique due to its strong local culture. In most communities in Sabah, a dower is known as a gift (Buxbaum, 1968, p. 117). However, for most of the Malay community in Tawau the term that is often used is dower. The rate, according to guidelines in Sabah, is RM100.00 for unmarried women (virgins) and RM80.00 for previously married women (widowed) (Kadar mas kahwin setiap negeri di Malaysia).

21.3.1 Research questions

This study addresses three main questions:

(a) What are the characteristics of dower-giving among Muslims? Is it prompt or deferred?
(b) How is dower interpreted by women? Is it in terms of kind, value, amount and usage of dower or its spending purposes?
(c) What is the role of dower among Muslim women?

21.3.2 Research method

The interview method was used in collecting data to identify dower practices among Muslims in Sabah. We interviewed 13 individuals, married and divorced women, who had volunteered to participate in the study. Twelve of these women were married and one was a single parent. They represented various ethnic Muslims in Tawau, Sabah, and the group comprised different socio-economic backgrounds.

The selection of respondents who were married can help to provide more practical answers to the questions submitted, based on experience

Table 21.1 Demography of respondents.

Respondent	Marital status	Ethnicity	Occupation	Education	Monthly income
R1	Married	Tidung	Housewife	High school	None
R2	Single mother	Jawa	Tailor	Primary school	RM400
R3	Married (2009)	Banjar	Religious teacher	High school	RM850
R4	Married (1990)	Buton	Businesswoman	Secondary school	RM700
R5	Married (2012)	Bugis	Businesswoman	High school	RM350
R6	Married (1970)	Bugis	Housewife	Secondary school	None
R7	Married (1979)	Bajau	Housewife	Secondary school	None
R8	Married (2012)	Visaya	Teacher	Bachelor degree	RM2500
R9	Married (2012)	Suluk	Housewife	High school	None
R10	Married (2011)	Jawa	Marketing executive	Diploma	RM1,500
R11	Married (2011)	Bugis	Religious teacher	High school	RM850
R12	Married (2007)	Cocos	Teacher	Diploma	RM1,800
R13	Married (2012)	Bugis	Teacher	Bachelor degree	RM2,500

and practice in their marriages. There were 3 respondents educated to SPM level; followed by 4 respondents educated to primary level; 2 who passed STPM; 2 who obtained diplomas; and 2 who obtained Bachelor's degrees. There were 5 respondents who worked in the government sector; 1 was in the private sector; 3 were self-employed; while the 4 remaining did not work due to their low educational background but were full-time homemakers. There were 3 respondents who earned below RM500; 3 who earned between RM500 and RM1,000; 1 who earned between RM1,501 and RM2,000; another earned between RM2,001 and RM2,500; 2 earned RM2,501 and RM3,000; and 4 respondents had no income (Table 21.1).

21.3.3 Results

(1) Respondents' perceptions of dower: The results show that the majority of respondents (12 of the women) thought that a dower was a mandatory grant from husband to wife upon marriage, paid either in cash, cheque or other. Only one of the respondents felt that it was a

wedding gift to the wife in the context of a requirement to give it, rather than a gift conferred voluntarily. Respondents appeared to have a good knowledge of the meaning of dower, probably due to their background as all were or had been married and had received a dower.

Based on our interviews, the results show that 12 of the 13 respondents received *mahr* in cash at the *mahr* rate of RM100, following the guidelines issued by the Islamic Religious Council of Sabah (MUIS), and only 1 respondent received dower in the form of a necklace and a pair of gold bracelets worth more than RM100. This assertion is supported by one of the respondents who stated that:

> *Initially, my family was not happy with the dower. However, as explained gently to my family, they finally understand. My neighbours are weird and awkward with my marriage because my dower is higher than normal. But, that's our right. After all, my husband was the one who happily gave the necklace as a dower. R13*

Based on the interviews, the typical practice in the community in Sabah was found to be payment of the dower in cash. This is attributed to the fact that the rate of dower in Sabah is lower and because payment in cash has become a local tradition that must be followed. Therefore, when respondents were asked questions about deferred dower (debt) in order to identify their perceptions and understanding of it, three respondents said that dower could not be given on credit and that this would invalidate the marriage, while the others took the opposite view because they thought that giving dower was a condition of marriage. In addition, they offered the perceptions that the giving of dower should be in cash and it brought shame if it was deferred.

> *If it is paid deferred (debt) then it is not the dower. This is because the dower should be given at the time of marriage. R2*

> *It is shameful if given deferred dower. R3*

21.3.4 Dower rate received by respondents

The respondents married between 1970 and 2012, and 12 of the 13 respondents received the dower rate in line with the guidelines. Between 1990 and 2012, 9 respondents received RM100, while the 3 other respondents received a dower of RM88 which was the dower given in the guidelines current in

1970 and 1979. Only 1 respondent received a dower outside the usual rate, namely a necklace and a pair of gold bracelets. She stated that:

> *The cash money of RM100 is not perpetual. For me, gold is good, 'memorable' and beneficial. R13*

Data show that the majority of respondents adopted the determination of dower rates based on the guideline provided by MUIS. This practice was the result of a misunderstanding by the respondents as to the recommended rate. Although they were of the view that the rate was not relevant, they seem to have followed the dower rate guide.

> *Yes, I received dower when I think it was too low, but the rate has been set. So, we take it ... R1*

The guideline dower rates have not changed over the past few decades. This means that the amount of dower received did not increase for most of the respondents, those married between 1990 and 2012.

In addition, the study found that ethnic influences limit women's right to demand or receive, "an additional amount of dower", the relevant portion on their own. This practice stems from the beliefs and ethnic traditions that are still strongly adhered to in the community, especially by the elderly in the family. They believe that a change in the existing dower rate would revoke the marriage blessing and bring possible calamity upon the marriage. Thus, they ensure that their children maintain the traditions and beliefs. Consequently, brides who want to get married must conform to the rate out of respect for other family members and to preserve the traditions of their faith.

> *People are very concerned about our old dower. For us, if we are adding or increasing the dower, there will be bad things, or things that are not good will happen to a couple. Blessings will already be gone. If we follow our faith also, if we add a little more dower money that exceeds what the rate should be, we will be faced with calamity. R4*

In addition, we found that the respondents' answers concerning a change in the existing rate of dower identified it as not being a good practice in the community, and one that would give a bad impression of the woman. Thus, it was not easy for a woman to set the rate herself in a society deeply rooted in an adherence to the dower rates. This assertion is supported by the testimony of the respondent R13 mentioned previously.

The respondents argued that the rates of dower set by the Council (MUIS) also had to be met. Although the guide is only a recommendation to the community, there was misunderstanding among the women regarding the rate. Most respondents were of the opinion that it had to be followed and that adding to or changing existing rates of dower would be illegal under Islam. This was found in the opinion expressed by 10 of the respondents who stated that the rate must be followed by every individual, against 3 respondents who disagreed.

> *Yes, that is the rate that should be followed because it is the rate determined by MUIS (Islamic Religious Council of Sabah) ... R2*

> *Dower rates are displayed in the marriage certificate and we cannot change it. R7*

> *Most importantly, it should not burden the man. In Tawau, RM100 is the best, so women should not ask more than that. R3*

21.3.5 Views of respondents on the appropriateness of the amount of the current guided dower rate

Out of the 13 respondents, 10 felt that the current dower rate of RM100 and RM80 for virgins and widows, respectively, was adequate and relevant to the current situation, while the remaining 3 felt otherwise.

Based on analysis of the interviews with respondents, we conclude that three reasons are given for contending that the dower was still relevant and did not need to be changed.

(1) Raising the dower would overburden husbands: If the current dower rate were raised, the men would become increasingly overburdened. Respondents to this research thought that their husbands had to bear the burden of wedding expenses, which would negate the importance of dower. R3 stated that:

> *... no need to demand a high dower as they also need to provide/pay for many other things for the wedding ... R3*

(2) No direction to change the rate has been issued by MUIS: Respondents were also very compliant with the guidelines issued by MUIS, believing that they could not be altered and must be followed.

We cannot escape from paying that value. Because it is already set by the Department of Religion, as stated in the marriage certificate. So, it is not good to change what has been set. R8

(3) Raising rates would lower the dignity of women and undermine the marriage blessings.

Putting a high dower was like selling a child as a bargaining chip. What is important is the blessing. For me and our Javanese culture, the lower the dower, the higher the dignity of women. R2

The respondents who felt that the current guided dower rates were no longer appropriate or adequate gave two possible reasons: the dower rates were too low compared to wedding expenses; or they did not reflect the current economic situation:

For me it is not adequate. It's necessary to balance between the dower and hantaran. As we can see now, the hantaran rises but the dower is still the same. R7

We must also take into account the economic needs of today. The fact that the cost of living is higher now must also be considered. In the past, perhaps RM100 was huge, but now the situation is no longer the same. R1

21.3.6 Women's perceptions of the best dower according to Islam

Most of the respondents believed that Islam prescribed[2] that the lower the dower rate the better since it would not be burdensome to the man. However, this is not the correct interpretation of the *hadith*, as mentioned earlier.

The lowest portion is the most good. I do not agree with the high dower. Not only it burdened men, but I think it can be vulgar and show-off. R2

Best dower is the lowest. Why should we ask for a high dower? It will only inconvenience the guy ... R11

However, there were some respondents who felt that a dower of high value, given according to the ability of the man, was more appropriate.

[2]Based on *hadiths* mentioned earlier.

Not necessarily the most expensive dower is the most favourable prices. It is better if the dower was raised slightly it will be more valuable and beneficial to women. R1

If the husband is able to provide a higher dower and give something valuable and more permanent, it is better. R13

To summarize, many of the women saw the giving of a dower as a blessing, and that the value of the blessing was associated with the low rate of the dower received. They felt that the lowest rate of dower was the best since it rendered the woman's dignity and the blessings of the marriage. On the questions and responses submitted regarding women's perception and understanding of dower, the study shows that the women generally saw giving dower simply as a typical ritual in weddings. They also displayed a lack of understanding regarding the deferred dower. This is because some saw the deferred dower as a shameful practice that could invalidate the marriage. This is in contrast to the custom in other places, such as India, Pakistan and the Middle East, where dower-giving is practiced in order to give women economic security in case of widowhood or divorce. The findings also show that there has been a misconception among people regarding the guidelines of the dower rates. Most women assumed that the rate must be followed, and that any change in it was not good as it would revoke the marriage blessings. Although the guide rate was designed only as a recommendation for the community, in reality it has become a socially mandatory rate. At the same time, women see the current rate of dower (the *mahr* rate guide) as still relevant since the groom has to bear other wedding expenses. This indicates that women prefer to help marriages by not burdening the men with high dowers. However, this preference is confined to the marriage dower only and not to other marriage expenses. On the basis of dower being viewed as a gift that symbolizes a blessing to women, the dower at the lowest rate is the best for women.

21.3.7 The use of dower among the respondents

Some of the respondents used the dower received to buy something valuable, such as gold or other essentials, while other respondents simply kept the dower and did not use it. Details of the data are recorded in Table 21.2.

Table 21.2 Use of dower.

Res.	Usage of dower	Reason
R1	Buying gold	Never thought of buying anything other than gold
R2	Buying gold	Can be kept permanently
R3	Buying gold	Keeping gold is better than keeping money
R4	Buying gold	Customary practice
R5	Kept in savings	Just married
R6	Kept by mother	No idea what to do with the dower
R7	Buying bed	customary practice
R8	Buying gold	Initial intention to buy sewing machine but the money was not sufficient
R9	Wedding expenses	Customary practice
R10	Buying gold	Commemoration of marriage
R11	Kept in savings	Just married
R12	Buying gold	Husband's suggestion
R13	Gold kept	Commemoration of marriage

21.3.8 Role of dower

It is reiterated that dower in Islam consists of something very beneficial and valuable that must be given by a husband to his wife. However, the study found that dower received by women in Tawau, Sabah acted only as a token and was complementary to the wedding itself. These findings differ from the study by Mehdi (2003, p. 120) which found that dower plays a very significant role for women because of the potential socio-economic security it gives them when there is a divorce or the husband dies. It also differs from Korson's findings (1967, pp. 527–533), according to which dower functions largely as a form of insurance to provide a degree of economic security to the wife should the couple separate or either party seeks divorce. The respondents also thought that what matters most was for the marriage to be easily contracted without burdening the husband.

The purpose of dower is to legalize the wedlock. R11

I do not know the importance of the dower. It is just for validating the marriage ... R6

For me, dower is for validating the marriage. Because for me, I do not consider dower as a gift that can secure women ... R3

In answering the question of whether the dower can provide economic security for women in the household in the event of a disaster such as widowhood or divorce, only 3 respondents felt that dower gave security, if received at high rates. Typically, respondents thought that dower could not function as a source of economic security. They gave the following reasons for this: dower values were too low and could not be an economic guarantee for women; and awareness and knowledge of the importance of dower.

In terms of the first reason, as mentioned earlier, guidelines for dower rates in Tawau, Sabah are set at RM100 for unmarried women and RM80 for widows (Kadar mas kahwin setiap negeri di Malaysia). The *mahr* rate has not changed for decades, with the result that the dower received at present is unable to provide great benefit to women but functions only as a complement to the wedding contract.

> *For me my dower cannot be enough to guarantee my economic needs because the dower is too low. To buy gold, I need to add our own money ... R1*

> *With the RM100, what can we do? R8*

> *For me, the dower is simply not enough to warrant or support the needs of our current trouble. R9*

> *The value of RM100 is unable to accommodate economic reasons nor is it enough to ensure women's economic welfare ... R2*

> *In terms of security, it does not secure the wife. Because, for us, a dower is only for fulfilment of the marriage ... R10*

> *Before this I had never heard that dower can give an advantage and security to women. Because of all this I am assuming that dower was only given to honour the wife ... R5*

> *The purpose is to legalise wedlock ... R11*

> *Do not know the importance and usefulness of the dower. Just for mandatory marriage alone ... R6*

> *For me, enough dower for the marriage to be valid. Because for me, I do not consider dower as grants aimed at guaranteeing women ... R3*

This result is similar to that of a study by Rahman (2007, pp. 1–18) who found that dower rates guidelines were too low and not commensurate with current conditions. Thus, they do not seem to be of any value to women compared with the potential dower in other countries, such as those in the Middle East.

Differences in the standards of living and the degree of economic independence also appear to influence the needs of women for economic security. Respondents who had economic independence through salaries from employment, whether in government or the private sector, explained that they could secure and maintain themselves without the need for a high *mahr*, while also getting monthly maintenance from their husbands.

> *I think I don't need it because my salary is enough to cover my daily needs. I also do some saving for the future ... R3*

This study found that women's need to see dower as security against difficult times was influenced by demographic variables, such as the experience of facing calamity in their marriage and the ability to have a job that paid a sufficient monthly salary. These findings are in line with the study conducted by Mir-Hosseini who found that among the factors influencing the value of dower was the woman's socio-economic situation. "Modern" women with high socio-economic status in the sense of being able to support themselves, who were highly educated and thus in a strong economic position, could face any calamity in the marriage without having to rely on the dower from the husband. In addition, the study confirms that experiencing unfortunate events during marriage increases women's awareness of dower as a form of socio-economic security.

The practice in India, Pakistan and the Middle Eastern countries implies that dower should be given at a higher rate because it constitutes security within marriage. This is unlike the practice in Malaysia where giving *mahr* at a low rate is not considered awkward or unusual since dower is seen only as a complement to the marriage tie. In the event of divorce, women will accept the development more readily. Also, women in Malaysia do not have their status downgraded by society if they become widows. Many Malaysian women have a good education and a guaranteed good job.

As for awareness and knowledge of the importance of women's dower, this is because even if the woman receives a valuable dower of benefit to her, the perception that dower exists just to preserve memories, or as a gift, limits the role of dower to that of a token of appreciation. For this group, the dower must still be kept as a memento of the marriage and will not be used even when unfortunate events in the marriage arise.

> *I did not think to use this dower even in desperation. This is because the dower is a sign of remembrance and love to my husband. So, I'll try to keep it. R3*

This statement was reinforced by the experience of a single mother whose husband had died. She explained that:

> *I never thought to use it let alone consider dower as economic security to me. For me it is just a memorable gift from my late husband to me ... R2*

21.4 Conclusion

The practice of dower in Islam symbolizes the esteem which husbands have for their wives and the respect that Islam has for women. In some countries, dower plays a bigger role as economic security for women in marriage; however, this is not the case in Malaysia.

This study found that the majority of women in the Muslim community in Tawau received dower at rates conforming to guidelines issued by the Sabah Islamic Religious Department, and that it was given in the form of cash. Dower is regarded as a complement to the marriage ties and as a memento of the wedding for the wife from husband. Members of the community in Tawau also believe that giving a dower can bless a marriage. Responses to this study indicated that the lower the rate of dower the most blessed the marriage was. The value and rate of dower was not a priority; the objective was for the marriage to take place without burdening the future husband. Despite the guidelines being recommendations only, it is believed that the prescribed low rate of RM100 cannot be changed. This belief is closely associated with the tradition that any changes or additions to the dower rates beyond the guidelines for current practice are not good and can bring bad luck to a marriage. Unlike social practices in other countries, such as those in the Middle East that have high dower rates, not only is there a very low rate in Malaysia but the rate has also not been reviewed in the last 30 years. However, women in Malaysia do not consider this a problem since for them their dower is no more than a complement to the marriage ties and a token gift from the future husband to a woman who is to be his wife.

References

English

Abdul Hak, Nora (2012), Right of women to mahr(dower) under Islamic Law and Malaysian family law: some suggestions for reform. *Journal of Islamic Law Review*, 8(12), 215–229.

Agnes, F. (1996), Economic rights of women in Islamic law. *Economic and Political Weekly*, 31, 2832–2838.

Buxbaum, D. C. (1968), *Family Law and Customary Law in Asia: A Contemporary Legal Perspective*, Netherlands: Martinus Nijhoff Publishers.

Coulson, N. J. (1964), *A History of Islamic Law*. Edinburgh: University Press.

Engineer, A. A. (2008), *The Rights of Women in Islam* (3 vols.), New Delhi: Sterling Publishers Private Limited.

Esposito, J. L. and De Long-Bas, N. J. (2001), *Women in Muslim Family Law*, New York: Syracuse University Press.

Fournier, P. (2010), *Muslim Marriage in Western Courts: Lost in Transplantation*, England: Ashgate Publishing.

Freeland, R. (2011), "The Islamic Institution of Mahr and American Law", available at http://www.law.gonzaga.edu/files/GJIL-Vol4-IslamicInstitution.pdf.

Glassé, C. and Smith, H. (2001), *The New Encylopedia of Islam*, Walnut Greek, CA: AltaMira Press.

Haddad, Y. Y. and Esposito, J. L. (1998), *Islam, Gender, & Social Change*, New York: Oxford University Press.

Hassan, S. Z. S. and Cederroth, S. (1997), Managing Marital Disputes in Malaysia: Islamic Mediators and Conflict Resolution in the Syariah Courts. Richmond. *Surrey: Curzon Press for Nordic Institute of Asian Studies*, Hawaii: University of Hawaii Press.

Hussain, J. (2004), *Islam: Its Law and Society*, Sydney: The Federation Press.

Khan, M. W. (2000), *Woman in Islamic Shariah*, New Delhi, India: Goodword Books.

Korson, J. H. (1967), Dower and social class in an urban Muslim community. *Journal of Marriage and Family*, 29(3), 527–533.

Kumar, R. (2010), Law of dower (mahr) in India. *Journal of Islamic Law and Culture*, 12(1), 58–73.

Løvdal, L. (2009), *Private International Law, Muslim Laws and Gender Equality: The Adjudication of Mahr in Scandinavian, English and French Courts*, Oslo: University of Oslo.

Mehdi, R. (2003), Danish law and the practice of mahr among Muslim Pakistanis in Denmark. *International Journal of the Sociology of Law*, 31(2), 115–129.

Mir-Hosseini, Z. (1993), *Marriage on Trial: Islamic Family Law in Iran and Morocco Compared*, London: I.B. Tauris & Co. Ltd.

Moon, R. (2008), *Law and Religious Pluralism in Canada*, Canada: UBC Press.

Moors, A. (1994), Women and dower property in twentieth-century Palestine: The case of Jabal Neblus. *Islamic Law and Society*, 1(3), 301–331.

Mutahhari, M. (1980), *The Rights of Women in Islam*, Tehran: World Organization for Islamic Services.

Qaisi, G. G. (2000), A student note: Religious marriage contracts: Judicial enforcement of mahr agreements in American courts. *Journal of Law and Religion*, 15(1), 67–81.

Rahman, Z. Abdul (2007), Mahar in Malaysia: The law revisited. *Shariah Law Reports*, pp. 1–18.

Rapoport, Y. (2000), Matrimonial gifts in early Islamic Egypt. *Islamic Law and Society*, 7(1), 1–36.

Umar, M. (1998), *Bride Burning in India: A Socio Legal Study*, New Delhi: A.P.H. Publishing Corporation.

Welchman, L. (2004), *Women's Rights and Islamic Family Law: Perspectives on Reform*, London: Zed Books.

Zilfi, M. C. (1997), *Women in the Ottoman Empire: Middle Eastern Women in the Early Modern Era.*, London, Brill.

Arabic

Al-Bassam (2003), 'Abdullah bin Abdul Rahman. *Taudhihul Ahkam min Bulughil Maram* (Vol. 5), Mekkah: Dar Al-Asadi.

Al-Hibri, Azizah and El Habti, Raja' M. (2006), "Islam" al, in Don S. Browning *et al.* (eds.), *Sex, Marriage, and Family in World Religions*, New York: Columbia University Press.

Al-Sabuni, Muhammad 'Ali (2007), *Rawa'i 'al-Bayan: Tafsir Ayat al-Ahkam 'Ain al-Qur'an*, Kaherah: Dar al-Sabuni.

Al-Tabari, Abu Ja'far Muhammad ibn Jarir (2000), *Jam'i Al-Bayan fi Ta'wil al-Qur'an*, Beirut: Muassasah Al-Risalah.

Al-Zuhayli, Wahbah (1989), *Al-Fiqh al-Islami Wa Adillatuhu* (Vol. 7), Damsyiq: Dar al-Fikr.

Qudamah, Muwaffaq al-Din 'Abd. Allah Ibn Ahmad Ibn (1997), *Al-Mughni*, Riyadh: Dar al-Alam al-Kutub.

Sabiq, al-Sayyid (2000), *Fiqh al-Sunnah*, Kaherah: Dar al-Fath li-al-'Ilam al-'Arabi.

Zaydan, 'Abdul Karim (1993), *Al-Mufassal fi Ahkam al-Mar'ah wa al-Bait al-Muslim fi as-Syari'ah al-Islamiyyah* (Vol. 7), Beirut: Muassasah al-Risalah.

Malay

Abd Manan, Mazlan (2010), "Kesalahan-Kesalahan Matrimoni Kalam Kes Perceraian Di Luar Mahkamah Dan Tanpa Kebenaran Mahkamah: Kajian di Mahkamah Syariah Negeri Selangor Darul Ehsan." Tesis Sarjana: Akademi Pengajian Islam Universiti Malaya.

Abd. Rahman, Azman and Musa, Zahari (2006), "Nilai Mas Kahwin Dan Hantaran Dan Kesannya Kepada Kebahagiaan Rumahtangga." *Seminar Falsafah Perkahwinan.* Mac. 1–13.

Azahari, Raihanah *et al.* (2009), Hubungan di antara faktor demografi dengan penentuan kadar mahar. *Jurnal Fiqh*, 5, 107–124.

Azahari, Raihanah (2006), Pengaruh Budaya Dalam Penentuan Kadar Mahar." Mohd. Salleh Haji Md and Haji Ahmad *et al.* (eds.). *Hukum Islam Dan Budaya Tempatan*, Kuala Lumpur: Jabatan Fiqh dan Usul, Akademi Pengajian Islam, Universiti Malaya, pp. 315–323.

Kasimin, Amran (1989), *Istiadat Perkahwinan Melayu: Satu Kajian Perbandingan Dewan Bahasa dan Pustaka*, Malaysia: Kementerian Pendidikan Malaysia.

Kasimin, Amran (1989), "Kadar mas kahwin setiap negeri di Malaysia." *Jabatan Kemajuan Islam Malaysia* (4 May 2011), available at http://www.islam.gov.my/maskahwin-negeri-negeri. Accessed on 25th April 2019.

Chapter 22

The Complexity of Measuring Women Empowerment and its Role in Nutritional Status of Bangladeshi Children

Rana Ejaz Ali Khan and Muhammad Ali Raza

Abstract

Measuring the woman empowerment and its impact on various aspects of woman and child welfare is still an enigma. The same measures of woman empowerment may be utilized for analyzing its role in different aspects of welfare of household members. This is the reason that a number of studies have shown no significant effect of woman empowerment on household welfare. This chapter has discussed different measures of woman empowerment and has attempted to see the impact of woman empowerment measured by an index on nutritional status of children in Bangladesh. The Composite Index of Anthropometric Failure (CIAF) has been calculated from Bangladesh Demographic and Health Survey 2007 (BDHS). The Binary logistic regression results have illustrated that the woman empowerment has no significant effect on child's nutritional status. It may be conferred that measure of woman empowerment has some flaws. The other explanatory variables like child's birth order and age, duration of breastfeeding, mother's education, mother's BMI, incidence of Diarrhea and fever, household wealth and number of children (5 or under 5 years) in the household have shown significant impact on nutritional status of children. For women empowerment a revised set of indicators related with child's nutritional status (similarly other areas of woman and child welfare) is required, which may reveal its impact on nutritional status of children (and other areas of woman and child welfare).

Keywords: Woman empowerment, Household economics, Woman autonomy, Child health, Child nutrition

Women empowerment is a multi-dimensional and multi-level concept. Psychological, legal, political, socio-cultural, economic and family/ interpersonal are the dimensions of women empowerment. They are measured at national, community and household levels. Women empowerment matrix measured by Charmes and Wieringa (2003) has six dimensions, i.e., physical, socio-cultural, religious, economic, political and legal. They are measurable at global, regional, state, community, household and individual levels. Millennium Project Task Force on Education and Gender Equality adopted three domains of empowerment, (i) the capability domain (through indicator of education, health and nutrition), (ii) the access to resources and opportunities domain, which referred to political decision-making and economic assets, and (iii) security domain which contains violence and conflict matters (Grown *et al.*, 2008).

Sen (1994) defined empowerment as altering relations of power, which constrain women's options and autonomy and adversely affect their well-being. There are many dimensions and definitions of it such as (i) control over resources like physical, human, intellectual and financial (see Kabeer, 1994), and ideology like values, believes and attitudes (see Batliwala, 1994), (ii) women's agency, i.e., women themselves have right to make choices about them and their families (Kabeer, 1999), (iii) the process and move from being without power to having power, and (iv) the outcome, such as improvement in education, health, economic and political participation.

Women empowerment connotes economic empowerment which implies a better quality of material life through sustainable livelihood owned and managed by women, social empowerment that means a more equitable social status of women in society, legal empowerment that suggests the provision of an effective legal structure that is supportive for women's empowerment, and political empowerment that means political system favoring the participation and control of political decision-making process and governance by women. All these aspects are of national level and by implementation and achieving these objects the effects may reach to households. At the household level participation in decision-making by the woman represents her empowerment. It is related with legal, psychological, economic, religious as well as political dimensions. The women empowerments at different levels are inter-connected and mutually reinforcing. For instance, empowerment at the national level or community level in the form of organizing around a particular objective is likely to affect the women empowerment at household level and individual level in the form of increased self-esteem and sense of agency. On the other hand, when empowerment at individual and household level occurs, it affects the women empowerment at community and national levels. For instance, empowerment in the form of geographic mobility by women, that is, empowerment at household level may affect the increased political participation of women at the national level.

Defining and measuring the women empowerment at the household level is challenging. The key underlying concepts that define woman's empowerment at household level relate to choices, control and power (Malhotra and Schular, 2005). It also refers to notion of power, agency, control and decision-making. Women's empowerment is conceptualized as a function of women's access to and control over resources, which extends to their decision-making capabilities regarding household decisions, employment, income, household assets and expenditures, fertility, sexuality, and freedom of movement (physical mobility) and their control over material and intangible resources such as property, information and time; their position within the household *vis-à-vis* other male and female household members; their experience of domestic violence; and their education (Gurumurthy, 1998).

A number of studies have recognized the need of direct measure of women empowerment (Cunningham *et al.*, 2015). The UN (2008) has developed indicators to measure women empowerment. They fall into five categories: woman's sense of self-worth; the right to have and determine choice; the right to have access to resources; the right to have the power to control their lives; and the ability to influence the direction of social change to create a more just social and economic order. These measures have been used in the literature for a variety of research areas.

The United Nations Development Program (UNDP) has identified three key areas of gender inequality to create gender empowerment measure (GEM). The key areas included are: political participation and decision-making power as measured by the percentage share of seats in parliament held by women *vis-à-vis*; economic participation and decision-making power as measured by the percentage of positions such as legislators, senior officials, managers, technocrats and other professionals held by women *vis-à-vis*; and power over economic resources as measured by relative share in estimated earned income held by women and men.[1]

[1]Beteta (2006) has questioned the GEM and described it an incomplete and biased index of women empowerment which measures inequality among the most educated and economically advantaged population. It failed to include important non-economic dimensions of decision-making power both at individual and household level.

At the household level Bloom *et al.* (2001) have used freedom of movement and decision-making power for women empowerment. Smith *et al.* (2003) measured the women empowerment as the woman's age at her time marriage. Kravdal (2004) used the women empowerment index (sum of binary response variable, such as, whether a husband is justified beating his wife in certain situations) and average women's education to find its effect on child mortality. Gaiha and Kulkarni (2005) measured the women empowerment as the wage gap between women and women to find out its effect on malnutrition in children. Lee-Rife (2010) included several dimensions of women empowerment like mobility, financial decision-making, experience of violence and threats of abandonment or homelessness. Mahmud *et al.* (2012) constructed the women empowerment index by using five indicators, i.e., self-esteem (two indicators — justification of wife beating and women should participate in decision-making), household decision-making, freedom of mobility and control of material resources. Khan *et al.* (2016) have taken women decision-making index and woman violence index to capture the effect of women empowerment on child vaccination in Pakistan (see also Sado *et al.* (2014) for maternal health care in Albania).

There are other literature proxies of women empowerment based on women's access and control over household resources. The women's decision-making power is proxied by work status, husband–wife age difference at marriage, age at first marriage and education. The assets of the woman at marriage have also been taken as a measure of women's decision-making power at household level. It is based on the fact that in South Asia, the cultural settings of marital union make women and men's assets at the time of marriage important for the future relation between wives and husbands (Quisumbing and Maluccio 2000; Thomas *et al.*, 2002).

The autonomy of woman in the household in the perspective of social and cultural norms of India has been measured by Pande (2003) as endogamy and exogamy marriages. It is an indicator of woman's position in marriage and family structure. Kinship endogamy (marrying blood relations) was directly measured while spatial endogamy (marrying within the village) was measured by whether the woman currently resides in her village of birth or not. Exogamy is associated with lesser autonomy than endogamy.

Generally, empowered women contribute to well-being and productivity of families and improve prospects for the next generations (NIPORT *et al.*, 2009). Woman empowerment is also generally associated with child anthropometry (Cunningham *et al.*, 2015). It is associated with child nutrition through social and economic autonomy in the household (Sethuraman, 2008). However, empirical evidences are mixed regarding impact of woman empowerment on nutritional status of children. For instance, that women empowerment enhances nutritional status of children has been found by Ramalingaswami *et al.* (1996) for tribal and rural community in India, Smith *et al.* (2003) for developing economies, Haddad (1999) for developing economies, Luke and Xu (2011) for India, Bhagowalia *et al.* (2012) for Bangladesh, Imai *et al.* (2012) for rural India, Heaton (2015) for developing economies and Khan *et al.* (2016) for child vaccination in Pakistan. It has positive impact on HIV in Tanzania (Bashemera *et al.*, 2013), antenatal and postnatal care utilization in Albania (Sado *et al.*, 2014).

On the other hand, Bloom *et al.* (2001) evidenced no effect of decision-making power of women on utilization of post-natal care (see also Mumtaz and Salway (2007) for Pakistan). Begum and Sen (2009) for Bangladesh has shown no significant effect of woman empowerment illustrated by an index of decision-making about her own health care, child health care, large household purchases, daily household purchases and her freedom to visit relatives and friends on stunting, wasting and under-weight. Similar are the results by Bose (2011) for India. Desai and Johnson (2005) concluded that children whose mothers had final decision-making power had children with higher height-for-age in India but not in Nepal. For Pakistan Zubia and Salway (2005) concluded that woman's unaccompanied mobility has no effect on her contraceptive behaviour and antenatal care practices. As concerns the measures of anthropometric measures, the evidences are varying. For instance, Shroff *et al.* (2011) disclosed that household decisions by the women are positively associated with the weight-for-age and weight-for-height but not with height-for-age. The inconsistencies and variations are attributed by population characteristics, analytical methods, conceptualization of woman's empowerment and specific domains of anthropometry (Cunningham *et al.*, 2015). Khan and Raza (2013a) documented that decision-making done by women has no significant effect on Tetanus Toxoid vaccination of pregnant women in India. Khan and Raza (2013b) have shown ambiguous effect of woman's say on maternal health care in the form of iron supplementation in India (see also Morgan *et al.* (2002) for Muslim and non-Muslim Asian population; Mumtaz and Salway (2007) for reproductive health care in Pakistan).

One of the important reasons may be that there is not a generally accepted approach to define and measure woman empowerment. Secondly, several studies have included a small number of measures of women empowerment from only one domain, that may be decision-making, freedom of mobility, economic security, social security and emotional security, irrespective of which domain or measure women empowerment are relevant. Thirdly, many studies consider only one context while political, economic and cultural contexts are ignored (Heaton, 2015). Fourthly, different domains of women empowerment like social support, workload and time, and control of resources and autonomy differently influence child nutrition (Cunningham *et al.*, 2015) and other aspects of woman and child welfare.

The fundamental hypothesis of the current study is whether women empowerment contributes in nutritional status of children. The stunting, wasting and under-weight children are alarmingly high at 43.2%, 17.4% and 41%, respectively, in Bangladesh so it may be a good case study for the purpose.

22.1 Women empowerment and different areas of household welfare

The literature on women empowerment covers different areas of household welfare like child health and nutrition, child schooling, fertility, maternal health and nutrition. The studies have used various indicators, proxies and indices of women empowerment and its association with malnutrition in children.

Osmani and Sen (2003) argued that one of the important factors of malnutrition in children is lack of women empowerment. In South Asia, marriage in adolescence remains a widespread practice. It is relevant with women's empowerment. At early stage of their life cycle, married adolescent girls are least empowered members in their marital homes. They are unable to provide optimum care to their children due to low status in their households. Maitra (2004) explained that child health is outcome of usage of health care, that is determined by woman's education and control over the household resources and bargaining power. Smith *et al.* (2003) through a meta-analysis of 36 developing economies concluded that women's empowerment measured by empowerment index has significant positive effect on nutritional status of children.

The mother's employment has been used as a proxy of women empowerment in the literature. It has diverse impact on nutritional status of children. When a child is in infancy during its first 6 months, mother's working status may affect child's nutrition negatively due to lack in child care. After that age, increase in income provides better milk and food for child which may boost infant's health (Mukuria *et al.*, 2005). In the empowerment perspective the women employment becomes effective in the case of formal sector employment where the women are literate. Kishor and Parasurman (1998) found that poor women who work as daily wage laborers, their employment increases the risk of child mortality and malnutrition. It is supported by the findings of Desai and Jain (1994) that as women's wages are so low the families prefer for women to stay home to be more productive for the household welfare including children nutrition. On the other hand, studies have shown that mothers who contribute more to household income are less likely to have malnourished children as majority of the mother's incomes are used to provide food to their children (Mencher, 1988).

Bose (2011) found that women empowerment index comprised decision-making of women on own health care, major household purchases, daily household purchases, visiting family or friends and freedom of movement to market, health facility and outside of village had no association with children's nutritional status.

Sethuraman (2008) explored the relationship between women's empowerment measured by women's decision making and physical mobility, and maternal nutrition, child nutrition and growth of children. The findings suggested that women's lack of empowerment and existence of violence adversely affect child nutrition and growth. Imai *et al.* (2012) concluded that mother's empowerment measured by her relative bargaining power (to her husband) has a positive impact on nutritional status of children in rural India.

Studies have also shown that education of women as an indicator of women empowerment confers the greatest benefit (Malhotra *et al.*, 2003). Heaton (2015) using a broad sample of 28 countries concluded that nutritional status of children is associated with the improved status of women. Increased control over reproduction, freedom from violence, legislation and enforcement of women rights, and greater political representation improve child health. However, decision-making has minimal impact and female employment, status of job and control of income has only modest impact on child health.

To see the impact of women empowerment on nutritional status of children we will use women empowerment index for measuring the women empowerment and CIAF for malnutrition. It will be an addition to the literature on malnutrition in children in the perspective of women empowerment.

22.2 Methodology

22.2.1 Data and principal variables

For the estimation the micro-data has been extracted from BDHS 2007 which provides complete information on components of empowerment and malnutrition.

(1) *Measuring CIAF*

The stunting, wasting and under-weight children have been defined as the children whose height-for-age, weight-for-age and weight-for-height Z-Score are less than −2.0 SD, respectively. CIAF represents the malnourished children who are suffering from either stunting, wasting, under-weight or any combination.

(2) *Women empowerment*

The limitations of indirect and proxy measures have been recognized in the literature. The direct measures of women empowerment having its multidimensionality is designed and utilized by the studies (Smith *et al.*, 2003; Begum and Sen 2009; Bose 2011).[2] Keeping in view all these aspects and availability of data from BDHS, we have included three indicators of women empowerment at household level to create index, i.e., wife beating, sex refusal to husband and decision-making in the household.[3] The indicator of wife beating is included as a component of women empowerment on the basis of theoretical and conceptual support from Sen (1994) regarding empowerment as a removal of the constraint from women welfare, Kabeer (1999) regarding the right to make choices about themselves, Grown *et al.* (2008) regarding the security domain which contains violence (see also Gurumurthy, 1998; NIPORT *et al.*, 2009) and legal dimension given by Charmes and Wieringa (2003).

The decision to include the component of refusal of sex in women empowerment index has the theoretical support from physical and socio-cultural dimensions of Charmes and Weiringa (2003), right of fertility and

[2]However, in the case of maternal health, reproductive events affect the women empowerment. For instance, in India, the women who have had abortion experience domestic violence and those who have had experience of mistimed pregnancies face lower domestic violence (Lee-Rife, 2010).

[3]The pathway for effect of domestic violence on child growth and nutrition is well documented by Yount *et al.* (2011).

sexuality (Gurumurthy, 1998) and reproductive life participation by woman (NIPORT *et al.*, 2009).

Regarding decision-making in the household, researchers recognized that women's participation in domestic decision-making affects their ability to make health decisions (Bloom *et al.*, 2001). Decision-making by the woman at the household level is an important component of women empowerment. It covers conceptual support about woman's option (Sen, 1994), choice about themselves and their families (Kabeer, 1999), freedom of movement, decision-making for household assets and expenditures, position within the household (Gurumurthy, 1998) and level of choice (Malhotra and Schular, 2005).

The woman empowerment index comprising three indicators represents the woman's empowerment at household level.[4] Such type of empowerment measures, indicators or components have been used by researchers for health-seeking behavior of women, maternal health, fertility and child health care (Bloom *et al.*, 2001; Dixon-Mueller, 2003; Larsen and Hollos, 2003; Bashemera *et al.*, 2013; Khan *et al.*, 2016). According to our knowledge none of the studies have used such type of index to see the impact of women empowerment on nutritional status of children in Bangladesh. It is speculated that woman empowerment increases the nutritional status of children.

22.2.2 Model estimation

Andersen and Newman (1973) developed the behavioral model for utilization of health care. The model gives the conceptual framework for determinants of health care.

The estimation equation based on Andersen and Newman (1973) model is expressed as follows:

$$\begin{aligned}\text{CIAF} = f(&\text{AGE}_{\text{ij}}, \text{SEX}_{\text{ij}}, \text{BORD}_{\text{ij}}, \text{MEDU}_{\text{ij}}, \text{MBMI}_{\text{ij}}, \text{WEM}_{\text{ij}}, \text{BF}_{\text{ij}},\\ &\text{DIAR}_{\text{ij}}, \text{FEVER}_{\text{ij}}, \text{COUGH}_{\text{ij}}, \text{WEALTH}_{\text{ij}}, \text{NCH}_{\text{ij}}) \qquad (1)\end{aligned}$$

Equation (1) is a general form of function to assess the impact of woman empowerment along with other socio-economic factors on malnutrition in

[4]The index covers majority of the theoretical aspects of women empowerment but economic and political aspect remains out of the net of this index. It is limitation of the study on account of data constraint.

Table 22.1 Operational definitions of variables.

Variables	Definitions
Dependent variable	
CIAF (Composite Index of Anthropometric Failure)	1 if the child falls in CIAF, 0 otherwise
Explanatory variables	
AGE (Child's Age)	Child's age in completed months
SEX (Child's Sex)	1 for Male, 0 for Female
BORD (Child's Birth order)	Child's Birth order
MEDU (Mother's Education)	0 for illiterate, 1 for primary, 2 for secondary, 3 for collage and higher
MBMI (Mother's Body Mass Index)	0 for $<$18.5, 1 for $\geq$18.5
WEM (Woman Empowerment Index)	Range 0–3 showing the incremental change in woman empowerment
BF (Breastfeeding)	Number of months of breastfeeding to child
DIAR (Diarrhea)	1 if diarrhea in the last two weeks, 0 otherwise
FEVER (Fever)	1 if fever in the last two weeks, 0 otherwise
COUGH (Cough)	1 if cough in the last two weeks, 0 otherwise
WEALTH (Wealth Index)	0 for Poorest, 1 for Poorer, 2 for Middle, 3 for Richer, and 4 for Richest.
NCH (Number of Children 5 or under 5 years)	Numbers of children in household as continuous variable

children. The binary logistic regression is applied for estimating the probability of CIAF. The operational definitions of dependent and explanatory variables are given in Table 22.1.

22.3 Results and discussion

The percentage estimates and results of binary logistic regression for CIAF of Bangladeshi children are presented in Tables 22.2 and 22.3, respectively.

Majority of the results are consistent with theoretical dimensions. First of all, we will discuss the principal variable, i.e., woman empowerment then the other variables in the order of the results.

22.3.1 Woman empowerment

There are a number of ways by which women empowerment may be associated with child's improved nutrition. Firstly, many actions that lead to better nutritional status emerged from day to day health enhancing behaviors, such as better personal hygiene, regular access to preventive

Table 22.2 Percentage estimates of malnutrition in Bangladeshi children.

Background characteristics		Percentage of malnutrition in children
Child's Age in Months	<6	38.4
	7–11	41.3
	12–17	48.4
	18–23	59.0
	24–35	61.5
	36–47	61.4
	48–59	58.1
Sex of Child	Male	55.3
	Female	54.5
Birth Order of Child	1	50.1
	2–3	53.7
	4–5	61.9
	6 ≥	67.5
Mother's Education	No Education	65.1
	Primary	61.2
	Secondary	47.1
	Collage and Higher	28.9
Mother's BMI	<18.5	64.5
	≥18.5	50.5
Woman Empowerment Index	0–5	61.3
	6–10	55.5
	11–15	52.7
	16–20	57.0
Breastfeeding in Months	≤6	40.2
	7–12	46.2
	13–36	58.8
	37 ≥	66.4
Incidence of Diarrhea in the last two weeks	No	54.1
	Yes	62.3
Incidence of Fever in the last two weeks	No	53.4
	Yes	57.5
Incidence of Cough in the last two weeks	No	54.0
	Yes	56.6
Wealth Index	Poorest	67.9
	Poorer	62.7
	Middle	56.7
	Richer	51.4
	Richest	37.6
Number of Children Under 5 Years	≤2	54.8
	>2	56.4

Table 22.3 Results of binary logistic regression for CIAF Bangladeshi children.

Variables	Coefficient	Standard error	p-value
Child's age in months [continuous]			
	0.007	0.002	0.002*
Sex of child [female as reference]			
Male	0.032	0.058	0.587
Birth order [continuous]			
	0.037	0.019	0.057**
Mother's education [no education as reference]			
Primary	0.019	0.081	0.817
Secondary	0.319	0.088	0.000*
Collage and Higher	−0.780	0.141	0.000*
Mother's BMI [thinness < 18.5 as reference]			
Normal ≥ 18.5	−0.374	0.065	0.000*
Woman empowerment index			
	−0.004	0.007	0.533
Breastfeeding in months			
	0.018	0.003	0.000*
Incidence of diarrhea [no as reference]			
Yes	0.304	0.100	0.002*
Incidence of fever [no as reference]			
Yes	0.154	0.077	0.045*
Incidence of cough [no as reference]			
Yes	0.006	0.077	0.935
Wealth index [poorest as reference]			
Poorer	−0.117	0.094	0.213
Middle	−0.330	0.096	0.001*
Richer	−0.426	0.099	0.000*
Richest	−0.778	0.102	0.000*
Number of children in under 5 years [continuous]			
Constant	0.047	0.038	0.214
	0.173	0.163	0.288

Note: Number of observations = 5,254.
*represents 5% and **represents 10% level of significance.

treatment such as timely vaccination, frequency of breastfeeding and initiation of supplement food, etc. When women have efficient decision-makings, it leads to better nutritional status of the children than when decisions are controlled by men. Secondly, at any given income, households must choose where resources would be spent. For poor households, some implicit trade-offs occur between quality of housing, food expenditure, health and education expenditures, and purchase of large consumer durables, etc. Literature documented that households in which women have more power devote a greater proportion of resources to child-centered expenditures (Bruce *et al.*, 1995). Lastly, when children are seriously ill, all family members may recognize the need to obtain medical care and will do it if they can afford it and if care is available. However, if the primary caregiver, i.e., mother needs to consult with husbands and family elders, it is possible that the child may not receive immediate care.

Despite the aforementioned pathways, by which women empowerment is linked with nutritional status of children, our results have shown no significant effect of women empowerment on nutritional status of children in Bangladesh. The explanation may be as: the highly empowered women living in a community where women have little say in decision-making may find their power diminished. For example, in highly patriarchal areas, doctors may refuse to carry out emergency treatment at the mother's sole discretion. Secondly, the community attributes and norms are far more important in determining health outcomes than individual attitudes. For example, when a woman is dealing with a sick child, and her husband is not present, the neighbors might encourage her to make an independent decision to take the child for treatment. Thus, a community that views women as capable for making independent decisions might positively influence a woman who has little power in her day-to-day life. Kabeer (2001) argued that when women do not act collectively to challenge the existing normative structures, their individual efforts often have a limited impact.

There emerged another notion of women empowerment at household level that may be incorporated with community settings. In the community like Bangladesh the women with lower empowerment may be able to do better about child health through other family members. This may include the activities related with nutrition and health care, special food for infants and hygienic material. This factor may neutralize the women empowerment effect on nutritional status of children.

The results support the idea of women's centrality within the household rather than empowerment or autonomy from the household. White (1992) explained that autonomy paradigm within household or empowerment at the household level is under-emphasized by the autonomous actions like unaccompanied mobility and final decision-making at the household level. Such an approach ignores the fact that household members, both men and women are tied together by strong emotional and structural bonds. Their relationships strengthen the interests of women toward their families. The women make the decisions with consultations of family members, family heads or their husbands. They perceive that these members would not only help them in decision-making but the decision would be better for the households. It implies domestic role for women and acts to reinforce patriarchal relations and women's subordinate status. The lack of female education and awareness about the health care further strengthen the phenomenon.

Women empowerment is a multi-dimensional concept, possibly woman may be empowered in one dimension but not in other (Hashemi *et al.*, 1996). It neutralizes the effect of women empowerment on child nutritional status. The scholars also argue that domestic violence is not the measure of empowerment but rather a determinant of empowerment (Allendorf, 2009). It may also be argued that the decision-making at the household level included in women's empowerment index is a different dimension of woman' autonomy from that dealing with decision-making for child health and nutrition. The relevant decision-making should include the questions regarding postnatal-care, immunization, fertility, infant supplement food, hygiene material and doctor's visit in emergency, etc. It may be concluded that the measure of women empowerment for it effect on nutritional status of children is weak. Cunningham *et al.* (2015) have also argued that there is a need to harmonize the definition of empowerment and key domain. Heaton's (2015) concluding remarks also stress for devising correct measures of women empowerment. The study narrated that it would be a mistake to make a general claim about the importance of mother's empowerment using the variables available in DHS because some of the indicators are partially or completely non-related to the child health. For instance, child health and decision about daily household purchases, visit to relatives and friends, refusing sex and justification of wife beating are non-related.

22.3.2 Child characteristics

The results have shown that by increase in child's age the risk of malnutrition increases in Bangladeshi children (see also, Das and Rahman (2011) for Bangladesh; Khan and Raza (2014a) for urban and rural areas of Bangladesh). It is supported by percentage estimates. It reveals that most parents in Bangladesh are failing to fulfill optimal food requirements of their children with the increase in children's age. However, the gender of the child has statistically no significant effect; so, gender discrimination does not exist in nutritional status of children.

22.3.3 Mother characteristics

In the literature, empirical evidences exist on relationship between child's birth order and allocation of resources to children which consequent to malnutrition (Ukwuani *et al.*, 2003; Biswas and Bose, 2010). The estimates show that birth order of the child increases the probability of CIAF in children (see also Khan and Raza (2014a) for urban and rural areas of Bangladesh; Khan and Raza (2014b) for CIAF in Bangladeshi children). The percentage estimation supports the results. It explains that less nutrition, health care and attention is available for high birth-order children.

The mother's secondary levels of education, and college and higher level of education decrease the risk of malnutrition (see also Khan and Raza, 2014a). It explains that acquiring knowledge and information about child health and nutrition by mother through education enhances the nutritional status of children.

The longer duration of breastfeeding has been found to increase the probability of malnutrition. It is corroborated by the percentage estimates and explains that mothers have been breastfeeding for long duration to fulfill the nutritional requirements of the children as a substitute of food supplements which results into decreased nutritional status of children.

The nutritional status of mother (BMI) has been found an important determinant of child's nutritional status. The probability of the children to fall in CIAF increases by lower BMI of mothers (see also Khan and Raza (2014a) for urban and rural areas of Bangladesh). It is also supported by the percentage estimates.

22.3.4 Disease-related characteristics

The estimates have shown that incidence of Diarrhea and fever that lasts for two weeks increase the probability of malnutrition (see also Das and Rahman (2011) for wasting and under-weight children in Bangladesh; Khan and Raza (2014a) for urban and rural areas of Bangladesh). The short-run and urgent measures may lessen the incidence of disease and ultimately reduce malnutrition in children.

22.3.5 Household characteristics

The wealth index has been taken as a proxy of socio-economic status of the household which shows that the risk of being malnourished in Bangladeshi children is negatively related with last three highest quintiles (middle, richer and richest). The result is corroborated with percentage estimates. It confirmed that wealth index is key determinant of nutritional status of children.

22.4 Conclusion

The empirical evidence emerged from this study has important research proposals and implications for policy formulation. The major variable, i.e., women empowerment was focused to see its effect on nutritional status of children. The study concluded that women empowerment has no significant effect on nutritional status of children. It has made conceptualization and dimensions of empowerment problematic. It weakened the general perception that women empowerment enhances the household welfare. The explanation may be linked to the measure of empowerment. The measure of women empowerment used in the analysis was derived from the question asked in DHS. The popularity of this measure rests on the fact that it is derived from the questions which are easy to ask in a large-scale survey. It is not completely obvious that they are proxies for women to have a greater control over their lives because they can be answered much more ambiguously than a standard survey is able to capture because at least some of these freedoms can coexist with severe constraints.

For measuring women empowerment it is proposed to include the decision-making of women regarding child health. For instance, decision for child's examination from a doctor, food for child, vaccination of child, fertility behavior particularly for the number of children and the birth interval, the mother's personal hygiene and nutrition, having information regarding child's health and nutrition from any source of media should be included as indicators of women empowerment. Women empowerment may be classified into dimensions like the mother and child's health dimension, which may explain its effect on child health. The general empowerment as measured by the current study and proposed by DHS studies is insufficient to explain the particular relationship between women empowerment and other socio-economic variables like mother's health and child schooling. There should be separate dimension of women empowerment for each of them. Kishor (2000) argued that capturing the impact of women empowerment requires indicators relevant to the end product of the process. Kishore and Subaiya

(2008) narrated that when studying women empowerment, there is a need to be specific about what is to be measured and for whom to be measured. Cunningham *et al.* (2015) also argued that key domain of the women empowerment relevant to the area of analysis should be included (in the analysis) and women empowerment should be measured in the relevance. It augments the notion that there is a need for measuring the women empowerment based on dimensions. Further research is proposed to see the impact of women empowerment on nutritional status of children through other measures of women empowerment.

It is further proposed that Bangladesh should focus on compulsory secondary education for all, mother's nutritional status and measures to diminish incidence of diarrhea and fever to increase the nutritional status of children. Policy is also needed to enhance the socio-economic status of the household.

References

Allendorf, K. (2009), The Quality of Family Relationships and its Effect on Women's Agency in India. Presented at the annual meeting of the Population Association of America in Detroit, MI.

Andersen, R. and Newman, J. F. (1973), Social and individual determinants of medical care utilization in the United States. *Milbank Memorial Fund Quarterly*, 51, 95–124.

Bashemera, D. R., Nhembo, M. J. and Benedict, G. (2013), The Role of Women's Empowerment in Influencing HIV Testing. DHS Working Papers. ICF International, Calverton, Maryland, USA.

Batliwala, S. (1994), "The meaning of empowerment: new concepts from action", in Sen, G., Germain, A. and Chen, L. C. (eds.), *Population Policies Reconsidered: Health, Empowerment and Rights*, Cambridge: Harvard University Press, pp. 127–138.

Beteta, K. C. (2006), What is missing in measures of women's empowerment? *Journal of Human Development and Capabilities*, 7(2), 221–241.

Bhagowalia, P., Menon, P., Quisumbing, A. R. and Soundararajan, V. (2012), What Dimensions of Women's Empowerment Matter Most for Child Nutrition? Evidence Using Nationally Representative Data from Bangladesh. IFPRI Discussion Paper 01192, Poverty, Health, and Nutrition Division. International Food Policy Research Institute, Washington, DC.

Biswas, S. and Bose, K. (2010), Sex differences in the effect of birth order and parents' educational status on stunting: A study on Bengalee preschool children from eastern India. *HOMO — Journal of Comparative Human Biology*, 61, 271–276.

Bloom, S. S., Wypij, D. and Das Gupta, M. (2001), Dimensions of women's autonomy and the influence of maternal health-care utilization in a north Indian city. *Demography*, 38(1), 67–78.

Bose, S. (2011), The effect of women's status and community on the gender differential in children's nutrition in India. *Journal of Biosocial Science*, 43(5), 513–33.

Bruce, J., Llyd, C. and Leonard, A. (1995), *Families in Focus: New Perspectives on Mothers, Fathers and Children*, New York: The Population Council.

Charmes, J. and Wieringa, S. (2003), Measuring women's empowerment: An assessment of the gender related development index and gender empowerment index. *Journal of Human Development*, 4(3), 419–435.

Cunningham, K., Ruel, M., Ferguson, E. and Uauy, R. (2015), Women's empowerment and child nutritional status in South Asia: A synthesis of the literature. *Maternal and Child Nutrition*, 11, 1–19.

Das, S. and Rahman, R. M. (2011), Application of ordinal logistic regression analysis in determining risk factors of child malnutrition in Bangladesh. *Nutritional Journal*, 10, 124.

Desai, S. and Jain, D. (1994), Maternal employment and changes in family dynamics: The social context of women's work in south India. *Population and Development Review*, 20, 115–136.

Desai S. and Johnson, K. (2005), Women's decisionmaking and child health: familial and social hierarchies. in Kishor, S. (ed.). *A Focus on Gender – Collected Papers on Gender Using DHS Data*, pp. 15–33. ORC Macro: Calverton.

Dixon-Mueller, R. (2003), *Female Empowerment and Demographic Process: Moving Beyond Cairo. In IUSSP Contribution to Gender Research*, Paris: International Union for Scientific Study of Population, pp. 1089–1108.

Gaiha, R. and Kulkarni, V. (2005), Anthropometric failure and persistence of poverty in rural India. *International Review of Applied Economics*, 19(2), 179–197.

Grown, C., Chandrika, B., Jesse, H. and Diane, E. (2008), "The financial requirements of achieving gender equality and women's empowerment", in Buvinic, M., Morrison, A. R. Waafas Ofosu-Amaah, A. W. and sj blom, M. (eds.). *Equality for Women: Where Do We Stand on Millennium Development Goal 3?* Washington, DC: The World Bank.

Gurumurthy, A. (1998), *Women's Rights and Status: Questions of Analysis and Measurement.* Gender in Development Monograph 7, New York: United Nations Development Program (UNDP).

Haddad, L. (1999), Women's status: levels, determinants, consequences for malnutrition, interventions, and policy. *Asian Development Review*, 17(1,2), 96–131.

Hashemi, S. M., Schuler, S. R. and Riley, A. P. (1996), Rural credit programs and women's empowerment in Bangladesh. *World Development*, 24(4), 635–653.

Imai, K. S., Anuim, S. K., Raiha, R. and Kulkarni, V. S. (2012), Does Women Empowerment Reduce Prevalence of Stunted and Underweight Children in Rural India? Discussion Paper Series. Research Institute for Economics and Business Administration, Japan: Kobe University.

Kabeer, N. (1994), *Reversed Realities: Gender Hierarchies in Development Thought*, London: Verso.

Kabeer, N. (1999), *The Conditions and Consequences of Choice: Reflections on the Measurement of Women's Empowerment.* UNRISD Discussion Paper No. 108, Geneva: United Nations Research Institute for Social Development.

Kabeer, N. (2001), Reflections on the Measurement of Women's Empowerment. In Discussing Women' Empowerment-Theory and Practice. Sida Studies No. 3, Stockholm: Novum Grafiska A. B.

Khan, R. E. A. and Raza, M. A. (2014a), Child malnutrition in developing economies: A case study of Bangladesh. *Quality and Quantity*, 48, 1389–1408.

Khan, R. E. A. and Raza, M. A. (2014b), Nutritional status of children in Bangladesh: measuring composite index of anthropometric failure (CIAF) and its determinants. *Pakistan Journal of Commerce and Social Sciences*, 8(1), 11–23.

Khan, R. E. A. and Raza, M. A. (2017), Utilization of quality source of prenatal care in India: An evidence from IDHS. *Social Indicators Research*, 131, 1163–1178.

Khan, R. E. A. and Raza, M. A. (2013a), Maternal health-care in India: The case of tetanus toxoid vaccination. *Asian Development Policy Review*, 1, 1–14.

Khan, R. E. A., Bari, K. M. and Mehmood, S. (2016), Women education and empowerment: The implications for child vaccination in Pakistan. *Journal of Educational Research*, 19(11), 10–23.

Khan, R. E. A. and Raza, M. A. (2013b), Maternal health-care: The case of iron supplementation in India. *Pakistan Journal of Commerce and Social Sciences*, 7, 263–275.

Kishor, S., and Subaiya, L. (2008), Understanding Women's Empowerment: A Comparative Analysis of Demographic and Health Surveys (DHS) Data. DHS Comparative Reports No. 20. Calverton, Maryland, USA: Macro International Inc.

Kishor, S. and Parasuraman, S. (1998), Mother's Employment and Infant and Child Mortality in India. National Family Health Survey Subject Report No. 8, Calverton: Macro International.

Kishor, S. (2000), "Empowerment of women in Egypt and links to the survival and health of their infants", in Presser, H. B. and Sen, G. (eds.). *Women's Empowerment and Demographic Processes*, New York: Oxford University Press, pp. 119–156.

Kravdal, O. (2004), Child mortality in India: the community level effects of education. *Population Studies*, 5(8), 177–192.

Larsen, U. and Hollos, M. (2003), Women empowerment and fertility decline among the Pare of Kilimanjaro Region, Northern Tanzania. *Social Science and Medicine*, 57, 1099–1115.

Lee-Rife, S. M. (2010), Women's empowerment and reproductive experiences over the life-course. *Social Science and Medicine*, 71, 634–642.

Luke, N. and Xu, H. (2011), Exploring the meaning of context for health: Community influences on child health in south India. *Demographic Research*, 24, 345–374.

Mahmud, S., Shah, N. M. and Becker, S. (2012), Measurement of women's empowerment in rural Bangladesh. *World Development*, 40(3), 610–619.

Maitra, P. (2004), Parental bargaining, health inputs and child mortality in India. *Journal of Health Economics*, 23(2), 259–291.

Malhotra, A. and Schuler, S. (2005), "Measuring women's empowerment as a variable in international development", in Narayan, D. (ed.). *Measuring Empowerment.* Washington, DC: World Bank.

Malhotra, A., Pande, R. and Grown, C. (2003), *Impact of Investments in Female Education on Gender Equality*, Washington, DC: International Center for Research on Women.

Mencher, J. (1988), "Women's work and poverty: Women's contribution to household maintenance in south India", in Dwyer, D. and Bruce, J. (eds.). *A Home Divided: Women and Income in the Third World*, Stanford: Stanford University Press, pp. 99–119.

Morgan, S., Stash, S., Smith, H. L. and Mason, K. O. (2002), Muslim and non-Muslim differences in female autonomy and fertility: Evidence from four Asian countries. *Population and Development Review*, 28(3), 515–737.

Mukuria, A., Cushing, J. and Sangha, J. (2005), *Nutritional Status of Children: Results from the Demographic and Health Surveys 1994–2001*, Calverton: Macro International.

Mumtaz, Z. and Salway, S. (2005), I never go anywhere': Extricating the links between women's mobility and uptake of reproductive health services in Pakistan. *Social Science and Medicine*, 60(8), 1751–1765.

Mumtaz, Z. and Salway, S. M. (2007), Gender, pregnancy and the uptake of antenatal-care services in Pakistan. *Sociology of Health and Illness*, 29, 1–26.

NIPORT, Maitra and Associate and Macro International (2009), *Bangladesh Demographic and Health Survey 2007*, National Institute of Population Research and Training (NIPORT), Bangladesh: Maitra and Associates, and Calverton: Macro International.

Osmani, S. and Sen, A. (2003), The hidden penalties of gender inequality: Fetal origins of ill-health. *Economics and Human Biology*, 1, 105–121.

Pande, R. P. (2003), Selective gender differences in childhood nutrition and immunization in rural India: The role of siblings. *Demography*, 40(3), 395–418.

Quisumbing, A. and Maluccio, J. (2000), Interhousehold Allocation and Gender Relations: New Empirical Evidence from Four Developing Countries. FCND Discussion Paper No. 84, Washington, DC: International Food Policy Research Institute.

Ramalingaswami, V., Jonsson, U. and Rohde, J. (1996), *The Asian Enigma' in Progress of Nations.* New York: United Nations Children's Fund.

Sado, L., Spaho, A. and Hotchkiss, D. R. (2014), The influence of women's empowerment on maternal health care utilization: Evidence from Albania. *Social Science and Medicine*, 114, 169–177.

Sen, G. (1994), "Women's empowerment and human rights: The challenge to policy", in Graham-Smith, F. (ed.). *Population — The Complex Reality*, London: Royal Society, pp. 363–372.

Sethuraman, K. (2008), The Role of Women's Empowerment and Domestic Violence in Child Growth and Undernutrition in a Tribal and Rural Community in South India. Research Paper No. 2008/15. Helsinki: UNU/WIDER.

Shroff, M. R., Griffiths, P. L., Suchindran, C., Nagalla, B., Vazir, S. and Bentley, M. E. (2011), Does maternal autonomy influence feeding practices and infant growth in rural India? *Social Science and Medicine*, 73(3), 447–455.

Smith, L., Ramakrishnan, U., Ndiaye, A., Haddad, L. and Martorell, R. (2003), *The Importance of Women's Status for Child Nutrition in Developing Countries*, Washington, DC: International Food Policy Research Institute and Department of International Health, and Atlanta: Emory University.

Thomas, D., Contreras, D. and Frankenberg, E. E. (2002), *Distribution of Power within the Household and Child Health*, Mimeo, UCLA.

Ukwuani, F. A. and Suchindran, C. M. (2003), Implications of women's work for child nutritional status in Sub-Saharan Africa: A case study of Nigeria. *Social Science and Medicine*, 56(10), 2109–2121.

UN (2008), *Guidelines on Women's Empowerment*, UN Population Division, New York: United Nations Population Information Network, United Nations.

White, S. (1992), *Arguing with the Crocodile: Gender and Class in Bangladesh*, Dhaka: The University Press Ltd.

Yount, K. M., DiGirolamo, A. M. and Ramakrishnan, U. (2011), Impacts of domestic violence on child growth and nutrition: A conceptual review of the pathways of influence. *Social Science and Medicine*, 72, 1534–1554.

Chapter 23

Does Parents' Education Matter in Inter-Generational Transmission of Human Capital? — A Case of Female Population in Saudi Arabia

Toseef Azid and Sara Aldowsari

Abstract

This chapter discusses the phenomenon of inter-generational transmission of education inequality in Saudi Arabia. Saudi Arabia has a unique position in the world, particularly in the Islamic World. This is the first study on this topic. It addresses separately the effect of father and mother's education on educational attainment of daughters, as well as whether there is an interactive effect of mother and father on daughters' outcomes, in order to address the possibility of assortative mating, and thus the endogeneity of the wife's education with respect to her husband's education. Findings indicate that, while both mothers' and fathers' education influence daughters' educational outcomes, mothers' education has a stronger impact. Conversely, fathers' education has a stronger impact on sons.

Keywords: Intergenerational transmission, Education, Human capital, Saudi Arabia, Daughter's outcome

After the remarkable contribution of Schultz (1961) and Becker (1964, 1975), the researchers have taken their interest in the inter-generational mobility across the generations. It is observed that parents and family mend the behavior of next generations. It is consensus among the social scientists that socio-economic status of the parents and family plays a vital role in the formation of human capital. This chapter will try to explore the issue of education transmission across generations and inequality in the educational achievements. This chapter will concentrate on the impact of the educational attainment of the parents of the female students and female faculty members especially in Saudi Arabia. From its cultural aspects, Saudi Arabia has a unique position in general in the world and particularly in the Islamic World. This is a first study which opens the door for this type of research. This chapter will investigate the following dimensions: (i) What is impact of fathers' education on their daughters? (ii) What is the association between the mothers' education and their daughters' education, (iii) Does the interaction of mothers' and fathers' education have any association with the ability of their daughters'? Considering the cultural aspects of Saudi Arabia, it is not possible to conduct a household survey especially for the female respondents. Traditionally, Qassim University is located in the religious center of Saudi Arabia, so it becomes more attractive for the female students (also for their parents) to get admission in this university and also female faculty members feel comfortable to work in this peaceful environment. Consequently, it represents female students and faculty members who approximately belong to all the geographical areas of Saudi Arabia. Keeping this in view, we selected female campus of the Qassim University for this current study.[1]

Generally, Western media have painted a picture which shows that women in Saudi Arabia does have not the facilities and opportunities which are enjoyed by the developed countries or even in the other Muslim countries. However, it was observed by the authors of this chapter and their own experience of the Western and other Muslim countries that Saudi women have many opportunities which are not available to the women belonging to other countries. Even according to the observations of the authors of this chapter, Saudi women are enjoying those luxuries which are not possible for most of the females in the rest of the world. For example, a good number of female students are proceeding to the Western/developed world for the higher studies which is sponsored by the Saudi government. Moreover, Saudi female population feels honored to be the citizen of a rich oil-based country. They have also the pride of living in a country which has still preserved its culture and their government is the custodian of both the Holy Mosques. The same observation was mentioned by Dunham (2013). Particularly, the current regime of the kingdom also creates a significant space for its female population in the socio-economic sphere. At present one can see women standing behind the counters in most of the shopping

[1]In Saudi Arabia almost all universities have separate independent campus for the female students.

malls in the kingdom. Especially, most of the workers and administrative staff is female in those businesses which are dealing the products related to women and kids. The current regime also made an amendment in the law, thereby women are freely driving on the roads of Saudi Arabia. And it is also interesting to note most of the Acts of the government of Saudi Arabia are in the support of empowerment of every citizen and particularly the women.[2]

This chapter has the following arrangement: Section 23.1 discusses the socio-economic condition of Saudi Arabia. Section 23.2 reviews the literature on the different dimensions of the inter-generational transmission, while Section 23.3 presents the discussion related to data, methodology and empirical analysis. At the end conclusion will be presented.

23.1 Socio-economic state of women in Saudi Arabia

It is observed that government is continuously trying to improve its state of education. Particularly under the present regime there is a steep rise in the literacy rate. Predominantly, the government is launching many new programs for the empowerment of women. Moreover, Saudi society is giving high value to female education. It is also observed from the official statistics that a reasonable number of women owns their businesses. Approximately more than 40% of the nation's private wealth is owned by Saudi women. In the past, the female education was administered by the Directorate General of Girls Education. Initially the purpose was "to bring her up in a proper Islamic way so as to perform her duty in life, be an ideal and successful housewife and a good mother, ready to do things which suit her nature as teaching, nursing, and medical treatment" (Alireza, 1987). The wife of the former King Faisal, Princess Iffat, was an active supporter of female education. She convinced the religious segment of the society about the conventional education for the girls. Hamdan (2005) explains the views

---

[2]Article 8 states that, "The system of governance in the kingdom of Saudi Arabia is based on justice, consultation and equality according to the Islamic Sharia (the law of Islam)". Article 13 states that, The goal of education is to instill the Islamic faith in the brains of the young generation and to impart them with knowledge and skills so that they become useful members in building their society, who love their homeland and be proud of its history". Article 22 states that, "Economic and social development shall be achieved in accordance with a systematic and fair plan". Article 28 states that, "The state shall provide job opportunities to all able-bodied people and shall enact laws to protect both the employee and the employer". Finally, Article 26 states that, "The state shall protect human rights in accordance with Islamic Shari'ah" (Vogel, 1999), Islamic law in the modern world: the legal system of Saudi Arabia, Leiden: Brill.)

of Princes Iffat as: "Iffat maintained that God would judge women as he would judge men, with no preferences for either sex. Men and women, said Iffat, were equal in the eyes of God. King Faisal supported his wife, maintaining that Saudi Arabia's future included equal education for men and women". Al Munajjed (1997) expressed that government of Saudi Arabia was actively involved in the promotion of female education. It is not only limited to the young female population but government has also provided the education facilities to a significant segment of old women. At present one can see that approximately every university has a female campus and all types of conventional courses are offered to the female students. Similarly, thousands of schools can be seen everywhere without considering their geographical location. In Saudi Arabia, every type of education is sponsored by the government and government supports all the educational activities. Government even offers stipend to the female students. Government also encourages the female population to participate in all the economic and social activities provided, if those do not conflict with the basic Islamic norms.

Moreover, in the Islamic history women performed a very key role in the transmission of knowledge, for example, the wife of Prophet (pbuh) Aysha (R.A.) transmitted a chain of sayings and traditions of Prophet (pbuh) and it is always highly appreciated by all the Muslim scholars. Similarly, Khadija (R.A.), the first wife of Prophet (pbuh) was a very successful and prominent businesswomen (Badawi, 1995). Currently in many Muslim countries the prime ministerial position is held by Muslim women, for example, in Bangladesh, Pakistan, Turkey and Indonesia. Prophet (pbuh) was always convincing his companion for acquiring the knowledge. He said: "The search of knowledge is a duty for every Muslim male and female", and "seek knowledge from the cradle to the grave" (cited in Hamdan, 2005). It is also observed from the teaching of *Qur'an* and the traditions of Prophet (pbuh) that women in Islam have many rights like right to education, right to inherit, property rights, and the Prophet (pbuh) encouraged women to participate in all the fields of life. Even at the time when women in the rest of the world were not able to enjoy these rights (Al Munajjed, 1994, Yamani, 1996). At present, in all the Muslim countries the wave of acquiring knowledge can be seen, especially the enrollment of the female students has tremendously increased in the kingdom. It is not a new phenomenon; El-Sanabary (1994) and Kapiszewski (2001) mentioned that a number of female students are going to either educational institution or work. According to Jawad (1998) that veiling does not create any hurdle in the achievement of education whereas acquiring knowledge do not have any conflict with the religious norms of the Islamic system. Even in 1990s, it was observed in the kingdom that mothers were putting an effort to enroll their daughters in the school (Al-Munajjed, 1997). The authors of this chapter have also observed during their survey that most of the women were very happy due to the sex segregation in the country. They informed that because of this segregation there are more jobs in the market thereby they are not competing with their male counterparts in the job market. According to them this is a big advantage for the educated women to get jobs very easily than their male counterparts especially in the professional institutions, for example, banks, universities and in other educational institutions. The same were observed in the past by Fakhro (1996) and Huyette (1985). Consequently, women are now working in the malls, hospitals and in different government offices. For example, in the early years of 2000, a Saudi women Thoraya Obaid was appointed as an Executive Director of the United Nations Population Fund (Qantara.de, 2003). A number of Saudi female students are sponsored by the government for the higher education in the universities of developed countries.

It is reported in different reports of the World Bank that literacy rate of female aged between 15 and 24 is approximately 100%. According to the International group of World Bank, Saudi Arabia is the role model for the other countries. Saudi ministry of education is trying to increase the number of educational institutions all over the country and is aiming to achieve the 100% literacy rate by 2024.

The demographic survey of 2016 which was conducted by the General Authority of Statistics describes: "The figures show that 103 percent of the gross enrollment ratio joined the primary schools, while the net enrollment rate at the same educational stage hit 96.1 percent. The Saudi gross and the net enrollment in the secondary education (intermediate and secondary stages according to the international standards) hit 109.9 percent and 83.1 percent respectively. At the university education stage, Saudi gross and the net enrollment hit 90.1 percent and 46.4 percent respectively. The Saudi gross and net enrollment at all public education stages hit 106.3 percent and 90 percent respectively. The gross enrollment rate for Saudi male population increases in the primary and secondary stages (103.6 percent and 117 percent respectively), higher that the gross enrollment of Saudi female population (102.4 percent and 116.6 percent respectively). On the contrary, the gross and net enrollment rate of Saudi female population is higher at the university stage (97.5 percent and 51.6 percent respectively) than the male population (83.1 percent and 41.6 percent respectively). The change may be reasoned by the fact that male students join labor work after secondary school while female students continue to join the university" (General Authority for Statistics, Demographic Survey 2016, stats.gov.sa).

Currently due to the policies of the present regime, the women are taking responsibilities from minor jobs to major jobs. Government is encouraging them to participate in different economic and social activities. Women are enjoying their right as a citizen as well as the right of their economic and social agent. One of the reports of the *Economist* (10 January 2014) stated that in 2012, 370,000 Saudi women were performing their duties in the public sector, however most of them are in the sector of education, health and administration whereas 216,000 were performing their duties in the private sector. Government is pursing the private sectors for offering more jobs to women. The economic development plans of Saudi government are also emphasizing the changing lifestyle of their citizens through education and economic participation; especially the 9th plan explicitly mentions about it. Generally, it is observed that most of the Saudis want to serve in the government sector because it is secure, more flexible, fully segregated and also guaranteed for life (Al-Asmari, 2008; Al-Shammari, 2009; Ramady, 2013; Al-Asfour and Khan, 2014). It is also observed that the performance of women is better than their male counterparts especially the younger generation. Before 2000, a reasonable number of jobs were occupied by the expatriate, however, after 2000 the policy of Saudisation significantly implemented (Al-Dosary and Rahman, 2009) particularly under the administration of this current regime. However, it is worthwhile to note that the natives are not ready to work in some special jobs (laboring and services) and they prefer to work in the financial, tourism and hospitality companies (Al-Munajjed and Sabbagh 2011). Saudi government also announced a new program known as Nitaqa. The main objective of this program is to impose the quota of Saudi employees in a forceful manner. In 2013, the government was also feminizing the Nitaqat program and instructed to the private sector to offer more jobs to the female labor force (*Arab News*, 8 January 2013). It is also very interesting to note that women are performing their duty with their religious dress, i.e., Islamic garments and covering their full face (Fakkar, 2014). There is no doubt that Saudi women have a desire to participate in the economy with their Islamic garments, provided the work environment and work conditions are comfortable (Al-Shammari, 2009; Ramady, 2013; Abeer Alfarran, 2016). Elamin and Omair (2010) conducted a survey and collected the opinion of Saudi men toward the work of women outside their homes. It is very interesting to note that young and educated were in favor of women working outside the home. Al-Ahmadi conducted a study related to the work responsibilities of Saudi women and he found that highly educated women have highly responsible jobs and a significant number has the managerial positions in different government and private institutions. Despite of the marvelous support from the government still these women are not comfortable because of their natural disadvantage of being a women. Why these women feel like this? According to Al-Ahmadi (2011) this is because women are generally not involved in major decision-making processes and also not significantly involved in the development of the strategic plans.

23.2 Education and intergenerational transmission

It is observed from the different research studies that education plays a very important role in increasing the welfare of the economy and society. It is also empirically observed that there are more chances for the educated to earn more than the uneducated persons. Also, there is more opportunity for the educated to find a good job compared to the uneducated one. Furthermore, education creates a very good environment in the economy. In this chapter, an effort is made to discuss how the education level of parents has impact on their children.

It is discussed in the literature that human capital[3] can be developed through providing health, education and job training facilities. Simultaneously, work experience also plays its significant role in developing the human capital. In the current literature, one can see a number of attempts which discuss the relationship between the parents' education and the state of the education of their children. This inter-generational mobility has different dimensions, such as the transfer of socio-economic status, differences in the gender, mobility in the social life and so on. The inter-generational

[3]Although human capital takes many forms, including skills and abilities, personality, appearance, reputation, and appropriate credentials" (Becker and Tomes, 1994, p. 262).

transmission of education and its effect on the new generations is reviewed in the following sub-sections.

23.2.1 Inter-generation transmission of education

The characteristics of a family and its background have a significant impact on the abilities and the attainment of the education. Many attempts can be seen in the series of publications, i.e., Leibowitz (1974), Haveman and Wolfe (1995), Lavecchia *et al.* (2014), Becker and Tomes (1994), Abbott *et al.* (2013), Solon (2013), Fletcher and Han (2018), Olivetti *et al.* (2013), Sharif *et al.* (2016) and many others.

Haveman and Wolfe (1995) have given a comprehensive breakdown on the educational achievement of the child. They considered three variables, i.e., ability, final schooling and adult income. They discussed in detail about these three variables. According to them the ability is influenced by two significant variables, i.e., the environment which is given by the family and the other factor is genetics. On the other hand, family income is correlated with that investment which is spent on the achievement of education. Over and above, the family income is generally determined by the level of parents' education and experience. Becker (1976) expressed in his detailed discussion that family income, abilities of the parents, home investment and level of parents' education have impact on the abilities of the children and their achievement in the field of education besides the genetics. Olivetti *et al.* (2013, p. 2) are of the opinion that children are mending their behavior through these three ways, "reinforcement by parents of gender appropriate behavior, children modeling their behavior on same sex parents, and children learning the rules of appropriate behavior from observing adults in a society". The same was observed by Hyde and Rosenberg (1980) and Williams (1977).

The difference of gender in the inter-generational studies (education of father vs. education of mother) got significant attention in the literature. Behrman (1997), Johnston *et al.* (2005) and Olivetti *et al.* (2013) discussed this phenomenon in detail. It was empirically observed that the degree of mothers' influence is more than the fathers' on the abilities and achievement of the children in the field of education (quality and quantity). It is interesting to note that even if the level of educational qualification of both the parents is same, the impact of mother's education is still stronger than the father's. It is worthwhile to note that the relationship between mother and daughter is stronger than the relationship in between father and son and has its own significance in the achievements, whereas the mother and son relationship is not observed as significant. The final year of school was discussed by a number of studies, especially on the developed countries, for example, Baxter (2002) examined it for Australia, Heineck and Riphahn (2007) test this hypothesis for Germany, Ermish and Francesconi (2002) studied the case of the U.K. whereas Bjorkman *et al.* (2007) analyzed the case of Sweden. They developed their model by considering the different variables like as number of siblings, immigrants, the level of gender qualification, etc. It was discovered that mother's education has insignificant effect on the performance of sons' whereas it has positive significant effect on the daughter's performance. The same was observed by Baxter (2002) and Ermish and Francesconi (2002) and they found that the father's education is more important for the sons than mother's education, for Australia and the U.K., respectively. Dearden *et al.* (1997) found the same results that father's education is more important for the sons in the process of education attainment compared to daughters; however, their results are not significant. Another interesting study was conducted by Bjorkman *et al.* (2007) for Sweden. Their sample was very large with 65,000 individuals. In their sample they had taken different combinations of parents, for example, natural mothers and fathers, step-mothers and step-fathers. They found very interesting results. According to their findings the natural parents have a significant impact on the educational achievements of their children even when they did not raise their children. It shows that genetics play its role in child-rearing process. They also found that natural fathers' educational achievements have more impact on their sons compared to the daughters and natural mothers' educational achievements have more impact on their daughters compared to their sons. It shows that there is a stronger correlation between the education of fathers and sons and similarly between mothers and daughters. Lavecchia *et al.* (2014) are of the opinion that because of the strong family background, children have more information and they also emphasized that one can always make better decisions if he has more information. In their opinion, there are more opportunities for improvement if someone has more information. Belley and Lochner (2007) found that income has a positive impact on the schooling of the children even if the family background is controlled. They also observed that family income has a positive and significant impact on the selection of the educational institutions, i.e., children who have high quality of environment at their homes are always attending the good and well-reputed educational institutions. Elwood and Kane (2000) and Carneiro and Heckman (2002) observed that family income has a positive impact on the cognitive abilities of the children. Carneiro and Heckman (2002) expressed that "quality of the home environment" and "early investment in children" have a significant impact on the learning abilities of the children. Becker and Tomes (1994, p. 260) said: "Some children have an advantage because they are born into families with greater ability, greater emphasis on childhood learning, and other favorable cultural and genetic attributes". And they further expressed (p. 261): "Parents not only pass on some of their endowments to children, but they also influence the adult earnings of their children by expenditures on their skills, health, learning, motivation, 'credentials,' and many other characteristics". Abott *et al.* (2013, p. 45) are also supporting the arguments of Becker and Tomes and concluded: "The capacity of people to optimally invest in education is crucial for economic prosperity and social mobility, and is an important determinant of the cross-sectional and intergenerational distribution of income". Blanden *et al.* (2005) examined the impact of income and education of the parents on the achievement of their children in the U.K. and the period of study was from 1958 to 1970. They found that children's education is highly sensitive to the education and income of their parents. They also found an association between the income of parents and education of the children and they have shown that there is a positive influence on the future income of the children. Olivetti *et al.* (2013, p. 2) concluded, "As expected, we find that there is a positive relationship between the labor supply of mothers and daughters: the more mothers work, the more they represent a role model for their daughters (i.e., the more their daughters work). The horizontal effect of peers' mothers is also positive and significant ... That is, the long lasting effects of others' work behavior is strongest when daughters become mothers themselves, with the mother's role model effect being strongest for college educated women". Whereas Currie and Moretti (2003) found that in the developed as well in the developing countries the education of mother has a positive and significant impact on the education and health of the children compared to their father's education. They suggested that governments should emphasize more on the education of mothers and give more grants for the achievement of their targets.

It is observed from the aforementioned review of the literature that most of the literature supports that parents' income, education, family background, quality of home environment and early investment on child education has a positive impact on polishing the abilities of the next generation.

23.3 Data, methodology and model specification

For this study we collected the primary data from the female students and female faculty members who are studying and working in the Qassim University, Saudi Arabia. The sample size is 100. For the collection of data, we applied purposive sampling which suits to the given environment. We selected the female population of Qassim University because of two reasons. First, Qassim is predominantly considered as a religious center of the whole kingdom. Therefore, most of its inhabitants are practicing religious norms and rituals very strictly. Due to this reason this is a good sample for us to examine the empowerment of the women, i.e., in the religious center how women are behaving. Second, because of aforesaid reason, most of the parents prefer that their daughters should get their education and training in the Qassim University. As a result, most of the female faculty and students belong to different regions of the kingdom. Because of the aforementioned reasons these female students and faculty members are representatives of entire the kingdom (approximately). Over and above, it is also difficult to conduct the household survey on the phenomenon of inter-generational mobility and transmission because of the social and cultural status of the country. For the empirical analysis we follow those models which were used by Sharif *et al.* (2016) for Pakistan.

By using education as a continuous variable, the human capital base model has been estimated. These models have been estimated by applying the OLS technique.[4]

23.4 Empirical results

This section presents the empirical findings along with the interpretations and discussion of the results. Both standardized and unstandardized coefficient were considered for the empirical analysis.

Human capital base model 1: Father's education effect — Biological and psychological studies have found that genetics endowments are transmitted from one generation to another. And these are positively associated among the generations. It has been observed from the results that father's education has a positive impact on the educational achievements of their daughters. Nevertheless, we controlled the income of the parents. However,

[4]For the detail of these models see Sharif *et al.* (2016)

it is always assumed in the literature that those parents who are highly educated have reasonable level of income, are able to provide better home environment, have enough material resources and consequently they can provide better facilities to their children. It is also observed from our findings that fathers who have graduated from the developed countries have stronger impact on the educational achievements of their daughters compared to those fathers who have obtained their degrees from the local universities or from the Gulf states. We also use an alternative method to measure the inter-generational educational mobility by using the partial correlation and the variance of fathers' and children' education. Results show that the attainment of educational inequality is reducing among the new generation. It may be because of those variables which we did not include in our regression analysis, for example, the facilities which are provided by the government for upgrading the education especially for the female students. Family size has a negative impact on the educational attainment of the respondents. May be parents are allocating their resources in the best way if the family size is not enough large and also they are able to provide better quality home environment.

Human capital base model 2: Mother's educational effect — The results of this model explain that mother's education has significant impact on her daughter's educational attainment. However, the value of standardized coefficient of mother's education is higher than the father's. It supports our argument that mothers have a significant influence on their daughters particularly in the Islamic and traditional culture. Particularly, in a country like Saudi Arabia this relationship is stronger because society is following Islamic traditions more than the other Muslim countries. The other findings are same as we have in human capital base model 1.

For examining the degree of inequality among the generations, we used one minus the coefficient of mother's education (β). The value of $1 - \beta$ is 0.690, which is the sign of high mobility among the generations. However, this also depicts that inequality is reducing across the generations in the process of educational attainment. May be other factors also have its influence which were considered as constant during the process of estimation, for example, quality of home environment, genetic endowment, other facilities provided by the family and parents, family background, etc. However, this coefficient gives us an absolute value. For relative measure we used the partial correlation coefficient ρ. This is an alternative measure for estimation the inter-generational mobility. If mother and daughter's education have the same level then the correlation coefficient of their education level will be similar to the coefficient of mother's education which is β. On the other hand, if the level is different then β should be adjusted. The β was adjusted "by the ratio of variances of both the generations" to measure the inter-generational relative mobility. The lower variance of daughters and high partial coefficient depicts that inequality in the educational attainment across the generation is reducing. The higher variance in the education of mothers in Saudi Arabia is a natural phenomenon because of certain reasons, for example, lower degree of awareness during the past period, less facilities available in general and particularly to the women and some cultural and religious constraints during the past period, etc.

Human capital base model 3: parental educational effect — In this model, we consider both fathers' and mothers' education as independent variable with other variables like family size and the income of the family. It is interesting to note that due to socio-economic structure of the society, daughters are closer to their mothers and they are also trying to follow them as much as they can. So, in this model it is observed that standardized coefficient of mother's education is greater than the father's education coefficient. However, both of these variables are significantly different from zero.

Education model with interacting terms: assortative mating — This model is developed on the assumption that interaction of fathers' and mothers' education has influenced on the education of their children. It is also assumed that by considering this interaction the assortative mating bias will be eliminated. It is generally assumed that if woman is educated then she will try to marry an educated man, so keeping that in view in this study an effort is made to include the interaction of the education of both parents. In this way, we are incorporating the assortative mating factor. In this model, for measuring the impact of interacting term we tried to estimate two regressions. One with the original interacting term and in the other regression a variable is constructed by taking the deviation from the mean of the interacting term. In this study, we have observed that the mother's education has a significant impact on the daughter's education. However, the results of this model suggest that if both parents are highly educated then there is a positive significant impact on the educational attainment of their daughters. Whereas the standardized coefficients depict that the impact of mother's education is stronger than the father's education in a society like Saudi Arabia.

We have also tried to regress income of the female respondents on the income of their fathers. Here we transformed the variables into the logarithmic form.

It is observed from the findings that log-income of the respondents have been taken as dependent variable. Results suggest that income of the respondents is positively related with the father's income. The impact of the father's income is highly statistically significant at 0.01 level of significance. The coefficient of this variable is 0.55 implying that 1% increase in income of the father brings 0.55% increase in the income of the respondents. It shows that either because of gender differences or still this is an early stage of the earing of the respondents, age at the time of final degree is having a positive impact on the income. Number of siblings has a positive impact on the income. May be due to higher family size the income earner is trying to put more efforts and supplying more labor and trying to search the good jobs for the welfare of his family. Father's education from the local educational institutions has less impact on income of their daughters. This coefficient shows that income of the respondents whose father was educated in GCC countries was lower as compared to foreign qualified fathers.

We have also tried to estimate the impact of different occupation of father and mother on the income of their daughters. On the basis of the occupations of the respondents we categorized occupation into four categories, i.e., 1 for managerial job, 2 for the skilled workers, 3 for teaching-related jobs and 4 for the self-employed. Kurksal Wallis test computes the ranks of the different categories and then provides results about the significant/insignificant differences among the groups. This test is for non-parametric variables and more than 2 categories. Results show that we cannot reject the null hypothesis of homogenous groups because of 0.692 value of asymptotic significance level. Therefore, there is no significant difference in the income of respondents involved in alternate occupational groups. This may be due the economic status (rich oil based) of the country or may be the financial support of government to overcome the other effects.

23.5 Conclusion

Authors of this chapter observed during the survey that female students and faculty members of the Qassim University are feeling proud to be a Saudi. They are very happy from the policies of the government. As we have said that all of these are educated so their opinion has a significant weightage. By constitution Saudi Arabia is a Muslim country and the members of the society are trying to follow the rules and laws of *Shari'ah*. In the true spirit of Islam, women have a significant role in the development of the society, especially mothers are playing a very important role and they are responsible for providing the moral training to their children. There are a number of instructions given in *Qur'an* about the value of mothers in the Islamic society and also Prophet (saw) emphasized on the role of mothers. Allah (swt) says in *Qur'an* as: "We have enjoined on man kindness to his parents; in pain did his mother bear him, and in pain did she gave him birth" (*Qur'an* 46:15). There is one saying of Prophet (pbuh) which emphasized that the paradise is the under the feet of the mothers (Ahmad and Nasai). A man came to the Prophet and said, "O Messenger of God! Who among the people is the most worthy of my good companionship? The Prophet said: Your mother, the man said then who? The Prophet said: Then your mother. The man further asked, then who? The Prophet said: Then your mother. The man asked again, Then who? The Prophet said: Then your father" (Al-Bukhari, 2008; Muslim, 2007). In the light of these teachings, it is observed that Saudi society follows the basic norms of the teaching of Islam, so mothers have a too much importance especially for the daughters and they are considered as a role model for them. From the results which we have from our survey it was observed that female students and faculty members of Qassim University are too much inspired from their mothers. Particularly educated mothers have more impact on their daughter's education than the educated fathers.

References

Abbott, B. Gallipoli, G. Meghir C. and Violante, G. L. (2013), Education Policy and Intergenerational Transfers in Equilibrium, Working Paper 18782, National Bureau of Economic Research, Cambridge, MA, USA, available at http://www.nber.org/papers/w18782, 30 April 2019.

Abeer, A. (2016), Increasing Women's Labour Market Participation in Saudi Arabia: The Role of Government Employment Policy and Multinational Corporations, PhD Thesis (unpublished), Victoria University, College of Business, Canada.

Al-Ahmadi, H. (2011), Challenges facing women leaders in Saudi Arabia. *Human Resource Development International*, 14(2), 149–166.

Al-Asfour, A. and Khan, S. (2014), Workforce localization in the Kingdom of Saudi Arabia: Issues and challenges. *Human Resource Development International*, 17(2), 243–253.

Al-Asmari, M. G. (2008), Saudi labor force: Challenges and ambitions. *Arts & Humanities*, 16(2), 19–59.
Al-Bukhari, Muhammad Bin Ismail (2008), *Sahih al-Bukhari*, Darussalam, Saudi Arabia.
Al-Dosary, A. and Rahman, S. M. (2009), The role of the private sector towards Saudisation (localisation), *International Journal of Arab Culture, Management and Sustainable Development*, 1(2), 131–143.
Alireza, M. (1987), Women of Arabia. *National Geographic*, 172(4), 423–453.
Al Munajjed, M. (1997), *Women in Saudi Arabia Today*, New York: St. Martins Press.
Al-Munajjed, M. and Sabbagh, K. (2011), Youth in GCC Countries: Meeting the Challenge, Booz & Co., available at http://www.booz.com/media/uploads/BoozCo-GCC-Youth-Challenge.pdf. Retrieved on 28 December 2013.
Al-Shammari, S. (2009), Saudisation and Skill Formation for Employment in the Private Sector, PhD thesis, Business and Organisation Division, University of Stirling, Stirling, Scotland.
Badawi, J. (1995), *Gender Equity in Islam: Basic Principles*, Plainfield, Indiana: American Trust Publications.
Baxter, J. (2002), How Much Does Parental Education Explain Educational Attainment of Males and Females in Australia? Negotiating the Life Course, Discussion Paper No. DP-015, Australian National University, Canberra.
Becker, G. S. (1964), *Human Capital*, New York: National Bureau of Economic Research.
Becker, G. S. (1975), *Human Capital: A Theoretical and Empirical Analysis, with Special Reference to Education*, New York: Columbia University Press.
Becker, G. S. (1976), *The Economic Approach to Human Behavior*, Chicago: University of Chicago Press.
Becker, G. S. and Tomes, N. (1994), "Human capital and the rise and fall of families", in Becker, G. S. (ed.), *Human Capital: A Theoretical and Empirical Analysis with Special Reference to Education* (3rd edn.), Chapter 9, Chicago: The University of Chicago Press, pp. 257–298.
Behrman, J. R. (1997), *Women's Schooling and Child Education: A Survey*, Mimeo, University of Pennsylvania, Philadelphia, PA.
Belley, P. and Lochner, L. (2007), The Changing Role of family Income and Ability in Determining Education Achievement, Working Paper 13527, National Bureau of Economic Research, Cambridge, MA, USA, available at http://www.nber.org/papers/w13527, accessed on 30 April 2019.
Bjorkman, I., Fey, C. and Park, H. J. (2007), Institutional theory and MNC subsidiary HRM practices: Evidence from a three-country study. *Journal of International Business Studies*, 38(3), 430–446.
Blanden, J., Gregg, P. and Machin, S. (2005), Intergenerational mobility in Europe and North America. Sutton Trust Report.
Carneiro, P. and Heckman, J. J. (2002), The evidence on credit constraints in post-secondary schooling. *Economic Journal*, 112 (October), 989–1018.

Currie, J. and Moretti, E. (2003), Mothers' education and the intergenerational transmission of human capital: Evidence from college openings. *Quarterly Journal of Economics*, 118(4), 1495–1532.

Dearden, L., Machin, S. and Reed, H. (1997), Intergenerational mobility in Britain. *Economic Journal*, 107(440, January), 47–66.

Dunham, A. E. (2013), Silence, Declaration, and Circumstance: Rethinking Women's Roles in Saudi Arabia, Master of Arts Thesis (unpublished), Department of Anthropology, Western Michigan University, Michigan, USA.

Elamin, A. M. and Omair, K. (2010), Males' attitudes toward working females in Saudi Arabia. *Personnel Review*, 39(6), 746–766.

El-Sanabary, N. (1994), Female and education in Saudi Arabia and the reproduction of gender Division. *Gender and Education*, 6(2), 141–150.

Ellwood, D. and Kane, T. (2000), "Who is Getting a College Education? Family Background and the Growing Gaps in Enrolment", in S. Danziger and J. Waldfogel (eds.). *Securing the Future: Investing in Children from Birth to College*, Russell Sage Foundation.

Ermish, J. and Francesconi, M. (2002), "Intergenerational mobility in Britain: New evidence from BHPS", in Miles Cora (ed.), *Generational Income Mobility in North America and Europe*, Cambridge: Cambridge University Press: Cambridge.

Fakhro, M. (1996), "Gulf women and Islamic law", in M. Yamani (ed.). *Feminism and Islam: Legal and Literary Perspectives*, New York: New York University Press, pp. 251–262.

Fakkar, G. (2014), "Ministry Says Face Veil a Must for Workers in Women Shops", *Arab News*, 21 May, available at http://www.arabnews.com/news/574291?quicktabs_stat2=0. Retrieved on 21 August 2014.

Fletcher, J. and Han, J. (2018), Intergenerational Mobility in Education: Variation in Geography and Time, Working Paper 25324 National Bureau of Economic Research, Cambridge, MA, USA, available at http://www.nber.org/papers/w25324.

Hamdan, A. (2005), Women and education in Saudi Arabia: Challenges and achievements. *International Education Journal*, 6(1), 42–64.

Haveman, R. and Wolfe, B. (1995), The determinants of children's attainments: A review of methods and findings. *Journal of Economic Literature*, 33(4), 1829–1878.

Heineck, G. and Riphahn, R. T. (2007), Intergenerational Transmission of Educational Attainment in Germany: The Last Five Decades, Discussion Paper No. 2985, Institute for the Study of Labor (IZA), Bonn.

Huyette (1985), *Political Adaptation in Saudi Arabia: A Study of the Council of Ministry*, Colorado: Westview Press.

Hyde, J. and Rosenberg, B. G. (1980), *Half the Human Experience: The Psychology of Women*, Washington, DC: Heath and Company.

Jawad, H. (1998), *The Rights of Women in Islam: An Authentic Approach*, London: Macmillan Press.

Johnston, A., Ganzeboom, H. and Treiman, D. (2005), "Mothers' and Fathers' Influences on Educational Attainment", paper presented at RC28 Conference, Oslo.

Kapiszewski, A. (2001), *Nationals and Expatriates: Population and Labor Dilemmas of the Gulf Cooperation Council States*, Lebanon: Ithaca.

Lavecchia, A. M., Liu, H and Oreopoulos, P. (2014), Behavioural Economics of Education: Progress and Possibilities, Working Paper 20609, National Bureau of Economic Research, Cambridge, MA, USA, available at http://www.nber.org/papers/w20609. Accessed on 30 April 2019.

Muslim, Abul HussainIbn Al-Hajjaj (2007), *Sahih Muslim*, Darussalam, Saudi Arabia.

Oreopoulos, Philip, Robert S. Brown and Adam M. Lavecchia (2014), Pathways to Education: An Integrated Approach to Helping At-Risk High School Students. NBER Working Paper 20430, National Bureau of Economic Research.

Leibowitz, A. (1974), Home investments in children. *Journal of Political Economy*, 82(2), S111–S131.

Olivetti, C., Patacchini, E. and Zenou, Y. (2013), Mothers, Friends and Gender and Gender Identity, Working Paper 19610, National Bureau of Economic Research, Cambridge, MA, USA, available at http://www.nber.org/papers/w19610. Accessed on 30 April 2019.

Qantara.de (2003), "Thoraya Obaid Working for Women", *Qantara.de*, available at http://www.qantara.de/webcom/show_article.php. Accessed on 30 April 2019.

Ramady, M. (2013), Gulf unemployment and government policies: prospects for the Saudi labour quota or Nitaqat system. *International Journal of Economics and Business Research*, 5(4), 476–498.

Schultz, T. (1961), Investment in human capital. *The American Economic Review*, 51(1), 1–17.

Sharif, F. Khawaja, M. J. and Azid, T. (2016), Does education transmit across generations? An evidence from Multan district (Pakistan). *International Journal of Social Economics*, 43(7), 760–778, available at http://dx.doi.org/10.1108/IJSE-11-2014-0222.

Solon, G. (2013), Theoretical Models of Inequality Transmission Across Multiple Generations, Working Paper 18790, National Bureau of Economic Research, Cambridge, MA, USA, available at http://www.nber.org/papers/w18790. Accessed on 30 April 2019.

Vogel, F. (1999), *Islamic Law in the Modern World: The Legal System of Saudi Arabia*. Leiden: Brill.

Yamani, M. (1996), "Some observations on women in Saudi Arabia", in M. Yamani (ed.). *Feminism and Islam: Legal and Literary Perspectives*, New York: New York University Press, pp. 263–282.

Chapter 24

Women in OIC Countries: State of Participation, Freedom and Supportive Legislation

Salman Ahmed Shaikh

Abstract

In this chapter, we discuss the current state of women's rights and their socio-economic participation in Muslim majority countries. The chapter also sheds light on effective legislation for promoting gender equality. Secondly, the chapter also presents the Islamic perspective of the gender equality and difference debate. It highlights the Islamic teachings, required social attitudes and the rationale for having certain prescribed differences in assigning roles to both the genders in the Islamic institution of family. We find that there is a difference in relative importance and strength of the institution of family in Organisation of Islamic Cooperation (OIC) and non-OIC countries. Nevertheless, in some of the conservative OIC countries in Gulf Cooperation Council (GCC) and Africa, there are specific attitudes toward socio-economic participation and mobility of women, which require a revisit. We find that the labor force participation and the upward mobility in the corporate hierarchy is lower for women than men; however, it is nonetheless not insignificant.

Keywords: OIC, Women's rights, participation, freedom, supportive legislations

Hammami (2014) argues that the desire for equality with recognition of difference is a basic dilemma in the discussion on Islam and rights of women. Islam grants equal rights to all humans in almost all matters irrespective of gender. On the other hand, Islam identifies certain natural differences which entail that there can be effective institutionalization of the family system by having specialization of roles. It does not mean that the roles remain completely non-overlapping. Cultural practices, norms and socio-economic context of one period when economic development was standing at a particular state are not to be mixed up with the divine guidance on the roles and responsibilities of both genders.

It is often alleged that norms in Muslim communities do not empower women and hence Muslim communities will underperform economically relative to non-Muslim communities (Adida *et al.*, 2012). Economic well-being alone might be insufficient to achieve gender equality. For ensuring gender equality, participation in the political structures is also important (Spierings *et al.*, 2009). As per some empirical research by Kucuk (2013), institutional quality, education and penetration of Information and Communication Technology better explain the effect on development than religion.

Muslim countries are not a homogeneous group. Muslim countries show tremendous political, economic and cultural heterogeneity (Spierings *et al.*, 2009). It is not entirely true that Muslim women in Muslim majority communities are challenged by religious norms. Rather, women embrace, preach and lead Islamic discourses and movements in countries, such as Indonesia (Widani, 2007).

Hashim (1999) contends that Islam provides generous rights to women in many matters and Muslim societies do not need to look beyond their faith toward providing women human, civil and socio-economic freedoms. Warren (2008) opines that distinctions between religion and culture will provide a flexible basis of legal and cultural changes in the Muslim society.

This chapter looks into the aforementioned issues by discussing the current state of women rights and their socio-economic participation in Muslim majority countries. The chapter also sheds light on effective legislation for promoting gender equality. Secondly, the chapter also presents the Islamic perspective of the gender equality and difference debate. It highlights the Islamic teachings, required social attitudes and the rationale for having certain prescribed differences in assigning roles to both the genders in the Islamic institution of family.

24.1 Current state of women socio-economic participation

This section looks at the current state of women rights and their socio-economic participation in Muslim majority countries. In Table 24.1, it can be observed that only in Chad, the net enrollment for females in primary education falls below the average by 10%. In other Organisation of Islamic Cooperation (OIC) countries, the difference is lower whereas, it is also negative in some cases as well. This shows that as per the recent statistics, the access to basic education has been made fairly equally available to both males and females as compared to the past. On the labor force participation, it is interesting to see that women in African Muslim

Table 24.1 Education and economic participation of women.

Country	Net enrollment rate (primary)	Net enrollment rate (primary) — female	Female LF participation
Afghanistan	N/A	N/A	19.19
Albania	95.92	95.25	40.28
Algeria	98.81	96.43	16.92
Azerbaijan	94.26	92.96	61.98
Bahrain	98.00	98.48	38.89
Bangladesh	94.93	99.98	43.19
Benin	95.87	88.20	69.98
Bosnia	N/A	N/A	34.39
Brunei	N/A	N/A	50.77
Burkina Faso	69.66	67.86	76.59
Cameroon	95.11	90.60	71.05
Chad	79.12	68.70	64.00
Comoros	81.30	79.88	35.51
Cote d'Ivoire	79.25	74.71	52.46
Djibouti	57.37	53.98	36.53
Egypt	98.94	99.36	22.93
Gambia, The	75.97	79.63	72.21
Guinea	78.02	72.24	79.45
Guinea-Bissau	69.23	67.55	67.34
Guyana	85.03	83.57	41.85
Indonesia	90.57	90.07	50.93
Iran	99.25	99.83	16.24
Iraq	92.31	86.59	15.20
Jordan	89.32	89.18	14.39
Kazakhstan	99.74	99.92	66.23
Kuwait	98.70	99.33	48.07
Kyrgyz Republic	97.93	97.44	49.56
Lebanon	83.52	80.80	23.64
Libya	N/A	N/A	27.83
Malaysia	98.09	98.36	49.31
Maldives	94.84	96.00	57.57
Mali	60.73	57.27	50.29
Mauritania	79.90	81.71	29.19
Morocco	98.92	98.81	25.46
Mozambique	89.13	86.83	82.34
Niger	63.28	58.31	40.30
Nigeria	65.67	59.97	48.47
Oman	98.04	98.01	30.11
Pakistan	73.85	67.88	24.57
Qatar	96.57	97.25	53.30
Saudi Arabia	97.69	98.46	20.06
Senegal	72.99	76.38	45.16
Sierra Leone	99.38	99.32	65.07

(Continued)

Table 24.1 (*Continued*)

Country	Net enrollment rate (primary)	Net enrollment rate (primary) — female	Female LF participation
Somalia	N/A	N/A	33.28
Sudan	54.75	56.06	24.32
Suriname	94.66	95.12	40.52
Syria	70.87	70.14	12.28
Tajikistan	98.89	99.62	59.55
Togo	97.46	89.79	81.05
Tunisia	99.61	98.26	25.12
Turkey	94.24	93.80	30.36
Turkmenistan	N/A	N/A	47.33
Uganda	93.80	95.27	82.33
UAE	95.96	95.71	41.81
Uzbekistan	97.13	96.02	48.44
W.B. and Gaza	92.25	92.70	18.09
Yemen	85.33	78.25	26.01
Low income	80.95	78.60	70.01
Middle income	92.35	91.75	46.96
High income	97.16	97.36	52.08

majority countries participate actively in the labor force and in relatively much better proportions. Most of the Arab World countries fall below the median on this rank. It is quite interesting to note that almost half of the OIC countries rank better than the average for the middle-income countries on this indicator. It implies that half of the Muslim majority countries in the sample outperform the middle-income countries on this indicator. It suffices to say that despite the room for improvement on this indicator, Muslim countries cannot be all clubbed together as having very low and insignificant female labor force participation.

Table 24.2 presents the proportion of seats in the parliament held by women in the OIC countries. Interestingly, African Muslim majority countries have much better standing in terms of having a greater proportion of women holding seats in the parliament. As per expectations, Muslim majority countries in the Arab World have a lower proportion of women holding seats in the parliament. The average for Muslim countries is lower than the low income, high income and middle-income countries. Nonetheless, there are 16 out of 52 countries in the sample whose proportion of women parliamentarians exceeds the average of middle-income countries. Thus, roughly one-third of the Muslim majority countries in the sample outperform middle-income countries on this indicator.

Table 24.2 Seats held by women in parliament.

Country	Seats held by women in parliament (% of total)
Afghanistan	27.70
Albania	20.70
Algeria	31.60
Azerbaijan	16.90
Bahrain	7.50
Bangladesh	20.00
Benin	7.20
Bosnia	21.40
Burkina Faso	9.40
Chad	14.90
Comoros	3.00
Cote d'Ivoire	9.20
Djibouti	12.70
Egypt	14.90
Gambia	9.40
Guinea	21.90
Guinea-Bissau	13.70
Guyana	30.40
Indonesia	17.10
Iran	3.10
Iraq	26.50
Jordan	12.00
Kazakhstan	26.20
Kuwait	1.50
Kyrgyz Republic	19.20
Lebanon	3.10
Libya	16.00
Malaysia	10.40
Maldives	5.90
Mali	8.80
Mauritania	25.20
Morocco	17.00
Mozambique	39.60
Niger	13.30
Nigeria	5.60
Oman	1.20
Pakistan	20.60
Qatar	0.00
Saudi Arabia	19.90
Senegal	42.70
Sierra Leone	12.40
Somalia	13.80
Sudan	30.50
Suriname	25.50

(*Continued*)

Table 24.2 (*Continued*)

Country	Seats held by women in parliament (% of total)
Syria	12.40
Tajikistan	19.00
Togo	17.60
Turkey	14.90
Turkmenistan	25.80
Uganda	35.00
UAE	22.50
Uzbekistan	16.00
Low income	24.19
Middle income	20.70
High income	26.67

24.2 Effective legislation for gender equality

On the legal front, there is a need for effective legislation and its effective execution to legislatively safeguard the rights of women in Muslim majority countries. Table 24.3 shows that in 36 countries, there is yet to be a legislation for ensuring equal remuneration, while in 17 Muslim majority countries, such legislation has been made. In 37 countries, there is yet to be legislation for ensuring non-discrimination in hiring, while in 16 Muslim majority countries, such legislation has been made. Except in Suriname, there has been legislation to provide maternity leave. Such legislation can ensure long-term stay in labor force as well as re-entry into the labor force. In 14 countries, there is yet to be legislation for ensuring no child marriage, while in 38 Muslim majority countries, such legislation has been made. Finally, in half of the OIC countries in the sample, there is yet to be legislation on banning domestic violence.

Having said that, doing such legislation is not impeded by Islam. Rather, Islamic principles are favorable to equal remuneration to same quantity and quality of work, non-discrimination in hiring and providing personal and social freedoms to women in planning their families.

24.3 Islamic perspective on gender equality and difference

24.3.1 Islam and contemporary paradigm for women's rights

The institution of family is highly respected in Islam. Women are an indispensable part of this institution. As per Islamic worldview, mental and physical capabilities that we enjoy are the blessings of Allah and we

Table 24.3 Legislation for gender equality in the OIC countries.

Country	Equal remuneration	Non-discrimination in hiring	Maternity leave	No child marriage	No domestic violence
Afghanistan	No	No	Yes	No	No
Albania	No	Yes	Yes	Yes	Yes
Algeria	Yes	No	Yes	Yes	No
Azerbaijan	Yes	Yes	Yes	Yes	Yes
Bahrain	No	No	Yes	No	No
Bangladesh	Yes	No	Yes	Yes	Yes
Benin	No	Yes	Yes	Yes	Yes
Bosnia	Yes	Yes	Yes	Yes	Yes
Brunei	No	No	Yes	Yes	Yes
Burkina Faso	No	No	Yes	No	No
Chad	Yes	Yes	Yes	Yes	No
Comoros	Yes	Yes	Yes	No	Yes
Cote d'Ivoire	Yes	Yes	Yes	Yes	No
Djibouti	Yes	Yes	Yes	Yes	No
Egypt	No	No	Yes	Yes	No
Gambia	No	No	Yes	Yes	Yes
Guinea	Yes	Yes	Yes	Yes	No
Guinea-Bissau	No	No	Yes	Yes	Yes
Guyana	Yes	Yes	Yes	Yes	Yes
Indonesia	No	No	Yes	Yes	Yes
Iran	No	No	Yes	No	No
Iraq	No	No	Yes	Yes	No
Jordan	No	No	Yes	Yes	Yes
Kazakhstan	No	Yes	Yes	Yes	Yes
Kuwait	No	No	Yes	Yes	No
Kyrgyz Republic	No	No	Yes	Yes	Yes
Lebanon	No	No	Yes	N/A	Yes
Libya	Yes	No	Yes	Yes	No
Malaysia	No	No	Yes	Yes	Yes
Maldives	No	Yes	Yes	No	Yes
Mali	No	No	Yes	Yes	No
Mauritania	No	Yes	Yes	No	No
Morocco	Yes	Yes	Yes	No	No
Mozambique	No	No	Yes	Yes	Yes
Niger	Yes	Yes	Yes	Yes	No
Nigeria	No	No	Yes	Yes	Yes
Oman	No	No	Yes	No	No
Pakistan	No	No	Yes	Yes	Yes
Qatar	No	No	Yes	Yes	No
Saudi Arabia	No	No	Yes	No	Yes
Senegal	No	No	Yes	Yes	Yes

(*Continued*)

Table 24.3 *(Continued)*

Country	Equal remuneration	Non-discrimination in hiring	Maternity leave	No child marriage	No domestic violence
Sierra Leone	No	No	Yes	Yes	Yes
Somalia	N/A	N/A	N/A	N/A	N/A
Sudan	No	No	Yes	No	No
Suriname	No	No	No	Yes	Yes
Syria	No	No	Yes	Yes	No
Tajikistan	Yes	Yes	Yes	Yes	Yes
Togo	Yes	No	Yes	No	No
Turkey	Yes	No	Yes	Yes	Yes
Turkmenistan	N/A	N/A	N/A	N/A	N/A
Uganda	Yes	No	Yes	No	Yes
UAE	No	No	Yes	No	No
Uzbekistan	No	No	Yes	Yes	No
W.B. and Gaza	No	No	Yes	Yes	No
Yemen	No	No	Yes	Yes	No

hold them as a trust. Therefore, based on the differences in these mental and physical capabilities alone, no one is superior and powerful in the eyes of Allah. As per Islam, following is a brief summary of women's rights.

- Muslim women must educate themselves like men. Education is not only allowed, it is compulsory for women like for men.[1]
- Women can choose an occupation and earn their livelihood. They are allowed to do that. But they are not made responsible for it. Men are made responsible for it in the Islamic family system.
- Women have the right to own property and engage in trade. The first wife of Holy Prophet (PBUH) was a business woman. It was not until the late 1870s onward in Europe that married women achieved the right to enter contracts and to own property. In France, this right was not recognized until 1938. Also, women got the right to vote in the U.S.A. less than 100 years ago only.
- Women have the right to choose their husbands and the right to separate from their husbands.

[1]Sunan Ibn-e-Majah, *Book of Sunnah, Hadith* No. 224.

- Married women are entitled to "Mehr" (wealth at the start of marriage) as well as "Wirasat" (prescribed share in wealth at the death of husband, children and parents).
- Mother must be respected three times more than the father according to a *Hadith*.[2]
- In another *Hadith*, it is said that "paradise lies beneath mother's feet" as a symbolic representation to highlight the importance of how critical one's attitude toward mother really is for having eternal success in the life Hereafter.[3]
- As per a *Hadith*, best men are considered those who are best to their wives.[4]
- No man is allowed to have extra-marital relationships with any other woman. Adultery and prostitution are severe crimes in Islam and can lead to capital punishment.

In fact, one of the arguments of non-believers in Arab was to say that how can we accept this religion which gives such rights to women. Prophet Muhammad (PBUH) Himself married an old widow to set an example. Several non-Muslim historians for this reason hold the view that Islam modernized the Arab world in terms of human rights and especially the women rights. Gustave Le Bon (Le Bon, 1974) says in his book *Arab Civilization*:

> "The principles of inheritance which have been determined in the Qur'an have a great deal of justice and fairness. The person who reads the Qur'an can perceive these concepts of justice and fairness in terms of inheritance through the verses I quoted. I should also point out the great level of efficiency in terms of general laws and rules derived from these verses. I have compared British, French and Islamic Laws of inheritance and found that Islam grants the wives the right of inheritance, which our laws are lacking while Westerners consider them to be ill-treated by the Muslim men."

But, in reality, we also see things like honor killing and discouragement of education and social mobility of women in some parts of the Muslim world. Moreover, we also see strong encouragement for complete body covering in some Muslim societies. Briefly, we give an answer to these issues.

---

[2]Sahih al-Bukhari, *Book of Manners*, *Hadith* No. 5971).
[3]Sunan Al-Nisai, *Book of Jihad*, *Hadith* No. 3106).
[4]Jam-et-Tirmizi, *Chapters on Suckling*, Hadith No. 1162).

Honor killing has nothing to do with Islam. It is to do with ignorance and especially about Islam (Aliyu, 2005). Education is a religious responsibility for all Muslims, men and women included. Regarding social mobility, there is no strict restriction, but a set of etiquette. The etiquette is also prescribed for men (*Qur'an*, 24:29). Women are also prescribed to cover themselves modestly in public (*Qur'an*, 24:29).

With this modesty, they play socio-economic and even political roles as well in most parts of the Muslim world. Regardless of how much the Muslim societies conform or do not conform to the Islamic ideals, the Islamic standpoint does not negate socio-economic mobility of women. Islam asks both men and women to lead their lives virtuously and it is only God-consciousness and good actions which make one person more successful than the other in the grand purpose of this life in the Islamic worldview.

The Islamic family system makes husbands responsible as head of family. This also means that they have an additional responsibility since husbands are made primarily responsible for their family's financial sustainability. In Muslim societies, low labor force participation by women is not because of strict prohibitions by Islam. The economic and social role of women had remained important, especially in building the social capital.

The primary contribution and expected responsibility of women as mothers is to inculcate right values as first nursery and learning institution for their children. Undocumented labor that women provide in agrarian economies understates their economic role in some Muslim countries where agriculture is still a significant contributor to the national income. As Muslim economies become more knowledge-based and industrialized in future, the labor force participation of women will further increase.

The institution of family brings social capital into existence. It ensures empathy and responsibility. It brings a very lasting and durable social safety net. Islamic injunctions about how to treat orphans foster social security for individuals with special circumstances. Furthermore, the Islamic inheritance laws ensure that the wealth of the deceased is distributed widely among the members of the family of the deceased and this permanently and systematically ensures reducing the concentration of wealth in every generation.

Empirical evidence shows that more crimes happen against women in societies where the family institution had been ignored or established with different norms. An international report from the Social Trends Institute highlights that the frequency of unwed mothers is much less in the OIC countries of Asia and Africa as compared to non-OIC countries, especially in Europe. In addition to that, divorce rates are considerably higher in non-OIC countries as compared to the OIC countries (Harrendorf and Heiskanen, 2010). Also, reported crimes against women are more in numbers in regions with less Muslim population.

Most definitely, these societies can have a market for daycare, old homes, free and paid sex experiences, but they may lack a strong family system, social capital and ethical standards which can make a human society any different from non-human ones.

24.3.2 Inheritance law of Islam and women

In the ancient world, women inherited nothing and even when they inherited, they were treated like a minor. Women usually had no independent legal personality. The pre-Islamic Arabs were opposed to inheritance by woman, who could not inherit as long as a male member of the family existed.

These Arabs were greatly surprised when the *Qur'an* explicitly said:

> *For men is a share of what the parents and the near relatives leave, and for women is a share of what the parents and the near relatives leave...*
> (*Qura'an* Chapter An-Nisa, 4:32)

Islam has given women a share in inheritance. Before Islam, women were not only deprived of that share but were also considered a property to be inherited by men. In Islam, whether a woman is a wife or mother, a sister or daughter, she receives a certain share from the wealth of the deceased close relative.

This share is hers by divine injunctions, and no one can take it away or disinherit her. Even if the deceased wishes to deprive her by making a will to other relations or in favor of any other cause, the Islamic law will not allow that to happen.

According to the Islamic law of inheritance distribution, a son receives twice as much a daughter, a brother twice as much as a sister and a husband twice as much as a wife. But, this does not mean that the shares of men and women are unequal in all circumstances. In the case of father and mother, the share of both is the same in the wealth left by their deceased children.

Even if a deceased only leaves behind female heirs, they will be given their prescribed share. In one of the cases, the only daughter the deceased leaves behind may receive as much as half of the inheritance and if there are more than two daughters, they together get two-third (2/3) of the remaining inheritance.

Muslim mothers, wives, daughters and sisters had received inheritance rights roughly 1,400 years before Europe recognized that these rights should even exist in the first place. According to the *Encyclopedia Americana*, in English Common law, all the real property held by a woman at the time of her marriage became the property of her husband. He was entitled to the rent from the land and any profit that might be made from managing it. It was not until the late 1870s onward in Europe that married women achieved the right to enter contracts and own property. In France, this right was not recognized until as late as 1938.

As per Islamic inheritance law, a son receives twice as much as a daughter, a brother twice as much as a sister and a husband twice as much as a wife. In order to understand the rationale behind this rule, one must take into account the fact that the financial obligations of men in Islam far exceed those of women.

As per Islam, Muslim women can own property and wealth. They are entitled to have "Mehr" (wealth at the start of marriage), "Wirasat" (share in inheritance upon the death of husband, children, father and in some cases brother[s]). Islam does not make it obligatory on women to earn for their family. However, they can earn for the family and yet they are not obliged to spend their earnings on the family. They have a right to choose an occupation and earn. However, men are obliged to spend their earnings on the family and they are made primarily responsible for earning the livelihood for their family.

Besides, it needs to be realized that Islam highly regards family life. It strongly encourages young individuals to get married and Islam does not regard celibacy as a virtue. Hence, one could appreciate that Muslim men, in general, have greater financial burdens than Muslim women. Male heir is burdened with all financial responsibilities; whereas, a female heir is burdened with no financial responsibilities.

References

Adida, C. L., Laitin, D. and Valfort, M. A. (2012), Gender, Economic Development and Islam: A Perspective from France. Discussion Paper Series, IZA DP No. 6421.

Aliyu, B. A. (2005), Status of Woman In Islam: Equality or Divine Balance? International Seminar on Muslim Women: The Future and Challenges in Shaping the Ummah (SEWANI).

Hammami, R. (2014), *Gender Equality and Muslim Women: Negotiating Expanded Rights in Muslim Majority and Immigrant Contexts. Development and Equity: An Interdisciplinary Exploration by Ten Scholars from Africa, Asia and Latin America*, Leiden: Brill, pp. 84–95.

Harrendorf, S. and Heiskanen, M. (2010), "Drug crime", in Malby, S. (ed.). *International Statistics on Crime and Justice*, Helsinki: European Institute for Crime Prevention and Control.

Hashim, I. (1999), Reconciling Islam and feminism. *Gender & Development*, 7(1), 7–14.

Kucuk, N. (2013), Gender inequality in the MENA: Myths versus facts. Topics. *Middle Eastern and North African Economies*, 15(2), 71–104.

Le Bon, Gustave (1974), *The World of Islamic Civilization*, New York: Tudor Publishing Company.

Spierings, N., Smits, J. and Verloo, M. (2009), On the compatibility of Islam and gender equality. *Social Indicators Research*, 90(3), 503–522.

Warren, C. S. (2008), Lifting the veil: Women and Islamic law. *Cardozo Journal of Law & Gender*, 15, 33–65.

Widani, A. (2017), Gender Equality and Women's Participation in Islamic Fundamentalist Groups: A Case Study of Indonesia (Master's thesis).

Chapter 25

Compulsory Schooling in Turkey, Educational Attainment, and the Gender Gap

Jennifer Ward-Batts and Kaitlin Nowacki

Abstract

Education is one of the factors widely understood to affect women's empowerment. Gender-neutral compulsory schooling requirements can decrease gender gaps in education in some circumstances. Compulsory schooling in Turkey was increased in 1997 from 5 years to 8 years. We examine the effect of this change on educational attainment, and in particular investigate whether there was a differential effect of this change on females relative to males. Using 2003 Demographic and Health Surveys data, we find an overall positive effect on the probability of completion of 8 years, as well as a positive differential effect for females of the change on both years of education and probability of completion of 8 years. We also find, as predicted, that the gender gap narrowed in low-wealth families in particular. However, we find a persistent gender gap in the country's more traditional, less-developed eastern region.

Keywords: Turkey, Gender gap, Compulsory schooling, Families wealth

Education is one of the factors widely understood to affect women's empowerment. Thus, the gender gap in education is often a policy target when women's empowerment is the goal. However, we argue that gender-neutral policies can reduce gender gaps in schooling under certain circumstances. A case in point is compulsory schooling requirements. Compulsory schooling in Turkey increased in 1997 from 5 years to 8 years for all children. We examine the effect of this change on educational attainment, and in particular investigate whether there was a differential effect of this change on females relative to males.

Turkey is a middle-income country, with a population of about 70 million. It is predominantly a Muslim country with a secular system of government and law. Turkey ranks relatively low in terms of gender equality, according to the *Global Gender Gap Report* that publishes an index of gender equality based on education, economic participation, political representation, and health (Hausmann *et al.*, 2009). Female labor force participation has declined since the 1950s and was flat for single women between 1988 and 1998, while it declined slightly over that period for married women (Tunali and Baslevent, 2006). Large sections of the country remain rural. There are large differences across regions of the country in the level of educational attainment generally, as well as in the gender gap in education. These differences are consistent with our expectations given cultural differences across those regions, especially between the east and the west.

As in many middle- and low-income countries, there is a gender gap in educational attainment in Turkey, with males' attainment exceeding that of females. There is also a literacy gap. In 1988, 1 out of 3 females, but only 1 out of 10 males, aged 12 years and over was illiterate. By 1998, male literacy had improved to 95% while female progress was more modest, reaching 80% (Tunali and Baslevent, 2006).

We examine the effect of the change in compulsory schooling on both males and females, with particular attention to the gender gap, as well as to region and wealth differences. We find that the education reform increased educational attainment and decreased the gender gap generally, but that the gender gap remains large in the relatively less-developed eastern region of the country.

25.1 Educational attainment and substantial gender gap

Studies too numerous to mention have found low educational attainment as well as a substantial gender gap in education and literacy in less-developed countries. However, the substantial gender gap in many countries has been declining recently (Behrman, 1993; King and Hill, 1993; World Bank, 1993).

Many factors contribute to low educational attainment and to a substantial gender gap in education. Psacharopoulos (1997) examines the relationship between child labor and schooling attainment in Bolivia and Venezuela. He finds a substantial difference of about 2 years of educational attainment between children who work and those who do not. Low household income or wealth may result in children getting less schooling for several reasons, including adult decision makers in those households are more likely to have low levels of education. In addition, Jensen and

Nielson (1997) found that in Zambia the need for child labor, especially in low-income households, affects the educational attainment of children.

Accessibility to schools in rural areas of less-developed countries is another hurdle (Alderman *et al.*, 1996). In Turkey, the location of the school has a significant effect on the quality and the years of education the child will receive. Development of urban centers and proximity to a major city also affect the probability that a child will go to school (Tansel, 2002). The western region of the country is more developed than the eastern region, and thus accessibility may be more of an issue in the eastern region.

Increasing labor market opportunities for females would tend to increase the benefits of educating girls. However, Behrman *et al.* (1999) observed that female educational attainment increased along with that of males in India during the Green Revolution, a time when there were few labor market opportunities for women. The authors attribute the increase in women's schooling to the increased demand for educated sons, who are better able to take advantage of the new agricultural technologies. Thus, demand for educated wives increased because they educate their young sons at home.

The increase in compulsory schooling in Turkey occurred at a time when women's labor force participation was quite low and not rising. It is therefore not an alternative factor driving an increase in female educational attainment at this time. According to Tunali and Baslevent (2006), female labor force participation in Turkey had declined since the 1950s, and they show that it was flat between 1988 and 1998 at 25.5% for single women, while declining slightly over that period for married women from 13.1% to 11.7%.

Dayioğlu *et al.* (2009), used data from the 1998 Turkish Demographic and Health Survey (TDHS), to examine educational attainment in Turkey. They examine the roles of sibship size, birth order and sibling sex composition in determining school enrollment probabilities. They found a substantially lower enrollment rate for females than males, and that the gender gap is important at all ages. They concluded that children with more siblings, with less educated and older parents, and who come from poorer households are less likely to be enrolled. And both low and high birth order children are more likely to be enrolled than those born in the middle, and that this a u-shaped relationship between birth order, and enrollment is stronger in lower-income households. Sex composition matters only for females and particularly in poor households, where, given sibship size, having more brothers decreases a girl's probability of being enrolled.

Kirdar (2009) used 1993 and 1998 TDHS data to examine ethnic disparities in school enrollment in Turkey. Ethnic Turks are in majority, while there is a substantial Kurdish minority population and smaller Arab and Caucasian groups. The ethnic Kurds are somewhat concentrated in the eastern region, while there are concentrations of Arabs in both the east and the south, with Caucasians more prevalent in the north and west. Kirdar found that Kurds and Arabs are significantly less likely to be enrolled, and that girls from these groups have even lower enrollment compared to their male counterparts, relative to other groups. After controlling for a set of family characteristics, including household wealth, sibship size, father's schooling, and mother's literacy and Turkish language ability, the negative effect for Kurds and Arabs disappears, but the differential negative effect for girls in these groups persists.

25.2 Theoretical framework

We assume family decisions about children's education are made by unitary households, given costs and benefits of education. Behrman *et al.* (1995) suggest that systematic differences in education for boys versus girls stem from three possible sources: (1) differences in expected wages, (2) differences in the costs of human capital investments and (3) differences in parental preferences.

Children may help to do household work and light farm work, such as caring of animals, from quite a young age. In cities, they may sell things on the street and provide services, such as carrying groceries purchased in the farmer's market to individuals' homes. The resulting opportunity cost of children's time is in addition to other schooling costs, such as school fees, the costs of books or school supplies, and the cost of transportation to and from school. The opportunity costs of time for boys versus girls may differ, and the difference may vary across space (i.e., in rural versus urban areas, or in more versus less traditional areas). We do not make any assumptions about the relative magnitude of those costs by gender.

However, there are several reasons that psychic costs of education of daughters for parents in Turkey may be higher than that for sons. First, while traveling to and from school, there is a risk of children being abducted or abused, and this may be of greater concern for female children. This issue may be more of a concern in rural areas where children may have to travel longer distances to school. Second, especially among conservative families and perhaps especially in rural areas, concern for virginity and honor of daughters may make traveling to school problematic for them. Third, among religious families, girls generally begin to cover their hair from an age around puberty or earlier. Until 2012, wearing a head covering was forbidden in schools in Turkey, and so girls (or their parents) faced the choice of the head covering or continuing in school.

The benefits of educating children may include higher future earnings, higher social status and perhaps better marriage prospects. Given the much higher labor force participation rate for males, labor market earnings are a more important (and larger) benefit for males than for females.

Finally, as Behrman *et al.* (1995) suggest, the pure preferences of parents may differ regarding education for boys versus girls. These differential preferences may stem from cultural and religious norms, and may differ across regions, by education of parents, and across ethnic groups. Hereafter, for convenience, we will in some passages use the term "preference" loosely to mean optimal levels, given pure preferences, costs, and benefits.

To the extent that the net benefits of the costs of educating boys is greater than that of girls, we would expect families to choose higher levels of education for boys relative to girls. This is commonly observed in many less-developed countries. This is likely due in large part to the limited labor market opportunities for women and thus the small return on investment in education of girls. However, there may be persistent cultural norms that result in slow progress in closing the gender gap in education, even when the gender gap in earnings prospects narrows. All parents are not identical and do not face identical costs, and so there will be a distribution of the preferred level of educational attainment for boys and for girls. If the distributions of the preferred levels of schooling for boys and girls differ, such as is shown in Figure 25.1, then a change in compulsory schooling may have a differential effect on boys and girls.

If the preferred level of schooling for girls is generally less than for boys, the initial compulsory schooling of 5 years represents a binding constraint for a larger fraction of the population of girls than boys, i.e., more boys than girls would have received at least 5 years of schooling in the absence of the compulsory schooling law. If compulsory schooling is perfectly enforced, then more girls than boys will attain exactly 5 years, while more boys than girls will attain more than 5 years. Similarly, after the reform, we would observe more girls than boys with exactly 8 years, more boys than girls with more than 8 years, and that the gender gap will have narrowed in

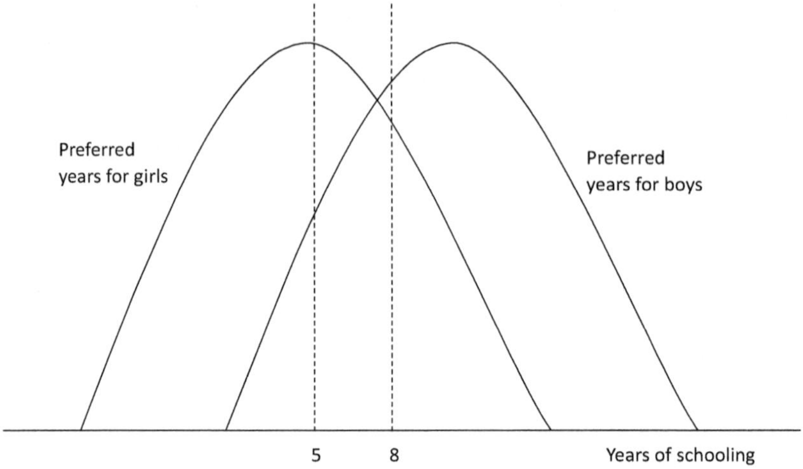

Figure 25.1 Distributions of preferred education levels for boys and girls.

both mean attainment and in the relative probability of attaining at least 8 years.

The "preferences" we refer to in this discussion are the levels of schooling families would choose for their children, given prices and resource constraints that they face. Many previous studies, including some we have discussed earlier, find that education for females appears to be a luxury good of sorts: Families with higher wealth tend to educate their daughters and sons to similarly high levels, but families who are more resource constrained tend to educate boys more than girls.

We use data on earlier cohorts (before the change in compulsory schooling) to estimate the revealed-preferred distributions of schooling for males and females in time periods prior to the change. Assuming compulsory schooling is perfectly enforced, we would see a spike at 5 years, and the portion of the distribution that lies to the right of it. Those who make up the portion of the preference distribution to the left of 5 years would be observed at exactly 5 years of schooling.

While we hypothesize that females may have disproportionately benefited from the increase in compulsory schooling, there are alternative narratives that might instead result in larger gains for males. For example, if the change in law provided new information to individuals and their families about the changing educational requirements in an evolving labor market, then there may have been increases in education even by children who were not directly constrained by the new law. If education is an important signal of ability in the labor market, then the new requirement will prod higher ability males to attain a higher level of schooling after the reform in order to signal their higher ability to employers. Both may result in attainment increases in cohorts not affected by the law, and may also affect probability of attainment of levels not targeted by the new law. These are more likely to affect males due to their higher labor force participation, and would make it less likely for us to find a significant empirical effect on the gender gap.

25.3 Background on Turkey and compulsory schooling

Prior to the change in law increasing compulsory schooling in 1997, schools were divided into primary (5 years), middle school (3 years) and high school (3 or 4 years, depending on type). Examinations after the eighth year determine which high schools one may attend, should one desire to continue.

Terminology referring to school was changed as well. The first 5 years of school were "ilk okul" (first school) and the sixth through eighth years "orta okul" (middle school). Under the new law, the first 8 years would be "ilkogretim okul" (first education school, or primary school). We refer to the first 5 years as "primary school" throughout this chapter to avoid confusion.

In August 1997, the new law was instituted. Students who had completed the fifth year of primary school in the 1996–1997 academic year were not required to continue. Students completing the fourth year of primary in the 1996–1997 academic year are the first affected cohort, and are required to continue and to complete the eighth grade. Given the flexibility in the starting age, identifying treated (affected by the policy) and untreated individuals is not so straightforward.

Those who enrolled in school for the first time in the fall of 1992 would complete the fifth year of school just prior to the policy change, and will not be required to continue on. Those enrolled for the first time in 1993 would complete the fourth year of school just prior to the policy change, and thus be the first cohort to be affected.

Children should start school in the September after their fifth birthday, or during which it occurs.[1] However, school starting age was historically

[1] In 1983, rules changed regarding school starting age, so that students were to start school 1 year earlier than had previously been the rule.

flexible in practice. Using the TDHS data for 1993, 1998 and 2003, we calculated enrollment rates for children aged 6, 7, and 8 years in each survey year. There were no children reported to be enrolled who were 5 years old in any of these 3 survey years, perhaps due to a survey design issue. However, attainment of children aged 6, 7, and 8 indicate that a few did enter at age 5. Over time, enrollment rates at the earlier ages have increased.

In 1993, only 21% of girls and 19% of boys were enrolled at age 6, while 60% and 64% of 7-year-olds and 90% and 92% of 8-year-olds were enrolled. If the pattern was the same 1 year prior, then about 42% of the 7-year-olds (39% of girls, 45% of boys) enrolled for the first time when they were seven, i.e., in 1993.[2] Those plus the 40% of girls and 36% of boys among the 7-year-olds, who were not yet enrolled in 1993 will therefore be part of the treated group. Thus, 79% of girls and 81% of boys aged seven in 1993 are affected by the policy change. We take those aged seven in 1993 (aged 17 in 2003) as the first treated cohort for our analysis. Those 18 and older in 2003 are considered the untreated (control) group. Assuming the enrollment rate pattern by age was the same in 1991–1993, two-thirds of those aged eight in 1993 who were enrolled by that time had enrolled prior to 1993, and would thus not be affected by the policy change. This implies that about one-third will have first enrolled in 1993 or after, and are therefore affected by the policy. Since less than half are so affected, we will put them in the control group. Some of them being treated implies that our estimate of the effect on the gender gap may be underestimated.

25.4 Data and methods

Demographic and Health Surveys (DHS) data was collected in Turkey in 1993, 1998, 2003 and 2008.[3] DHS data have been collected in 130 or more less-developed countries over time. These data collections are largely consistent across countries, but may differ in some ways to make them appropriate and relevant in different settings. In this study, we use primarily the 2003 data collected in Turkey, but also some data from 1993 and 1998 for some descriptive statistics. Married women were interviewed face-to-face.

[2]That is, 39% of girls and 45% of boys. If enrollment rates at age six were lower the prior year, then these numbers would be higher.

[3]At the time of our initial analyses, 2008 data were not available to us. We have since obtained the 2008 data and used them in the ongoing research on this topic. Preliminary results are consistent with our findings in this chapter.

For the 2003 data, interviews were conducted from December 2003 to May 2004. Interviews include a household interview, aimed at collecting information about individuals in the household and about household characteristics, and individual interviews with any married women in the household aged 15–49 years. The latter gather information about marital and birth histories, and various information relevant to maternal and child health. The household interview collects information about all household members, including age, gender, marital status, educational attainment and current school enrollment.

We use individual-level data, along with household characteristics, such as household size (i.e., the number of people living in the household), and household wealth. Summary statistics of the primary variables we utilize in our analysis of children are given in Table 25.1. Household wealth is an index based on owned assets and durable goods, such as vehicles and household appliances. We report the wealth index values in tens of thousands for convenience.

Unlike some earlier studies, we do not use data on sibship size and composition, and characteristics of parents. Those variables are only

Table 25.1 Summary statistics for key variables, aged 14–20 years sample.

Variable	Obs.	Mean	Std. Dev.
Household size	4065	6.579	3.242
Household wealth index	4065	−1.120	9.516
Child age	4065	15.547	1.128
		Proportion	
5+ years of schooling	4065	0.8817	
8+ years of schooling	4065	0.6308	
At least some high school	4065	0.3169	
Female	4065	0.4959	
South	4065	0.1419	
Central	4065	0.1601	
North	4065	0.1058	
East	4065	0.3788	
West (omitted in analysis)	4065	0.2133	
Small city	4065	0.3670	
Town	4065	0.1188	
Rural	4065	0.3105	
Large city (omitted in analysis)	4065	0.2037	

Notes: Large city category includes Ankara, Istanbul and Izmir.
Source: Data are from TDHS 2003.

available for individuals who currently live in the same household with their mother. In Turkey, marriage is virtually universal (Tunali and Baslevent, 2006), and one typically moves out of the parental home only upon marriage. Those individuals who marry relatively early tend to get less education. If they have married and moved out, then they will be excluded from the sample if we use the additional variables that are only available for those still residing with their mother. By using that information, we would create a select sample, which would tend to have more education and perhaps a lower gender gap than exists in our more representative sample, in which we include all individuals at the relevant ages. We would also miss more females than males in our target age range by using that information. The TDHS 2003 final report (Hacettepe University Institute of Population Studies and General Directorate of Mother and Child Health/Family Planning, Ministry of Health, 2004, Table 2.4) shows that, in these data, among children under age 18, females are more likely than males to not live with either parent. We will consider the omission of this family background information, and findings of previous research that have used these variables, when interpreting our results.

25.5 Results

25.5.1 Graphical analyses

First, we return to the distribution of preferences for female education relative to that for male education. We illustrated the hypothesized relationship in Figure 25.1. Using TDHS 2003 data on adult men and women, we constructed distributions of observed educational attainment for adults, none of whom would have been constrained by the new higher compulsory schooling requirement. Figure 25.2 shows the distribution of years of education for four different age groupings of adults, by sex, from our data. Unlike the smooth distributions shown in Figure 25.1, we see spikes at particular levels equating to completion of the three levels of schooling: 5 years is completion of primary school, 8 years is the end of middle school, and 11 years represents completion of high school for most high schools. We have simplified the histograms by lumping together years of education that lie between the completion milestones, i.e., 1–4, 6–7, 9–10, and 13–15.

The four panels of Figure 25.2 tell us something about the distribution of preferred education levels over time, and about the gender gap in those

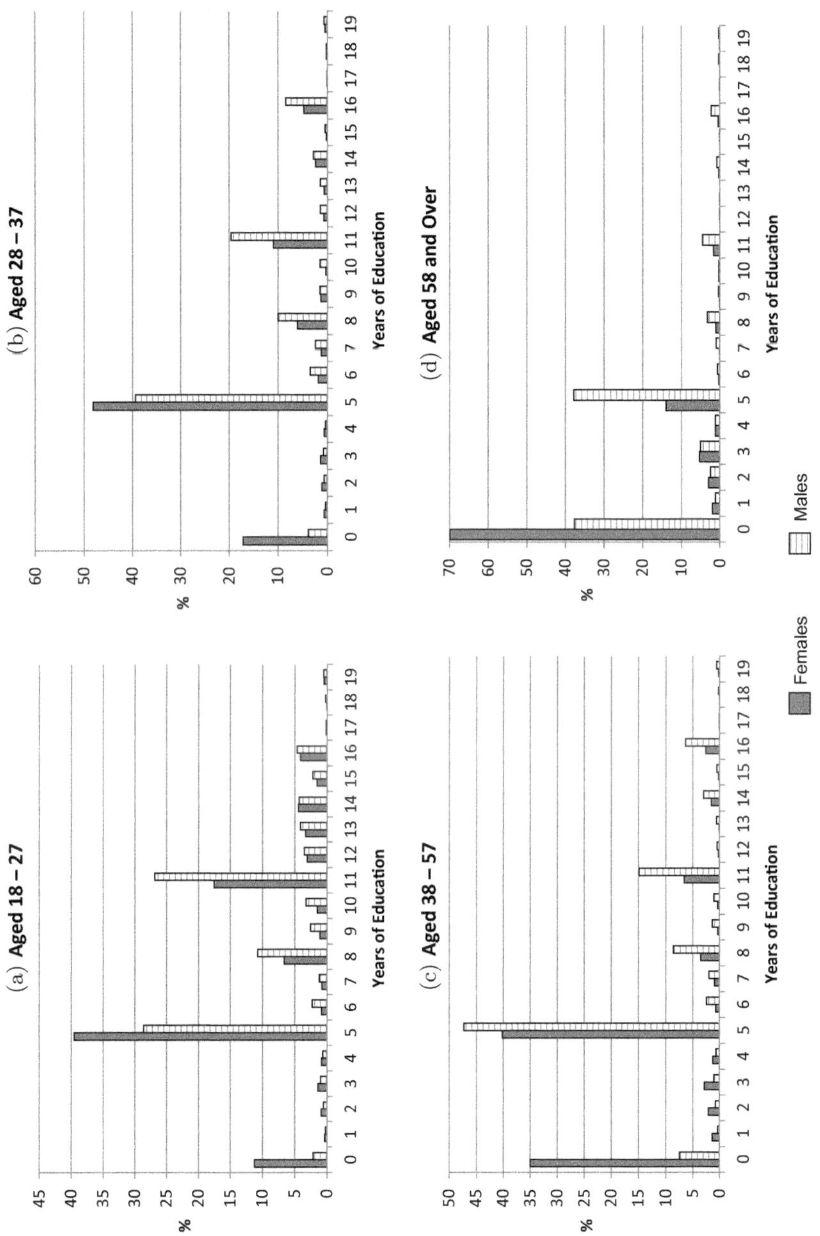

Figure 25.2 Percent of adults by sex and age group with each level of education — Nationwide.

levels. In all four age groups we see that the distribution of women's education lies more leftward than that of males. Females are more heavily represented in lower levels of education and males in higher levels. Those aged 18–27 may not have all completed their education, so representation at higher levels (especially university and above) may be downward biased.

By comparing older and younger cohorts, we see that, over time, educational attainment increased in Turkey, but that the gender gap has been quite persistent. In the oldest two cohort groupings (Panels A and B), many more women than men have zero education, and more men than women have education levels of 5 years and above.[4] For the younger two groupings (Panels C and D), women are more likely to have 5 years of education than men. However, there are still substantial numbers of women with zero education, and men are more likely than women to have attained any given level higher than 5 years. A Kolmogorov–Smirnov test rejects equality of the distributions for males and females at a very high level of significance ($p < 0.001$) for each of the age groups.

Next, we examine graphical representations of the data for birth cohorts affected by the new compulsory schooling law. The gender gap remains persistent even among these younger cohorts.

Our next aim was to estimate the effects that the law had on educational attainment and on the gender gap in educational attainment. The law, implemented in 1997, made it a requirement to complete 8 years of schooling. As we discussed earlier, children aged 17 in our 2003 data represent the first (oldest) cohort to be directly affected by the policy change. Our strategy is to look for effects among the first cohorts to be directly affected by the new law, in that the completed educational attainment of those cohorts would be significantly larger than those of cohorts that came just before them. Upward time trends move comparing cohorts further away from each other in age and is problematic for this purpose, so we will focus our analysis on the two cohorts who should have finished 5 years of education just before the change in law (those aged 16–17 in 2003) and compare them to the two cohorts just after them (those aged 18–19 in 2003).

[4]If education improves longevity, then education at the oldest ages is biased upward relative to the original population. This may tend to narrow the observed gender gap at a given age. However, the longer life-expectancy of women, and lower education levels of the oldest cohorts, will tend to exaggerate the gender gap in the oldest age grouping due to over-representation of very old women relative to very old men.

In additional graphical analyses (not shown here due to space constraints) we see a gender gap in completion of 8 years among the older two cohorts who were not directly affected by the law. However, in the younger (treated) cohorts, females appear as likely to have attained 8 years (7 years in the case of those aged 14) as males. Birth month is not reported in our data, so we cannot be as precise as we otherwise might. Most children aged 14–15 would have just completed 7 and 8 years of schooling, respectively, at the time of the survey. When we compare regions in similar graphical explorations, we find larger gender gaps in the east region than in the west region, as we expected. We explored detailed further using regression analysis.

25.5.2 Multivariate regression analyses

First, we estimate multivariate regression models using ordinary least squares (OLS) and probit in order to get baseline models of relationships of various variables to education in the pre-change period. We include individuals in two birth cohorts who should have finished 5 years of schooling before the new law was implemented in August 1997. We run two versions of each model — one excluding and one including a household wealth index and its square. We first run an OLS model with years of education as the dependent variable. We then run probit models, for binary dependent variables on three different attainment thresholds — 5 years (completion of primary school), 8 years (completion of middle school), and 9 years (whether has any high school education). Results of these models are shown in Table 25.2.

Generally, we see results consistent with our expectations. For example, years of education and probabilities of having attained each of the three threshold levels tends to be lower for females than males, education is negatively associated with household size, and education tends to be lower in the more traditional east region than in other regions of the country. One interesting result that we see, which is the reason why we run two separate models for each dependent variable, is that household wealth and whether the household lives in area type 4 (rural) appear to be strongly negatively correlated. When we exclude wealth from the model, we find that those living in rural areas tend to have lower education than others. However, when we add wealth and its square to the model, the coefficient on "rural" becomes positive and is generally weakly statistically significant. This suggests that, controlling for their generally lower wealth, those in

Table 25.2 Baseline estimates for two birth cohorts just before change in schooling law.

	(1)	(2)	(3)	(4)	(5)	(6)	(7)	(8)
	OLS models		Probit models					
	Years of education		5+ years of education		8+ years of education		9+ years (some HS)	
Family size	−0.303***	−0.266***	−0.0968***	−0.0913***	−0.147***	−0.131***	−0.125***	−0.102***
	(0.0194)	(0.0183)	(0.0114)	(0.0120)	(0.0118)	(0.0121)	(0.0122)	(0.0124)
Female	−1.346***	−1.354***	−0.668***	−0.738***	−0.760***	−0.848***	−0.355***	−0.402***
	(0.112)	(0.104)	(0.0830)	(0.0888)	(0.0647)	(0.0687)	(0.0582)	(0.0610)
Age	0.0727	0.0934	−0.0958	−0.0877	−0.259***	−0.278***	0.153***	0.178***
	(0.111)	(0.104)	(0.0795)	(0.0844)	(0.0639)	(0.0672)	(0.0580)	(0.0605)
South	0.00473	0.162	−0.139	−0.108	0.0218	0.163	0.102	0.229**
	(0.202)	(0.189)	(0.158)	(0.171)	(0.116)	(0.125)	(0.102)	(0.108)
Central	0.643***	0.562***	0.598***	0.481**	0.339***	0.339***	0.184*	0.189*
	(0.196)	(0.184)	(0.199)	(0.211)	(0.121)	(0.128)	(0.0997)	(0.104)
North	0.777***	0.590***	0.636**	0.610**	0.430***	0.389**	0.486***	0.452***
	(0.241)	(0.225)	(0.260)	(0.288)	(0.153)	(0.163)	(0.126)	(0.132)
East	−0.797***	−0.487***	−0.545***	−0.475***	−0.301***	−0.173	−0.265***	−0.140
	(0.197)	(0.184)	(0.152)	(0.166)	(0.113)	(0.120)	(0.101)	(0.106)
Small city	0.238	0.351**	0.128	0.233	0.185*	0.297**	0.117	0.205**
	(0.189)	(0.177)	(0.158)	(0.171)	(0.113)	(0.120)	(0.0966)	(0.102)
Town	0.297	0.676***	0.102	0.375*	0.378***	0.646***	0.0881	0.305**
	(0.226)	(0.213)	(0.185)	(0.204)	(0.138)	(0.149)	(0.116)	(0.122)
Rural	−0.479**	0.326*	−0.0591	0.347**	−0.210*	0.215*	−0.381***	0.0236
	(0.191)	(0.185)	(0.157)	(0.173)	(0.111)	(0.122)	(0.0974)	(0.106)
Wealth		0.103***		0.0510***		0.0627***		0.0562***
		(0.00606)		(0.00635)		(0.00517)		(0.00388)
R-squared	0.283	0.376						

Notes: Standard errors in parentheses $^{***}p < 0.01$, $^{**}p < 0.05$, $^{*}p < 0.1$.
Constant included but not shown. Wealth squared included in models 2, 4, 6, and 8. 2,137 observations.

rural areas get more education than we would expect, compared to those living in large cities.[5]

Next we run regression (OLS and probit) models for these same four dependent variables using a sample that includes two cohorts who were the last to be subjected to the old rules (requiring just 5 years) and two cohorts who were the first to be subjected to the new rules (required to complete 8 years). Results from these models are shown in Tables 25.3–25.6. We control for age and age squared, household size, region, rural/urban area type, and household wealth index and its square in all models. We run various models adding variables to capture effects of the law change, beginning with a simple binary variable, and then adding various interaction terms to allow for differential effects for females (Models 2 and 4), and then for differential effects for females across different rural/urban area types (Model 5) and finally, differential effects for females by wealth of the household (Model 6).

Table 25.3 includes these results from OLS models for years of education. After controlling demographics, we see from Model 1 that the change in law does not appear to have had a significant effect on years of education. The coefficient is positive and indicates an additional 0.4 years of education on average after the law change, but is not statistically different from zero. However, when allowing for differential effects, we find that there was a statistically significant increase in female relative to male coincident with the change in law. This supports our hypothesis that the change in law disproportionately benefited girls. Models 3 and 4 repeat Models 1 and 2, but allow for differences across regions in educational attainment of females relative to males. The basic results from Models 1 and 2 are robust enough to allow for this difference. We also checked whether there were differential effects for females relative to males across regions. Since the gender gap is particularly large in the east, we had expected that we might see a catching-up effect for females in the east region. We did not find any significant differentials across regions in the effects for females relative to males, so we have not shown those results here. The large gender gap in the east persists despite the new law, raising concerns that enforcement may be laxer, especially regarding females, in that region. In Model 5, we allow for differential effects for females relative

[5]One concern is that location may be endogenous with respect to educational preferences of the family. We do not address this issue here, but are examining it in other work.

Table 25.3 Years of education (OLS).

	(1)	(2)	(3)	(4)	(5)	(6)
After	0.396	0.150	0.401	0.147	0.0660	0.0833
	(0.307)	(0.317)	(0.303)	(0.313)	(0.312)	(0.309)
Female × after		**0.487*****		**0.506*****	−0.161	**0.475*****
		(0.158)		(0.156)	(0.270)	(0.170)
Female × after X rural					**1.452*****	
					(0.311)	
Female X wealth X after						**−0.0770*****
						(0.0115)
Female	-1.075^{***}	-1.195^{***}	-0.488^{***}	-0.605^{***}	-0.378^{**}	-0.694^{***}
	(0.0681)	(0.0784)	(0.145)	(0.150)	(0.177)	(0.149)
Age	5.711^{**}	5.683^{**}	5.923^{**}	5.896^{**}	5.227^{**}	5.494^{**}
	(2.642)	(2.639)	(2.605)	(2.602)	(2.590)	(2.572)
Age squared	-0.170^{**}	-0.169^{**}	-0.177^{**}	-0.176^{**}	-0.155^{*}	-0.163^{**}
	(0.0825)	(0.0824)	(0.0813)	(0.0812)	(0.0808)	(0.0803)
Household size	-0.223^{***}	-0.223^{***}	-0.221^{***}	-0.221^{***}	-0.223^{***}	-0.223^{***}
	(0.0120)	(0.0120)	(0.0118)	(0.0118)	(0.0117)	(0.0117)
South	0.143	0.141	0.293^{*}	0.295^{*}	0.285^{*}	0.211
	(0.125)	(0.125)	(0.166)	(0.166)	(0.169)	(0.164)
Central	0.437^{***}	0.434^{***}	0.424^{***}	0.421^{***}	0.413^{**}	0.374^{**}
	(0.122)	(0.122)	(0.163)	(0.163)	(0.168)	(0.161)
North	0.390^{***}	0.386^{***}	0.247	0.251	0.268	0.221
	(0.145)	(0.145)	(0.186)	(0.186)	(0.196)	(0.184)
East	-0.632^{***}	-0.635^{***}	0.101	0.103	0.107	−0.0574
	(0.121)	(0.121)	(0.148)	(0.148)	(0.161)	(0.148)
Female X east			-1.503^{***}	-1.514^{***}	-1.465^{***}	-1.165^{***}
			(0.182)	(0.182)	(0.226)	(0.186)
Small city	0.269^{**}	0.277^{**}	0.251^{**}	0.259^{**}	0.119	0.258^{**}
	(0.117)	(0.117)	(0.116)	(0.115)	(0.159)	(0.114)
Town	0.486^{***}	0.501^{***}	0.470^{***}	0.486^{***}	0.408^{**}	0.471^{***}
	(0.140)	(0.139)	(0.138)	(0.138)	(0.194)	(0.136)
Rural	0.307^{**}	0.314^{***}	0.301^{**}	0.308^{**}	0.615^{***}	0.305^{***}
	(0.121)	(0.121)	(0.120)	(0.120)	(0.162)	(0.118)
Female X rural					-0.985^{***}	
					(0.243)	
Wealth	0.0853^{***}	0.0850^{***}	0.0843^{***}	0.0840^{***}	0.0840^{***}	0.0569^{***}
	(0.00404)	(0.00403)	(0.00398)	(0.00398)	(0.00395)	(0.00532)
Female X wealth						0.0730^{***}
						(0.00777)
R-squared	0.364	0.365	0.382	0.383	0.392	0.399

Notes: Standard errors in parentheses.
Statistically significant coefficients on our main variables of interest (those reflecting effects of the law change) are shown in bold for convenience of the reader.
$^{***}p < 0.01$, $^{**}p < 0.05$, $^{*}p < 0.1$.
All models also include a constant and wealth index squared not shown for space reasons. Models 3–6 in each table also include females who interacted with each of south, central and north regions. Model 5 in each table also includes female × small city and female X town and each of these interacted with "after". Model 6 in each table also includes female X after X wealth.[2]
Sample size for all models is 4,065 individuals between the ages of 14 and 17 years, inclusive.

Table 25.4 Probability of five or more years of education (probit).

	(1)	(2)	(3)	(4)	(5)	(6)
After	0.169	0.179	0.159	0.159	0.123	0.124
	(0.280)	(0.297)	(0.281)	(0.296)	(0.298)	(0.298)
Female × after		−0.0152		−0.000002	−0.466*	−0.0555
		(0.153)		(0.152)	(0.249)	(0.169)
Female × after X rural					**0.710*****	
					(0.266)	
Female X wealth X after						−0.0319***
						(0.0103)
Female	−0.736***	−0.732***	−0.588***	−0.588***	−0.434**	−0.512***
	(0.0655)	(0.0742)	(0.166)	(0.168)	(0.195)	(0.171)
Age	1.163	1.163	1.110	1.110	0.825	0.911
	(2.394)	(2.393)	(2.396)	(2.396)	(2.411)	(2.414)
Age squared	−0.0379	−0.0379	−0.0362	−0.0362	−0.0273	−0.0301
	(0.0747)	(0.0747)	(0.0748)	(0.0748)	(0.0752)	(0.0753)
Household size	−0.0827***	−0.0827***	−0.0831***	−0.0831***	−0.0847***	−0.0840***
	(0.00860)	(0.00860)	(0.00863)	(0.00863)	(0.00868)	(0.00866)
South	−0.159	−0.159	−0.218	−0.218	−0.229	−0.219
	(0.127)	(0.127)	(0.194)	(0.194)	(0.205)	(0.194)
Central	0.391**	0.391**	0.240	0.240	0.207	0.235
	(0.160)	(0.160)	(0.254)	(0.254)	(0.269)	(0.253)
North	0.584***	0.584***	0.442	0.442	0.379	0.416
	(0.221)	(0.221)	(0.338)	(0.338)	(0.352)	(0.334)
East	−0.601***	−0.602***	−0.413**	−0.413**	−0.418**	−0.422**
	(0.125)	(0.125)	(0.172)	(0.172)	(0.207)	(0.173)
Female X east			−0.286	−0.286	−0.265	−0.269
			(0.185)	(0.185)	(0.255)	(0.188)
Small city	0.272**	0.272**	0.258**	0.258**	0.185	0.255**
	(0.127)	(0.127)	(0.127)	(0.127)	(0.205)	(0.127)
Town	0.418***	0.418***	0.414***	0.414***	0.539**	0.403***
	(0.152)	(0.152)	(0.152)	(0.152)	(0.263)	(0.152)
Rural	0.379***	0.379***	0.375***	0.375***	0.503**	0.375***
	(0.129)	(0.129)	(0.128)	(0.128)	(0.208)	(0.129)
Female X rural					−0.382	
					(0.270)	
Wealth	0.0483***	0.0483***	0.0480***	0.0480***	0.0483***	0.0458***
	(0.00447)	(0.00447)	(0.00446)	(0.00446)	(0.00451)	(0.00742)
Female X wealth						0.0147*
						(0.00840)

Notes: Standard errors in parentheses.
Statistically significant coefficients on our main variables of interest (those reflecting effects of the law change) are shown in bold for convenience of the reader.
$^{***}p < 0.01$, $^{**}p < 0.05$, $^{*}p < 0.1$.
All models also include a constant and wealth index squared not shown for space reasons. Models 3–6 in each table also include females who interacted with each of south, central and north regions. Model 5 in each table also includes female X small city and female X town and each of these interacted with "after". Model 6 in each table also includes female X after X wealth.[2]
Sample size for all models is 4,065 individuals between the ages of 14 and 17 years, inclusive.

Table 25.5 Probability of eight or more years of education (probit).

	(1)	(2)	(3)	(4)	(5)	(6)
After	−0.220	−0.480**	−0.206	−0.443**	−0.478**	−0.451**
	(0.212)	(0.218)	(0.213)	(0.219)	(0.220)	(0.221)
Female × after		**0.524*** **		**0.488*** **	**0.435** **	**0.506*** **
		(0.102)		(0.103)	(0.174)	(0.113)
Female × after X rural					**0.359* **	
					(0.205)	
Female X wealth X after						−0.0393***
						(0.00843)
Female	−0.488***	−0.635***	−0.199**	−0.335***	−0.237*	−0.297***
	(0.0461)	(0.0546)	(0.0986)	(0.103)	(0.123)	(0.104)
Age	6.510***	6.542***	6.711***	6.727***	6.482***	6.675***
	(1.839)	(1.847)	(1.846)	(1.854)	(1.862)	(1.872)
Age squared	−0.205***	−0.206***	−0.212***	−0.212***	−0.204***	−0.211***
	(0.0574)	(0.0577)	(0.0576)	(0.0579)	(0.0581)	(0.0584)
Household size	−0.120***	−0.120***	−0.122***	−0.123***	−0.124***	−0.124***
	(0.00870)	(0.00876)	(0.00880)	(0.00885)	(0.00891)	(0.00889)
South	0.140*	0.142*	0.260**	0.270**	0.241**	0.243**
	(0.0840)	(0.0843)	(0.117)	(0.118)	(0.122)	(0.118)
Central	0.341***	0.339***	0.428***	0.440***	0.395***	0.419***
	(0.0868)	(0.0871)	(0.123)	(0.124)	(0.130)	(0.124)
North	0.255**	0.250**	0.253*	0.273**	0.208	0.254*
	(0.102)	(0.102)	(0.135)	(0.137)	(0.147)	(0.137)
East	−0.273***	−0.277***	0.00790	−0.00163	−0.0390	−0.0372
	(0.0815)	(0.0818)	(0.102)	(0.103)	(0.115)	(0.103)
Female X east			−0.560***	−0.540***	−0.456***	−0.482***
			(0.123)	(0.123)	(0.158)	(0.126)
Small city	0.156*	0.167**	0.154*	0.164**	0.172	0.171**
	(0.0810)	(0.0813)	(0.0809)	(0.0812)	(0.118)	(0.0817)
Town	0.406***	0.426***	0.408***	0.426***	0.620***	0.426***
	(0.0984)	(0.0986)	(0.0985)	(0.0986)	(0.148)	(0.0993)
Rural	0.110	0.121	0.109	0.120	0.291**	0.127
	(0.0827)	(0.0830)	(0.0826)	(0.0829)	(0.118)	(0.0833)
Female X rural					−0.423**	
					(0.171)	
Wealth	0.0448***	0.0447***	0.0446***	0.0445***	0.0445***	0.0387***
	(0.00295)	(0.00295)	(0.00295)	(0.00296)	(0.00297)	(0.00416)
Female X wealth						0.0262***
						(0.00616)

Notes: Standard errors in parentheses.
Statistically significant coefficients on our main variables of interest (those reflecting effects of the law change) are shown in bold for convenience of the reader.
$^{***}p < 0.01$, $^{**}p < 0.05$, $^{*}p < 0.1$.
All models also include a constant and wealth index squared not shown for space reasons. Models 3–6 in each table also include females who interacted with each of south, central and north regions. Model 5 in each table also includes female × small city and female × town and each of these interacted with "after". Model 6 in each table also includes female × after × wealth.[2]
Sample size for all models is 4,065 individuals between the ages of 14 and 17 years, inclusive.

Table 25.6 Probit models of the probability of at least some high school.

	(1)	(2)	(3)	(4)	(5)	(6)
After	0.0864	0.160	0.111	0.208	0.202	0.237
	(0.213)	(0.224)	(0.214)	(0.225)	(0.225)	(0.225)
Female × after		−0.182		−0.238	−0.859**	−0.0417
		(0.176)		(0.177)	(0.406)	(0.199)
Female × after X rural					**1.530*** **	
					(0.444)	
Female X wealth X after						−0.0739***
						(0.0184)
Female	−0.261***	−0.245***	0.0921	0.114	0.164	0.0796
	(0.0484)	(0.0506)	(0.0999)	(0.101)	(0.116)	(0.103)
Age	9.423***	9.430***	9.695***	9.711***	9.433***	9.692***
	(1.694)	(1.694)	(1.702)	(1.702)	(1.713)	(1.710)
Age squared	−0.280***	−0.281***	−0.289***	−0.289***	−0.280***	−0.288***
	(0.0528)	(0.0528)	(0.0531)	(0.0531)	(0.0534)	(0.0533)
Household size	−0.0915***	−0.0917***	−0.0930***	−0.0932***	−0.0954***	−0.0943***
	(0.0103)	(0.0103)	(0.0104)	(0.0104)	(0.0105)	(0.0104)
South	0.160*	0.159*	0.365***	0.364***	0.357***	0.338***
	(0.0853)	(0.0853)	(0.115)	(0.114)	(0.117)	(0.114)
Central	0.124	0.126	0.233**	0.234**	0.236**	0.220**
	(0.0823)	(0.0824)	(0.112)	(0.111)	(0.115)	(0.111)
North	0.288***	0.287***	0.408***	0.402***	0.420***	0.389***
	(0.0989)	(0.0989)	(0.128)	(0.128)	(0.135)	(0.127)
East	−0.118	−0.118	0.188*	0.189*	0.202*	0.154
	(0.0849)	(0.0850)	(0.105)	(0.104)	(0.113)	(0.105)
Female X east			−0.671***	−0.680***	−0.689***	−0.614***
			(0.133)	(0.133)	(0.166)	(0.136)
Small city	0.0971	0.0964	0.0955	0.0944	0.0331	0.0970
	(0.0797)	(0.0798)	(0.0799)	(0.0800)	(0.109)	(0.0804)
Town	0.210**	0.207**	0.208**	0.204**	0.107	0.200**
	(0.0951)	(0.0952)	(0.0954)	(0.0956)	(0.134)	(0.0960)
Rural	−0.0151	−0.0146	−0.0162	−0.0155	0.126	−0.0175
	(0.0837)	(0.0837)	(0.0839)	(0.0839)	(0.113)	(0.0841)
Female X rural					−0.430**	
					(0.167)	
Wealth	0.0450***	0.0450***	0.0451***	0.0452***	0.0455***	0.0381***
	(0.00302)	(0.00302)	(0.00303)	(0.00303)	(0.00305)	(0.00395)
Female X wealth						0.0204***
						(0.00586)

Notes: Standard errors in parentheses.
Statistically significant coefficients on our main variables of interest (those reflecting effects of the law change) are shown in bold for convenience of the reader.
$^{***}p < 0.01$, $^{**}p < 0.05$, $^{*}p < 0.1$.
All models also include a constant and wealth index squared not shown for space reasons. Models 3–6 in each table also include females who interacted with each of south, central and north regions. Model 5 in each table also includes female × small city and female × town and each of these interacted with "after". Model 6 in each table also includes female × after × wealth.[2]
Sample size for all models is 4,065 individuals between the ages of 14 and 17 years, inclusive.

to males across urban/rural area types. Here we find that there was a large and statistically significant positive effect for females relative to males in rural areas. However, family wealth and rural residential status are strongly negatively correlated. Therefore, in Model 6 we instead allow for differential effects for females relative to males by family wealth. Here we see that females in wealthy families made smaller gains relative to males coincident with the policy change compared to their less-wealthy counterparts. An alternate way to phrase this is that females in low-wealth households gained more relative to their male counterparts compared to females in wealthier families. This is consistent with the interpretation of female education as a luxury good. If wealthier families were already educating girls as much as boys, then girls in those families have relatively little to gain from the change in law — both boys and girls in wealthy families were likely already getting well above compulsory levels. We will continue to look at the two possible explanations for these differences that we see in Models 5 and 6 in future research to try to ascertain how much of the differential effect is in fact due to wealth versus due to the population density of the area.

In Table 25.4, we repeat these analyses using a probit model on a binary variable indicating having attained at least 5 years of schooling. We would not expect the law change to have any effect on this outcome if compulsory schooling law was well-enforced prior to the change. Indeed, in Models 1–4 we do not see any evidence of such effects. However, we do see results in Models 5 and 6 that are fairly similar to those in the previous tables with respect to differential effects for females associated with rural or low wealth status. This may suggest increased access or enforcement of compulsory schooling after the law change, which might have particularly affected females, for whom the 5-year requirement was more likely to be a binding constraint. We also see a puzzling negative and marginally significant result for females relative to males overall in Model 5. It is possible that this can be explained by endogeneity of rural status, and it does not appear in Model 6.

We expect to see an effect on the probability of attaining 8 years of schooling of this law change. Probit results for at least 8-years are shown in Table 25.5. The "after" variable is not statistically different from zero in Models 1 and 3. However, the differential effect for girls is positive and significant, indicating some closing of the gender gap in attainment of this level of schooling. Again, we see positive differential effects for females in rural locations, as well as by family wealth.

Finally, in Table 25.6 we examine the impacts of the new law on whether individuals get at least some high school education. If the new law increases schooling only through directly affecting constraints, then we would expect no effect here. Finding no effect here would support our claim that the effects we find in Table 25.5 are due to the law change rather than to time trends or increased development and job opportunities generally over time. We find no significant effects of the policy in Models 1–4. However, we still see the persistent apparent effects of the law change differentially affecting females relative to males that appears to occur either for those in rural locations, or for those in low-wealth households, along with a puzzling negative effect of the policy variable for girls relative to boys in Model 5, like what we found in Table 25.4. These results could possibly be explained by some indirect effects of the policy due to information value or signaling, coupled with increased access and/or enforcement in rural areas.

25.6 Conclusions and discussion

As we hypothesized, we find that females appear to have benefited disproportionately relative to males in terms of increased education after the change in compulsory schooling. We see effects most prominently for the outcomes where we would expect to see them, namely the probability in completing 8 years of schooling, and in years of education. However, we also see some effects for females in the probability of completing 5 years of education, which may stem from increased attention to enforcement of compulsory schooling rules that occurred at the same time that the new law was implemented.

The gender gap in the more traditional eastern region is persistent, even after the increase in compulsory schooling. Additional research is needed to look into this area in particular, as well as to identify households who migrated to other regions from the east in order to ascertain whether those families maintain a larger gender gap than their neighbors. There has been significant migration in Turkey since the 1950s, mainly to large cities in the western region (Tunali, 1996). Alderman *et al.* (1996) assert that biases must be broken at the local policy level, as well as within communities, such as within ethnic groups, in order for change to be effected in the gender gap in education. Optimal design of policies to address the gender gap depends upon whether migrants carry their gender preference with them when they migrate.

We find differential effects of the law change for females among low income households, and in households living in rural areas. The implied gains in closing the gender gap in rural areas and among low-income households are encouraging. We hope to investigate these effects in more detail in future work.

To the extent that education implies empowerment, our findings suggest that gender neutral compulsory schooling policies *can* foster advances in women's empowerment. However, they may not always do so, and understanding why this change did not more substantially narrow the gender gap in the east region of Turkey could contribute important knowledge in designing future policies. In the ongoing work, we hope to further address this and other important questions.

Acknowledgments

The authors are grateful to Heather Royer, conference attendees at the 2012 ASSA meetings, and seminar participants at Wayne State University, Eastern Michigan University, Western Michigan University and Oakland University for their helpful comments, and to DHS/TDHS, IPUMS and the Turkish Statistical Institute for providing the data used herein. All errors are our own.

References

Alderman, H., Behrman, J., Ross, D. and Sabot, R. (1996), Decomposing the gender gap in cognitive skills in a poor rural economy. *The Journal of Human Resources*, 31(1), 229–254.

Behrman, J. (1993), Investing in female education for development. *Journal of Educational Planning and Administration*, 7(4), 393–412.

Behrman, J., Foster, A., Rosenzweig, M. and Vahsishtha, P. (1999), Women's schooling, home teaching, and economic growth. *Journal of Political Economy*, 107(4), 682–714.

Behrman, J., Pollak, R. and Taubman, P. (1995), Do parents favor boys? *International Economic Review*, 27(1), 33–54.

Dayioğlu, M., Kirdar, M. and Tansel, A. (2009), Impact of sibship size, birth order, and sex composition on school enrollment in urban Turkey. *Oxford Bulletin of Economics and Statistics*, 71(3), 399–426.

Hacettepe University Institute of Population Studies and Ministry of Health General Directorate of Mother and Child Health and Family Planning (2004), Turkey Demographic and Health Survey, 2003, Ankara: Hacettepe University Institute of Population Studies, (Final Report, October 2004).

Jensen, P. and Nielsen, H. S. (1997), Child labour or school attendance? Evidence from Zambia. *Journal of Population Economics*, 10(4), 407–424.

King, Elizabeth M. and Hill, M. Anne (eds.), (1993), *Women's education in developing countries: barriers, benefits, and policies.* Baltimore, MD. http://documents.worldbank.org/curated/en/849491468740172523/Women s-education-in-developing-countries-barriers-benefits-and-policies.

Kirdar, M. (2009), Explaining ethnic disparities in school enrollment in Turkey. *Economic Development and Cultural Change*, 57(2), 297–333.

Minnesota Population Center. Integrated Public Use Microdata Series, International (2000 Census of Turkey): Version 6.3 [Machine-readable database]. Minneapolis: University of Minnesota, 2014.

Psacharopoulos, G. (1997), Child labor versus educational attainment: Some evidence from Latin America. *Journal of Population Economics*, 10(4), 377–386.

Tansel, A. (2002), Determinant of school attainment of boys and girls in Turkey: Individual, household, and community factors. *Economics of Education Review*, 456–457.

Tunali, I. (1996), Migration and remigration of male household heads in Turkey. *Economic Development and Cultural Change*, 45(1), 31–67.

Tunali, I. and Baslevent, Cem (2006), "Female labor supply in Turkey", in Sumru Altug and Alpay Filiztekin (eds.). *Routledge Studies in Middle Eastern Economics*, London and New York: Routledge, Taylor and Francis.

Hausmann, R., Tyson, L. D. and Zahidi, S. (2009), *The Global Gender Gap Report*, Geneva: World Economic Forum.

Chapter 26

Women Empowerment Through Islamic Microfinance Schemes in Bangladesh

Abul Hassan, Salah Al Shalhoob and Yaser Ahmad Fallatah

Abstract

Islamic microfinance programs have been used, for some time in Bangladesh, as an instrument to empower women and fight poverty. Women are specifically targeted by Islamic microfinance under the rural development scheme of Islami Bank Bangladesh Limited (IBBL), which provides interest-free loans and many other benefits to the women groups involved. The main aim of this chapter is two-fold: firstly, to check for a positive relationship between Islamic microfinance and the socio-economic empowerment of women and secondly, to explore the perspective in which Islamic microfinance packages function in Bangladesh and how the system of their performance can be enhanced. A structured questionnaire survey method was employed to see the socio-economic empowerment of the women through Islamic microfinance program and under what circumstances would such a program be more useful? The results of this study show that the growth in women's revenues and resources plays an important role in improving women's financial freedom and sense of self-possession. However, a significant policy lesson from this study is that, it is essential to redirect Islamic microfinance to more sectors and more beneficiaries, in order to spread its benefits in the developmental activities, which will drive the contribution toward the socio-economic empowerment of the recipients and toward the socio-economic development of the country, in the long-run.

Keywords: Socio-economic empowerment, Islamic microfinance, Poverty, Health

The utmost benefit of microfinance, targeting the economic progress of women in deprived society, is their empowerment and the self-employment it generates with the creation of small and micro-entrepreneurships against the wage-based employment. The task here is to advance entrepreneurship and generate enough productive employment and income prospects for the deprived people. Financing small and micro businesses through the banking system as well as developing entrepreneurship are the two main agents in the route of economic development. The contribution of Islami Bank Bangladesh Limited (IBBL) in promoting Islamic microfinance and women entrepreneurship through its Rural Development Scheme (RDS) started in 1995. More than 30% of the people in Bangladesh live with poverty. Presently, the RDS scheme is being implemented in 60 districts of the country and benefiting some 520,000 members that are involved in this scheme (Rahman and Ahmad, 2014).

The performance of RDS has been remarkable over a long period of time and across other mainstream; foremost is the Microfinance Institutions (MFIs) that have been operating in Bangladesh. The Islamic microfinance under RDS has used a very effective model for eliminating poverty, the Grameen Bank Model, but with an Islamic social perspective of the Muslim society of Bangladesh. Like Grameen Bank Model, it has boarded on enabling women, with 80% of its clientele being economically poor women. However, Islamic microfinance has been endeavored in a *Shari'ah* compliant manner that endorses family integration and cohesiveness. This scheme has also endeavored to encourage the healthy social practices by ensuring the participation of all members in the group activities.

The plan of operational adjustment guidelines of the World Bank shows mixed impacts on the well-being of women. The socio-economic context before the last 2–3 decades imposed huge restrictions on women's occupation and can occasionally reduce their socio-economic standing, and compel them to intersect in the labor marketplace under severe conditions.

Given the rise of awareness on Islam in Bangladeshi political discourse and social life, the role of women in the society are gradually recognized in the light of Islamic principles. Therefore, the participation of women in economic activities has attracted a significant level of attention in the socio-economic development of the country. In this situation, Islamic microfinance is used by IBBL and some other Islamic non-government organizations to promote entrepreneurship as an instrument to alleviate poverty.

To explain why women are explicitly targeted by several microfinance packages in Bangladesh, some studies submit that the involvement of women in microfinance programs have a multiplier outcome since women devote most of their incomes to their households (Akter, 2001). The RDS scheme of IBBL came out with a scientific *Shari'ah*-based program with an objective of economic empowerment of women in particular and rural people in general, to alleviate poverty by providing credit for financing their investment in farm and non-farm activities and thereby raising the level of their incomes and improving their standards of living.

This program is characterized by different distinctive features, techniques and mechanisms, which have prompted to undertake this study expected to provide insights on the well-being of women that can be achieved through Islamic microfinance program. It, also, gives some visions for future policy and programs to be undertaken for the betterment of RDS of IBBL before it goes for further expansion.

26.1 Overview of Islamic microfinance program

The RDS — a popular Islamic microfinance program implemented under the umbrella of IBBL provides the investment requirements of the rural sector especially for agriculture to generate opportunities for employment and to raise the incomes of village people in order to eliminate poverty. All branches of the IBBL are directed by their authorities to invest their deposits at their respective zones and specifically for the economic uplifting of the people in the rural areas. The main purposes of RDS, as cited in the Annual Report 2013 of the IBBL, are:

- To provide investment facilities to agrarian, rural farming and off-farming activities in the rural areas.
- To provide finance for self-employment and income generating events of the village people, particularly for the unemployed of rural youths and the rural poor.
- To lighten rural poverty through integrated rural development approach.
- To spread investment facilities for hand tube-wells and rural housing, keeping in view the needs of safe drinking water and housing facilities of the rural dwellers.
- To deliver education and medicare services to the people of down-trodden society.

The IBBL is one of the biggest Islamic microfinance providers in Bangladesh. It provides Islamic microfinance facilities by its RDS (Ahmad, 2011). Through its RDS, IBBL has designed a *Shari'ah* compliant model of poverty alleviation, ensuing the value of group loaning and participating management technique. The target group or cluster comprises needy women and economically poor people, a family with 0.50 acres of property either possessed or hired for farming or the families involved in a small off farm activities within rural areas. The pattern of micro-credit cluster creation and associated activities are identical to those of the Grameen model (a pioneer microfinance bank) in Bangladesh. Groups are homogenous and self-motivated. The members of a microfinance group form a homogenous group, which elects 4–5 members in their management committee. The first and foremost condition to be part of the group is that the members should essentially bear an excellent character with promising to the principle and wisdoms of Islam.

26.1.1 Islamic financial plan of RDS and its growth

The RDS is a poverty alleviation scheme of IBBL, which has its own *Shari'ah* Department and a strong *Shari'ah* Board comprising renowned Islamic scholars of Bangladesh. There is also a National Shari'ah Supervisory Board for all the Islamic banks operating in Bangladesh. This Board monitors the investment and other activities of RDS (Rahman and Ahmad, 2014). The official documents of IBBL claim that all the products of the RDS are compliant with *Shari'ah* (Annual Report of IBBL, 2013). Under RDS, three types of funding are provided to the beneficiaries:

(a) Collateral-free microfinance up to Bangladesh Taka (BDTK) 50,000 to the poor in diverse income making activities;
(b) Microenterprise finance, i.e., collateralized finance up to BDTK 300,000 to the graduated and other micro-clients;
(c) Benevolent loan (*Qard-hasan* program) up to BDTK 10,000 to the hard-core poor and distressed people for water, sanitation and rehabilitation.

Under the scheme of RDS, there is no collateral required for the flagship program for the poor. A member can request for financing, which may be considered within eight weeks after the date of her or his enrollment as a member of the group. A qualified member is entitled to obtain initial financing to the tune of BDTK 10,000.00 ($145.00). The upper limit for financing under the scheme is BDTK 50,000.00 ($725.00). The total debt (principal amount plus profit) is needed to be cleared by the client over a 1-year period in 44 equal weekly installments.

Each and every member of Islamic microfinance groups under the RDS are required to save weekly at least Bangladesh Taka (BDTK) 20.00 ($0.30) in their savings account at the IBBL. The branches of IBBL have the responsibility to implement the scheme. Investment in specified sectors is made in four modes, *Bai' Mu'ajjal*, *Bai' Murabahah*, *Bai' Salam*

Table 26.1 Growing of RDS — Islamic microfinance program.

Year	2008	2009	2010	2011	2012	2013
No. of villages	10,676	10,751	11,482	12,857	15,507	17,401
No. of centers	21,193	22,261	20,833	22,206	24,623	27,800
No. of beneficiaries	577,740	492,475	523,941	608,703	733,520	897,000
No. of investment clients	321,848	312,036	319,859	382,319	474,766	584,000

Source: IBBL Annual Report (2013).

and Hire Purchase under *Sharikat al-Mulk* or *Ijarah* (leasing). The parent organization, IBBL gives a profit of 12.50% (increased from 10.00%) on the investment. Well-timed refund is encouraged by offering 2.50% discount. Each group members need to contribute BDTK 2.00 per week at the center fund. Instalment is fixed on weekly basis as mentioned earlier. The Field Officers make collections of the instalments, personal savings, center fund, etc. in the weekly center gatherings. As on 2013, there are 2,499 Field Officers, who are trained by the IBBL at their headquarters. These field officers are engaged in the supervision of the Islamic microfinance programs.

This RDS program has been implemented by the branches of IBBL all over the country since 1995. Under this scheme, an investment of BDTK 98,259.07 million to 569,426 persons of which 80% are women and 20% men have been made through 242 branches in 17,488 villages in 64 districts of the country, as of 30 November 2014. The Recovery rate is 97.10% (BDTK 16,462.20 million). This indicates that within a decade of time, Islamic microfinance program under IBBL covers 69% villages in Bangladesh.

26.1.2 Objectives of the study

The two main objectives of the study are:

(1) Refuting or confirming a positive link between Islamic microfinance and social as well as economic well-being of women and,
(2) Discovering the background in which the Islamic microfinance programs operate in Bangladesh and how their performance can be enhanced.

Keeping in view of the above two aims, two main research questions addressed in the study are:

(1) What is the expectation from the offer of Islamic microfinance program on the welfare of beneficiaries?
(2) Under what circumstances would such an offer be more useful?

The rest of the chapter is structured as follow. Section 26.2 presents a brief literature review. In Section 26.3, the choices of variables of the study have been determined. Section 26.4 discusses the methodology and data collection of the study. Section 26.5 offers the empirical results. Section 26.6 discusses the financial and social development of the beneficiaries. Section 26.7 provides an analysis of the microfinance experts' opinion, which is followed by conclusion and policy recommendations in the Section 26.8.

26.2 Microfinance, development and poverty

In the developing economies, women are rarely possessors of significant economic means. Usually, they are marked as very destitute when facing financial crisis. In this regard, a few studies have indicated that for the economically poor, such as women, the lack of fiscal resources is a vast limitation in undertaking economic events. Therefore, it is desired to apply the theory of "added worker effects" (Cerrutti, 2000) by engaging women to produce extra income. On the other hand, the pressure, put by economic conditions on governments, has led to the preponderance of the national "labor" policy over the traditional "gender" policy in the developing countries.

Also, today the majority of the Muslim scholars tend to say that women's employment does not contradict the traditional Islamic ethics, as it is a prolongation of their role as mothers in providing the basic needs of their families. In this situation, the application of microfinance is an instrument used in developing economies to alleviate poverty on one side and to correct market disappointments on the other (Khandker *et al.*, 1995). It is a suitable scheme to engage women in income-generating activities.

People in the very poor families, where savings are expensive because of small incomes and where consumption is minimal, lack basic existence necessities. In this situation, microfinance could play a significant role in improving the family's well-being (Ahmad, 2007). Moreover, the idea of empowerment is vital in the foundation of the deal of microfinance to women. It inspires the capability of women to adopt new economic initiatives. In respect of "poverty combat", this terminology is demarcated as the procedure of offering more economic power to the financially poor, irrespective of age, sex and ethnicity in order to give them advantage from the benefit of development (Jahur and Quadir, 2010).

In Bangladesh, microfinance programs are reinforced by different non-governmental organizations (NGOs) and by groups of specialists, each executing its own agenda according to its own creed. The proponents argue that microfinance places people in the sentiment of the route of development as well as policy expansion. The defenders of women's rights believe that Islamic microfinance allows women to work, since it endorses progress while focusing on eradicating gender discernment. The policymakers approach is of poverty reduction. They encourage the adoption of microfinance programs because it allows the poor to make them financially independent and less susceptible when facing financial crises. The economic experts support the microfinance program since it encourages the growth of the less advanced areas and less privileged clusters of folks within the society and encourages economic development over the long term.

The microfinance research activities have revealed that the usefulness of microfinance in easing poverty depends upon how far the microfinance association is penetrating in dealing with clients' demand. The necessity to put emphasis on demand-driven financial services persuade them to take optimum benefit from development-oriented suitable products and services with operation efficiency and more outreach enhancement. For example, the space of lending facilities presented to the poor people should address not only production and income-oriented activities but also other needs such as education, health care, water, sanitation and other social requirements. Subsequently, the improved financing products will produce superior financial benefits for economically poor customers and eventually lead to greater effects to the society, predominantly the poor people (Seibel and Parhusip, 1998; Zeller and Meyer, 2002).

There is a lot of literature on microfinance, which focus on developmental issues. The MFIs are principally prepared to realize the social welfare objective with specific goal of poverty alleviation and to provide benefit to the beneficiaries. Studies in this area emphasize on the involvement of women and its emerging effect in terms of poverty eradication. Furthermore, some experimental studies, typically from Bangladesh, offer suggestions on the welfare and endowing effects of microfinance on women (Kabeer, 2001; Lakwo, 2006; Osmani, 2007; Pitt *et al.*, 2006).

Brau and Woller (2004) give a lucid example on some important development matters such as the involvement of MFIs in women's deliverance and the varied impact of women's contribution on the productivity of MFIs. Regarding the growing impact of women's involvement, Brau and Woller (2004) study specifically mentions the gender contribution, the borrower's solvency and poverty eradication. Islam, as a faith and as a system of living, is grounded on a customary of religious dogmas and economic standards that emphasize on the inclusive welfare of humankind, particularly for the distressed and economically poorer classes of the society. In combination with the spiritual vision and objective of well-being, Islamic microfinance appeared as a novel financial instrument and different from mainstream microfinance. Researchers in Islamic finance frequently claim that the religious dogmas in Islamic countries is in contrast to mainstream microfinance, which is why *Shari'ah*-based or Islamic microfinance is needed to clarify why it is booming (Ahmad, 2007; Obaidullah and Khan, 2008).

Ahmad (2007) reveals that the importance of Islamic microfinance as a tool is to boost economic development, respond to the effects of economic uncertainty and empower women in the society. It is true that, once women, who used to stay at home and devote their time to multiplicative tasks, will have new opportunities open to them. Microfinance programs based on Islamic values are specifically significant for women since they could get interest-free loans to start some legitimate income-making activities. In fact, financially weaker class women frequently lack the essential guarantees and pre-condition to get loans from official lending institutions.

Islamic microfinance packages are increasingly targeting women due to following reasons:

(1) First, for a cost-efficiency rationale since, women's repayment rates are higher than that of men,
(2) Second, for equity reason, since women have fewer access to fruitful occupation in the emerging countries and
(3) Third, for multiplier outcome that expands the usefulness of the capitals because women devote themselves wholly to the welfare of their children and families.

It is generally understood that Islamic microfinancing is a word that specifies "the deal of financial facilities to clients with small income levels without charging interest or *riba*" (Ahmad, 2011). Thus, Islamic microfinancing targets groups of people with very low income who have no access to the official lending system. Saad and Duasa (2010) has come out with the characteristics of Islamic microfinance as follows:

(i) Microfinance products could serve as guidelines to MFIs in designing Islamic microfinance products.
(ii) Reasonable service charges.

(iii) Easy and speedy evaluations.
(iv) Flexibility in payment of arrears.

In addition to this, there are several initiatives taken to strengthen the Islamic MFIs (Obaidullah and Khan, 2008):

(i) Participate in equity of Islamic financial institutions with a view to create specialized microfinance divisions.
(ii) Create *qard al-hasan* (interest-free loan) specific funds to support various interest-free-based MFIs across the globe.
(iii) Create refinance facility to act as a wholeseller of Islamic microfinance products for a chain of Islamic microfinance retailers.
(iv) Participate in equity of *takaful* (Islamic insurance) and *retakaful* (Islamic re-insurance) companies with a view to develop micro-*takaful* products and services.
(v) Design a Credit Guarantee Scheme (CGS) for Islamic microfinance providers.
(vi) Promote dialogue among *Shari'ah* scholars for collective resolutions of *fiqhi* issues related to microfinance (Attia, 2010).

The implementation of microfinance should be based on concepts of human well-being (*falah*) and good life (*hayat tayyibah*) that emphasize the utmost importance of brotherhood and socio-economic justice. This in turn would require a balanced satisfaction of both the material and the spiritual needs of all human beings (Chapra, 1992).

Not many of the existing literature on Islamic microfinance provide empirical evidence in respect of the well-being of women through Islamic microfinance. Only recently, Ashraf *et al.* (2014) analyzed how common socio-economic factors such as income, assets, health care, etc., may explain the socio-economic well-being of women who enrolled in microfinance. Also a few studies (Jahur, 2010; Alamgir *et al.*, 2010; Rahman and Ahmad, 2014) show that family income, productivity of harvests and livestock, spending and employment had enlarged significantly due to the effect of invested money through Islamic microfinance scheme like RDS.

However, there is lack of studies on well-being and socio-economic empowering effects of Islamic microfinance on women. In other words, so far, there is no study that focuses on the socio-economic well-being of women through Islamic microfinance — RDS — since more than 80% members or beneficiaries under the scheme are women. Therefore, a study on the role Islamic microfinance (RDS) in eradicating poverty and in improving the socio-economic well-being of women will be more appropriate in the current situation.

26.3 Different variables of Islamic microfinance model

Two different methods exist in measuring the effects of the microfinancing (Cerrutti, 2000). First, the "welfarist" method that highlights on progresses gathered by microfinance on the receivers' well-being. Second, the "institutionist" method, which focuses, on the other hand on the practical/formal aspects of the application, namely the financial sustainability and outreach of microfinance schemes (Chaves and Gonzalez-Vega, 1996; Buckley, 1997).

The first method is more appealing to donors and researchers, while the second method is used to economically validate the use of the capitals dedicated to the Islamic microfinance schemes. The "welfarist" method is the one that may conceptually escort our own investigational work. Actually, two diverse styles exist to associate between microfinance and women's empowerment (Hashemi *et al.*, 1996). This research represents a summative evaluation of Islamic microfinance business model under RDS scheme of Islamic Bank Bangladesh Limited, more explicitly; a socio-economic outcome study on women welfare following the methodology employed by Nader (2008).

A study conducted by Khandker (1998) displays that, in spite of the significance of the assessment of microfinance packages in matter of their economic sustainability and outreach, such norms do not essentially echo the real effect on the society and the recipients. Consequently, this study as well as the selection of the variables falls within the "welfarist" method in evaluating the effect of Islamic microfinance business model of IBBL. The variables have been selected to signify the socio-economic welfare of women. These variables are: income, possession of assets, health, schooling of children, and harmony in the family. The reasons of choosing these variables are:

26.3.1 Income

It is a general perception that obtaining Islamic microfinance loan would increase the income of the recipients while enabling them to widen their activity and to increase the quantity of the goods they sell. The income outcome is predominantly significant in Bangladesh in the perspective of the eradication of poverty. It may be stated that more than

27% of the families depend on women as the main sources of revenue (Ahmad, 2011).

26.3.2 Assets

The ownership of assets has been kept provision as a second variable since this variable echoes the sustainability outcome of Islamic microfinance. The growth in the revenue would not have a sustainable effect on women if the assets they hold should rise at the upper level. After apprehension of bigger profit, it appears that women would one day discontinue relying on the Islamic microfinance when sufficient capital would be accumulated, the credit/investment being accordingly used for culminations not for consumption and nevertheless for production.

26.3.3 Health

Health care is chosen as one of the variables because health problem is an acute problem in Bangladesh and threaten people's productivity. So, health care is an important variable as a development indicator of the third world countries. This sector needed further improvement. As a result, Islamic microfinance should make it promising to women who may get better treatments and more health care. This is very important in the situation of Bangladesh since insurance and social security systems in Bangladesh are not much efficient.

26.3.4 Schooling of children

The education of children is another most significant variable to measure human progress of a country (Sinha, 1998). Certainly, this variable echoes the greatest outcome of Islamic microfinance, that of the multiplier outcome, when the effects of a simple lending is provided over many generations. This is mostly stimulating since the struggle against illiteracy is one of the priority agendas of Bangladesh government for some years. Governmental movements and programs are set up to inspire parents to send their children to school. If the proposal to provide interest-free loan influences the schooling of the children of the beneficiaries, then the resources of the governmental and efforts might be transmitted toward other purposes. Furthermore, the education of girls is particularly significant in the circumstances of Bangladesh where boys frequently come first.

26.3.5 Family harmony

The understanding of harmony in the family is selected as a fifth variable of the research because harmony in the family means the degree to which most of the members of a family are living with tranquility without facing any major problems and worrying events. While this variable has not been largely considered in the past researches, it is revealed that "harmony" is well considered by Islamic microfinance, if it could reduce the household problems by enlightening the financial situation of the family.

26.4 Methodology of the study

In this study, the research hypothesis tests whether Islamic microfinance (RDS) is confidently associated with the socio-economic welfare of women in Bangladesh with regard to: income, possession of assets, children's schooling, health and harmony in the family. The used methodology relies mostly on regression analysis and doing correlation of cross-sectional data. A few other inquiries are comprised in the interviews to reflect the details regarding the happiness of the women *vis-a-vis* Islamic microfinance. Interviews were also conducted with the Field Officers of Islamic microfinance program managed by IBBL and with Islamic microfinance specialists/experts in Bangladesh. The main purpose of these interviews is to offer a qualitative dimension to the investigation and to support the explanation of the outcome or results. This will provide the response of the second question relating to the operation of Islamic microfinance scheme and offer policy recommendations. It would, therefore, be of immense importance to examine the poverty and socio-economic welfare of women and their household by executing RDS — a prominent Islamic microfinance model in Bangladesh.

26.4.1 Sampling

This study aims at authenticating the relationship between Islamic microfinance and the socio-economic welfare of the recipients, and the unit of investigation — the women who benefited from a *Shari'ah* compliant investment. In a domain of plentiful resources, a bigger sample might have been selected. However, the means and time for the completion of conducting the survey of this study were limited, the sample totaled 700 women, customers of our sample Islamic microfinance program.

This study shows the effects of the program or policy and links the observed changes of the program, which may be called "treatment group" in term of statistical analysis (Sinha, 1998). In our case, women benefiting from Islamic microfinance (RDS) and on the same time, a control cluster, women who do not get benefit from Islamic microfinance (i.e., same RDS) but who are otherwise analogous to the members of the treatment group. Subsequently, finding women within the society with same class of likenesses is difficult, in this study the sample was separated equally into two groups following the same method employed by Nader (2008):

(1) Group 1 (treatment group or experimental): Comprising 350 women who benefited from Islamic microfinance program for at least 3 years to ensure that it got minimum time to have effect on their lives.
(2) Group II (comparison group): Covering 350 women who have recently joined the Islamic microfinance program in order to confirm that they have wished their likenesses with the treatment group not being immediately profited by Islamic microfinance program (RDS).

Since the treatment and control group could ideally vary only by the point that one group received the credit and the other group did not or just get the credit. Any observed changes might then, with some reasons, be mostly may be attributed to Islamic microfinance program.

The sample of participants was selected through the Field Officers of Islamic microfinance program (RDS) by means of the Islamic microfinance program database of 7,500 customers. The search and enrolment were operated by the Islami Bank Field Officers with concealment. Also, five key microfinance specialists were interviewed; out of them two were university professors and three microfinance officers, who were from other microfinance organizations.

26.4.2 Data collection

By following the same methodology as adopted by the study of Nader (2008), data have been collected by the ensuing process:

(1) Verifying the program documents and archives to collect information about membership rules, mechanisms and running.
(2) One-to-one interviews carried out with members employing open-ended and closed-ended survey questionnaires. The survey questionnaires were tested to confirm their transparency and understanding skill by the members who came from very poor background and different literacy stages.

The researchers met with key specialists of the microfinance area, specifically with university professors who conducted academic studies in the microfinance area, and Microcredit Officers of Grameen Bank. The limitations of this study include the fact that, some women were unwilling to respond to some of the queries regarding their education and income levels. In some other cases, the details and clarification of the purpose of this study motivated some of them to cooperate. In addition, if women believed that giving constructive comments about the program might increase their likelihoods of receiving more credits, the study would be prejudiced.

To overcome these issues, a detailed demonstration about the nature and type of the study facilitated the understanding of the target group of our sample, helped clear the understanding and reduce mistakes. Furthermore, the recklessness ratio of the Islamic microfinance program would have signified a limitation of the investigation. Subsequently it would have caused a variance between the profiles of the two groups and made them unhealthy for comparison. The fact is that this rate remained very small and made this risk irrelevant.

26.4.3 Regression equation and statistical test

Most of the previous studies aimed at examining the impact of conventional microfinance on the socio-economic welfare of the recipients have used simple quantitative methods in the form of regression analyses and correlation tests where the indicators of welfare signified the dependent variables (El-Solh, 1999; Doumato and Posusney, 2003). In this study, firstly the correlation is made in order to investigate the existence of relationships between the Islamic microfinance and selected dependent variables and to show the possible size effect. Secondly, the regressions were done in order to examine the causality and importance of such relations. It may be pointed out that because the sample of this study is relatively small, simplification should be avoided. Even though, a few studies have previously measured the effect of Islamic microfinance packages on recipients; our expectation is to shed some focus on the following research questions:

- What is to be anticipated from the Islamic microfinance model in Bangladesh on the well-being of beneficiaries?
- Under what circumstances will such offer add extra benefit?

To respond to these research questions, the recipients of Islamic microfinance were questioned, on the one hand, with a varied kind of queries like:

What is the purpose of availing Islamic microfinance? What type of small activities or entrepreneurships they are themselves operating? How much they earn of that activity/entrepreneurship? Do they have other source of earnings? The purpose of these questions was to distinguish it from the money they earn from Islamic microfinance-linked entrepreneurship. The beneficiaries were also questioned about the properties or asset they hold and the method of use of the money they earn, i.e., whether it is used for buying or investment of new assets or they use the earnings for consumption purposes.

On the other hand, the participants were asked to state the number of their children, who were going to school and why others did not go. The beneficiaries were also asked about their health conditions, and were asked to rank the level of their health status. In case, they were receiving any treatments, then in what way they met the expenditure of such treatments? The purpose of asking these questions was to ascertain their views — whether Islamic microfinance helped to improve their health.

Other queries related to harmony in family affairs with husband and sons have been addressed by requesting the beneficiaries to rank their situations with respect to "stability or lack of problems". Further, the beneficiaries were requested to answer whether the income from Islamic microfinance helped them improve the relations within their families — added steady and harmonious circumstances. They were also asked to offer any comments or suggestions they desired to make in respect of the aforementioned subjects or any supplementary Islamic microfinance/conventional microfinance related issue.

The Microfinance Specialists were requested to give their opinion or assessment about the efficiency of Islamic microfinance programs in Bangladesh, in terms of planning, outreach and operation; and effect on both microfinance recipients and on the economy.

The regression equations have been replicated from Nader (2008) as follows:

(1) Income = A1 + B1 Islamic microfinance + C1 age + D1 education + F1 marital status + G1 number of children + e_1.
(2) Assets = A2 + B2 Islamic microfinance + C2 age + D2 education + F2 marital status + G2 number of children + e_2.
(3) Schooling of girls = A3 + B3 Islamic microfinance + C3 age + D3 education + F3 marital status + G3 number of children + e_3.
(4) Schooling of boys = A4 + B4 Islamic microfinance + C4 age + D4 education + F4 marital status + G4 number of children + e_4.

(5) Perception of health = A5 + B5 Islamic microfinance + C5 age + D5 education + F5 marital status + G5 number of children + e_5.
(6) Observation of the harmony in household = A6 + B6 Islamic microfinance + C6 age + D6 education + F6 marital status + G6 number of children + e_6, where Islamic microfinance used the independent variable in the last 3 years. The designated control variables were education, age, married status and children.

26.5 Results

The results in Tables 26.1A, 26.1B and 26.2 show that Islamic microfinance has been positively linked to income ($r = 0.737$), assets ($r = 0.267$), education of girls ($r = 0.382$) and education of boys ($r = 0.405$), but the correlation is not statistically significant between Islamic microfinance and the awareness of health and the awareness of harmony in the household. These results were confirmed by the regression coefficients.

The results, further, show that the "income" equation in matter of income of the recipient is inclined to rise on average by BDTK (Bangladesh Taka) 2,040.00 per month when taking the Islamic microfinance loan. As per the survey results, the average income of women, who did not obtain/newly receive Islamic microfinance loan was BDTK 4,010.00. An increase of BDTK 2,040.00 represents about 49% increase, which gives evidence that Islamic microfinance has a significant economic outcome on the women getting the loans. In the "assets" equation, getting Islamic microfinance loan is linked with a normal growth of assets of BDTK 4,850.00 as compared to those who did not get advantage from Islamic microfinance loan. The equation of "schooling of girls" is linked with an average rise of 29% in the number of girls going to school from each family benefiting from Islamic microfinance loan. Similarly, the equation of "schooling of boys", is linked with an average rise of 31% in each family benefiting from Islamic microfinance loan. Regarding the equation of the "perception of health", it is observed that Islamic microfinance coefficient is not at the significant level, suggesting a lack of a strong relationship between the two variables.

As regards to the equation of the "perception of harmony in the family", the Islamic microfinance coefficient is also not at the statistically significant level. The results suggest that there is lack of a significant relationship between the harmony in the household and the fact of getting Islamic microfinance loan.

Table 26.1A Results of correlation.

	Age	No. of children	Income of the members	Assets	Health	Harmony within the family
Age	1	0.472**	0.014	−0.011	−0.395**	−0.146
No. of children	0.472**	1	0.232*	−0.251*	−0.295**	0.028
Income of the members	0.014	0.232*	1	0.454**	−0.056	0.227*
Assets	−0.011	0.251*	0.454**	1	0.068	0.214*
Health	−0.393**	−0.295**		0.066	1	0.366**
Harmony within the family	−0.146	0.028	−0.056	0.214*	0.366**	1
Islamic microfinance	0.000	0.172	0.737**	0.267**	−0.033	0.123
Girls' schooling	−0.020	−0.058	0.208	0.232*	0.018	0.014
Boys' schooling	−0.042	0.019	0.371**	0.228*	−0.098	0.092
Education	−0.306**	−0.238*	0.51	0.111	0.210*	0.149
Marital status	−0.367**	0.068	0.088	0.192	0.186	0.578**
Sample (Table 1A + 1B)	700	700	700	700	700	700

Significance levels: ** at 5% and * at 10%, respectively.

Table 26.1B Results of correlation.

	Islamic microfinance	Schooling of girls	Schooling of boys	Education women	Marital status
Age	0.000	−0.021	−0.044	−0.308**	0.365**
Number of children	0.172	−0.059	0.019	−0.238*	−0.066
Income	0.736**	0.208	0.373**	0.051	−0.088
Assets	0.267**	0.232	0.228*	0.111	−0.192
Health	−0.032	0.018	−0.097	0.210*	−0.188
Harmony in the family	0.121	0.014	0.094	0.147	−0.578**
Islamic microfinance	1	0.382**	0.405**	0.023	0.000
Schooling of girls	0.382**	1	0.164	0.155	0.097
Schooling of boys	0.405**	0.164	1	0.064	−0.136
Education	0.023	0.155	0.066	1	−0.154
Marital status	0.000	−0.099	0.152	0.152	1
Sample (Table 1A + 1B)	700	292	298	700	700

Significance levels: ** at 5% and * at 10%, respectively.

Table 26.2 Regression analysis.

Coefficient	Income	Assets	Health	Family harmony	Girls' schooling	Boys' schooling
Age	0.037	−2.802	−0.029	0.021	0.003	0.002
	(0.023)	(−2.89)	(−2.171)	(1.369)	(0.601)	(0.215)
Islamic microfinance	2040.499	4850.699	−0.017	0.376	0.295	0.311
	(9.222)	(2.281)	(−0.015)	(1.633)	(3.588)	(4.688)
Education	19.666	255.225	0.221	0.227	0.107	0.055
	(0.456)	(1.325)	(0.777)	(0.837)	(1.192)	(0.648)
Marital status	30.901	272.137	0.263	2.399	−0.083	0.118
	(0.955)	(1.311)	(0.855)	(6.712)	(−0.844)	(1.198)
No. of children	9.586	99.021	−0.095	−0.059	−0.021	−0.008
	(1.376)	(2.188)	(−1.399)	(−0.875)	(−0.967)	(−0.374)
Constant	252.098	1033.212	7.729	5.502	0.334	0.364
	(2.611)	(2.834)	(12.988)	(10.102)	(1.728)	(2.178)
Adjusted R^2	0.551	0.129	0.141	0.331	0.132	0.142
Standard error	120.27138	779.58812	10.09321	1.14762	0.3417	0.34175
F-score	24.379	3.599	4.209	10.811	3.489	3.913
F-probability	0.000	0.003	0.002	0.000	0.006	0.001

While examining the effect of Islamic microfinance investment/loan on women's well-being, some interesting results were found. First of all, it is imperative to see how much of the change is due to the intervention in these women's lives. In the study, if we employ the Cohen's benchmark for the economics field to interpret r of size-effect estimation, we observe that the consequence of Islamic microfinance on income is huge while its influence on the schooling of boys, girls and ownership of assets is average. When we personify the power of this measure of the effect of size by the proportion of variance clarified by squaring the correlation coefficients in assessing the affiliation in the context of the total variance, we see that Islamic microfinance accounts for almost 54% of the variance on income.

In the following sections, details of economic and social implication of these results are given. The outcomes are, in fact, enormously important and decisive, which may be clarified in the light of the socio-economic settings in which Islamic microfinance is presented, from which the women get benefit from Islamic microfinance when they avail it. The interpretation of the results and their implications are as follows.

(1) **Income — positively associated with Islamic microfinance loan and hypothesis confirmed in the results (Table 26.3):** The income effect was extremely bad when the women availed private loans before benefiting from Islamic microfinance. At that time, women did not join Islamic microfinance yet and they were forced to follow their dealers' terms and conditions, among which was getting sub-standard goods.

There are many cases of exploitation of the poor women by private loan suppliers or money lenders. One female member exposed through the interviews that she was confronted with severe difficulties in her vegetable-selling business before joining the Islamic microfinance program: "The private dealer was very harsh, as I did not possess adequate money; so he provided me with only faulty goods of last stock. I did not have right

Table 26.3 Validation hypothesis.

Variables	Correlation with Islamic microfinance	Regression coefficient of Islamic microcredit	Hypothesis validation
Income	0.737**	2040.499 (9.222)	Confirmed
Assets	0.267**	4850.699 (2.281)	Confirmed
Schooling of boys	0.405**	0.311 (4.688)	Confirmed
Schooling of girls	0.382**	0.295 (3.588)	Confirmed
Health perception	−0.033	−0.017 (−0.015)	Rejected
Harmony in the family	0.123	0.376 (1.633)	Rejected

Significance levels: ** at 5%, respectively.

to select the goods or vegetables I want. So I was forced to take the rotten vegetables. If I did not take it, then I would be given nothing. As a result, I always suffered losses because of sub-standard goods, which I had to take from the suppliers. By becoming a member of the Islamic microfinance group (RDS), I do not face extortion anymore. I can select what I want!"

After availing Islamic microfinance, the women can now pay dealers immediately after receiving goods and henceforth do not necessarily need to face severe circumstances. The malicious circle is, thus, cracked with their capacity to make their own choices that would absolutely increase their volumes of trade as well as incomes.

There were some other cases earlier, where some women borrowed some cash from their friends or their families and neighbors to pay for their acquisitions of goods. Sometimes, some women got humiliated as a result for not been able to repay on time or just for borrowing from them in the first place. This led to humiliation in society. One woman spoke in the interviews saying: "My parents-in-law termed me 'useless' and forced me to do their housework since they loaned me the cash that I needed for the buying the goods I needed to purchase. Certainly, I paid them back".

Now self-confidence and self-reliance are boosted after the women joined the group and obtained Islamic microfinance loans. With these loans, the women involved with microfinance have increased their income, and feel economically liberated. The increase in their revenues also permitted them to achieve basic requirements of consumption as well as meeting their daily expenses that otherwise were unaffordable in the past. In view of this, it seems that the Islamic microfinance programs have enhanced the well-being of the woman involved and definitely empowered them.

Another significant fact to note when speaking about incomes, is one question that was asked to the women contributing in this research. The question was related to the kind of projects or activities they started with after getting Islamic microfinance loans from the group. The responses were separated into five types of activities and the outcomes display that practically, 50% of the sample women work in the retail trade of household objects such as bedsheets and homemade handicraft articles in narrow geographic zones. Some of the women earned smaller incomes as they faced severe price competition.

The survey also included some other questions associated with the other sources of income of women. Their responses were used to distinguish what were their motivations to avail Islamic microfinance loan. It was found that almost 79% of the women who answered the questions were monetarily unstable. They did not have other sources of income and therefore, they suffered consequently, because of the husband's unstable income from unstable occupation. Hence, the result displays that there was a shift of economic role. This was the role of supplementing the household with an extra income provided by the wife in the family.

(2) **Assets — positively associated with Islamic microfinance and hypothesis confirmed in the results (Table 26.3):** The result of this hypothesis echoes a long-term improvement of the recipients' welfare. This betterment is sustainable since the growth in their revenues is financed with the assets which they own. Nevertheless, one must notice that the occasional growth in households and individual assets (like TV, computer and others) did not increase production. Some of the recipients spent all their revenues and proceeds for consumption purposes. Some even did not understand how to capitalize their additional income in a project since they lacked the suitable talents. Indeed, one woman believed: "No practical difference in the magnitude of my venture occurred after getting Islamic microfinance loan. But it simply facilitated my life to have an extra liquidity for sufficient spending at home and on my children."

Another woman admitted during the survey interview that: "I categorically availed of Islamic microfinance loan as my children's wants are limitless. A good sum of money is needed for their day-to-day subsistence and wants; such as private tuition, schooling of children and preparations for girls' marriage when they reach the teenager stage. I used to borrow money from family and friends in the past, but now I meet these expenditures from the income I earn from my micro-business which is quite adequate".

(3) **Schooling of children — positively associated with Islamic microfinance and confirmed the hypothesis in the result (Table 26.3):** The result of this test is one of the most interesting of this study. The improvement of the schooling of children signifies a multiplier outcome of providing Islamic microfinance loans to women. During the interview, most of the women announced that the education of their children is the greatest significant investment they made in their lifetime. This is a precedence since in their own lifetime they did not get such an opportunity to get education during their young age. Therefore, they want to provide opportunity to their children to become educated. The participants also believe that their children can have a better

> future with better education. One woman, who recently joined Islamic microfinance program, has five sons and a girl. She stated during the interview: "My kids were not receiving any education because earlier my modest revenue did not permit me to meet the expenditure. I felt very bad. After availing Islamic microfinance loan, I would invest the money in the education of my children." Another woman also confirmed that the cause for which she was asking for a loan from Islamic microfinance was to provide education for her children: "I will provide education for my children!".

It may be noted here that the very vital result exposed by this study is correlated to the link between getting an Islamic microfinance loan and progress in schooling of the beneficiaries' children, both boys and girls. Furthermore, it shows that no major variance occurs between the rise in the improvement of schooling of girls and boys. This result is certainly encouraging in respect of education in general and human resources development in particular.

In this regard, some women also stated that an advanced level of education of their children is redirected by an advanced volume of private coaching needed in Bangladesh since private coaching became essential for good success at the school examinations. As stated earlier, the key stimulating result of this research was that there was no key difference among the coefficients of schooling for girls and boys, which have echoed a deep transformation in the community.

In Bangladesh, conventionally a head of the household preferred the education of boys to girls, since girls would be married outside the households and would take care of their husbands and new households, whereas the boys are engaged as only the future bread-winners of their families. However, the trend is changing. Currently guardians ponder that the education of both boys and girls are equally vital since learning will benefit girls to get better marriage with "better" grooms, henceforth a decent life, while boys want "job oriented" education and extra "practical" skills to secure a superior job. This reflects the social and cultural dimension of the choices they make.

In summary, the aforementioned results are mainly motivating in the circumstance of Bangladesh as the combat against illiteracy has been a priority on the government program for some years now. In this respect, the governmental actions and packages are set up to inspire families to direct their children to schools. Consequently, the governmental resources and determinations could be transmitted toward some other purposes.

(4) **Health awareness — no significant link with Islamic microfinance and the hypothesis is not confirmed in the result (Table26.3):** This result shows that women take less care of their health. They give preference to the education of their children and to the provision of food to the family members with certain extravagant stuff such as purchasing superior clothes, etc. Most of the women are brought up with an understanding that they are lower in ranking than men and ought to sacrifice themselves and attend to their households. The women contemplate that the expenses associated with their individual medical or health care may be taken care of with the service run by the government, which is free even though it is normally not very adequate due to secondary quality of facilities used.

(5) **Opinion about harmony in the family — positively non-significant associated with Islamic microfinance and hypothesis is rejected in the result (Table 26.3)**

Actually, this hypothesis needs a bigger sample to test, to see that the hypothesis can be accepted or rejected, since minor effects need bigger samples to confirm. However, the objective of the selection of this variable in the research was due to the special situation of women in Bangladesh where in the past, it was considered that women's labor outside of the house was offensive and that women's key role should solely be caring for their family members. In this regard, a desire, to test in what way a variation in this role would upset the harmony of the family was felt. The outcome could be one or the other, as reflected by the growing encounters because of the disapproval of husbands regarding their women's new roles, or by increasing the family solidity as a consequence of the family income rise.

The responses were considerably expanded concerning this issue among the women interviewed. Some of the women stated that the Islamic microfinance programs endangered their family solidity since the husband disliked the work activity of his wife. Certain others believed that stiffness in the family diminished because of the enhanced economic situations they enjoyed. Another woman stated: "I desired to accept an income making activity to evade the difficulties and family disparities caused by the need for money", while certain women thought that they possibly could not report any noteworthy change in this aspect of their lives.

(6) **Financial and social development (harmony) among beneficiaries:** The performance of Islamic microfinance has been quite promising. In this study, the results reveal that the performance of RDS of IBBL was better in terms of growth (12.50%), dropout rate (5.00%), and operational efficiency as compared to three conventional leaders in microfinance; Grameen Bank, Association for Social Advancement (ASA), and Bangladesh Rural Advancement Committee (BRAC). Having lower rate of return charged (10.00% with 2.50% rebate for on time payment) than other microfinance (16.00% to 22.50% of interest), has proved advantageous for the poor (Obaidullah, 2008a). The Islamic microfinance also offers active spiritual development programs with the purpose to improve members' awareness of social rights and responsibilities in order to improve better relationships with others (Obaidullah, 2008a). These programs have not been provided by conventional MFIs.

Concerning the impacts of Islamic microfinance, based on the empirical evidence of this study, it can be discussed into two areas: economic and social aspects.

In general, it is expected that the provision of financial access to poor people will enable them to increase their income and enhance their economic well-being, develop assets, decrease weaknesses and get involved in economic development. The latest empirical study on economic impact on rural poverty presented by IBBL found that loans affected considerably the improvement of household earnings, output of harvest and cattle, disbursement and employment (Obaidullah, 2008b; Rahman and Ahmad, 2010). In particular, based on a field survey of 1,024 respondents, Rahman and Ahmad (2010) found that the family income increased by more than 33%, the expenditure for health increased 50%, family employment increased from 1.91 to 2.1 working members, and all types of assets have also increased.

Moreover, the impressive economic impact based on the study of three Islamic MFIs in Bangladesh was explored by Ahmed (2002). He found that the economic impacts include increasing time spent on productive activities by beneficiaries and other family members, output of economic activity, improving amounts of goods/services, innovation of new products, increasing assets and other properties. In line with this study, he revealed that these economic aspects might imply that Islamic microfinance has an advantage to offer, although it still has weaknesses to overcome.

Social development impacts might include improvement of Islamic knowledge and relationships with others and health care. This study found that the health awareness of the respondents increases with an increase in the number of people consuming clean drinking water and using hygienic sanitation facilities. Besides, the clients also have positive opinions toward improvement of their skills and social and economic well-being. These findings are similar to the study of Rahman and Ahmad (2010).

Ahmed (2002) also revealed that the beneficiaries of Islamic microfinance not only get financial advantages but also improvement in other aspects through social development programs: improvement of Islamic knowledge, improving relationship with spouses and other group members. These two studies support the results of this survey and it can be implied that Islamic microfinance considers social aspects including family harmony, although more attention should be emphasized.

Above all, it can be inferred from the results of this study that Islamic microfinance has considerable social aspects, although it requires more attention. Hence, in order to have a wider impact, Dusuki (2008) argues that microfinance should provide market-based services, creativity to innovate new programs and product differentiation, efficient operation, and broader outreach, offering not only productive loans but also loans for consumption purposes to cover the cost of health, education and social responsibility.

(7) **Diversification of the scheme — experts' opinion:** There are two Islamic microfinance strategies that exist to answer the needs of two different targeted groups. Firstly, the "protectionist" or "survival" strategy which targets the very poor recipients to whom survival is the main concern. In this case, low amounts of loan are offered, allowing them to address the very urgent and basic needs of consumption through very modest economic activities. Secondly, the "promotional" approach which is when the amount of loan is higher and targets less poor recipients permitting substantial investment in income generating activities. This differentiation is very important in analyzing the outcomes of Islamic microfinance program, as we will see in the discussion of the results.

Most of the microcredit programs in Bangladesh are working for the "survival" programs of the poor since these programs could only help women to survive by generating some extra income through the activities they undertake for meeting their daily expenses (Ahmad, 2011).

No substantive investment is made in most of the programs and thus has no real sustainable effect. Most of the microfinance programs only offer credit without any other accompanying services such as training or marketing. Coupled with the women's lack of skills, RDS (Islamic microfinance) program helps to increase the first effect (survival not promotional). According to a former economic professor of a local university who is a devoted researcher in the area of interest free microfinance program in Bangladesh, explained the reason why Islamic microfinance program does not offer "start-ups". This program requires that the project applying for the loan must be running for at least six months. In fact, according to him and other experts in the field of Islamic microfinance program, he mentioned that: "it is necessary to provide other non-financial services to women to help them better manage Islamic microfinance loan. This can significantly improve the products the Islamic microfinance offers and increases the chances of success of the project. If the program is limited to the offer of Islamic microfinance, and if the only concern of the beneficiary is to have the loan and reimburse it, then one will face a simple vicious circle of loan".

According to the experts, the objective should rather be the success of the projects via high quality need-based entrepreneurship training and services. Even if the program does not directly offer the services, it could make available information about it and provide a network of useful services. Furthermore, there is a big competition between different programs offering conventional microcredit and Islamic microfinance program in the same geographic zones. Therefore, there is a chance of the group members to switch from one program to another for no specific reason and consequently limits the positive impact of such programs. Sometimes some regions have a surplus offer of credit and others have a lack of such an offer. There is therefore a need for a better planning of the existing Islamic microfinance programs in Bangladesh so that these anomalies do not exist in the future.

26.6 Summary and Policy Recommendations

Islamic microfinance run by Islami Bank Bangladesh has become a very important tool to combat poverty. This has been used in Bangladesh, Egypt, Indonesia, Iran, Nigeria, Pakistan, Turkey and Yemen to combat poverty and enhance the social and economic well-being of the recipients. Women are specifically targeted because they are very vulnerable. They lack the necessary resources to change their pathetic economic conditions. However, evidence shows that when women are involved in any income generation activities they exhibit greater courage in venturing into experiences and has proved to be productive. Investing largely in beneficiaries' families and increasing family member's involvement with income-generating activities would reflect in borrowers' well-being. In this regard, Islamic microfinance program is an important input.

The aim of this research was two-fold: Firstly, it wanted to confirm or refute a positive link between Islamic microfinance business model RDS under IBBL and the socio-economic well-being of women in Bangladesh. Secondly, to explore the context in which Islamic microfinance program (RDS) functions under IBBL and the way their performance can be improved. The research also addresses the following two questions:

(1) What can be expected from the offer of Islamic microfinance business model of IBBL on the welfare of recipients?
(2) Under what conditions would such an offer be more beneficial?

The outcomes exposed some interesting facts and important policy implications. It was important to notice that the increase in women's income and assets played a very important role in enhancing women's economic independence and sense of self-confidence. It helped in breaking the cycle of poverty they lived in and allowed them to have more control over their lives and economic decisions. Moreover, both Islamic microfinance loan recipients' answers and interviews with the experts were analyzed.

The results show that Islamic microfinance (RDS) has been found to exert a positive and significant influence on the gross monthly income of the borrowing members. This means that Islamic microfinance program can influence the socio-economic factors mentioned in the study. The strategy followed by Islamic microfinance business model of Islamic Bank Bangladesh resembles the subsidies system to the targeting beneficiaries, which definitely helped in a limited way in transforming the women's lives. Moreover, this was supplemented by the small amount of Islamic microfinance loan offered to the women of this group. These women lacked the skills needed to engage in highly profit-making activities or entrepreneurship. Lack of opportunity to pursue diversified income-generating activities in the villages is one of the major causes of poverty. Therefore, there is a need to establish small and cottage industries in the rural areas. Necessary technical support should also be given to the village entrepreneurs.

A very important policy recommendation is the necessity to review the existing programs in respect of the way Islamic microfinance is offered by IBBL. The program should shift from the simplistic "survival" goal to pluralistic goal that offers services besides Islamic microfinance (such as marketing, match-making, training, etc.). It is also necessary to redirect Islamic microfinance toward developmental activities that will contribute to the improvement, in the long run, of the well-being of the recipients.

Furthermore, IBBL should increase the size of investment in order to cope with the change in the value of currency because of inflation and other economics reasons. The scheme should project their value of activities for future, then all parties should be involved in managing Islamic microfinance scheme and be held responsible for job assigned at the beginning of the year.

Further, the performance of the Islamic microfinance should be subjected to balance scorecard system. The development would be possible when an Islamic microfinance loan allows real and substantial investments in the production/investment capital and assets, not only personal assets.

References

Ahmed, H. (2002), Financing microenterprises: An analytical study of Islamic microfinance institutions. *Islamic Economic Studies*, 9(2), 27–64.

Ahmad, H. (2007), Waqf Based Microfinance: Realising the Social Role of Islamic Finance. Paper Presented at the International Seminar on 'Integrating Awqaf in the Islamic Financial Sector'. Singapore, 6–7 March.

Ahmad, M. (2011), "The role of RDS in the development of women entrepreneurship under Islamic microfinance: A case study of Bangladesh", in Obidullah, M. and Salma, H. (eds.). *Islamic Microfinance for Micro and Medium Enterprises*, Jeddah: IRTI and UBD.

Akter, S. (2001), Rural women in micro credit programs for poverty alleviation in bangladesh-participants and constraints to their activities. *Parikarama*, XXV, 7–19.

Alamgir, D. A. H., Hassan, M. K. and Dewan, H. H. (2010), A Comparative Review of Islamic Versus Conventional Microfinance in Bangladesh, a paper present at the 8th International Conference on Islamic Economics and Finance held in Doha, Qatar in 2010.

Ashraf, A., Hassan, M. K. and Hippler III, W. J. (2014), Performance of microfinance institutions in Muslim countries. *Humanomics*, 30(2), 162–182.

Attia, G. (2010), *Towards Realization of the Higher Intents of Islamic Law-Maqasid al Shariah: A Functional Approach*, Herdon (USA): IIIT.

Brau, J. C. and Woller, G. M. (2004), Microfinance: A comprehensive review of the existing literature. *Journal of Entrepreneurial Finance and Business Ventures*, 9(1), 1–26.

Buckley, G. (1997), Microfinance in Africa, is it either the problem or the solution? *World Development*, 25, 23–34.

Cerrutti, M. (2000), Economic reform, structural adjustment, and female labor force participation in Buenos Aires, Argentina, *World Development*, 28, 879–891.

Chapra, M. U. (2002), *Islam and Economics Challenge*, Leicester: The Islamic Foundation.

Chapra, M. U. (2009), *The Islamic Vision of Development in the Light of Maqasid Al-Shari'ah.* IRTI-IDB, Jeddah, available at http://zulkiflihasan.files.wordpress.com/2009/11/ppp-vision-7.pdf. Retrieved 29 May 2015.

Chaves, R. and Gonzalez-Vega, C. (1996), The design of successful rural financial intermediaries: Evidence from Indonesia, *World Development*, 24, 211–225.

Choudhury, M. A. (2015), Res extensea et res congitans de magasid as-Shari'ah, *Humanomic*, 57(6), 662–693.

Doumato, E. and Posusney, M. (2003), *Women and Globalization in the Arab Middle East, Gender, Economy and Society*, New York: Lynne Rinner Publishers.

Dusuki, A. W. (2008), Banking for the poor: The role of Islamic banking in microfinance initiatives, *Humanomics*, 24(1), 9–66.

El-Solh, C. (1999), *Feasibility and Operationalization of Microcredit Finance Facilities Targeting Poor Women in Urban and Rural Areas in Selected Arab Countries: Theoretical Perspectives and Practical Considerations*, New York: ESCWA, United Nations.

Hashemi, S., Schuler, S. and Riley, A. (1996), Rural credit programs and women empowerment in Bangladesh. *World Development*, 24, 432–442.

IBBL (2013), *Annual Report 2013*, Dhaka: Islamic Bank Bangladesh Limited.

Jahur, M. S. and Quadir, S. M. N. (2010), Rural development scheme of Islamic Bank Bangaldesh Limited — A study on its growth, effectiveness and prospect in Bangladesh. *Economia*, 13(2), 283–299.

Kabeer, N. (2001), Conflict over credit: Re-evaluating the empowerment potential of loan to women in rural Bangladesh. *World Development*, 29(1), 63–84.

Khandker, S. R. (1998), Microcredit program evaluation: A critical review. *IDS Bulletin*, 29, 25–32 (University of Sussex, UK).

Khandker, S. R., Khalily, B. and Khan, Z. (1995), Grameen Bank: Performance and Sustainability, World Bank Discussion Paper No. 306. World Bank, Washington DC.

Lakwo, A. (2006), *Microfinance, Rural Livelihoods, and Women's Empowerment in Uganda.* Unpublished doctoral dissertation, Radboud University Nijmegen.

Nader, Y. (2008), Microcredit and well-being of women and their families in Cairo. *Social Economics Journal*, 37, 644–656.

Obaidullah, M. (2008a), *Role of Microfinance in Poverty Alleviation*, Jeddah, IRTI- Islamic Development Bank.

Obaidullah, M. (2008b), *Introduction to Islamic Microfinance*, New Delhi: International Institute of Islamic Business and Finance.

Obaidullah, M. and Khan, T. (2008), *Islamic Microfinance Development: Challenges and Initiative*, Jeddah: IRTI-IDB.

Osmani, K. A. (2007), Breakthrough in women's bargaining power: The impact of microcredit. *Journal of International Development*, 19, 695–716.

Pitt, M., Khandker, S. R. and Cartwright, J. (2006), Does micro-credit empower women? Evidence from Bangladesh. *Economic Development and Cultural Change*, 54, 791–831.

Rahman, M. M. and Ahmad, F. (2004), Impact of microfinance of IBBL on the rural poor' livelihood in Bangladesh: An empirical study. *International Journal of Islamic and Middle Eastern Finance and Management*, 3(2), 168–190.

Saad, N. M. and Duasa, J. (2010), Determinants of economic performance of micro-credit clients and prospects for Islamic microfinance in Malaysia ISRA. *International Journal of Islamic Finance*, 2(1), 37–48.

Seibel, H. D. and Parhusip, U. (1999), Rural bank Sinta Daya, Attaining Outreach with Sustainability: A Case Study of a Private Microfinance Institution in Indonesia, Working Paper, No. 1999, 2, Universitätzu Köln, Arbeitsstelle für Entwicklungsländerforschung (AEF), Köln.

Sinha, S. (1998), Micro-credit: Impact, targeting and sustainability. *IDS Bulletin* 29, 34–42.

Zeller, M. and Meyer, R. L. (2002), "Improving the performance of microfinance: Financial sustainability, outreach and impact", in Zeller, M. and Meyer, R. L. (eds.), *The Triangle of Microfinance: Financial Sustainability, Outreach and Impact*, Baltimore: The Johns Hopkins University Press, MD.

PART D
Special Issues

Chapter 27

Wife Beating in Islamic Law: Re-Evaluating the Illocutionary Force of the Imperative Verb in *Qur'an* 4:34

David Solomon Jalajel

Abstract

Verse 4:34 is the primary source of evidence cited in Islamic legal literature to permit wife beating. The injunction *wa-ḍribūhunna* (literally: "and hit them") is seen as giving the husband permission to hit his wife in response to her rebellion. The necessity of this interpretation has been challenged by contemporary thinkers who argue that the interpretive community's biases precluded other interpretive possibilities. Attention has been given to interpreting the verb in question, *ḍaraba*, to mean something other than "to hit". Problems have arisen with this approach, since the interpretations suggested have required the use of dependent prepositions before the object of the verb which are absent in the verse. However, classical Islamic legal scholars have recognized that the imperative verb tense has a wide range of senses, listing several possibilities which are determined by context, some of which are far removed from the issuing of commands. Evaluating the function of the verb from this angle allows for a viable, robust interpretation of the verse that disallows wife beating while remaining faithful to classical interpretive methods. As a result, it can be argued that the insistence of classical scholars on asserting the husband's right to beat the wife is a result of cultural perspectives limiting interpretive possibilities.

Keywords: Wife, *Wa-ḍribūhunna*, Islam, Classical interpretive methods, Husband's right

Classical Islamic scholars have understood that the *Qur'an* permits a husband to beat his wife to discipline her if she disobeys him. This conclusion is taken from *Sūrah al-Nisā'* (4) verse 34, which can be translated as follows:

> Men are responsible (*qawwāmūn*) over women because God has favored some over others and because they spend out of their property; the good women are, therefore, obedient, guarding the unseen as God has guarded; and (as to) those on whose part you fear rebellion, admonish them, and leave them alone in the sleeping-places and beat them; then if they obey you, do not seek a way against them; surely God is High, Great.

Many contemporary thinkers are troubled by this interpretation, and are not willing to accept that the *Qur'an* allows a husband to beat his wife. They rightly argue that an interpretive community's biases can influence their interpretations and cause them to disregard or fail to recognize other interpretive possibilities.[1]

Much attention has been focused on re-evaluating the meaning of the verb *ḍaraba*, generally translated as "to hit, to beat", with less than satisfactory results. The verb appears in the verse in the imperative form with the attached feminine third-person plural pronoun *hunna* as its direct object: *iḍribūhunna*. Classical commentators have, without exception, understood the phrase to mean "beat them". Some contemporary thinkers have suggested that it might be possible to interpret the verb according to one of its many other meanings. However, as Chaudhry points out, the verb "does not have most of these meanings without a specific direct object, preposition, or other verbal indicator" (Chaudhry, 2013, p. 12). It is safe to say that all the alternative meanings require a preposition before the object, an adverbial modifier, or a specific intangible direct object. For instance, Laleh Bakhtiar in her translation of the *Qur'an*, renders the phrase as "go away from them" (Bakhtiar, 2007). It is true that the verb can mean "to go away", but this meaning is expressed in Arabic only when its object comes after the appropriate preposition (D'Silva, 2014, p. 110). In 4:34, the verb has an immediate direct object, the attached feminine plural pronoun referring back to the women. Therefore, interpreting the verb to mean anything other than "to hit/beat" in this context is not a simple matter.

---

[1]See Chaudhry (2013, p. 195). This work explores both classical and modern interpretations of verse 4:34, providing an exhaustive survey of classical legal and exegetical thinking, as well as examining the wide variety of approaches of modern thinkers. It is an excellent and indispensable work. See also: Kausar *et al.* (2011, p. 96).

In English, a person can "hit someone", "hit *on* someone", and "hit *upon* an idea". These all mean different things. However, when someone says "Sally hits John" it means she struck him with her hand, fist or car. It does not mean she tried to pick him up at a bar, nor that she chanced upon him on the street. Those meanings are only conveyed by the verb when it comes together with the right preposition or modifier. Arabic functions in much the same way.

This chapter seeks to demonstrate another interpretive possibility that does not require reinterpreting the meaning of the verb *ḍaraba*, but which disallows wife beating and, moreover, conforms with what is possible and valid according to the dictates of the Arabic language and classical interpretive methods. Once that is accomplished, the reasonableness of the proposed interpretation must be shown to depend upon the underlying assumptions and values of the interpretive community. This final step is necessary to argue that cultural biases and subjectivities prevented pre-modern jurists and exegetes from realizing other possible and valid interpretations.

This research does not examine the Prophetic traditions relating to wife beating. Classical jurists admitted that those traditions contradict each other, so they applied various hermeneutical strategies at their disposal for reconciling apparently contradictory textual evidence, which they did in light of their interpretation of the verse.[2] As a consequence, those traditions were reconciled and contextualized by the scholars to accord with their understanding that the verse permits beating. It could just as easily have gone the other way, had the interpreters allowed for a different interpretation of the verse.

27.1 The classical interpretation of the passage

From the outset, it must be understood that classical interpreters did not take a strictly literal approach to this verse. They interpreted much of it

[2]Al-Māwardī describes three approaches that jurists have used to reconcile this conflicting evidence. The first is to take the verse and the Prophetic reports that permit beating and apply them to cases of disobedience, while applying the reports that prohibit beating to cases where there is no disobedience. The second is to say that the texts permitting beating indicate legal permissibility, while those prohibiting it indicate what is preferable. The third is to consider the reports prohibiting beating to be abrogated by the other reports permitting it. Then the verse serves to explain why the original ruling of prohibition was abrogated. See Al-Māwardī (2009, 12:176).

at variance to its literal meaning. For instance, most of them understood the "fear" of rebellion to mean actual evidence of rebellion, and not just a suspicion that rebellion could take place. Likewise, most of them understood that the conjunction between the three verbs does not mean the three actions could be engaged in simultaneously, but rather in a certain sequence. They also understood that the three imperative verbs do not entail obligation.

Regarding the first issue of "fear", this sets the condition for enacting the tricolon of imperative verbs that follow. Literally, this would mean that the moment fear is felt, even in the absence of any action or substantial behavioral change on the part of the woman, the recommended actions would be carried out. Though classical exegetes and jurists have differed as to its implications, most of them have opted that it does not mean mere suspicion of rebellion, but interpret it to mean "those on whose part you *know* rebellion" (Al-Ṭabarī, 2001, 6:696). "Fear" is used metaphorically for "knowledge" due to the close resemblance between knowing something dreadful and fearing it.[3] This is clearly a figurative interpretation of the term. Abū Ḥayyān explains the context for adopting this metaphorical meaning is that the verse continues by saying "then if they obey you, do not seek a way against them" (Abū Ḥayyān al-Andalusī, 2002, 3:342). Since obedience requires the cessation of enacting these options, it follows that the options can only be adopted in the face of actual disobedience. Some scholars interpret it closer to the literal meaning, that if a woman behaves in a way that makes the husband suspicious of her rebellion, like making indiscreet and injudicious glances, and by going in and out of her home with indiscretion, then the husband can start admonishing her.[4] Even in this interpretation, it is the woman's outward actions, though possibly not enacted as open rebellion to start with, which bring about the condition for the husband to respond and make her desist from those actions. The literal meaning of fear, a feeling in the husband's heart, is not accepted to be the intent of the verse. There are some scholars who adopt a literal reading of "fear", but they take a different approach on how it relates to the second two imperative verbs, which will be discussed in the following paragraphs.

[3] Al-Ṭabarī (2001, 6:696). He cites classical poetry as a precedent for this usage: "Do not bury me in open country, for indeed I / Fear that when I die, I will not taste it." The poet knows that when he dies, he will not taste it.

[4] At-Tabari cites the opinion of Muhammad b. Ka'b al-Qurtubi on this matter. See: Al-Ṭabarī (2001, 6:696).

Regarding the second issue of sequence, the three imperative verbs are joined by the conjunction *wa*, which is usually equivalent to the English word "and". Literally, the passage reads: "admonish them, and leave them alone in the sleeping-places and beat them". The language of the verse does not necessarily indicate that one action must be completed before the other. Therefore, it is possible to interpret the verse to mean that the husband can carry out any one of these actions, or do all of them together, as a response to a woman's rebellion.[5] However, this is not the understanding of most classical scholars. They regarded the sense of verse 4:34 to strongly indicate that the options are listed in order of preference. Al-Rāzī asserts: "The apparent meaning of the words indicates that they can be enacted together, but the sense of the verse indicates they are sequential."[6] The prevailing view is that each option must be exhausted before the next can be enacted.[7] Some are of the opinion that the second option can be skipped altogether or can be enacted along with the beating, but they almost all agree that admonition must first be exhausted as an option.[8] The fact that they differ about the last two options shows the amount of subjective interpretation that is exercised in understanding how the conjunction is used.

[5]Abū Ḥayyān al-Andalusī (2002, 3:342). He writes: "The apparent sense of the verse indicates he should admonish, leave alone in the sleeping place, and beat the woman from whom he fears disobedience. This is because the conjunction 'and' is not sequential." The view of some Shāfiʿī jurists is that the husband can choose any of the options he wishes, including beating, if the woman engages in open rebellion. See: al-Rāzī (2000, 10:74). Al-Shāfiʿī himself says it is a "possible interpretation" that if the she rebels, and her rebellion is clear in her disobedience to him, that he may combine between admonishing them, leaving them, and beating them. See: al-Shāfiʿī (n.d., p. 1034). Later Shāfiʿī jurists were divided on matter, with some of them disallowing beating until the woman persisted in disobedience. However, the revisionist jurist al-Nawawī, adopted the opinion in *al-Minhāj* that hitting was allowed at the first instance of her open disobedience, due to the literal meaning of the verse. See: (al-Shirbīnī, 1997, 3:343; al-Ramlī, 2003, 6:390). Al-Nawawī argues that "this accords with the apparent language of the Qur'an" (al-Nawawī, 2002, p. 1313).

[6]al-Rāzī (2000, 10:73). See also: al-Kāsānī (2000, 2:650) where he says: "Whereas the apparent meaning of the verse has the conjunction 'and' literally bringing things together in an absolute sense, but the intent here is to bring them together in a sequential order. The conjunction "and" allows for this meaning."

[7]This is stated by most exegetes. See: Ilkiyā al-Harrāsī (2001, 1:450), as well as Ibn al-ʿArabī (2001, 1:44) and al-Qurṭubī (2001, 5:165). It is the position that the Ḥanafī, Mālikī, and Ḥanbalī schools of law have adopted. See: al-Kāsānī (2000, 2:650), as well as ʿUlaysh (2003, 3:352), and al-Bahūtī (1999, 5:226).

[8]See: al-Ṭabari (2001, 7:709–710). Al-Nawawī lists three differing opinions in the Shāfiʿī school, the first being that the husband can employ all three options at once, the second that he can apply any one he wishes without combining them, and the third being that he must follow the sequential order. See: al-Nawawī (2002, p. 1313).

Scholars who explain "fear" to mean the suspicion of the wife's rebellion differ in their understanding of the sequential nature of the verse. For instance, the Ḥanbalī jurist Ibn Qudāmah argues that the admonishment applies in the case of suspicion, whereas leaving her alone in her sleeping place applies to her manifest disobedience, and then beating can be resorted to if she persists in her disobedience.[9] This position was later rejected by the Ḥanbalī school, which insists that admonition must come first (Al-Bahūtī, 1999, 5:226). It is important to note that Ibn Qudāmah's opinion shows a willingness to apply different legal rulings to the various commands, even though they are all joined by the same conjunction.

Regarding the third issue of the elocutionary force of the verb, most classical jurists see the three actions listed as being merely permissible, the right of the husband, and not an obligation.[10] This is clearly an interpretive move on their part. This is because most jurists and legal theorists regard the Arabic imperative tense to literally indicate obligation (Al-Zarkashī, 1992, 2:365). In other words, when God commands something, the default assumption is that it is obligatory to carry it out. Any other understanding of the imperative tense, accordingly, requires interpreting it as a metaphor, and therefore needs some contextual evidence (*qarīnah*) to show that the metaphorical meaning is intended. Another opinion held by a substantial minority of jurists is that the imperative tense is equally indicative of more than one possible literal sense (Al-Zarkashī, 1992, 2:367–369; al-Muḥallī, 2006, 1:589–592). Most of the jurists who hold this view identify obligation and encouragement as the two senses, with a few of them adding permission as a third. According to this view, the only way to resolve which of these is intended is through interpretation by relying on contextual indicators, without which no meaning can be specified.[11] In either case, classical jurists and exegetes agree that taking an imperative verb to mean permission

---

[9]Ibn Qudāmah (1997, 10:260). He explains that additional clauses are understood in the verse by way of implication. He cites 5:33, dealing with the punishment of highway robbers, as another example of such language use. He also mentions that there is a narration from Aḥmad b. Ḥanbal implying that the husband can beat the wife at the first instance of manifest disobedience without first leaving her alone in her sleeping place, but Ibn Qudāmah does not adopt this view himself.

[10]This is the position of all four schools of law. See: al-Kāsānī (2000, 2:650), ʻUlaysh (2003, 3:352), al-Shāfiʻī (n.d., p. 1034) and Ibn Qudāmah (1997, 10:260).

[11]For instance, al-Zarkashī says: "If there is no contextual indicator for the homonym and it is impossible for it to simultaneously carry both of its meanings, its meaning is indefinite (*mujmal*) and requires a determinative factor to specify it" (Al-Zarkashī, 1992, 2:126).

as opposed to obligation is an act of subjective interpretation, since it requires either taking the imperative verb off its literal indication onto a metaphorical one, or isolating the correct sense from its two or three equally viable literal senses.

In summary, the prevailing interpretation of this verse entails that when the husband knows or has clear evidence of the wife's rebellion, he is permitted to admonish her. If she desists, well and good. Otherwise, he can take the second step and shun her bed. If that is not effective, he is permitted to beat her. There are other issues that could be discussed, like the exact nature of the woman's rebellion,[12] the meaning of leaving them alone in their sleeping places,[13] and the nature and conditions of the man's responsibility/authority (*qiwāmah*). However, what is important for our purposes is to see that classical scholars were not literalists in their interpretation of the verse. They interpreted it according to what made sense to them and even disagreed with one another on the implications of most of the terms. Importantly, they did not take the imperative tense of the verbs to mean an obligation, nor did most of them take the literal conjunction of the verbs to mean that the three options could be enacted simultaneously.

27.2 Revisiting the elocutionary force of the imperative verb

It has already been demonstrated that classical exegetes and jurists have interpreted the imperative verb *iḍrib* away from its default sense of obligation to one of permissibility. This is a clear and subjective interpretive move. However, obligation, encouragement, and permission are not the only three possibilities. Classical scholars have identified at least thirty additional senses for the imperative tense, and concede that there are many more, "the large number of which cannot be pinned down and all of which are known through the circumstances, context, and indicative factors

[12]The majority of classical scholars took this to mean disobedience (*ma'ṣiyah*) of the husband and dissention (*khilāf*) and failure to obey his commands. See: al-Ṭabarī (2001, 6:697–698).

[13]The prevailing view is that it means to abstain from sexual intercourse with them, though some exegetes have opined that it means to avoid speaking to them, or to speak to them harshly. See: al-Ṭabarī (2001, 6:705). Al-Ṭabarī himself holds the strange view that it means the woman can be tied up and confined in her house. 6:707. This interpretation is fiercely rejected by other exegetes and jurists. See: Ibn al-'Arabī (2001, 1:439).

associated with the speech act" (Al-Zarkashī, 1992, 2:364). Some of these indicate that the action in question should not be carried out. Among those identified are: to call for some other command to be fulfilled,[14] to disparage the action,[15] to warn against it,[16] to threaten,[17] and to give warning.[18] Therefore, it is possible for the positive imperative tense to indicate that the action of the verb should not be carried out. Importantly, jurists also assert that two imperative verbs in the same sentence can have two different rhetorical senses, even when they are joined together by a conjunction.[19]

In the case of this passage, most classical scholars agree that the three options are somehow ranked in a sequential order, and therefore do not have the same status. They also agree that the imperative verbs are to be interpreted off their literal sense. This opens up the possibility of another interpretation: that hitting is not an option at all, but that the other options that precede it should be sought instead. The question is whether the particular language of this verse can convey such a meaning.

As already discussed, a strictly literal interpretation of the verse would be: "Those on whose part you fear rebellion, you must do to them one or more of the following: admonish them, leave them alone in their sleeping places, and/or beat them." Sensibly, most classical jurists and exegetes did not understand it in this way. The prevailing interpretation could be rendered: "Those on whose part you fear rebellion, you should first admonish them, and if that does not work, you should leave them alone in their sleeping-places, and if that does not work, you can beat them."[20]

---

[14]For instance, the tradition where the Prophet is reported to have said: "Be Allah's servant who is slain; do not be Allah's servant who kills." Al-Zarkashī observes: "He does not intend by the command that the person should get himself killed, but rather to be resigned and not engage in strife." (Al-Zarkashī 1992, 2:363).

[15]For instance, Moses challenge to the magicians: "Cast what [spells] you are going to cast" (Qur'an 10:80). See: Al-Zarkashī (1992, 2:358).

[16]For instance, "The truth is from your Lord. So whosoever wishes, then believe, and whosoever wishes, then disbelieve" (Qur'an 18:29).

[17]For instance, "So worship what you wish besides Him" (Qur'an 39:15). See: Al-Zarkashī (1992, 2:358).

[18]For instance, "Enjoy yourselves, for indeed, your destination is the Fire". [Qur'an 14:30].

[19]Two examples of this are: "Eat of their fruit when they give fruit, and render the proper dues on the harvest day" (*Qur'an* 6:141). Here the first command indicates a permission to eat of the fruit, while the second indicates the obligation to pay Zakāh on it. The same pattern can be observed in: "Divorce them for their waiting period and keep count of the waiting period" (Qur'an 65:1). See: Al-Zarkashī (1992, 2:364).

[20]Paraphrasing the interpreted meaning of the verse is quite common in classical texts of law an exegesis, going back to at least the Successor Sa'īd b. Jubayr. See Ibn al-'Arabī (2001, 1:440).

According to this interpretation, the beating is not carried out in anger. It is not a lashing-out on the part of the husband, but rather a calculated, deliberate move. It is a disciplinary action, like when a parent spanks a child. This, however, is not how beatings between adults usually take place. Beating is an emotional response, born of anger. Beating the wife is not something that is planned and deferred for a prolonged period of time until after the husband takes other steps, and then administered formally, almost ritualistically, like interpreters have traditionally tried to present it. Therefore, it could be argued that by telling men what they should do before letting themselves hit their wives, it is instructing them not to hit their wives at all. The understanding of the verse would be: "Those on whose part you fear rebellion, you should first admonish them, and if that does not work, you should leave them alone in their sleeping-places, instead of beating them."

The listing of options, with the final option being disparaged, is in fact a normal, everyday way of speaking when talking to someone who is about to do something injudicious. For instance, a parent might say to a child who wants to drop out of school: "First, look at what jobs are available for dropouts, then look at your friend who dropped out and now cleans toilets for a living, then go drop out of school!" Likewise, a person could say to someone contemplating suicide: "First, think about your little children who depend on you for support. Then think how much those children — and your parents — love you and how you are going to hurt them. Then consider that it is a mortal sin to kill yourself. Then go jump!"

In both cases, the imperative tense is used throughout, but it is obvious that the speaker is telling the person to take other steps so that they do not quit school and do not jump. In the context of verse 4:34, it could be argued that it is addressing a husband whose wife is being disobedient, telling him that he should reason with her and then avoid her company if he is upset with her, and not beat her.

Some exegetes and thinkers, past and present, have indeed sensed this meaning in the verse, especially in light of evidence in the Prophetic traditions that disparages the beating of wives. A hint of this understanding can be seen in the opinion of the Successor and senior *Qur'an* commentator 'Aṭā, who said "He should not hit her, even if he commands and prohibits her and she does not obey, but he can get angry with her" (Ibn al-'Arabī, 2001, 1:441).

Al-Qāḍī 'Iyād's comment on this saying is insightful: "This shows 'Aṭā"s legal acumen. It comes from his understanding of Islamic Law and his grasp of the possibilities of juristic reasoning to see that the imperative verb "to hit" is an imperative indicating (mere) permissibility, whereas he sees by way of the Prophet's tradition, that it is something disliked" (Ibn al-'Arabī, 2001, 1:441).

In other words, since the elocutionary force of the verb is for permission and not obligation, and other evidence clearly shows that beating is disliked, then the indication here is that it should not be taken as an option. This, admittedly, falls short of prohibiting wife beating, but does show that the idea that beatings should not be carried out was sensed from the verse by certain classical scholars.

Some contemporary Muslim thinkers have seen the same meaning. Hamza Yusuf argues that violence occurs in anger and not after a progression of steps like those understood from the verse, saying "Nobody has ever hit their wife working out some progressive thing". Though he argues that the verse is meant to prevent domestic violence by imposing a process where the husband has to "stop and think", he concedes soon thereafter that a light beating without anger and without leaving a bruise is not altogether prohibited, just extremely disliked (Yusuf, 2009). Chaudhry cites Rashad Khalifa as another modern thinker who came to the same conclusions as Yusuf, but who still stops short of seeing the verse as prohibiting wife-beating altogether.[21] None of these thinkers, past or present, have connected this understanding with the elocutionary force of the imperative verb *iḍrib*. Consequently, they still maintained that beating the wife is, at the final reckoning, a permissible act for the husband.

Nevertheless, these examples show that people, past and present, have sensed the final imperative verb is deprecated, proving that it is something the verse's language can communicate. When this is taken in conjunction with the fact that Muslim jurists and legal theorists recognize the imperative verb's elocutionary force to have many possible senses, some of which are prohibitive of the action expressed by the verb, it allows for a valid interpretation of the verse that prohibits beating.

27.3 Enabling assumptions

Classical exegetes and jurists overwhelmingly accepted the idea that husbands have the right to beat their wives in cases of open rebellion,

[21] Chaudhry (2013, pp. 169–170). She says: "Khalifa confirmed that husbands have divine sanction to hit their wives, but the sequence in the verse practically bars them from ever doing so."

at least after exhausting the other options. They differed in the details, like how hard a beating could be administered, while agreeing that it must be a beating that does not break bones or disfigure limbs.[22] The notion that the husband ultimately has a right to beat his wife was reasonable to them. It accorded well with their general outlook on the husband–wife relationship and the male–female relationship in general. This is something they readily expressed when discussing the meaning of *qiwāmah* "responsibility, agency, authority" at the beginning of 4:34: "Men are responsible (*qawwāmūn*) over women". Classical scholars understood the term *qawwāmūn* to mean that men have been put in charge of the household in an absolute sense. Ibn 'Ābidīn writes that husbands: "are in charge of their [wives] the way rulers are in charge of their subjects, so therefore the man is the commander of his wife" (Ibn 'Ābidīn, 1902, 1:68; al-Bayḍāwī, 1998, 2:72). As a consequence, husbands have authority in the household and can use force on occasion to enforce that authority and ensure obedience. This interpretation made sense to them in their societal context. One's cultural outlook enables various interpretive possibilities and obscures others.

However, the verse is not explicit in giving men such categorical authority. The term *qawwāmūn* is quite broad in its meaning. Kecia Ali makes this point by surveying how the major English *Qur'an* translations differ in rendering *qawwāmūn* as: " 'bread earners', 'maintainers', 'protectors and maintainers', 'the managers of the affairs of', 'in charge of', 'have authority over', or 'shall take care of' ". In her note on this passage, she adds: "These are the translations of, respectively, Ahmed Ali, Shakir, Abdullah Yusuf Ali, Arberry, Pickthall, Dawud, and Asad". Ultimately, she opts to define *qawwām* literally as: "one who 'stands over' or 'stands up for,' thus potentially encompassing both authority and responsibility. These dual elements were recognized by classical commentators on this verse" (Ali, 2006,

[22]This is how many jurists and exegetes define the phrase "a beating which is not severe" found in some Prophetic traditions. See: 'Ulaysh (2003, 3:352), al-Qurtubī (2001, 5:165), and Ibn 'Aṭiyyah al-Andalusī (2002, p. 432). Al-Shāfi'ī put four conditions on the beating in *al-Umm*, 1034, which al-Māwardī explains as follows: "The beating should not be severe, meaning lethal, nor should it draw blood, nor should it disable a limb, and it should avoid the face which would disfigure her and destroy her appearance." See: al-Māwardī (2009, 12:175). The Ḥanbalī jurist Ibn Qudāmah (1997, 10:260) defines it more vaguely as "a beating which is not severe, where he has to avoid the face and vulnerable areas". As for statements of the Companions that refer to beating with a toothstick or a cloth, these are generally taken as recommendations and are not understood to define the legal limits of a sanctioned beating. The qualification that the beating should be done "lightly" found in many English translations of the *Qur'an* is neither in the language of the verse, nor is it understood by most classical commentators and jurists.

pp. 117–118, 184, n24). *Qiwāmah* does not connotate authority in the same way that *sulṭān* or *wilāyah* does. Its meaning compasses more of an idea of responsibility toward something and maintenance for it. This concords with the context of the verse that continues "and because they spend out of their property". The linguistic meaning of the word gives connotations of both responsibility and authority. Its full linguistic sense needs to be kept in mind when considering how medieval Muslim jurists understood the term, since how people perceive this responsibility/authority depends on their cultural backgrounds.

Classical scholars make their understanding clear when they elaborate on the phrase "because God has favored some over others" which is the justification for men's *qiwāmah.* Many exegetes elaborate on this by listing a number of legal rulings where men are given preference to women and by elaborating on men's "greater possession of reason and organized thinking", to quote al-Qurṭubī (Al-Qurṭubī, 2001, 5:162; Al-Bayḍāwī, 1998, 2:72). Indeed, some commentators use this opportunity to propound at length on all the ways men are better than women, with Ibn Kathīr going as far as to proclaim categorically that "men are preferable to women and the man is better than the woman" (Ibn Kathīr, 2002, 2:261).

In the same way, al-Qurṭubī discusses *qiwāmah* as comprehending a broader understanding of authority, saying: "It means that they [the men] spend on them [the women] and protect them. Also, included among [men] are those who are rulers, governors, and soldiers, and this is not to be found among women" (Al-Qurṭubī, 2001, 5:161). It must be kept in mind that he is reading these meanings back into the verse, not deducing them from it, and he presents these disparate meanings in the context of clarifying the rationale for the *qiwāmah* of men over women in the marital relationship.

For people who accept that men have been put in charge of the household in an absolute sense, it would appear obvious that husbands might sometimes need to use force to maintain that authority and ensure obedience. It was easy for them to compare a husband beating his wife to a parent disciplining a child (Ilkiyā al-Harrāsī, 2001, 1:405; al-Qurṭubī, 2001, 5:165). Some went further and saw it as the husband's prerogative to safeguard his own marital rights and interests.[23] Ḥanafī jurists express this

[23]Al-Shirbīnī (1997, 3:343). He writes: "It is better for [the husband] to withhold from beating ... This is different in the case of a child. It is better not to withhold, since beating him to discipline him is for the child's own good, while the husband beating the wife is for his personal interests."

principle as "the authority to discipline the wife".[24] All of this makes sense in the world of the classical scholars, a world where women went from the authority of their fathers to the authority of their husbands and never took complete control of their own lives. Interpreting 4:34 to permit beating the wife would be obvious to them, since that interpretation was enabled by their cultural assumptions.

However, that interpretation does not make sense in a worldview where women are seen as complete adults, full partners of men, who are as equal in marriage and society as they are equal in their accountability before their Lord on the Day of Resurrection. It is this changed outlook on the woman's inherent status and role in society that causes many people today to find the classical interpretation of the verse difficult to accept. This, in turn, enables people to consider other interpretive possibilities while making those which were previously accepted as obvious to appear less apparent and less likely. Essentially, the way the verse is understood depends on the interpreter's assumptions about the levels of autonomy and authority that men and women have in the marital relationship. These assumptions determine what does and does not make sense.

To make this clearer, it might help to look again at the earlier example of the person advising a friend about suicide. It is clear to any modern person reading the statement that the speaker is telling the friend not to jump. The final imperative verb in that sequence is not intended as a command, but is completely deprecated by the speaker. This is obvious to anyone coming from a culture that has no tolerance of suicide or one wherein suicide is regarded as a mortal sin. Yet, one can imagine the same statement being made within a culture where suicide is seen as an honorable way of responding to shame, dishonor, or dereliction of duty, or as a way of sacrificing oneself for the nation, as has indeed been the case with some cultures in the past. A listener from that culture might regard the advice differently, especially if the person intending suicide has reasons to do so that are justified by the culture. The advisor would then be merely asking the person to consider the other matters before making

[24]Al-Kāsānī (2000, 2:650). The Arabic term for authority used here is *wilāyah.* He compares this to the master's authority to punish a slave, saying: "It is the husband's right to discipline his wife in the same way that a master has the right to discipline his slave." 2/651. The Ḥanbalī jurist Ibn Taymiyah also compares the authority (*wilāyah*) of the husband over the wife to that of a master over a slave, "and this is why Allah permits the man, in the text of the Qur'an, to beat her". Ibn Taymiyah (1998, 17:190).

such a final and momentous decision. The final option to jump would not be understood as deprecated, but only as something to be weighed against other considerations. In this case, the prevailing cultural assumptions enable an interpretation that would not be possible in a modern context, while obscuring the interpretation that our modern minds would consider obvious.

Likewise, if a speaker — whom the listener assumes to be someone who cares about their welfare and the welfare of others — begins by reminding them that they are in a position of responsibility, and goes on to advise them that they should reason with the individual to whom they have that responsibility and then avoid their company if they are upset with them, a modern listener would be certain that this speaker is not telling them to beat that individual if they do not come right. This would be obvious, and it could very well be a way of understanding verse 4:34.

It should be clear that how the verse is interpreted is sensitive to the interpretive community's cultural attitudes about women and the institution of marriage. The verse does not stand as decisive proof that men can hit their wives, since it is possible to interpret it to prohibit such beatings.

References

Arabic

Al-Bahūtī, Manṣūr b. Yūnus (1999), *Kashshāf al-Qunnāʿ ʿan Matn al-Iqnāʿ*. Muḥammad ʿAdnān Yāsīn Darwīsh (ed.), Beirut: Dār Iḥyāʾ al-Turāth al-ʿArabī.

Al-Bayḍāwī, ʿAbd Allah b. ʿUmar (1998), *Anwār al-Tanzīl wa Asrār al-Taʾwīl*. Muḥammad ʿAbd al-Raḥmān al-Marʿashlī (ed.), Beirut: Dār Iḥyāʾ al-Turath al-ʿArabī.

Al-Kāsānī, Abū Bakr b. Masʿūd (2000), *Badāʾiʿ al-Ṣanāʾiʿ fī Tartīb al-Sharāʾiʿ*. Muḥammad Adnān Yāsīn Darwīsh (ed.), Beirut: Muʾassasat al-Tārīkh alʿArabī.

Al-Māwardī, Abū al-Ḥasan ʿAlī b. Muḥammad b. Ḥabīb. al-Ḥāwī al-Kabīr (2009), *Abd Allah Muḥammad Najīb ʿAwwāmah*, Beirut: Dār Iḥyāʾ al-Turāth al-ʿArabī.

Al-Muḥallī, Muḥammad b. Aḥmad (2006), *Sharḥ Jamʿ al-Jawāmiʿ*. Published with al-Banānī's marginal notes. Muhammad ʾAbd al-Qādir Dārshāhīn (ed.), Beirut: Dār al-Kutub al-ʿIlmiyyah.

Al-Nawawī, Abū Zakariyyā Yaḥyā b. Sharaf (2002), *Rawḍah al-Ṭālibīn*, Beirut: Dār Ibn Ḥazm.

Al-Qurṭubī, Aḥmad b. ʿUmar. al-Jāmiʿl (2001), *Aḥkām al-Qurʾan*. ʿAbd al-Razzāq al-Mahdī (ed.), Beirut: Dār al-Kitāb al-ʿArabī.

Al-Ramlī, Aḥmad b. Ḥamzah (2003), *Nihāyat al-Muḥtāj fī Sharḥ al-Minhāj*. Muḥammad 'Alī Bayḍūn (ed.), Beirut: Dār al-Kutub al-'Ilmiyyah.

Al-Rāzī, Muḥammad b. 'Umar (Fakhr al-Dīn) (2000), *Mafātīḥ al-Ghayb*, Beirut: Dār al-Kutub al-'Ilmiyyah.

Al-Shirbīnī, Muḥammad b. al-Khaṭib (1997), *Mughnī al-Muḥtāj fī Sharḥ al-Minhāj*. Muḥammad Khalīl 'Aytānī (ed.), Beirut: Dār al-Ma'rifah.

Al-Shāfi'ī, Muḥammad b. Idrīs (n.d.), *al-Umm*. Ḥassān 'Abd al-Mannān (ed.), Amman: Bayt al-Afkār al-Dawliyyah.

Al-Ṭabarī, Muḥammad b. Jarīr. Jāmi' (2001), *al-Bayān fī Tafsīr Āy al-Qur'an*. Dr. 'Abd Allah b. 'Abd al-Muḥsin al-Turkī (ed.), Giza: Dār Hajar.

Al-Zarkashī, Badr al-Dīn Muḥammad b. 'Abd Allah (1992), al-Baḥr al-Muḥīṭ. 'Abd al-Qādir 'Abd Allah al-'Ānī (ed.), Kuwait: Ministry of Endowments and Islamic Affairs.

Abū Ḥayyān al-Andalusī, Muḥammad b. Yūsuf (2002), *al-Baḥr al-Muḥīṭ*, Beirut: Dār Iḥyā' al-Turath al-'Arabī.

Ibn 'Ābidīn, Muḥammad Amīn (1902), *Majmū'ah Rasā'il Ibn 'Ābidīn*, Cairo: al-Maktabah al-Hāshimiyyah, 1:68.

Ibn al-'Arabī, Muḥammad b. 'Abd Allah (2001), Ahkām al-Qur'an. 'Alī Muḥammad al-Bajjāwī (ed.), Beirut: Dār Iḥyā' al-Turāth al-'Arabī.

Ibn 'Aṭiyyah al-Andalusī (2002), *'Abd al-Ḥaqq. al-Muḥarrar al-Wajīz fī Tafsir al-Kitāb al-'Azīz*, Beirut: Dār Ibn Ḥazm.

Ibn Kathīr, Ismā'īl (2002), *Tafsīr al-Qur'an al-'Aẓīm*. 'Abd al-Razzāq al-Mahdī (ed.), Beirut: Dār al-Kitāb al-'Arabī.

Ibn Qudāmah al-Maqdisī, 'Abd Allah b. Aḥmad b. Muḥammad (1997), *al-Mughnī Sharḥ Mukhtaṣar al-Khiraqī*. 'Abd Allah b. 'Abd al-Muḥsin al-Turkī and 'Abd al-Fattāḥ Muḥammad al-Ḥilū (eds.), Riyādh: Dār 'Ālam al-Kutub.

Ibn Taymiyah, Aḥmad (1998), *Majmū' al-Fatāwā*, Riyadh: Maktabah al-Obeikan.

Ilkiyā al-Harrāsī, 'Imād al-Dīn b. Muḥammad al-Ṭabarī (2001), *Aḥkām al-Qur'an*, Beirut: Dār al-Kutub al-'Ilmiyyah.

'Ulaysh, Muḥammad b. Aḥmad. Minaḥ al-Jalīl Sharḥ (2003), *'Alā Mukhtaṣar al-'Allāmah al-Khalīl*. 'Abd al-Jalīl 'Abd al-Salām (ed.), Beirut: Dār al-Kutub al-'Ilmiyyah.

English

Ali, K. (2006), *Sexual Ethics and Islam: Feminist Reflections on Qur'an, Hadīth, and Jurisprudence*, Oxford: Oneworld Publications.

Bakhtiar, L. (2007), *The Sublime Quran*, Chicago: Kazi Publications.

Chaudhry, A. S. (2013), *Domestic Violence in the Islamic Tradition*, Oxford: Oxford University Press.

D'Silva, P. J. (2014), "Social agency and translating the *Qur'an*: The case of Laleh Bakhtiar's The Sublime *Qur'an* and 4:34" in Said Faiq, Ovidi Carbonell and Ali Almanna (eds.), *Culguage in/of Translation from Arabic*, Munich: LINCOM GmbH.

Kausar, S., Hussain, S. and Idriss, M. M. (2011), "Does the *Qur'an* condone domestic violence?" in Mohammad Mazher Idriss (ed.), *Honour, Violence, Women and Islam*. London: Routledge.

Yusuf, H. (2009), "Sermon: Removing the Silence on Domestic Violence" Berkeley: Zaytuna College (YouTube), 21 February, available at https://www.youtube.com/watch?v=BDEKJDgXO-U. Retrieved on 20 October 2017.

Chapter 28

Dimensions of Women Empowerment and Gender Inequality: A Muslim World Perspective

Toseef Azid and Jennifer Ward-Batts

Despite much recent attention to gender inequality and empowerment of women and girls, gender inequality persists in both developed and developing countries. We maintain after considering the chapters herein that gender inequality is not a consequence of religion per se, but of various dimensions of culture and social norms, institutions, laws and policies of the society, and the interaction of these factors with economic development. Culture and social norms contain much variation in interpretation of religion across time and space, and religion is often used as a rationale to support social rules, common practices, and law, even when these predate arrival of the religion. Nevertheless, these vary widely over space and time, so cannot be claimed to stem directly from a single religion.

We know from much research that poverty is a global problem, and that it is particularly a problem for women and children. However, in some cases, there is less gender imbalance in the poorest of the poor communities. In some such communities, neither boys nor girls are able to attend school. As another example, among poor families in rural Pakistan, there is much less inequality and sex segregation than is observed in cities and better-off families. Some data show that women work in agriculture as much or more than men, and *purdah* (the practice of seclusion of women) is not practiced by tenant farmers, small landowners and lower castes. However, "small landowners who achieve prosperity start forcing their women to observe *purdah*. Even a slight improvement in prosperity permits peasant families to hire paid labor as a replacement for the work done previously by their female members" (Rahman, 1987, p. 249). It seems that restrictions on women and girls are somewhat of a luxury at the low end of the income spectrum. However, after some point, economic development and growth tend to allow greater freedoms and more empowerment for women, and better living conditions for families generally. As income per capita of a country rises, (non-agricultural) job opportunities for women outside the home tend to increase, as do opportunities for them to participate in public life more generally. This takes various forms — in many cases sex segregation decreases, but in others it is maintained with a parallel set of markets, offices and other spaces for women versus for men (as in Saudi Arabia, as per Ferdoos, 2005). Returning to the example of Pakistan, most of the rural population and those living in the suburbs of the urban areas are poor, less educated and are unable to achieve more than a subsistence standard of living. Male and female alike are restricted by these life conditions. As income rises, the population overall benefits, but as we said in the introduction to this volume, women's participation in the labor market outside the home first decreases as incomes rise, and then increases as they rise further.

Gender discrimination and gender gaps in outcomes, such as education, literacy, and other measures of empowerment, are especially pronounced in developing (low and middle-income countries), which includes most of the Muslim world. Pursuing economic development, along with programs and policies to target women's welfare, can make significant impacts on the well-being of women and girls in these countries in myriad ways.

We began by calling attention to commonly held stereotypes among Westerners regarding Muslim women that they are not allowed to participate in economic, social and political activities. In contrast, in the introduction and in chapters herein, counter arguments are presented that Islam provides for women's rights to participate in these activities — i.e., that 1,400 years ago, Islam explicitly gave rights to women that other religions and cultures denied them. The diverse collection of chapters in this volume present theoretical foundations, empirical evidence and various country studies covering various dimensions of the relevant issues. While we are aware of significant restrictions on the freedoms of women in some ways in certain settings, we also highlight herein some very significant achievements of Muslim women, both historically and in more recent times. Muslim women can and do participate in the economic, social and political sphere. They are prime ministers, minsters, CEO, Doctors, professors, entrepreneurs, other professionals and so on, in additional to providing care for their families.

The eight chapters that are included in Part A discussed the theoretical foundations and true philosophy of Islam in the context of women's empowerment. These chapters described the multi-dimensional role and rights of Muslim women, i.e., guarantee of expenses of women's maintenance, property right, right to their own dowry and gifts, inheritance rights, right to work and earn, measures prescribed for economic empowerment after divorce, their political and leadership role, women as judge and head of the state, as a witness, women in the workplace, Islamic feminism, women's citizenship rights, and others.

Previous studies tend to presume that sex segregation automatically implies gender discrimination. However, it is not the researcher's prerogative to decide what increases individual welfare. In the context of a given culture, preferences of individuals may be such that they prefer something that individuals from a different society would find less than desirable. Again, we are reminded to keep our ethnocentric judgments in check and consider the welfare of the subjects under study in their own views, rather than in our view. In fact, many Muslim women are happy with sex segregation, as it provides them their own spaces to work and socialize without being scrutinized by men. They feel happy that they are treated with a special honor by their families and by others in society. Given a particular culture, having separation of men and women may very well maximize utility of both, and perhaps especially women. Of course, under other conditions, in a different culture, women might prefer not to have such segregation. If women begin to desire less segregation, they are increasingly able to assert their preferences and make their opinions known thanks to the Internet and other modern technologies. This in itself is empowering. As women and girls are also able to learn about the life conditions of others, and to converse with others from around the world due to these same technologies, the next generation may develop different preferences regarding seclusion, the extent that they work inside versus outside the home, etc.

Countries, and even regions within a country, each have their own culture. This culture is often intertwined with religion, but is not the same as religion, and is different even across places that profess to subscribe to the same religion. For example, the culture of Malaysia is completely different than that of Iran, which is different from Saudi Arabia, even though these three countries are, by constitution, Islamic countries. Every country has its own laws and economic and social policies regarding employment, education, training, legal protection, health care, family issues, and regulations of various other dimensions of society. Though Islam prescribes a default assignment of responsibilities in the households that are different for men than for women (as do other religions), it is not religion per se that compels women to stay at home and raise the children in countries where this is the norm. Rather it is a combination of culture, laws, social policies, educational opportunities (or lack thereof), job opportunities (or lack thereof), the level of economic development, and the industry mix (even in rich Western countries, women make up a tiny share in certain industries and occupations). All of these factors can interact to result in restrictions on women and their choices. Indian and Pakistani culture are virtually the same, but the religion of most Indians is Hindu. Both countries have a rigid caste system, making it difficult to have social and economic mobility within the society. The rich classes in the two countries behave more or less the same, and the same can be said if we compare the poor classes across the two countries (though India is a huge country with diversity across provinces, and this claim may be truer for some than others).

We would also encourage future work on women's empowerment generally, and that on Muslim women in particular, and take a broad view of empowerment and welfare. While much previous work in economics shows that greater income control within the household tends to increase various measures of welfare of women and children, the measures that have traditionally been used are often imperfect measures of welfare (see Ward-Batts 2008 for a survey). It is impossible for us to measure individual welfare directly, so we have used proxy measures, including health and education outcomes, and consumption of various goods within the household. If a mother maximizes her utility by raising her child or serving her family and avoiding market work, then we would ideally measure this state for her as a positive outcome, and we would also ideally take account of the productive work she does even though is not transacted in the market. Our analyses have historically been quite limited due to data limitations. However, as the world has become richer overall, and technology has increased for such efforts, we have increased data collection, and developed new methods for doing so. As a result, we have much more detailed data available to address some of these questions or welfare and empowerment of women. One example is research on individual's own self-reported well-being, measured as happiness, life-satisfaction and related concepts. We also now have regular collections of time-use data in a growing list of countries, which allow us to examine time spent on home production and child care, which would then allow us to calculate values of the work done by unpaid care workers. These time-use data can also be used to examine leisure time, which is an important element of consumption that increases individual welfare. We also have very detailed longitudinal data sets that allow us to follow the same families and individuals over time, and to examine a wide set of issues for those subjects. These longitudinal data sets include two in populous Muslim countries: the Malaysian Family Life Surveys and the Indonesian Family Life Surveys.[1] Research literatures using all of these rich data are growing rapidly. There are incredible opportunities for empirical researchers to examine questions around empowerment of women and girls generally, and of Muslim women and girls in particular, using such data. Researchers could examine various measures of well-being, including leisure time, physical health, mental health, extent of one's social network, mortality, morbidity and life expectancy, among others. Research on Muslims versus others is hampered by lack of data to distinguish individual religion, so studies often focus on Muslim countries compared to non-Muslim countries. We need more and better data, like those collected by the Pew Research Center (referenced elsewhere herein), that allow us to examine Muslims versus non-Muslims in different countries.

We might criticize previous researchers for using narrow measures of well-being and empowerment, and point out the inadequacy of those measures. We can criticize generations of economists for not including the value of unpaid care work in their GDP statistics. However, issuing these critiques does not solve the problem. Researchers today must do the work and also must argue with governments and NGOs to fund these researches for more data collection, and to include such alternative measures in official statistics. However, doing such research and making these calculations is much easier said than done. There are many complications in valuing the outputs of unpaid work. Should we count the value of a home-cooked meal as the same as a meal one could purchase in the market? The home-cooked meal might be valued more by the family. In particular, it seems less than ideal to value the care and training that a mother provides for her child as equivalent to the care and training provided in market-based child care. As the mother, she cares more about the outcomes and the child, and the

[1]See RAND Family Life Surveys at https://www.rand.org/well-being/social-and-behavioral-policy/data/FLS.html. Retrieved on 30 April 2019.

everlasting emotional bond between mother and child has immense value. Alternatively, we could simply use the time inputs to value the outputs, but this is both inconsistent with measures of outputs traded in the market, and requires that we place a value on the time of the worker, which requires that we also make assumptions and difficult choices in those assumptions. It is neither easy nor obvious how to come up with these measures, even given the time-use data are available. But we must try.

The economic model of the family presented by Becker (1993) is the traditional family model in which the husband and wife specialize in traditional gender roles: he earns the income while she does household production and raises the children. This is consistent with the traditional Muslim family model as well. However, we have seen that, as economies develop further, moving to higher technologies and away from agriculture as the primary employment, the nature of families, and marriages, has changed. As fewer children are desired due to those changes in the economy and due to decreases in infant mortality, and as the technology available to assist in home tasks has increased, women's time available for other endeavors has increased. At the same time, the nature of marriage has moved away from a model of specialization in traditional gender roles. However, we still see gender gaps in income in rich countries, even though women's education exceeds that of men on average. One reason these gaps are believed to persist is that women are now doing both market work and the housework and childrearing. Having their own incomes comes at this price — they have very little leisure time.

Thus, we advocate for a more holistic view of women's status than just looking at relative wages, income and education. It is possible that Muslim women, holding other things equal, may be better off than other women due to family rules in Islam that release wives from responsibility from providing financial support for the family. Making this comparison empirically is obviously near to impossible due to the different circumstances in which Muslim and non-Muslim women live today, including the various social norms and laws that are not derived only from the *Qu'ran*. Actual conditions women face differ in many ways, some of which we can measure, and some of which are very difficult to measure. Arguing that Muslim women are not empowered because we see low labor force participation in many Muslim countries is due to a reliance on a narrow view of empowerment. Similarly, arguing that women in the Muslim world constitute an underemployed resource is taking a narrow view. Without a measure of their contribution to society, we cannot say whether their contribution would be greater if they were employed in the market to a larger degree. Furthermore, it does not take account of the value of their leisure time, which would be sacrificed if they participate more in market work. Finally, in contrast to the neo-classical economic assumption, having more material goods to consume does not always bring greater happiness or life-satisfaction, so should not be so heavily relied upon as a measure of well-being. Because Muslim women have, according to true Islamic law, greater control of their own individual wealth than many non-Muslim women, as well as having a rightful claim on the market income of their husband's to provide for the support of their household, including themselves and their children. They may be more empowered than the traditional measures of empowerment are capable of showing. In the standard economic model, an individual will choose to work less when his or her wealth or income from another source rises. This could explain much of the low participation of Muslim women in the labor market.

Education is one of the most important factors in reducing wage disparities between groups, including the gender wage gap. However, education and literacy alone are not a sufficient condition regarding this issue. For example, Sri Lanka has a high literacy rate but still discrimination among the different segments prevails. The earning differentials are always there if there is no legal protection and if justice does not prevail. It is not the matter of gender, the ground reality is the process of development and the legal system of the country.

In the chapters herein, it is argued that Muslim women have approximately equal rights with men, and they feel more productive when they are performing their duties according to the principles of Islam. In Islam mothers, wives, sisters and daughters have, in many ways, more value than their male counterparts. It is not fair to judge the inequality only in terms of easily measured economic aspects. In a broader view, other aspects of life that contribute to well-being are also very important, including social, psychological and religious well-being, in addition to the arguments for expending measures of production we have made previously. Through their position in the family, women contribute not only to human capital but also to social, psychological and moral capital of her family and her local community. Though culture may restrict her movements and actions in some countries, the mother is a highly valued matriarch in her family, where she is revered, valued and generally obeyed. Traditional narrow views of women's empowerment do not capture the empowerment this position in the family implies.

There is substantial evidence that discrimination against women existed in every society and culture and that it continues in myriad ways, both in rich and poor countries. There is evidence that women's status had declined in the last two decades, or at least that their progress has stalled. However, because culture is difficult to measure, most of the literature could not draw any conclusions about the impact of culture on women's empowerment. They are also under-represented in the well-paid and prestigious professions. However, if we redefine the prestigious positions to include the title of mother, which we can argue is accurate, then most of the prestigious positions will be held by women. If we move away from thinking of humans in an overly simplistic way, move away from a view espoused by using narrow measures available to us to make strong statements about empowerment and well-being, then we would likely come to a different understanding. Human beings are not machines, but have emotional ties, sentiments, culture, and widely differing utility of material goods. Paid jobs and participation in the labor market are not the main determinant of their individual welfare. Satisfying all of their individual needs according to Maslow's hierarchy of needs does not necessarily require participating in paid work. By assuming that paid work is important for welfare and empowerment, are researchers imposing an ethnocentric measuring stick?

In conclusion, we wish to emphasize three main points. (1) After considering the chapters and other information herein, we are unable to conclude that women in one country are more or less empowered than those in another country. This is in part because we view the definition of empowerment to be too narrow and ethnocentric. We encourage a more holistic view of empowerment of humans generally, and of women and girls relative to those of the male gender. (2) From the evidence presented, we believe that the religion of Islam itself is not responsible for low levels of women's welfare and empowerment, however it is defined. If anything, Islam is more progressive than other religions in guaranteeing basic rights of women. Instead, other factors determine the status of women. In many cases when Islam is used as a justification for behavior, social norms, laws, and policies that negatively impact women, the arguments for the basis of these in Islam are misguided, or more blatantly in contradiction to true Islam. (3) Further research on the welfare of Muslim women and girls by researchers who are either Muslim themselves, or who are well-meaning non-Muslims who are able to put aside their ethnocentrism, would be welcomed by contributors to this volume. Our hope is that this volume will generate interest in such research and in more discussion and interaction surrounding the topics considered and issues raised herein, in addition to many other issues that affect the welfare of Muslim women and girls, and of Muslims generally.

A final hope is that this volume and the discussions and additional research that may stem from it will generate greater dialogue and understanding between Muslims and non-Muslims, which will help to dispel stereotypes about Muslim women and allow more understanding of them and their issues and concerns.

References

Becker, G. (1993), *A Treatise on the Family* (2 edn.), Harvard University Press: Cambridge, MA.

Ferdoos, A. (2005), *Social Status of Rural and Urban Working Women in Pakistan — A Comparative Study*, doctoral dissertation, Universität Osnabrück, available at https://d-nb.info/980210313/34. Retrieved on 30 April 2019.

Rahman, M. (1987), Women in rural development in Pakistan. *Journal of Rural Studies*, 3(3), 247–253.

Ward-Batts, J. (2008), Out of the wallet and into the purse: Using micro data to test income pooling. *Journal of Human Resources*, 43(2), 325–351.

Index

A

B

C

D

E

I

Q

T

U

Lightning Source UK Ltd.
Milton Keynes UK
UKHW051833230620
365408UK00006B/258

9 789811 212147